DATE DUE

			PRINTED IN U.S.A.

The Blackwell Guide to
Soul Recordings

The Blackwell Guide to
Soul Recordings

edited by

Robert Pruter

BLACKWELL
Reference

Copyright © Basil Blackwell Ltd 1993
Editorial organization © Robert Pruter 1993

First published 1993

Blackwell Publishers
108 Cowley Road
Oxford OX4 1JF
UK

238 Main Street,
Cambridge, Massachusetts 02142
USA

British Library Cataloguing in Publication Data
A CIP catalogue record for this book is available from the British
Library.

Library of Congress Cataloging-in-Publication Data
The Blackwell guide to soul recordings / edited by Robert Pruter.
  450p. (Blackwell reference)
  Includes bibliographical references and index.
  ISBN 0-631-18595-X (hardback : alk. paper) : £17.99
  1. Soul music–Discography. 2. Soul music–Reviews. I. Pruter,
Robert, 1944–
ML156.4.S6B6   1993
016.781644' 0266–dc20   93-12312
                                                           CIP
                                                           MN
Typeset in Plantin and Univers
by TecSet Ltd, Wallington, Surrey
Printed in Great Britain by T J Press Ltd, Padstow

Contents

Contributors

GEOFF BROWN, a former professional drummer in UK soul bands, is now a freelance writer and journalist living in London. He was a feature writer for *Melody Maker*, editor of *Black Music* and *Black Music and Jazz Review* magazines, and music and senior editor of *Time Out* magazine, and he contributes to numerous newspapers and magazines on music and sport. Published books include *Diana Ross* (1981) and *Michael Jackson: body and soul* (1984, 1988).

BILL DAHL is a freelance writer and journalist and a resident of Chicago. He has a BA (1977) degree from Columbia College in mass communications. He has written extensively on soul and blues for *Goldmine, Chicago Tribune, Illinois Entertainer, Living Blues, Downbeat, Guitar World,* and many other publications. His liner notes are found on releases from Rhino, Blind Pig, Delmark, Flying Fish, Rooster, and Alligator. Dahl was a contributor to a Tina Turner biography, *T*I*N*A* (1985), and co-writer of *Rock n'Roll Trivia* (1985). He also has worked as a disc jockey in the Chicago area.

PETER GRENDYSA is a freelance writer from Caledonia, Wisconsin, near Milwaukee. More than 400 of his articles, reviews, and columns have appeared in specialist music magazines, including *Goldmine, Bim Bam Boom, Record Collector's Monthly,* and *Yesterday's Memories.* He was the principal researcher for the books *Top R&B Singles, 1942–1988* (1988), *Top Country Singles, 1944–1988* (1989), and *Top Videocassettes, 1979–1991* (1992). Since 1979 he has been United States liaison for European record companies engaged in reissuing vintage rock-and-roll, and since 1989 he has been a member of the Awards Committee of the Association of Recorded Sound Collections. He was the producer and host of local and syndicated radio programs from 1980 to 1983.

JEFF HANNUSCH is a freelance writer and journalist, and a resident of New Orleans. He has a BA degree from the University of Western Ontario and has written innumerable articles on soul and blues, generally on artists from the South and especially from New Orleans. His articles have appeared in *Billboard, Rolling Stone, Juke Blues, Elle, Baseball America,* and the *New Orleans Times-Picayune,* and his liner notes have appeared on releases from Rounder, Rhino, EMI, and many other labels. He is the author of the award-winning *I Hear Your Knockin': the sound of New Orleans rhythm and blues* (1985).

RANDAL C. HILL is a high-school teacher and freelance writer from Upland, California. He received a BA in radio–TV production in 1964, and an MA in education in 1978. He has been teaching since 1965, but his most passionate interest is popular music. He was a part-time deejay in 1959 and 1960. He is a frequent contributor to the record collector specialist magazine *Goldmine,* and the author of *Rock Hall of Fame* (1981), *Music Hall of Fame* (1986), *Spotlight on Rock Stars* (1989), *Superstars of Rock* (1989), and the *Official Price Guide to Collectible Rock Records* (1979–82). He was a contributor to *Contemporary Music Almanac, 1980/81.*

WAYNE JANCIK is a family therapist in Chicago. He received an MA degree from University of Chicago in 1977 and an MSW degree in social work from Loyala University in 1986. As a freelance writer he has contributed articles in all areas of popular music for such publications as the *Chicago Sun-Times, Illinois Entertainer, Goldmine, RPM, Discoveries,* and *Record Review.* Jancik is the author of *The Billboard Book Of One-Hit Wonders* (1990).

DAN NOOGER is an album reissue producer and music business attorney living in Flushing, New York. He is employed at Tuff City Records in New York City. He has produced reissue albums for the Chess Blues Masters series for All Platinum, the Swingtime reissues for Night Train International, and for various artists on Savoy Jazz and Ace (UK). Four of his projects appeared in the *Blackwell Guide to Recorded Blues* – Little Esther's **Complete Savoy Recordings**, Big Maybelle's **Blues, Candy And Big Maybelle**, J. B. Lenoir's **Chicago Golden Years**, and Jimmy Rogers's Chicago blues set. His writing experience includes stints at *Cash Box* and at Atlantic Records publicity department, and as a longtime freelancer, contributing to such publications as *Goldmine, Blues and Rhythm,* and *Shades of Soul.*

ROBERT PRUTER is the senior editor of social sciences for New Standard Encyclopedia in Chicago, Illinois. He resides in suburban Elmhurst. He received his BA (1967) and MA (1976), both in history, from Roosevelt University. Since 1977 Pruter has been a columnist and features writer for *Goldmine* and since 1985 its R & B editor. He has been a regular contributor to *Time Barrier Express*, *Juke Blues*, *Living Blues*, *Record Collector's Monthly*, *Illinois Entertainer*, *Soul Survivor*, and *It Will Stand*, and has written liner notes for releases from Atlantic, Rhino, Chess/MCA, Epic, Kent (UK), and Rooster Blues. He is the author of the award-winning *Chicago Soul* (1991).

Discographical Information

With the growth of the box-set market, we were faced with the problem of providing a readable listing of artists and titles in large various-artists sets, some of which have included more than 200 titles. Rather than run the listing as presented on each set, which usually was a chronological order, we have opted for a different arrangement by listing each artist followed by his or her song titles. For consistency's sake we have followed this format into every various artists compilation. Note also that releases other than those from the United States have a notation as to the country of origin. They are as follows:

Ger   Germany

Jap   Japan

Neth   The Netherlands

Swe   Sweden

UK   United Kingdom

Introduction

Robert Pruter

S oul music is such an integral part of popular culture today that it is sometimes taken for granted. Turn on the television, and a popular situation comedy uses classic Motown hits for story lines or simply soundtrack ambience. Break to a commercial and one hears a soul song selling grapes (Marvin Gaye's *I Heard It Through The Grapevine*), cars (Doris Troy's *Just One Look*), or spark plugs (James Brown's *I Got You*). Turn to a late-night show and a mail-order album commercial comes on selling hit soul songs of the 1960s or the greatest funk songs of the 1970s. Radio in every major market is filled with stations that mix in classic 1960s soul with soft-rock hits, trying to reach the 25–40 audience. And record companies since the advent of the CD in the late 1980s have been working overtime trying to fulfill the demand for old soul songs. What an amazing development this is, when one considers that soul arose in the late 1950s and early 1960s as a mostly unknown form of the widely despised rock-and-roll.

It was in the late 1950s that soul music records originally appeared, first as a mere trickle, with a Ray Charles disc here, an Isley Brothers record there, amid the torrent of rhythm-and-blues records that was then the staple of black radio. What made these early soul records "soul" was mainly the employment of a more gospelized approach. The record in question may only have hinted at black church origins or it may have been a pure gospel number that had been secularized with profane lyrics, but in any case the term "soul" came into currency to describe this new style. Most of the soul records in the late 1950s and early 1960s were usually only heard on the four-figures' end of the radio dial, on obscure black stations that were unknown to most of the populace. The few soul songs that crossed over onto teen-oriented Top 40 radio were considered at first as a part of rock-and-roll. It took a number of years before soul music emerged in the consciousness of wider American culture as a distinctive style.

On the other hand, in the African American community the popularity of soul by the early 1960s built so quickly that there was a flood of soul records reaching the market, so that by 1964 the term was on everyone's lips and the old terms used by blacks to discuss their popular music, "rock-and-roll" and "rhythm and blues," had fallen well by the wayside. Hundreds of new soul records each week were fighting for space on the broadcast dials, and by the late 1960s, sociologists were discussing the "soul culture" of the black community, which encompassed food, dress, religion, and other aspects. At this time, paradoxically, soul music had reached its highest crossover appeal in the white community, so that up to a third of the Top 40 in a major city market would be soul records.

Beginning in the early 1970s, soul began modifying and transforming itself into new soul styles called variously funk, disco, and disco-funk. Soul began to lose crossover appeal as well, and the virulent reaction against disco was directed as much against black music in general as at the reputed failings of disco itself. By the early 1980s a new, youthful African American music culture called hip-hop, centered on rap records, had replaced the concept of "soul" in popular consciousness. Cultural commentator Nelson George, in a reflective essay in the *Village Voice* in 1992, calls the 1980s an era of "postsoul black culture."

The period from 1960 to 1975, the core years of the soul phenomenon, were the final years of the regional recording industry. Made up of several major labels and hundreds of independents, from mom-and-pops to multimillion dollar operations, the record industry at the beginning of the era was flourishing across the country in a multitude of recording centers. These included Detroit, Philadelphia, Chicago, Memphis, Houston, New Orleans, Nashville, and Los Angeles, as well as the national recording center in New York. Two decades later the regional scenes had disappeared as the recording industry coalesced into a half-dozen majors operating out of three national centers – New York, Nashville, and Los Angeles.

Reflecting the regionalization of soul music, the *Blackwell Guide to Soul Recordings* uses a regional format for most of the chapters. The regions covered are New York/New Jersey, Philadelphia, Detroit, Chicago, the South, and the West Coast (Los Angeles and the Bay Area). The South is divided into two chapters – Louisiana (New Orleans and Shreveport), the Gulf of Mexico literal of Texas (Houston), Florida (Miami), and Mississippi (Jackson); and the largely inland centers, which include Tennessee (Memphis and Nashville), Alabama (Muscle Shoals), Georgia (Atlanta), Virginia (Newport News), and Carolinas. The defining judgment as to where to place the artists was the cities in which they recorded, or more precisely the cities where the producers recorded them, and artists were roughly assigned to each region on that basis.

"Roughly" is the key word here, because a number of compromises and exceptions had to be made. On some collections, it is evident that the artist recorded in a number of regions, as did Detroit native Barbara Lewis, who recorded first in Detroit, then in Chicago, and finally in New York. We placed her in New York (chapter 2). Producer Phil Spector began producing regularly in New York but later switched to Los Angeles, where most of his output was recorded. Thus, we opted to put the Spector box set in the West Coast chapter (chapter 8). Then there is the Aretha Franklin situation, in which musicians from a Muscle Shoals, Alabama, studio were brought to New York studios to back the singer. We decided the artistic approach in this case was Southern and placed these recordings in a Southern chapter (chapter 6). Many more anomalies and difficulties arose from this regional division of the chapters, but in the end we found this organization scheme made the best sense.

By the mid-1970s the regional scenes had largely broken down and it is difficult to discuss most artists as coming from a particular recording scene. We have listed artists from this later, non-regionalized period in two broad chapters (chapters 9 and 10) on the international scene and on the United States national scene that extend to the present day (at this writing, 1993). And to recognize that soul music did not come out of a vacuum, that it grew out of a substantial body of rhythm-and-blues music, we have added a chapter (chapter 1) on 1950s releases called "rhythm and blues" to cover those kinds of artists – including those whose styles would make them "soul precursors," although some had more of that "precursor" element than others. Due to the fluid nature of the recording industry some readers might object here and there to the organization, but again keep in mind the chapter division exists to provide a framework for discussion, not to provide metaphysical certainty.

Each chapter is divided into two review sections – an "Essential Recordings" section listing 5–15 releases and a "Basic Recordings" section listing 30 releases (20 in the short chapter 9). Each reviewer has selected the essential releases as the preeminent ones deserving of the most extended comments. Generally these are by the recording artists best recognized by the public and almost universally considered the most important. There are a total of 105 essential releases reviewed in this guide, give or take a couple. The basic entries are designed to supplement the essential listings, covering some of the so-called "lesser" artists, certain classic albums that augment essential best-of collections, and some of the tangents and byways of a regional scene, such as Latin soul, low-rider music, and soul-blues. There are 290 basic entries. What brought the most anguish to our contributors was relegating many of their favorite collections into the basic section. One contributor in jest even suggested reversing the numbers devoted to each section, so he could have 30 releases he could deem essential.

The "Recommended Reading" list toward the end of the book brings together the recommendations of the contributors to this volume for further reading. Possibly unfamiliar soul and music-industry terms are explained in the glossary.

Despite the ascendency of rap, new jack swing, house, and other postsoul styles, soul music remains a hot commodity in the CD stores. In a visit to such a store the consumer will find an immense display of racks and racks of the latest releases of almost all the soul greats, an awesome demonstration that people are buying soul music in the 1990s. Why is this? Most African American buyers of popular music are youths who are not interested in artists of the past. They are the buyers who keep black music progressive and advancing toward new avenues. So who is buying all this older black music? I hate to use the "Y" word, but yes, it is young urban professionals, yuppies, as well as buppies, black young urban professionals. These are people who are no longer attuned to many of the latest sounds, and are buying the classic sounds they fondly remember from their youth, or maybe what their older brothers and sisters may have remembered from their youth.

This guide was put together by some of the most knowledgeable British and American experts on soul music in order to aid both the casual and the more dedicated buyer of soul. The guide perhaps reflects more encompassing tastes than those of the typical soul consumer. So it is hoped that the buyer might be led to discover some great, fairly obscure recordings along with the commonplace, some of which unfortunately are not easily obtainable.

"Why include difficult-to-obtain, obscure discs?" we anticipate will be the oft-asked question. One of the brutal truths evident to most soul fans is that if one were to take any Top 40 list from an R & B radio station of the mid-1960s and compare what was broadcast then and what is available today in the record stores, the gulf would be enormous. In some chapters up to half the chart entries, both top and bottom, can no longer be heard. Many of the artists were one- or two-hit wonders or regional phenomenons and have simply been overlooked in reissue projects. Many of the more dedicated fans of soul music remain collectors of singles only, because it is in that medium they can find the music for which they are looking. When the editor approached one highly respected writer on soul music to contribute, his offer was declined: the writer was a collector of singles and did not feel qualified to discuss soul music in an album format.

At the beginning of the soul era, a little record entrepreneur with $700 could get a group of street-corner singers or harmonizers or an ingénue high-schooler with a poem in her pocket into the studio, and within 30 days get a million-seller. A group might be discovered in New York by a producer who, in his cubby-hole office in the Brill Building, answered the knock on the door by four or five young lads who had been traipsing around the building all day with on-the-spot auditioning. Or a producer might be riding past Washington Park on Chicago's South Side and discover a terrific ensemble singing under the street lamp. Or a soul artist might be discovered at the amateur contests at one of the nation's many chitlin' circuit theaters, such as the Apollo (Harlem), the Uptown (Philadelphia), the Howard (Washington, DC), the Fox (Detroit), or the Regal (Chicago). It was easy to get a record out, so soul records could come out of just about any city in the country that had a halfway decent studio. And there were tens of thousands of them made.

Given that reality and the ability of the public to absorb only so much, the recording industry today finds itself in a quandary in which it must meet the demand for soul music but at the same time try to determine what soul-music artists can be sold in sufficient number to be profitable. Thus, a critic must tread lightly in faulting reissue programs that miss much of the music that made an impact in the past. During the late 1980s and early 1990s, there has been an avalanche of reissues and the companies have done a tremendous job in putting out superbly mastered, well-produced, well-packaged CD sets on soul and other forms of popular music. New reissues hit the market daily and in compiling this guide we had the old problem of trying to hit a moving target. Additions were made right up to the point of going to press.

Yet what remains to be reissued is substantial. One cannot find much of Sony's catalog of 1960s soul on CD. There are no CDs by Major Lance, Walter Jackson, Peaches and Herb, and the Spellbinders. None of the Warner Brothers/Loma product from the mid-1960s is currently available, though notable among it are the releases by the famed Lorraine Ellison and the Los Angeles vocal groups. There are no O'Jays and Jimmy McCracklin CDs of their great Imperial output, and one cannot find famed Southern soul singer Jimmy Hughes on CD from either his Atlantic or his Vee Jay years. Bobby and James Purify, of *I'm Your Puppet* fame, are likewise not available.

Many of the classic soul albums may never again see the light of day. While Atlantic has been exemplary in reissuing on CD the great Stax albums of yesteryear, other companies have decided the market does not warrant straight reissues of old LPs. Thus, such great LPs as the Artistics' **Get My Hands On Some Lovin'**, Garnett Mimms and the Enchanters' **Cry Baby**, McKinley

Mitchell's **End Of The Rainbow**, Lou Rawls's **Live!**, Brenda and the Tabulations' **Dry Your Eyes**, and Funkadelic's **One Nation Under A Groove** remain unavailable. The omissions seem boundless.

Thus the philosophy in compiling these reviews is not to provide a guide as to what is currently available in the stores, because obviously a lot of great music is not. Rather, it is to provide a timeless listing of the best recordings in album form, whether or not they are currently or easily available. Therefore, the reader will find among the listings a substantial number of vinyl and obscure CD releases. Some of the old vinyl records we have listed may seem impossible to obtain, but who is to know whether one will find them in a used record store, or whether a company will soon come out with the very same LPs in a CD format? Since we started this project some vinyl releases have already come out on CD. Note, the assumption of the compilers is that CD is the standard format. Therefore, if a release that is listed is only available on vinyl, we have put a notation "LP" in parentheses to tell the reader it is not a CD.

The jobs of the editor and contributors were made much easier by the assistance given by a number of record companies in supplying review copies and offering other support. These representatives and their companies are James Austin (Rhino), John Broven (Ace/Kent), Marion Carter (Ripete), Donn Fileti (Relic), Bob Fisher (Sequel), Bob Koester (Delmark), Andy McKaie (MCA), Bob Porter (Atlantic), Kirk Roberts (Specialty/Fantasy), Tim Whitsett (Urgent), and Jean Luc Young (Charly). On behalf of the contributors I warmly thank these companies for taking the time and making the effort to respond to all our requests and entreaties.

As editor I would like to extend a grateful thanks to all the contributors, who responded to my invitation to become a part of the project. Needing only a little prodding on my part, they enthusiastically tackled their chapters and persevered to completion. The knowledge and expertise (as well as the fine-tuned ears) they brought to their essays made my job as editor so much easier. The contributors also made use of original interviews with artists and record industry people to add inside insight to their reviews. Finally I must thank the senior editor who conceived the project, Alyn Shipton, who saw a need for a companion volume on soul music to the previously published *Blackwell Guides* to jazz and blues.

Rhythm and Blues 1

Peter Grendysa

The story of black music in America is one of endless innovation and experimentation. At times moving close to the mainstream of popular music, then pulling away again, the music and its practitioners have always avoided following the lead of the mass market. As a living mosaic, black music is a kaleidoscope of hues and shades, ever changing in fractional bits and pieces, but always maintaining elements of the forms that have come before.

The style that became known as rhythm and blues in the late 1940s was an amalgam of earlier blues, gospel, and hot jazz sounds, molded into a new shape by factors equally external and internal. The cultural trauma of the war years effected countless changes in public tastes and attitudes, all reflected in music. Influenced by society, music also influences the listeners, and change is intensified and reinforced.

Among the circumstances leading to the development of rhythm and blues were the breakup of the big swing bands into smaller, more economically viable units, the growing popularity of vocalists, the urbanization of large numbers of African Americans, and the sudden growth of the small independent recording companies. Many of the players in rhythm-and-blues combos were veterans of big bands, and singers took the spotlight. Urban blacks only lately removed from farms and small towns enjoyed a brief, happy prosperity in the defense industries, and their demand for entertainment was filled by entrepreneurs who recorded a music that retained enough of blues and gospel to be familiar while mirroring the frenetic and sometimes lonely city life.

The result defies easy description. Rhythm and blues has encompassed leather-lunged shouters in sharkskin suits and their curvaceous female counterparts. It has embraced crooning vocal groups just minutes away from their favorite street corner. Included are the last vestiges of the big bands with their swaying lines of golden saxophones and relentless heavy beat – playing for people who love to dance. There are expatriates from sanctified churches singing of hot worldly love and cold heartbreak, and refugee cotton farmers plugged into up-to-the-minute electrified blues. If there is a common thread at all, it is exuberance and authenticity.

Essential Recordings

(i) Jumpin' In The Midnight Hour

Small combo jump blues, piano–bass–drum trios patterned after the leading light of Nat "King" Cole, and highly individualistic vocalists marked the first stirrings of rhythm and blues. The songs were built on simple blues progressions, stylized arrangements from standard pop tunes, and jazzy riffs. When the bands jumped, the dancers jived to new variations of the jitterbug and Lindy Hop; when the crooners sang of broken hearts and newfound loves, it was cheek-to-cheek time. Recordings of this new music sold in quantities that astonished many old hands in the record business, and each success bred imitators, clones, and innovators, all swept up in the excitement of a genuine phenomenon of popular culture.

One of the first small labels to leap headlong into the new music was Atlantic Records, headquartered in New York City, but constantly searching all over the country for material. After a shaky beginning, Atlantic survived turmoil in the industry to reach a position of importance in rhythm and blues in 1950. Always looking to build a small, eclectic artist roster, the label took a chance on Ray Charles.

Although Atlantic unblushingly call their Ray Charles tribute **The Birth Of Soul**, it could just as easily have been entitled "The Birth Of Ray Charles," as it represents the transformation of the artist over relatively few years. It is an extraordinary documentation of a rich source of raw material for soul music, performed by a man who is many things to many people. A "genius" perhaps, but more importantly a survivor in a fickle business where survival is the greatest talent of them all.

The symbiosis of Atlantic and Ray Charles is the real revelation of **The Birth Of Soul**. Producers at Atlantic (not even called producers in the early years) quickly discovered that the best way to record Ray Charles was to stay in the background and attend to engineering chores while Charles directed his backing band, coached the vocal groups, and bent and blended his lyrics to some sort of master mental blueprint known only to him.

Born Ray Charles Robinson in Albany, Georgia, on September 23, 1930, Charles knew enough poverty and heartbreak in his early years to fuel a dozen "blues" singers. A steady decline in vision left him totally blind by age six and he was orphaned in his early teens. He was raised as a ward of the state at the St Augustine (Florida) School for the Deaf and Blind until he was 15 years old. He spent his time at the school learning Braille and piano, and also played several other instruments.

Charles's first professional experience was with local blues and hillbilly bands in Florida, playing for the people whatever they wanted to hear. In 1948 he moved to Seattle, Washington – as far away from Florida as he could get. There the 18-year-old assembled a combo, the McSon Trio (later called the Maxime Trio), to work the clubs. With G.D. McKee on guitar and Milton Garred on bass, the trio landed a radio spot on station KRSC and appeared in some primitive TV broadcasts.

The men traveled to Los Angeles in February, 1949, to cut their first tracks for the Downbeat/Swingtime label. At that time, the trio was a virtual carbon copy in sound and style of that of Nat "King" Cole and Johnny Moore's Three Blazers, both intensely popular and influential small groups among blacks and whites.

Three minor hit records resulted with this style, *Confession Blues, Baby Let Me Hold Your Hand*, and *Kiss-A Me Baby*, and Charles otherwise occupied his time by touring with label-mate Lowell Fulson in place of Fulson's regular accompanist, Lloyd Glenn. As early as 1951 trade-paper reviewers were commenting appreciatively on his "soulful style" and his unique approach to standard blues fare.

The best of his early material allowed the pent-up anguish in his heart to show, and sales of his Swingtime records were brisk enough – he made 17 singles for the label in three years. With the Swingtime company suffering from a recession in the business that claimed many small independents in the early 1950s, Charles's contract was made available. Atlantic, one of the few R & B labels strong enough to survive, bought the artist for $2,500, a substantial sum for the time.

The company had no immediate plans for their new artist when he reported for work in May, 1952, so they sent him on the road with the Joe Morris Blues Cavalcade on that big musical revue's endless circuits of the South. Charles played piano with the Morris band and was permitted to pick up any session work he could find along the way, including the now-famous *Things That I Used To Do* hit with Guitar Slim (Specialty 482), recorded in New Orleans in October, 1953. By the time that record hit the streets, Charles had already banked three sessions for Atlantic (two in New York, one in New Orleans) without coming up with a hit of his own.

The relentless chronological order of **The Birth Of Soul** is, in this case, the perfect form for hearing the artist develop. At his first session for Atlantic, Charles remained very close to his earlier style, and three of the four songs are his own compositions: *The Sun's Gonna Shine Again, Roll With My Baby,* and *Jumpin' In The Morning* contain the spare piano and patented Charles "holler". *Roll With My Baby* finds the singer in his best Nat Cole garb, while in *The Midnight Hour* he is in his Charles Brown suit.

Jumpin' In the Morning, a fast boogie shuffle, breaks the mold, primarily with the addition of a fine band backing and ensemble vocal. Six months later, *It Should've Been Me* produced his first chart hit for his new label, and the novelty lyrics by songwriter Memphis "King" Curtis are given a satisfying, wry treatment. *Losing Hand* is virtually a duet between Charles and the guitar of Mickey Baker, with the slight natural echo adding to the haunting quality of this standard blues by Jesse Stone. *Funny But I Still Love You* has the singer still entwined with Charles Brown vocal mannerisms.

During his time in New Orleans, Charles did a couple of sessions not recognizable as "New Orleans" in style. The most musically exciting product of this period was *Don't You Know,* a churchy, medium-tempo tune that opens with a wail and is filled with squeals and shouts; the harbinger of the Ray Charles to come. *Nobody Cares, Ray's Blues,* and *Mr. Charles Blues,* from the same session, did not appear until a late 1950s LP release. Disc 1 of this set ends with *Blackjack,* from a wild session in Atlanta with Charles's own band.

Ray Charles "arrived" with *I've Got A Woman,* worked out by trumpeter Renald Richard and Charles on a long road trip. While the lyrics were familiar in content and intent, Charles added a touch of sweat and stained-glass fervor seldom heard before in R & B. The choppy shuffle beat and repetitious sax figure laid the foundation for the singer's barely restrained screams and shrieks. Although white and black rock-and-roll was already a nationwide sensation at the time the single was released in early 1955, Charles's approach had shifted from the cocktail and novelty blues of Charles Brown and Louis Jordan to a tangibly "blacker" sound.

Songs such as *Greenbacks, Come Back* (shown as *Come Back Baby*), and *A Fool For You* were aimed directly at the black audience, as the amazed and bemused owners at Atlantic stood back and let their genius follow his own path. They did not know where he was going; all they could do was smooth the way for him. Quasi-spirituals were what he wanted to do for a while, and success in the black community came from *This Little Girl Of Mine* and *Hallelujah I Love Her So* in this genre. *Hard Times,* a reversion to Charles Brown, and the instrumental *A Bit Of Soul* were held back from release until a more enlightened fandom was ready to appreciate some vintage Charles.

Where the addition of a backing vocal group or chorus skewed the performances of other Atlantic artists into the white pop camp,

Charles took on his own group, the Raelets, in his own good time, and molded them to his master plan. The dirge-tempoed *Drown In My Own Tears* and the upbeat Latin rhythm number *Mary Ann* show Charles's conception of a backup vocal group as just another delightful tool in his musical bag, not a concession to changing tastes.

Swanee River Rock broke into the Top 40 in late 1957; the first Ray Charles number to go pop. For the next year-and-a-half he was unable to recapture the ears of the mass market and experimentation continued during this time. *Talkin' About You, I Want A Little Girl, Yes Indeed, My Bonnie,* and his reprise of Nappy Brown's *The Right Time* are so exquisite in rehearing as to make one wonder what the mass market was thinking of when it passed them by the first time around. On the other hand, such hack renditions as *Tell All The World About You, You Be My Baby,* and *Tell Me How Do You Feel* are best forgotten.

Charles scored his first Top 10 pop hit with *What'd I Say,* recorded in February, 1959, as a 6-minute, 30-second jam with the Raelets and Charles's own band. Edited into two parts for the single, the joyful funk original hit both charts simultaneously in July and reached number 1 in R & B a month later. Undoubtedly, the hefty sales of this number attracted the attention of the major pop labels, and many fans consider it one of the first soul records.

Not surprisingly, *I'm Movin' On,* a reprise of the Hank Snow country hit of 1950, found greater favor in the pop charts than in the R & B market when it was released in late 1959. Charles's interpretation was straight-ahead, rocking R & B, but the presence of a steel guitar may have made the tune just too country for black buyers. After leaving Atlantic in 1960, Charles had great success in adapting country songs to his own style on ABC–Paramount and has frequently used country material ever since.

Everything Charles did worked well, whether it was country, pop, gospel, jazz, or R & B; he had an extremely broad base in all types of music to draw upon. In addition, his perfectionism and perfect pitch are legendary in the business. The soul artists of the 1960s and 1970s found a lot worth copying in the stark intensity of his vocal style and his technique of secularizing church music.

Even more adept than Ray Charles in turning gospel intensity and passion into scorching rhythm and blues, Nappy Brown came by his vocal fervency the right way – by singing in sanctified quartets. With the ability to heat and contort notes and a wide vocal range, Brown did tormented blues that cut like a knife.

Born Napoleon Culp Brown in Charlotte, North Carolina, on October 12, 1929, Brown was plucked from the amateur ranks of gospel singers by the Golden Bells and later worked with the famous Selah Jubilee Singers. The Selahs were a highly polished stage act and the young singer picked up a lot of dramatic presence while with that group. While in Newark, New Jersey, with the Heavenly Lights, Brown was asked if he could sing blues by Savoy Records president Herman Lubinsky.

Savoy recorded Brown solo in March, 1954, and all of Brown's first session is on **That Man**. Brown's dark voice conveys the right mix of menace and anguish on *That Man*, a classic playlet of unfaithful love. In a different approach to the same eternal subject, *Is It True – Is It True*, Brown strains with emotion that boils over into despair. The gentle blues *I Wonder (What's Wrong With Me)* builds relentlessly but the singer never breaks his restraint. The final song from this session, *Two Faced Woman (And A Lyin' Man)*, is a lightweight jump blues with a big-voiced, somewhat pedestrian delivery by Brown.

Despite a few rough edges, this session was good enough to prove to Savoy that their new vocalist had something different to offer the R & B field. Brown's second session for Savoy produced the chart hit *Don't Be Angry*, a contrived pop tune that attracted the attention of Mercury's cover-artist specialists, the Crew-Cuts, who turned it into a number 14 chart hit. Brown's original version did some selling in the pop market, too. Another session in 1955 generated an even more mainstream pop effort, the novelty *Piddly Patter Patter*, unsuccessful even for Patti Page.

Open Up That Door (And Walk Right In My Heart) was recorded in February, 1956, at the height of the R & B–rock-and-roll crossover rage. Relentless backbeat by Panama Francis and sax by Sam "The Man" Taylor helped impart the rock flavor, with Brown's powerful tones belting out the lyric. Much more finely honed, *Little By Little* has a charming Latin beat, inspired baritone sax, and Brown in superb voice. The single moved into the pop chart in January, 1957, and probably outsold a lackluster pop cover by Micki Marlo, although not by much. Brown's strongest release, it was a bit too pop to dent the stubborn R & B charts.

Attempts to crack into the mass market having proved fruitless, Brown now had to regain some prominence in the R & B arena. *Bye Bye Baby* spotlights rambling piano and vocal backup from Brown's old group, the Heavenly Lights, on a melodic, medium-beat love song by Billy Myles. As a sign of the times, the Heavenly Lights were billed as the "Zippers" on the single labels. By the end of 1956, rock-and-roll was in full flower, and R & B was regrouping to head in a different direction.

Brown responded to these changes by leaving the candy-store lyrics and teenage themes for harder, adult-oriented material. Recorded in October, 1957, *The Right Time* was a startling departure for the singer. His craggy voice soars, swoops, and hollers over the persistent beat and yammering choir in a performance that harks back to his gospel days. *The Right Time* was adapted by Brown from Roosevelt Sykes's 1937 recording *Night Time Is The Right Time*, and in 1958 Ray Charles did a version based on Brown's interpretation that sold well.

The gospel elements in Brown's later recordings are what make him a pivotal figure in the early development of soul music. The moody *My Baby* casts its spell via Brown's delicate phrasing and the brilliant arrangement by Teacho Wiltshire. *A Long Time* and *Down In The Alley* have prominent guitar-work as a counterpoint to the singer's sizzling delivery. In 1960, *Baby I Got News For You* was totally unlike anything else in the R & B field. Brown's voice is full of threat and hurt as he takes leave of his woman, and the ominous tone of the lyric is echoed in the instrumental backing.

Lighter pieces such as *Baby-Cry-Cry-Cry-Baby* are overshadowed by the intimidating force of *What's Come Over You, Baby* with its intoxicating, complex arrangement. Seldom has the tragedy of a dying love been so evocatively presented. The equally strong *Coal Miner*, by contrast, is a showcase of saxophone artistry with conga accompaniment by Ray Barretto.

I've Had My Fun is Brown's version of St Louis Jimmy's *Going Down Slow*, masterful in its use of vocal squalls and squeals as Brown out-blues the bluesmen, and *Didn't You Know* is everything Ray Charles was trying to do in secular gospel – carried to perfection. With this reaffirmation of his church roots, Brown left Savoy. Disgruntled over the constant loss of songwriting credits and royalties, he returned to the church choir in Charlotte.

In recent years, Brown has come back to the concert and recording circuit, doing his old hits and many other trademark songs on both sides of the Atlantic. During his active period of the late 1950s, he brought a strong church tone to the changing sound of rhythm and blues and his influence was far more extensive than his sparse representation in the hit charts would indicate.

In contrast to the well-recorded and far-travelling Ray Charles and Nappy Brown, Billy Wright made few records during his career and always returned to his home town of Atlanta, Georgia, where he was born on May 21, 1918 (he told some interviewers he was born in 1932, one of the more extreme examples of age-shaving in show business). Where Ray Charles dabbled in country in his early days and Nappy Brown was an accomplished gospel quartet singer, Wright brought little in the way of folk- or church-singing experience to his style, although he possessed one of the most thrilling voices in rhythm and blues.

Wright began in show business as a dancer at the age of nine and was soon touring the South and Midwest as part of a road show. In addition to his dancing in the chorus line, he developed a knack of imitating popular vocalists and was given a closing spot as a singer. After a brief stint as a soloist in Washington, DC, he returned to Atlanta, where he became a revered and respected fixture of the black community night life both as a performer and as a master of ceremonies.

Working as an opening act and announcer for the big stage shows, Wright came into contact with many of the superstars and budding talents of the postwar R & B movement and he in turn influenced them in vocal techniques and stagemanship. B.B. King called him "the greatest blues singer there was" and Little Richard borrowed much of the older man's style, including his dramatic pompadour. There was also a lot of Wright in the singing of Bobby Bland and Chuck Willis.

Starting in 1949, the Savoy label recorded Wright whenever they came down to Atlanta, and Wright was expected to provide fresh material and a band. The quality of the musical accompaniment on these tracks is a tribute to the professionalism of those local musicians. Much of his written material was a derivative patchwork of old, half-remembered blues lyrics from prewar days, but Wright always added his own touches and, however hoary the lyrics, his funky and preaching delivery made each tune sound brand-new.

This set is the first compilation by Wright, since his recording career ended before R & B albums became marketable and he was virtually unknown to the blues fans who sparked the later reissue album fervor. The opening cut, *After Dark Blues*, recorded in 1950, is a hand-clapping boogie excursion with the singer bending notes to good effect. Boogie blues such as this were a staple on Southern juke-boxes. *Thinkin' Blues* is standard blues in format and Wright's reedy, strained vocal matches perfectly the jazzy instrumentation.

The smooth sound of *Fore Day Blues* is a conscious attempt to fit into the mainstream of R & B as it was in 1950, with elaborate orchestration and careful enunciation. The song itself was taken from Ida Cox's *Fore Day Creep*, with a piece from *When You Feel Low Down* by Lonnie Johnson. Once again, Wright is able to create new gold from old ore. *Billy's Boogie Blues* owes a lot to Louis Jordan's jump boogie style, still all the rage in 1949 when this was recorded. A bewildering amalgam of common blues lines, it is saved from mediocrity by the heavy beat and Wright's uninhibited vocal.

The "real" Billy Wright comes to the fore in *Mercy, Mercy*, a tormented declaration of misery issued as the flip side of *Stacked Deck*, perhaps the most special of Wright's material. *Stacked Deck* uses the deck-of-cards metaphor to expose the heartbreak between a man and his woman, building slowly to a climax punctuated by Tom Hatton's surreal piano and a droning baritone sax. Like most of Wright's recordings, this one only made a moderate showing on the national charts, but was very popular in the Southeast.

Turn Your Lamps Down Low cemented Wright's reputation as a purveyor of the unusual in R & B. A call-and-response reprise of Big Joe Williams's *Baby Please Don't Go*, the tune spotlights lazy sax and muted trumpet melding with wistful vocalizing. *Keep Your Hands On Your Heart* remains true to the Lil Green–Bill Broonzy original, brought up-to-date with drawling tenor sax and Wright's consummate note-bending. Wright teamed with pianist Cleve Lyons for the engaging *Four Cold, Cold Walls* in May, 1953, wherein Wright's crystal-clear enunciation of despondency is soothed by the sympathetic Lyons.

The shouting vocal on the stop-time rhythm *Live The Life* is evidence of Wright's influence on Little Richard and features a searing guitar solo by Wesley Jackson. *I Remember*, a torchy blues ballad from the same session in 1954, was based on Cecil Gant's *I'll Remember You*, but while the basic idea came from Gant, Wright's version is completely in the vernacular of rhythm and blues, 1950s style.

The most rewarding cut on this set is a noisy acetate of a live performance from the early 1950s. Recorded at Atlanta's Harlem Theater, *Do Something* was used as a radio advertisement for the stage shows. Wright on stage is a revelation, as he drives his audience wild with screams and shrieks, cutting to the heart of the lyric in a way Clyde McPhatter and the Dominoes, who recorded it first, had never captured on record.

Wright never received more than a small portion of the fame and critical acknowledgment he deserved during his lifetime, but among those who count – his fellow musicians – he is regarded with envy and admiration. Wright died in Atlanta in October, 1991.

Little Richard – The Georgia Peach is 25 tracks – one hour – of unrelenting rock-and-roll by one of the few artists who can truthfully be called an originator of the form. Richard Penniman is the essence of all those who came before – Ray Charles, Nappy Brown, and Billy Wright – and much more besides. The personification of rock-and-roll with his wild eyes and fright-wig hair, Little Richard is still a constant and refreshing presence in these days of corporate rock – an archetypal reminder of the way things are supposed to be in the music with the big beat.

Born in Macon, Georgia, on December 5, 1932, Richard moved into the shadowy and colorful world of shake dancers, transvestites, and blues musicians at an early age, working the medicine shows and seamy juke joints of the Southeast with a scant repertoire of tunes lifted from Louis Jordan, Leadbelly, Nat Cole, and pop ballads. Like Billy Wright, his mentor, Richard made frequent appearances at the 81 Theater in Atlanta as an opening act for the black headliners and big bands.

On stage, his flamboyant dress and wildman antics drew crowds, but when he first recorded in 1951 for RCA-Victor the excitement did not carry over. With a vocal delivery and hairdo patterned after Wright's and a pounding piano style learned from the enigmatic Esquerita (Eskew Reeder, an eccentric and flamboyant rock-and-roller), Richard slowly built his popularity on the club circuit in the very early 1950s, but two sessions for Peacock with his own band, the Tempo Toppers, were also not successful.

In February, 1955, Richard started petitioning Specialty Records for a record deal. Finally, in exasperation, Art Rupe of Specialty instructed his music director, Robert "Bumps" Blackwell, to record the persistent vocalist in New Orleans. Blackwell set up studio time for a double session. Richard's reputation as a club-wrecker was not evident in the studio, however, and after a while Blackwell suggested everybody take a break. Despairing of getting a saleable track, Blackwell and Richard went to the Dew Drop Inn, where Richard promptly took over the stage.

The crowd's wild reaction to Richard's uninhibited piano thumping and screaming vocal was astonishing to the classically trained Blackwell. One number that particularly charmed the audience was *Tutti Frutti*, in its original configuration a bawdy song absolutely unfit for airplay. The lyrics could be changed – it was the excitement that Blackwell wanted to capture on wax. Back in the studio, local songwriter Dorothy La Bostrie was given a few minutes to come up with new words and Richard was installed at the piano bench in place of the session pianist. *Tutti Frutti*, a rock classic, was completed in 15 minutes.

The record hit the charts in late November, 1955, two months after it was recorded. *Tutti Frutti* rose to number 2 on all of the R & B charts and sold strongly for over five months. Right from the demented scat beginning, the listener knew nothing in music would ever be the same. Richard shouts the simple lyrics to his own ragged piano; the raw edge to his voice was due to "wrecking it" at the Dew Drop Inn earlier that evening. The thumping piano, honking sax figures, and shrieking vocal made a combination that had no precedent in R & B and became part of the Little Richard hit record formula.

I'm Just A Lonely Guy, from the same session, shows Richard's idea of a blues ballad, delivered with unparalleled emotional intensity. Drawing on the success of his first record, Richard formed a touring band with Chuck Connors (drums), Grady Gaines and Clifford Burks (tenor saxes), Sammy Parker (baritone), and Lee Diamond (sax and piano). Seeing and hearing the overwhelming power of this sax-heavy group in person helped spur public demand for Little Richard records.

Tutti Frutti crossed over into the pop charts and narrowly missed outselling a lackluster cover version by Pat Boone in the white market. Only competition from such classics as *The Great Pretender* by the Platters and *At My Front Door* by the El Dorados kept it from reaching the top slot in the R & B chart, but this was quickly rectified by Richard's next release. *Long Tall Sally* came from another young female writer, Enortis Johnson, but the packaging was pure Little Richard. The rapid-fire singing was done with the specific intent of making it harder for white artists to cover the song.

Recorded in February, it was on the R & B chart by April and hit number 1 two weeks later. *Long Tall Sally* whipped cover specialist Pat Boone in the pop charts this time, illustrating an increasing trend among young white buyers towards R & B originals. The flip side of the single, *Slippin' And Slidin' (Peepin' And Hidin')*, a Little Richard–Eddie Bo collaboration, also sold strongly in both markets. The next two releases were both double-sided smash hits. *Rip It Up* and *Ready Teddy* were summertime successes, while *She's Got It* and *Heeby-Jeebies* carried the teenagers back to school in the fall of 1956. All four were carefully contrived distillations of the Little Richard formula sound, but *She's Got It* is special in that it was the first time Richard used his own band at a recording session, this one in Hollywood instead of New Orleans.

Richard's bizarre onstage image was also enhanced to dramatize the radical nature of his music. No cute teenage idol could have generated the scenes of frenzy in the audience that became a fixture of Richard's numerous theater appearances. National audiences finally got a good look at their hero in the films "Don't Knock The Rock," wherein he sang *Tutti Frutti* and *Long Tall Sally*, and the big-budget "The Girl Can't Help It," starring pneumatic Jayne Mansfield and nerdy Tom Ewell.

Richard had only a moderate hit with *The Girl Can't Help It* despite its being one of his finest performances to date. The song was written by Bobby Troup, a pop and film-score composer, and it is the material and not the medium that is not up to par. On the other hand, *She's Got It*, also featured in the film, is one of the most stirring visual and aural delights from the early rock era.

The pounding *Lucille* returned Richard to the top position in the R & B list in April, 1957, and *Jenny, Jenny*, one of the most feverish excursions into rock madness ever captured on record, made it to number 2 later in the summer. By early 1958, his final great hits had been released: *Keep A Knockin'* and *Good Golly, Miss Molly. Keep A Knockin'* is based on an early Louis Jordan tune and was originally only a snippet of tape 57 seconds long, carefully looped into a fairly respectable length of 2 minutes 17 seconds. *Good Golly, Miss Molly* bears a melodic pedigree that includes Jackie Brenston's *Rocket 88* and Jimmy Liggins's *Cadillac Boogie*.

When Richard left Specialty in 1957 the hits stopped coming and a little bit of the music died, too. The company kept up a stream of new releases for a short time by using material from the vaults with overdubbed female choruses and additional instrumentation on tracks that sounded dated. Richard has also redone his classic hits many times, but these are the real thing – music that did not merely open the door to rock-and-roll, but knocked the house down.

When he first went to Los Angeles, Little Richard left his band, the Upsetters, holding the bag of some unfulfilled bookings, and his manager, Clint Brantley, hurriedly filled the vacuum with a young singer whose band had played intermissions for Richard in South Carolina. James Brown thus spent a few weeks of his early career billed as "Little Richard" even though the future Mr Dynamite shared little in common with Mr Tutti Frutti aside from a somewhat similar hairstyle.

Born in South Carolina in 1928 and raised in Georgia, Brown played many of the same venues as Richard, starting in 1953. From a beginning in extreme poverty, he had scuffled as a dancer, boxer, ball-player, and, finally, a jailbird. While doing time for burglary, Brown began singing gospel with Johnny Terry, and upon his release joined the Gospel Starlighters vocal quartet. With Terry and Bobby Byrd, he then formed an R & B trio patterned after Johnny Moore's Three Blazers.

First earning their way via renditions of other people's hits, the Famous Flames expanded in size and repertoire with the addition of vocalists Nashville Knox and Sylvester Keels and guitarist Nafloyd Scott. Brown developed an extremely extroverted and emotional singing style, playing upon the sanctified hollers and Holy-Roller physical movements of his gospel background. In November, 1955, Brown and the Flames cut a demo disc of a song he and Terry had written, *Please, Please, Please*. Manager Brantley sent copies to Leonard Chess of Chess Records and Don Robey of Duke Records in hopes of securing a recording contract.

Robey wanted the record, but did not offer enough money. Chess, too, was excited by what he heard but delayed coming down to Macon to sign the artist. In the meantime, Ralph Bass, talent scout for King Records, heard the demo at a radio station in Atlanta and drove to Macon to find the artist. Bass signed the group before he ever saw them perform. Where Bass had heard gold in Brown's visceral dynamism, Syd Nathan, the tightfisted owner of King, found only dross, and threatened to fire Bass for signing the artist and advancing him money to come to Cincinatti to record.

Bass put Brown and the Flames with sax men Clifford Scott, Wilbert Smith, and Ray Felder, plus Clarence Mack on bass and drummer Edison Gore to record *Please, Please, Please* on February 4, 1956. Bobby Byrd played piano and Nafloyd Scott was guitarist for this momentous occasion. Brown opens the song with a heartfelt plea in a quavering, angst-laden voice, and is joined by the rest of the group repeating the title in standard doo-wop fashion. Brown's stuttering repetition of "I-I-I" leads into a whispering reprise of the first verse, the "hook" that captures the listener (and record buyer).

The jump tune, *I Feel That Old Feeling Comin' On*, written by Knox and Scott of the Flames, makes heavy use of the "I-I-I" gimmick, leading one to think that this was Brown's specialty at the time. A whoop or two borrowed from Little Richard's bag of tricks and the party-shout backing by the group enhance the sax break. Also from this first session, *I Don't Know* gives full view of Brown's guttural and tortured voice over blow-notes (blown exhalations that build a solid wall of sound behind the lead singer) and droning reiteration of the title phrase by the group. Brown does a talking bridge in lieu of the instrumental break.

Success came immediately with the release of *Please, Please, Please*, and then vanished with the breeze. Brown's first record spent 19 weeks in the national charts and transformed the singer into a superstar for a brief time, although it failed to climb any higher than number 5. Once in a while, the public balks at follow-up records that are too similar to the hits, and this was one of those times. *I Feel That Old Feeling Comin' On* was coupled with *I Don't Know* for Brown's second record and sales were disappointing. It was over two years before he could achieve another smash hit.

For the most part, the tracks on **Please, Please, Please** chronicle forgotten and hitless years – hitless but not without great musical merit. With his first hit still a big seller, Brown was called back into the studio in March, 1956. *I Walked Alone* is another plea for love, with unison singing behind Brown's coarse, preachy lead. *No, No, No, No* makes use of the repetition that developed into Brown's sparse funk vocals years later, but *Chonnie-On-Chon* is the real gem of this session.

The tune kicks off with determined drums and melodic sax providing an inexorable boogie backdrop to Brown's manic and rasping vocal, combining to produce a brilliant jump blues. All of the elements of highly stylized doo-wop are present on *Just Won't Do Right*, including a dual lead with Bobby Byrd and propulsive piano by Lucas "Fats" Gonder, but Brown goes beyond the typical with his impassioned vocal. *Let's Make It* is based on Bill

Doggett's instrumental *Honky Tonk* and begins with a sax figure lifted note for note from part 2 of that great hit.

By the time this recording was released in October, 1956, it was apparent that R & B was changing to reflect the tastes of the mass white market. Still, Brown moved in a different direction and, despite the fact that none of his Federal recordings was a national hit, he was pulling black music behind him. The stark beauty of *Love Or A Game* is an early indication of Brown's desire to put the band and vocal backing in a subordinate position to his theatrical emoting. *That Dood It* is a rapping novelty reminiscent of Ray Charles's *Greenbacks*, with little else to recommend it.

That's When I Lost My Heart is an exquisite tune from the singer's prolific pen, and it is evident that the vocal group is now considered just part of the orchestra. The schizophrenic state of the national R & B charts in May, 1958, when *That's When I Lost My Heart* was released, is reflected in the fact that the number 1 R & B record in the country was *Wear My Ring Around Your Neck* by Elvis Presley.

Black music finally broke free from the influence of the white market in late 1958, thus setting the stage for the rise of soul. The record that accomplished this feat was *Try Me*, recorded in New York City by Brown in September. Abandoning all the white teenager trappings of rock-and-roll, Brown's eloquent appeal for love struck a responsive nerve among urban blacks. After hitting the charts in November, it rose to number 1 in February, 1959. The singer's career was revitalized just as he revitalized the music. Under the watchful eye and fearless leadership of "The Godfather Of Soul," soul music was launched.

The doomed angel of rhythm and blues, Little Esther was discovered by Johnny Otis when she was just 13 years old, belting out Dinah Washington songs. By the time she was 15, she had a national number 1 hit record and was on cross-country tours with Otis's big band. Before she left her teen years she was also a heroin addict.

Born Esther Mae Jones in Galveston, Texas, on December 23, 1935, her early life was filled with music, and she could play drums, trumpet, and piano. Moving with her family to Los Angeles, she was swept up in the whirlwind of the new music, rhythm and blues, as performed by Charles Brown, Amos Milburn, Lowell Fulson, and T-Bone Walker. Her major vocal influence was Dinah Washington, but aside from a certain breathy, insinuating tone, there is little similarity between the two.

Esther's effect on the R & B market of 1950 cannot be overstated. In that single year, she had three number 1 records, and monopolized the top spot for 14 weeks. Unable to work a better deal with Savoy's Herman Lubinsky, who was reaping thousands of dollars from those hits, Otis first took his entourage to Modern Records and then made an arrangement sending Esther to Federal in early 1951. **Better Beware** collects the lesser-known recordings that resulted from this association.

It should be noted that Esther never sounded like a "kid" singer; right from the first, the depth and breadth of her voice conveyed completely adult yearnings. The tracks on this set were all made before she turned 18 years old. Her first session for Federal was held on January 26, 1951, in Cincinnati with Otis's band and the Dominoes in attendance. *Looking For A Man* is a mellow jump with delightful alto sax by Earl Warren and an evocative guitar break by Pete Lewis.

The cocktail-lounge torch song *Other Lips, Other Arms* has Esther bringing her husky voice close to the mike, while Devonia Williams trills up and down the ivories. *The Deacon Moves In*, the final track from this session, brings on the Dominoes in an attempt to recreate the boy–girl patter of Esther's biggest hit, *Double Crossing Blues*. Despite the wonderful rocking background, party chatter, and wild climax, there is no disguising the 40-ish origins of the song. "Deacons" were no longer sure-fire record subject material in 1951.

I'm A Bad, Bad Girl offers the same instrumental and vocal group lineup, with Esther wringing every nuance out of the lyrics. The smooth and swinging Otis band reaches new heights of big-band R & B. *Crying And Singing The Blues* is cut from the same cloth, but the market was looking for a harder sound and remained resistant to giving her another hit. Finally, at the end of 1951, Esther returned to the charts with the moderate jump *Ring-A-Ding Doo*. Another duet, this time with Mel Walker, her partner on several Savoy hits, the song owed a lot to Paul Williams's giant dance hit from 1949, *The Hucklebuck*, but only managed to reach the bottom rungs of the chart ladder. This mediocre showing was to be her best for Federal.

The previously unreleased *Hold Me* is, ironically, one of her finest performances of this period. Esther dissects the lyric with delicacy and feeling. The blues shout *Better Beware*, which was ignored at the time, is a finely honed production both musically and vocally. In addition to Esther's expressive piping, the start of this track are saxman Lorenzo Holderness and the guitar of Pete Lewis.

Life on the road with Otis was grueling and demanding. The band never stopped touring, doing one-nighters from New York to Detroit and Los Angeles. The package got a minimum of $600 per night, plus a percentage of the gate, so it is doubtful whether Esther was making a lot of money. In May, 1951, she sued Savoy for back royalties and was promptly countersued for damages from breach of contract to the tune of $50,000. She was unable to prevent Savoy from issuing new and recoupled tracks from their vaults.

When Otis switched from Savoy to Mercury in November, 1951, he was unable to bring Esther with him, although his band continued to moonlight behind her on Federal. After *Ring-A-Ding Doo*, she had no further chart hits. *Aged And Mellow Blues*, with its clever lyrics, the scatting *Ramblin' Blues*, and the melodramatic *The Storm*, complete with thundering sound effects, are three of her most persuasive offerings, the last providing magnificent counterpoint between Esther and Pete Lewis. *Saturday Night Daddy*, an early Jerry Leiber and Mike Stoller composition that is considered a classic today, recreated the excitement of her first duet with Bobby Nunn, but with liberal doses of steamy and direct sex. Also from Leiber and Stoller, *Mainliner* is a real rocker, although the scratchy sound-effects record used to create the train theme adds an unintentional camp flavor. Using Leiber–Stoller material helped put the songs, at least, back on the cutting edge of rhythm and blues.

Another denizen of the Los Angeles R & B scene, Little Willie Littlefield, joins Esther on *Last Laugh Blues* and *Turn The Lamps Down Low*, but neither the material nor the contrast in their singing styles works well. *Flesh, Blood and Bones* shows Esther to be easily a match for the better-selling female shouters of the era, and it is amazing that this record was not a big hit. Whatever personal demons were pursuing her at the time, they obviously did not affect her singing. Esther made her final session for Federal in Cincinnati on March 11, 1953, with studio musicians. *Cherry Wine* was a regional success but failed to make the restricted and short list of national hits. Her rendition of *Hound Dog* can only be described as uncomfortable. The singer tries too hard to imitate Big Mama Thornton's original version and the musical backing is uneven and dull. After leaving Federal, Esther spent 1954 recording for Decca, but without success. At the age of 18, sick and broke, she returned to Texas to stay with her grandfather.

In 1956, Esther made a highly touted comeback for Savoy, but sales of the two releases from this association did not warrant having her do a second session. She again dropped from sight, this time until early 1959, when she recorded once more for Savoy. In 1960 she did an abortive session for Morty Craft's Warwick label and, finally, with her drug habit in remission, recorded the country hit *Release Me* for Lelan Rogers's Nashville-based Lenox Records. From this she moved to Atlantic for a series of records that sold well. The remainder of her career included a hit live album in 1970 and a reunion with Johnny Otis. Club work and tours of Europe helped rebuild her fame over the next decade, but her wracked body finally succumbed in August, 1984.

During a time when R & B was first declaring its independence from pop and jazz, Little Esther was the top female singing star, and her themes of love and loss were delivered from the heart of a tortured soul. Small wonder she has finally been elevated to legendary status – her followers are legion.

In a musical world where black female singers sang the blues and torch songs or were gospel-tinged shadows of their white pop counterparts, Etta James was a hot blast from the West Coast. She rocked, she rolled, she jumped the boogie just like the best of the male shouters. She was street-tough and brassy, a blonde bundle of talent who was a sensation wherever she appeared. **R & B Dynamite** collects her earliest material, recorded between 1954 and 1958 for the Los Angeles-based Modern Records.

Jamesetta Hawkins was born in Los Angeles on January 25, 1938, and was just 16 years old when she made her first session. *The Wallflower* (listed as *Roll With Me, Henry* on this CD) is an answer to Hank Ballard's *Work With Me Annie*. With Richard Berry and the Peaches (Abbye Mallory and Jean Mitchell) in support, James delivers the lyrics in a self-assured manner, her rich voice showing little trace of her tender years. The single moved up the charts quickly after its release in early 1955 and claimed the top spot in R & B in April, displacing Johnny Ace's *Pledging My Love*.

The Wallflower stayed at number 1 for a month and sold heavily for 19 weeks, weeks that were crowded with controversy over the lyric content. The objections were directed at the use of the word "roll" so prominently in the song. A more acceptable version substituting the word "dance" was a number 1 pop smash by Georgia Gibbs, and James also did a *Dance With Me, Henry* that appeared only on LP somewhat later.

The young singer immediately left on a series of cross-country tours with various R & B package shows, usually in the company of Johnny Otis. A follow-up release, the contrived *Hey Henry*, again with Richard Berry doing second lead, failed to excite buyers. *Be Mine* (titled *Be My Lovey Dovey* and incorrectly designated as unissued on this set) was the flip side of *Hey Henry* and is a pleasant, medium-tempo jump, with James giving a breathy and sweet interpretation over chanting vocal backing. Her third release, *Good Rockin' Daddy*, storms along from start to finish with a choppy boogie beat and inspired work by the Dreamers, Richard Berry's vocal group. The tune hit the national charts in November, 1955, but failed to register any higher than number 6 for an anemic three-week stay. It was her last chart hit for Modern and she was not to return to the star spotlight for five long years.

The torchy *Crazy Feeling* (listed as *Do Something Crazy*) was coupled with *Good Rockin' Daddy* and unjustly ignored by record buyers. Her superb performance over strong big-band backing and wailing vocal chorus pulls out all the stops with smooth, sensuous note-bending. *That's All*, released at the end of 1955, is a reworking of the Sister Rosetta Tharpe hit of 1942, complete with biting guitar.

W-O-M-A-N is a salacious and withering answer to Bo Diddley's *I'm A Man*. The rolling *I'm A Fool* appeared in March, 1956, by which time the singer was struggling with a drug addiction that affected her onstage performances very little and is not discernible on record. *Tears Of Joy* (track 11, not track 10 as the CD indicates) is reminiscent of the Lavern Baker style, but James injects a raw squall. Sounding like a female Little Richard, James rollicks and sputters through the hand-clapper *Tough Lover*, recorded in New Orleans with Lee Allen and Dave Bartholomew's hot band in early 1956 in an attempt to get a harder rocking sound on her records.

The Pick Up (track 12, listed as 11) is a hilarious "conversation" with the tenor sax of Plas Johnson, with a melody line very close to that of Ruth Brown's *Smooth Operator* of a few years before. The tempo-changing *Market Place*, chosen as the flip side of *The Pick Up*, works hard to attain a more commercial sound. When the coupling was released in March, 1957, *Jim Dandy* by Lavern Baker and *Love Is Strange* by Mickey and Sylvia were topping the charts, and James was struggling for her share of the attention.

The Modern label was discontinued in early 1958 and James and several other artists were switched to the Kent logo. On *Baby, Baby Everynight* she sounds a great deal like her close friend, Ruth Brown, and *Sunshine Of Love*, the reverse side, is likewise aimed at the mainstream R & B market. James's usual exuberance is somewhat muted on these otherwise good songs. *How Big A Fool* (track 10, not 12 as shown) is an experiment in double-tracking James's vocal, but her performance is uneven, rough and vaguely unsatisfying. Later in 1958 James hooked up with Harvey Fuqua and he took her music in a different direction. The duets on the charming *I Hope You're Satisfied* and the engaging *We're In Love* are products of this association.

James left Modern and went to Chess with Fuqua in late 1959, and promptly scored a stunning comeback record with *All I Could Do Was Cry*. In the ensuing years she has proven that she has the resilience to overcome the twin devils of drug addiction and a tough and heartless business. Now a spokesperson against substance abuse, Etta James is a familiar sight on TV and stages across the country. Despite annoying inaccuracies in notes and track listing, this set is a fine document of the roots and development of a remarkable talent.

Discographical Details

1 The Birth Of Soul
Ray Charles
Atlantic 7 82310-2 (3-disc set)
The Sun's Gonna Shine Again/Roll With My Baby/ The Midnight Hour/Jumpin' In the Mornin'/It Should Have Been Me (sic) /Losing Hand/Heartbreaker/Sinner's Prayer/Mess Around/Funny But I Still Love You/Feelin' Sad/I Wonder Who/Don't You Know/Nobody Cares/Ray's Blues/Mr. Charles Blues/Blackjack/I Got A Woman (sic)/Greenbacks/Come Back Baby (sic)/A Fool For You/This Little Girl Of Mine/ Hard Times/A Bit Of Soul/Mary Ann/Drown In My Own Tears/Hallelujah I Love Her So/What Would I Do Without You/Lonely Avenue/I Want To Know/Leave My Woman Alone/It's Alright/Ain't That Love/Get On The Right Track/Rockhouse, Pts 1 & 2/Swanee River Rock/That's Enough/Talkin' About You/What Kind Of Man Are You/I Want A Little Girl/Yes Indeed/I Had A Dream/You Be My Baby/Tell All The World About You/My Bonnie/Early In The Morning/The Right Time/Carryin' The Load/Tell Me How Do You Feel/What'd I Say, Pts 1 & 2/Tell The Truth/I'm Movin' On/I Believe To My Soul

2 That Man
Nappy Brown
Mr R & B 10C (Swe) (LP)
That Man/I Wonder (What's Wrong With Me)/ Is It True – Is It True/Two Faced Woman (And A Lyin' Man)/Open Up That Door (And Walk Right In My Heart)/ Little By Little/Bye Bye Baby/My Baby/The Right Time/A Long Time/Down In The Alley/Baby I Got News For You/Baby-Cry-Cry-Cry-Baby/What's Come Over You, Baby/Coal Miner/I've Had My Fun/Didn't You Know

3 Stacked Deck
Billy Wright
Route 66 KIX-13 (Swe) (LP)
After Dark Blues/Thinkin' Blues/Fore Day Blues/Billy's Boogie Blues/Mercy, Mercy/ Married Woman's Boogie/Keep Your Hands On Your Heart/Stacked Deck/Turn Your Lamps Down Low/Every Evening/Four Cold, Cold Walls/Live The Life/I Remember/ Do Something

4 The Georgia Peach
Little Richard
Specialty SPCD-7012-2
Tutti Frutti/Baby/I'm Just A Lonely Guy/True Fine Mama/Kansas City – Hey-Hey-Hey-Hey (medley)/Slippin' And Slidin' (Peepin' And Hidin')/Long Tall Sally/ Miss Ann/Oh Why/Ready Teddy/Hey-Hey-Hey-Hey/Rip It Up/Lucille/Heeby-Jeebies/Can't Believe You Wanna Leave/Shake A Hand/All Around The World/ She's Got It/Jenny Jenny/Good Golly, Miss Molly/The Girl Can't Help It/Send Me Some Lovin'/Ooh! My Soul/Keep A Knockin'/Whole Lotta Shakin' Goin' On

5 Please, Please, Please
James Brown and the Famous Flames
Polydor 1847 (Jap)

Please, Please, Please/Chonnie-On-Chon/Hold My Baby's Hand/I Feel That Old Feeling Coming On/Just Won't Do Right/Baby Cries Over The Ocean/I Don't Know/ Tell Me What I Did Wrong/Try Me/That Dood It/Begging Begging/I Walked Alone/ No No No No/That's When I Lost My Heart/Let's Make It/Love Or A Game

6 Better Beware

Little Esther

Charly CD 248 (UK)

Looking For A Man/Other Lips, Other Arms/The Deacon Moves In/I'm A Bad, Bad Girl/Crying And Singing The Blues/Ring-A-Ding Doo/Hold Me/Better Beware/Aged And Mellow Blues/Ramblin' Blues/The Storm/Hollerin' And Screamin'/Saturday Night Daddy/Mainliner/You Took My Love Too Fast/Last Laugh Blues/Flesh, Blood And Bones/Turn The Lamps Down Low/Cherry Wine/Hound Dog

7 R & B Dynamite

Etta James

Flair/Virgin 2-91695

W-O-M-A-N/Number One/I'm A Fool/Strange Things Happen/Hey Henry/[I]Hope You're Satisfied'/Good Rockin' Daddy/Sunshine Of Love/That's All/Tears Of Joy/The Pick Up/How Big A Fool/Market Place/Tough Lover/Do Something Crazy (sic)/Be My Lovey Dovey (sic)/Nobody Loves You (Like Me)/Hickory Dickory Dock/You Know What I Mean/Roll With Me, Henry (sic)/Baby, Baby Everynight/We're In Love

(ii) Why Do Fools Fall In Love?

The dawn of the R & B era had very little to do with vocal harmony groups. The biggest names in the black vocal group field were the Mills Brothers and the Ink Spots, pioneers with extensive experience dating back to the early 1930s. While extremely popular, the Mills Brothers and Ink Spots did not reflect the black lifestyle in their songs. Neither group was grounded in gospel or church music; the Mills Brothers were radio stars and the Ink Spots were originally a hot jazz ensemble.

Being black was the greatest contribution the two supergroups made to black music. When the new and exciting R & B sound was being developed, most groups were vocal/instrumental combinations loosely based in swing music or jazz. Straight vocal quartets such as the Delta Rhythm Boys, the Golden Gate Quartet or the Charioteers stuck very close to popular music in their repertoires. The Ravens, whose 1946 appearance on the scene has been considered the origination of the R & B vocal group sound, merely carried the Ink Spots' high-tenor–deep-basso formula a bit further.

The Orioles, who came into prominence in 1948, brought a dreamy, untutored elegance and charm to black music, again without a grounding in gospel. There is no doubt that Sonny Til's marvelous voice and stage presence did much to further acceptance of the modern black vocal quartet, but the music was still basic pop.

The Five Royales of Winston-Salem, North Carolina, brought the elements of gospel, jazz, and blues to the vocal group style in 1951, one of the very first groups to do so. The group had been singing gospel since 1938 and made their first recordings in that genre in 1951. It was constructed around the extraordinary songwriting talents of Lowman Pauling (bass singer and guitar player) and the dramatic dual lead voices of brothers Johnny and Eugene Tanner. Doubling in the tenor or baritone parts as needed were Obediah Carter and Jimmy Moore. **Baby Don't Do It** chronicles some of the earliest recordings and major hits by the group.

Let Nothing Separate Me is a glimpse of the group in its gospel phase. The careful rhythm accompaniment and heartfelt group backing effectively bracket Johnny Tanner's enraptured and soaring lead voice. It was that performance, no doubt, that induced Apollo Records executives to have the group try rhythm and blues. After two gospel releases as "The Royal Sons," *Too Much Of A Little Bit* was recorded in October, 1951. A Lowman Pauling composition, the drinking theme is enlivened by infectious boogie piano, handclapping, and joyous ad-libs from the group behind Pauling's smoky lead.

Sales of the first two R & B waxings by the Five Royales were only moderate, but the group found the magic key a year later. *Baby Don't Do It* is a strong combination of gospel piano, jazz orchestra backing, and exhilarating lead voice by Johnny Tanner. Tanner swoops and soars in high-energy, dramatic fashion. The powerful song found a place on the charts in early 1953 and was number 1 in the nation by the end of February. The other side of the single, *Baby Take All Of Me*, is an uninhibited rocker enhanced by superb tenor and baritone sax interplay, with the group casting aside all restraints.

Also recorded in 1952, although not released until 1954, *Let Me Come Back Home* is a run-of-the-mill ballad lifted above dullness solely by Tanner's high-register piping and wailing. The previously unissued *I Wanna Rest*, probably recorded a bit earlier, features a gang-sing vocal and is a curious amalgam of gospel and 1940s pop styles, in an obvious attempt to add some excitement to an old spiritual.

The next hit by the Five Royales, *Help Me Somebody*, starts out as a slow, heavy-beat blues but is saved by a tricky tempo change and truly remarkable lead vocal. A compelling performance, it too reached the top spot on the charts, displacing Willie Mabon's *I'm Mad* in June, 1953. The Five Royales never had a better year than 1953 and their popularity drove the flip side of the single, *Crazy, Crazy, Crazy*, to number 5 on the Juke Box sales chart. The same instrumental lineup that was a highlight of their *Baby Take All Of Me* is again used to good effect.

All Righty and the unreleased *I Am Thinking* are from July, 1953. The first is a tenor-sax–vocal-lead duet with pronounced backbeat. Apollo relied heavily upon the musical talents of tenor saxman Charlie "Little Jazz" Ferguson rather than the usual New York studio bands with Sam "The Man" Taylor, giving a fresh, special sound to their recordings. *I Am Thinking*, on the other hand, is a contrived, sentimental blues with neither the band nor the group really getting together.

By the time 1954 rolled around, the Five Royales' star was already descending in the face of stiff competition from such groups as the Midnighters, the Drifters, and a host of younger aggregations. The teenage movement in R & B left many of the more seasoned performers behind. *I Do*, released in January, 1954, made a brief chart appearance, but the close harmony style was out of vogue by then and some of the creative energy seems to be gone from their performance.

Cry Some More has a competent lead vocal on a pedestrian ballad that never seems to take off, while *I Like It Like That*, a rocking riff number, has all the rousing party flavor of their earlier material. The group left Apollo for King Records in June, 1954, in a flurry of lawsuits for back royalties and claims of broken contracts. Apollo issued two more singles by the Five Royales, including *(Put Something In It) With All Your Heart*, heard here as an alternate take.

While with King, the group did some brilliant and unjustly neglected recordings, among them *Think, Tears of Joy*, and the original of Lowman Pauling's most famous composition, *Dedicated To The One I Love*, but their former fame was never recovered. The group finally disbanded in the mid-1960s; their great guitarist/songwriter Lowman Pauling died a forgotten man in 1974. Among the select few true innovators, the Five Royales made a great contribution in moving black group singing away from pop traditions, and they also pioneered in featuring adult themes, a mode that was gratefully embraced once again some years later by soul music.

The Moonglows rode the crest of the first wave of rock-and-roll to become a nationally known R & B vocal group, under the guidance of influential disc jockey Alan Freed. The style they brought to the music had its roots in jazz and the harmony technique of blow-notes. The kingpins of the Moonglows, Harvey Fuqua and Bobby "Bobby Lester" Dallas, were born in Louisville, Kentucky, where they first met in high school.

Fuqua's famous uncle, Charlie Fuqua of the Ink Spots, provided the impetus for Harvey to enter show business, and Harvey and Lester sang as a duet and also performed as a piano–

vocal combo with Lester singing to Fuqua's accompaniment. The duo toured briefly with Ed Wiley's band in the early 1950s but by 1952 Fuqua was in Cleveland and Lester still in Louisville.

While in Cleveland, Fuqua formed a jazz vocalese trio called the Crazy Sounds. Attracting the attention of the up-and-coming disc jockey Alan Freed, the group began performing rhythm-and-blues material and was renamed the Moonglows by Freed, who was then working as "Moondog." After a single release on Freed's own label, Champagne, the group was reformed to include Harvey Fuqua, Bobby Lester, Alexander "Pete" Walton, Prentiss Barnes, and guitarist Billy Johnson. It was this lineup that recorded their most famous tunes, collected on **Sincerely**.

Their first major recording contract was with Chicago's Chance Records, where they made a series of lovely ballads and rough-edged jump tunes from 1953 to 1954. When Chance went under, they moved to Chess. All of their records were heavily promoted by Alan Freed in New York City and they made frequent appearances on his live shows. Their first release on Chess became their biggest hit.

Sincerely, written by Fuqua and Freed, opens with one of the most recognizable vocal riffs of the era, the basso imitating a saxophone. Following this, the second tenor and baritone lay down a blow-note backdrop for Lester's impassioned and dramatic lead reading. The song ends with the Moonglows' formula "oow-wah" in harmony. The simplicity of the song and its skillfully woven tapestry of voices proved very popular. After appearing on the chart in December, 1954, *Sincerely* bumped the Penguins' *Earth Angel* out of the number 1 spot just one month later.

All told, *Sincerely* spent 20 weeks on the national R & B chart and sold strongly for months afterward. It even made a brief appearance on the pop juke-box list, but sales in the mainstream market went to the cover version by the McGuire Sisters, a version that held onto the number 1 pop position for 10 weeks. Nonetheless, the Moonglows were catapulted into the top ranks of R & B performers overnight.

The exciting Moonglows ballad technique continued to delight fans with *Most Of All*, released in March, 1955, and a number 5 on *Billboard's* Jockey's chart measuring radio play. Lester's gliding lead is bracketed by warm bass and soaring falsetto in this virtual twin to the Moonglows' first hit. Subsequent releases did not do as well despite their uniform excellence. *In My Diary*, on the market by the end of 1955, is a jazz-weighted love song with all the tricks of the trade – close harmony, high second tenor, burbling bass, and forceful lead.

With the rock-and-roll movement in full flood, *We Go Together* brought the group back to the charts in June, 1956. Written by

Cleveland songwriters, Shelley Haims and Percy Stevens (composer of *Come Spring*), the song captured the hearts and dollars of love-struck teenagers all across the country. Using a dual lead punctuated by an ethereal falsetto tenor, the catchy melody is given enough twists, turns, and tempo changes to keep the listener enthralled.

The two-sided hit *See Saw* and *When I'm With You* followed the jump/ballad format used on most R & B records in the middle 1950s. *See Saw*, written by Billy Davis, is a rock-and-roll jewel that gives full exposure to Billy Johnson's twangy guitar. Backing here is provided by James Moody's band, with Moody himself delivering a marvelous alto sax break, proving once again that jazz artists could rock with the best of them. Topping it all off, Fuqua's yodeling lead adds interesting complexity. The ballad side was written by Lester and Fuqua and features tricky, scale-climbing harmony from the group behind Fuqua's choking cries.

The Moonglows continued their unenviable string of once-a-year hits followed by flops with *I Knew From The Start*, a medium-beat ballad performed in the film "Rock, Rock, Rock." Despite the impressive rendition by the group and publicity generated by the film appearance, the song was unable to break into a chart dominated at the end of 1956 by Elvis Presley, Fats Domino, and Ivory Joe Hunter. *Please Send Me Someone To Love*, *Don't Say Goodbye*, and *Love Is A River* are all from the same session, representing a major change in direction for the group.

Please Send Me Someone To Love is a beautiful reading of the Percy Mayfield hit song from 1950 with its plea for universal peace and understanding. Piano triplets maintain the R & B tradition, but Fuqua's crystalline diction and subdued group-work is aimed at the major market. Other songs from this session, intended for a Moonglows' LP that was never issued, were overlaid with strings.

Don't Say Goodbye is virtually a solo performance by Bobby Lester that had little to recommend it to either pop or R & B buyers. Perhaps Chess was trying to make the group into another Platters. The same comments apply to *Love Is A River*. Both songs fell into the cracks and found little airplay. *The Beating Of My Heart* is a gentle R & B ballad unfortunately eclipsed by changes in public tastes by the time it was released in September, 1957.

The original group broke up in November, 1958, a split precipitated by the departure of Bobby Lester. *Ten Commandments Of Love* was a chart hit at the time, billed as by "Harvey and the Moonglows." This melodramatic reading made inroads in both the pop and R & B markets but marked the decline of the Moonglows. In later years various former members have kept the name alive with new groups, but there is no doubt that the Chess material recorded between 1954 and 1958 is all anyone ever needs to hear by the group.

Harvey Fuqua has carved a remarkable and successful career in singing and record production since he left the group and continues to be a force in music. The great ballad voice of the Moonglows, Bobby Lester, died in 1980.

After a period of domination totaling five years, the heyday of the rhythm-and-blues vocal group was over by the late 1950s. Groups did not disappear, but the old singing styles, bowdlerized into doo-wop, fell out of favor. Those groups that remained had to make the transition into the newer, harder, urban music forms or they did not survive. Making the change was a difficult proposition for many groups, and those first attempts often sound awkward and contrived in retrospect.

Detroit's Falcons managed to bridge the gap between doo-wop and soul and even made a couple of hits while doing it. **You're So Fine** is a musical journal of their earliest tracks, more than half of which remained unreleased until the tapes were pulled from the producer's closet 30 years later. The Falcons were an integral and influential part of the pre-Motown Detroit music scene.

The group was formed in 1955 as a quintet containing two white members, an unusual content for the time. In August, 1956, their first recording, *Baby That's It*, was released by Mercury with Eddie Floyd doing the lead. A straight, up-tempo rhythm number with a Latin flavor, the tight harmonies are overshadowed by erratic drumming, with the result only an average doo-wopper. The original lineup disbanded after this recording and their manager, Eddie Floyd's uncle Robert West, reformed the Falcons as a quartet with guitar accompaniment.

The roster then consisted of Eddie Floyd and Joe Stubbs (lead tenors), Mack Rice (baritone), Willie Schofield (bass), and Lance Finnie (guitar). West decided to record the group for his own labels with an eye to leasing the masters to other companies. The bluesy boogie *Sent Up*, with lead by Mack Rice, appeared late in 1957 on the Silhouette logo. Lance Finnie's dynamic string-work easily steals the show from the singers on this early track.

Eddie Floyd's reedy squall dominates the previously unissued *I Wonder* from the same period, with the band substituting raw enthusiasm for musicality on a driving rocker. The barnyard parody *No Time For Fun* also reposed in the can undisturbed for a few decades, West being astute enough to detect little commercial fodder on the track. All of the experimentation and false starts finally bore fruit with *You're So Fine*, the kind of hit record that independent producers daydream about.

Joe Stubbs takes the lead on this track recorded in early 1959, coming in after an exquisite guitar introduction from Finnie. Stubbs, a brother of the Four Tops' Levi Stubbs, had worked with

Finnie in the Fabulous Four, a short-lived high-school group from Detroit. After *You're So Fine* began to be a success in Detroit and Chicago, West leased the master to United Artists, and national distribution boosted the record into the pop and R & B charts in April, 1959.

Selling for over 20 weeks on both charts added up to a huge hit, even though the disc was unable to nudge the competition from the number 1 spot. It first hovered at the heels of Wilbert Harrison's *Kansas City*, then dogged *Personality*, Lloyd Price; *There Goes My Baby*, the Drifters; and *What'd I Say*, Ray Charles. Perhaps if United Artists had been a stronger label or the other contenders less formidable, the record would have made number 1.

West retained the tapes of his Falcons' material and his closet vault yielded *Juke Hop*, a standard rocking party story, and *Anytime, Anyplace, Anywhere*, a reprise of the old Joe Morris–Laurie Tate hit from 1950, done in a curiously old-fashioned, mellow style. *Goddess Of Angels* is an atmospheric weeper done with commendable delicacy by Eddie Floyd, and was used as the flip side of their giant hit. Chess was holding some leased Falcons' tracks and decided to have the group redo the sides. *Just For Your Love* as heard here is a previously unissued alternate take of the Chess version that made a brief entry into the charts.

On *Just For Your Love*, the expressive Joe Stubbs leads the group in a pleasant jump tune that unfortunately lacks the emotional power of *You're So Fine*, although it contains a lyrical allusion to that hit song. *You're Mine* is a more blatant attempt to strike gold again with a close sound-alike, this time layered with the currently popular string section. The weak United Artists organization was unable to place this fine release anywhere in the hit ranks.

From the pile of unissued tapes, *Girl Of My Dreams* is the most promising, showcasing Joe Stubbs at his penetrating best. With the arrival of Wilson Pickett in the summer of 1960, Stubbs was gradually phased out of the group, which then stepped full stride into soul. Pickett, Floyd, and Rice all carved out careers for themselves as solo soul performers in subsequent years. The Falcons anticipated soul, and their moving and forceful technique lighted the way for dozens of vocal groups that followed.

Discographical Details

8 Baby Don't Do It

The Five Royales

Relic 7010

Baby Don't Do It/Baby Take All Of Me/(Put Something In It) With All Your Heart/ All Righty/Too Much Of A Little Bit/I Am Thinking/I Like It Like That/Help Me

Somebody/Crazy, Crazy, Crazy/I Wanna Rest/Let Me Come Back [Home]/I Do/Cry Some More/Let Nothing Separate Me

9 Sincerely
The Moonglows

Blues Journey SSI 865

Sincerely/Most Of All/We Go Together/See Saw/When I'm With You/Please Send Me Someone To Love/Ten Commandments Of Love/The Beating Of My Heart/In My Diary/I Knew From The Start/Don't Say Goodbye/Love Is A River

10 You're So Fine
The Falcons

Relic 7003

You're So Fine/Please Don't Leave Me Dear/Just For Your Love/(When) You're In Love/Girl Of My Dreams/Let It Be Me/Goddess Of Angels/Sent Up/You're Mine/Baby That's It/Anytime, Anyplace, Anywhere/I Wonder/Juke Hop/No Time For Fun/Whose Little Girl Are You/I'll Never Find Another Girl Like You

(iii) Harlem Hit Paraders

While the ranks of rhythm-and-blues artists swelled with ex-gospel shouters and quartets, bringing a thrilling, hard edge to the music, acceptance of this style by the multitudes of pop and rock-and-roll fans remained fragmentary. In R & B itself, the "blues" ingredient was usually represented by down-home or urban guitar and harmonica wailers. Major solo artists were shouters or urbane crooners such as Ivory Joe Hunter. What was lacking was a ballad crooner who sang the blues, and that vacuum was filled in 1952 by Johnny Ace.

Collections of Johnny Ace will necessarily be short since he only released ten singles, and four of those were posthumous. Such was his effect on listeners that he scored eight hits (three number 1s) in three years and Johnny Ace songs were in the charts for a total of 92 weeks during that time. He accomplished this feat through some of the most tear-drenched lyrics in the business, all delivered in a voice of deepest blue.

Johnny Ace's **Memorial Album** is a direct CD reissue of a 1956 album and remains the best view of this musical phenomenon. John Marshall Alexander was born in Memphis on June 9, 1929, a member of a large family headed by a preacher. He began playing piano at a very young age and after a short stint in the US Navy started working with the Beale Streeters, which included Bobby Bland and B.B. King. By 1950, this band was a top draw in the Memphis area. He first used his voice in addition to his piano on a radio broadcast with the Beale Streeters.

Now called Johnny Ace, the singer signed with Duke Records in early 1952 and his first release brought him instant fame. *My Song* is based on the Russ Morgan hit *So Long*, given a rhythm-and-blues style in 1949 by Ruth Brown and altered just enough by Ace and his then manager James Mattis to avoid copyright infringement. The simple lyric is laid out by Ace's smooth baritone while he noodles on the piano, and the pathos is perfectly matched by reedy, mournful tenor sax from Adolph Duncan.

Substantial regional sales of *My Song* brought the singer and his label under the wing of Don Robey's Peacock label, based in Houston, and improved distribution moved it into the national charts in August, 1952. By the end of September it had swept aside the Clovers' *Ting-A-Ling* to take the top spot, where it remained for nine weeks, eventually outselling all 1952 R & B records except the Dominoes' *Have Mercy Baby*.

Cross My Heart was shipped to eager Johnny Ace fans as the follow-up to this enormous hit in January, 1953. Recorded in the same radio studio as *My Song*, the song has an identical dreamlike sound quality, due more to studio acoustics than to creative engineering. A tubby bass is further anchored by Ace's Hammond organ, an instrument he played for the first time at that session, plus two horns and vibes. After achieving the number 3 position on the Juke Box charts, it provided Ace with another 10-week chart run.

In March, *The Clock* very nearly repeated the success of Ace's first release. After a mood-setting introduction of a ticking "clock" and Ace's gentle piano, the overwhelming gloom of the lyric is convincingly interpreted. There are few other R & B performances that can compare with the poignancy of *The Clock*, and the record buyers of the time apparently recognized this. Ace had found his niche, and he held tight in it for the rest of his recording career.

Saving My Love For You was recorded in Los Angeles in August, 1953, with the Johnny Otis Band, while Ace was on a lengthy tour with Willie Mae Thornton. Otis's celesta-like vibes carry the diaphanous mood to new heights (or depths) of melancholy. Like Ace's previous releases, this song remained a saloon juke-box favorite for many weeks, being especially suitable for those dark, depressing moments just before closing time.

Johnny Board's orchestra provides the sophisticated backdrop for Ace's torchy vocal and dramatic piano runs on *Never Let Me Go*, a lovely ballad from the pen of trumpeter Joe Scott. Despite the enhanced production values, it did not sell well and may have marked an inevitable decline in public acceptance of Ace's languorous style. Rock-and-roll was on the rise when this was released near the end of 1954, with *Hearts of Stone* by the Charms showing the direction in which R & B was going to travel.

No one will ever know whether the career of Johnny Ace would have simply withered away in 1955. His shocking accidental death on Christmas Day, 1954, propelled him overnight from the ranks of fine singers into the category of "legend." As news of his death while playing Russian Roulette sped around the country, his next release was already in the stores.

Pledging My Love, a composition attributed to Don Robey and Ferdinand Washington, seems tailor-made as a "last" record by a deceased superstar. Pledging love forever, not an uncommon theme in popular song, takes on an entirely different importance when the person singing it is dead. The track was recorded nearly one year earlier, however, and released before the singer's death. Objective hindsight reveals it to be just another superb Ace weeper, very much like the others that had come before.

In the hysteria that followed his death, a public outpouring of anguish encouraged in no small way by Duke's promotion department, the demand for this record was overwhelming. It climbed to number 1 in the R & B chart within three weeks after it first appeared, and it took ten weeks to finally dislodge it. Sales spilled over into the pop market, where Ace's original outsold the cover version by Teresa Brewer, an unprecedented feat. Through his tears, Robey managed to regain his composure long enough to make a deal with a major New York publishing firm to market the tune to other labels, and publishing and writer royalties eventually added up to far more than profits from record sales.

Tightfisted Robey had never kept much of a master backlog on his artists, even his major star, and Ace's unexpected exit caught the record company with little in reserve. Of the material released after the death of the singer, *Anymore* was the most successful, and is the most satisfying. Over a plodding dirge tempo, Ace's voice quavers and strains at the desolate lyrics with the pervasive mood of surrender unrelieved by the vibraphone counterpoint.

So Lonely is a standard blues ballad and *Don't You Know* is a hot, Southern-style jump number. *I'm Crazy Baby* belongs to the Charles Brown school of after-hours torch songs. Ace's straightforward approach to his songs let his marvelous voice carry the message. Singing from his heart, he touched a responsive nerve in the listener and it was this direct appeal that made his music so compelling.

One of the most expressive and identifiable voices in rhythm and blues is that of Clyde McPhatter, a gospel-bred vocalist who had brought great success to two vocal groups, the Dominoes and the Drifters. Sporting surprising strength in his thin natural tenor, McPhatter added drama and emotion to his renditions by gospel phrasing, note-bending, and stretching. From the very beginning, he was determined to become a pop star and he did much to acculturate the masses to the fervent music of the black churches.

Like Ace, McPhatter was the son of a preacher. Born in Durham, North Carolina, on November 15, 1932, he grew up in

New York City and while still a teenager joined a gospel quartet, the Mount Lebanon Singers. From there he moved into Billy Ward's disciplined and professional Dominoes. The trade-paper raves over the unnamed lead singer of that group's hits convinced him to form his own group. His Drifters caused such a sensation in the R & B field that the name and the group lived on long after he had left.

McPhatter's stint in the US Army interrupted the hit string of the Drifters and provided a convenient punctuation mark for him to end one phase of his career and pursue his dream. With several months still remaining in his service commitment, he recorded his first solo tracks. Clyde McPhatter's **Deep Sea Ball** begins at that point in his career. *Seven Days*, a heavy-beat ballad, has "pop hit" written all over it, from the muted piano triplets and relatively mild sax break to the obviously oh-so-white mixed chorus background.

Recorded in August, 1955, on one of McPhatter's weekend furloughs from his base near Buffalo, New York, the song broke into the R & B chart in early January, 1956, and climbed to the number 2 spot. More important to the singer and his label, it went pop a month later. Clearly, his goal of major stardom was not unattainable. The declamatory self-penned paean to love, *I'm Not Worthy Of You*, is from the same session.

With the curtain drawn and the stage set, McPhatter walked into the pop spotlight propelled by *Treasure Of Love*, a stop-time rhythm ballad distinguished by guitar introduction and tempo changes. McPhatter's crystalline voice projects the lyric with a minimum of trickery. It hit number 1 in R & B in late July, 1956, but was immediately supplanted by Little Richard's *Rip It Up*. More records were sold pop this time, and surprisingly no white cover versions even found a place in the Top 100.

Two days before *Treasure Of Love* completed its climb to number 1, McPhatter was in the studio cutting a fresh follow-up record. *Thirty Days* was released in September, but the tricky tempo and busy arrangement by Ray Ellis added up to a hybrid sound that was not alluring to either pop or R & B buyers, and the record failed to chart nationally on either list. The flip side of the single, *I'm Lonely Tonight*, is typical of what the trade papers called a "rockaballad" at the time, but McPhatter seems unsteady and overwhelmed by all the business going on around him.

Danny Small's theatrical *Without Love (There Is Nothing)* pushed the singer back into the spotlight. First moving forward, then dropping back, the drama builds until the spine-tingling finale. Throughout, McPhatter overpowers the background orchestra and chorus. Perhaps Ray Ellis had learned something about R & B in the three months since the previous session and held back the trite pop embellishments. The song barely crossed over into the pop Top 40, but these improved results were encouraging to McPhatter, who now publicly professed his intention to be a star as big as Nat Cole or Perry Como.

Rock And Cry, a dreadful pseudo-calypso recorded at the same session, was held back a year before release, by which time even good calypso was a dead issue. McPhatter's red-hot, soulful voice was obviously being wasted by being forced into a pop mold of the worst kind, but the nature of the record market only allowed him two choices, R & B or pop. R & B was moving into harder rock-and-roll sounds while pop hardly noticed yet another ballad crooner, even one as talented and special as Clyde McPhatter.

My Island Of Dreams is one of the best ballads from the hit-making pens of Doc Pomus and Mort Shuman. It provides a fine showcase for McPhatter's craftsmanship, as he draws out every nuance of the lyric. The singer developed a smooth and sprightly delivery for ballads, avoiding the overly moody or maudlin. That refreshing style and the ubiquitous Ray Ellis chorus produced an identifiable flavor in his records from the late 1950s. *No Matter What,* recorded in February, 1957, is typical of this mild-mannered approach to a Tin Pan Alley song.

Just To Hold My Hand, a cover of the Paul Perryman original on the Duke label, allows the singer to stretch out a little on a mid-beat Southern rocker, with the light and easy texture reinforced by alto sax. It sold better than *Without Love* on the pop chart but was still far from the big hit for which McPhatter was striving. Another cover, *Long Lonely Nights,* struck gold on the R & B charts, reaching number 1 in September, 1957, easily seeing off competition from the original by Lee Andrews and the Hearts. In many ways, it is a throwback to McPhatter's glory days as an R & B vocal group lead singer, with only a marimba as a concession to pop sensibilities.

Despite the impressive showing in the R & B charts, the song did not move the mass market, where it sold neck-and-neck with Lee Andrews's original. By early 1958, with less than a year to go on his Atlantic contract, McPhatter was still not divorced from his R & B origins. He toured the country with one of the big package shows, sharing top billing with Fats Domino and Lavern Baker – somewhat degrading for a would-be pop icon. Gossamer ballads such as *No Love Like Her Love* went unnoticed by record buyers, and *Deep Sea Ball,* a novelty jump recorded in February, 1958, was not even released until two years later.

Come What May brought the singer back to the charts in June, 1958. The rolling New Orleans rhumba beat and lyric hook kept the tune in the pop charts for 15 weeks. The hit McPhatter had been waiting for came at long last in October. The Brook Benton–Clyde Otis tune *A Lover's Question* has an infectious and memorable lilting bounce well suited to McPhatter's swoops and melodic swings. Listeners are caught first by the a cappella bass voice of Nigel Hopkins and the finger-popping introduction supplied by the songwriters themselves. Another number 1 on the R & B chart, the song lasted nearly six months on the pop list after entering it in October, 1958.

This, the biggest hit of his career, was moving off the charts when McPhatter started shopping around for a new label. He chose MGM from a variety of suitors primarily because they offered the largest advance but also because MGM was a respected adult pop label. Atlantic continued a trickle of releases after the singer was gone but it has only been in recent years that the label has recognized his importance in the world of black music.

I Can't Stand Up Alone, a white gospel number by Martha Carson, brings McPhatter back to his roots, and his earnest shout would not be out of place in a sanctified church. It is one of the few instances in his career where he recorded gospel. *Lovey Dovey* is a pulsating reprise of the Clovers' R & B hit and a last backward glance at the world he was trying to leave behind. The chattering sax of King Curtis adds interest and timeliness.

McPhatter's final Atlantic session was on February 27, 1959, and produced *You Went Back On Your Word* and *Since You've Been Gone,* two jump tunes that made modest inroads in the latter half of 1959. Both did better nationally than the first releases on McPhatter's new label, to the dismay and chagrin of the people at MGM. Although McPhatter was at the peak of his vocal prowess with MGM and, later, Mercury, he suffered in the first instance from poor material and heavy-handed arrangements and then from an unresponsive pop market.

During his early career, at least, Clyde McPhatter influenced a wide number of vocalists. He was not the only one igniting secular songs with religious fire, but his limber tenor and dramatic flash made him a unique presence in a crowded field. After racking up his last major hit, *Ta Ta,* in 1962, he spent the next decade on a downward slide, propelled by alcohol and an increasing bitterness towards a public that had forgotten him. He died on June 13, 1972, at the age of 41.

What Clyde McPhatter had strived for in vain, Sam Cooke got, seemingly without effort. He placed 43 songs in the top pop charts between 1957 and 1966 and was one of the best-selling artists on that most major of major labels, RCA–Victor. The backgrounds, training, and even the physiognomies of the two men were similar. Both were born in the South of preacher fathers; both moved to big Northern cities to sing in gospel quartets; and both had matinee-idol good looks and stage presence.

Where McPhatter moved from gospel to R & B as a springboard for his pop aspirations, Cooke jumped directly from gospel into a number 1 pop hit. This phenomenal feat has never been duplicated, but, then again, there has never been another singer quite like Sam Cooke. Born in Clarksdale, Mississippi, on January 22, 1931, Cooke was raised in Chicago from the age of two. When he was 15 years old he took over the lead spot of the Highway QCs, an understudy group under the wing of the Soul Stirrers.

The Soul Stirrers, founded in Texas in 1926, lost their longtime lead singer, Rebert H. Harris, in 1950, and Cooke was recruited to take his place. **Sam Cooke With The Soul Stirrers** is a chronological document of his development as a singer and carries his career from the beginning right up to the threshold of his breakthrough as a pop star. All of the magic of his later well-known pop hits is found in these tracks. There is no mystery surrounding his success – it was inevitable.

On his earliest tracks, such as *Peace In The Valley* and *It Won't Be Very Long*, Cooke is cradled in the group, his soaring voice somewhat cautious, as befits his place as the youngest member of an old and revered gospel institution. *How Far Am I From Canaan*, from February, 1952, is suddenly all Sam Cooke, and he impresses with extraordinary range and power, even though he is still consciously trying to imitate the raw-edged shouts of his predecessor. Second lead Silas Crain settles into providing that cutting quality on *Just Another Day*, leaving Cooke to deliver a bluesy, cracked introduction.

By the end of his first year with the Soul Stirrers, Cooke was attracting a new, younger audience to their performances, an audience whose fervid response to his singing left no doubt who they had come to see and hear. On *Any Day Now*, recorded in 1954, Cooke's virtually solo performance over muted backing from the group shows masterful control and thrilling vocal range. *He'll Make A Way* from the same session has connections to the Clyde McPhatter school of note-bending, but Cooke's voice has a fuller spectrum.

His first major hit was *Nearer To Thee*, released in April, 1955. A stinging organ and tinkling piano lead into Cooke's floating vocal over chanting by the rest of the group. Cooke's yodel, later so familiar in his pop hits, is used to good effect. The more traditional *Be With Me Jesus* was chosen as the reverse of the single and both sides were written by Cooke. James Cleveland's lovely hymn *One More River To Cross* and the jubilee-flavored *I'm So Glad (Trouble Don't Last Always)* followed in September.

During those years, Cooke and the Soul Stirrers were on the road constantly, playing the one-nighter circuit of churches and concert halls throughout the United States and Canada. Each record release and personal appearance spread the fame of the group and its handsome and theatrical lead singer. *Wonderful*, while traditional in form, is given a rapturous turn that enables it to be easily visualized as a secular love song.

The gently rolling lilt of *Touch The Hem Of His Garment*, a major hit in the summer of 1956, is animated by the singer's unbridled passion. Around this time, Cooke began flirting with the idea of transforming his wide gospel acceptance into pop stardom. His primary impetus was to make more money than the $150 a week the religious venues could offer. Under the tutelage of Robert "Bumps" Blackwell, Specialty's main producer, his first solo mainstream record was released in February, 1957.

Sales of *Lovable* and *Forever*, issued under the pseudonym "Dale Cook," were dismal. Both songs are mediocre and Cooke is nervous and tentative, perhaps thinking of the enormity of the step he is taking away from his gospel fans. The second pop single, *I'll Come Running Back To You*, starts out with an Ink Spots' guitar riff, and even Cooke's heavy use of his "woe-oh-oh" yodel cannot rescue him from the material. Cooke was discouraged by the lack of response to his efforts, Specialty was unhappy at the prospect of losing one their major gospel artists, and gospel fans, who brook no deviation into "sinful" music by their people, were getting disgruntled.

Cooke and Blackwell left Specialty in the fall of 1957, taking with them a pile of pop tracks that Specialty had no interest in releasing. A home for the cuts was found at Keen Records. After two lackluster singles were fielded, Keen released *You Send Me*, which propelled the singer to a number 1 hit that sold strongly for over half a year into 1958. This was followed by a steady stream of pop and R & B hits for Keen and RCA–Victor. (For discussion of Cooke's Keen and RCA–Victor work, see chapter 8.)

During the next five years, Cooke had 15 Top 10 R & B hits, including a number 1 for the re-released *I'll Come Running Back To You* on Specialty. None of his records repeated the pop success of *You Send Me*, but his influence on black singers was enormous. Although his career had slowed in 1964, his sudden and bloody death on December 11 caused a repeat of the public hysteria that had accompanied the passing of Johnny Ace.

Completing the legend with his death, Cooke was the epitome of the black folk hero. He rose to wealth and fame in the tough white business world after a long upward struggle, and was snuffed out on the threshold of a musical form that was to dominate black music for years to come, a form he had done much to define. His vocal mastery provided the inspiration for a whole generation of soul singers.

Little Willie John looked as though he had just stepped off the top of a wedding cake – a dapper, smooth-faced little man in a tailored suit, topped off with a snappy homburg hat. But when he opened his mouth and sang, it became apparent that this David had the voice of a Goliath. William John was born in Arkansas in 1937, and raised in Detroit. He sang with his family gospel quintet, the United Four, and by 1951 he was making the rounds of the amateur shows on his own.

After doing a single Christmas record at the age of 16, he was taken on tour with the big Paul Williams band. Williams was the first to discover the fiery and mercurial side of his nature and dumped his difficult employee in New York City. After he brashly collared King Records' Henry Glover for an audition he was given a recording session later that same day.

For the next eight years, John recorded exclusively for King, producing a body of work that included some of the most soul-stirring outpourings of wretched bad luck and heartbreak laid to wax, interspersed with jaunty readings of old standards, light opera, teenage rockers, and pop sentimentality, all with that unmistakable Little Willie John stamp. **Fever** collects 20 tracks that sample most of John's styles, avoiding only the more obviously pop renditions.

John's first session on June 27, 1955, consisted of only two tracks, both included here. One of these, *All Around The World*, had just been released the same day by singer/songwriter Titus Turner. While one might expect a 17-year-old newcomer to the business to make a slavish copy of that original, John made it all his own, turning Turner's comic lyrics into a sly, streetwise blues jump. John shouts and wails his love over outstanding backing which includes Jack Dupree, Willis Jackson, and Mickey Baker, in the studio for a Jack Dupree session.

This first record made big sales, reaching number 6 on the R & B bestseller chart and hanging on for 16 weeks. *Are You Ever Coming Back*, recorded two days later, is a strong lament, with John squeezing out moans and cries at the top of his voice. The follow-up to his hit was *Need Your Love So Bad*, a timeless, self-written love song in which the singer's distinctive nasal voice commands attention with its crystalline intensity. He entered 1956 with two minor hits, but the major breakthrough was just around the corner.

Written by Otis Blackwell and Eddie Cooley, *Fever* took John to the top of the R & B chart and made great inroads in the pop market. It was a major hit for nearly six months, without any competition in either market. Two years later, Peggy Lee made it one of her trademark songs with a slightly different lyric. This disc contains the lesser-known version released in 1962 with over-dubbed strings and chorus, neither of which does anything to improve on the original. Luckily, the original hit is available on numerous other compilations.

It was at this time that John began using James Brown as his opening act on stage shows, a professional association that turned into a lifelong friendship. Brown has acknowledged his debt to John in showmanship and musicianship in a tribute album and numerous public statements since then. *Drive Me Home*, from the *Fever* session, is a pounding plea for understanding for the singer's wicked ways that was not released until 1961, by which time it had lost none of its appeal.

Although John stayed away from the pop charts for nearly two years after *Fever*, he remained a sensation in the black community, building a reputation for hard themes delivered with knife-edged clarity. *Suffering With The Blues* was cut with the Bill Doggett combo, Doggett's pulsing organ tones providing a delicate backdrop to a spine-tingling story of heartbreak. The fast boogie *Look What You've Done To Me* works its mood with a male chorus and ripping Willis Jackson tenor horn, but found no room in an R & B chart dominated by the first wave of rock-and-roll artists.

If I Thought You Needed Me, released in September, 1957, takes a formula R & B riff ballad to new heights of emotion. *Person To Person*, a reprise of the Eddie "Cleanhead" Vinson original, offers no compromises to its blues theme but is held back by an obtrusive and yammering chorus. The straight-ahead rock-and-roll *Uh Uh Baby* appeared in the last weeks of 1957, and lacks the necessary electricity and "hook" to compete on the same ground with Jerry Lee Lewis and Elvis Presley.

It took a dramatic departure from both R & B and rock-and-roll to bring Little Willie John back to the big leagues in sales. John runs the emotional gamut from tender pleas to fierce demands in *Talk To Me, Talk To Me*, a lovely and melodic ballad from the pen of Joel "Joe Seneca" McGhee. The mood is further underscored by the singer's straining, forceful swings up and down the scale. Pop buyers brought the song to number 20 and it remained active for 17 weeks.

Let's Rock While The Rockin's Good is another attempt at joining the rock-and-roll mainstream in August, 1958, but the hackneyed dance-call lyrics are perhaps the least effective vehicle for John's soulful voice. The enjoyable *Why Don't You Haul Off And Love Me*, which started off as a country song and was turned into an R & B hit by Bullmoose Jackson in 1949, has more substance and propulsive drumming from Panama Francis, although John's voice is barely adequate for the material.

Heavily produced and intricate, *Leave My Kitten Alone* is one of the high points of John's career – not in sales, perhaps, but as a virtuoso performance. He wails, bends notes, and injects sly

Rhythm and Blues   43

humor into every line. By the time this track was released in the fall of 1959, John was experiencing trouble on the road due to his bellicose behavior off stage. Drinking was taking a toll on his disposition – and he had never been an easy man to work with.

The remainder of this set contains no chart hits, although John managed to make brief appearances on the bestseller lists from time to time through 1961. Of the also-rans and near-misses, the gaunt *You Hurt Me* is the most soulful, and *My Baby's In Love With Another Guy* is a gratifying exposure of the singer's talent and range. Unable to regain any measure of his past glory in a changing musical world, Little Willie John gave in to his wild side, and his mental and physical health began to suffer.

In August, 1964, he was arrested in a Miami nightclub for attacking a man with a beer bottle. He jumped bail and fled to the West Coast. In October a cloudy series of events left him charged with murder. His natural arrogance won him no friends at his trial in Seattle in January, 1965, and he was given an 8–20-year sentence, finally entering prison in July, 1966. His health further deteriorated in prison, and he died there on May 26, 1968.

Always combative and competitive, whether pouring everything he had into his songs or defending his pride in a dingy bar, John brought a dynamism to the music that transcended gospel fervor. He sang songs of the dark and light sides of love, and behind them all was the specter of the reality of street life in the black ghettos. When urban black music came of age, it was because Little Willie John had demonstrated that there are roots other than red-dirt farms and whitewashed churches.

The inroads into pop music that began so tentatively with Clyde McPhatter reached a peak with Sam Cooke, but there was a price to pay. While it was impossible to completely mask the gospel origins of Sam Cooke's singing style, his success was due to material that was unmistakably pop in content. It was left to Jackie Wilson to meld rhythm and blues, gospel, and rock-and-roll into a theatrical and multifaceted vocal technique that cut across racial barriers without compromise.

The Jackie Wilson Story collects Wilson's output between 1957 and 1972, with emphasis on his early solo years, and offers glimpses of the straight-ahead rockers, the sultry torch songs, and those uncategorizable rhythm numbers that earned him the nickname "Mr Excitement." The momentum of his talent carried him headlong into the soul era (see chapter 5).

Detroit-born on June 9, 1934, Wilson sang in church and in the Ever Ready Gospel Singers quartet before he was out of high school. After becoming a prominent member of Detroit's R & B community, Wilson was tapped by Bill Ward as the replacement for the departing Clyde McPhatter in the

Dominoes. Little of Wilson's dynamism was allowed to shine through under the tight rein of classically trained Ward, and the quartet format likewise gave him scant opportunities to stretch out vocally.

After serving in the Dominoes from 1953 to 1956, he was signed as a solo act to Brunswick in 1957. Many of the tracks on this set are accompanied by session bands under the direction of Dick Jacobs, a pop composer and resident musical director at Coral and Brunswick. Jacobs, unlike his counterpart Ray Ellis, was able to infuse his arrangements with a large measure of freshness and vitality, and was a genuine fan of rock-and-roll.

The first product of this association was *Reet Petite*, released in October, 1957. An inauspicious beginning, the showy boogie romp failed to chart in the R & B market but hovered in the nether reaches of the pop chart for ten weeks. The nonsense lyrics leave the spotlight to Wilson, who climbs the octave ladder and shouts his part with total abandon over a relentless rock beat. In retrospect, the song is a rock-and-roll prize, flawless in construction and well suited to that musically unstable period.

This first hit was written by a young songwriting team comprising Wilson's cousin Billy Davis and Berry Gordy, Jr. His next four chart records were also from those prolific and talented pens. *To Be Loved*, after its release in March, 1958, did much better than *Reet Petite*. The full-flowering orchestration by Milton DeLugg props Wilson's dramatic reading with comparable strength, and the singer makes thorough use of his operatic vocal power.

A Davis–Gordy ballad, *Lonely Teardrops*, was transformed during the recording session into a Latin-flavored, medium-beat rocker, and stormed into the charts in late 1958. It bumped fellow Dominoes' alumnus Clyde McPhatter's *A Lover's Question* from the number 1 R & B hit spot in mid-December. Wilson handles the tune's transformation with confidence, his tightly wired voice soaring above the chanting chorus and minimal instrumentation. Guitar arpeggios and amplified tambourine add sparkle.

With a number 1 hit as a draw, the singer began a whirlwind year of tours and personal appearances, during which he drove audiences to the heights of ecstasy with a stunning stage routine including physical acrobatics that mirrored his high-energy vocals. Cut from the same cloth as *Lonely Teardrops*, *That's Why (I Love You So)* made a lesser showing on the charts. The stop-time rhythm *I'll Be Satisfied* followed in the summer of 1959 and again hit both R & B and pop charts.

Wilson appeared in the Alan Freed movie "Go Johnny Go," wherein he sang *You Better Know It*, a relatively tame performance that somehow managed to strike number 1 in the R & B charts. Pop buyers gave it scant attention. *Talk That Talk*, written by the great black songwriter Syd Wyche, brought 1959 to a close, and the frantic and tense vocal by Wilson overshadows the clumsy arrangement. While Wilson continued to sell strongly in the black marketplace, his pop presence finally returned to the Top 10 with a two-sided smash in March, 1960.

Sounding like nothing less than a black Mario Lanza, Wilson thrilled his fans with *Night*, as mainstream as white bread and mayonnaise. Based on a Saint-Saëns aria, the rich orchestration and lofty choral backing lay the ideal groundwork for Wilson to pull out all the stops. It was a superb vehicle for this talented singer, and the sound was right for the times, too. The schizophrenic pop market was buying hundreds of thousands of copies of *The Theme From A Summer Place*, *Greenfields*, *Sink The Bismarck*, and *Stuck On You*.

R & B buyers did not exactly turn up their noses at *Night*, which moved to number 3, but they dearly loved the flip side, *Doggin' Around*, awarding this languid blues the top spot in the nation. The coupling of two powerful, dissimilar performances sold strongly for five months. This healthy showing was immediately followed by another top hit, *A Woman, A Lover, A Friend*, a scorching love song aimed directly at the hearts of Wilson's largest cadre of fans. Who among his thousands of female admirers did not feel that the lyrics fit her to a tee?

Wilson's sex-choked vocals and electrifying stage shows brought him a base of diehard fans that gave him the latitude to sing light opera classics, blues, and rhythm numbers with equal success. Brunswick issued several albums to capitalize on the performer's versatility, among them **You Ain't Heard Nothin' Yet** (1961), a tribute to Wilson's idol, Al Jolson, and a set of opera and classical themes transformed into pop numbers, **The World's Greatest Melodies** (1962). Albums of this type were not intended to sell as well as collections of hit tracks, but rather to give the performer a certain cachet.

Am I The Man, which appeared in late 1960, sold very well in the black community, but the melding of raw vocal and sugary strings was too confusing for the mass market. In contrast, the straight-ahead vocal on *The Tear Of The Year*, a hit in early 1961, should have done better on the pop chart than it did. The flip side of that single, *My Empty Arms* (not included here), was based on a classical theme, and did better in the pop market. *Please Tell Me Why*, an engaging blues, is sung with cracks and sobs that reveal a debt to blues shouter Roy Brown. The summer of 1961 brought *I'm Comin' On Back To You*, a hit return to the up-tempo, rock-and-roll style on which Wilson had built his career.

By this time Wilson had begun a collaboration with writer Alonzo Tucker, a veteran of the Detroit R & B scene who had been with the Royals/Midnighters in the early 1950s. Tucker's first contribution was the minor bluesy hit, *You Don't Know What It Means*, in August, 1961, and he also supplied the 1962 chart hit *I Just Can't Help It*, a successful blending of gospel and jump with a burbling bass singer as its bottom.

The collaboration struck gold in early 1963 with *Baby Workout*, a muscular rock-and-roller that went to the top of the R & B charts and also proved to be one of Wilson's biggest pop hits, peaking at number 5 and rivaling *Lonely Teardrops* and *Night* in crossover success. *Baby Workout* was arranged by Detroit trumpeter Gil Askey, an alumnus of the Buddy Johnson Band, who in the 1970s attained prominence writing arrangements for Diana Ross at Motown. Tucker and Wilson next collaborated on an entire album, **Somethin' Else**, but when the LP was released in 1964, the arrangements and songs sounded dated in comparison to the sounds emerging from Chicago and Detroit.

Wilson slipped into the soul form with ease, providing the continuity between rhythm and blues and the new music. Turning the passion and truth of gospel into torrid themes of carnal desire was no mean feat; it took a consummate performer to put it over, and Jackie Wilson was the man who did it first.

Discographical Details

11 Memorial Album

Johnny Ace

MCA MCAD-31183

Pledging My Love/ Don't You Know/ Never Let Me Go/So Lonely/I'm Crazy Baby/ My Song/Saving My Love For You/The Clock/How Can You Be So Mean/Still Love You So/Cross My Heart/Anymore

12 Deep Sea Ball

Clyde McPhatter

Atlantic 7 82314-2

I Can't Stand Up Alone/Seven Days/Treasure Of Love/Rock And Cry/I'm Lonely Tonight/Without Love (There Is Nothing)/Deep Sea Ball/Just To Hold My Hand/My Island Of Dreams/No Matter What/Come What May/Lovey Dovey/I'm Not Worthy Of You/A Lover's Question/Thirty Days/You Went Back On Your Word/No Love Like Her Love/Long Lonely Nights/Since You've Been Gone

13 Sam Cooke With The Soul Stirrers

Sam Cooke and the Soul Stirrers

Specialty SPCD-7009-2

Peace In The Valley/It Won't Be Very Long/How Far Am I From Canaan/Just Another Day/Come And Go To That Land/Any Day Now/He'll Make A Way/Nearer To Thee/Be With Me Jesus/One More River [To Cross]/I'm So Glad (Trouble Don't Last Always)/Wonderful/Farther Along/Touch The Hem Of His Garment/Jesus Wash Away My Troubles/Must Jesus Bear This Cross Alone/That's Heaven To Me/Were You There/Mean Old World/Lord Remember Me/Lovable/Forever/I'll Come Running Back To You/That's All I Need To Know/I Don't Want To Cry

14 Fever

Little Willie John

Charly CD 246 (UK)

All Around The World/Suffering With The Blues/Need Your Love So Bad/If I Thought You Needed Me/Let's Rock While The Rockin's Good/Are You Ever Coming Back/ Person To Person/Drive Me Home/Fever/ Uh Uh Baby/Like Boy, Like Girl/Look What You've Done To Me/Talk To Me, Talk To Me/My Baby's In Love With Another Guy/Bo-Da-Ley Didd-Ley/Inside Information/Rock Love/Why Don't You Haul Off And Love Me/You Hurt Me/Leave My Kitten Alone

15 The Jackie Wilson Story

Jackie Wilson

Epic EGK 38623

Reet Petite/To Be Loved/Lonely Teardrops/That's Why (I Love You So)/I'll Be Satisfied/Talk That Talk/Baby Workout/Please Tell Me Why/Doggin' Around/Passin' Through/A Woman, A Lover, A Friend/You Don't Know What It Means/Night/The Tear Of The Year/You Better Know It/I Just Can't Help It/I'm Comin' On Back To You/Danny Boy/Am I The Man/Whispers (Gettin' Louder)/Your Love Keeps Lifting Me (Higher And Higher)/No Pity (In The Naked City)/She's All Right/You Got Me Walking

Basic Recordings

Jumpin' In The Midnight Hour

16 The Best Of Louis Jordan

Louis Jordan

MCA MCAD-4079

Choo Choo Ch'Boogie/Let The Good Times Roll/Ain't Nobody Here But Us Chickens/ Saturday Night Fish Fry, Pts 1 & 2/Beware/Caldonia/Knock Me A Kiss/Run Joe/ School Days (When We Were Kids)/Blue Light Boogie, Pts 1 & 2/Five Guys Named Moe/What's The Use Of Getting Sober (When You Gonna Get Drunk Again)/Buzz Me/Beans And Corn Bread/Don't Let The Sun Catch You Cryin'/Somebody Done Changed The Lock On My Door/Barnyard Boogie/Early In The Mornin'/I Want You To Be My Baby/Nobody Knows You When You're Down And Out

Louis Jordan (b. July 8, 1908, in Brinkley, Arkansas) was the undisputed king of black music for a decade, with 18 number 1 hits between 1942 and 1949, a feat accomplished via a combination of good humor and superb musicality. No artist before or since has had such a far-reaching influence on the evolution of the music. Jordan graduated from playing alto sax in Chick Webb's hot band and spent three years gathering a large cadre of fans before his first big hit. Jordan died in 1975 at the age of 66.

17 Blues And Boogie

Amos Milburn

Sequel NEX CD132 (UK)

After Midnite/Anybody's Blues/It Took A Long Long Time/Empty Arms Blues/ Chicken Shack Boogie/Good Good Whiskey/Bewildered/One Scotch, One Bourbon, One Beer/Bad Bad Whiskey/Hold Me Baby/In The Middle Of The Night/Roomin'

House Boogie/Let's Make Christmas Merry, Baby/Real Pretty Mama/Everybody Clap Hands/Tears Tears Tears/Let's Rock Awhile/Thinkin' And Drinkin'/Let Me Go Home Whiskey/Walkin' Blues/Sax Shack Boogie/Birmingham Bounce/Chicken Shack

Bridging the gap between piano blues boogie and R & B, the genial piano man Amos Milburn (b. April 1, 1927, in Houston, Texas) had an unprecedented string of national hit records between 1948 and 1954 – four number 1 and nine more Top 5 hits are included here. Milburn made good use of hard-blowing sax, and his inventive and soulful blues are balanced by some of the most searing jump scorchers in rock history. A stroke in 1970 prevented him from participating in the rhythm-and-blues revival in the United States and Europe, and he passed away in Houston at the age of 52 in 1980.

18   The "3B" Blues Boy

Bobby "Blue" Bland

Ace CDCHD302 (UK)

No Blow, No Show/Wise Man's Blues/Army Blues/Lost Lover Blues/It's My Life, Baby/Honey Bee/Time Out/Million Miles From Nowhere/Woke Up Screaming/You've Got Bad Intentions/I Can't Put You Down Baby/I Don't Believe/I Learned My Lesson/I Smell Trouble/Don't Want No Woman/Further Up the Road/Teach Me (How To Love You)/Bobby's Blues/You Got Me (Where You Want Me)/Loan A Helping Hand/Last Night/Little Boy Blue/You Did Me Wrong/I Lost Sight On The World (undubbed)/*Wishing Well*

Brassy urban blues and bop provided the framework for Bland to invoke his paranoid images of distrust and heartbreak. Bland (b. January 27, 1930, in Rosemark, Tennessee) got his start in the fertile Memphis rhythm-and-blues scene in 1949, but did not score his first national hits until 1957. He has remained a prominent figure in black music ever since. These cuts from 1952 to 1959, fraught with squeals, squawls, and hollers, show him at the crest of his vocal powers.

19   Good Rocking Tonight

Wynonie "Mr Blues" Harris

Charly CD 244 (UK)

Good Rocking Tonight/She Just Won't Sell No More/Blow Your Brains Out/I Want My Fanny Brown/All She Wants To Do Is Rock/Lollipop Mama/Baby, Shame On You/I Like My Baby's Pudding/Wynonie's Boogie/Sittin' On It All the Time/Good Morning Judge/I Feel That Old Age Coming On/Lovin' Machine/Mr. Blues Is Coming To Town/Quiet Whiskey/Rock Mr. Blues/Bloodshot Eyes/Luscious Woman/Down Boy Down/Keep On Churnin' (Til The Butter Comes)

Exclusively concerned with the eternal truths of whiskey and women, the songs of Wynonie Harris (b. August 24, 1915, in Omaha, Nebraska) mirrored his wild (and short) life. During his hectic career he became the leader of the R & B revolution, and his jump blues laid the foundations for rock music. As the reigning "Mr Blues," he was a big draw on the personal appearance circuit during the growing-up years of rhythm and blues. His wild lifestyle caught up with him and he left music from 1953 to 1960. The songster was just 53 years old when he died in 1969. These King tracks from the early 1950s are his best.

20   Good Rocking Tonight

Roy Brown

Route 66 KIX-6 (Swe) (LP)

Good Rocking Tonight/Long About Midnight/Whose Hat Is That/Fore Day In the Morning/Butcher Pete, Pt 2/Dreaming Blues/Old Age Boogie, Pts 1 & 2/Good Man Blues/Miss Fanny Brown Returns/Brown Angel/Grandpa Stole My Baby/Teenage Jamboree/Black Diamond/This Is My Last Goodbye/Mighty, Mighty Man

Brown's composition of the title track is sufficient to earn him a place in rock history, but he was also a competent and innovative blues balladeer, with an angst-ridden approach to traditional love themes. Brown (b. September 10, 1925, in New Orleans) was one of the key movers and shakers of the Crescent City's rhythm-and-blues night life for many years, and his 17 national hits made his influence widespread. Brown was active in music until his sudden death in Los Angeles in 1981. This volume carries him from his New Orleans origins in 1947 to 1954.

21   Risque Rhythm

Various Artists

Rhino R2 70570

Moose Jackson: *Big Ten-Inch Record*; Dinah Washington: *Big Long Slidin' Thing/ Long John Blues*; The Five Royales: *Laundromat Blues*; Fluffy Hunter: *The Walkin' Blues*; Wynonie Harris: *Wasn't That Good/Keep On Churning*; Roy Brown: *Butcher Pete, Pt 1*; The Swallows: *It Ain't The Meat*; The Dominoes: *Sixty-Minute Man*; The Sultans: *Lemon Squeezing Daddy*; The Royals (Midnighters): *Work With Me Annie*; Myra Johnson: *Silent George*; Eddie Davis: *Mountain Oysters*; Julia Lee and Her Boyfriends: *My Man Stands Out*; The Bees: *Toy Bell*; Connie Allen: *Rocket 69*; The Toppers: *Let Me Bang Your Box*

The "blue" in rhythm and blues kept a lot of songs off the airwaves back when sex had to be implied, not explicit, but they received heavy juke-box play. Artists such as Bullmoose Jackson and Wynonie Harris built a reputation for bawdy material, but almost all early rhythm-and-blues artists had one or two raunchy numbers in their bag of tricks. The underlying theme then was good humor and good times, and some hilarious and rare examples from the 1950s are collected here.

22   Poet Of The Blues

Percy Mayfield

Specialty SPCD-7001-2

Please Send Me Someone To Love/Prayin' For Your Return/Strange Things Happening/Life Is Suicide/What A Fool I Was/Lost Love/Nightless Lover/Advice (For Men Only)/Cry Baby/Lost Mind/I Dare You, Baby/Hopeless/The Hunt Is On/ The River's Invitation/The Big Question/Wasted Dream/Louisiana/Bachelor Blues/Get Way Back/Memory Pain/Loose Lips/You Don't Exist No More/Nightmare/Baby You're Rich/My Heart Is Cryin'

When Mayfield got the blues, he got them real bad. Despondency, suicide, and a general sense of impending doom are the images on his lyrical canvas. Gloomy and threatening, *Please Send Me Someone To Love* was the biggest R & B hit of 1950. Born August 12, 1920, in Minden, Louisiana, the pianist/songwriter moved to Los Angeles in 1942, just in time to be on the scene when rhythm and blues was born. His career was derailed by a tragic auto accident, but he recovered and spent several years in the 1960s as an exclusive writer for Ray Charles. He died of a heart attack in 1984.

23 Roy Milton And His Solid Senders

Roy Milton and the Solid Senders

Specialty SPCD-7004-2

Milton's Boogie/R.M. Blues/Camille's Boogie/Big Fat Mama/Keep A Dollar In Your Pocket/Hop, Skip, And Jump/Porter's Love Song/The Hucklebuck/Information Blues/ Bartender's Boogie/Oh Babe/Christmas Time Blues/The Numbers Blues/So Tired/ Night And Day (I Miss You)/Blue Turning Gray/True Blues/Thrill Me/Everything I Do Is Wrong/Where There Is No Love/Junior Jives/It's Later Than You Think/I Have News For You/T-Town Twist/Best Wishes

One of the ignitors of the postwar R & B explosion, Milton (b. July 31, 1907, in Tulsa, Oklahoma) and his tough little band had 19 chart hits from 1946 to 1953, with the aid of an incomparable boogie pianist, Camille Howard, and a sometimes whimsical approach to standard blues matters. *R.M. Blues* dominated the charts for half of 1946. Milton was one of the earliest practitioners of rhythm and blues in Los Angeles and the drummer's knack of melding the big-band sound with blues made him an extremely popular attraction well into the 1960s. Milton played right up until his death in 1983.

24 Got My Mojo Working

Ann Cole

Krazy Kat KK782 (UK) (LP)

Got My Mojo Working/Easy Easy Baby/Each Day/Are You Satisfied/You're Mine/ My Tearful Heart/I'm Waiting For You/I've Got Nothing Working Now/Darling Don't Hurt Me/I've Got A Little Boy/In The Chapel/Brand New House/Nobody But Me/That's Enough

Scion of the famous gospel Coleman family, Cole stepped right from the church into the R & B limelight by virtue of intense and dramatic vocal stylings. Her version of the title track predates the more famous Muddy Waters rendition, and she was equally at ease with rock-and-roll and rhythm ballads. Born Cynthia Coleman in Newark, New Jersey, on January 24, 1934, she had her own gospel group of Coleman youngsters before changing her name to sing rhythm and blues. The lovely singer has been confined to a wheelchair since an auto accident in the 1960s, but still sings in church.

25 Blues, Candy And Big Maybelle

Big Maybelle

Savoy Jazz ZDS 1168

Candy/Ring Dang Dilly/Blues Early, Early/A Little Bird Told Me/So Long/That's A Pretty Good Love/Tell Me Who/Ramblin' Blues/Rockhouse/I Don't Want To Cry/ Pitiful/A Good Man Is Hard To Find/How It Lies/Goin' Home Baby

The undisputed queen of female shouters, with lungs of steel and hips of jelly, Big Maybelle (b. Mabel Louise Smith, May 1, 1924, in Jackson, Tennessee) delivered every song with vein-popping intensity, no matter if they were winsome Tin Pan Alley standards, gritty blues, or flat-out rockers. She worked with the Sweethearts Of Rhythm before striking out on her own. As much a visual delight as a superlative singer, Maybelle never achieved a great deal of success in the record charts but remained a popular stage attraction until illness forced her retirement in 1968. A diabetic coma claimed her life in 1972. These tracks from 1956–9 have the added attraction of backing by some superlative jazz musicians. The playing of *Candy* on an American television broadcast, "The Bill Cosby Show," precipitated the release of this album.

26 I'm Goin' To Leave You

Faye Adams

Mr. R&B 110 (Swe) (LP)

You Ain't Been True/I'm Goin' To Leave You/You're Crazy/Cry, You Crazy Heart/ Somebody Somewhere/Sweet Talk/No Way Out/So Much/My Greatest Desire/I'm So Happy/Johnny Lee/Shake A Hand/That's All Right/Look Around/Step Up And Rescue Me/Keeper Of My Heart/I'll Be True To You/It Made Me Cry/It Hurts Me To My Heart/Somebody, Somewhere (Prayin' For Me)/I Don't Want Your Love (No More)

Her doll-like beauty contrasting with a compelling voice, Faye Adams came from a church background, and returned there when her career in R & B turned sour. In between time, her sensational hit *Shake A Hand* and follow-ups made her a nationwide R & B attraction. Born Faye Tuell in New Jersey in the mid-1920s, she looked much younger than her years and had no problem appealing to the younger crowd. She was featured on several coast-to-coast tours during the heyday of rhythm and blues, but never achieved her goal of becoming a mainstream pop star. Since her retirement from secular singing in the early 1960s her voice continues to delight the congregation at her husband's church in New Jersey. These tracks were recorded between 1952 and 1961.

27 Mellow Mama

Dinah Washington

Delmark Apollo Series DD-451

Mellow Mama Blues/All Or Nothing Blues/Rich Man's Blues/Chewin' Mama Blues/ Blues For A Day/Wise Woman Blues/My Voot Is Really Vout/Pacific Coast Blues/ Beggin' Mama Blues/Walking Blues/No Voot No Boot/My Lovin' Papa

Urbane and deeply blue, Dinah Washington redefined the art of the torch song and commanded the R & B charts in the 1950s before becoming a pop favorite. Born Ruth Jones in Tuscaloosa, Alabama, on August 29, 1924, she was raised in Chicago from an early age. After singing with the Sallie Martin Gospel Singers in 1940, she worked local clubs, and then joined Lionel Hampton in 1943. Critical acclaim for her refreshing style followed. She left Hampton in late 1945 and recorded three sessions in Los Angeles, all included here, with Lucky Thompson and an array of jazz luminaries. As a soloist she had 25 R & B hits from 1948 to 1952, and her popularity increased with mainstream material thereafter. An accidental drug overdose claimed her life in 1963.

28 Soul On Fire

Lavern Baker

Atlantic 7 82311-2

Soul On Fire/Tomorrow Night/Tweedle Dee/That's All I Need/Bop-Ting-A-Ling/Play It Fair/Jim Dandy/My Happiness Forever/Get Up Get Up (You Sleepy Head)/Still/I Can't Love You Enough/Jim Dandy Got Married/I Cried A Tear/Whipper Snapper/I Waited Too Long/Shake A Hand/How Often (with Ben E. King)/You Said/Saved/ See See Rider

The most productive years of the lady with the voice that could blow down walls are gathered here. Born Delores Baker in Chicago on November 11, 1929, she worked as band vocalist for Todd Rhodes in 1952–3. After a tour of Europe on her own, she started her solo career in 1954. Her dynamic performances appealed to the teenagers who were attracted to R & B in the mid-1950s, but her career did not survive the coming of soul. After many years in the Philippines, she made a triumphant return in 1990. There was no song she could not make uniquely her own, although her biggest hits were booming rockers. A sprinkling of mournful ballads and torch songs fills out this set covering the years 1953–62.

Why Do Fools Fall In Love?

29 Down In The Alley
The Clovers
Atlantic 7 82312-2
One Mint Julep/Good Lovin'/Don't You Know I Love You/Wonder Where My Baby's Gone/Ting-A-Ling/Crawlin'/Hey, Miss Fannie/Lovey Dovey/Middle Of The Night/ Fool, Fool, Fool/I've Got My Eyes On You/I Confess/Your Cash Ain't Nothin'/But Trash/Little Mama/Down In The Alley/Nip Sip/Devil Or Angel/Blue Velvet/In The Morning Time/Love Bug/If I Could Be Loved By You

After starting out as Ink Spots clones in 1946, the Clovers (John "Buddy" Bailey, Matthew McQuater, Harold Lucas, Harold Winley, and guitarist Bill Harris) developed into skilled purveyors of hard-edged jump and dreamy rhythm ballads. The group from Washington, DC, had a stinging bite to their up-tempo rockers that made them stand apart from competitors with gospel backgrounds. Likewise, their bluesy ballads were earthy and sincere. Longtime lead singer John "Buddy" Bailey made room for Billy Mitchell, making them a quintet in 1954. Always present was the superb jazz guitarist, Bill Harris. A succession of R & B chart hits made them the first Atlantic supergroup and all of their hits and B sides from 1952–6 are included, plus the original 1953 version of the title track.

30 Shirley And Lee
Shirley and Lee
EMI CDP-7-92775-2
I'm Gone/Sweethearts/Baby/Why Did I/Confessin'/Keep On/Comin' Over/Takes Money/Feel So Good/Lee's Dream/Deed I Do/That's What I'll Do/Let The Good Times Roll/I Feel Good/When I Saw You/I Want To Dance/Rock All Night/Don't You Know I Love You/I'll Thrill You/Everybody's Rockin'

The original boy–girl duo in R & B, these teenagers from New Orleans were hyped as "The Sweethearts Of The Blues" through a series of lovin' and leavin' songs from 1952 to 1958. Shirley Goodman (b. June 19, 1936) and Leonard Lee (b. June 29, 1936) were just 16 years old when they were plucked from a large group of auditioning high-schoolers and teamed up. The combination of their youthful voices and the always thrilling New Orleans rhythm backing added up to numerous hits until the duo finally split in 1963. Lee died in 1976, but Shirley had a few soul era hits on her own. This set is evenly divided between poignant ballads and rockers, some of the latter a bit too cute. Still, once heard, Shirley's cracked-ice voice is never forgotten.

31 My True Story

The Jive Five

Relic 7007

My True Story/When I Was Single/Rain/Johnny Never Knew/Hurry Back/The Girl With The Wind In Her Hair/I Don't Want To Be Without You Baby/These Golden Rings/Do You Hear Wedding Bells/What Time Is It/Lily Marlane/Beggin' You Please/ Hully Gully Callin' Time/Never Never/People From Another World/No Not Again/ You Know What I Would Do/She's My Girl/My True Story (stereo underdub)/ *Never Never Never* (stereo alternate)

With one foot firmly in doo-wop and the other in soul, the Jive Five were successful with all types of tunes from romantic ballads to novelties, pulled along by one of the best lead voices of the era, Eugene Pitt (other members: Jerome Hanna, Billy Prophet, Richard Harris, and Norman Johnson). They formed in Brooklyn in 1959, and their brief time in the limelight started with the title track in 1961. The success of this number 1 blockbuster was never repeated and this set wraps up in 1963. Since that time, they have continued to parlay their proto-doo-wopping into a successful personal appearance career.

32 In The Still Of The Night

The Five Satins

Relic 7001

In The Still Of The Night/Wonderful Girl/When Your Love Comes Along/To The Aisle/A Million To One/A Nite To Remember/The Jones Girl/Shadows/Love With No Love In Return/The Time/Pretty Baby/Candlelight/When The Swallows Come Back/A Nite Like This/Skippity Doo/You Must Be An Angel/Toni My Love/I'll Be Seeing You

Tricky harmonies and soulful leads show this group to be much more than their one superhit would suggest. Hailing from New Haven, Connecticut, the group recorded *In The Still Of The Night* in a church basement and had their big hit while their lead singer Fred Parris was in the army. During his absence, Bill Baker substituted on records and stage shows. Their dreamy, sentimental approach to songs of young love was just right for the times, and by 1960 they had passed into memory. As balladeers they had few equals but their up-tempo tracks are merely adequate. Covering the period from 1956 to 1958, several tracks are heard here in true stereo for the first time.

33 The Best Of Frankie Lymon And The Teenagers

Frankie Lymon and the Teenagers

Rhino R2 70918

Why Do Fools Fall In Love/Please Be Mine/Love Is A Clown/Am I Fooling Myself Again/I Want You To Be My Girl/I'm Not A Know It All/Who Can Explain/I Promise to Remember/The ABC's Of Love/Share/I'm Not A Juvenile Delinquent/Baby Baby/Paper Castles/Teenage Love/Out In The Cold Again/Goody Goody/Creation Of Love/Thumb Thumb/Portable On My Shoulder/Little Bitty Pretty One

The prototype "kid-lead" vocal group opened a whole new field in popular music and it is easy to share the excitement of 1956 with this flawless set. Love songs aimed at teens and driving rockers were exactly in the spirit of the times. Herman Santiago (tenor), Jimmy Merchant (tenor), Joe Negroni (baritone), and Sherman Garnes (bass) formed the original group in the Bronx in 1955, but it was not until they added 13-year-old Frankie Lymon the following year that they were able to launch a recording career on George Goldner's Gee label.

Lymon's schoolboy piping as well as the exuberant support by saxophonist Jimmy Wright and other great New York session musicians added excitement and interest to otherwise pedestrian material. Efforts to let Lymon "grow up" ended in disaster and by 1960 his career was over. In 1992, Frankie Lymon and the Teenagers were the first true doo-wop group to be inducted into the Rock And Roll Hall of Fame, but only Merchant and Santiago were still alive to receive the honor.

34 The Vocal Group Collection
Various Artists
Mercury 830 283-2

The Platters: *Bark, Battle And Ball/Winner Take All/You'll Never, Never Know/It Isn't Right/On My Word Of Honor/One In A Million/Helpless*; The Penguins: *Be Mine Or Be A Fool/Don't Do It/It Only Happens With You/Walkin' Down Broadway/Devil That I See/Promises, Promises, Promises/She's Gone, Gone*; The Del Vikings: *Cool Shake/Come Along With Me/A Sunday Kind Of Love/When I Come Home/You Cheated/Flat Tire/How Could You*; The Danleers: *One Summer Night/ Wheelin' And A-Dealin'/I Really Love You/My Flaming Heart/A Picture Of You/ Prelude To Love/Your Love*

Four of the vocal groups that found considerable favor with the mass market record buyers via impeccable harmony and classy productions in the mid-1950s are heard here in an assortment of hits and fine B sides. The Platters and the Penguins represent the West Coast school of group harmony, the former always overshadowed by the exquisite lead voice of Tony Williams and the latter forever typecast by their eternal favorite, *Earth Angel*. Likewise, the Pittsburgh-based Del Vikings and New York's Danleers are known primarily for single big hits. That there was much more to these groups is ably proved on these tracks. Digital mastering by Dennis Drake means crystalline clarity and enjoyable listening.

35 Sixty Minute Man
Billy Ward and the Dominoes
Charly CD 242 (UK)

Sixty Minute Man/Chicken Blues/Don't Leave Me This Way/Do Something For Me/ That's What You're Doing To Me/Weeping Willow Blues/How Long How Long Blues/ I Am With You/Have Mercy Baby/If I Never Get To Heaven/Pedal Pushin' Papa/I'd Be Satisfied/'Deed I Do/The Bells/My Baby's 3-D/Tenderly/I Ain't Gonna Cry For You/You Can't Keep A Good Man Down/I Really Don't Want To Know/I'm Gonna Move To The Outskirts Of Town

Such stellar lead voices as Clyde McPhatter, Jackie Wilson, and Bill Brown kept the Dominoes in the upper reaches of the R & B charts from 1951 to 1953, but it was the unrelenting professionalism of pianist/songwriter Ward that provided the backbone of the group. He assembled his group in 1950 with Clyde McPhatter as lead tenor and Bill Brown as bass. When McPhatter left in 1953, Ward had Jackie Wilson waiting to take his place. Most of their hits were written by Ward, and the fervid lead singing came straight out of church. The Dominoes were the leaders in the vocal group revolution of the 1950s but later moves into the pop field met with scant success.

36 Best Of The Cadillacs
The Cadillacs
Rhino R2 70955

Gloria/No Chance/Down The Road/Window Lady/Speedoo/Zoom/You Are/Woe Is Me/Betty My Love/The Girl I Love/Sugar-Sugar/My Girl Friend/Speedoo Is Back/ Peek-A-Boo/Zoom-Boom-Zing/Please, Mr. Johnson/Romeo/Tell Me Today

The first bigtime street-corner group, the Cadillacs brought a rough-edged, tough charm to vocal harmony that touched a responsive chord in young listeners. Coming straight from public school in Harlem, the group put Earl "Speedy" Carroll in the lead spot. As the first R & B group to make extensive use of choreography in their stage routines, they gave a visuality to the music. Their sax-laden upbeat numbers and heart-on-sleeve weepers were eminently suited to dancing and both styles are represented on this compilation of tracks from 1954 to 1960. Carroll left the group to join the Coasters in 1958 and the Cadillacs did not survive much longer.

37 Let 'Em Roll

Hank Ballard and the Midnighters

Charly CD 240 (UK)

Work With Me, Annie/It's Love Baby (24 Hours A Day)/Tore Up Over You/Annie Had A Baby/In The Doorway Crying/The Twist/Rock and Roll Wedding/Kansas City/ Teardrops On Your Letter/Sexy Ways/Let 'Em Roll/Crazy Lovin'/Deep Blue Sea/ Hoochie Coochie Coo/Let's Go, Let's Go, Let's Go/Sugaree/Look At Little Sister/ Switch-A-Roo/I'm Gonna Miss You/Daddy Rolling Stone

Detroit's Midnighters pushed the envelope of R & B vocal harmony a bit farther with their hilarious and ribald "Annie" series, but the group always highlighted sizzling guitar where the rest used saxophones, and Ballard's impassioned lead vocals worked wonders with moody blues ballads (other members: Henry Booth, Charles Sutton, Lawson Smith, Sonny Woods). Formed as the Royals in 1952, the group first concentrated on ethereal slow songs until the entrance of Ballard, who was born in Detroit in 1936. After disbanding in 1965, Ballard carried on with a solo career that included work with the James Brown Revue.

38 Play It Cool

The Spaniels

Charly CD 222 (UK)

I Like It Like That/Hey, Sister Lizzie/You're Gonna Cry/Play It Cool/False Love/ Crazee Baby/(You Gave Me) Peace Of Mind/Great Googley Moo/Automobiles/Tina/ House Cleaning/Baby It's You/Why Won't You Dance/(Get Away Child) You Don't Move Me/I Need Your Kisses/Goodnight, Sweetheart, Goodnight/I'm Gonna Thank Him/Jessie Mae/Lucinda/I.O.U./Bounce/Red Sails In The Sunset/Please Don't Tease/ You Painted Pictures/Baby Sweets/Everyone's Laughing

The suave voice of lead singer James "Pookie" Hudson set this group apart from the multitudes in the early 1950s, and this evenly balanced collection of laments and jumps gives him the perfect showcase. Formed in Gary, Indiana, in 1952, their style was tougher than that of their East Coast counterparts but no less expressive. Hudson's unique voice was instantly recognizable and the burbling, dark-brown bass of Gerald Gregory provided a firm foundation. Hudson left the group in 1961, but formed a new Spaniels in 1975. The best of their Vee Jay tracks from 1953–60 are heard here.

39 The Best Of The Heartbeats/Shep And The Limelites

The Heartbeats/Shep and the Limelites

Rhino R2 70952

The Heartbeats: *A Thousand Miles Away/Crazy For You/Darling How Long/Your Way/People Are Talking/I Won't Be The Fool Anymore/Everybody's Somebody's Fool/ I Want To Know/After New Year's Eve/500 Miles To Go/Down On My Knees/I Found A Job/One Day Next Year/Lonely Lover/Sometimes I Wonder*

Shep and the Limelites: *Daddy's Home/Three Steps From The Altar/What Did Daddy Do/Ready For Your Love/Our Anniversary*

The pleading, romantic lead voice of James "Shep" Sheppard is the common thread in these two superb New York sound vocal groups. Formed in high school in 1955, the Heartbeats perfected a polished harmony style that brought them to national notice in late 1956. Internal dissension caused their breakup in 1960, but Sheppard rebounded with his Limelites trio in 1961. Where the Heartbeats had brought the traditional vocal group style to full flower, the Limelites, comprising three tenors, had a fresh and distinctive sound. Sheppard was also the primary songwriter for his groups, and his lyrics wove a coherent tale of a man enduring separation and reunion and, finally, celebrating marriage to the one love of his life. He died in January, 1970.

Harlem Hit-Paraders

40 Hail! Hail! Rock 'n' Roll

Chuck Berry

Charly CD 5035 (UK)

Maybellene/Thirty Days/No Money Down/Roll Over Beethoven/Brown Eyed Handsome Man/Too Much Monkey Business/You Can't Catch Me/School Day (Ring Ring Goes The Bell)/Rock And Roll Music/Sweet Little Sixteen/Reelin' And Rockin'/Johnny B. Goode/Around And Around/Beautiful Delilah/Carol/Sweet Little Rock And Roller/Almost Grown/Little Queenie/Back In The USA/Memphis, Tennessee/Too Pooped To Pop/Let It Rock/Bye Bye Johnny/I'm Talking About You/ Come On/Nadine (Is It You)/No Particular Place To Go/You Never Can Tell/Little Marie/Promised Land/Tulane/My Ding-A-Ling

Always in a category of his own, Berry (b. October 18, 1926, in San Jose, California) produced deceptively simple and enchanting depictions of teenage concerns – cars, money, and girls. His accessible style was carefully replicated by black and white artists alike, all across the world, to the greater glory of rock-and-roll. Raised in St Louis, Berry grabbed the spotlight with his very first recording and has not let it go since then. Showing no signs of retiring, he continues to dazzle audiences on two continents with his guitar-work and receives homage from rockers who are only one-fourth his age.

41 Raging Harlem Hit Parade

Various Artists

Relic 7009

Elmore James: *Dust My Broom/The Sky Is Crying/Shake Your Moneymaker*; Gladys Knight and the Pips: *Every Beat Of My Heart/Letter Full Of Tears*; King Curtis: *Soul Twist*; Bobby Marchan: *There Is Something On Your Mind, Pts 1 & 2*; Tarheel Slim: *Number Nine Train*; The Charts: *Deserie*; Buster Brown: *Fannie Mae/Is You Is Or Is You Ain't*; Red Prysock: *Wiggles*; Lee Dorsey: *Ya Ya/Do Re*

Mi; Dr Horse: *Jack, That Cat Was Clean*; Don Gardner and Dee Dee Ford: *I Need Your Lovin'*; The Velvets: *At Last*; Lightnin' Hopkins: *Mojo Hand*; Tarheel Slim and Little Ann: *Much Too Late*; Wilbert Harrison: *Kansas City*; Les Cooper: *Wiggle Wobble*; Arthur "Big Boy" Crudup: *That's All Right*

From the copious vaults of Bobby Robinson, an excellent cross-section of the many shades of R & B, this time from the perspective of a New York independent label. Stretching from the early 1950s to 1962, there are hot sax instrumentals, deep blues, rockers, love songs, and novelties galore, in super-clean sound. Robinson started his first label, Red Robin, in the back of his Harlem record shop in 1951, drawing upon local talent. His biggest hits were by Wilbert Harrison and Buster Brown in the early 1960s, but Robinson and his record store were still doing business in the early 1990s.

42 Mercury R & B '46–'62

Various Artists

Mercury 838 243-2 (2-disc set)

Dinah Washington: *Evil Gal Blues/I Know How To Do It/Salty Papa Blues/New Blowtop Blues/Trouble In Mind/Fat Daddy/I Don't Hurt Anymore/I Just Couldn't Stand It No More*; Eddie "Cleanhead" Vinson and his Orchestra: *Cherry Red Blues/Just A Dream/Cleanhead Blues/When A Woman Loves Her Juice/Kidney Stew Blues/Old Maid Boogie/Some Women Do/You Can't Have My Love No More*; Roy Byrd and his Blues Jumpers: *Her Mind Is Gone/Baldhead/Oh Well/Byrd's Blues*; The Eagles: *Trying To Get To You*; Buddy and Ella Johnson: *That's How I Feel About You/Hittin' On Me/Shut Your Big Mouth (Girl)/A Pretty Girl (A Cadillac And Some Money)/(Gotta Go) Upside Your Head/I Don't Want Nobody (To Have My Love But You)/That's What You Gotta Do/I Still Love You*; Louis Jordan: *Caldonia/Let The Good Times Roll/Big Bess/Cat Scratchin'/Salt Pork, W. Va./Fire/Ella Mae/Sweet Hunk Of Junk*; Clyde McPhatter: *Ta Ta/I Never Knew/Lover Please/Little Bitty Pretty One*

A fine sampling of the various flavors of R & B, from New Orleans blues-rhumba piano, big-band jumps, doo-wop, and jazz-tinted vocals to the proto-soul of Clyde McPhatter. The Mercury Record Company, founded in Chicago in 1945, always had a presence in rhythm and blues, somewhat overshadowed by the label's prominence in pop, jazz, and classical. Some of the biggest names in the field recorded for Mercury and the talent represented here is awesome.

43 Lawdy!

Lloyd Price

Specialty SPCD-7010-2

Lawdy Miss Clawdy/Mailman Blues/Chee Koo Baby/Oo-Ee Baby (alternate)/*So Long/Operator* (alternate)/*Laurelle* (alternate)/*What's The Matter Now/If Crying Was Murder/Walkin' The Track/Where You At/Lord, Lord, Amen/Carry Me Home/Froglegs* (alternate)/*Froglegs/I Wish Your Picture Was You/Let Me Come Home, Baby/Tryin' To Find Someone To Love/Night And Day Blues/All Alone/What A Fire/Rock 'N' Roll Dance/I'm Glad, Glad/Baby Please Come Home/Forgive Me, Clawdy*

The man from New Orleans enjoyed a brilliant comeback as a rock-and-roll singer in the late 1950s, but these are the true grit tracks from 1952 to 1956. Price (b. March 9, 1933, in Kenner, Louisiana) had his career interrupted by army service 1953–6. Upon his return he changed musical direction and also began producing records and managing talent. Right from the beginning, his reputation was built on pounding jump tunes, and rightly so, although he delivered ballads with sincerity and charm.

44   My Story

Chuck Willis

CBS Special Products A 36389

Don't Deceive Me (Please Don't Go)/I Feel So Bad/My Story/Two Spoons Of Tears/ Caldonia (What Makes Your Big Head So Hard)/You're Still My Baby/Need One More Chance/Going To The River/Change My Mind/I Rule My House/Charged With Cheating/It Ain't Right To Treat Me Wrong/My Heart's Been Broke Again/Salty Tears

These are the earliest tracks by the skilled singer/songwriter whose career was cut short by his untimely death in 1958. Willis (b. January 31, 1928, in Atlanta) worked his way up to a recording contract with Columbia's OKeh label in 1951. After five hits in three years he switched to Atlantic, where he enjoyed even greater acclaim. He also wrote numerous songs that were hits for other artists. Few artists could match his facility with doleful themes and exuberant jump blues and these songs from 1952–4, almost all written by Willis, include his first five chart hits.

45   Miss Rhythm: Greatest Hits And More

Ruth Brown

Atlantic 7-82061-2 (2-disc set)

So Long/Hey Pretty Baby/I'll Get Along Somehow (Pt 1)/I'll Come Back Someday/ Sentimental Journey/ R.B. Blues/Teardrops From My Eyes/Standing On The Corner/ I'll Wait For You/I Know/Don't Cry/The Shrine Of St. Cecilia/It's All For You/Shine On/Be Anything/5-10-15 Hours/Have A Good Time/Daddy Daddy/Mama He Treats Your Daughter Mean/Wild Wild Young Men/Ever Since My Baby's Been Gone/Love Contest/Oh What A Dream/Old Man River/Somebody Touched Me/Mambo Baby/I Can See Everybody's Baby/As Long As I'm Moving/It's Love Baby/I Gotta Have You (with Clyde McPhatter)/Love Has Joined Us Together (with Clyde McPhatter)/I Wanna Do More/Lucky Lips/One More Time/This Little Girl's Gone Rockin'/Why Me/I Can't Hear A Word You Say/I Don't Know/Takin' Care Of Business/Don't Deceive Me.

Comedienne, actress, chanteuse, and star on television and Broadway, Ruth Brown was the top female R & B singer from 1950 to 1955. Brown (b. January, 30, 1928, in Portsmouth, Virginia) went from nightclubs to the top of the charts via a jaunty, exuberant lyrical approach to jump numbers that earned her the title "Miss Rhythm." She was a reluctant rocker, however, and preferred torch songs. Some of each are on this collection, including 20 Top 10 R & B hits, and are still featured in her nightclub sets. The consummate professional remains a welcome presence with no signs of slowing down.

New York and New Jersey   2

Wayne Jancik

N ew York City was the center of the United States recording
industry for those peak years – between the late 1950s and
early 1970s – when soul in all its permutations was a dominant
force. However, no such thing as a unified "New York Sound"
has ever existed. New York City was far too large, far too diverse,
and far too uncontrollable to ever merge into an identifiable
signature styling. But for a moment, in the early 1960s, New York
did have the chart-dominating "Brill Building Sound."

The Brill Building in mid-Manhattan, at 1619 Broadway, was
the capital of Tin Pan Alley back in the days of big bands, big
ballads, and the coast-to-coast "Your Hit Parade," the nation's hit
barometer. All of these crumbled in 1956 when rock-and-roll
became important. Although the term "Brill Building sound"
lingered, the action largely shifted to 1697 Broadway and across
the street to 1650 Broadway. Located at the latter was the mighty
Aldon Music, formed in 1958 by Al Nevins, a guitarist formerly
with the Three Suns, and Don Kirshner, an ambitious song-
plugger.

Aldon hired teams of young songwriters and demo artists, who
often functioned as producers and sometimes as recording acts.
Most successful of these were Neil Sedaka–Howie Greenfield,
Barry Mann–Cynthia Weil, and Gerry Goffin–Carole King. Brill
Building pop-rock is usually loosely defined to include Jerry
Leiber–Mike Stoller, Ellie Greenwich–Jeff Barry, Hal David–Burt
Bacharach, Doc Pomus–Mort Shuman, and Bert Berns, among
others. Together the "Brill Building bunch" had a lot to say about
what was recorded, how, and by whom. And if for a flicker of time
there was a sound radiating from New York's music district that
produced chart hits, it was largely a black-pop, girl-group sound.

Aldon's clients were the majors such as Columbia and RCA and
a large number of indie labels that required a constant stream of
quality teen tunes. Dimension Records was formed by Kirshner,

with Goffin and King supplying much of the writing and producing, for the firm's Little Eva, Big Dee Irwin, and the Cookies. In less than a year, Kirshner was head of Colpix, the Columbia Pictures music division responsible for the Marcels, Earl-Jean, Nina Simone, Freddie Scott, and the early Ronettes. In 1964, Leiber and Stoller, with industry kingpin George Goldner, formed Red Bird/Blue Cat Records. Some of the prized works to emerge from this era were cut for the label by the Shangri-Las, the Dixie Cups, the Jellybeans, and the Ad-Libs.

In the 1950s, Goldner had formed the Rama, Gee, Roulette, Gone, and End labels largely to meet the need for New York's home-grown street-corner doo-wop. Among his empire's influential charges were the Three Degrees, the Chantels – the girl-group prototype – and Little Anthony and the Imperials, who managed the transition into the 1960s with a string of plush soul ballads for the New York-based Don Costa label DCP.

Laurie Records, formed by Gene and Bob Schwartz in 1958 and noted for their early success with Dion and the Belmonts, supplied the girl-group sound with the Chiffons, their alter ego the Four Pennies, the less successful Bernadette Carroll, and a mix of Italian neo-doo-wop and novelty pop.

Florence Greenberg formed Scepter Records in 1959 and had continued chart hits due largely to one of the most appealing of all pop-soul groups, the Shirelles, and the soft soul sounds of Dionne Warwick. These successes in large part stemmed from the production skills of Luther Dixon and of Hal David and Burt Bacharach. Chuck Jackson, Maxine Brown, Tommy Hunt, the Joe Jeffrey Group, and the Isley Brothers fleshed out the hits for the label.

Bobby Robinson had been filling East Coast airwaves with dozens of classic doo-wop discs, cut for his Red Robin and Whirlin' Disc labels, when in 1959 he opened the Fire/Fury/Enjoy complex of labels. Most of his rough recordings were gems that ranged from throwback R & B to urban blues. Don Gardner and Dee Dee Ford, Les Cooper, Buster Brown, Bobby Marchan, Wilbert Harrison, King Curtis, Elmore James, and Lightnin' Hopkins were signed.

In 1958 Sue Records was created by Juggy Murray, later the Symbol subsidiary. Murray's stable included Ike and Tina Turner, Jimmy McGriff, and the soul sounds of Baby Washington, Inez and Charlie Foxx, the Mighty Hannibal (James T. Shaw), the Poets, and the Soul Sisters.

Dave Kapp, with his Kapp label (formed in 1955), had much success with MOR acts such as Jane Morgen, Jack Jones, and Roger Williams. The firm also had recorded a small stable of soul acts, including Ruby and the Romantics, the Hesitations, the Unifics, and, on Kapp subsidiary Congress, Shirley Ellis.

Under the productive skills of Jerry Ragavoy, New York-based United Artists (formed in 1957) had chart hits with Jive Five, the Exciters, and the gospel-gripping Garnet Mimms and the Enchanters. In 1961, Art Talmadge left United Artists and, with Aaron Schroeder, formed Musicor/Dynamo. With producer Luther Dixon's aid the Platters' faltering career was revived on Musicor; that of Inez Foxx and Tommy Hunt were continued.

Atlantic Records was formed in New York in 1948 by Herb Abramson and Ahmet Ertegun. During the soul era they found unheard-of success with the Drifters, recording in New York. Other New York-produced acts include Ben E. King, Solomon Burke, Donny Hathaway, Roberta Flack, Esther Phillips, the Persuaders, the Sweet Inspirations, Doris Troy, and Barbara Lewis.

The Amy/Mala/Bell complex of labels under Larry Uttal began as Amy/Mala in 1959. The company got its first hit with Al Brown and the Tunetoppers' *The Madison* the following year. Uttal joined the company in 1963 and formed Bell as the parent label in 1964. The stable of New York soul artists directly on Amy/Mala/Bell was not that large, but through distribution agreements with many small New York labels and with Southern producers, the company made a formidable impact during the soul era. On Larry Maxwell's Maxx label, Gladys Knight and the Pips got a spate of hits; on Burt Bacharach's Hilltop (later Big Hill), Lou Johnson became a hitmaker (notably with *There's Always Something There To Remind Me*); and on Luther Dixon's Gold imprint there was a lovely hit by Brooks O'Dell (*Watch Your Step*). Another small Bell-distributed label, Aurora, produced one of the great songs from New York, *My Ship Is Coming In*, by songwriter Jimmy Radcliffe.

Amy/Mala/Bell's Southern output was substantial, with distribution deals with Goldwax in Memphis, Elf in Nashville, and the Sansu and Tou-Sea labels in New Orleans. Also, the label complex directly put out Southern productions on Lee Dorsey, Bobby and James Purify, and the Van Dykes (see chapters 6 and 7). In 1975 Clive Davis took over Bell and reorganized the company into Arista Records. During the 1970s and 1980s he got hits from such artists as Dionne Warwick, Jermaine Stewart, and Whitney Houston.

Big Top, a creation of the Hill & Range music publishing company in 1958, produced a few hits in the soul era, notably by Lou Johnson (*Reach Out For Me*) and the VIPs (*You Pulled A Fast One*). By 1967, the company had essentially come under the Amy/Mala/Bell umbrella. Another small label, Diamond, was formed in 1961, and had hits with Johnny Thunder (*Loop De Loop*) and Ruby Winters (*I Don't Want To Cry* and *Guess Who*).

Buddah, formed by Art Kass and Neil Bogart in 1967, began its history with a string of "bubblegum" rock hits, but in the 1970s settled down to become a specialist in soft soul. Its biggest hitmakers were Gladys Knight and the Pips, but other notable artists were Norman Conners, Michael Henderson, the Five Stairsteps, and Barbara Mason.

While the majors may have focused on MOR, rock, country, or Broadway show tunes, Columbia did well by recording Aretha Franklin on its own imprint and Peaches and Herb on its subsidiary, Date. In addition, the Spellbinders and O.C. Smith made some notable releases on the label. Chicago-based Mercury, through its New York offices, had a long string of chart hits with Brook Benton, and also recorded Dinah Washington, Sarah Vaughn, and Dee Dee Warwick. Early on, RCA had the Isley Brothers, Jessie Belvin, and the Metros; later the company had success with the Friends of Distinction, Main Ingredient, and Nona Hendryx.

Producer Joe Evans, once a musician with "Hot Lips" Page and Lionel Hampton, formed Carnival Records in Newark, New Jersey, in 1961. Evans was primarily responsible for the success of the Manhattans and of Lee Williams and the Cymbols. In 1968, in nearby Englewood, Joe and Sylvia Robinson started All-Platinum; Stang, Turbo, and Vibration were subsidiaries. Acts signed included the Moments, Donnie Elbert, Phillip Wynne, the Whatnauts, Brother-To-Brother, Linda Jones, and co-label owner Sylvia (half of the famed Mickey and Sylvia).

The New York/New Jersey area, while in no way unified as were Memphis, Chicago, or New Orleans, and while not thought of as soulful, did in its unique and energy-filled ball of confusion create an impressive quantity of some of the finest soul to ever find captivity on disc.

Essential Recordings

(i) Scepter/Wand

One of the most successful independent New York labels of the 1960s was Scepter/Wand, the creation of Florence Greenberg – an energetic housewife with no music business experience. When she was ready to venture forth, her daughter, Mary Jane, nagged four singing classmates from Passiac, New Jersey, into auditioning for her mother. The girls – Shirley Owens (b. June 10, 1941), Doris Coley (b. August 2, 1941), Addie "Micki" Harris (b. January 20, 1940), and Beverly Lee (b. August 3, 1941) – all 16 or 17 years of age, had performed as the Poquellos at a school talent show.

Renamed the Shirelles, Shirley, Doris, Micki, and Bev became one of the first in a long trail of successful girl groups; and one of the longest lasting. In just under a three-year period, between late 1960 and the summer of 1963, the Shirelles earned 13 Top 50 pop hits, two of which – *Will You Still Love Me Tomorrow* and *Soldier Boy* – topped the pop charts, becoming immortal oldies.

It was in Greenberg's living room late in 1957 that the girls auditioned what became their debut disc, the self-penned *I Met Him On A Sunday* (1958). Greenberg recorded it for her short-lived Tiara label, and when the disc started to receive a positive response, Decca Records bought the master and the Shirelles' contract. After two failed singles for the major, the Shirelles were released.

Greenberg formed Scepter Records and signed the act to her new label. The Shirelles had played the Uptown Theater with the Five Royales and overheard their now classic but non-charting *Dedicated To The One I Love*. Issued first in the summer of 1959, the Shirelles' version of *Dedicated* only made the lower reaches of the pop listings. The Owens' co-penned *Tonight's The Night* (1960) was next. Despite cover competition from the Chiffons, the original 45 did well in the charts.

With their next several releases, the Shirelles became the best and most popular female act in the country. The recordings were utter perfection, and came in quick succession in 1961: the Gerry Goffin–Carole King tune *Will You Still Love Me Tomorrow*, the reissued *Dedicated To The One I Love*, and *Mama Said*, all went into the Top 10, both R & B and pop. *A Thing Of The Past* and *Big John* fleshed out the year.

In 1962, after getting to the Top 10 with the Hal David–Burt Bacharach–Barney Williams *Baby It's You* (later remade and a hit by the hard-rocking Smith group) the Shirelles got into the charts with the biggest disc of their near-40-year career. This was the song from their "F. Green" (a.k.a. Florence Greenberg) producer Luther Dixon, *Soldier Boy*. Major black-pop hits – *Welcome Home Baby, Everybody Loves A Lover*, and *Foolish Little Girl* – were to follow in 1963 right up to the British Invasion and Luther Dixon's departure from Scepter.

In admiration and for their first UK LP, the Beatles did remakes of the girls' *Baby It's You* and *Boys*. Despite the accolades and some fine tracks between 1964 and their departure from the label in 1968 – such as *Sha-La-La* (covered by Manfred Mann, for whom it was a bigger hit), *Tonight You're Gonna Fall In Love With Me*, and *Maybe Tonight* – the Shirelles' girl-group sound had been replaced by nearly anything long-haired and British.

The Shirelles continued to perform and record into the late 1960s, and reformed in the early 1970s to work revival shows and, sporadically, to record. Addie Harris suffered a heart attack and died June 10, 1982.

"To Blacks, Chuck Jackson was a superstar – he was rightfully called 'Mr Excitement' – but it hurt me bad that I couldn't have done more for him," said Florence Greenberg. "He should still be a star, yet to this day white people only know Chuck for *Any Day Now*. Such a waste – even to his own, he's one of the most underrated of all soul singers."

At the age of 11, Chuck Jackson (b. July 22, 1937, in Winston-Salem, South Carolina) made his first public performance, singing and playing piano for 15 minutes over a Sunday radio program. He won a scholarship to South Carolina State College, but ran away to join a Cleveland gospel group, the Raspberry Singers. In 1958, he joined the Del Vikings. While Jackson was touring with the act known for *Come Go With Me* and *Whispering Bells* (neither of which Jackson appears on), Jackie Wilson took notice of his talent and encouraged him to drop out of the group and become his opening act. It was at one of these early performances that producer/songwriter Luther Dixon spotted Jackson and offered him a contract with the newly formed Scepter off-shoot, Wand Records.

I Don't Want To Cry (1961), Jackson's emotion-drenched Wand debut – written in one evening over dinner by the producer and his charge, about the young singer's heart-hurtin' woman – was not his first record. Jackson had recorded several 45s with the Del Vikings, in duets with the group's Kripp Johnson, and under his own name and those of "Chuck Flamingo" and "Charles Jackson" for such labels as Petite, Clock, and Beltone. With Jackson's success, numerous early demos were later offered by Amy, Logo, and others.

In rapid succession, Jackson had chart hits in 1961–2 with *(It Never Happens) In Real Life*, and two Jackson classics, Leiber and Stoller's *I Wake Up Crying* and the Burt Bacharach–Bob Hilliard *Any Day Now*. The last was written especially for him, though it lingered in the can for a year; Greenberg had decided that labelmate Tommy Hunt needed a hit, and he was given the song. Bacharach insisted on Jackson and the Hunt recording was never issued. *Any Day Now* became Jackson's first and only million-seller.

After his undanceable, futuristic, and overlooked *I Keep Forgettin'* and solid R & B hits with *Tell Him I'm Not Home* (featuring a frantic call-and-response chorus between Jackson and the song's creator, Doris Troy) and *I Will Never Turn My Back On You*, Jackson's recording career cooled for two years. His handling in 1963–4 of William Bell's *Any Other Way*, the Skyliners' classic *Since I Don't Have You*, and the frenzied *Beg Me* lacked nothing but higher chart positions.

Jackson's teaming with Maxine Brown, beginning in 1965 with a reworking of Chris Kenner's *Something You've Got*, did much to revive his career. The duo got into the charts in 1967 with remakes of Sam and Dave's *Hold On, I'm Comin'* and Shep and the

Limelites' *Daddy's Home*, among others. On his own at this time he found success with *I Need You, If I Didn't Love You*, and *Shame On Me*, before leaving the label for a disappointing stay with Motown/VIP, and later even less successful stops at Dakar, ABC–Dunhill, All Platinum, and EMI–American.

What Whitney Houston is to 1990s pop music, her first cousin Dionne Warwick (b. Marie Dionne Warwick, December 12, 1941, in East Orange, New Jersey) was to the 1960s. Warwick is one of the art form's most successful female singers. Accordingly, Joel Whitburn's *Top R & B Singles: 1942–1988* ranks Warwick as twenty-second among the top 200 R & B artists of all time. Over 50 of her singles have earned positions on the R & B listings; 29 were Top 40 pop hits.

The Warwick family was steeped in the gospel-music tradition. Dionne's mother had been a manager and member of the Drinkard Singers; her father had been the promotional director for the gospel-music division of Chess Records. From the age of six on, she studied music, eventually gaining a scholarship at Hartt College of Music in Hartford, Connecticut. In the early 1960s, Warwick, sister Dee Dee, and aunt Cissy Drinkard-Houston (Whitney's mother) were the Gospelaires on sacred days; on workdays – occasionally joined by Doris Troy – they were one of the most active units of backing singers in New York City.

Hal David and Burt Bacharach brought Florence Greenberg a demo of their *Make It Easy On Yourself*. Greenberg's response was "To hell with the song, who's the girl?" Warwick was tracked down and, before her solo debut, was often utilized as yet another voice on the successful Shirelles recordings. Late in 1962, David and Bacharach presented her with *Don't Make Me Over* (1963), intended to be a Leiber-and-Stoller-like lush production with full orchestra. Her debut was everything it was meant to be and more. Its pervasive, brooding, quasi-classical feel goes beyond words. Greenberg considers it her label's finest release. "Thirty years later, I still cry on hearing it," said the label owner.

Before repeating this success in 1963 with *Anyone Who Had A Heart*, Warwick aroused only mild interest with her *This Empty Place* and *Make The Music Play*, both grade-A efforts. There was no looking back for ten years following the issue of *Walk On By* (1964). David and Bacharach, who by the mid-1960s were writing the majority of Warwick's material, consistently supplied her with nothing but the best. *You'll Never Get To Heaven, Message to Michael, Trains And Boats And Planes, Alfie, The Windows Of The World, I Say A Little Prayer, Do You Know The Way To San Jose, Promises, Promises* – David and Bacharach 1964–8 compositions and classics, all; and standard lite-FM fare ever since.

Who could ask for more of a package of Dionne Warwick soft soul? All of the mentioned songs are contained therein, with the unfortunate exceptions of *This Empty Place* and *Make The Music Play*. Still, Warwick was so productive and David and Bacharach were not only unique but in such peak form that a double-CD, to include such other hits as *Who Can I Turn To* (from the Broadway play "The Roar Of The Grease Paint"), her remake of Jerry Butler's *Make It Easy On Yourself*, and the sensual and sweeping *I Just Don't Know What To Do With Myself* – not to mention some of her equally winning B sides and album tracks – would have been much appreciated.

Discographical Details

46 Anthology 1959–1964
The Shirelles
Rhino 5897

Dedicated To The One I Love/Tonight's The Night/Will You Still Love Me Tomorrow/ Boys/Mama Said/A Thing Of The Past/What A Sweet Thing That Was/Big John/ Baby It's You/Soldier Boy/Stop The Music/Everybody Loves a Lover/Foolish Little Girl/Don't Say Goodnight And Mean Goodbye/Sha-La-La/Maybe Tonight

47 Good Things
Chuck Jackson
Kent 935 (UK)

Tell Him I'm Not Home/Beg Me/I Keep Forgettin'/Millionaire/Hand It Over/Two Stupid Feet/Make The Night A Little Longer/I Wake Up Crying/I'm Your Man/ Castanets/Who's Gonna Pick Up The Pieces/Good Things Come To Those Who Wait/I Don't Want To Cry/The Breakin' Point/Any Day Now/Since I Don't Have You/They Don't Give Medals To Yesterday's Heroes/Where Do I Go From Here/These Chains Of Love/What's With This Loneliness/Forget About Me/I Just Don't Know What To Do With Myself/I Can't Stand To See You Cry

48 Anthology 1962–1969
Dionne Warwick
Rhino 75898

Don't Make Me Over/Anyone Who Had A Heart/Walk On By/You'll Never Get To Heaven/A House Is Not A Home/Reach Out for Me/Are You There With Another Girl/ Message To Michael/Trains And Boats and Planes/Alfie/The Windows Of The World/I Say A Little Prayer/Valley Of The Dolls/Do You Know The Way To San Jose/ Promises, Promises/I'll Never Fall In Love Again

(ii) Atlantic/Atco

The Drifters came into being in 1953 as a vehicle for Clyde McPhatter, already much noted in the African American community for his lead-work with the successful R & B group the Dominoes. McPhatter surrounded himself with Andrew and Gerhart Thrasher and Bill Pinkney, and garnered a contract with

Atlantic Records. Their name, incidentally, came about because all the members had previously "drifted" from group to group; a foreshadowing and surely a warning.

Promptly, the Drifters got into the 1953–5 charts again and again – *Money Honey, Such A Night, Honey Love, Bim Bam, What'cha Gonna Do, Adorable* – but exclusively with R & B fans. McPhatter was drafted in 1955 and already numerous members had drifted off, but the Drifters' name continued to be in the charts into the early months of 1957. Later recordings like *Fools Fall In Love* (1957) and *Drip Drop* (1958) failed to get into the R & B charts, despite promising placings on the pop listings.

Discouraged by dwindling sales, the group's manager and owner of the Drifters' name, George Treadwell, fired them. To meet multiyear contracts, Treadwell persuaded the little-known Five Crowns to become the "new" Drifters. It is this latter group that the mass of appreciative listeners think of when the Drifters' name is reverently mentioned; and it is with this formation and its later constellations that the Atlantic set is exclusively concerned.

The rechristened Five Crowns comprised Ben E. King, Elsberry Hobbs, Reggie Kimber, Charlie Thomas, and Johnny Lee Williams. Greatly assisted by writers/independent producers Mike Leiber and Jerry Stoller, the new Drifters created *There Goes My Baby* (1959), their debut disc, a number 2 pop hit and undisputed world classic. Some pop-culture historians have claimed the disc to be a genre-altering archetype – it is the first R & B recording, they say, to make an extensive use of strings, to utilize a large percussion section, to top the pop listings. *There Goes My Baby* was a lushly produced track whose style became a Drifters trademark.

The follow-up proved double-sided. *(If You Cry) True Love, True Love* backed with *Dance With Me* (1959) won individual top 5 positions on the R & B listings and Top 40 pop places, and established the act in England. Suddenly, the Drifters could do little wrong. Hit followed hit. In 1960, *This Magic Moment* and *Lonely Winds* went into the R & B Top 10, and then the Latin-flavored *Save The Last Dance For Me* topped both the R & B and pop charts. King's lead vocal on this track won such acclaim that he left the group to work as a soloist. Rudy Lewis, a comparable singer, filled in for King and the hit string continued.

The list of cherished classics produced by this group, one of the most successful African American acts in all of pop music history, is insurmountable. Possibly only the Temptations or the Supremes have created more golden greats than the Drifters. The Lewis-fronted Drifters did well in both R & B and pop charts with – among others – *I Count The Tears, Some Kind Of Wonderful, Please Stay, Sweets For My Sweet, Roomful Of Tears, Up On The Roof, On Broadway,* and *I'll Take You Home* (all 1961–3).

Through this peak period the Drifters often worked with Phil Spector, Burt Bacharach, and Bert Berns, among others. Following Lewis's death in 1964, a mid-1950s member, Johnny Moore, rejoined as lead vocalist. Moore sang the lead on *Under The Boardwalk* (1964), the group's last major North American hit. The Drifters managed to continue through the 1960s with medium-sized chart hits, such as *I've Got Sand In My Shoes* (1964), *Saturday Night At The Movies* (1964), and *At The Club* (1965).

When their Atlantic contract ran out in 1972, the Drifters (ever-revising, though always fronted by Moore) experienced a full-blown revival in England, where they scored Top 10 hits in 1973–6 with various Atlantic reissues and *Like Sister And Brothers, Kissin' In The Back Row Of The Movies, Down On The Beach Tonight, There Goes My First Love, Can I Take You Home Little Girl,* and *You're More Than A Number In My Little Red Book,* for Bell Records.

When the soul music ratings are firmly in place, former Drifters' lead Ben E. King (b. Benjamin Earl Nelson, September 23, 1938, in Henderson, North Carolina) will surely be ranked at the top, with Aretha Franklin, Solomon Burke, and Chuck Jackson. From his very first recording with the "new" Drifters (the Five Crowns) – his co-authored *There Goes My Baby* (1959) – King left an indelible mark on rock-and-roll and R & B. With the visionary aid of Jerry Leiber and Mike Stoller, King created some of the premier soul recordings of the early 1960s, not the least being later Tom Jones million-seller *I (Who Have Nothing)* (1963), *How Can I Forget* (1963), and *The Record (Baby I Love You)* (1965) – all *not* included in this allegedly ultimate packaged set.

It was with the chart-topping success of the Drifters' *Save The Last Dance For Me* (1960) that King decided to forge a solo career. *Spanish Harlem* and the self-penned and now pop standard *Stand By Me*, his initial, 1961 singles, went into both R & B and pop Top 20s. After *Amor* (1961) and *Don't Play That Song* (1962), King fared markedly better on the R & B listings. Nearly a decade and a half passed before he resurfaced high on the pop listings with *Supernatural Thing, Part 1* (1975).

Ultimate is quite erroneously titled. It is the best available CD compilation, but it is marred. Besides the aforementioned sins of omission, it passes over such R & B notables as King's *Tell Daddy* (1963), *Seven Letters* (1965), *It's All Over* (1964), *Too Bad* (1962), *What Is Soul* (1967), and *Do It In The Name Of Love* (1975), and his successful pairings with the Average White Band, *Get It Up* (1977) and *A Star In The Ghetto* (1977) – all of which were in the R & B or pop charts – in favor of such lesser recordings and atypical pop-puffery as *I Could Have Danced All Night* (1963) and LP tracks *On The Street Where You Live* and *Moon River*.

The roots of Solomon Burke (b. 1936, in Philadelphia, Pennsylvania) are as deep in gospel as possible. Burke was embedded in a highly religious family and was such a precocious talent that he became a soloist in his church by the age of nine. By 12, he had his own radio program, "Solomon's Temple," and was known in the African American community as "The Wonder Boy Preacher." Noting young Burke's vocal prowess, Philadelphia deejay Kae Williams brought the lad to the attention of the small Apollo label. Four singles, including *Christmas Presents From Heaven* (1957), a small local hit, were issued before Burke decided to shelve the music in favor of mortuary school. After his return and a few sides for Singular Records, Burke signed with Atlantic Records, on a handshake. With *Just Out Of Reach (Of My Two Empty Arms)* (1961), his second single for the label – and two years before Ray Charles had a big hit with the very country *I Can't Stop Loving You* – Burke made both the R & B and pop listings with a glorified, gospelized country-and-western ballad; a musical merger such as few had heard before.

For the remainder of the decade, Burke was an original, a secular-sacred integrator and first-rank soul star, dubbed "King Of Rock And Soul" by Baltimore deejay Round Robin. Hits were continuous and at the time such future chart entries seemed sure to be endless for this ebullient emoter and man of God.

Opening in 1962, he had chart hits with the intense *Cry To Me* and the double-sided *Hangin' Up My Heart For You* backed with *Down In The Valley*. The next year saw Burke issue two of his biggest and most cherished 45s, *You're Good For Me* and the competitive Wilson Pickett cover *If You Needed Me*. In 1964 Burke reworked and gospelized Jim Reeves's *He'll Have To Go* and worked out what later became a Rolling Stones live-performance staple, *Everybody Needs Somebody To Love*.

Although years of success were to follow, Burke seemed to peak in popularity in 1965 with his R & B chart-topping *Got To Get You Off My Mind* and its successor *Tonight's The Night*. Before his departure from the label late in 1968, Burke did well in the charts with *Baby Come On Home*, *Keep A Light In The Window Till I Come Home*, *Take Me (Just As I Am)*, and his last for Atlantic, the socio-soul ballad *I Wish I Knew (How It Would Feel To Be Free)*.

For a brief time, Burke moved to Bell Records where he got into the charts with a cover of Creedence Clearwater Revival's *Proud Mary* (1969). Next on MGM, Burke found success with *The Electronic Magnetism (That's Heavy, Baby)* (1971) and *Love's Street And Fool's Road* (1972). Thereafter, the hits were harder to come by and less well received. By the 1980s, Burke's name was unfamiliar to the next generation of rock and soul fans.

Discographical Details

49   All The Greatest Hits and More: 1959–65
The Drifters

Atlantic 81931-2 (2-disc set)

There Goes My Baby/Oh My Love/Baltimore/Hey Senorita/Dance With Me/(If You Cry) True Love, True Love/This Magic Moment/Lonely Winds/Nobody But Me/Save The Last Dance For Me/I Count The Tears/Sometimes I Wonder/Please Stay/Roomful Of Tears/Sweets For My Sweet/Some Kind Of Wonderful/Loneliness, Loneliness/ Mexican Divorce/Somebody New Dancing With You/Jackpot/She Never Talks To Me That Way/When My Little Girl Is Smiling/Strangers On The Shore/What To Do/Up On The Roof/Another Night With The Boys/I Feel Good All Over/Let The Music Play/ On Broadway/I'll Take You Home/If You Don't Come Back/Didn't It/One Way Love/He's Just A Playboy/Under The Boardwalk/I Don't Want To Go On Without You/I've Got Sand In My Shoes/Saturday Night At The Movies/At The Club/Come On Over To My Place

50   The Ultimate Ben E. King
Ben E. King

Atlantic 80213-2

Stand By Me/That's When It Hurts/I Could Have Danced All Night/First Taste Of Love/Dream Lover/Moon River/Spanish Harlem/Amor/Don't Play That Song/Young Boy Blues/It's All In The Game/Supernatural Thing (Pt 1)/On The Street Where You Live/Will You Still Love Me Tomorrow/Show Me The Way/Here Comes The Night

51   The Best Of Solomon Burke: Home In Your Heart
Solomon Burke

Rhino/Atlantic 702084 (2-disc set)

Home In Your Heart/Down In The Valley/Looking For My Baby/I'm Hanging Up My Heart For You/Cry To Me/Just Out Of Reach (Of My Two Empty Arms)/ Goodbye Baby (Goodbye Baby)/Words/Stupidity/Send Me Some Loving/Go On Back To Him/Baby (I Wanna Be Loved)/Can't Nobody Love Me/Got To Get You Off My Mind/Someone To Love Me/You're Good For Me/Dance Dance Dance/Everybody Needs Somebody To Love/Tonight's The Night/Baby, Come On Home/If You Needed Me/The Price/Get Out Of My Life Woman/Save It/Take Me (Just As I Am)/When She Touches Me (Nothing Else Matters)/I Wish I Knew (How It Would Feel To Be Free)/Party People/Keep A Light In The Window [Till I Come Home]/I Feel A Sin Coming On/Meet Me In Church/Someone Is Watching/Detroit City/Shame On Me/I Stayed Away Too Long/It's Just A Matter Of Time/Since I Met You Baby/Time Is A Thief/Woman, How Do You Make Me Love You Like I Do/It's Been A Change/ What'd I Say

(iii) Other New York Labels

Brook Benton (b. Benjamin Franklin Peay, September 19, 1931, in Camden, South Carolina) grew up in a rural area. As a child he sang in the church choir, later traveling the South with the Camden Jubilee Singers. In 1948 he moved to New York City, earning his money pushing a hand-truck round the city's garment district. For a time he was a member of the Bill Landford Spiritual Singers, the Golden Gate Quartet, and later the Jerusalem Stars.

Back in New York, in the mid-1950s Benton drove a truck by day and lingered around recording studios and small clubs. He formed an R & B group called the Sandmen and earned the opportunity to record demos for Clyde McPhatter, Roy Hamilton, and lifelong influences Nat "King" Cole and Billy Eckstine. Some unsuccessful sides followed for OKeh, Epic, and Vik. *A Million Miles From Nowhere* (1958), recorded for Vik, was a minor hit.

Benton's career turning-point came with his signing with Mercury Records and their teaming him with A & R/producer Clyde Otis and arranger Belford Hendricks. His first release for them, *It's Just A Matter Of Time* backed with *Hurtin' Inside* (1959), opened the floodgates. *Endlessly* backed with *So Close*, and *Thank You Pretty Baby* backed with *With All Of My Heart* did well in both the pop and R & B listings; all were co-written by Benton, a feat seldom achieved in the late 1950s.

Benton was a popular success and had a phenomenal run – 21 gold records and 40 Hot 100 pop chart entries within a five-year period, 16 of the latter in the first 18 months! This double-CD package makes no false claims – **Forty Greatest Hits** is just that. All of Benton's *Billboard* pop and R & B chartings for the Mercury label (1959–66) – both A sides and the B sides that got into the charts, plus his two classic duets with Dinah Washington, *Baby (You've Got What It Takes)* and *A Rockin' Good Way* – are included (except one *Lost Penny*), and all is presented in near-perfect chronological order. Also included, on lease from Cotillion, is Benton's most cherished and last major hit, Tony Joe White's *Rainy Night In Georgia* (1970).

Leaving Mercury, Benton signed with RCA, Cotillion, Brut, All Platinum, and Stax, among others. Aside from a lone chart entry in the late 1970s with an atypical disco disc, *Makin' Love Is Good For You*, the hits stopped for him in 1971. By this point, apparently, there was no longer any room for his rich baritone and that staple, lush, string backing. Benton died on May 9, 1988, of complications from spinal meningitis.

The original three Isley Brothers – Rudolph (b. April 1, 1939), O'Kelly (b. December 25, 1937), and lead vocalist Ronald (b. May 21, 1941) – began as gospel vocalists performing with their pianist mother Sallye Bernice Isley around their home town of Cincinnati, Ohio, in the early 1950s. In 1957, with their mother's blessing, they trekked to New York City to seek out a career singing secular music. After several unsuccessful rock-and-roll, doo-wop, and R & B efforts for Teenage, Cindy, Mark-X, and Gone Records, the brothers were discovered by a representative for RCA. Their initial release for the major label went nowhere. RCA A & R heads Hugo Peretti and Luigi Creatore convinced the act to record an improvised interpretation of Jackie Wilson's *Lonely Teardrops*. The result, *Shout, Pts 1 & 2* (1959), has become a world-wide standard, despite its failure to make the national R & B listings and its only modest pop chart placing at number 47. *Shout* has been revived by many artists, with sales now totaling in the millions.

Although they recorded some fine follow-ups for RCA – here represented by *Open Up Your Heart* (1960), an update on Bill Haley's rock-and-roll anthem *Rock Around The Clock*, and the turntable classic *Respectable* (1960) – the Isleys failed to get into the charts; R & B or pop. In 1961, the act moved to Atlantic Records, where, despite handling by the legendary Leiber and Stoller, the dry spell continued. An energized *Your Old Lady* (1961) and two further singles were issued. Late in the year, they moved their operations to Florence Greenberg's Wand label. After a false start with a lame dance ditty called *The Snake* (1962), the brothers went solid gold and coast-to-coast with the Bert Berns-produced *Twist And Shout* (1962). Many months later the Beatles reintroduced the song into the charts.

Further efforts for Wand – including *Twistin' With Linda* (1962) and *Nobody But Me* (1963), later a Top 10 remake for the Human Beinz – sold poorly. Through a technical error, Greenberg lost the Isleys to United Artists Records. In 1963–4 the label rapidly released *She's Gone, You'll Never Leave Him* and their first cut of *Who's That Lady* – ten years later a Top 10 R & B and pop hit remade as *That Lady* – but to no avail. Next, the brothers formed their own label, an unheard-of practice in 1964. Their first and only issue on their own T-Neck – at this time – was *Testify, Pts 1 & 2* (1964). Atlantic Records picked up their label's distribution and within months the Isleys were recording again for the major. Inexplicably, the Isleys were yet to be superstars. *Move Over And Let Me Dance* (1965) and the touching *Last Girl* (1965) failed, like far too many of their former offerings, to sell.

During 1965, the brothers made appearances with the Motown Review. Berry Gordy offered them a contract and handed them over to his hit machine, Holland–Dozier–Holland. Despite their Motownization, the Isley Brothers escaped with integrity intact, and finally found a winning streak. *This Old Heart Of Mine* (1966) is a Motor City classic. *Take Some Time Out For Love* (1966), *I Guess I'll Always Love You* (1966), *Got To Have You Back* (1967), and *Take Me In Your Arms (Rock Me A Little While)* (1968) rapidly paraded onto the charts.

By the decade's end, the Isley Brothers were well on their way to becoming one of the most successful African American acts the world has ever known. Their T-Neck label was re-established. With the addition of brothers Ernie (guitar) and Marvin (bass), and cousin Chris Jaspers (keyboards), the act became a dark-skin hippy dream, a self-contained funk machine. The successes are staggering – *It's Your Thing, Love The One You're With, Fight The Power Pt 1* – and yet to be terminated.

Jeanette "Baby" Washington (b. Justine Washington, October 13, 1940, in Bamberg, South Carolina) was one of the finest female singers in the R & B/soul idiom, one of the most underrated and underappreciated singers of her era. She was a mere "baby," a Manhattan high-school student, when discovered in 1956 in a neighborhood voice and dance school by Zell Sanders, owner of the J & S record firm. Sanders needed a replacement for her ever-changing doo-wop act, the Hearts, then popular with *Lonely Nights*. Washington agreed to sing with the Hearts and sometimes was called upon to do so with label-mates the Jaynetts, later noted for their eerie *Sally Goes Round The Roses*. In a year's time, Washington was given her first solo single. Neither *Everyday*, nor its three successors for Sanders, got into the charts.

The Time backed with *You Never Could Be Mine* (1959), her debut disc for producer Donald Shaw's Newark, New Jersey, Neptune label, was a success with R & B fans. *The Time* is a classic; a rockaballad with soulful wails and a heavy, tick-tock beat. Months later, Washington repeated her success with a similar dirge, *The Bells (On Your Wedding Day)*. *Workout* backed with *Let's Love In The Moonlight*, a change-of-pace rocker backed with an easy-listening number, followed the same year. Neither side, nor the next three discs for Neptune, got into the charts.

Nobody Cares (1961), a doo-wop ballad, was Washington's final single for Neptune; the label folded within months. *Nobody Cares* became her largest hit thus far, placing her for the first time on the pop airwaves and listings. Two overlooked 45s were issued by ABC–Paramount before Washington found her hit-making home with Juggy Murray's Sue label. In 1962, after a false start with the bluesy *Go On*, Murray recorded her soul-like *Handful Of Memories*, which got into the Top 20 in the R & B charts. The gospel-based *Hush Heart* was passed over, but rapidly followed by Washington's biggest ever, the lushly orchestrated, double-sided perennial *That's How Heartaches Are Made* backed with *There He Is*. The B side was tough, fever-pitched, pure 1960s soul.

All of Washington's remaining pop-chart entries happened in the next 18 months. In near-unbroken succession, there was *Leave Me Alone, Hey Lonely One, I Can't Wait Until I See My Baby, The Clock, It'll Never Be Over For Me*, and *Only Those In Love*. A few further singles were issued before Washington took a year off and Murray sold Sue Records to United Artists.

By 1967, R & B had completed its transition to modern 1960s soul. Washington made the change, with sporadic chart hits in the late 1960s and early-to-mid-1970s for Cotillion and Master Five. Numerous notable soul sides were cut, none yet available in compilation form. The two collections here contain the best of Washington's Sue recordings and for purposes of review are considered as one entry.

The Manhattans' original five-man lineup consisted of Edward "Sonny" Bivens, Jr (b. January 15, 1942), Kenneth "Wally" Kelly (b. January 9, 1942), Winfred "Blue" Lovett (b. November 15, 1943), George "Smithy" Smith, and Richard Taylor. They were formed in the late 1950s from the most enthusiastic individuals of rival street-corner doo-wop groups in Jersey City, New Jersey, and named after their favorite skyline. Bivens and Taylor, who had met while enlisted in the air force, had previously recorded as members of the Dorsets.

As Ronnie and the Manhattans, the five Jersey City guys recorded for Piney in 1962 and Bobby Robinson's Enjoy in 1964 – with no results. Their big break came when singer Barbara Brown recommended them to producer and former member of the Lionel Hampton and Louis Armstrong bands Joe Evans, now owner of the Newark-based Carnival label. *For The Very First Time* and *Call Somebody Please*, their first and second single for Carnival in 1964, sold well locally but did little to stir a national interest. The third single, *I Wanna Be (Your Everything)* (1965), did everything. Orders for 6,000 copies poured in on the first day of its release.

Despite Evans's lack of any major-label distribution throughout the act's stay with the label, their immediate follow-up, *Searchin' For My Baby* backed with *I'm The One That Love Forgot*, sold well where found, peaking on the R & B listings at number 20. Back-to-back, they moved from progressive doo-wop to sweet soul: in 1965–6, *Follow Your Heart, Baby I Need You, Can I,* and *I Bet'cha (Couldn't Love Me)* all did equally well. In 1967, the Manhattans found success again and then again, with *When We're Made As One* and *I Call It Love*. The seasonal perennial *It's That Time Of The Year* backed with *Alone On New Year's Eve*, which featured female label-mates the Lovettes, did not. The best of the Manhattans' Carnival output is included on two Collectables discs, considered as one entry here.

Following a lull in the late 1960s, the Manhattans signed with King Record subsidiary Deluxe. A new string of chart hits followed, despite the death of lead vocalist George Smith during the winter of 1970. Gerald Alston, from the New Imperials, joined as Smith's replacement and the act signed with Columbia Records late in 1972. (For discussion of the Manhattans' Columbia years, see chapter 3.)

Discographical Details

52   Forty Greatest Hits
Brook Benton

Mercury 836 755-2 (2-disc set)

It's Just A Matter Of Time/Hurtin' Inside/Endlessly/So Close/Thank You Pretty Baby/ With All Of My Heart/So Many Ways/This Time Of The Year/The Ties That Bind/ Hither and Thither And You/Kiddio/The Same One/Fools Rush In/Someday You'll Want Me To/Think Twice/For My Baby/The Boll Weevil Song/Frankie And Johnny/ It's Just A House Without You/Revenge/Baby (You've Got What It Takes) (with Dinah Washington)/*A Rockin' Good Way* (with Dinah Washington)/*Shadrack/ Walk On The Wild Side/Hit Record/Lie To Me/Hotel Happiness/Still Waters Run Deep/I Got What I Wanted/Dearer Than Life/My True Confession/Two Tickets To Paradise/Going Going Gone/It's Too Late To Turn Back Now/Another Cup Of Coffee/ A House Is Not A Home/Lumberjack/Do It Right/Love Me Now/Rainy Night In Georgia*

53   The Isley Brothers Story, Vol. 1: Rockin' Soul 1959–1968
The Isley Brothers

Rhino R2-70908

Shout, Pts 1 & 2/Respectable/Rock Around The Clock/Open Up Your Heart/Your Old Lady/Twist And Shout/Twistin' With Linda/Nobody But Me/She's Gone/You'll Never Leave Him/Who's That Lady/Testify, Pts 1 & 2/The Last Girl/Move Over And Let Me Dance/This Old Heart Of Mine/Take Some Time Out For Love/I Guess I'll Always Love You/Got To Have You Back/Take Me In Your Arms (Rock Me A Little While)/Behind A Painted Smile

54   The Best of Baby Washington
Baby Washington

Collectables COL-5040

The Time/Only Those In Love/Move On Drifter/There He Is/You Never Could Be Mine/The Clock/That's How Heartaches Are Made/Nobody Cares/Leave Me Alone/ Handful Of Memories/Let's Love In The Moonlight/The Bells (On Your Wedding Day)

Only Those In Love
Baby Washington

Collectables COL-5108

Only Those In Love/I Can't Wait Until I See My Baby's Face/Who's Going To Take Care Of Me/It'll Never Be Over For Me/Your Fool/Hey Lonely One/Careless Hands/ Go On/Run My Heart/Money's Funny/White Christmas/Silent Night

55   Dedicated To You: Golden Carnival Classics, Pt 1
The Manhattans

Collectables COL-5135

Follow Your Heart/That New Girl/Can I/The Boston Monkey/I've Got Everything But You/Manhattan Stomp/Searchin' For My Baby/Our Love Will Never Die/I'm The One That Love Forgot/What's It Gonna Be/Teach Me (The Philly Dog)/Baby I Need You

For You And Yours: Golden Carnival Classics, Pt 2
The Manhattans
Collectables COL-5136
I Call It Love/I Bet'cha (Couldn't Love Me)/Sweet Little Girl/There Goes A Fool/
Alone On New Year's Eve/All I Need Is Your Love/I Wanna Be (Your Everything)/
When We're Made As One/Call Somebody Please/For The Very First Time/It's That
Time Of The Year/Baby I'm Sorry

Basic Recordings

56   The Best Of Little Anthony and the Imperials
Little Anthony and the Imperials
Rhino 70919
Tears On My Pillow/Two People In The World/It's Not For Me/So Much/The Diary/
Wishful Thinking/A Prayer And A Juke Box/I'm Alright/Shimmy Shimmy Ko-Ko-
Bop/My Empty Room/I'm Taking A Vacation From Love/Please Say You Want Me/
Traveling Stranger/I'm On The Outside (Looking In)/Goin' Out Of My Head/Hurt
So Bad/Take Me Back/I Miss You So

Anthony Gourdine (b. January 8, 1941) and his Imperials – Clarence Collins (b. March 17, 1939), Ernest Wright (b. August 24, 1941), Tracy Lord (b. 1940), and Glouster "Nat" Rogers (b. 1940) – were a premier Brooklyn doo-wop group in the late-1950s. With Anthony's falsetto sailing over the rest, the act entered the pop and R & B listings with most of the tracks provided by this Rhino compilation; particularly their ethereal *Tears On My Pillow*, super-stupid *Shimmy Shimmy Ko-Ko-Bop*, and a classic reworking of the Schoolboys' *Please Say You Want Me*. Like Frankie Lymon and the Teenagers (a major influence), Anthony and his Imperials separated in 1962, for what proved to be unsuccessful solo endeavors. Unlike their musical models, the Imperials managed to reform – without Lord and Rogers, who were replaced by Sam Strain (b. December 9, 1940) – to successfully adapt their style to the soulful 1960s, and to drive their career to a pinnacle undreamed of before.

Beginning with *I'm On The Outside (Looking In)* (1964) – under the tutelage of Don Costa and producer/songsmith Teddy Randazzo – the group found success with a classy line of dramatic, string-encased soul ballads. *Goin' Out Of My Head* and *Hurt So Bad*, both 1965, are classics. Unfortunately, while this trilogy of plush productions is included on this set, only two other soul-era hits are provided, *Take Me Back* (1965) and *I Miss You So* (1965). A double package is needed, each disc to document a phase – the End label rock-and-roll classics (1958–62) and the pathos pieces from their mature DCP–Veep–United Artists years (1964–70).

57   The Oh So Fine Fiestas
The Fiestas
Ace CH173 (UK)
So Fine/Dollar Bill/That Was Me/Mr Dillon, Mr Dillon/Come On And Love Me/
Mexico/Last Night I Dreamed/The Lawman/Our Anniversary/The Railroad Song/Try
It One More Time/Mama Put The Law Down/Fine As Wine (unissued)/*You Can Be*
My Girlfriend/Anna/I'm Your Slave

The Fiestas (Sam Ingalls, Preston Lane, Eddie Morris, and lead singer Tommy Bullock) may have been more influential than successful. Their name is usually identified with little more than the late 1950s rock-and-roll hit, *So Fine*. But they were there at the moment of change. They were a transitional group, present when Jerry Butler and the Impressions, Ray Charles, and Brook Benton were fundamentally altering R & B into soul in all its variety. Fiestas' music ranged from the doo-wopping (*Last Night I Dreamed* and *You Can Be My Girlfriend*) through the teen-oriented Coasters/Olympics niche (*Lawman, That Was Me*, and *Mr Dillon, Mr Dillon*) to out-and-out, gospel-linked soul ballads and shouters (*Try It One More Time*, Arthur Alexander's *Anna*, and the unissued *Fine As Wine*).

The Oh So Fine Fiestas is a good package of turn-of-the-age music. All of the aforementioned tracks are included. The set lean towards the act's rock-and-roll and pop roots: such 1960s soul-styled recordings as *All That's Good, Gotta Have Your Loving*, and their only other pop and R & B chart entry, *Broken Heart* (1962), are not reproduced here.

58 Greatest Recordings
The Chiffons

Ace CDCH 293 (UK)

He's So Fine/My Boyfriend's Back/Stop, Look And Listen/Oh My Lover/One Fine Day/A Love So Fine/Nobody Knows What Is Going On (In My Mind But Me)/Out Of This World/Mystic Voice/Up On The Bridge/Dream Dream Dream/My Block/Did You Ever Go Steady/March/Keep The Boy Happy/When The Boy's Happy (The Girl's Happy Too)/The Real Thing/Sweet Talking Guy/I Have A Boyfriend/Sailor Boy/I'm Gonna Dry My Eyes/Open Your Eyes (I Will Be There)/The Heavenly Place/Teach Me How/He's A Bad One/If I Knew Then (What I Know Now)/Lucky Me/Why Am I So Shy/Tonight I Met An Angel/When I Go To Sleep At Night/Tonight I'm Gonna Dream/Down Down Down/My Sweet Lord

Girl groups were popular in 1963, and Judy Craig (b. 1946), Barbara Lee (b. 1947), Patricia Bennett (b. 1947), and Sylvia Peterson (b. 1946) were South Bronx high-schoolers who, with the aid of Ronnie Mack, a neighbor, piano player, and aspiring songwriter, managed to provide just what the trend-conscious nation needed: a teen-oriented, doo-wop tune with the never-to-be-forgotten hook, "Doo-lang, doo-lang, doo-lang . . ." Their adolescent exuberance shot *He's So Fine* to the top of the pop and R & B listings, where it remained for four weeks. They returned again and again, well into the Motown era, with similar, minimally soul-sounding records: *One Fine Day* (1963), *A Love So Fine* (1963), *I Have A Boyfriend* (1964), *Sweet Talking Guy* (1966), and such lesser lights as *Sailor Boy* (1964), *Out Of This World* (1966), *Stop, Look And Listen* (1966), and their eerie *Nobody Knows What Is Going On (In My Mind But Me)* (1965).

All of their pop-soul successes and seemingly every musical drop ever squeezed out for Gene Schwartz's Laurie Records is included in this package – even their pleasing but little noted recordings as the Four Pennies, *When The Boy's Happy (The Girl's Happy Too)* (1963) and the atypically earthy *My Block* (1963).

59 Oh No Not My Baby
Maxine Brown

Kent 949 (UK)

Since I Found You/Gotta Find A Way/I Wonder What My Baby's Doing Tonight/Let Me Give You My Lovin'/It's Torture/One In A Million/Oh No Not My Baby/You're In Love/Anything for A Laugh/Coming Back To You/Yesterday's Kisses/Ask Me/All In My Mind/Little Girl Lost/I Want A Guarantee/The Secret Of Livin'/Baby Cakes/One Step At A Time/I've Got A Lot Of Love Left In Me/I Don't Need Anything/Oh Lord, What Are You Doing To Me/I Cry Alone/Funny/Misty Morning Eyes/Love That Man/Losing My Touch/Put Yourself Together In My Place/It's Gonna Be Alright

Fans have freely referred to Maxine Brown (b. August 18, 1939, in Kingstree, North Carolina) as the premier female soul singer. Some wags assert that *All In My Mind*, her self-penned debut, was the first crossover soul single. Both assertions are arguably off the mark, but not by much. From that initial release on the tiny Nomar label in 1960 – after years of dues-paying gospel through her departure from Wand Records in 1967 for a planned career extension under Otis Redding's tutelage at Volt, which ended with his untimely death, Brown created some of the most poignant soul ever.

While the many hit-making duets with label-mate Chuck Jackson are absent, all of Brown's distinctive sweet-soul ballads are included in this remastered Kent offering. In addition to the chart-moving *Ask Me* (1963) and *Coming Back To You* (1964), the Gerry Goffin–Carole King *It's Gonna Be Alright* (1965), and Brown's most noted number, *Oh No Not My Baby* (1965) are here. There are numerous passed-over gems, such as *Little Girl Lost, I Don't Need Anything*, and the now-classic Maxine Brown–Ed Townsend composition *Since I Found You*. Also included are seven unissued tracks, among them the Otis Redding-produced *Baby Cakes* and an impassioned reading of Luther Dixon and Bert Keyes's underappreciated *Oh Lord, What Are You Doing To Me*.

60   Jazz To Soul
Aretha Franklin
Columbia C2K 48515 (2-disc set)

Today I Have The Blues/(Blue)/By Myself/Maybe I'm A Fool/All Night Long/Blue Holiday/Nobody Like You/Sweet Lover/Just For A Thrill/If Ever I Would Leave You/Once In A While (previously unreleased)/*This Bitter Earth/God Bless The Child/Skylark* (alternate take)/*Muddy Water/Drinking Again/What A Difference A Day Makes/Unforgettable/Love For Sale/Misty/Impossible* (alternate take)/*This Could Be The Start Of Something/Won't Be Long/Operation Heartbreak/Soulville/Runnin' Out Of Fools/Trouble In Mind/Walk On By/Every Little Bit Hurts/Mockingbird/You'll Lose A Good Thing/Cry Like A Baby/Take It Like You Give It/Land Of Dreams/Can't You Just See Me/(No, No) I'm Losing You/Bit Of Soul/Why Was I Born?/Until You Were Gone/Lee Cross*

There is a myth in pop music circles that Aretha Franklin (b. March 25, 1942, in Memphis, Tennessee) made little of note prior to her signing with Atlantic Records in 1967, and especially little in the way of outstanding soul music. A mere glance at the *Billboard* singles charts (seven R & B and eight pop chart entries) or a casual hearing of nearly any of her Columbia efforts – most particularly, perhaps, her **Soul Sister** – should dispel this. Better yet, listen to Franklin's **Jazz To Soul**, a compilation of her very best while with the label.

Franklin came from Detroit's East Side, the same area that produced Jackie Wilson, Smokey Robinson, and the Four Tops. Her father, Reverend C.L. Franklin, was a civil rights activist and fiery preacher at the New Bethel Baptist Church. Franklin sang with, toured with, and was totally engulfed by the sounds of the gospel. At the age of 18 – with the familial blessing – she made a demonstration tape of secular songs. It was heard by John Hammond, who was responsible for Bessie Smith's last sessions and Billie Holiday's first, and who is credited with bringing Bob Dylan, Bruce Springsteen, and others to the label. He immediately signed her to a Columbia contract.

Ten albums were recorded for Columbia between 1961 and 1967. Much effort was made in shaping Franklin as a classy pop star. Large orchestras and strings, big-time arrangements, show tunes, jazzy numbers, and sheer sentimentality peppered her Columbia catalogue. Still, it is hard to deny – and a sin to overlook – the soulful brilliance found in tunes like *Cry Like A Baby*, *Lee Cross*, *(No, No) I'm Losing You*, *Can't You Just See Me*, *Until You Were Gone*, and *Runnin' Out Of Fools*.

61 In the Beginning
Gladys Knight and the Pips

Bell 1323 (LP)
Letter Full Of Tears/Either Way I Lose/If Ever I Should Fall In Love/Daybreak/ Maybe, Maybe Baby/Every Beat Of My Heart/Giving Up/Stop And Get A Hold Of Myself/Lovers Always Forgive/Tell Her You're Mine/Operator

In the Beginning is the most apt title for this 1974 release that collects all of Gladys Knight and the Pips' hits during their years on Bobby Robinson's Fury label (1961–2) and Larry Maxwell's Maxx label (1964–5). This Atlanta family group – Gladys (b. May 28, 1944), her brother Merald (b. September 4, 1942), and her cousins William Guest (b. June 2, 1941) and Edward Patten (b. August 2, 1939) – got their first national hit, *Every Beat Of My Heart* (1961), in two versions, on Vee Jay and Fury. Vee Jay obtained its version by purchasing the original from Atlanta-based Huntom, and Fury by signing the group and working up a new version (contained here). The group's next hit was the remarkable *Letter Full Of Tears* (1961), for which Robinson, with a pocketful of money from the previous hit, was able to invest in a great string arrangement. The energetic *Operator* (1962) was Fury's last chart record from the Pips. Van McCoy wrote both of the Maxx hits, *Giving Up* (1964) (perhaps the most dramatic ballad the group ever recorded) and *Lovers Always Forgive* (1964), another worthy ballad. Three other fine Maxx songs are here: another McCoy ballad, *Either Way I Lose* (1964), the lovely mid-tempo *If Ever I Should Fall In Love* (1965), and the up-tempo *Tell Her You're Mine* (1965).

In 1966 Gladys Knight and the Pips moved to Motown, which made them international recording artists. In some Motown collections, re-recordings of these songs appear. It is best to look for the originals. Arista, which is sitting on this album, has by now sold enough Whitney Houston albums to spare a few dollars to re-release this on CD.

62 His Golden Classics
Tommy Hunt

Collectables COL-5246
Lover (unissued)/She'll Hurt You Too/Didn't I Tell You/This and Only This (unissued)/It's All A Bad Dream/I Am A Witness/Make The Night A Little Longer (unissued)/Oh Lord, What Are You Doing To Me (unissued)/Human/Your Man (unissued)/Don't Make Me Over (unissued)/Promised Land (unissued)

Tommy Hunt (b. Charles Hunt, June 18, 1933, in Pittsburg, Pennsylvania) was a smooth powerhouse of a singer, who never received his just share of cash and fame. In the early 1950s he recorded rarities with one of the most bluesy of Chicago's vocal harmony ensembles, the Five Echoes (whose lineup included Johnnie Taylor). For his three most visible years in the late 1950s, Hunt was a member and often lead singer of the Flamingos, appearing on four of their albums and their classics *Lovers Never Say Goodbye* (1959) and *I Only Have Eyes For You* (1959).

Hunt's solo career began months after his exit from the Flamingos in 1961. *Human* (1961) was his debut, and inexplicably his only major R & B or pop hit. From this first burst through to his flight to Germany in 1967, Luther Dixon, Scepter/Wand's classically trained producer, lovingly placed Hunt's recordings in spine-tingling, symphonic-like arrangements.

His Golden Classics includes one of his two other chart entries, *I Am A Witness* (1963); *The Biggest Man*, a Top 30 R & B hit for Symbol, is not to be found. Fleshing out the excellent package are a few of his overlooked singles (*Didn't I Tell You* and *It's All A Bad Dream*) and a number of first-rate, never-issued sides, among them *Lover* (the identical track was used for Chuck Jackson's *Any Day Now*), a soul-expanding version of Dionne Warwick's debut *Don't Make Me Over*, and a pair that should have been hits: *Make The Night A Little Longer* and *Oh Lord, What Are You Doing To Me.*

63   Need Your Lovin'

Don Gardner and Dee Dee Ford

Collectables COL-5155

I Need Your Lovin'/Now Is Too Late/Nobody But You/Make The Girl Love Me/I Can't Stand By/Morning, Noon And Night/You Said/Tell Me/T.C.B. (Taking Care Of Business)/I Need You/I'm Coming Home To Stay/What A Thrill/Honey Sweet/ Don't You Worry/Lead Me On

Don Gardner had been working the Philadelphia bars (and dashing off singles for Gotham, Bruce, Deluxe, Kaiser, and Val-ue, among others) for years prior to his teaming with keyboardist Dee Dee Ford. The pair's dialogue of screeching and screams happened at the right moment. The intense edginess found in gospel music was making itself felt in the R & B and pop works of Ray Charles, the Isleys, and others. The Gardner–Ford union was quite brief, not exceeding 12 months.

This Collectables package includes all of the known sides cut for Bobby Robinson's Fire label. Their only chart entries are not included – their initial follow-up, *Don't You Worry* (1962), and an unofficial previous effort for KC Records, *The Glory Of Love* (1962). Both artists went their separate ways, recording numerous other singles for numerous other labels. Despite the vocal chemistry and efforts to get the twosome to return to the studio, Gardner and Ford never recorded together again. Sometime in the late 1980s, Dee Dee Ford died of cancer.

64   Tell Him

The Exciters

EMI CDP-7-95202-2

Tell Him/Hard Way To Go/Drama Of Love/I Dreamed/It's Love That Really Counts/ Are You Keeping Score/Say It With Love/He's Got The Power/Remember Me/So Long, Goodnight/Handful Of Memories/Get Him/It's So Exciting/If Love Came Your Way/Do-Wah-Diddy/We Were Lovers (When The Party Began)/Having My Fun/All Grown Up/Tell Him (unedited version)/*He's Got The Power* (unedited version)

The Exciters were pure, exciting New York pop-soul. Carol Johnson (b. 1945), Lillian Walker (b. 1945), Herb Rooney (b. 1941), and lead singer Brenda Reid (b. 1945) were from Jamaica, a section of Queens, New York.

Despite Reid's energized voice – a voice that songstress Ellie Greenwich told girl-group expert Alan Betrock was "one of the best female voices ever heard . . . she could do no wrong" – arrangements by Teacho Wiltshire, the magical productive fingers of Leiber and Stoller, and songs by the best of the Brill Building writers, the Exciters' *Tell Him* (1962) remained their one hit. Other rousing pop-shouters followed but none – not the overly similar *Get Him* (1963), the pre-Manfred Mann work-up of *Do-Wah-Diddy* (1964), nor *He's Got The Power* (1963), which is the Exciters' finest – managed to return their name to the pop or R & B Top 40s.

The EMI package contains each of the Exciters' five United Artists singles (both A and B sides), all the tracks from their lone UA LP, unedited versions of *Tell Him* and *He's Got The Power*, and a cut on *All Grown Up* (later a small hit for the Crystals) unissued in the US.

65 Greatest Hits
Ruby and the Romantics
MCA MCAC-541

Our Day Will Come/Hey There Lonely Boy/Baby Come Home/Our Everlasting Love/ Does He Really Care For Me/Your Baby Doesn't Love You Anymore/Young Wings Can Fly (Higher Than You Know)/My Summer Love/How Deep Is The Ocean (How High Is The Sky)/When You're Young and In Love/Nobody But My Baby/We'll Meet Again

They were pop-soul, very soft and distinctive. Graced with the smooth, sensuous, and seemingly effortless lead vocals of Ruby Nash Curtis (b. November 12, 1939), the Romantics – Leroy Fann (bass, d. 1973), George Lee (second tenor), Ronald Moseley (baritone), and Ed Roberts (first tenor) – who had recorded unsuccessfully as the Supremes, topped the R & B and pop charts with their 1963 debut, *Our Day Will Come*. The Akron, Ohio, quintet successfully worked their niche for three years. All eight of their *Billboard* pop chart entries are included in this MCA compilation. *Hey There Lonely Boy* (1963), and *When You're Young And In Love* (1964) were later more successfully reprised by Eddie Holman and the Marvelettes, respectively. By 1966, the hits stopped.

66 Hello Stranger
Barbara Lewis
Solid Smoke SS-8014 (LP)

Hello Stranger/Think A Little Sugar/Spend A Little Time/Please, Please, Please/On Bended Knees/Does Anyone Want A Lover?/Make Me Belong To You/Someday We're Gonna Love Again/Stand By Me/My Moma Told Me/Pushing A Good Thing/How Can I Say Goodbye/Baby I'm Yours/Sho-Nuff/I'm Thankful For What I Got/Make Me Your Baby

Between 1963 and 1969, Barbara Lewis (b. February 9, 1943, in South Lyon, Michigan) had four major pop/R & B hits, and a half-dozen more pop chart entries. Her voice – often flowing over a gentle cha-cha sway – was a silk-smooth coo; her lyrics, usually, were submissive and uncritically devoted as in her three hits recorded in New York under producer Bert Berns, *Baby, I'm Yours* (1965), *Make Me Your Baby* (1965), and *Make Me Belong To You* (1966). Lewis did have a range and could, if pushed, get a touch rougher and sing like a mellow Motowner (*My Mama Told Me*), make a teen-topic "girl-group" sound (*Someday*

We're Gonna Love Again), and, near the end of it all, showed off the nuances of a seasoned soul singer (*I'm Thankful For What I Got*).

Lewis's five Atlantic albums have long been unavailable. While some of her chart hits, notably *Snap Your Fingers* (1964), *Puppy Love* (1964), and *I'll Make Him Love Me* (1967) are not included in the Solid Smoke package, **Hello Stranger** does contain her three big New York-recorded hits as well as her first smash single, *Hello Stranger* (1963) which was recorded in Chicago under her first producer, Detroit record-man Ollie McLaughlin.

67   Just One Look And Other Memorable Selections
Doris Troy

Atlantic 8088 (LP)

What'cha Gonna Do About It/Bossa Nova Blues/Just One Look/Trust In Me/Lazy Days (When Are You Coming Home)/Somewhere Along The Way/Draw Me Closer/A School For Fools/Be Sure/Someone Ain't Right/Stormy Weather/Time

Troy was born Doris Payne (January 6, 1937), the daughter of a New York City preacher. Her childhood was spent singing in church choirs. Her teens were spent with the Halos, a jazz-bar trio, and recording Shirley-and-Lee-ish duets as the "Dee" half of Jay and Dee. In her spare time she wrote *How About Me*, a fair-sized hit for Dee Clark. Chuck Jackson and Solomon Burke made use of her voice on their recordings. James Brown walked her into Atlantic Records. The gospel-edged but teen-touched *Just One Look* was her first single – and went into the Top 10, on both the R & B and pop charts, in 1963. The equally moving and likewise self-penned *What'cha Gonna Do About It* was a small hit, twice (1964 and 1965); but only in England, where Troy moved out of desperation in 1969.

This long-out-of-print 1964 Atlantic album is one of but two Troy LPs ever issued. In 1970, a self-titled package was issued by Apple. Guest appearances were made by George Harrison and Ringo Starr, who co-authored tunes with Troy.

Troy still occasionally records backgrounds – most notably, Troy and Claire Torry were the backup voices to be heard on Pink Floyd's legendary **Dark Side Of The Moon** – and still wonders why her promising career never made the heights pundits had predicted. The story of her life is the subject of "Mama, I Want To Sing, Pt 1," a long-running musical in New York.

68   The Best Of Charlie and Inez Foxx
Charlie and Inez Foxx

EMI 4XQ-17243 (LP)

Mockingbird/Searching For My C.C./Broken Hearted Fool/My Momma Told Me/Don't Do It No More/I Wanna See My Baby/If I Need Anyone/Here We Go Round The Mulberry Bush/Hurt By Love/Sitting Here/La De Da I Love You/I Fancy You/Down By the Seashore/Ask Me/Confusion/Jaybirds

They were a brother-and-sister duo from Greensburg, North Carolina. Charlie (b. October 23, 1939) was a basketball player; Inez (b. September 9, 1942) a dressmaker. Both were church-reared. Inez first performed as a member of the Gospel Tide Chorus. After two failed secular singles for Brunswick (as "Inez Johnston") in 1960–1, the duo approached Juggy Murray, owner of Sue and Symbol Records. Murray signed them up, noting similarities between the siblings and his chart hits Ike and Tina Turner – both males played guitar and wrote songs, while Tina and Inez shared an aggressive approach complete with soul-shaking rasps and screeches.

Unlike the Turners, the Foxx duo was viewed as a novelty act – a one-hit-wonder – by pop listeners. *Mockingbird* (1963), their nursery-rhyme-like debut, went into the Top 10 on both the R & B and pop listings. Over the next decade, nearly a dozen efforts sold well to soul seekers. Of these, the only available compilation, the EMI **Best of** . . . set, unfortunately features only *Mockingbird* and two other chart entries, *Ask Me* (1964) and *Hurt By Love* (1964). The package draws only from the years 1963–5, and too often opts for weak LP tracks (including a rare *Here We Go Round The Mulberry Bush*, a one-off solo by Charlie as "Chuck Johnson") over the chart entries *Hi Diddle Diddle* (1963) and the more credible single releases. None of the more mature, emotive sides for Musicor/Dynamo and Volt – such as *No Stranger To Love* (1966), *You Shouldn't Have Set My Soul On Fire* (1970), and the teasingly suggestive *Circuit Overload* (1974) – is to be found.

69   The Best Of Garnet Mimms: Cry Baby
Garnet Mimms

EMI-USA E-2-80183

Cry Baby/Don't Change Your Heart/A Quiet Place/For Your Precious Love/Baby Don't You Weep/Until You Were Gone/I Keep Wanting You/The Truth Hurts/Anytime You Want Me (all preceding songs w/the Enchanters)*/Tell Me Baby/One Girl/Look Away/Every Time/A Little Bit Of Soap/I'll Make It Up To You/As Long As I Have You/It Was Easier To Hurt Her/Welcome Home/Prove It To Me/Looking For You/Thinkin'/Keep On Smilin'/I'll Take Good Care Of You/It's Been Such A Long Way Home/My Baby*

Garnet Mimms and the Enchanters (Zola Pearnell, Charles Boyer, and Sam Bell) were a Philadelphia-based group and all had extensive gospel experience before recording these 1963–67 sides. The sound of the group was centered around the magnificently soulful voice of Mimms and the gospel-styled arrangements by producer Jerry Ragovoy working in New York studios with fellow producer Bert Berns. Mimms (b. November 26, 1933, in Ashton, West Virginia) began his singing career in such Philly gospel ensembles as the Norfolk Four and the Evening Stars (led by Little Joe Cook), but by the late 1950s had switched to secular music when he and Sam Bell were in a proto-soul group called the Gainors. After recording unsuccessfully for several Philadelphia labels, the Gainors broke up in 1961 and Mimms and Bell formed the Enchanters.
   The collection includes selections from three albums and a couple of extra singles all produced by Ragovoy. The first nine tracks are from the **Cry Baby** album, and includes the fabulous debut title hit, plus two other hits from 1963, the near frenzied *Baby Don't You Weep* and the electrifying remake of Jerry Butler and the Impressions' *For Your Precious Love*. Notable inclusions are the excellent *Anytime You Want Me* and the urban tale-of-woe *A Quiet Place*, a belated hit in 1964. The next seven selections are from Mimm's first solo LP, **As Long As I Have You**, which includes four modest chart records – *Tell Me Baby, One Girl, Look Away*, and a remake of the 1961 hit by the Jarmels, *A Little Bit Of Soap*. The next seven selections are from the **I'll Take Good Care Of You** solo LP, and includes the magnificent title track and the should-have-been-a-hit *It Was Easier To Hurt Her*. The compilers erred, however, by omitting the chart hit *That Goes To Show You* and the delicious *More Than A Miracle* for several exceedingly weak tracks. This collection is close to being essential.

70   Set Me Free
Esther Phillips

Atlantic 81662-2

All God Has Is Us/Brand New Day/Catch Me I'm Fallin'/Cheater Man/Crazy Love/
Double Crossing Blues/Fever/He Knows/Hello Walls/I Saw Me/I'm In Love/Just Like
A Fish/Let Me Know When It's Over/Mojo Hanna/Set Me Free/Some Cats Know/
Some Things You Never Get Used To/Somebody Else Is Taking My Place/Tomorrow
Night/Try Me/Ups And Downs/When A Woman Loves A Man/When Love Comes To
The Human Race/Woman Will Do No Wrong/I'm Sorry

Between 1963 and 1970, Esther Phillips (b. Esther Mae Jones, December 23, 1935, in Galveston, Texas) recorded many superb sides that ran the gamut from soul to blues and jazz. Most notable to pop Top 40 listeners was the cover the Beatles' *And I Love Her* (1965) (not included in this set) and the "answer" to Percy Sledge's *When A Man Loves A Woman* (1966).

The self-billed "Little Esther" was discovered at a talent contest at band-leader Johnny Otis's Barrelhouse Club when she was all of 13. Several 1950 discs – utilizing Otis's band, often with Mel Walker and sometimes the Robins – in rapid succession made *Billboard's* R & B listings. Phillips signed with Atlantic in 1965 and that alignment produced the cuts in the **Set Me Free** package, all largely and in retrospect surprisingly commercially unsuccessful.

Phillips was one of the most distinctive singers in black history. Time – and a mere listener's dip into this offering – will sustain the belief that her talents were of far greater magnitude than her chart success would imply. In 1973, when Phillips lost the "Best Female R & B Singer" Grammy award, the winner – Aretha Franklin – accepted the trophy and quickly gave it to her, saying Esther Phillips was the rightful winner. She died August 7, 1984.

Her final recordings for Mercury (1977–9) and Kudu (1972–7) – including the Top 10 disco-fied R & B remake of Dinah Washington's *What A Diff'rence A Day Makes* (1975) – have yet to be compiled. The Lenox sides – featuring her definitive version of Ray Price's *Release Me* – are collected in the long unavailable LP **Release Me**. Savoy Jazz is offering **Little Esther Phillips: The Complete Savoy Recordings, 1949–50**, which includes her work with Johnny Otis. Charly Records has issued **Better Beware**, the 1951–3 tracks for Federal (see chapter 1, "Essential Recordings").

71   We Got Latin Soul!
Various Artists
Charley 91 (UK)

Ray Barretto: *El Watusi/Soul Drummers/Boogaloo Con Soul;* Ralph Robles: *Taking Over;* Joe Cuba: *Sock It To Me/Bang Bang/Oh Yeah (!);* Tito Puente: *TP Treat/ Pata Pata;* Joe Bataan: *It's A Good Feeling (Riot);* The Fania Allstars: *Son Cuero Y Boogaloo*

"Ahh beep beep, ahh beep beep" goes the rousing opening chant for the archetypal and biggest-selling Latin soul record of all time, *Bang Bang* (1966) by Joe Cuba (born in Spanish Harlem of Puerto Rican parents). The chant – derived from the 1946 R & B tune *Hey! Baba-Re-Bop* – is used to create a good-time party atmosphere in which hot Latin rhythms are flavored by English lyrics and the backbeat of rhythm and blues. And in the 1960s, this infectious sound crossed over into the R & B charts as Latin soul, first in New York, where the largest Puerto Rican and African American populations were cross-fertilizing their musical cultures, and then nationwide. Cuba had a second party-atmosphere hit the same year with *Oh Yeah!*. Its flip, *Sock It To Me*, was co-written by Hector Rivera, who achieved recording success on his own with the hit *At The Party* (1966) (unfortunately not included in this collection, which is of only Tico and Fania label hits). Some R & B artists also jumped on the bandwagon by creating hits in the Latin soul style, notably Ramsey Lewis with *One Two Three* and the Young–Holt Trio with *Wack Wack*.

The earliest Latin soul record is the compelling *El Watusi* (1963), with its menacing Spanish recitation/dialogue that sounds like street-gang threats. A big hit in pop, soul, and Latin charts, the song was something of a novelty number by the Brooklyn-born conga player Ray Barretto, who in the late 1960s created hits that sustained a dance craze of black origin called the "bugalú." There was an endless stream of bugalú records, and the three here by Barretto, the Fania Allstars, and Ralph Robles are most representative. Although strongly soul flavored, none crossed over into the soul market. One must jump a couple of decades to discern the importance of *Soul Drummers*, from Barretto's 1967 **Acid** album, which in the 1990s became a motherlode source for rap artists to mine for samples. By 1970, Latin soul, an exciting precursor to the Salsa rage of the last two decades, was dead.

72 16 Greatest Hits
The Platters

Trip 16-11 (LP)

All My Love Belongs To You/Delilah/The Great Pretender/Harbor Lights/Heaven on Earth/I Love You 1,000 Times/I Love You, Yes I Do/I'm Sorry/The Magic Touch/My Prayer/Only You (And You Alone)/Red Sails In The Sunset/Smoke Gets In Your Eyes/Sweet, Sweet Lovin'/Twilight Time/Washed Ashore (On A Lonely Island In The Sea)

Without a doubt, the Platters – David Lynch, Herb Reed, Paul Robi, Zola Taylor, and their spirited lead Tony Williams – were the most successful, best-selling vocal harmony act of the 1950s. Now, nearly 40 years after their chart hits, their seminal Mercury recordings of *Only You, My Prayer*, and *The Great Pretender* are still prized as international pop standards.

Williams left the fold in 1960 for what proved an unsuccessful solo career, and Taylor and Robi had left the era's most chart-dominating group by 1966. It was then, with the input of young blood – Sandra Dawn, Nate Nelson from the Flamingos, and lead singer Sonny Turner – that the Platters entered their third phase. Recording for Musicor, with production assistance from Luther Dixon, Charlie Foxx, and Gerry Sherman, the revamped Platters forged a contemporary, up-beat, and soul-oriented sound. In 1966–7 *I Love You 1,000 Times, With This Ring* (inexplicably not included), *Washed Ashore (On A Lonely Island In The Sea)*, and the Motown-influenced *Sweet, Sweet Lovin'* brought the act's name back to the airwaves and to the R & B and pop charts – for the last time.

Currently, no well-balanced package of these Musicor releases is available. The label and those acquiring a lease of the materials have notoriously stuffed their sets with the usually inferior remakes of the "original" Platters classics. One day, when money is a lesser concern, a second-phase Platters CD set will exist that includes *their* hits – not remakes of the first-phase Platters hits – and *their* could-have-been hits, *I Get The Sweetest Feeling, Alone In The Night*, and possibly their finest effort, *Devri*.

73 Stay With Me
Lorraine Ellison

Line CD 9, 01011 (Ger)

Only Your Love/Try (Just A Little Bit Harder)/I'm Gonna Cry Till My Tears Run Dry/I Want To Be Loved/The Hurt Came Back Again/Stay With Me/You Don't

Know Nothing About Love/You're Easy On My Mind/No Matter How It All Turns Out/A Good Love/Heart Be Still

When Frank Sinatra cancelled a recording session at New York's A & R Studios at the last minute, the time and the 48 assembled musicians were used by producer Jerry Ragovoy to create, with gospel-singer extraordinaire Lorraine Ellison, one of the most emotionally devastating recordings in the history of soul music.

Ellison (b. 1935, in North Philadelphia, Pennsylvania) was raised on gospel music. In 1965, Sam Bell – her manager and once a member of the Enchanters – made arrangements for her to record her first secular sides (including *I Dig You Baby*, a Top 30 R & B entrant) for Mercury. Dissatisfied, Ellison signed with Warner Brothers. *Stay With Me* was the result of that defaulted Sinatra session.

Inexplicably the pop-gospel, symphonic-soul single only made number 69 in the *Billboard* pop charts and number 11 in the R & B listings. The climactic classic was included on both **Heart And Soul** (1966) and a second LP (1969), named after this, Ellison's highest chart hit. In the mid-1970s, a third, self-titled, final album was issued.

Reportedly filled with bitterness, Ellison seldom performed. **Stay With Me**, a German re-release of her 1969 LP, contains scalding readings of Bell's *I Want To Be Loved*, Ragovoy's *You Don't Know Nothing About Love*, and some particularly fine Ellison compositions: *The Hurt Came Back Again*, a later Janis Joplin retread *Try (Just A Little Bit Harder)*, and *Heart Be Still*, a reworking of James Cleveland's *Peace Be Still*. Ellison died August 17, 1985.

74   Are You Lonely For Me?

Freddie Scott

Shout SLPS 501 (LP)

Are You Lonely For Me/Let It Be Me/Open Up The Door To Your Heart/Where Were You/Spanish Harlem/Shake A Hand/He Will Break Your Heart/Who Could Ever Love You/Cry To Me/For Your Love/The Love Of My Woman/Bring It On Home To Me

Freddie Scott (b. April 24, 1933, in Providence, Rhode Island) was a child gospel singer who eventually became a Brill Building tunesmith and demo singer. His big moment happened when Chuck Jackson declined to record Gerry Goffin's and Carole King's *Hey Girl*. After sitting on the shelf for a year, Scott's dusty demo – complete with his emotional, pleading vocal and the voices of the Sweet Inspirations singing "bye, bye baby" – was seasoned with strings and a touch of Phil Spector on the tympani. The song became a hit in 1963 on the Colpix label, which unfortunately could not see the emergence of soul in *Hey Girl*. On his album for the label, **Sings And Sings And Sings**, he is saddled with old standards and inappropriate early 1960s-style pop-rock arrangements.

It took New York producer Bert Berns, who produced Solomon Burke's sides for Atlantic, to bring out the deep soul in Scott's singing. He signed Scott to his own Shout label in 1966, and immediately got a number 1 hit with *Are You Lonely For Me*, one of the transcendent sounds of New York soul. Berns got Scott into the charts five more times, once with a remake of Burke's *Cry To Me*. Because this album came out at the same time as his first single, the above two are the only chart hits in the collection. The remaining selections are mostly excellent remakes of other artists' soul tunes, done New-York style (attributable in part to Gary Sherman's perceptive arrangements). Particularly good are *Let It Be Me* (made famous by Betty Everett and Jerry Butler), *Spanish Harlem* (Ben E. King), *For Your Love* (Ed Townsend), and *Bring It On Home To Me* (Sam

Cooke). **Are You Lonely For Me?** is a perfect slice of mid-1960s New York soul, once it had escaped from Brill Building pop conventions.

75 Peaches And Herb's Greatest Hits
Peaches and Herb

Date TES-4012 (LP)

United/Let's Fall In Love/Two Little Kids/We've Got To Love One Another/For Your Love/Close Your Eyes/What A Lovely Way (To Say Goodnight)/Love Is Strange/I Need Your Love So Desperately/The Ten Commandments Of Love/It's True I Love You

They were one of the most popular duets of the late 1960s; they were "the sweethearts of soul." Legend tells that Francine Barker (b. Francine Hurd, 1947, in Washington, DC) and Herb Fame (b. Herb Feemster, 1943, in Washington, DC) met one night by accident. Both were signed to Date Records and on tour. Fame was a solo; Barker was the leader of the three-girl Sweet Things (known individually as Peaches, Plum, and Cherry). Neither act's single was having much success and, after witnessing an impromptu duet between Fame and Barker, excited observers assured them their vocal combination had real chemistry.
  A string of successful, soft, sweet-soul love ballads followed their rushed debut – a take on Eddie Duchins's 1934 chart-topper, *Let's Fall In Love* (1967). Their early formula involved updating magic moments – the Five Keys' *Close Your Eyes*, Mickey and Sylvia's *Love Is Strange*, the Intruders' *United*, Harvey and the Moonglows' *Ten Commandments Of Love*, and Ed Townsend's *For Your Love*, all 1967–8. Other winners included *Let's Make A Promise* (1968) and *When He Touches Me (Nothing Else Matters)* (1969). All but the last two are contained in **Peaches And Herb's Greatest Hits**, a currently unavailable set.
  In 1968, Barker married and withdrew from the duo for a year, to be replaced by Marlene Mack. The Peaches and Herb name was shelved in the early 1970s, while Fame worked as a DC police officer. Herb and Linda Greene, a third Peaches, reactivated the act in 1977, only to create an equally long list of chart entries, among them the massive club hit *Shake Your Groove Thing* (1979) and the international chart hit *Reunited* (1979).

76 Hypnotized And 19 More
Linda Jones

Collectables COL-5120

Hypnotized/I Can't Stop Lovin' My Baby/Give My Love A Try/You Can't Take It/What've I Done (To Make You Mad)/I Can't Stand It/The Things I've Been Through/If Only (We Had Met Sooner)/Make Me Surrender (Baby, Baby, Please)/A Last Minute Miracle/Seeing Is Believing/I'll Take Back My Love/Fugitive From Love/Ooh Baby You Move Me/For Your Precious Love/Not On The Outside/Stay With Me Forever/I'll Be Sweeter Tomorrow/You Hit Me Like TNT/Take This Boy Out Of The Country

Gladys Knight called her one of her three favorite singers; Al Goodman of the Moments called her the most exciting female artist to come along in years. Linda Jones (b. January 14, 1944, in Newark, New Jersey) went full out in live performance, was wildly uninhibited in her vocal style, and died before many appreciative listeners even knew her name.
  From the age of six on, Jones was singing, preaching, and breathing gospel, and for the remainder of her 28 years she sang spirituals on waking every

morning as a vocal exercise. It was the teaming in 1967 of Jones with producer George Kerr, who wrote most of her hits with Jerry Harris, that made her artistry blossom. Her first three singles for Loma – *Hypnotized*, *What've I Done*, and *Give My Love A Try*, all 1967–8 – entered both the R & B and pop listings. After Loma shut down, and after two singles for Neptune – included in this collection, with both the A and B sides of the aforementioned Loma discs – Jones signed with Joe and Sylvia Robinson's Turbo label, for *Stay With Me Forever* (1971) and perhaps the ultimate deep-soul performance – complete with a sermon-like introduction – Jerry Butler and the Impressions' *For Your Precious Love* (1972).

Both Turbo sides and the Moments' reworked *Not On The Outside* (1972) – her last and posthumous A side – are included in this fine package, along with Jones's unsuccessful early sides, *You Hit Me Like TNT* (1965) and *Take This Boy Out Of The Country* (1964). Missing are *I Do*, *Doggin' Me Around*, and others of the spine-tingling pieces of histrionic desolation Jones recorded in a last-minute dash. Linda Jones died March 14, 1972.

77   The Soul Of Big Maybelle
Big Maybelle

Scepter SLP 522 (LP)

Oh Lord, What Are You Doing To Me/Put Yourself In My Place/I Will Never Turn My Back On You/I Cried For You/Only You/I Won't Cry Anymore/Don't Let The Sun Catch You Crying/I Know Love/I Just Don't Know What To Do With Myself/In The Still Of The Night/That's All/Same Old Story

No one could squeal, shout, and cry about it just the way Big Maybelle could. She was born Mabel Louis Smith, in Jackson, Tennessee, on May 1, 1924. Smith sang in church choirs, won amateur contests, and at 14 joined the all-girl band Sweethearts of Rhythm. As Maybelle Smith, she recorded a few sides in the 1940s with Christine Chatman's orchestra and Hot Lips Page. Despite some hard-core, bluesy R & B treats – *Gabbin' Blues*, *Way Back Home*, *My Country Man*, and *Candy* (all not included) – which found places in the R & B Top 10 listings in the mid-1950s, Big Maybelle remained largely an in-person act and undiscovered by the later record-buying public.

In the 1960s, Smith was dubbed the "Mother of Soul." She became a crowd-pleasing staple at the Apollo Theatre, but had only one chart entry in the pop market with a remake of ? and the Mysterians' *96 Tears* (1967). These Scepter sides are out of print, like the comparable records done for Epic, Brunswick, Paramount, Rojac, and Savoy. Smith's rendering of *Don't Let The Sun Catch You Crying* is untouchable, and all the tracks here are left with the Big Maybelle imprint. Sadly, Maybelle slipped into a diabetic coma and died on January 23, 1972.

78   The Moments' Greatest Hits
The Moments

Sequel 614 (UK)

Lovely Way She Loves/My Thing/If I Didn't Care/Nine Times/To You With Love/ Girls/Jack In The Box/Gotta Find A Way/All I Have/Sexy Mama/Love On A Two-Way Street/With You/Life And Breath/I Do/Not On The Outside/Lucky Me/What's Your Name/Dolly My Love/Look At Me (I'm In Love)/Girls (French version)

Considering the Moments (original lineup: Mark Greene, Richie Horsley, and John Morgan) were a group put together by the owners of All Platinum, Joe and Sylvia Robinson, to open a new subsidiary, the act has done quite a job – even getting into the charts with their first ever release, *Not On The Outside* (1968). The group's original members scattered within 15 months, but their replacements remained together for more than 20 years.

As the Moments, Harry Ray (b. Long Beach, New Jersey), Al Goodman (b. Mississippi), and Billy Brown (b. Atlanta, Georgia) made a series of successful sweet-soul singles in the 1970s. By the end of the decade, African American music had little room for delicacy. In the 1980s, they left Stang – and their name, owned by the Robinsons – and carried on as Ray, Goodman, and Brown, altering their style and their tempo to adapt to changes in the market. All in all, 37 of their recordings have been in *Billboard's* R & B listings, and 14 in the pop charts. Harry Ray died in 1992.

Twenty of their melodic, lushly orchestrated, falsetto ballads are included in **The Moments' Greatest Hits**. Contained within are all of their R & B Top 10 cuts – *I Do* (1969), *Love On A Two-Way Street* (1970), *If I Didn't Care* (1970), *All I Have* (1970), *Sexy Mama* (1974), and *Look At Me (I'm In Love)* (1975) – plus numerous other fan favorites that got into the charts, such as *Lovely Way She Loves* (1970) and *My Thing* (1973), and some Top 10 British-only hits, *Dolly My Love* and *Jack In The Box*.

79 Donnie Elbert Sings
Donnie Elbert

Trip TLP-9514 (LP)

Where Did Our Love Go/What Can I Do/Get Myself Together/Sweet Baby/If You Love Me/I Can't Help Myself (Sugar Pie, Honey Bunch)/Can't Get Over Losing You/If I Can't Have You/Will You Ever Be Mine/[A] Little Piece Of Leather/1,970 Years

Despite a career spanning three decades and numerous chart hits, Donnie Elbert (b. May 25, 1935, in New Orleans, Louisiana) has remained something of a mystery. He was a rare bird – a distinctively talented falsetto singer, who could write, produce, and arrange, and played most of the instruments on many of his recordings. With Lenny O'Henry, he formed the Vibraharps in 1955, and first entered the charts with the pre-soul *What Can I Do* (a remade version is included) in 1957. He made his first impact in the soul market in 1964 with two fine, up-tempo numbers on his own Gateway label, *Run Little Girl* and *A Little Piece of Leather*. (The latter was remade for All Platinum in 1972, and is included here in a better mix, without strings.)

His finest cuts are scattered over nearly a dozen labels. An adequate presentation of this prolific talent has yet to be compiled. This long-out-of-print Trip package, however, offers a hint of what Elbert became most widely known for – his reworkings of Motown classics. Present are his versions of the Four Tops' *I Can't Help Myself* (1972), the Supremes' *Where Did Our Love Go* (1971), and his well-studied Motown-ish chart entries, *Sweet Baby* and *If I Can't Have You*, both 1972. Elbert died January 17, 1989.

80 Best Of Donny Hathaway
Donny Hathaway

Atco 38107

The Ghetto/Someday We'll All Be Free/Song For You/Valdez In The Country/Where Is The Love (with Roberta Flack)/*You Were Meant For Me/You've Got A Friend* (with Roberta Flack)/*Giving Up Your Love Is Like (Givin' Up The World)/This Christmas*

Hathaway (b. October 1, 1945, in Chicago, Illinois) was raised in St Louis by his grandmother, Martha (Pitts) Cromwell, a noted gospel performer. From the age of three, he accompanied her on tours, billed as "the World's Youngest Gospel Singer." He attended Howard University, Washington DC, on a scholarship as a music major.

Curtis Mayfield had him recording duets with June Conquest as June and Donnie. Hathaway held a staff job with Chess before working freelance as a producer/arranger for Kapp, Uni, and Stax. King Curtis introduced him to the powers at Atlantic/Atco, and it was there that Hathaway successfully worked his fusion of R & B, jazz, and rock.

This inaccurately titled **Best Of . . .** package contains three Hathaway solo hits, *The Ghetto* (1970), *You Were Meant For Me* (1978) and *Giving Up Your Love* (1972), and two of his most noted duets with classmate Roberta Flack, *Where Is The Love* (1972) and their remake of James Taylor's *You've Got A Friend* (1971), but where are such major chart hits and fan favorites as *I Love You More Than You'll Ever Know* (1972), *Love, Love, Love* (1973), and his R & B Top-10 duets with Flack, *The Closer I Get To You* (1978) and *You Are My Heaven* (1980)? Hathaway died from a fall or jump from the fifteenth floor of New York City's Essex Hotel on January 13, 1979.

81 Best Of Roberta Flack
Roberta Flack

Atlantic 19317

The Closer I Get To You (with Donny Hathaway)/*Feel Like Makin' Love/The First Time Ever I Saw Your Face/If Ever I See You Again/Jessie/Killing Me Softly With His Song/Where Is The Love* (with Donny Hathaway)/*Will You Still Love Me Tomorrow/You Are My Heaven* (with Donny Hathaway)/*You've Got A Friend* (with Donny Hathaway)

Roberta Flack (b. February 10, 1939, in Black Mountain, North Carolina) attended Howard University, Washington DC, on a music scholarship and was a friend and classmate of Donny Hathaway. Later, he was her duetist and introduced her to the pop and R & B charts with their remakes of James Taylor's *You've Got A Friend* (1971) and the Righteous Brothers' *You've Lost That Lovin' Feelin'* (1972). In the late 1960s, Flack worked as a piano accompanist to an opera singer and performed five nights a week at an R & B club. It was there that a passing Atlantic producer discovered her.

In 1972, Flack did fairly well in the charts with her remake of the Shirelles' *Will You Still Love Me Tomorrow*, but it was the success that year of *The First Time Ever I Saw Your Face* – from her two-and-a-half-year-old debut album, and popularized by its inclusion in the Clint Eastwood film "Play Misty For Me" – that gave Flack her first number 1 hit, a Grammy award for Record Of The Year, and an international audience. Thereafter, numerous of her sensuous and soft ballads have graced the pop and R & B listings; among these are *Killing Me Softly With His Song, Jessie, Feel Like Makin' Love*, and *If Ever I See You Again*, all 1973–4.

While including four of the ever-popular Flack duets with Donny Hathaway, this **Best Of . . .** set does not contain many of her chart entries after 1980. Notably absent are *Making Love, I'm The One*, and the huge successes she has had in duet with Peabo Bryson, like *Make The World Stand Still* and *Love Is A Waiting Game*, both 1981.

82 Thin Line Between Love And Hate
The Persuaders
Collectables COL-5139

Thin Line Between Love And Hate/Let's Get Down Together/Blood Brothers/You Must Put Something In Your Love/Thanks for Loving Me/Bad, Bold And Beautiful Girl/Love Gonna Pack Up (And Walk Out)/If This Is What You Call Love (I Don't Want No Part Of It)/Mr. Sunshine/Thigh Spy/Can't Go No Further And Do No Better/Peace In The Valley Of Love

The Persuaders – James "B.J." Barnes, Willie "B.B." Holland, Charles Stoodghill, and lead singer Douglas "Smokey" Scott – were born of the ashes of a failed New York City group called the Internationals. Two raw singles, produced by the songwriting team of Richard and Robert Poindexter, were issued by Bell in 1970. No one seemed to – as one of the failed discs was titled – *Give A Damn*, and the Internationals folded. Months later the Poindexter brothers made an arrangement with Atlantic Records to release their Win, Lose Or Draw Productions. To commemorate the event, the brothers persuaded the reformed act to alter their name. As the Persuaders, their first release was *Thin Line Between Love And Hate* (1971), a huge hit. It is a classic, slow, somber ballad. Featuring the starkest of piano introductions and atop a morbid plodding beat, Scott wails a solemn narrative of illicit womanizing and the consequences that landed our lead in "a hospital, bandaged from feet to head." An equally catchy and morose *Love Gonna Pack Up (And Walk Out)* (1972) – complete with death-march percussion – did well in the charts. Their rapid rise to fame, however, left the group at a loss. Can a lively career be carved of such ponderous pieces?

The Collectables package includes in its entirety the short-lived act's first and best album, **Thin Line Between Love And Hate**, plus two further tracks that entered the charts – *Peace In The Valley Of Love* (1972) and *Bad, Bold And Beautiful Girl* (1973) – from their self-titled follow-up album. By this point all the original members had left the group but Scott. The Persuaders' name existed into the late 1970s, entering the R & B listings a few more times.

83 We Came To Play
The Persuasions
Collectables 5234

Chain Gang/Man, Oh Man/It's You That I Need/The Sun/Don't It Make You Want To Go Home/Walk On The Wild Side/Another Night With The Boys/Gypsy Woman/Don't Know Why I Love You/Let It Be

Lead baritone Jerry Lawson (b. January 23, 1944, in Fort Lauderdale, Florida), baritone Herbert "Tubo" Rhoad (b. October 1, 1944, in Bamberg, South Carolina), bass Jimmy "Bro" Hayes (b. November 12, 1943, in Hopewell, Virginia), and tenors Joseph "Jesse" Russell (b. September 25, 1939, in Henderson, North Carolina) and Jayotis Washington (b. May 12, 1941, in Detroit, Michigan) are a successful oddity, an a cappella act. They gathered together in the Bedford-Stuyvesant area of Brooklyn in the early 1960s. In 1966 Minit Records issued a one-off single from the group – with a musical accompaniment. Thereafter, except for a few accompanied efforts for A & M that resulted in two minor R & B singles chart entries, the Persuasions have remained true to their unique mix of doo-wop, pop, and soul.

We Came To Play was the group's first studio album and includes their distinctive reworking of such classics as Sam Cooke's *Chain Gang*, the

Impressions' *Gypsy Woman*, the Drifters' *Another Night With The Boys*, and an incredible alteration of Joe South's *Don't It Make You Want To Go Home*. Other equally enticing efforts include **Chirpin'** (Elektra), **Comin' At Ya** (Flying Fish), and two 1980s issues for Rounder, **Good News** and **No Frills**.

84   Soul Survivors: The Best of Gladys Knight And The Pips
Gladys Knight and the Pips

Rhino R2 70756

Where Peaceful Waters Flow/Midnight Train To Georgia/I Got To Use My Imagination/Best Thing That Ever Happened To Me/Make Yours A Happy Home/ The Makings Of You/On And On/I Feel A Song (In My Heart)/Love Finds It's [sic] Own Way/The Way We Were – Try To Remember/Part Time Love/Baby Don't Change Your Mind/Landlord/Save The Overtime (For Me)/You're Number One (In My Book)/Love Overboard/Lovin' On Next To Nothin'

After a six-year superstar stand with Motown's Soul subsidiary that produced such Top 5 R & B and pop classics as *I Heard It On The Grapevine* (1967) and *Neither One Of Us (Wants To Be The First To Say Goodbye)* (1973) (all not included on this set), Gladys Knight and the Pips collected yet another chain of huge hits for the Buddah label. **Imagination**, their first LP for Buddah and their biggest seller to date, produced three gold singles in *Midnight Train To Georgia* (1973), *I've Got To Use My Imagination* (1974) and *Best Thing That Ever Happened To Me* (1974). Their movie soundtrack to "Claudine" with Curtis Mayfield included the songs *On And On, Make Yours A Happy Home*, and *The Makings Of You* (1974). The following year the hits continued with *I Feel A Song (In My Heart), Love Finds Its Own Way*, and the matching of *The Way We Were* with *Try To Remember*.

Problems were on the horizon. Knight made her acting debut in the financially disastrous "Pipe Dreams" – a tall tale about lust in Alaska and the pipe-line, in which Knight had invested heavily – and after some merely mild chart successes in the late 1970s, the group found themselves embroiled in a bitter lawsuit with Buddah. For three years they were legally kept from recording or performing together. When the matter was finally settled and the reunited act was signed to Columbia Records, many insiders thought that Knight and the Pips were yesterday's news.

Initially it seemed the detractors were right. Aside from a Top 10 R & B charting with *Landlord* (1980), their first two LPs were not notably successful. Then, in 1983, the group hit the big time yet again with the back-to-back Top 5 R & B chart hits *Save The Overtime (For Me)* and *You're Number One (In My Book)*. Knight and her Pips continued consistently to make the listings with sporadic, near-chart-topping successes, like the 1988 *Love Overboard* and *Lovin' On Next To Nothin'*.

85   Greatest Hits: 1979–1990
Dionne Warwick

Arista 8540

That's What Friends Are For (with Elton John, Gladys Knight, and Stevie Wonder)/*Heartbreaker/Love Power* (with Jeffery Osborne)/*I'll Never Love This Way Again/How Many Times Can We Say Goodbye* (with Luther Vandross)/*Walk Away/Take Good Care Of You And Me/Deja Vu/Friends In Love* (with Johnny Mathis)/*No Night So Long/I Don't Need Another Love/All The Time*

As the 1970s were blooming, the Dionne Warwick–David and Bacharach hit-making machine was rapidly falling apart. In 1971 Warwick left Scepter, the company responsible for *Anyone Who Had A Heart*, *Walk On By*, and *Alfie* – all of her pop and R & B hits thus far. After one lackluster David-and-Bacharach-produced album for Warner Brothers, the incredible songwriting/production team parted. Warwick was now without her regular, consistent, and top-notch producers and songwriters, who had tailored their material especially for her.

Warwick continued on as a top draw in concerts, on world tours, and in Las Vegas and Reno, Nevada. Aside from a Top 5 R & B cut in *Once You Hit The Road* (1976), and *Then Came You* (1974) (her first-ever chart-topper, a shared vocal with the Spinners), the 1970s produced few successes for her. By the decade's end most insiders, including Warwick, thought her career had run its course.

This Arista package starts with her signing to the label early in 1979. Barry Manilow was assigned the task of producing and recapturing the emotional elements that had made Warwick's Scepter work among the most notable pop artifacts of the 1960s. *I'll Never Love This Way Again* (1979) and *Deja Vu* (1979) were issued from her label debut. Both earned positions in the pop Top 20, a feat Warwick had been unable to accomplish in ten years. While not as regular now in her chart entries, Warwick has had many notable hits, solo and in duet, such as *No Night So Long* (1980), *Heartbreaker* (1982), *Friends In Love* (1982), *How Many Times Can We Say Goodbye* (1983), *Love Power* (1987) and *That's What Friends Are For* (1986).

Philadelphia 3

Dan Nooger

Philadelphia, Pennsylvania, is unfairly tagged as the home of "American Bandstand"/Cameo/Chancellor/Swan "teen idols" – namely Frankie Avalon, Fabian, and Bobby Rydell – and the 1970s Gamble and Huff Philadelphia International label. Actually, the city has rich musical traditions in all kinds of roots music, from jazz and blues to doo-wop, R & B, and even country and rockabilly. The thriving 1950s–1960s doo-wop and soul scene was centered on the legendary Uptown Theater and powerful deejays such as Jimmy Bishop, Georgie Woods, and Kae Williams.

Philadelphia's jazz scene boasted such leading lights as saxophonists John Coltrane and Jimmy Heath, drummer Philly Joe Jones, and organists Bill "Honky Tonk" Doggett and Jimmy McGriff. McGriff scored hits like *I Got A Woman* in the late 1950s on Sue Records, and is still popular. The early 1950s blues/R & B era is well covered by Interstate Records with its large Gotham Records reissue series. Gotham, originally founded by New York record store mogul Sam Goody, but quickly acquired by Philadelphia-based distributor Ivin Ballen, saw releases by performers like guitarist Tiny Grimes (his vocalists included Screamin' Jay Hawkins and a young Claudine Clark of later *Party Lights* fame), tenor sax honker Red Prysock, and blues shouters like the ex-Basie man Jimmy Rushing, Bobby Prince, and Jimmy Preston (who cut the original version of Bill Haley's first hit, *Rock The Joint*), and much excellent gospel material. Gotham also bought in recordings by Los Angeles drummer/bandleader Roy Milton, early Detroit blues sides by John Lee Hooker from producer Joe Von Battle, and even the first commercial sides (pre-Chess) by Muddy Waters!

Other early Philadelphia labels included Cadillac and 20th Century, which released the first sides – strongly influenced by blues and R & B – by future Cameo star Charlie (*Butterfly*) Gracie, and Jack Howard's Arcade Records. Howard was Bill

Haley's first manager, and recorded some interesting country and rockabilly material (reissued by Rollercoaster). Jerry Blaine's long-lived Josie label released classic early 1950s doo-wop by the Orioles, and Five Sharps, and many others. Red Top, partly owned by organist/bandleader Doc Bagby, released early sides by Harold Melvin's Blue Notes and other interesting doo-wop and soul material in the late 1950s and early 1960s. Legendary soulman Solomon Burke also came up in the Philadelphia area, although the early 1960s hits that made his reputation were cut for Atlantic Records in New York.

The top Philadelphia operation in the late 1950s/early 1960s period was undoubtedly the Cameo/Parkway group, founded by Bernie Lowe and Kal Mann. Although generally considered the home of "Twist"-derived dance-craze records (Chubby Checker) and teen idols (Bobby Rydell, Charlie Gracie), these labels issued a wide variety of material, ranging from out-and-out rock-and-roll by Vernon Wray (backed by his brother Link, the king of raunch guitar) and pop-doo-wop (*Silhouettes* by the Rays) to early sides by such solid soul performers as Patti LaBelle, Don Covay, and Eddie Holman. The late Neil Bogart, who later found fame and fortune with his Casablanca label (Donna Summer and Kiss), served as an A & R man and picked up a lot of 1960s Mid-Western rock including material by ? and the Mysterians (*96 Tears*) and early Detroit sides by future superstar Bob Seger (*East Side Story*). The Fairmount subsidiary also issued solid material from club soul stalwart Lonnie Youngblood and others. The pop-soul sounds of such performers as the Orlons (*Don't Hang Up*) and the Tymes (*Wonderful, Wonderful*) also make good listening. Sadly, most of this material, now owned by Allen Klein's ABKCO operation, remains unreissued. Cameo/Parkway's policy on vintage albums seems to have been to release a large number of albums by a small group of their most successful artists, such as Chubby Checker, Dee Dee Sharp, and Bobby Rydell, all of which are long out of print.

The seeds of Kenny Gamble's and Leon Huff's Philadelphia International Records (PIR), which dominated Philly's record industry in the 1970s, were planted in the Cameo/Parkway operation. Kenny Gamble himself, born in Kingston, Jamaica, but raised in Philadelphia, worked as a songwriter for Cameo/Parkway, and also had aspirations as a singer, fronting a group called Kenny and the Romeos. The group included his old school friend Thom Bell on keyboards, and guitarist Roland Chambers, who later became a mainstay of the PIR studio band MFSB ("Mother, Father, Sister, Brother"). The group also came to include his future partner Leon Huff, and even blue-eyed soulboy Daryl Hall of Hall and Oates mega-fame has recalled working with them. They recorded a few unsuccessful singles for Jimmy

Bishop's (longtime WDAS deejay) Arctic label in the mid-1960s. Arctic's big star was of course Barbara Mason (*Yes I'm Ready*).

Leon Huff, Philadelphia born and raised, got into the music scene as a session pianist. He played on some of the New York-based Leiber and Stoller productions, was involved with such hits as Len Barry's (ex-lead singer of the Dovells, of *Bristol Stomp* repute) *1-2-3* (1965), and also played on some Phil Spector productions. Some early Huff songs, such as Patty and the Emblems' *Mixed Up Shook Up Girl* and *(The Sound Of Music Makes Me Want To) Dance Dance Dance*, emerged on Al Silver's New York-based Herald label. Huff recently recalled to Vaughn Harper the beginning of their partnership:

> I was hired to play piano on Kenny's song *The 81* by Candy and the Kisses [which became a Top 50 hit for Cameo in 1964]. During the course of the session we started talking about collaborating on songs. The first time we got together at my house we wrote seven or eight songs and decided to keep doing it. We worked together in the group Kenny and the Romeos – the guys in the band were basically what became the MFSB band. We played college gigs with Little Anthony and the Imperials, Chubby Checker, Lloyd Price. It was destined to have a record company in Philly . . . during that time Kenny and I were hanging out a lot in the clubs every weekend. People like the Intruders, the Delfonics, Bunny Sigler, and Harold Melvin and the Blue Notes would come by. We signed a lot of artists just by going out and watching them perform. The best artists are the ones who can take it from the studio and have that same intensity on stage. We didn't want just recording artists.

By the late 1960s Gamble and Huff had built up a solid reputation as producers and writers (although not confining themselves to R & B – in 1968 they had produced sob-rock queen Lesley Gore on *I'll Be Standing By*). Motown was also checking them out – Gamble's *I'm Gonna Make You Love Me* (first cut by Dee Dee Warwick for Mercury in 1966, and a Top 30 hit for Madeline Bell in 1968 on Phillips) was covered by the Supremes/Temptations combination in 1969, reaching the number 2 position. Nineteen-sixty-six saw the launch of their first label, Gamble Records, which was built around the Intruders – *Together* became a million seller in 1968. In 1967 Gamble and Huff had their first hit in the Top 5 with the strongly Memphis/Stax-influenced *Expressway To Your Heart* (released on Crimson Records) by the Soul Survivors, a million-seller. The late 1960s also brought major hits with their writing/production efforts for major labels: Jerry Butler (their first shot at a blue-chip major soul artist) on Mercury with *Only The Strong Survive, Never Give You Up,* and *Hey, Western Union Man,* and Archie Bell and the Drells on Atlantic (*I Can't Stop Dancing, There's Gonna Be A Showdown*), while 1970 saw the now-classic Wilson Pickett sessions that produced the Wicked One's **In Philadelphia** album, as well as the underappreciated set **A Brand New Me** by the excellent British pop-soul singer Dusty Springfield (both for Atlantic Records).

Both Huff and Gamble have credited the ultra-polished, painstaking writing and production style of Burt Bacharach and Hal David as important early influences, and, as for Bacharach and David, a crucial aspect of Gamble and Huff's success was their custom-tailoring of songs for each artist, in contrast to the Motown "factory" approach in which several artists would be tried out on a song, with the best version then being released. Huff noted to Harper:

> All the artists we worked with had identifiable sounds, and it was easy for us to write songs for each particular artist we'd work with. Kenny's the lyric writer, so when we'd do our demos he'd usually sing, and he'd phrase something like the artist would. The phrasing, arrangements and chords would fit their characters.

In 1969 the Gamble label was joined by their new Neptune label, which was financed by Chess Records. Neptune Records, although it lasted only a little more than a year, was a crucial step in Gamble and Huff's development, because it brought together many of the talents that ultimately launched their Philadelphia International venture into the stratosphere. The label was built around the veteran vocal group the O'Jays, who provided Neptune with solid R & B hits like *One Night Affair* and *Branded Bad*. This was the beginning of an association that was to last more than a decade, continuing into the mid-1980s.

This period also saw the beginnings of their relationships with jazz-soul vocalist Billy Paul, still a few years away from hitting with *Me And Mrs Jones*, and Walter "Bunny" Sigler, a veteran Philadelphia musician, writer, and performer. Sigler had flirted with the charts since the mid-1960s with releases on Decca and Parkway – his *Let The Good Times Roll/I Feel So Good* medley attained R & B and pop Top 20 status in 1967, and Huff had worked on some of his Parkway releases – and he was a good singer in the mellow, Marvin Gaye tradition, but his real strength was in songwriting and production.

Competing against the up-and-coming Gamble and Huff operation in Philadelphia was a host of small labels, most notably Newtown, Phil-LA Of Soul, Arctic, and Philly Groove. Newtown, owned by Harold B. Robinson, produced the first hits by Patti LaBelle and the Bluebelles (outstanding was *Down The Aisle*) under the aegis of arranger/producer Bobby Martin, making his debut. Phil-LA Of Soul, a subsidiary label of Jamie Records, produced a host of exciting acts, namely the Fantastic Johnny C. (*Boogaloo Down Broadway*), Helene Smith (*A Woman Will Do Wrong*), and the People's Choice (*I Likes To Do It*). People's Choice later went on to much greater success recording for Gamble and Huff's TSOP label, with the giant hit from 1975, *Do It Any Way You Wanna*. Jimmy Bishop's Arctic label was competing in the city with such acts as Barbara Mason (*Yes I'm Ready*), the Volcanos (*Storm Warning*), and the underrated Honey and the Bees. Stan Watson's Philly Groove operation produced hits by the Delfonics (*La-La-Means I Love You*) and First Choice (*Armed And Extremely Dangerous*), and helped launch the career of longtime Gamble and Huff consort Thom Bell as a wildly successful songwriter/arranger/producer in the 1970s.

By the late 1960s Gamble and Huff were basing their productions in Joe Tarsia's Sigma Sound Studios. Sigma was housed in the former Cameo/Parkway studios, where Tarsia had been chief engineer. Quite possibly the first time most modern rock fans heard of Sigma Sound was when David Bowie recorded most of his **Young Americans** album there in 1975. Producer Tony Visconti recalled in the book *The Record Producers*: "This was a studio where they had built their own mixing desk, and there wasn't a word of English on it, just red knobs and blue knobs and yellow knobs . . . so I had to learn it, just like learning a new alphabet!"

Gamble and Huff also whipped their house band into a hitmaking machine, built around the talents of drummer Earl Young, bassist Ronnie Baker, guitarists Norman Harris, Roland Chambers, and Bobby Eli, organist Lenny Pakula, vibist Vince Montana, percussionist Larry Washington, and arrangers Bobby Martin, Thom Bell, and Don Renaldo. Bell and Martin doubled on keyboards, while Baker, Harris and Pakula also doubled as arrangers. Every man in the band was a star musician and many attained later success in their own rights. Thom Bell is indelibly associated with the Spinners' superstar achievements of the 1970s for Atlantic, and also forged many hits for such soft-soul performers as the Stylistics and the Delfonics. Harris and Eli branched out on their own in writing/production partnership with Al Felder, creating the hits of Blue Magic, First Choice, and others, while the Baker–Harris–Young team was the force behind the Trammps. Vince Montana became a top producer for Salsoul/Gold Mind Records, creating the disco classics of the Salsoul Orchestra, Loleatta Holloway, and Double Exposure, as well as more way-out dance projects for Philly Soundworks with the Montana Orchestra.

The Neptune label was wound up in 1970 soon after the death of Leonard Chess, and the following year saw the launch of Philadelphia International Records (PIR) in collaboration with CBS Records. Gamble and Huff brought with them the O'Jays, Bunny Sigler, the Intruders, Billy Paul, and their crack studio crew. They signed up Harold Melvin and the Blue Notes and the Three Degrees, and with CBS's promotional muscle behind them, they started producing some huge hits.

The 1970s were Gamble and Huff's gold and platinum decade – heading the list were hits by the O'Jays, Harold Melvin and the Blue Notes, Teddy Pendergrass, the Three Degrees, Lou Rawls, Billy Paul, even the house band MFSB, alongside solid efforts from such new acts as McFadden and Whitehead, the Jones Girls, and Dexter Wansel, not to mention their short-lived liaison with the Jacksons (released on Epic). They also tried more straight-ahead jazz and blues, recording Bobby Rush and Monk Montgomery, as well as the Thad Jones/Mel Lewis Big Band, and even some gospel (live recordings of choirs from the National Black College Gospel Festival) and the raw-edged funk of People's Choice.

There were some records laden with strong social comments – the O'Jays' *When The World's At Peace* ("will it still be in one piece?"), *For The Love Of Money*, and *Rich Get Richer*, Harold Melvin and the Blue Notes' *Wake Up Everybody*, Billy Paul's *Bring The Family Back*, and the Philadelphia All Stars (an *ad hoc* supergroup) with *Let's Clean Up The Ghetto*. As the liner notes of many a PIR album proclaimed, "there's a message in our music." But PIR most succinctly billed itself as the "Sound of Philadelphia."

The end of the 1970s marked the beginning of the downslide in Gamble and Huff's pop chart fortunes, despite continuing R & B chart success with Teddy Pendergrass, the O'Jays, Patti Labelle, and the Jones Girls. Styles were changing and some of their biggest artists had departed for other labels, were looking elsewhere for new production ideas, or were otherwise out of action – Pendergrass was crippled in an automobile accident in 1982 – and by this time most of the original studio crew had also moved on. In 1983 the CBS distribution deal was terminated, bringing to an end the classic PIR era. Other labels continued to operate in Philadelphia, some, like WMOT (distributed by Atlantic), with national success, others (Philly World, Renaissance) mostly confined to the local markets. In the early 1990s Gamble and Huff recorded with the jazz-influenced singer Phyllis Hyman and the veteran Chicago vocal group the Dells (whose style was the template for the success of Harold Melvin and the Blue Notes).

But the classic "Sound Of Philadelphia" remains a powerful force in modern music. Such star pop/R & B stylists as Lisa Stansfield, Simply Red, and Soul II Soul (and their many imitators) constantly acknowledge the Philly soul sound as their roots. The influence of Philadelphia on house and garage music has been incalculable. As top dance producer Frankie Knuckles told *Soul Underground*, "the whole house thing was based on what came out of Philadelphia," while Chicago's Marshall Jefferson drafted in drummer Earl Young to play on his productions by Ten City (getting Young in, he said, was "a dream come true"). Not only the polished dance scene but the streetwise rap posses have paid tribute to Philadelphia soul. MFSB's *Love Is the Message* was used as the backing track for a couple of the seminal old-school rap classics: *Rock The Message Rap* by Grand Master Chilly-T, and The Incredible Mr Freeze's *Back To The Scene Of The Crime*. More recent hip-hop borrowings have included Marky Mark and the Funky Bunch's *I Need Money* (the O'Jays' *For The Love Of Money*) and *Good Vibrations* (Loleatta Holloway's *Love Sensation*), and EPMD with *Give The People What They Want* (sampled wholesale, again from the O'Jays, with Gamble and Huff even sharing the writing credits). Visit any house/dance/specialist record shop and you will still see those Philadelphia Sound 12-inches stocked, either on high-priced originals or on bootleg re-pressings – imitation *is* the sincerest form of flattery!

Essential Recordings

(i) Gamble and Huff – Laying the Foundations

Although Jerry Butler's musical career of over more than four decades is mostly associated with the Chicago soul sound, the core of **Iceman: The Mercury Years**, a 44 track gala presentation of his 1966–75 Mercury years is clearly the 1967–70 collaborations with Gamble and Huff (*Lost* through *I Could Write A Book* – 15 tracks plus one new remix). Butler (b. December 8, 1939, in Sunflower, Mississippi), together with Curtis Mayfield and the Impressions, made a Top 20 pop and R & B debut in early 1958 with *For Your Precious Love* (Vee Jay). Soon leaving the group for a solo career, Butler built a sophisticated catalog of soul and pop hits in the early 1960s. (See chapter 5, "Essential Recordings", for discussion of his Vee Jay catalogue.)

Upon Vee Jay's bankruptcy in 1966 Butler switched to Mercury. The earlier half of the first CD in this set covers his somewhat experimental efforts in New York, Chicago, and Hollywood studios to keep developing his sound in perhaps the most fruitful period in the soul era. Butler continued to turn out some fine work, but his commercial luck had become erratic. The best tracks from this period include the hit *Mr Dream Merchant*, his previously unreleased version of *The Right Track*, first cut by his brother Billy's group the Enchanters, and Jerry Ross's productions of the Lorraine Ellison song *I Dig You Baby* and Butler's own *(Nobody Ever Loved Anybody) The Way I Love You*.

Butler's first connection with Gamble and Huff surfaced in these 1966 sessions in Gamble's song *You Don't Know What You Got Until You Lose It*. Their first session together in September 1967 (which was actually recorded in New York) yielded the fine *Lost* and *Beside You*, paving the way for the Philadelphia-recorded Top 5 R & B and Top 20 pop hit *Never Give You Up*, which, with its shimmering textures set against the singer's now rough-edged baritone, established a new image for Butler: "The Iceman."

In contrast to the heavily produced late 1960s Motown style, Gamble and Huff created a sonic soufflé with Butler, using a full range of instrumentation, but mixing in as much air as sound and fury. And the songs, written by Gamble, Huff, and Butler together, with occasional help from Thom Bell, were among the greatest of their careers, not hung up on Broadway or Hollywood fantasies but deeply felt, drawn from love of real life and experiences. *Only The Strong Survive* (a number 1 R & B and top 5 pop hit in early 1969) even earned the ultimate accolade of being the only Gamble and Huff song ever to be cut by Elvis Presley, on his superb "comeback" album **From Elvis In Memphis**. With hit songs like *Moody Woman, Are You Happy*, and *Hey, Western Union Man* (again, a number 1 R & B hit and pop Top 20 item), and even B-sides and album tracks like *Can't Forget About You Baby, A Brand New Me*, and *Go Away – Find Yourself*, Butler had no need to indulge in the sweaty histrionics that make so many soul recordings of the era sound dated. Decades later, these recordings exude taste, polish, and just the right amount of class to reach everyone.

Gamble and Huff severed their connection with Mercury in 1970 over a royalty dispute during the sessions for Butler's **You And Me** album (although they later briefly reunited with Butler in the late 1970s at PIR and produced such further hits as *The Best Love I Ever Had* and *Don't Be An Island*). Butler completed the album with Curtis Mayfield's protégé Donny Hathaway (*Life's Unfortunate Sons*), and went on to work with Bobby Scott (the writer of *A Taste Of Honey* and *He Ain't Heavy, He's by Brother*, and creator of the unforgettable charts for Marvin Gaye's **Romantically Yours/Vulnerable** sessions) on the soundtrack for the movie "Joe." Butler sang some memorable duets with fellow Chicago soul veteran Gene Chandler, including *You Just Can't Win (By Making The Same Mistake)*, and set up the Butler Music Workshop to keep himself supplied with good songs, taking on such talented staff songwriters as his brother Billy, Holmer

Talbert, Hershalt Polk, Terry Callier, James Blumenfeld, and Chuck Jackson (not New York's Wand hitmaker, but the man who was responsible for hits by Natalie Cole, among others). The great results included further Butler hits like *Walk Easy My Son*, and such superb duets with Brenda Lee Eager as the million-selling *Ain't Understanding Mellow* and *Can't Understand It*. His 1972 cut of the O'Jays' hit *One Night Affair* became a club classic, and a collaboration with ex-Motown producer Johnny Bristol (of *Hang On In There Baby* fame) yielded such fine mid-1970s cuts as *Power Of Love* and *Memories Don't Leave Like People Do* to fill out his Mercury years. The collection ends with a marvelous 1967 live cut of *For Your Precious Love* that brings Butler's story back to its beginning.

Wilson Pickett was already well established as a top-line star of soul by 1970 when he came to Philadelphia to record under Gamble and Huff. Since first notching the Top 100 in 1962 as lead singer on the Falcons' *I Found A Love*, he had achieved no fewer than 28 Top 100 entries. These included a mixture of his own material (*In The Midnight Hour* and *Don't Fight It*) and carefully chosen treatments of the best writers' work in soul and rock, including *Mustang Sally* by his old Falcons' mate Sir Mack Rice, *Funky Broadway* by Arlester Christian (Dyke of Dyke and the Blazers), *Land Of 1000 Dances* by New Orleans' Chris Kenner, *I'm In Love* by Bobby Womack, and even the Beatles' *Hey Jude*. After his early, relatively unsuccessful, carefully arranged New York sessions, Pickett had achieved his biggest successes working with the loose approach of the Southern studios at Stax (Memphis) and Fame (Muscle Shoals) where, as Pickett has recalled, "sometimes we have wasted half a night in the studio just trying a little bit of this and a little bit of that." By 1970 soul music production styles were polishing up – it was time for a change. Pickett, never slow to recognize commercial realities, headed for Philadelphia.

Wilson Pickett In Philadelphia was in every way a triumph both for Pickett, who successfully brought his gospel-drenched shouting style into the more polished 1970s soul era, and for Gamble and Huff, who once again, as with Jerry Butler, took on a major, experienced artist rooted in the earlier era of soul and did not overpower him but placed him in exactly the right setting. The whole was brought together by the sterling performance of the Gamble and Huff studio band and the writing workshop built around Gamble and Huff themselves – Jerry Akines, Johnnie Bellmon, Victor Drayton, Reginald Turner, Bobby Eli, Bunny Sigler, and Ugene Dozier. Although the album credits read "Produced by The Staff for Gamble–Huff Productions," Pickett himself has left no doubt who was in charge of the sessions: "Everybody worked – they had complete control over the musicians. There was never a time when there was any disagreements or arguments."

Run Joey Run provides an up-tempo, rocking opener, similar to Pickett's Southern material. *Help The Needy* is more typical Gamble and Huff fare, carefully arranged with strings and a double-tracked vocal, with Pickett answering his own phrases. *Bumble Bee (Sting Me)* again goes up-tempo, with raunchy rhythm section work and punching horn lines – Pickett is right up front – together with some prominent guitar-work. *Don't Let The Green Grass Fool You* was understandably a large hit from these sessions. It recalls some of the Butler material, jazz-tinged, built around guitar, horns, and some mellow organ (played by Thom Bell) cushioning Pickett's hard-core gospelized shouting – sheer class and perfection packed into its two minutes and forty-six seconds.

Get Me Back On Time, Engine Number 9, although listed as two cuts, is run together into one long track (split for single release). It is impossible to say enough good things about the rhythm-section work of bassist Ronnie Baker and drummer Earl Young. It builds up into a strong vamp for the band to blow on, with Pickett interjecting "keep on moving" and his personal shouts. The guitar-work is about as excessive as Gamble and Huff ever got, yet the whole track is perfectly controlled.

Strings come on again for the ballad *Days Go By*, with Wilson, unencumbered by backing voices, wailing up front. With its air of regret for a lost love, it is a very sophisticated piece of material, which one can easily imagine Teddy Pendergrass tackling in his Harold Melvin and the Blue Notes days.

International Playboy sounds custom-made for Pickett, boasting "I'm a legend in my own time," with a girl in every town. It was written by longtime Philly consort Bunny Sigler with pianist Ugene Dozier, who soon afterwards produced a version by Little Carl Carlton on Backbeat, which was included on his album **You Can't Stop A Man In Love**. The triumphant love song *Ain't No Doubt* is a medium-paced shuffle, with punching horns and a laid-back male chorus backing Pickett's "ain't no doubt about it, you're just what I need" verses.

With this superb album as a starting point, what Pickett and the Gamble and Huff team could have achieved on further collaborations can unfortunately only be guessed at. The album gave Pickett a million-seller with *Don't Let The Green Grass Fool You*, while *Engine Number 9* also entered the Top 20 and went into the R & B Top 3. However, Pickett, although professing the greatest respect for Gamble and Huff's abilities, refused to record further with them, telling me: "Back then I had been cutting a whole album for $18,000. That one cost me $60,000, and I didn't have a piece of publishing in it, I didn't have a song I wrote in it, they took everything. And I told Gamble and Huff I would never cut with them another day in my life because of that." Pickett went on to achieve another million-seller, *Don't Knock My Love*, with producers Brad Shapiro and Dave Crawford, eventually signed with RCA, and subsequently recorded for EMI and Motown, and even returned to Atlantic's Big Tree imprint, without recapturing his former success.

Discographical Details

86 Iceman: The Mercury Years
Jerry Butler

Mercury 314 510 968-2 (2-disc set)

Love (Oh How Sweet It Is)/Loneliness/Alfie/The Right Track/You Make Me Feel Like Someone/I Dig You Baby/You Walked Into My Life/(Nobody Ever Loved Anybody) The Way I Love You/You Don't Know What You Got Until You Lose It/Mr Dream Merchant/I've Been Loving You Too Long/Lost/Beside You/Never Give You Up/Hey, Western Union Man/Can't Forget About You, Baby/Are You Happy/Only The Strong Survive/Moody Woman/Go Away – Find Yourself/Only The Strong Survive (stronger version)/A Brand New Me/What's The Use Of Breaking Up/Don't Let Love Hang You Up/I Forgot To Remember/Got To See If I Can't Get Mommy (To Come Back Home)/I Could Write A Book/Life's Unfortunate Sons/Where Are You Goin'?/Special Memory/You Just Can't Win (By Making The Same Mistake) [w/ Gene Chandler]/How Did We Lose It/If It's Real What I Feel/Walk Easy My Son/ Ain't Understanding Mellow/Windy City Soul/Radio Promo/One Night Affair/I Only Have Eyes For You/(They Long To Be) Close To You/Can't Understand It/Power Of Love/Memories Don't Leave Like People Do/For Your Precious Love (live)

87 Wilson Pickett In Philadelphia
Wilson Pickett

Atlantic SD 8270 (LP)

Run Joey Run/Help The Needy/Come Right Here/Bumble Bee (Sting Me)/Don't Let The Green Grass Fool You/Get Me Back On Time, Engine Number 9 (Pts 1 & 2)/ Days Go By/International Playboy/Ain't No Doubt About It

(ii) Thom Bell – The Classic Sessions

The Stylistics (lead Russell Thompkins, Jr, Airrion Love, James Smith, Herb Murrell, and James Dunn, all born in Philadelphia) were Philadelphia's top soft-soul group. Their five million-sellers – *You Make Me Feel Brand New*, *Betcha By Golly Wow*, *Break Up To Make Up*, *You Are Everything*, and *I'm Stone In Love With You* – still guarantee the Stylistics work today, over twenty years after their breakthrough hit with *You're A Big Girl Now* (all represented on this **Best of the Stylistics** collection). They reached their artistic peak in the early 1970s with the songwriting and production work of Thom Bell, but the group's members had been performing since the mid-1960s.

In 1968 Thompkins, Love, and Smith from the Monarchs joined with ex-Percussions members Murrell and Dunn to form the Stylistics. Their backup guitarist and road manager Robert Douglas wrote their first record, *You're A Big Girl Now*, which harkened back to the 1950s group sound that had always remained popular in Philadelphia, led by Thompkins' skyscraping falsetto against the group's pin-point harmonies and a simple, organ-dominated background. Originally released on Bill Perry's local Sebring label, the record was picked up by Avco for national release, repaying the company's faith by going into the Top 10 R & B and breaking into the Hot 100.

Label heads Hugo and Luigi (Sam Cooke's producers in his RCA days) put the Stylistics together with up-and-coming Thom Bell (the Delfonics, Jerry Butler, etc.) for the all-important follow-up. Bell recalled in *Black Music* that his first step was to slightly lower Thompkins's falsetto, "because when you sing up there you're just making noise"; then the hit machine started rolling. As Bell told it, "For their first session the Stylistics needed an hour a side. The first thing was *Stop, Look, Listen (To Your Heart)* (unfortunately not included in this collection). The second time I recorded them we did *Betcha By Golly Wow*, *You Are Everything*, and *People Make The World Go Round* " (think about this – three million-sellers in one session!). Bell had penned the songs together with his writing partner and former Philly Groove singer, Linda Creed. *You Are Everything* had already been recorded as an album track by Joe Simon on **Drowning In The Sea Of Love**, but Bobby Martin's arrangement failed to bring out the song's hit potential. With Bell's own arrangement and production the song became a smash hit, and later (in Diana Ross and Marvin Gaye's duet version) twice became a successful single hit in England, in 1974 and 1976.

Linda Creed, who sadly passed away April 10, 1986, aged only 37, had written, in collaboration with Bell, for artists ranging from the Spinners and Teddy Pendergrass to Dusty Springfield (*Free Girl*) and Johnny Mathis (*I'm Coming Home*), while her composition *The Greatest Love Of All*, sung by Whitney Houston, has become a modern standard.

Successful follow-ups for the Stylistics included *I'm Stone In Love With You* and *Break Up To Make Up*. Bell started varying the sound as well, introducing dual leads by Thompkins and Airrion Bell on *You Make Me Feel Brand New*, and an up-tempo change of pace with *Rockin' Roll Baby* (which went into the pop Top 15 in 1973). By 1974 Bell was so busy with his work with the Spinners that production/writing chores were taken over by Hugo and Luigi. The great results were *Heavy Fallin' Out* and *Let's Put It All Together*, with arrangements by longtime New York writer/producer Van McCoy. Although McCoy is only remembered by general pop fans for his disco hit *The Hustle*, in his long career he was a crucial player in the development of soul. David Ruffin

(*Walk Away From Love*) and Aretha Franklin (*Sweet Bitter Love*) are only two of the many soul giants to benefit from his writing and production skills.

Unfortunately after their 1974 hits the quality of the Stylistics' material fell off rapidly, slipping over the line from soulful to slick and sentimental, although they remained very popular in Europe and on the touring circuit. This collection contains virtually all of the Bell–Creed gems and comes highly recommended, even to those who are not big fans of the soft-soul style.

When the Spinners (lead Philippe Wynne, Bobbie Smith, Henry Fambrough, Billy Henderson, and Pervis Jackson) signed with Atlantic Records in 1972, the basic quartet of Smith, Fambrough, Henderson, and Jackson had been together since 1955, had first hit the Top 30 way back in 1961 on Harvey Fuqua's Tri-Phi label, and had just completed a frustrating eight-year tenure with Motown. The Motown years yielded only one substantial hit, in *It's A Shame* (1970). Atlantic, except for its powerhouses the Clovers, the Coasters, and the Drifters in the 1950s and 1960s, and later Archie Bell and the Drells, had never been very strong on vocal groups. The new Spinners' combination was very much unproven, and their first recording for the label, *(Oh Lord) I Wish I Could Sleep*, written by ex-Motown producer Jimmy Roach, went unreleased until its inclusion in this collection. Longtime Atlantic executive Henry Allen teamed the group with Philadelphia producer/writer Thom Bell, who had already created orchestral soul masterpieces with the Delfonics and the Stylistics and had collaborated with Gamble and Huff on hits by the O'Jays, Jerry Butler, Wilson Pickett, and others.

The next five years were, indeed, historic. Their first album together, **Spinners**, yielded no fewer than four smash hits by Bell and his collaborators Yvette Davis, Phil Hurtt, Mervin and Melvin Steals, Joe Jefferson, and the late Linda Creed: *I'll Be Around* (number 1 R & B and Top 3 pop), *Could It Be I'm Falling In Love* (a million-seller), *One Of A Kind (Love Affair)* (number 1 R & B and number 11 pop), and the touching *Ghetto Child* (Top 5 R & B, number 11 pop). Inside of one year the group was boosted to superstar status. They also reworked Wilson Pickett's smash hit from his 1970 **In Philadelphia** session, *Don't Let The Green Grass Fool You*, as a big-band, jazz-flavored showcase for Wynne (a direction which was, unfortunately, never followed up).

Working with basically the same studio band that Gamble and Huff used for their contemporary PIR hits by the O'Jays, Harold Melvin and the Blue Notes, Billy Paul, and the Intruders, Bell created a unique sound for the Spinners, lusher than Gamble and Huff (reflecting his early classical training) but more danceable than his work with the Stylistics and the Delfonics. *I'll Be Around* featured a gorgeous lead by Smith, but beginning with *Could It Be*

I'm Falling In Love Bell paired the leads of Smith and Wynne, setting the pattern that would give the group many hits in the years to come (as Smith recalled, "I'd set up the play, he'd hit the home run").

No one lucky enough to have seen Wynne perform with the Spinners will ever forget him. Their second album, **Mighty Love**, produced the hit ballads *I'm Coming Home* and *Love Don't Love Nobody*, and the rocking masterpiece that will forever be associated with Wynne and the Spinners, *Mighty Love*. Not since her first hits with Bacharach and David had Dionne Warwick sounded as genuinely soulful as on her chart-topping duet with the group, *Then Came You* (the Spinners' only number 1 pop hit). The **New And Improved** album contained the hit *Living A Little, Laughing A Little* and the tender ballad *Sadie*. Further hits with Wynne in the lead included the danceable *Rubberband Man* and the classy *Games People Play* and *Wake Up Susan*. A fine live album from 1975, **Spinners Live** (represented here by *How Could I Let You Get Away*), was also released and merits attention both for its showcasing of the group's excellent harmonies, which were often overshadowed by female backups on their studio recordings, and for the humorous *Superstar Medley*.

In 1977, in the wake of *Rubberband Man*, Wynne left the group for an erratic solo career (which included some memorable recordings with George Clinton's P-Funk Mob) prior to his death at age 43 on July 13, 1984. His replacement was John Edwards, a gospel-trained Chicagoan. Edwards had released an album of tough Southern soul – produced by David Porter – on Atlantic's Cotillion label, and even briefly deputized on tour for Wynne prior to joining the group. The Thom Bell/Spinners collaboration ended after one more album, which most notably produced *You're Throwing A Good Love Away* and *Heaven On Earth (So Fine)*, and a planned duet collaboration with Elton John that did not work out (Elton got a Top 10 hit from it, *Mama Can't Buy You Love*). The group returned to the charts in a big way during the disco era with a revival of the Four Seasons' *Working My Way Back To You – Forgive Me, Girl*, produced by Jerry Zager, and later in the mid-1980s recorded, unmemorably, for the Atlantic-associated Mirage label.

This collection, which includes a few snippets of studio chat and an a cappella Wynne coda on *Could It Be I'm Falling In Love*, is indeed the best of the Spinners and, by definition, some of the best 1970s pop-soul music from any source. If this whets your appetite, also pick up the **Spinners** album, which includes one gem, *Just Can't Get You Out Of My Mind*, that did not make this collection.

Discographical Details

88   Best Of The Stylistics, Vol. 1
The Stylistics
Amherst AMH 9743
You Make Me Feel Brand New/Betcha By Golly Wow/Rockin' Roll Baby/Break Up To Make Up/You're A Big Girl Now/I'm Stone In Love With You/Heavy Fallin' Out/ Let's Put It All Together/You Are Everything/People Make The World Go Round

89   A One Of A Kind Love Affair (The Anthology)
The Spinners
Atlantic 7-82332-2 (2-disc set)
That's What Girls Are Made For/I'll Always Love You/It's A Shame/(Oh Lord) I Wish I Could Sleep/How Could I Let You Get Away/I'll Be Around/Could It Be I'm Falling In Love/One Of A Kind (Love Affair)/Don't Let The Green Grass Fool You/ Ghetto Child/Mighty Love/I'm Coming Home/ He'll Never Love You Like I Do/Love Don't Love Nobody/Then Came You (with Dionne Warwick)/*Living A Little, Laughing A Little/Sadie/Games People Play/I Don't Want To Lose You/Honest I Do/ Love Or Leave/Sweet Love Of Mine/How Could I Let You Get Away* (live)/*Wake Up Susan/The Rubberband Man/Me And My Music/You're Throwing A Good Love Away/Heaven On Earth (So Fine)/Working My Way Back To You – Forgive Me, Girl/Funny How Time Slips Away*

(iii) The Philadelphia International Records Superstar Groups

The O'Jays (the PIR-era lineup was lead Eddie Levert, Walter Williams, William Powell – d. 1977, replaced by Sammy Strain) had been together some 11 years by the time they joined up with Gamble and Huff in 1969, having had hits on Imperial in Los Angeles and Bell in New York. (The O'Jays' early recording history and their Imperial years are covered in chapter 8.)

At Bell, the O'Jays got a Top 10 R & B hit with *I'll Be Sweeter Tomorrow* and two modest follow-ups during 1967–8. This success encouraged Gamble and Huff to sign the group to their newly activated Neptune label, and the O'Jays became their mainstay act. Their hits with Neptune from 1969 to 1970 (*One Night Affair, Branded Bad, Looky Looky (Look At Me Girl)*, and *Deeper (In Love With You)* are collected on the **O'Jays In Philadelphia** album. After Neptune's distributor, Chess Records, ran into financial trouble, the O'Jays made a couple of one-shot releases on small indie labels, and then, revamped as the trio of Levert, Williams, and Powell, signed with Gamble and Huff's new PIR venture. The group is not represented well on the CD review here, in that **Collectors Items** omits many of the hits and great album tracks discussed here. The best the buyer can do, until a two- or three-disc package is released on the group, is to search out some of the various albums mentioned below.

The combination of PIR and the O'Jays exploded on the charts beginning with 1972's million-selling ode to paranoia, *Back Stabbers* ("they smile in your face, all the time they want to take your place"). With a more wide-screen production style than that of the Neptune days framing the group's powerful vocals in churning dance rhythms, the **Back Stabbers** album also rolled up hit singles like *992 Arguments, Time To Get Down,* and the chart-topping *Love Train.* The title cut was later housed to perfection by Britain's Pressure Zone.

The socially conscious *When The World's At Peace* was a harbinger of changes to come on the follow-up album **Ship Ahoy**, which also marked a move from R & B into the new black rock. Top New York session man Anthony Jackson (inventor of the five-string bass) was drafted in for the sessions, and his unforgettable throbbing introduction to *For The Love Of Money* earned him a co-writing credit on this all-time classic (recently sampled by Marky Mark and the Funky Bunch for *I Need Money*, and reworked into Carole Davis's club favorite *Serious Money*). *Ship Ahoy* was a powerful evocation of the days when slave ships brought the first Africans to America, while *Don't Call Me Brother* continued in the vein mined by *Back Stabbers*. This album was just chock-full of winners. The tender *Now That We Found Love* was revived successfully by the reggae group Third World and more recently by rap stars Heavy D and the Boyz. *For The Love Of Money* and the lighter-toned *Put Your Hands Together* both attained Top 10 status.

The **Survival** album again took strong social stands, with the astonishing *Rich Get Richer, Give The People What They Want,* and the title cut. By this time the O'Jays were taking Europe by storm, and an excellent **Live In London** album resulted. The hits kept rolling with the anthemic *I Love Music* and *Livin' For The Weekend.* During this period original member William Powell became too ill to continue, and was replaced by Sammy Strain (a former member of the Chips, of *Rubber Biscuit* fame, who had also put in a long stint with Little Anthony and the Imperials). In the late 1970s production concepts were opening out, and the 1978 album **So Full Of Love**, which led off with the Top 5 ballad *Use Ta Be My Girl,* also included contributions from Thom Bell and his Spinners' writing team Joe Jefferson and Carl Simmons (*Brandy*) as well as the group's self-written and produced *Help (Somebody Please)* – a harbinger of things to come.

Gamble and Huff worked hard to keep the O'Jays sound fresh – for example, drafting in Stevie Wonder and Mtume to add some new colors to 1979's **Identify Yourself** – and kept coming up with top-shelf songs like the ballad classics *Forever Mine* (later a jazz classic in the hands of the soulful sax master Hank Crawford) and *Girl Don't Let It Get You Down.* The **Love Fever** set added co-producer Reggie Griffin, who had worked with such early rap stars as Grandmaster Flash. Their later recordings (since 1987 they have been with EMI), such as **Solid** and the superb **Emotionally Yours**, show how well the group learned from Gamble and Huff. In the early 1990s the O'Jays were deeply involved in the writing and production of much of their material, still casting a wide net for outside songs – the title cut of **Emotionally Yours** is by Bob Dylan – and sounding totally contemporary, even incorporating a rap from Eddie's son Gerald (leader of his own successful group Levert) on *Lies*.

The hitmaking incarnation of Harold Melvin and the Blue Notes consisted of lead Teddy Pendergrass, Harold Melvin, Bernard Wilson, Lawrence Brown, and Lloyd Parkes, all from Philadelphia. Parkes had previously sung on Stax with the Epsilons (*The Echo*), who also included future PIR writers/producers/performers Gene McFadden and John Whitehead (*Ain't No Stopping Us Now*), later responsible for several of the Blue Notes' biggest hits including *Where Are All My Friends, Bad Luck*, and *Wake Up Everybody*. Billy Paul of *Me And Mrs Jones* fame also served a stint in the Blue Notes.

Prior to their affiliation with Gamble and Huff, the Blue Notes had first recorded for Josie in 1956, then in 1960 for the Red Top/Val-ue labels, run by Doc Bagby (longtime Philadelphia bandleader and A & R man for Gotham and other early Philadelphia labels) and Irv Nahan (who had managed such performers as the Dells, the Spaniels, Little Joe Cook, and Screamin' Jay Hawkins). The Blue Notes' cuts for Red Top included *Blue Star* and *My Hero*, which scraped the Top 100 in October 1960. Both are included on the **Best Of Red Top** collection on Relic. In 1965 *Get Out* (a favorite Northern soul stomper) on Landa went into the R & B charts, and the group also recorded for Jimmy Bishop's Arctic label and for Henry Stone's Miami-based Dash set-up. But making records was not then their main concern.

Basically during this period the Blue Notes had been making their living working the nightclubs, singing standards (witness their version of *Cabaret* on the **Black And Blue** album). Teddy Pendergrass was playing drums in their backup band – as Lawrence Brown told *Black Music*: "Around 1969 we heard Teddy sing something and we thought 'there's a voice the Blue Notes need.'" The man was not wrong, as evidenced by the string of hits the Blue Notes recorded on PIR. **Collectors Items** includes only eight songs and thus omits some hits and other top-notch tracks that belong in any essential collection. It will, however, have to suffice until a more representative collection comes along.

The group, after some initial reluctance (fearing that extended recording sessions would cut into their lucrative nightclub work) signed with Gamble and Huff in 1972 and found success with their first single, *I Miss You*. The pattern used on the group's PIR recordings was directly descended from the sound that Chicago producer Bobby Miller had created for the Dells and the Holland–Dozier–Holland Four Tops' hits – hoarse baritone lead voice (Pendergrass/Marvin Junior/Levi Stubbs), surging orchestral backdrop (Thom Bell arranged *I Miss You*), sweet harmonies, and, of course, superb songs. The innovation here was the addition of dramatic monologues *à la* Isaac Hayes. The follow-up, *If You Don't Know Me By Now* (in 1989 revived and taken up the charts all around the world by British pop-soulsters Mick Hucknall and Simply Red) was in similar vein, and also provided more than a little inspiration for the Eagles' smash hit *Take It To The Limit*.

The Blue Notes' second album, **Black And Blue**, was a solid advance, moving them into more up-tempo stylings with the hits *The Love I Lost* and *Satisfaction Guaranteed (Or Take Your Love Back)*. The third, **To Be True**, was if anything even stronger, with a wider mix of material, from the pulsating disco dancers *Bad Luck* and *Where Are All My Friends* to the deepest soul of *Hope That We Can Get Together Soon*, which added the bittersweet sound of Sharon Paige. **Wake Up Everybody** went from strength to strength, headlined by the socially conscious *Wake Up Everybody*, the super-smooth *Tell The World How I Feel About 'Cha Baby*, and *Don't Leave Me This Way*, a classic performance and song in every way, and later taken all the way to number 1 in Thelma Houston's roof-raising disco treatment. Billing on the third and fourth albums was amended to "Harold Melvin and the Blue Notes featuring Theodore Pendergrass." Huff recalled that *Wake Up Everybody* was "basically the song that launched Teddy's solo career, even though it was a Blue Notes track – his performance just filled that whole record up."

After this run of successes a combination of business problems and internal dissension led to a split, with Pendergrass becoming a solo artist for Gamble and Huff, and the group, with new lead singer David Ebo, switching to ABC (*Reaching For The World*). But where Pendergrass prospered, the Blue Notes declined (although their old hits still insured them plenty of work). The combination of Pendergrass/the Blue Notes/Gamble and Huff produced some of the all-time classics of the Philadelphia soul sound, and while this hits compilation includes most of their very best material, all four of their PIR albums are well worth acquiring for a more detailed collection.

Discographical Details

90 Collectors Items

The O'Jays

Philadelphia International 35024

Family Reunion/Survival/Give The People What They Want/Let Me Make Love To You/I Love Music/Stairway To Heaven/Back Stabbers/For The Love Of Money/ Sunshine/You Got Your Hooks In Me/Love Train/Livin' For The Weekend/ Wildflower/Darlin' Darlin' Baby (Sweet, Tender, Love)

91 Collectors Items

Harold Melvin and the Blue Notes

Philadelphia International ZK 34232

The Love I Lost/Bad Luck/If You Don't Know Me By Now/Be For Real/Wake Up Everybody/Hope That We Can Get Together Soon/Where Are All My Friends/I Miss You

(iv) After Midnight – The Balladeers

Jersey City's finest, and one of America's premier soul groups, the Manhattans produced some of the most successful recordings for Columbia in the 1970s. Of their Columbia hits, all except *I'll Never Find Another, Shining Star*, and *Do You Really Mean Goodbye?*, which were cut by producer Leo Graham in Chicago, were recorded at Sigma Sound under longtime Philadelphia producer/arranger Bobby Martin.

In their 1960s Carnival Records period (dealt with in chapter 2), the Manhattans, with George Smith as lead, had laid down some fine up-tempo material, such as *I Betcha, The Boston Monkey*, and *Searchin' For My Baby*, but by the time of these Columbia sessions they had established themselves as a ballad-oriented group, or, as "Blue" Lovett described it, doing "progressive doo-wop." Members at this time were Gerald Alston (lead), Winfred "Blue" Lovett (bass), Edward "Sonny" Bivins (first tenor), Kenneth Kelly (second tenor), and Richard Taylor (baritone).

The Manhattans in their Philadelphia period produced five albums and a brace of hit singles. The overall pattern was set with their first Martin-produced recording, *There's No Me Without You*. The formula consisted of a well-crafted song, often written from within the group, with a bass monologue by Lovett set against Alston's lead vocal and strong harmonies from the group. They did not need the female background singers and other embellishments lavished on other groups of this period. Martin's arrangements for the Philadelphia house band are tasteful and restrained – *There's No Me Without You* features some virtually a cappella passages, displaying what a truly fine harmony group the

Manhattans are. *It Feels So Good To Be Loved So Bad* is from the pen of Teddy Randazzo (ex-Three Chuckles), with the singer urging his girl to "move a little bit closer, follow me to ecstasy," while *We Never Danced To A Love Song* takes on the disco craze, as Alston sings "Please Mr Deejay, slow the music down, I want to dance to a love song," and even throws in a reference to the O'Jays' hit *I Love Music*. The Manhattans' biggest hit from this period, *Kiss And Say Goodbye* (which became the second single to be certified platinum for sales of over two million – Johnnie Taylor's *Disco Lady* was the first), was an adult, emotionally complex brew of longing and regret. *I Kinda Miss You* followed up *Kiss*, less successfully, but the group came back strong with their first Chicago/Graham production *Shining Star*, which won them a Grammy Award in 1981 for "Best R & B Performance, Group." The three Graham-produced Chicago recordings here closely follow the Martin/Philadelphia style, but rely on his own writing rather than the group's efforts – perhaps they were, after several years of successful songwriting, a little dry of ideas. The Manhattans have not scaled such heights since then, despite the occasional nice side like their treatment of Sam Cooke's *You Send Me*. Former lead singer Alston enjoyed a successful solo career in the early 1990s.

By the time Low Rawls signed with PIR in 1976, his style had mellowed considerably from the streetwise hipster image of his 1960s Capitol Records days, as captured by such albums as **Soulin'** and **Lou Rawls Live!** Rawls (b. December 1, 1935, Chicago, Illinois), was raised in a minister's family, and had come up singing hard gospel with the Chosen Gospel Singers (whose 1950s sessions for Specialty Records were recently reissued by Ace UK) and the Pilgrim Travelers. After early solo efforts with Herb Alpert and Jerry Moss's Carousel and Shardee labels (the predecessors of A & M Records), Rawls signed with the major Capitol Records label. His mixture of jazz and soul (providing the model for the success of such singers as Billy Paul and Al Jarreau) gave him major R & B and pop hits in the 1960s. (See chapter 8 for discussion of his Capitol work.)

Rawls's early 1970s recordings for MGM (*A Natural Man*) had failed to sustain his 1960s success, but with his 1976 signing to PIR his fortunes took a big upswing. With Rawls, Gamble and Huff updated their late 1960s Jerry Butler sound, letting more of their jazz leanings show. The beautifully mellow *You'll Never Find Another Love Like Mine* took Rawls to the top of the charts that year, and has been his signature song ever since.

Rawls's late-night style, romantic and sensitive, featuring his smooth purrs, octave climbs, and rounded tone, effectively picked up from Al Green's mid-1970s "love man" persona. Such PIR hits as *You'll Never Find Another Love Like Mine*, *Lady Love*, and

Groovy People provided the touchstone for modern balladeers like Freddie Jackson, Peabo Bryson, and Will Downing, and brought Rawls a 1978 Grammy Award as "Best R & B Male Performer." I well recall during this period attending several Rawls concerts, which were packed with attractive African American women of all ages throwing flowers and lacy undergarments on stage.

Long established by these recordings as a top-line star performer, Rawls in the early 1990s reverted to his looser, jazz-blues style on recordings for Blue Note, obviously feeling, as he titled one of his albums, "it's supposed to be fun."

Discographical Details

92 Greatest Hits
The Manhattans
Columbia 36861

I'll Never Find Another (Find Another Like You)/Shining Star/Kiss And Say Goodbye/Hurt/There's No Me Without You/Do You Really Mean Goodbye/We Never Danced To A Love Song/It Feels So Good To Be Loved So Bad/I Kinda Miss You/ Don't Take Your Love

93 The Best Of Lou Rawls
Lou Rawls
Sony Music 21522

You'll Never Find Another Love Like Mine/Lady Love/Groovy People/I Go Crazy/Let Me Be Good To You/This Song Will Last Forever/Sit Down And Talk To Me/One Life To Live/There Will Be Love/Ain't That Loving You

(v) Dance Express – Spreading The Love Epidemic

For most listeners, the Trammps (lead Jimmy Ellis, Stanley Wade, Harold Wade, Earl Young, and Robert Upchurch) are only remembered for *Disco Inferno*, which was prominently featured in the 1978 blockbuster film **"Saturday Night Fever"** (John Travolta danced to it twice) and its soundtrack album. In fact, the Trammps, a group concept created by famed Sigma Studio sessionmen Ron Baker, Norman Harris, and Earl Young, and featuring the lead vocals of Jimmy Ellis, were among the very best disco bands. Most of the members were originally from a group known as the Volcanos, whose *Storm Warning* achieved Top 30 R & B chart status in 1965 on Jimmy Bishop's Arctic label, where they had half-a-dozen releases. When the group were revamped as the Trammps in the early 1970s, they based their sound on an updated version of the Coasters' style, contrasting Ellis's leads with Earl Young's booming bass voice (as Young explained, "we decided to revive that sound, in addition to selecting music which has a strong dance beat and meaningful lyrics"). Three early

1970s singles were very successful in the discos – *Sixty Minute Man* (the 1951 Clyde McPhatter and the Dominoes hit), *Zing Went The Strings Of My Heart* (an old standard which the Coasters had themselves revived), and the gospel-based *Pray All You Sinners*. These were collected onto a Buddah album in 1975. The subsequent 1976 single release of the previously unissued *Hold Back The Night* brought them into the Top 40 for the first time, but is more familiar to rock fans in Graham Parker and the Rumour's version – either way, it is a brilliant song.

The Golden Fleece album under consideration here was released under the aegis of PIR/CBS, with both group and band (augmented by the MFSB crew) at their best, and reflects the stunning virtuosity of this group. In addition to the pulsating disco sounds of *Stop And Think, Love Epidemic,* and *Where Do We Go From Here* (the latter two had considerable success on the R & B charts), the Trammps also excelled on straight-ahead ballads (*Down Three Dark Streets* and *Every Dream I Dream Is You*) and the all-out R & B rave-up on the Isley Brothers' *Shout*. It is astonishing that Earl Young not only stands comparison with the likes of Benny Benjamin and Al Jackson as among the very best drummers in soul-music history, but is also a superb bass vocalist, and an excellent songwriter and producer.

For their later albums for Atlantic the group again turned their hands to classic soul (Wilson Pickett's *Ninety-Nine And A Half*), the occasional ballad (*Seasons For Girls*), and of course disco sounds (the Top 30 hit *Where The Happy People Go*), all leading up to the smash hit *Disco Inferno*. Unfortunately, they never had as successful a follow-up hit, despite considerable recording. The Atlantic **Disco Inferno** album or a now out-of-print **Best Of** set represents this period well. The Buddah album has recently been reissued on CD by the Unitron label. However, this Golden Fleece album represents the Trammps at their very best. More than a handful of today's top dance producers/remixers have singled this album out as "a record that really used to make us rock."

Finally, to round things off, **TSOP Dance Classics** is a neat little collection of extended 12-inch mixes of some of the very greatest Philadelphia floor-shaking favorites. *I Love Music* stands as perhaps the O'Jays' best dancer, while MFSB's ever-popular *Love Is The Message* has often been sampled and reused by both modern rap and dance artists. Harold Melvin and the Blue Notes' *Bad Luck* ranks behind only *The Love I Lost* as their most popular up-tempo number, and comes complete with Teddy Pendergrass's extended, heartfelt rap, ending with musings worthy of Marvin Gaye: "the only thing I got that I can hold onto is my God . . . Jesus be with me, give me good luck." The secret weapons of this collection are writers/performers Gene McFadden and John Whitehead. In addition to their own anthemic, transatlantic smash *Ain't No Stoppin' Us Now* (a highlight of George Michael's recent **Cover To Cover** tour and later revived by Mike Davis), they also penned *Bad Luck* and the Intruders' *I'll Always Love My Mama* on this set. As an introduction to the PIR dance sound this package cannot be beaten.

Discographical Details

94 Trammps
The Trammps

Golden Fleece KZ 33163 (LP)

Stop And Think/Trusting Heart/Every Dream I Dream Is You/Love Epidemic/Save A Place/Trammps Disco Theme/Where Do We Go From Here/Down Three Dark Streets/I Know That Feeling/Shout

95 TSOP Dance Classics
Various Artists

Sony Music 21540

The O'Jays: *I Love Music*; MFSB with the Three Degrees: *Love Is The Message*; Harold Melvin and the Blue Notes: *Bad Luck*; The Intruders: *I'll Always Love My Mama*; The Three Degrees: *Dirty Ol' Man*; McFadden and Whitehead: *Ain't No Stoppin' Us Now*

Basic Recordings

The Roots

96 The Golden Groups – Part 8: The Best Of Red Top
Various Artists

Relic 5021 (LP)

The Quintones: *Heavenly Father/The Letter (What Am I To Do)/Oh My Love/There'll Be No Sorrow/Down The Aisle Of Love/Please Dear*; Tony and the Twilighters: *Did You Make Up Your Mind/Key To My Heart/Yes Or No/Be My Girl/Gee But I'd Give The World/I Promise To Remember*; The Students: *Bye Bye Truly/Mary/My Heart Is An Open Door/Mommy And Daddy*; The Blue Notes: *My Hero/Blue Star*; The Ivytones: *Oo Wee Baby/Each Time*

Red Top Records was started in Philadelphia in 1957 by bandleader/organist/A & R man Harry "Doc" Bagby, promotion man Marvin Schwartz, and artist-manager Irv Nahan, and lasted into the early 1960s. Limited in distribution muscle, the label functioned mostly as a showcase for local Philadelphia talent, leasing tracks that had regional success to larger operations. Archetypal high-pitched lead vocals backed by tight harmonies in the inimitable Philly style come to the fore on the nursery-rhyme rock tracks of the Students (not the Chess *I'm So Young* group). The Quintones, a girl-led group, displayed as much warmth and charm as Arlene Smith and the Chantels on their tracks. Their sole hit, *Down The Aisle Of Love*, was placed with Dick Clark's Hunt label and made the Top 20 in late 1958. Of the two very early tracks by the Blue Notes – the group including Harold Melvin, Lawrence Brown, and Bernard Wilson, later members of the

1970s PIR hit-makers Harold Melvin and the Blues Notes – *My Hero* is a big production number, complete with overdubbed strings, and gave them their first small taste of national chart success (number 78 in late 1960) on the affiliated Val-ue label. Little Joe Cook of *Peanuts* fame sings with the Ivytones on the strong ballad *Each Time*, which, coupled with the jump side *Oo Wee Baby*, had national release on Liberty. Tony and the Twilighters, a white group, try hard, but their version of Frankie Lymon and the Teenagers' classic *I Promise To Remember* will never make anyone forget the original. Their slow-grinding *Did You Make Up Your Mind* and the Latin-rhythmed *Key To My Heart* do bring some originality to the "kid-group" style. Overall this set provides a rare and valuable look at the late 1950s Philadelphia R & B vocal group scene that was the precursor to the area's 1960s soul sound.

97 Meet The Majors
The Majors

Collectables COL 5249

A Wonderful Dream/Time Will Tell/She's A Troublemaker/Don't You Lose Your Cool/ A Little Bit Now (A Little Bit Later)/Ooh Wee Baby/I Wonder Who's Dancing With Her Now/Come On, Come On/Anything You Can Do (I Can Do Better)/Tra La La

The Majors (lead Ricky Cordo, with Ronald Gathers, Eugene Glass, Frank Troutt, and Idella Morris) were an early 1960s doo-wop-soul transitional group, like New York's Fiestas, Chicago's Sheppards, and Detroit's Falcons. Recording for Imperial and produced by Jerry Ragovoy, who had previously worked with the Castelles (*This Silver Ring*), their up-tempo *A Wonderful Dream*, fronted by Cordo's high tenor, reached the number 22 position in late 1962. The more soulful follow-up, *A Little Bit Now (A Little Bit Later)*, was toughened up with some gritty sax. Similarly *Anything You Can Do*, although having almost schoolyard/playground-type lyrics, features a fat sound with some deep-toned guitar twangs, an effect Ragovoy later used to greater effect on Garnet Mimms's *As Long As I Have You*. *I Wonder Who's Dancing With Her Now* leans toward the Drifters' Latin-tinged style, though with a sparser production. The Majors had no further hits, but Ragovoy's later efforts included Irma Thomas's original *Time Is On My Side*, Garnet Mimms's *Cry Baby*, Lorraine Ellison's epic *Stay With Me*, the Howard Tate sessions, and close collaboration with Bert Berns's New York Shout label on some of the best recordings of the soul era.

The Beginnings of Soul

98 Twist With Chubby Checker
Chubby Checker

Parkway P 7001 (LP)

Twistin' USA/The "Ooh Poo Pah Doo" Shimmy/The "C.C. Rider" Stroll/The Strand/The Chicken/The Hucklebuck/The Twist/The Madison/"Love Is Strange" Chalypso/The "Mexican Hat" Twist/The Slop/The Pony

Chubby Checker (b. Ernest Evans, October 3, 1941, in Philadelphia, Pennsylvania) is forever associated with his famous reworking of Hank Ballard and the Midnighters' *The Twist*, which topped the charts twice, in 1960 and again in 1962. His early 1960s string of dance-craze hits, *Pony Time*, *Limbo Rock*, *Slow Twistin'* with Dee Dee Sharp, and the rest, began with this album (*The Hucklebuck* and *Twistin' USA* also were chart material), which will be of especial interest to R & B fans, as he works out on songs drawn from Chuck Willis (*C.C.*

Rider), Jesse Hill (*Ooh Poo Pah Doo*), Mickey and Sylvia (*Love Is Strange*), and even Memphis bluesman Rosco Gordon (*The Chicken*). Those desiring just Checker's hits will be well served by one of his many **Greatest Hits** collections. Parkway issued over half-a-dozen such compilations.

99   Down The Aisle
Patti LaBelle and the Bluebelles

Relic 7044

I Sold My Heart To The Junkman/Tear After Tear/You Will Fill My Eyes No More/ Danny Boy/Decatur Street/One Phone Call/Go On (This Is Goodbye)/Where Are You?/Down The Aisle/What Kind Of Heart?/You'll Never Walk Alone/Love Me Just A Little/C'est La Vie/I Believe/Cool Water/Have I Sinned/Itty Bitty Twist/Island of Unbroken Hearts/Impossible/Academy Award/My Bridal Gown/When Johnny Comes Marchin' Home/I Walked Right In/Please Hurry Home/The Joke's On You/It's Written In Our Hearts/I Sold My Heart To The Junkman (unreleased version)

This CD is drawn from the early 1960s sessions of the group (lead Patti LaBelle, Cindy Birdsong, Nona Hendryx, Sarah Dash) for Harold Robinson's Newtown label. With arrangements and production by future PIR/G & H studio main man Bobby Martin, this CD spans the range from the uptempo girl-group sound found on their first hit from 1962, *I Sold My Heart To The Junkman* (which actually was recorded by the Chicago-based Starlets) and on *Decatur Street* (1964), to the doowopish styling of *Down The Aisle* (1963), to the big ballad stylings on the standards *You'll Never Walk Alone* (1964) and *Danny Boy* (1964). Martin keeps the focus firmly on LaBelle and the group's harmonies, with crisp, minimal backing on the uptempo items, augmented with tasteful strings for the ballad showcases.

Down The Aisle is indeed the roots of the Patti LaBelle sound that eventually won her a Grammy Award in 1991 for her solo hit, *Somebody Loves You*. After recording for Cameo/Parkway and Atlantic, the group (minus Cindy Birdsong, who replaced Flo Ballard in the Supremes), was reformed as LaBelle, hitting with *Lady Marmalade* in 1974.

100   Peanuts
Little Joe Cook and the Thrillers

Beantown 224891 (LP)

Peanuts/This I Know/Echoes Keep Calling Me/Lilly Lou/Let's Do The Slop/I'm A Fool/Run Little Girl/Lonesome/Peanuts (alternate take)/*Please Don't Go/Don't Delay/ Don't Leave Me Alone/Meet Me Down At Soulville/Cherry/I Love You For Sentimental Reasons/Stay*

Little Joe Cook (b. 1922, in Philadelphia) first recorded gospel between 1949 and 1952 for the Philadelphia labels Apex and Gotham with the Evening Star Quartet (which included Sam Bell, later of Garnet Mimms's Enchanters), and toured with such star gospel acts as the Soul Stirrers and the Dixie Hummingbirds. The original Thrillers group consisted of Cook with Farris Hill, Harry Pascle, Richard Frazier, and Donald Burnett. This album contains the cream of his 1956–61 OKeh recordings with the group, including an alternate take of his biggest hit *Peanuts* (number 22 in October, 1957) featuring his fabulous falsetto lead. Most of his other sides showcased his attractive natural high tenor, such as the ballad *This I Know*. His 1964 solo recording, the dance gem *Meet Me Down At Soulville*, was strongly influenced by Sam Cooke, with whom he toured in Cooke's early

1950s Soul Stirrers days. Indeed, Horace Ott, who co-wrote *Soulville*, arranged and conducted some of Cooke's finest RCA work.

Philadelphia Soul – the 1960s

01 Dry Your Eyes

Brenda and the Tabulations

Dionn LPM 2000 (LP)

Dry Your Eyes/Walk On By/God Only Knows/Who's Lovin' You/Summertime/Where Did Our Love Go/Just Once In A Lifetime/Forever/Stay Together Young Lovers/Hey Boy/Oh Lord, What Are You Doing To Me/The Wash

Brenda and the Tabulations (lead Brenda Payton, with Maurice Coates, Eddie Jackson, and Jerry Jones) were organized in 1966 and quickly came under the wing of top WDAS deejay Georgie Woods. Payton was only 18 when they made their debut on Dionn with the Top 20 pop and Top 10 R & B hit ballad *Dry Your Eyes* (co-written by Payton and Coates). They had over a dozen pop and R & B chart entries through the mid-1970s on Dionn, Top and Bottom, and later Epic with a mixture of original material and well-chosen covers (the Miracles' *Who's Lovin' You* and Dionne Warwick's *Don't Make Me Over*, the latter not included here). Payton was at her most effective on slower sides (*One Girl Too Late* on Epic – also not included here – although not a large hit, was among her very best performances). David Bowie had clearly listened closely to her stirring version of *God Only Knows* before cutting this Beach Boys tune (the flip side of *Wouldn't It Be Nice*) for his **Tonight** album. The Big Maybelle–Scepter soul classic *Oh Lord, What Are You Doing To Me* receives a fine treatment and was even recut for the group's 1969 Top and Bottom album. While a definitive collection of their Dionn sides would also have to include such later hits as *Just Once In A Lifetime* and *The Price You Have To Pay* and the non-hit but classic *I Can't Get Over You* (one of the all-time great Phil Spector imitations, complete with more echo than the Grand Canyon), this set represents state-of-the-art Philadelphia soul just prior to the Gamble and Huff explosion. Arranger Richard Rome later worked with the O'Jays and the Three Degrees at PIR. Payton later cut some fine dance tracks for Epic under ex-Motowner Mike Terry (*Walk On In*) and Casablanca's Chocolate City label, and in the mid-1980s recorded for Philadelphia's tiny Major label.

102 Yes I'm Ready

Barbara Mason

Arctic ALPS 1000 (LP)

Yes I'm Ready/Come To Me/You Got What It Takes/Misty/Something You Got/Come See About Me/Sad Sad Girl/Got To Get You Off My Mind/Keep Him/Girls Have Feelings Too/Moon River/Trouble Child

Barbara Mason (b. August 9, 1947, in Philadelphia), could be considered as Philadelphia–Arctic Records' counterpart to Detroit–Karen Records' Barbara Lewis. After recording in 1964 for Crusader, she approached Jimmy Bishop's Arctic label as a songwriter (as Mary Wells had originally come to Motown). Bishop liked her youthful, innocent sound and signed her as an artist. *Girls Have Feelings Too* brought her into the R & B charts and paved the way for her 1965 Top 5 pop and R & B classic tale of adolescent longing, *Yes I'm Ready*. This album, built around the hit, showcased her in a variety of styles, from a teen-beat version of the standard *Misty* and the New York uptown soul style of *Got To Get*

You Off My Mind to the obligatory Motown sound of *Come See About Me*, as well as several of her original compositions. Mason was a solid writer and did best with her own material, such as *Sad Sad Girl* and *Oh How It Hurts* (it would be nice if the latter one was included here). She later recorded for National General and had further hits on Buddah in the mid-1970s with a fine version of Curtis Mayfield's love theme from "Superfly," *Give Me Your Love*, and her answer to Shirley Brown's *Woman To Woman*. She went on to cut an album of duets with longtime Philadelphia writer/producer/performer Bunny Sigler for Salsoul, as well as recording for WMOT in 1980 (*You Did Not Stay Last Night*), trading the youthful longing of *Yes I'm Ready* for sophisticated, adult frustration.

103 I Love You
Eddie Holman

ABC 701 (LP)

I Love You/It's All In The Game/Since My Love Has Gone/I Cried/I'll Be Forever Loving You/Since I Don't Have You/Hey There Lonely Girl/Let Me Into Your Life/ Four Walls/Don't Stop Now/Am I A Loser

Eddie Holman (b. June 3, 1946, In Norfolk, Virginia) was a veteran of TV and off-Broadway performing before getting on record in the mid-1960s on Philadelphia's Parkway label, where *This Can't Be True* and his first version of *Am I A Loser* were both Top 20 R & B hits. He secured his claim to fame in 1969 with his hit falsetto ballad *Hey There Lonely Girl*. Producer/arranger Peter DeAngelis had earlier been involved in the careers of such Philadelphia teen-idols as Fabian and Frankie Avalon; this album, however, is not reruns of *Tiger* or *Venus*, but, led by Holman's reaching voice and occasional writing (*Don't Stop Now* and *Am I A Loser* are his), a solid set of late-1960s, string-sweetened, uptown pop-soul. In fact, *Lonely Girl* is an unusual track for Holman, being performed entirely in falsetto. On other tracks Holman sings in his normal high tenor, soaring into his falsetto to provide crucial emotional peaks – and *Let Me Into Your Life* has no falsetto at all. Highlights include the hits *I Love You* and *Don't Stop Now*, and his treatments of the Tommy Edwards hit *It's All In The Game* and the Skyliners' classic ballad *Since I Don't Have You*. Holman later recorded, less successfully, for Buddah and Salsoul Records in the 1970s.

104 Love
Honey and the Bees

Josie JOS 4013 (LP)

We Got To Stay Together/Make Love To Me/Please Have Mercy/Help Me (Get Over My Used To Be Lover)/It's Gonna Take A Miracle (medley)/*Do You Understand/ Now That I Know/What About Me/I'll Spend My Life Loving You/Love Is The Key*

After gaining early experience with the Superiorettes and the Yum Yums, Honey and the Bees' lineup was solidified in 1965-6 with Nadine Felder (lead), Gwen Oliver, Jean Davis, and Cassandra Ann Wooten. They first recorded for Jimmy Bishop's Arctic label (their *Dynamite Exploded* being a Northern soul favorite). Their Josie recordings featured the entire Gamble and Huff studio band lineup, with Huff himself playing piano, arrangements by Norman Harris, Bobby Martin, and Ronnie Baker, and songs contributed by Bishop and Wilbert Hart as well as Al Felder and Norman Harris, who went on to write and produce many hits for Blue Magic, First Choice, and others. *Have Mercy* is modeled closely on the Miracles' *Ooh Baby Baby*, while *Help Me* is a good dance groove, and their version of *It's Gonna Take A Miracle* (a Teddy Randazzo ballad which was also a big hit for the Royalettes) is fine. The overall style furnished a model for the later PIR hits of the Three Degrees, and this album shows the studio band coalescing into the well-oiled MFSB machine. All that was really needed was the addition of Gamble and Huff's songs and production work.

105 Get It While You Can
Howard Tate

Verve V-6 5022 (LP)

Ain't Nobody Home/Part Time Love/Glad I Knew Better/ How Blue Can You Get/ Get It While You Can/Baby I Love You/ I Learned It All The Hard Way/Everyday I Have The Blues/How Come My Bulldog Don't Bark/Look At Granny Run Run

Originally a gospel singer, and later a protégé of organist/bandleader Bill "Honky Tonk" Doggett Tate (b. 1943, in Macon, Georgia), is a strong, flexible singer who artfully straddles the line between uptown 1960s blues and soul. He is best remembered for his original version of the Janis Joplin classic *Get It While You Can* (written by Jerry Ragovoy and the late Mort Shuman, a frequent songwriting partner of Doc Pomus). Ragovoy, whose extensive oeuvre includes Irma Thomas's *Time Is On My Side* (which became the first Top 10 hit for the Rolling Stones) and, with his frequent collaborator Bert Berns, Erma Franklin's *Piece Of My Heart* (another famous Joplin cover-job), recalls this album with Tate as among his very favorites of his own work. While Tate brings his shouting style to bear on the B.B. King chestnuts *Everyday I Have The Blues* and *How Blue Can You Get*, he really shines on Ragovoy's original material. There's tender blues balladry (*Baby I Love You*), jumping, up-tempo soul (*Ain't Nobody Home*), and raunchy humor (*How Come My Bulldog Don't Bark*) aplenty. Tate later recorded for Lloyd Price's Turntable label, and (reunited with Ragovoy) for Atlantic and Columbia, and is ripe for rediscovery à la the great Memphis soul man James Carr.

Gamble and Huff Early Works

106 There's Gonna Be A Showdown
Archie Bell and the Drells

Atlantic SD 8226 (LP)

I Love My Baby/Houston Texas/(There's Gonna Be A)Showdown/Giving Up Dancing/Girl You're Too Young/Mama Didn't Teach Me That Way/Do The Hand Jive/My Balloon's Going Up/Here I Go Again/Go For What You Know/Green Power/ Just A Little Closer

Archie Bell and the Drells (lead Bell, with Lee Bell, James Wise, and Willie Pernell) came from Houston, Texas, in early 1968 with Bell's self-written dance smash *Tighten Up*, which topped the pop and R & B charts and sold over one million copies. However, they were not able to come up with another self-written hit, and their manager Skipper Lee Frazier joined them up with the ascendant Gamble and Huff team. They came up with the Top 10 follow-up *I Can't Stop Dancing* and were then given the opportunity to stretch out and produce this album (the group's third for Atlantic). It yielded four hit singles in 1969, the biggest and best-remembered being the title track, plus *Girl You're Too Young*, *My Balloon's Going Up*, and *I Love My Baby*. Also of note was *Go For What You Know*, penned by Melvin and Mervin Steals, who went on to write the Spinners' million-seller *Could It Be I'm Falling In Love*. Except for two tracks (*Mama Didn't Teach Me* and *Just A Little Closer*), which were Archie Bell compositions cut in

Houston and included as leftovers from earlier sessions, these recordings were roughly contemporary with Gamble and Huff's classic Jerry Butler Mercury sessions.

This album, like the Butler sessions, presents Gamble and Huff and their studio cadre in rare form, carefully tailoring their songs and sound for Bell's hard-edged tenor and dance orientation. (*There's Gona Be A*) *Showdown* was later revived by punk princes the New York Dolls on their **Too Much Too Soon** album (some might say in a rare attack of good taste). *Do The Hand Jive* (not the Johnny Otis 1950s classic) and *Here I Go Again* are also of note as rare examples of Gamble and Huff aiming for an out-and-out Motown sound, complete with burping baritone sax riffs. **There's Gonna Be A Showdown** stands as a fine showcase for the writers/producers/bandsmen, and of course for Archie Bell and the Drells. After a few more singles for Atlantic, and a couple for Henry Stone's Miami-based Glades label, the group signed with Gamble and Huff in 1974. The collaboration produced some modest R & B hits (*I Could Dance All Night, Soul City Walk*, and *Everybody Have A Good Time*), but their earlier success was not recaptured.

107   Super Hits
The Intruders

Philadelphia International KZ 32131

Cowboys To Girls/Together/United/Love Is Like A Baseball Game/Slow Drag/When We Get Married/A Love That's Real/Friends No More/Gonna Be Strong/Me Tarzan You Jane/Check Yourself

Gonna Be Strong and *United* by the Intruders (lead Sam "Little Sonny" Brown, with Eugene Daughtry, Robert Edwards, and Phillip Terry) were among Gamble and Huff's first productions for their own labels. *United*, which inaugurated the Gamble label, became both the Intruders' and Gamble and Huff's first Top 10 R & B hit in 1966. Although far cruder than their later productions, these sides showed them moving away from the then-dominant Motown sound of shrill highs and booming bass toward their own style, featuring solid, mid-tempo rhythms with vibes and piano prominent (the piano by Leon Huff himself), with strings and horns filling in but not dominating the backgrounds behind Little Sonny's vocals. True, he tended to wander off pitch at any opportunity, but if anything this gave the records a touching, youthful vulnerability, which was perfectly served by the metaphors of songs like *Cowboys To Girls* and *Love Is Like A Baseball Game*.

Cowboys became the first (and last) million-seller for the Intruders, being the second million-seller for Gamble and Huff in 1968 – their first was the Soul Survivors' *Expressway To Your Heart*. These early sides by the Intruders are among the first examples of the fully realized Gamble and Huff sound, which achieved full fruition in the classic 1968 Jerry Butler sessions. The Intruders were the mainstay of the Gamble label, as were the O'Jays on the companion Neptune label. Gamble and Huff kept the Intruders on for over a decade, and eventually brought them to their TSOP label, where they achieved further hits with the more adult, polished sound of (*Win Place Or Show*) *She's A Winner* and the rolling, up-tempo dancer *I'll Always Love My Mama*.

108   O'Jays In Philadelphia
The O'Jays

Philadelphia International KZ 32120 (LP)

One Night Affair/You're The Best Thing Since Candy/Branded Bad/I Should Be Your Lover/Looky Looky (Look At Me Girl)/Deeper (In Love With You)/Let Me In Your World/Just Can't Get Enough/I've Got The Groove/Little Green Apples – Something (medley)/*It's Too Strong*

These 1969–70 tracks, originally cut for Gamble and Huff's Neptune label, were not of course the O'Jays' biggest hits; that would begin in 1972 with *Back Stabbers*. But there are four successful singles included – the stomping *One Night Affair* and *Branded Bad, Looky Looky (Look At Me Girl)*, which captures the youthful vulnerability of the Intruders' material, and *Deeper (In Love With You)*, which has some of the feel of the group's earlier Imperial/Minit sides, like the Northern soul favorite *Working On Your Case*. The Gamble and Huff machine – fresh from triumphs with Jerry Butler and about to achieve success with Wilson Pickett – was in high gear for these sessions. Even the non-hit songs were excellent, such as *I Should Be Your Lover* (with Eddie Levert in particularly fine voice), *Let Me Into Your World* (soon revived for the first Harold Melvin and the Blue Notes PIR album), and Ugene Dozier's tender *You're The Best Thing Since Candy*. With arrangements by Thom Bell, Bobby Martin, and Richard Rome, these tracks fall short of the **Back Stabbers** material only in that they were more obviously tightly conceived for the dictates of R & B radio play.

109   Drowning In The Sea Of Love
Joe Simon

Sound Bound CDSEW021 (UK)

Drowning In The Sea Of Love/Glad To Be Your Lover/Something You Can Do Today/I Found My Dad/The Mirror Don't Lie/O'le Night Owl/You Are Everything/If/ Let Me Be The One (The One Who Loves You)/Pool Of Bad Luck

Joe Simon (b. 1943, Simmesport, Louisiana) made his first releases in the early 1960s – some with the vocal group the Goldentones – on Irral, Hush, and Vee Jay Records. Charly Records reissued some of this material. In 1966 he signed with the late WLAC air personality and entrepreneur John "John R" Richbourg's Sound Stage 7 label (a division of Monument Records). Sound Stage 7 was one of the crucial but underappreciated Southern soul labels, specializing in country-flavored soul stylings, and Simon was easily the most important and successful artist ever recorded by Richbourg.

In late 1970 Simon signed with the larger, New York-based Spring label (distributed by Polydor). His first releases continued in his country-soul style, with such tracks as the Kris Kristofferson classic *Help Me Make It Through The Night*. In late 1971 he went to Philadelphia to record under Gamble and Huff, and the result was one of his biggest hits, the loping *Drowning In The Sea Of Love*. The merger of Joe's mellow baritone, the marvelous studio band – by now veterans of the Jerry Butler and Wilson Pickett sessions – and excellent material from Gamble and Huff, Thom Bell, and others, produced a classic set that showed Gamble and Huff stretching out from their strictly singles orientation. Tracks like *Something You Can Do Today*, *The Mirror Don't Lie* (a ballad just oozing pure soul), *Pool Of Bad Luck*, and *I Found My Dad* all broke the four-minute mark (and the last two, edited to single length, later became hit singles). The album also includes the first version of *You Are Everything* (by Thom Bell and the late Linda Creed). Bell had played organ on the Simon sessions, and shortly afterwards radically rearranged the song and cut it with the Stylistics. It has now become a soul and pop standard. Simon went on from this album to other successes for Spring, including the disco stomper *Get Down, Get Down (Get On The Floor)*.

The Soft-soul Romancers

110   The Best Of The Delfonics

The Delfonics

Arista AR 8333

La-La Means I Love You/Break Your Promise/Ready Or Not Here I Come/You Got Yours/Trying To Make A Fool Of Me/Tell Me This Is A Dream/Didn't I (Blow Your Mind This Time)/I'm Sorry/You Are Gone/Hey Love/When You Get Right Down To It/Delfonics Theme

After early sides for Cameo and Moonshot (Thom Bell's first productions), the Delfonics (lead William Hart, with Wilbert Hart and Randy Cain, from Washington, Pennsylvania) made their debut on Stan Watson's Philly Groove label in 1968 with the million-selling ballad *La-La Means I Love You*. The Delfonics specialized in ballad stylings, such as *I'm Sorry* and *Break Your Promise*, but could also break out with an infectious dancer like *Ready Or Not Here I Come* or the enchanting, mid-tempo *When You Get Right Down To It*. The songs, usually written by Bell and William Hart, featured lush, quasi-classical orchestration by Bell, who recalled cutting the tracks utilizing up to 40 musicians, including French horns, bassoons, oboes, and flugelhorns, on "live" sessions. If the Intruders were Gamble and Huff's "breakthrough" group, the Delfonics served a similar purpose for Thom Bell, and helped cement a close working relationship between G & H and Bell. Major Harris (of future *Love Won't Let Me Wait* fame) replaced Randy Cain in the group in 1971.

111   Greatest Hits

Blue Magic

Atlantic/Omni 90527

Sideshow/Stop To Start/Spell/What's Come Over Me/Three Ring Circus/Tear It Down/Look Me Up (remix)/Welcome To The Club/Chasing Rainbows/Just Don't Want To Be Lonely/Summer Snow/Where Have You Been

With the decline of the Stylistics in the early 1970s, Blue Magic (lead Ted "Wizard" Mills, with Vernon Sawyer, Wendell Sawyer, Richard Pratt, and Keith Beaton, from Philadelphia) took over as Philadelphia's top falsetto soft soul group. Produced by longtime sessionmen Norman Harris and Bobby Eli under the WMOT ("We Men Of Talent") imprint, they combined a rootsy, neo-do-wop sound with polished modern soul style. Making their debut in late 1973 with *Spell*, Blue Magic specialized in ballads like the Top 40 hit *Three Ring Circus* and their 1974 million-seller *Sideshow*, but could also rock the dance floors with such infectious items as *Look Me Up* and *Welcome To The Club*. *Just Don't Want To Be Lonely* is the beautiful original recording of the song that became a million-seller for the Main Ingredient. Another high point for the group was singing backup vocals on the Rolling Stones' hit *Fool To Cry*. Later they recorded for Def Jam's OBR label.

112   My Way

Major Harris

Atlantic 18119

Each Morning I Wake Up/Love Won't Let Me Wait/Sweet Tomorrow/Sideshow/Two Wrongs/Loving You Is Mellow/Just A Thing That I Do/After Loving You/My Way

Former member of the Jarmels and the Delfonics (as replacement for Randy Cain), Harris (from Philadelphia) had recorded for OKeh in the late 1960s with little success, before scoring his million-selling ballad *Love Won't Let Me Wait* in the summer of 1975. Produced by Bobby Eli (longtime Gamble and Huff guitar-player and Blue Magic producer/writer), this album shows why Harris has long been known as "the mellow mellow Major." He delivers a nice version of Blue Magic's *Sideshow* and even essays Frank Sinatra's standard *My Way* (personally, the only version of this song I can stand is by Sid Vicious). Still popular in Europe, Harris went on to record less successfully for RCA, Streetwave, and the local Philadelphia label Renaissance.

That Philly Groove – the Dancers

13 Armed And Extremely Dangerous
First Choice

Philly Groove 1400 (LP)

Smarty Pants/Runnin' Out Of Fools/A Boy Named Junior/Love And Happiness/ Wake Up To Me/Newsy Neighbors/Armed And Extremely Dangerous/This Little Woman/This Is The House/One Step Away

Stan Watson's Philly Groove label was already well established with the Delfonics' hits (*La-La Means I Love You*) when PIR guitarist/arranger Norman Harris brought in First Choice (Rochelle Fleming, Annette Guest, and Joyce Jones). But where the Delfonics specialized in the smoothest of ballads, First Choice were firmly aimed at the dance floor. They tried more classic soul stylings like Aretha Franklin's *Runnin' Out Of Fools* or Al Green's *Love And Happiness*, and occasionally a ballad (the soppy *A Boy Named Junior*). But their hits came with the fun, impudent club classics *Smarty Pants*, *Newsy Neighbors*, *The Player*, and biggest of all, *Armed And Extremely Dangerous*. All but *The Player* are included here. Late 1970s recordings for Gold Mind (*Doctor Love*) and Warners only showed that the music had moved on and their raunchy but innocent spirit had, sadly, become passé.

14 Love Sensation
Loleatta Holloway

Gold Mind GA 9506 (LP)

Love Sensation/Long Hard Climb To Love/Short End Of The Stick/I've Been Loving You Too Long/Two Became A Crowd/Dance What 'Cha Wanna/My Way/I'll Be Standing There

Loleatta Holloway (b. Philadelphia, Pennsylvania) is one of the great voices in the gospel-shouting diva tradition to emerge from the disco field. (Another is her West Coast contemporary Martha Wash, ex-Two Tons Of Fun and the Weathergirls, of *It's Raining Men* fame, and the glorious voice on contemporary dance productions by C & C Music Factory, Black Box, and many others.) Holloway has been sampled for such modern club hits as Mass Order's *Lift Every Voice (Take Me Away)*, while teen pop/rap stars Marky Mark and the Funky Bunch borrowed from her dance-floor anthem *Love Sensation* for their first hit,

Good Vibrations. Holloway knows her roots – she dedicated this album to Albertina Walker, founder/leader of the top-ranked female gospel group the Caravans, with whom she began her career.

Several producers contributed to the excellent selection of material. The dance tracks are quite rootsy: Bobby Womack's up-tempo *Dance What 'Cha Wanna* is closely modeled on the similarly titled early 1960s single by Johnnie Taylor, cut by Womack's mentor Sam Cooke on his Derby label. *Love Sensation* (written and produced by Dan Hartman of Edgar Winter Group fame) is diva/disco at its most glorious. But it is on the ballads that Holloway really struts her considerable stuff. The elegaic *My Way* (not the Sinatra standard) was first cut by Womack himself on his great Muscle Shoals-produced album **Lookin' For A Love Again**. Longtime Philadelphia mainstay Norman Harris contributes *I'll Be Standing There*, in the Blue Magic tradition. To top it all off, Holloway wails out a church-wrecking *I've Been Loving You Too Long* (we can but dream of her duetting with its originator, Otis Redding). Do not dare to overlook this set as "just another disco album." The formidable Holloway has seen a number of other album releases on Spring and Gold Mind, all well worth picking up. But this set ranks as her masterpiece.

115   Feel It
Fat Larry's Band

WMOT WM 625 (LP)

Feel It/Nighttime Boogie/Down On The Avenue/Music Maker/Center City/Fascination/Life Of An Entertainer/We Just Want To Play For You

Fat Larry's Band – Larry James (drums, vocals), Ted Cohen (guitar), Darryl Grant (vocals, percussion), Larry LaBes (bass, vocals), Erskine Williams (keyboards, vocals), Doug Jones (saxes, vocals), Art Capeheart (trumpet, vocals), and Jimmy Lee (trombone, vocals) – was formed in Philadelphia in the mid-1970s. It carried on the urban funk tradition of Cliff Nobles and Co., People's Choice, and the Trammps. The band were always very popular in England (*Blues and Soul* hailed their first single, *Center City* as "very exciting . . . ideal disco music"), where they rolled up four Top 50 hits (their biggest being the atypical ballad *Zoom*). *Fascination* is a version of David Bowie's Philadelphia-recorded track from **Young Americans**, although owing more to its co-author Luther Vandross's original *Funky Music Is A Part Of Me*. They also recorded for Fantasy under the names Philly Cream and Slick (*Sexy Cream*). Larry James died of a heart attack in 1983.

The PIR Hit Machine

116   The Three Degrees
The Three Degrees

Philadelphia International KZ 32406 (LP)

Dirty Ol' Man/Can't You See What You're Doing To Me/A Woman Needs A Good Man/When Will I See You Again/I Didn't Know/I Like Being A Woman/If And When/Year Of Decision

The Three Degrees (Fayette Pinkney, Valeria Holiday, and Sheila Ferguson, from Philadelphia) first recorded in the mid-1960s for Philadelphia's Swan Records, under manager/producer Richard Barrett, a longtime fixture on the New York vocal group scene. Their first hit was *Gee Baby (I'm Sorry)*, while other tracks of this period included *Close Your Eyes* (the old Five Keys hit), *Look*

In My Eyes (a song Barrett had originally written for the Chantels), and their first version of *Maybe* (the Chantels' all-time classic). Brief stays on Warner Brothers, Metromedia, and Gamble and Huff's Neptune label preceded their hit version of *Maybe* for Roulette in 1970, complete with overheated monologue and Valerie Holiday's explosive, wailing lead.

The group signed with PIR in 1973, and *Dirty Ol' Man* paved the way for the million-selling *When Will I See You Again*. The group also supplied the vocals on MFSB's *TSOP* (*The Sound Of Philadelphia*), which became the theme song for the "Soul Train" TV show, and the club classic *Love Is The Message* (not included here). Surprisingly, the group had no other big successes, although *I Didn't Know* and *Year Of Decision* made some impact. The Three Degrees were not a hard-soul group, but polished nightclub entertainers whose cabaret-style act ensured them plenty of work, hit records or not. Hearing a group like the Nitecaps, long one of New York's best club bands, tearing into *When Will I See You Again* only brings home what Old Town Records founder Hy Weiss once told this writer: "*Songs* make artists – artists never made a song in their lives."

17   360 Degrees Of Billy Paul
Billy Paul

Philadelphia International KZ 31793

Brown Baby/I'm Just A Prisoner/It's Too Late/Me And Mrs Jones/Am I Black Enough For You/Let's Stay Together/Your Song/I'm Gonna Make It This Time

Billy Paul (b. Paul Williams, December 1, 1934, in Philadelphia) had a background based as much on jazz as on R & B. As a teenager he had performed locally with such artists as Charlie Parker and Dinah Washington, later gaining R & B experience alongside the Impressions, Kim Weston, Roberta Flack, and others, and serving a stint with Harold Melvin and the Blue Notes. His jazz background was reflected in an early album (reissued in the wake of *Me And Mrs Jones*'s success) titled **Feelin' Good At The Cadillac Club**, in which he scat-sings his way through such items as *Bluesette* and *That's Life* with jazz piano-trio backing. **360 Degrees** was Paul's third album for Gamble and Huff, and probably his best. With his mixture of jazz and soul, he was the precursor to the Lou Rawls sound of *You'll Never Find Another Love Like Mine* and Rawls's other PIR hits, as well as such contemporary performers as Al Jarreau. *Me And Mrs Jones* is simply a perfect combination of singer and song, and hard to top. Paul's eclectic approach led him to the up-tempo sound of *Am I Black Enough For You*, Al Green's *Let's Stay Together*, and Carole King's *It's Too Late*, and he was one of the first to cover an Elton John number (*Your Song* is very nice indeed and even became a hit in England). Paul's later hits ranged from the loping *Thanks For Saving My Life* to the soppy *Let's Make A Baby*. Paul later recorded for Total Experience and for John Abbey's Ichiban label, but it seems unlikely he'll ever score another perfect record like *Me And Mrs Jones*.

18   Jacksons
The Jacksons

Epic EK 34229

Enjoy Yourself/Think Happy/Good Times/Keep On Dancing/Blues Away/Show You The Way To Go/Living Together/Strength Of One Man/Dreamer/Style Of Life

The Jacksons, from Gary, Indiana, were one of the most successful "family" acts of the rock era, and the last great product of the 1960s Motown Artist Development machine. Known as the Jackson Five on Motown, brothers

Michael, Jackie, Marlon, Tito, and Randy (who replaced Jermaine when the group switched from Motown to Epic) had already scored 18 Top 100 hits in six years when the group signed with Epic Records in 1976. The Jacksons had been promised more artistic control, not having been permitted to write, produce, or even play their own instruments on Motown, and were given a chance to stretch out on *Style Of Life* and *Blues Away*, but this album's hits, *Show You The Way To Go* and the million-selling *Enjoy Yourself*, were firmly under the Gamble and Huff production/writing aegis. The combination may not have always worked – picks of the pack here would include the rocking, guitar-driven *Think Happy* and *Living Together* – but Michael Jackson's 1979 smash solo album **Off The Wall** clearly showed that he had absorbed much from this brief liaison. This album could have been even stronger if the superb stomper *Goin' Places* had been added for CD release.

119 Teddy Pendergrass

Teddy Pendergrass

Philadelphia International KZ 34390

You Can't Hide From Yourself/Somebody Told Me/Be Sure/And If I Had/I Don't Love You Anymore/The Whole Town's Laughing At Me/Easy Easy Got To Take It Easy/The More I Get The More I Want

When Teddy Pendergrass left Harold Melvin and the Blue Notes in 1976, the group switched over to ABC. Pendergrass stayed with Gamble and Huff and, from 1977 onwards, he went on to become one of the most successful male vocalists in soul history. This, his first solo outing, includes the hits *I Don't Love You Anymore* and *The Whole Town's Laughing At Me*. Gamble and Huff's approach was not very different from that of his earlier hits with the Blue Notes. Teddy's voice was well cushioned with harmonies on tracks like the throbbing, up-tempo stompers *I Don't Love You Anymore* and *The More I Get The More I Want*, while his romantic ballad sound came to the fore on *The Whole Town's Laughing At Me*, which set the pattern for many of his later hits – the million-selling *Close The Door*, *Turn Off The Lights*, *Love TKO*, and others. The "Teddy Bear" became the archetypal "love man" with his famous "ladies only" concerts. Sadly, in 1982 an automobile accident left him in a wheelchair. In the early 1990s he was recording for Elektra, singing well if less extravagantly, and doing some producing for his own label.

120 Jones Girls

The Jones Girls

Philadelphia International KZ 33575 (LP)

This Feeling's Killing Me/You Made Me Love You/Show Love Today/You're Gonna Make Me Love Somebody Else/Life Goes On/Who Can I Run To/We're A Melody/I'm At Your Mercy

The Jones Girls (sisters Valerie, Brenda, and Shirley, from Detroit, Michigan), having already sung backup on a number of records by Lou Rawls and Teddy Pendergrass and toured behind Diana Ross, came to the PIR stable in 1979. Perhaps they were viewed as a replacement for the Three Degrees. They were given some good material – the shuffling *You're Gonna Make Me Love Somebody Else* and *I Just Love The Man* (the latter not included here) both made the R & B Top 10. They were more out-and-out soulful than the Three Degrees, but, as befits a backup group pushed to the front, their strongest suit was their fine harmonies, cushioned in the lavish but funky productions. They could deliver some strong lead vocals, though, and attained further success with later productions such as *Nights Over Egypt.*

Gamble and Huff Side Trips

121 Rush Hour
Bobby Rush

Philadelphia International KZ 35509 (LP)
I Wanna Do The Do/I Can't Find My Keys/Let's Do It Together/Intermission/ Nickname/Evil Is/No Axe Ta Grind/Hey Western Union Man

Rush Hour was the first album by Bobby Rush (b. Emmett Ellis, Jr, November 10, 1940, in Homer, Louisiana), who is better known for his subsequent funky Southern soul-blues releases on La Jam (notably *Sue*). Producer Leon Huff and the Philadelphia house band clearly enjoyed cutting this set, reveling in the break from cutting contemporary sessions with the likes of Lou Rawls, Teddy Pendergrass, and the O'Jays. The band renders an extremely polished but gutsy performance. Rush's *I Wanna Do The Do* mixes *Wang Dang Doodle* and Junior Parker's *Feelin' Good* into a real devil's brew. *I Can't Find My Keys* is an outstanding modern *urban* blues: "Here I am all dressed up, clean as I can be, gotta pick up my baby 'bout a quarter to eight, I can't find my keys." *Let's Do It Together* is a hard-edge funk workout for Rush and the band, while *Hey Western Union Man* is reshaped from Jerry Butler's original, ice-cool soul style into an up-tempo blues shuffle. This is a superb, one-off, PIR *blues* album.

122 Boogie Down USA
People's Choice

TSOP KZ 33154 (LP)
Do It Any Way You Wanna/Are You Sure/Mickey D's/I'm Leaving You/The Sooner You Get Here/Boogie Down USA/Nursery Rhymes/Party Is A Groovy Thing/If You Want Me Back/Don't Send Me Away

People's Choice – Frankie Brunson (vocals and keyboards), Guy Fiske (guitar), Roger Andrews (bass), and David Thompson (drums) – could well be considered as Gamble and Huff's version of Junior Walker and the All Stars, a tough little funk band fronted by Brunson's occasional rough-voiced leads. *Do It Any Way You Wanna* and *Boogie Down USA* are two of the great 1970s Philadelphia funk instrumentals, in the tradition of the late 1960s hits *The Horse* and *Switch It On* by Cliff Nobles & Co. (actually the future MFSB band). Brunson and company had even recorded for Nobles' label Phil LA of Soul, where they had a small hit with *I Likes To Do It* in 1971. *Do It Any Way You Wanna* topped the R & B charts and reached number 11 in the pop charts in 1975. Only minimal sweetening was applied – a few blasts from the MFSB horns on *Are You Sure* and *If You Want Me Back*, a touch of female backing vocals on *I'm Leaving You* and the down-in-the-alley soul ballad *Don't Send Me Away*. As with Bobby Rush's blues album **Rush Hour**, Gamble and Huff obviously had fun cutting these sessions.

---

123   Travelin' In Heavy Traffic
Don Covay

Philadelphia International KZ 33958 (LP)

No Tell Motel/Chocolate Honey/You Owe It To Your Body/Travelin' In Heavy Traffic/Feelings/Right Time For Love/Six Million Dollar Fish (Jaws)/Swet (And You Shall Be Rewarded) (sic)

Born in 1938 in Orangeburg, South Carolina, and raised in Washington, DC, Covay began his career in a teenage doo-wop group, the Rainbows, which also housed the talents of Marvin Gaye and Billy Stewart. An early protégé of Little Richard, whose band the Upsetters backed Covay on his debut Atlantic single *Bip Bop Bip* (1958), Covay's career has encompassed songwriting (his Grammy Award winner *Chain Of Fools* for Aretha Franklin), performing (*I Was Checkin' Out, She Was Checkin' In, Mercy Mercy, See Saw*), and all-around R & B inspiration (the J. Geils Band's former frontman Peter Wolf often sang his praises, not to mention his songs, and even wrote the liner notes for Covay's 1973 Mercury album **Super Dude I**). Covay's brief affiliation with PIR yielded this self-produced set, which splits neatly into up-tempo and ballad sides. *No Tell Motel* is a typically humorous visit to a low-life place "where you can go and raise hell," while *You Owe It To Your Body*, featuring Covay's own "Jefferson Lemon Blues Band," is a really funky shuffle. The ballad side drags a little (notably Morris Albert's song *Feelings* – the late, great Chicago soulman Walter Jackson cut the definitive R & B version of this tune), but Covay redeems it with another humorous take-off, this time based on the "Jaws" movie, *Six Million Dollar Fish*, complete with sound effects (and a great couplet: "They'll catch up with you soon, in your own dining room"). Covay's classic albums for Atlantic (**Mercy!**, **See Saw**, and **House Of Blue Lights**) and Mercury (**Super Dude I** and **Hot Blood**) are out of print, but worth seriously searching for.

---

124   Happy 'Bout The Whole Thing
Dee Dee Sharp

TSOP PZ 33839 (LP)

Love Buddies/Touch My Life/Ooh Child/Real Hard Day/Make It Till Tomorrow/Happy 'Bout The Whole Thing/I'm Not In Love/Share My Love/Best Thing You Did For Me

Dee Dee Sharp (b. Dione La Rue, September 9, 1945, in Philadelphia) first got on record singing an uncredited duet with Chubby Checker on his soulful 1962 hit *Slow Twistin'*. Soon signed as an artist in her own right, Sharp's recordings for Cameo/Parkway were mostly in the dance-craze groove, such as *Do The Bird*, *Gravy*, and her biggest, *Mashed Potato Time* (number 1 R & B, number 2 pop in 1962). The song so closely resembled the big Motown hit *Please Mr Postman* by the Marvelettes that it was actually published by Motown's Jobete Music. Sharp dismissed her years as the "Mashed Potato Queen" in a *Soul Survivor* interview, noting: "I can't even dance!" Her future husband Kenny Gamble had a hand in writing a few of her Cameo/Parkway sides: *He's No Ordinary Boy, I Really Love You*, and the excellent dancer *There Ain't Nothing*. The British London label released a compilation of these sides back in the mid-1970s, but there have been no subsequent reissues. Sharp saw some more soulful singles releases, including the deep *My Best Friend's Man* and a strong duet with Ben E. King, *We Got A Thing Going On*, on Atco and Gamble in the late 1960s (a few of the Gamble sides even saw release in England on the Action label) before signing with Gamble and Huff's PIR complex in the early 1970s. **Happy 'Bout The Whole**

Thing, which produced a fine R & B hit version of 10 CC's *I'm Not In Love* (1976), showcased a far more mature Sharp, ranging from the disco-stomping title track and *Share My Love* to the torchy, ballad stylings of *Love Buddies, Best Thing You Did For Me*, and the Five Stairsteps' *Ooh Child*. However, after one further album, **What Color Is Love**, Sharp has apparently retired from active performing.

125 Reality
Monk Montgomery

Philadelphia International KZ 33153 (LP)

Reality/Me And Mrs Jones/Sippin' And Tippin'/Bump De Bump/I Love You Camille/ Little O's/Girl Talk/Close Your Face

Monk Montgomery (b. October 10, 1921, in Indianapolis, Indiana), a brother of jazz guitar great Wes Montgomery, was a pioneer of the Fender electric bass, having introduced it with the Lionel Hampton Orchestra in the early 1950s. His jazz credentials included work with Freddie Hubbard, George Shearing, Cal Tjader, and Red Norvo; he was also associated with Joe Sample and the Jazz Crusaders (who recorded with him for Motown's Chisa label), worked with Bill Cosby, and was a prominent jazz educator. Gamble and Huff, whose own work had always been informed by a jazz sensibility – witness Billy Paul, Lou Rawls, and Dexter Wansel; they even recorded the Thad Jones/Mel Lewis Big Band for PIR – signed Montgomery in 1974. This is a happy soul-jazz-funk set featuring Montgomery's bass, with a small group fronted by Bobby Martin's keyboards and, on some cuts, the PIR house band, including a lovely version of *Me And Mrs Jones* and the romping *Bump De Bump*.

Detroit

Detroit   4

Dan Nooger

For the general pop music fan, Detroit music is equated with Motown on the soul side; with the "bad boy" rock antics of Iggy and the Stooges, MC5, Mitch Ryder and the Detroit Wheels, and Ted Nugent and the Amboy Dukes; with being the launching pad for Bob Seger and boss bluesman John Lee Hooker; and with little else. Detroit in fact had an active black music scene – blues, jazz, and R & B – after World War II, centered on Hastings Street and venues like the Flame Show Bar, where such 1950s stars as Lavern Baker, Little Willie John, and Johnnie Ray (the first blue-eyed soulboy) emerged.

Record producers and labels such as Bernie Besman (John Lee Hooker, Sensation label), Joe Von Battle (JVB, the first to record a then 14-year-old Aretha Franklin, as well as her father Rev. C.L. Franklin – his series of sermons recorded "live" at his New Bethel Baptist Church sold for Chess Records for many years), and Jack and Devora Brown with their Fortune and Hi-Q labels, as well as others now obscure, were quite active. The scene was so localized and operations were so chaotic, however, that few artists were able to break out of the Detroit scene and make a national impact. Even the very existence of some labels, such as Morry Kaplan's Danceland (John Lee Hooker and others), has only recently been discovered by collectors. Such well-regarded jazzmen as pianist Barry Harris, the talented Jones family (trumpeter/bandleader Thad, drummer Elvin, of John Coltrane Quartet fame, and pianist Hank), and saxman Pepper Adams (who even recorded for Motown's Workshop Jazz label) also came from the area.

On the soul side, the single most important early performer in bringing the Detroit scene to prominence was the late Jackie Wilson. After a stint as lead singer with Billy Ward and the Dominoes (as replacement for Clyde McPhatter), Wilson broke through in the late 1950s in the pop and R & B markets with such hits as *Reet Petite*, *To Be Loved*, *Lonely Teardrops*, and *That's Why I*

Love You So. All were written by Berry Gordy, Jr, (together with his early associate Roquel "Billy" Davis, who went on to become an important writer/producer/A & R man for Chess Records). Wilson's crossover appeal, his mixture of extravagant gospel theatrics, dancing moves, and his ability to transform the hoariest of standards (such as *Danny Boy*), provided the blueprint for Gordy and Motown's future successes.

The most important early Detroit R & B/soul producer prior to Motown and Gordy's emergence was the late Robert West, with his Lupine, Flick, and Contour labels. West, a longtime record man, never achieved consistent national success, despite on-and-off associations with such major national labels as Atlantic, launching the careers of many important performers (including Wilson Pickett, Eddie Floyd, and even the Supremes), as well as cutting crucial pre-Motown sides by the likes of Eddie and Brian Holland. Relic Records, best known for their "Golden Groups" series of doo-wop reissues, have done sterling work in gathering up the important early West soul recordings.

Other early Detroit R & B labels of some importance include the Fortune operation and the Chex label. Fortune, which had actually been active since the late 1940s, was never confined to R & B, having also cut some fine country and rockabilly (Skeets McDonald, Roy "The Hound" Hall, and the ex-Sun rocker Johnny Powers), but is best known for the records of Nolan Strong and the Diablos (a crucial early influence on Smokey Robinson), and Andre "Bacon Fat" Williams (who went on to record for Motown, Ric-Tic, and Chess, and even produced bluesman Bobby Bland). Albums devoted to Strong and Williams, and a couple of odd **Fortune Of Hits** compilations, are sporadically available on vinyl, but Mrs Brown has steadfastly resisted the efforts of reissuers such as Ace, Charly, and Bear Family to license her holdings for wider distribution. Willie Ewing's tiny Chex label actually nudged the pop Top 20 in 1962 with the Volumes' *I Love You*, but was more important as a launching pad for such talents as producer/performer Richard "Popcorn" Wylie, and Lamont Dozier (formerly a vocalist on Anna Records as "Lamont Anthony"), who started as a producer here as well as working as a session drummer (reportedly, on certain sides, beating brushes on an upended suitcase!). Again, Relic Records have reissued the best of the Chex recordings.

Other Detroit labels of interest from the turn of the 1960s include Anna, Check-Mate, and Harvey/Tri-Phi. Anna and Check-Mate were Detroit "outposts" for the Chess brothers' Chicago-based operations. Billy Davis, together with Gwen Gordy, ran Anna, whose roster included David Ruffin and Lamont Dozier, and enjoyed a hit with *The Hunch* by ex-New Orleans bandleader and longtime Chess promotion man Paul

Gayten. Ex-Moonglows' leader Harvey Fuqua was a staff producer and used his young protégé Marvin Gaye as a session musician. Anna even distributed one of Gordy's best-remembered early hits, Barrett Strong's *Money*. After Anna went out of business, Fuqua launched his own Harvey label, which discovered the talents of the Spinners, Junior Walker, and Shorty Long, as well as recording the veteran bluesman Eddie Burns, whose *Orange Driver* became a staple for the J. Geils Band. Check-Mate was launched in 1961 by Billy Davis (who had, as with Anna Records, gotten financing for the label from Leonard Chess), and again recorded David Ruffin in his pre-Temptations days. Anna and Harvey were absorbed by Motown, and Check-Mate was folded back into Chess in the early 1960s. However, little of this material has been sensibly reissued or made available. The same fate befell the works of such other labels as Carmen Murphy's H-O-B (House of Beauty) and Johnnie Mae Matthews's Northern Records. Murphy's label launched the careers of the important Detroit vocalist Lee Rogers and top Motown producer Mickey Stevenson, among others, while Matthews was the first to record the Distants (later to develop into the Temptations) and discovered Mary Wells and Betty Lavette.

The success of Motown inspired a large number of local entrepreneurs to try their luck in the mid-1960s. The Detroit scene was thoroughly incestuous, with musicians, producers, and performers moving from label to label, sometimes without regard to contractual obligations. But all of this cross-breeding, mixing, and matching produced not a race of sniveling, pin-headed idiots, but some of the best soul music ever. Perhaps the most successful were Ollie McLaughlin with his Karen/Moira/Carla labels – whose association with Atlantic gained national success for Barbara Lewis, the Capitols, and Deon Jackson – and Ed Wingate, whose Golden World and Ric-Tic labels gave Motown such a run for their money that Gordy eventually bought up his whole operation. McLaughlin's best material has been reissued by Solid Smoke and more recently Collectables, while much of the Wingate canon (Edwin Starr, J.J. Barnes, Fantastic Four, etc.), has remained accessible only to dedicated collectors.

The Groovesville and Solid Hitbound labels were the product of Don Davis and LeBaron Taylor. Taylor was a former deejay on WCHB, while Davis had cut his teeth as a Motown session guitarist. Taylor and Davis then moved into producing and writing for Ed Wingate's group of labels. Out of this evolved the Revilot–Solid Hitbound group (some Golden World/Ric-Tic releases were Solid Hitbound productions). The roster included J. J. Barnes, Steve Mancha (b. Clyde Wilson, he later joined 100 Proof Aged In Soul), and early efforts by George Clinton's Parliaments, including their big hit *I Wanna Testify* (covered by

Johnnie Taylor on Stax, and more recently by Queen's drummer Roger Taylor as a solo artist). Again, very little of this material has been reissued. Davis later became a top producer at Stax Records.

Another important early Detroit entrepreneur was the late Mike Hanks. Starting out with the H-O-B label, Hanks later launched his own labels including Mah's, D-Town, and Wheelsville. His discoveries included the important vocalist Lee Rogers (*I Want You To Have Everything* was a Top 20 R & B hit in 1965) and the Fabulous Peps, who later became, under Norman Whitfield's guidance at Motown, the Undisputed Truth.

It must be remembered that all of this activity was not taking place in isolation. Many of Detroit's rockers were close to the R & B scene. As P-Funk main man George Clinton recalled in *Goldmine*, "The MC 5 and the Stooges were our favorite bands at one point. We even shared the same management. Us, the Stooges, the MC 5, and Ted Nugent and the Amboy Dukes used to all play the same shows, the same college towns together." Motown had experimented with white artists as early as 1961, with singers like the Valadiers (who even had a hit with *Greetings (This Is Uncle Sam)*), Debbie Dean, and most notably Chris Clark (of *Love's Gone Bad* fame), and in the mid-1960s recorded such rock groups as the Underdogs and the Mynah Birds (who included Neil Young, pre-Buffalo Springfield, and future punk-funk star Rick James). Ed Wingate's white groups included the pop-slanted Reflections (*Just Like Romeo And Juliet*), the funkier Flaming Ember (who later achieved success on Hot Wax with *Westbound #9*), and the Sunliners, who, renamed Rare Earth, scored Top 10 successes for Motown in 1970 with their roaring remakes of the Temptations' *Get Ready* and *(I Know) I'm Losing You*.

Many other labels were active in the area during this time. Names such as Buddy Lamp, the Masqueraders, La Beat Records, and Soul Hawk Records continue to excite collectors to this day. In the post-Motown period (after the company's move to Los Angeles at the turn of the 1970s), the most active labels were Invictus/Hot Wax, run by ex-Motown star producers Eddie and Brian Holland and Lamont Dozier (H–D–H), and Armen Boladian's Westbound Records. H–D–H enjoyed a large number of hits with Freda Payne, Laura Lee, the Honey Cone, 100 Proof Aged In Soul, and Chairmen Of The Board (led by General Johnson), while Westbound soldiered along with solid products from the Detroit Emeralds, Fantastic Four, Denise LaSalle, and George Clinton's acid-drenched Parliaments' spin-off Funkadelic. P-Funk's influence on modern rap and dance music has of course been incalculable – just ask Janet Jackson, De La Soul, Digital Underground, Public Enemy, the Jungle Brothers, and Gang Starr. The International P-Funk fan-club newsletter *New Funk Times* regularly carries long lists of modern productions that have sampled or borrowed from the Funk. As George Clinton recently told *Motorbooty* magazine: "there's nothing wrong with rap bands sampling our old songs. They sample, and we sample right back. They use my material, I use theirs." Modern star performers ranging from Keith Richards and Talking Heads to Deee-Lite have often drafted in crucial P-Funkers like bassist Bootsy Collins, sax-man Maceo Parker, and keyboardist Bernie Worrell for tours and recording projects, while Prince has recorded George Clinton for his Paisley Park label, and featured him in his film "Graffiti Bridge." The 1970s also saw nationally successful Detroit-based productions from performers including the Dramatics (*In The Rain*), Enchantment (*Gloria*), the Floaters (*Float On*), and Al Hudson and the Soul Partners (*Spread Love*).

Even now Detroit still has active producers and labels, such as Mike Hanks's son Donald Hanks and ex-Motowner Sylvia Moy's Michigan Satellite label, as well as small operations like R & R, Skylight, Spectrum X, and Watchman, which sadly are barely distributed outside of their local areas. Detroit was also the birthplace for the modern techno sound, pioneered by producers Juan Atkins, Derrick May, and Kevin Saunderson, but it seems unlikely the city will ever regain the glory days of the 1960s.

Essential Recordings

(i) Detroit Soul Roots – The Falcons

I Found A Love, along with its companion sets **The Soul Of The Falcons** and **You're So Fine**, and the various artists' compilations released by Relic, **Detroit Girl Groups** and **The Soul Of Detroit**, covers the late 1950s–early 1960s' activities of producer/entrepreneur Robert West and his Lupine/Flick/Contour Detroit label complex. That West's labels were not able to achieve the stature of his near-contemporary Berry Gordy was surely not due to musical shortcomings. Even a short list of the artists and producers to pass through his doors includes Brian and Eddie Holland, Wilson Pickett, Eddie Floyd, Joe Stubbs (Originals and 100 Proof Aged In Soul), the embryonic Diana Ross and the Supremes (as the Primettes), the Ohio Players (then known as the Ohio Untouchables and featuring guitarist Robert Ward, who in the early 1990s resurfaced with an excellent album for Black Top), Sir Mack Rice (author of *Mustang Sally* and the Staple Singers' *Respect Yourself*), Marv Johnson (pre-*Come To Me*), Betty Lavette, and the first-class bluesmen Eddie Kirkland and the B.B. King-styled Louis "Mr Bo" Collins (see the **Three Shades Of The Blues** set put out by Relic).

The Falcons' vast and complex decade-plus career encompassed three different incarnations and innumerable personnel changes. While their first album in this series, **You're So Fine** (covered in chapter 1), included their traditional group harmony sounds and classic sessions from the late 1950s, this album picks up the story with a few late 1959 sides featuring lead singer Joe Stubbs and the original lineup with Eddie Floyd (West's nephew), Willie Schofield, Mack Rice, and guitarist Lance Finnie. New lead singer Wilson Pickett had made his debut in 1960 with *Pow! You're In Love* (not included here), but this album starts with the immortal *I Found A Love* from 1962 with Pickett's amazing gospel-screaming lead. As with much of West's product, it was leased to Atlantic for national distribution, and is still the starting point for Pickett compilations today.

West's brand of Detroit proto-soul was rougher and rawer than Gordy's contemporary productions, with such artists as Marv Johnson, Mary Wells, or the Miracles – closer to the roots – although West was also a compulsive studio experimenter who would often re-record songs several times in different sessions before picking a final version for release.

The original Falcons' lineup with Joe Stubbs on lead is heard on *You Must Know I Love You*, a slab of up-tempo R & B, and the delightfully crude *That's What I Aim To Do*. Other Pickett leads included here are *Take This Love I Got* and *Let's Kiss And Make Up* (with Ward's guitar especially dynamic), both alternate versions to those included on his Atlantic **In The Midnight Hour** album. Bennie McCain and the Ohio Untouchables are backed by the Falcons on *She's My Heart's Desire*, *You're On My Mind*, and *What To Do*. McCain's voice is somewhat lighter than Pickett's, being heavily influenced, like so many Detroit singers, by Jackie Wilson. His best side, *I Don't Want No Part Time Love*, is included on the **Soul Of Detroit** album. Sir Mack Rice takes the lead on the sparsely accompanied *Feels Good*, backed by some strong harmonies from the rest of the group.

With both Pickett and Eddie Floyd busy developing their solo careers by 1963, West took a group called the Fabulous Playboys, who had recorded as far back as 1956 as the Ramblers, to be the "new" Falcons. Carlis Monroe (lead), James Gibson, Alton Hollowell, and Johnny Alvin comprised the Falcons group which appeared on the famous Atlantic **Apollo Saturday Night** album. As Pickett told this writer: "They came to the Apollo, bombed like a dog. They just didn't sound like no Falcons. Guy couldn't sing *I Found A Love*, couldn't nobody sing *I Found A Love* but me!" But in West's studios, they laid down some tough sounds in their own right, such as *Lonely Nights* (garage-level Jackie Wilson), *Has It Happened To You Yet*, and the doo-wop-soul hybrid *Oh Baby*. Later renamed the Firestones, they cut the super-soulful *Buy Now And Pay Later* (written by original Falcon Mack Rice) for Ollie McLaughlin (included on **Detroit Gold, Vol. 1**, discussed later in this "Essential Recordings" section).

In comparing the sounds that were being achieved in 1964 by Motown and by West (for example, *Lonely Nights*), it should be noted that the now classic "Motown Sound," polished, cohesive, and well recorded (exemplified by the Supremes' *Baby Love*, Mary Wells's *My Guy*, the Four Tops' *Baby I Need Your Loving*, and Marvin Gaye's *How Sweet It Is To Be Loved By You*) was coming on strong, while West's sounds were altogether cruder, both in arrangements and in recording quality. Maybe West's records would not have had a shot at the pop charts, but miss them at your peril. Detroit was far more than Motown and these recordings prove it. Top tracks on this album include, of course, *I Found A Love*, the transitional (though anachronistic for 1963) *Oh Baby*, Pickett again on *Take This Love I Got*, Bennie McCain's *She's My Heart's Desire*, and Joe Stubbs's raw, exciting wailing on *That's What I Aim To Do*, showing the promise that would take him way up the charts in later years with 100 Proof.

Discographical Details

126   I Found A Love
The Falcons
Relic 7012
I Found A Love/She's My Heart's Desire/You Must Know I Love You/Oh Baby/ You're On My Mind/Let's Kiss And Make Up/Feels Good/Lonely Nights/Take This Love I Got/That's What I Aim To Do/Anna/What To Do/Fine Fine Girl/Part Time Love/Has It Happened To You Yet

(ii) Motown's Superstar Male Groups – Smokey Robinson and the Miracles, the Temptations, the Four Tops

The Miracles (William "Smokey" Robinson on lead, Bobby Rogers, Warren "Pete" Moore, Ronnie White, and Claudette Rogers, all from Detroit) were the first group Berry Gordy signed to Motown. Originally formed in 1957 as the Matadors, the group joined up with Gordy, then a songwriter and independent producer, in 1958. Their first recordings, *Got A Job* (a take-off of the Silhouettes' hit *Get A Job*) and the ballad *Bad Girl*, were licensed to the End and Chess labels respectively. Robinson is credited with inspiring Gordy to form his own labels and, as he related in his autobiography, told him, "Why work for the man? Why not *you* be the man?" – which carried them both to places they could never have dreamed of. Their faith was soon repaid, with the Miracles' *Shop Around* becoming Motown's first million-seller in 1960. Smokey became Gordy's right-hand man, as artist, producer, and songwriter, being named a Motown vice-president in 1963.

A full listing of Smokey's songs and productions would easily fill this section to bursting. Consider just a few high spots, among the best-loved songs of the 1960s: the Miracles' *Tears Of A Clown, I Second That Emotion, Mickey's Monkey*, and *You've Really Got A Hold On Me* (covered by the Beatles – John Lennon named the Miracles as his favorite group) were all Top 10 hits; Mary Wells's *My Guy, Two Lovers, The One Who Really Loves You*, and *You Beat Me To The Punch*, again all Top 10 hits; the Temptations' *My Girl, The Way You Do The Things You Do, It's Growing*, and *My Baby* (all Top 20, including the chart topping *My Girl*); Marvin Gaye's classics *I'll Be Doggone, Ain't That Peculiar*, and *One More Heartache*; the Marvelettes' hits *Don't Mess With Bill, The Hunter Gets Captured By The Game*, and *My Baby Must Be A Magician*; superb efforts for Brenda Holloway (*Operator*), Kim Weston (*Looking For The Right Guy*), the Isley Brothers (*Little Miss Sweetness*), the Contours (*First I Look At The Purse*), Tammi Terrell (*He's The One I Love*), the Supremes (*The Composer, A Breath Taking Guy, Take Me Where You Go*) . . . and the beat goes on.

Smokey's marvelous lyric explorations, sometimes humorous, sometimes serious, of the joy, ambiguity, and pain of love earned him the accolade of "America's greatest living poet" from Bob Dylan (a view echoed by such modern rap stars as Big Daddy Kane), yet he has always said that he viewed songwriting as a job. As a producer, he stood somewhat apart from the Motown "factory" approach, his work always being tailored to the artist – cool and seductive for Mary Wells, giving full scope to the Temptations' gospel-rooted harmonies, letting Marvin Gaye find a pocket in the groove and ride with it, getting raw and funky with the Contours. The Marvelettes were not the greatest of singers, but they never sounded better or more sensual than on sides like *Don't Mess With Bill, The Hunter Gets Captured By The Game*, or *Here I Am Baby*.

In his songwriting catalog – over 400 songs, many composed with the other Miracles and long-time guitarist Marv Tarplin – Smokey took different approaches. Sometimes he could be straight ahead – *Ooh Baby Baby* is one of the sweetest little broken-hearted love odes ever – but always with those marvelously turned phrases. Or he could mix high-flown images with emotional directness, as in *The Love I Saw In You Was Just A Mirage*: "just like the desert shows a thirsty man a green oasis where there's only sand, you lured me into something I should have dodged, the love I saw in you was just a mirage." Many blues and soul songs have used the image of laughing to keep from crying, but few more poetically than Smokey's tales of the brokenhearted Pagliaccis in *Tracks Of My Tears* or *Tears Of A Clown*. Then he could shift gears and make the skin ripple with the wrathful simplicity and pounding beat of *I Gotta Dance To Keep From Crying*.

The Miracles were also excellent live performers. The 1963 **Recorded Live On Stage** set (part of a series which also included Mary Wells, Marvin Gaye, the Marvelettes, and Stevie Wonder) was something special. Smokey and the group's rapport with the audience, even at this early stage, was close to B.B. King's on **Live At The Regal**, or Sam Cooke's on the **Live At The Harlem Square Club** set. In contrast to their studio recordings, which were always tightly controlled, on this set Smokey *rocks* – the ballad *Way Over There* is taken at double speed, building to a frenzy of pure gospel shouting. Even more polished later sets, like 1968's **Smokey Robinson And The Miracles Live!**, where they are mixing standards like *You And The Night And The Music* and the modern pop of *Walk On By* or *Yesterday* (à la **Sam Cooke At The Copa**) with their own material, make good listening. The last few years of Smokey's time with the Miracles (1970–2) is generally considered a somewhat fallow period, but gems still emerged, like *We've Come Too Far To End It Now*, *Crazy Bout The La La La*, the smash hit *Tears Of A Clown*, and the album **One Dozen Roses**. A representative selection of Miracles' albums would also include their first set **Hi, We're The Miracles, Going To A Go-Go, Doin' Mickey's Monkey**, and **Tears Of A Clown**.

Robinson decided to leave the group in 1972 to devote more time to his family, and they went out on a high note with the valedictory farewell tour recording **1957–1972**. Bill Griffin replaced Robinson as lead singer, and the group continued for another five years, but their only substantial hits were *Do It Baby* and the 1976 chart-topper *Love Machine*, neither sounding much like the Miracles of old. A change to Columbia Records did nothing to restore their fortunes. Smokey Robinson's post-Miracles solo career (*Cruisin'*, *Baby That's Backatcha*, etc.) is covered in chapter 8.

The Temptations ("classic" lineup: David Ruffin, lead baritone, b. January 8, 1941, in Meridian, Mississippi; Eddie Kendricks, lead tenor, b. December 17, 1939, in Union Springs, Alabama; Otis Williams, b. Otis Miles, October 30, 1941, in Texarkana, Texas; Melvin Franklin, b. David English, October 12, 1942, in Montgomery, Alabama; Paul Williams, b. July 2, 1939, in Birmingham, Alabama, died August 17, 1973) were, along with the Four Tops, Motown's top male group. But unlike the Tops, together since 1954 without a single personnel change, the Tempts went through numerous changes, both in lineup and style, yet remained at the top.

The Temptations were transplanted Southerners, and their style was formed in the forge of gospel singing, although their performances and recordings were always polished to a gleam as bright as their shoes. Originating in the late 1950s from a merger of the Detroit groups the Primes (including Eddie Kendricks and Paul Williams) and the Distants (including Melvin Franklin and Otis Williams), they were first known as the Elgins (no connection with the later Motown group of *Heaven Must Have Sent You* renown). A few early recordings for local songwriter/entrepreneur Johnnie Mae Matthews's Northern label and session work for Robert West's Lupine operation provided experience if not fame. Adding Elbridge Bryant as lead singer, the group was signed by Berry Gordy in 1961. Early releases included *Oh Mother Of Mine*, the doo-wop-flavored *Paradise* and *Dream Come True* (with writing and production by Gordy and Smokey Robinson), and the raw, soulful *Check Yourself*, which was written by the group and featured a rare lead by Paul Williams. Only *Dream Come True* (which inaugurated the Gordy label) nudged the R & B charts in 1962. They became so desperate for a hit that they even did a cover of Nolan Strong's *Mind Over Matter* in late 1962 under the name the Pirates, on Gordy's little-known Mel-O-Dy label.

Bryant was soon replaced by David Ruffin, who had previously recorded with the Voice Masters for Anna Records and as a solo artist on the Chess label's Detroit "outpost" Check-Mate Records. *I Want A Love I Can See* (written and produced by Smokey) was his first lead. Most of their early recordings were collected on their first album, **Meet The Temptations**, which if light on hits still makes a fine addition to any soul collection. But it was the easy-swinging *The Way You Do The Things You Do* (again written and produced by Smokey) with Kendricks on lead that catapulted the group to star status at last, reaching number 11 on the Hot 100 in early 1964. Kendricks also fronted the group on the follow-up hits *I'll Be In Trouble* and *Girl (Why You Wanna Make Me Blue)* (the latter written and produced by Norman Whitfield). But it was the combination of Ruffin's emotive lead and Smokey's ethereal ballad *My Girl* that brought the Temptations their first across-the-board chart-topper and million-seller in 1965. This kicked off a three-year period in which the Tempts were rarely absent from the upper reaches of the charts. The one-two punch of Kendricks and Ruffin, a machine-tooled succession of custom-tailored hits ranging from dance-floor ravers (*Get Ready*) and pure funky soul (*Beauty's Only Skin Deep*) to heartbreakers like *(I Know) I'm Losing You, Ain't Too Proud To Beg*, and the stunning *I Wish It Would Rain*, and the reputation as the finest dancers to emerge from Motown's Artist Development school cemented the Tempts' reputation for the decades to come. This indeed was the first golden era for the group. These songs have been frequently revived (megastars like the Rolling Stones and Rod Stewart head the list) and often imitated, but their original beauty has never been equalled.

In the wake of *Wish It Would Rain*, David Ruffin left the Temptations (depending on whether you get an up-tempo version or a slow blues, he either jumped or was pushed out) for a solo career, inconsistent but with some real gems over the next decade – *My Whole World Ended (The Moment You Left Me)* and the 1976 superhit *Walk Away From Love* being high spots. Drafting Dennis Edwards from the Contours, the Temptations embarked on their second golden era. With producer Norman Whitfield picking up on the rock-infused stance of Sly and the Family Stone, they inaugurated their "psychedelic soul" period with the million-selling *Cloud Nine*, which earned them a Grammy Award for Best R & B performance by a group for 1968, and *Runaway Child, Running Wild*. Although Dennis Edwards was a tough vocalist in his own right, Whitfield's new wide-screen production style emphasized instrumentation in the overall sound, with vocals broken up and parceled out among the group members. But in among such spaced-out sounds as *Ball Of Confusion* and (the style's culmination) the 14-minute *Papa Was A Rolling Stone* (again a million-seller, and multi-Grammy Award winner for best R & B group performance, best R & B instrumental performance, and best R & B song for 1972), more traditional soul sounds were also successful for the Tempts during this period. Consider the bluesy *I Can't Get Next To You*, once again a chart-topper and million-seller in 1969 (it also kick-started the career of Al Green the following year as the top soul man of the 1970s), and Eddie Kendricks's ballad swan-song with the group, *Just My Imagination (Running Away With Me)*, which achieved the same success in 1971. The Tempts also recorded four albums with Diana Ross and the Supremes – *I'm Gonna Make You Love Me* provides a taste, but the Supremes came off better on their collaborations with the Four Tops.

The 1970s began a period of changes within the group. In 1971 Paul Williams left and was replaced by Richard Street, a former member of the Distants, who had previously performed with the Monitors on Motown's VIP imprint (*Greetings (This Is Uncle Sam)*). Eddie Kendricks also departed and was replaced by Damon Harris, born in Baltimore and with both gospel and R & B experience.

Kendricks enjoyed a quite successful solo career on Tamla. Especially popular were his dance/disco-oriented *Keep On Truckin'* (a million-seller in 1973), *Boogie Down*, and *Girl You Need A Change Of Mind*. (This work is covered in chapter 8.) Kendricks also wrote and produced the Northern soul floorshaker *Evil* for the otherwise little-known group Posse. One of top modern hip-hop producer Marley Marl's earliest efforts was a version of *Girl You Need A Change Of Mind* featuring vocalist Fred Fowler, renowned for his house favorite *Times Are Changing*.

The post-*Rolling Stone* period is, once more, generally regarded as a falling off from the Tempts' earlier peaks. Certainly during this time there were again a number of personnel changes. Damon Harris, who had replaced Eddie Kendricks, was in turn eclipsed by Glenn Leonard, while Dennis Edwards finally left for a solo career in 1976 and was replaced by Louis Price, a gospel-trained Chicagoan and nephew of the great Rebert H. Harris of the Soul Stirrers. Producer Norman Whitfield turned the bulk of his attention to other projects such as the Undisputed Truth (*Smiling Faces Sometimes*), who took the "cosmic soul" style to unprecedented heights (or depths, depending on your point of view). There were also business problems with the Motown organization, now relocated in Los Angeles and more focused on film projects. Scattered gems still emerged, such as the dance-oriented *Shakey Ground* and *Glasshouse*, but most interesting of all was their last album for the label in 1976, **The Temptations Do The Temptations**. After years of domination by producers and rock-inspired excesses, the Temptations went back to pure soul with this set of mainly original, self-produced material. Songs like *Why Can't You And Me Get Together* and the disco stomper *There's No Stopping (Til We Set The Whole World Rockin')* were strongly influenced by the now-dominant Philadelphia sound. Unfortunately, with the group preparing to leave Motown, this album received little promotional support and is now a lost treasure. It should have presaged a great renaissance for the Temptations, as upon signing with Atlantic in 1977 they were put with the Baker–Harris–Young team in Philadelphia. Things went badly and inexplicably wrong, and **Hear To Tempt You** was a disaster. The next album, **Bare Back**, pairing the group with the writing and production of Brian and Eddie Holland, promised much but delivered little, and sank like a stone in 1978's disco-fevered ocean.

The Tempts returned to Motown in 1980, with Dennis Edwards also rejoining. Homecoming albums **Power** and **The Temptations** (the latter produced by Thom Bell, again a minor masterpiece but a missed opportunity – what could this combination have accomplished seven or eight years earlier, when Bell had the golden touch?) paved the way for 1982's **Reunion**. Ruffin and Kendricks returned for several tracks, including the Rick James production *Standing On The Top*, a slab of prime funk (keeping it in the family, James is a nephew of Melvin Franklin). Sadly it was only a temporary reunion with Ruffin and Kendricks. However, 1984 tracks like the smooth *Sail Away* and *Treat Her Like A Lady* prove that those tempting Temptations have still had what it takes.

A representative selection of Temptations albums would include **Meet The Temptations, The Temptations Sing Smokey**, and **I Wish It Would Rain** from the early years (unfortunately, the "classic" lineup never recorded the first-rate *live* album they could have); **Puzzle People, Psychedelic Shack**, and **All Directions** from the "cosmic soul" period, plus **The Temptations Do The Temptations** and the **Reunion** set. Paul Williams died in 1973; David Ruffin in 1991; and Eddie Kendricks in 1992.

Now closing in on their fourth decade without a personnel change, the Four Tops (Levi Stubbs on lead, Renaldo "Obie" Benson, Lawrence Payton, and Abdul "Duke" Fakir from Detroit), who along with the Temptations stand as Motown's top male group, were originally known as the Four Aims when they first got together in 1954. Their first recordings in 1956 for Chess Records were written and produced by longtime Berry Gordy associate Roquel "Billy" Davis (a cousin of Lawrence Payton). Subsequent recordings for Columbia and Riverside went nowhere, and, much like Harold Melvin and the Blue Notes in their struggling days, the group made their living as a polished nightclub/cabaret act. While the Temptations were strongly rooted in the hard-core gospel tradition, the Four Tops were always based as much on jazz and pop styles as on R & B. Even their early track for Chess, *I Wish You Would*, featured some tongue-twisting jazz harmony backgrounds à la the Four Freshmen or the Hi Los. It is interesting to note that many of the early R & B vocal groups professed admiration for such jazz-based modern harmony groups. In fact, the Tops' first recordings for Motown after signing in 1963 were in a jazz vein, on the subsidiary Workshop Jazz label.

In 1964 Gordy matched the group with the Holland–Dozier–Holland (H–D–H) production team, and starting with *Baby I Need Your Loving* the group made 13 Top 10 hits. The focus was on Levi Stubbs's lead voice, but unlike H–D–H's contemporary work with the Supremes, in which every note and facet was tightly controlled, Stubbs's emotional shouting and wildness cut across their high-gloss productions like a switchblade through a silk scarf, giving these records their special edge. As an example, listen to the way Stubbs throws in "just look over your shoulder" in the penultimate verse of *Reach Out I'll Be There*, possibly their finest recording. The team created what came to be *the* sound of Motown – explosive drums and pounding rhythms set against swirling horns and strings, all held together by the roaring Stubbs and the Tops. Motown bass master James Jamerson remembered some of his favorite bass parts in all his years at Hitsville as being on the Tops' *Reach Out I'll Be There, Bernadette*, and *Standing In The Shadows Of Love*. The Tops seemed to be much less subject to production overkill than their contemporaries like the Supremes or the Temptations – perhaps because they themselves were such a strong unit. Once they had found their groove, they just kept at it, working successfully with other producers, including Mickey Stevenson and Ivy Hunter (*Sad Souvenirs, Ask The Lonely, Loving You Is Sweeter Than Ever*), Norman Whitfield (*Don't Let Him Take Your Love From Me*), and Smokey Robinson (*Then*). Even when they tackled outside songs like the Left Banke's *Walk Away Renee*, Tim Hardin's *If I Were A Carpenter*, or the Ike and Tina Turner/ Phil Spector extravaganza *River Deep Mountain High* (cut with the Supremes, produced by Ashford and Simpson), they made the songs their own. They never forgot their jazz/cabaret training either, and could throw in a well-turned classic or modern standard like *Climb Ev'ry Mountain* or Jim Webb's *MacArthur Park*. They were teamed with the Supremes for three albums in the late 1960s – **The Magnificent Seven, Return Of The Magnificent Seven**, and **Dynamite** – with arguably better results than the similar pairings of the Supremes with the Temptations.

While the departure of H–D–H to set up their own Hot Wax/ Invictus operation (which obviously saw 100 Proof Aged In Soul, featuring Levi Stubbs's brother Joe on lead, as their own version of the Tops) seemed to dry up the hits of their other top artists, the Four Tops formed a strong new affiliation with producer Frank Wilson, who had previously done top-class work with Marvin Gaye. The hits kept rolling, with a dramatic version of the Tommy Edwards's favorite *It's All In The Game, Just Seven Numbers (Can Straighten Out My Life)*, and the classic *Still Water (Love)*. The **Still Waters Run Deep** album, with its peaceful, spiritual feel, was a little-recognized predecessor to Marvin Gaye's magnum opus **What's Going On**.

When Motown moved out to Los Angeles, the Tops joined the general exodus from the label and signed with ABC–Dunhill. Again, the hits just kept rolling – *Ain't No Woman Like The One I Got, Keeper Of The Castle*, and *Are You Man Enough* (featured in the film "Shaft In Africa"), most notably. (Their work with ABC–Dunhill is covered in chapter 8.) They signed with the much-maligned Casablanca label in 1981 and against all odds again came up with an exceptional album, **Tonight**. The hit single was *When She Was My Girl* but the peak was *Something To Remember*, with Stubbs's hollering "just look over your shoulder" recalling the glory days of *Reach Out*.

A classic moment was their appearance at the 1985 Live Aid concert. Singing and dancing as well as ever, they blew the next act, Crosby, Stills and Nash, right off the stage. Stubbs also supplied the voice of the man-eating plant monster in the hit film "Little Shop Of Horrors." Their joint appearances with the Temptations were always crowd pleasers.

The Tops returned to Motown in 1983 with the solid album **Back Where I Belong**. Stubbs had contributed mightily to Aretha Franklin's "comeback" effort **Jump To It** and she repaid the favor, appearing on *What Have I Got To Lose*. A few more recordings emerged, but by this time Motown was going downhill, and the group has recently recorded for Arista. If the results were less than impressive, their sheer longevity has been amazing. If a hot modern soul producer joined up with them, the Tops could have a whole new run of hits. A representative selection of Four Tops albums would include: **Reach Out, Four Tops Live, On Top, Still Waters Run Deep**, and **Keeper Of The Castle** (the last, an ABC–Dunhill album, now available on Motown).

Discographical Details

127 Anthology
Smokey Robinson and the Miracles
Motown MODT 793 (2-disc set)
Shop Around/Tears Of A Clown/Love Machine/I Second That Emotion/You've Really Got A Hold On Me/Mickey's Monkey/Baby Baby Don't Cry/Abraham Martin And John/Choosey Beggar/Come On Do The Jerk/Darling Dear/Doggone Right/Got A Job/ Here I Go Again/I Can't Stand To See You Cry/I Don't Blame You At All/I Gotta Dance To Keep From Crying/I Like It Like That/I'll Try Something New/(Come Round Here) I'm The One You Need/I've Been Good To You/The Love I Saw In You Was Just A Mirage/A Love She Can Count On/More Love/My Girl Has Gone/Ooh Baby Baby/Point It Out/Satisfaction/Save Me/Special Occasion/That's What Love Is Made Of/The Tracks Of My Tears/Way Over There/We've Come Too Far To End It Now/What's So Good About Goodbye/Who's Loving You/Yester Love/Who's Gonna Take The Blame/You Can Depend On Me/Bad Girl/Going To A Go-Go/I'm Crazy 'Bout The La La La/Do It Baby/Don't Cha Love It

128 Anthology
The Temptations
Motown MODT 6189 (2-disc set)
My Girl/I Can't Get Next To You/Just My Imagination (Running Away With Me)/ Papa Was A Rolling Stone/I'm Gonna Make You Love Me/Beauty Is Only Skin Deep/I Wish It Would Rain/You're My Everything/Cloud Nine/Runaway Child, Running Wild/Psychedelic Shack/Masterpiece/Ain't Too Proud To Beg/All I Need/Ball Of Confusion (That's What The World Is Today)/Don't Let The Joneses Get You Down/Don't Look Back/Funky Music Sho Nuff Turns Me On/Get Ready/Girl (Why You Wanna Make Me Blue)/The Girl's All Right With Me/I Truly Truly Believe/I'll Be In Trouble/(I Know) I'm Losing You/The Impossible Dream/It's Growing/It's You That I Need (Loneliness Made Me Realize)/Love Woke Me Up This Morning/Mother Nature/My Baby/Ol' Man River/Please Return Your Love To Me/Since I Lost My Baby/Superstar (Remember How You Got Where You Are)/Try To Remember/The Way You Do The Things You Do/I Could Never Love Another (After Loving You)/I Ain't Got Nothin'/Shakey Ground/Power/Sail Away/Treat Her Like A Lady

129 Anthology
The Four Tops

Motown MOTD 2-809 (2-disc set)

I Can't Help Myself (Sugar Pie Honey Bunch)/Bernadette/Standing In The Shadows Of Love/Still Water (Love)/Walk Away Renee/River Deep Mountain High/Ask The Lonely/Baby I Need Your Loving/I Can't Quit Your Love/Climb Ev'ry Mountain/ Don't Let Him Take Your Love From Me/Everybody's Talkin'/For Once In My Life/ Helpless/Hey Man – We Got To Get You A Woman/I Got A Feeling/I'll Turn To Stone/I'm In A Different World/If I Were A Carpenter/In These Changing Times/It's All In The Game/It's The Same Old Song/Just Seven Numbers (Can Straighten Out My Life)/MacArthur Park/Nature Planned It (It's The Way)/A Place In The Sun/ Reach Out I'll Be There/Reflections/Sad Souvenirs/Seven Rooms Of Gloom/Shake Me Wake Me (When It's Over)/Something About You/Then/Without The One You Love (Life's Not Worthwhile)/Yesteday's Dreams/You Gotta Have Love In Your Heart/ You Keep Running Away/Loving You Is Sweeter Than Ever/Can't Seem To Get You Out Of My Mind/Don't Tell Me That It's Over/I Just Can't Walk Away

(iii) Motown's Premier Girl Group – the Supremes

There can be few readers who have not heard the story of "Dreamgirls" Diana Ross and the Supremes, so we will not hash it over unnecessarily here. Diana Ross (lead), b. March 26, 1944; Mary Wilson, b March 4, 1944; and Florence Ballard, b. June 30, 1943, died Feburary 22, 1976 (all from Detroit) can be compared only with Elvis Presley, the Beatles, and more recently Michael Jackson in record sales. For a substantial part of the 1960s the Supremes, more than any other Motown act, were truly "The Sound Of Young America."

Originally formed in the late 1950s as the Primettes – a "sister" group to the Primes, who later evolved into the Temptations – the group first recorded for Robert West's Lupine label as a quartet including one Barbara Martin. West's operation, best known for the hard early soul sounds of Wilson Pickett and the Falcons, was not really a good match for this young group, which even then had pop aspirations. Mary Wilson, in her book *Dreamgirl: my life as a Supreme*, recalled that their early performances included ballads like *Canadian Sunset* and *Moonlight In Vermont* alongside such R & B chestnuts as *Night Time Is The Right Time* and the early uptown soul sound of the Drifters' *There Goes My Baby*.

After signing with Motown in 1961, their early sessions reflected Gordy and his producers' sustained efforts to find the right sound for the group. *Let Me Go The Right Way*, set in the cha-cha groove popularized by the Marvelettes' *Please Mr Postman*, is almost a generic "girl-group" sound. The first seeds of future greatness are found in a few of these other early tracks – the smooth trade-offs in the choruses of the Smokey Robinson production *A Breath Taking Guy*; the up-tempo pop styling of *Run, Run, Run* (although Diana's lead is almost buried in the mix); and the first effort with the H–D–H crew *When The Lovelight Starts Shining Through His Eyes*, which provided their first Top 40 entry in 1963. One can sense the pieces of the puzzle being painstakingly fitted into place. Then came the first big success with *Where Did Our Love Go*, which had originally been offered to the Marvelettes, who turned it down – indeed the Supremes at first were not happy with it either, deeming it too "childish." In the tangled story of this song, Wilson and producer Eddie Holland also recalled that Wilson was originally slated to sing lead on this number. The rest is history . . . beginning with a string of five successive number 1 hits: following were *Baby Love, Come See About Me, Stop! In The Name Of Love*, and *Back In My Arms Again*. The number 1 hit string also included *You Can't Hurry Love* (later the first worldwide solo smash for Genesis frontman Phil Collins), *You Keep Me Hangin' On* (later a hit for Vanilla Fudge), *Love Is Here And Now You're Gone, The Happening, Love Child* and the last hit credited to Ross and the Supremes in 1970 (although by this time only Ross was appearing on the records), *Someday We'll Be Together*.

Through the hits one can trace the development of the Supremes' sound – from the gospel echoes of *Come See About Me* (Junior Walker and the All Stars' later version brought out the root feel of the song) to the playful girls' talk of *Back In My Arms Again* ("how can Mary tell me what to do, when she's lost her love so true? And Flo, she don't know, 'cause the boy she loves is a Romeo"), the heavy beats of the first hits giving way to the fluffier sonic soufflés of *My World Is Empty Without You* and *You Can't Hurry Love*. Diana rarely sounded more sensuous than in the rarefied but surprisingly bluesy atmosphere of *Love Is Like An Itching In My Heart*. Touches of psychedelia enliven *In And Out Of Love, The Happening*, and *Reflections*, alongside the social comment (daring for its time) of *Love Child* – perhaps the original inspiration for fellow Detroit native Madonna's *Papa Don't Preach*?

Yet at the same time the Supremes were making their hits there were other stylistic explorations, showing Gordy's ultimate aspirations – albums devoted to country and pop, Beatles and Merseybeat, a Sam Cooke tribute set, and most tellingly the **Supremes At The Copa** set, as well as albums devoted to the songs of Rodgers and Hart and the Barbra Streisand Broadway vehicle "Funny Girl."

In the late 1960s they were teamed up with both the Temptations and the Four Tops, achieving such hits with the Tempts as *I'm Gonna Make You Love Me* (co-written by Kenny Gamble and Jerry Ross and earlier a 1968 Top 10 hit for Madeline Bell – this is a strong version) and *River Deep Mountain High* with the Tops, which is included on the Four Tops' own anthology (but the original Tina Turner/Phil Spector blowout is unsurpassable).

Sounds and plans changed in the late 1960s with the departures of both H–D–H and Flo Ballard; the lighter, more MOR sound of *The Happening* and *No Matter What Sign You Are*, the change, beginning with *Reflections*, in billing to "Diana Ross and the Supremes." Most later sessions featured only Diana, with harmonies supplied by Motown's crack vocal backup group the Andantes (whose leader Marlene Barrow even subbed for Flo on a few shows). The last hit credited to the Ross/Supremes combination before Diana launched her solo career was the elegaic *Someday We'll Be Together*. The song had originally been cut in 1961 by Johnny Bristol and Jackey Beavers (as Johnny and Jackey) on Harvey Fuqua's Tri-Phi label. The trio produced the Supremes' version and Bristol's voice is heard on the track. Both Fuqua and Bristol (who had a later hit with *Hang On In There Baby*) became important Motown producers, while Beavers became a strong producer, writer, and performer with Southern soul doyen John "John R" Richbourg's Sound Stage 7 label. *Cash Box*, in reviewing the original Johnny and Jackey release, had presciently opined that the song "could develop into something."

In January of 1970 Ross left the group to begin her solo career, and Jean Terrell was added as replacement. The new Supremes had some success and hits, with *Stoned Love*, *Nathan Jones*, *Floy Joy*, and *Automatically Sunshine* all making the Top 40. Of course, Motown's attention was now on Diana Ross as a solo artist and budding film star. Ross's solo career is covered in chapter 8. But these are the recordings that created the "Dreamgirls" legend for all time. A deeper examination of the Supremes' extensive discography would include: **Meet The Supremes** (the original LP release of this album, showing the girls sitting on stools, is a collectable of considerable repute), **The Supremes Sing Holland–Dozier–Holland, Love Child, The Supremes At The Copa**, and, for some rare and previously unissued items, the **Never Before Released Masters** set or the wider-ranging **25th Anniversary** collection.

Discographical Details

130   Anthology

Diana Ross and the Supremes

Motown MODT 2-794 (2-disc set)

Let Me Go The Right Way/A Breath Taking Guy/When The Lovelight Starts Shining Through His Eyes/Standing At The Crossroads Of Love/Run, Run, Run/Where Did Our Love Go/Baby Love/Ask Any Girl/Come See About Me/Stop! In The Name Of Love/Back In My Arms Again/Nothing But Heartaches/I Hear A Symphony/My World Is Empty Without You/Love Is Like An Itching In My Heart/You Can't Hurry Love/You Keep Me Hangin' On/Love Is Here And Now You're Gone/The Happening/

Reflections/In And Out Of Love/Forever Came Today/Some Things You Never Get Used To/You Can't Hold On Too Long/Love Child/A Hard Day's Night/Funny How Time Slips Away/You Send Me/Falling In Love With Love/I'm The Greatest Star/I'm Gonna Make You Love Me/I'm Livin' In Shame/The Composer/I'll Try Something New/No Matter What Sign You Are/Someday We'll Be Together

(iv) Motown's Superstar Male Artists – Marvin Gaye and Stevie Wonder

Marvelous Marvin Gaye (b. April 2, 1939, in Washington, DC) is Motown's tragic genius. There are certain performers whose stories go beyond recitation of their successes. Gaye, who died April 1, 1984, enjoyed many successes in his lifetime – 40 Top 40 numbers including 18 Top 10 hits and four number 1s. But of all the Motown artists, and with no disrespect to any of the others, Gaye was the only one who *sang his life*. From the early jubilant shouts of *You're A Wonderful One*, my *Pride And Joy*, of the days when there *Ain't No Mountain High Enough* to keep me from *Your Precious Love*, to the questioning of love's foibles *Ain't That Peculiar*, the bitterness of coming to *The End Of Our Road* and asking *When Did You Stop Loving Me, When Did I Stop Loving You*, longing for the return of a *Distant Lover*, trying to fill the void by *Flyin' High In The Friendly Sky*, finally just asking *What's Going On*, and reaching an epiphany – *That's The Way Love Is*. Daniel Stone, the hero of Elaine Jesmer's book *Number One With A Bullet*, a Motown *roman à clef* (itself ill-fated, dogged by litigation, and now a literary collectable of a high order), was said to be based in large part on Marvin Gaye. But we are not here to detail Gaye's life problems, fascinating as an open wound though they are, but to celebrate his outpourings of musical genius.

The early days were prosaic enough. Raised in a minister's family which virtually prohibited secular music, Gaye had early church singing and playing experience, such teenage doo-wop groups as the Marquees and the Rainbows (the latter also variously housing the talents of future soul stars Don Covay and Billy Stewart) leading to the first big break of meeting Harvey Fuqua, which began a relationship that lasted to the end of his life. In short order the Marquees became Fuqua's new Moonglows. When the group crumbled, Fuqua took Gaye to Detroit, spent hours showing him all the chords he knew on piano, used him as a backup musician on sessions he was producing for Billy Davis and Gwen Gordy's Anna label, and groomed him. Eventually he joined the Gordy clan – Harvey and Marvin married the Gordy sisters Gwen and Anna – and came under the Motown wing. On to the music: at first, Gaye wanted to be the black Sinatra, singing ballads and standards, but three failed singles and an album mining this vein did not produce what Berry Gordy felt Marvin was capable of. His first sniff of a hit record was playing the drums on the Marvelettes' 1961 chart-topper *Please Mr Postman*.

Gaye finally broke through a year later with the rocking *Stubborn Kind Of Fellow* ("got my mind made up to love you") and then he was off. There was the gospelized blues of *Can I Get A Witness* and *You're A Wonderful One*, and the utterly funky *Hitch Hike*. Many of the 1960s' rock stars were paying close attention – the Rolling Stones covered both *Witness* and *Hitch Hike* (which Lou Reed and the Velvet Underground later transmogrified into *There She Goes Again*). His best rocker, *Baby Don't You Do It*, was borrowed by the Who – and interestingly, its falsetto harmonies uncannily presaged the sound that the Bee Gees took to the top of the worldwide charts in their "Saturday Night Fever" days. Then there were the sheer classy soul sounds of *Pride And Joy* and *How Sweet It Is (To Be Loved By You)*, the doo-wop-rooted *Forever*, and the strolling, jazz-tinged *Try It Baby* (a Top 15 hit in 1964), which featured the early Temptations lending vocal support – Eddie Kendricks's high tenor and Otis Williams's bass voices fall somewhere between background harmony and second leads. Other examples of Motown's famous "family atmosphere" (or incest, for the cynical) were Martha and the Vandellas' backup work on *Stubborn Kind Of Fellow* and the Supremes' appearance on *You're A Wonderful One*, only a few months before they crashed into the charts with *Where Did Our Love Go*.

Gaye's biography, *Divided Soul* by David Ritz, was aptly titled: he was always torn between sacred and secular, between his R & B-styled hits and his ever-present desire to sing smooth, supper-club fare (well examined in the 4-disc **Marvin Gaye Collection** box set). At the height of his 1960s fame he commissioned several arrangements of standards from jazz pianist Bobby Scott (composer of *A Taste Of Honey* and *He Ain't Heavy He's My Brother*), but spent years studying the tracks before even attempting to sing them.

The mid-to-late 1960s is rightly considered Gaye's first halcyon era. A few of the high spots were the so-tough *I'll Be Doggone*, *Ain't That Peculiar* with its ringing, Byrds-like guitars, the thumping *Take This Heart Of Mine*, the pure, raw *cri de coeur* of *You*, and the voodoo rock of *I Heard It Through The Grapevine*. Then there were the duets with his equally ill-fated soul-mate Tammi Terrell. Gaye had earlier teamed up successfully with songbird Mary Wells (*What's The Matter With You Baby*) and the tougher-voiced Kim Weston (*It Takes Two*), but *Ain't No Mountain High Enough*, *If I Could Build My Whole World Around You*, *Ain't Nothing Like The Real Thing*, and *Your Precious Love* were larger-than-life declarations of eternal love, and stand proudly among the very greatest recordings Gaye ever made. Terrell's illness – she collapsed in his arms in 1967 while performing – and subsequent tragic death at age 24 drove Gaye into seclusion. In 1969 he began to re-emerge, writing and producing the eerie *Baby I'm For Real* and *The Bells* for the Originals. His experiments with this veteran vocal group led him towards the style that emerged in the epochal **What's Going On**, using his own voice multi-tracked – crooning one line high and sweet, shouting another low and raw, then harmonizing his own backgrounds.

What's Going On marked as crucial a milestone in the early 1970s music scene as the Beatles' **Sergeant Pepper**, Dylan's electric experiments, or Miles Davis's **Kind Of Blue** had been in their eras. So different was it in style and stance to the "Motown Sound" that Berry Gordy initially refused to release it. **What's Going On** fused social commentary, Gaye's ever-present spiritual concerns, and all of the music he had been absorbing over the past decade. This was very much a collaborative effort – Renaldo "Obie" Benson of the Four Tops co-wrote *Save The Children, Wholy Holy* (fellow Detroit native Aretha Franklin included it on her classic 1972 gospel album **Amazing Grace**), and the title track. This was also the first Motown album on which the long-serving Hitsville musicians had their names listed for their contributions – the sessions were so emotionally and physically exhausting that bassman supreme James Jamerson is said to have played while laying flat on his back. Smokey Robinson recently recalled visiting Gaye, burning up in the very fever of creation, and being told the songs were coming from God. **What's Going On** lifted Gaye to another level, quoth a Motown biography of the era, as a "mysterious and exalted figure." It seemed he had managed to fuse all of his parts, the divided soul coming together at last. But it was not to be. Other great albums followed – the seethingly sensual **Let's Get It On** (the searing *Distant Lover* became his climactic live-show set closer) and the wide-screen sound painting of his sole film soundtrack **Trouble Man** (*Don't Mess With Mr T* became a jazz classic in the hands of tenor-sax master Stanley Turrentine), but the 1970s were a difficult and tragic time for Gaye, full of problems with drugs, business, taxes, his bitter divorce from wife Anna (chronicled in the album **Here, My Dear**), a second failed marriage, and the wild swings of his relationship with Berry Gordy – perhaps one of the great love/hate stories of the twentieth century.

If Marvin Gaye anthologies and hits collections (of which this set is probably the best) can be criticized, it is for being light on his mid-to-late 1970s recordings. To the general audience much of this material must have seemed patchy, and indeed after 1973's *Trouble Man* Gaye was absent from the Top 10 until 1977's chart-topping disco smash *Got To Give It Up*. The closest he came was the number 12 ranking in late 1973 of his duet with Diana Ross, *You're A Special Part Of Me*, but their duet album was an artistic disaster (they recorded their vocal tracks at separate sessions) except for the stirring and passionate *My Mistake*. But there is much to savor from this period. **I Want You** from 1976, despite its air of careless confusion (there are two more tracks on the record than are listed on the jacket) and padding with throwaway instrumentals, is worth getting for songs like the title track and *After The Dance* (recently revived by Fourplay featuring El DeBarge). The smoking hot **Live At The London Palladium** set from 1977 ranks as the best of his "in-performance" recordings, and is topped up with the full-length studio cut of *Got To Give It Up*. The 1978 album **Here, My Dear**, although sprawling and too diffuse, contains some of his best singing (listen to *Sparrow* or *Anger*), emotions rubbed blood-raw. Although Gaye damned the 1981 release of his last Motown album **In Our Lifetime**, saying it had been taken from him in an unfinished state, it is one of his most fascinating sets. *Praise* uniquely encapsulates the man's divided soul, starting out as a hot love song to a dancing girl, and ending with pure sacred purpose, with Gaye singing "praise Him from the mountain tops." Similarly *Love Party* begins in a Barry White groove ("to me you're extra special mellow baby"), then segues into apocalyptic references straight from the Book of Revelation, and a closing vamp of "you got to pray and meditate." *Far Cry* provides a unique view of Gaye's creative process, as he scats out lyrical ideas and pure vocal sounds over raw, unpolished beats and riffs. **In Our Lifetime** is out of print – it is well worth searching the remainder bins for it.

After a period of self-imposed exile in Belgium, Gaye signed with Columbia in 1982 and came back strong with the multimillion-selling single *Sexual Healing* and the last album released during his lifetime, **Midnight Love**, which earned him the first Grammy Awards of his career. His appearance on the 1983 "Motown 25" TV special was, along with Michael Jackson's performance of *Billie Jean*, the show's artistic high spot. The posthumous Columbia release **Romantically Yours** included his first (late 1960s) attempts at the Bobby Scott arrangements of *Why Did I Choose You, The Shadow Of Your Smile*, and *I Won't Cry Anymore*, although the later versions included on the **Collection** box set are superior – as Gaye himself said to his biographer David Ritz, "I didn't like the way I sounded . . . I had more suffering to do before I could get to the feelings." The last Columbia album, **Dream Of A Lifetime**, is just plain *weird*. Spanning a decade-long collection of sessions, it ranges from *Masochistic Beauty*, with its nasty S & M overtones and Gaye affecting an hilarious English accent, and the self-explanatory *Savage In The Sack*, which would make Luther Campbell blush, to Gaye's long rumored but clearly unfinished "masterwork" *Life's Opera* – overall best for addicts (like myself). Motown also released a set of previously unissued tracks, **Motown Remembers Marvin Gaye**, but with its crude and ill-advised overdubs, this album is not recommended unless you must have *everything*.

Most of Gaye's essential albums are available on CD, some coupled, with two albums on one CD. A representative selection would include, from the 1960s recordings: **Moods of Marvin Gaye, That's The Way Love Is, I Heard It Through The Grapevine**, and the duet collection **Marvin Gaye And His Women** (with a few Diana Ross tracks added to fatten up an earlier collection, **Marvin Gaye And His Girls**). There is also the Gaye/Terrell **Greatest Hits** set. From the 1970s there are: **What's Going On, Let's Get It On**, and **Live At The London Palladium**. **Midnight Love** is also essential, and the elaborately packaged, 4-disc **Marvin Gaye Collection** box set (with a CD each devoted to the Top 20 hits, the duets, live and rare recordings, and ballads, including 34 previously unreleased recordings) would make a fine present to yourself. Gaye's 1965 **Tribute To The Great Nat King Cole**, including his version of *Unforgettable*, flopped on its original release, but is now ripe for renewed appreciation.

Marvin Gaye was shot and killed by his transvestite father on April 1, 1984, a day short of his forty-fifth birthday. His personal problems, his failed marriages, his tragic death – all pale into insignificance compared to the music he made.

Stevie Wonder (b. Steveland Morris, May 13, 1950, Saginaw, Michigan) is Motown's longest-serving artist, signed to the label in 1962 and still there thirty years on. These two **Greatest Hits** albums, considered as one entry, neatly sum up his 1960s "Motown Sound" period – subsequent albums, self-produced by Stevie and beginning with the one-two punch of **Music Of My Mind** and **Talking Book**, are outside the scope of this section (which does not lessen their status as essential listening). The man is all music – singer, composer, producer, multi-instrumentalist – and, like his early idol Ray Charles, transcends such categories as soul, pop, blues, or jazz.

The ultimate product of Motown's Artist Development school, Wonder achieved all of the hit records included here – starting with the chart-topping, million-seller *Fingertips, Pt 2* at age *12* – before the age of 21! From the raw energy of that first hit, through the early social comment of his 1966 hit cover of Bob Dylan's *Blowin' In The Wind* and the tough funk of 1967's *I Was Made To Love Her*, to the ultra-polished balladry of *My Cherie Amour*, introducing the modern standard *For Once In My Life* and his lovely reading of the Beatles' *We Can Work It Out*, these 1962–71 recordings, great as they are, were only the groundwork for his even greater successes of the 1970s, 1980s, and 1990s. Of his many albums from this period, perhaps the brightest gems are

The 12 Year Old Genius Recorded Live, his third album for the label, which yielded the *Fingertips* hit, and the 1967 effort **I Was Made To Love Her,** which Wonder himself has described as his favorite from this era. His voice had matured from its earlier adolescent squeak (his new sound first being heard on the hard-rocking *Uptight*) and on this album, whether paying tribute to Ray Charles (*A Fool For You*), James Brown (*Please, Please Please*), Little Richard (*Send Me Some Lovin'*), or Bobby Bland (*I Pity The Fool*), he is absolutely in control and never less than brilliant. Since then he has of course gone from strength to strength, but the start of it all is contained in these matchless early recordings.

Discographical Details

131 Anthology
Marvin Gaye

Motown MOTD 791 (2-disc set)

Stubborn Kind Of Fellow/Hitch Hike/Pride And Joy/Once Upon A Time/Can I Get A Witness/What's The Matter With You Baby/You're A Wonderful One/Try It Baby/ Baby Don't You Do It/What Good Am I Without You/Forever/How Sweet It Is (To Be Loved By You)/It Takes Two/I'll Be Doggone/Pretty Little Baby/Ain't That Peculiar/Ain't No Mountain High Enough/One More Heartache/Take This Heart Of Mine/Your Precious Love/Little Darling (I Need You)/Your Unchanging Love/If This World Were Mine/You/If I Could Build My Whole World Around You/Chained/Ain't Nothing Like The Real Thing/How Can I Forget/Heaven Sent You, I Know/I Heard It Through The Grapevine/Good Lovin' Ain't Easy To Come By/Too Busy Thinking About My Baby/That's The Way Love Is/You're All I Need To Get By/The End Of Our Road/What's Going On/Mercy Mercy Me (The Ecology)/Inner City Blues (Make Me Wanna Holler)/Save The Children/You're The Man/Trouble Man/Let's Get It On/Come Get To This/Distant Lover/I Want You/Got To Give It Up/After The Dance

132 Greatest Hits, Vol. 1
Stevie Wonder

Motown MOTD 282

Uptight (Everything's Alright)/I'm Wondering/I Was Made To Love Her/Hey Love/ Blowin' In The Wind/A Place In The Sun/Contract On Love/Work Out Stevie, Work Out/Fingertips, Pt 2/Castles In The Sand/Hey Harmonica Man/Nothing's Too Good For My Baby

Greatest Hits, Vol. 2
Stevie Wonder

Motown MOTD 313

Shoo-Be-Doo-Be-Doo-Da-Day/Signed, Sealed, Delivered I'm Yours/If You Really Love Me/For Once In My Life/We Can Work It Out/You Met Your Match/Never Had A Dream Come True/Yester-Me, Yester-You, Yesterday/My Cherie Amour/Never Dreamed You'd Leave In Summer/Travelin' Man/Heaven Help Us All

(v) Motown's Greatest Import – Gladys Knight and the Pips

Gladys Knight (b. May 28, 1944, in Atlanta, Georgia) was, along with Brenda Holloway and Martha Reeves, the toughest female singer to record for Motown during the "Golden Era." Knight and the Pips (Gladys's brother Merald "Bubba" Knight and cousins Edward Patten and William Guest) had over a decade's experience together when they signed with Motown in 1965. Knight had won first prize on the Ted Mack Amateur Hour at age 7. Her father and mother had been members of the famous Wings Over Jordan choir. A family party at which Knight sang with Merald and several cousins led to the formation of the group. Patten's father had played piano with Atlanta blues shouter Billy Wright, who recalled young Edward watching the group rehearse. Atlanta was a hotbed of R & B activity in the 1950s, centered on the 81 Theatre and radio station WGST, spearheaded by deejay Zenas Sears, and it is no coincidence that the area launched the careers of such performers as Chuck Willis, Little Richard, James Brown, Otis Redding, and Willie "Dr Feelgood" Perryman – whose *Mr Moonlight* was covered by the Beatles. Knight had an eye for young talent – as recounted in Nelson George's *Where Did Our Love Go?*, it was she, not Diana Ross, who first discovered the Jackson Five.

Knight and the Pips were already a polished, road-trained act (having even performed with future Motown music director Maurice King's big band in Detroit and recorded, without Knight, for Brunswick in 1958) when they cut the old Johnny Otis blues ballad *Every Beat Of My Heart* (originally done by the Royals, predecessors of Hank Ballard and the Midnighters) for Atlanta's tiny Huntom label in 1961. New York R & B entrepreneur Bobby Robinson quickly signed the group to his Fury label and their recut was a number 15 R & B and Top 50 pop hit, while the original Huntom version, licensed to Vee Jay under the name "The Pips," reached number 6 pop. Fury's follow-up *Letter Full Of Tears*, a superb deep soul ballad by Don Covay, was a number 3 R & B and Top 20 pop hit in 1962. Switching to Maxx Records in 1964, they cut some fine material under producer/writer Van McCoy (*Lovers Always Forgive* and *If Ever I Should Fall In Love*), but only *Giving Up* made the Top 30. (The Fury and Maxx titles in this compilation are Motown remakes. The earlier material is reviewed in chapter 2.)

Although their Motown signing caused some dissension in the group (Knight later recalled that when Motown offered them a contract, the Pips voted yes but Knight, concerned about playing second fiddle to the label's established groups, voted no), their eight-year association yielded many classic recordings. Paired with producer Norman Whitfield, their debut on the Soul label *Take Me In Your Arms And Love Me* missed the charts, but was quickly followed by the one-two punch of the swaying *Everybody Needs Love*, which returned them to the Top 40, and the driving *I Heard It Through The Grapevine*, which topped the R & B charts and reached number 2 pop, becoming their biggest Motown-era hit. If Marvin Gaye's 1968 recut of *Grapevine* was, as the late Mike Bloomfield said, "voodoo music," Knight's version was pure, wailing, church rock that set the pattern for many of their later releases – not for nothing did their albums bear titles like **The Nitty Gritty** and **Feelin' Bluesy**. Hits like *Friendship Train* (1968) and *You Need Love Like I Do (Don't You?)* (1970) were more rootsy reflections of Whitfield's contemporaneous psyche-delic-funk productions for the Temptations, while the wailing *It Should Have Been Me* has Knight watching another woman wed her man (number 10 R & B and Top 40 pop in mid-1968).

Later productions with Clay McMurray, including *If I Were Your Woman, Make Me The Woman You Go Home To*, and the 1973 number 2 pop hit *Neither One Of Us (Wants To Be The First To Say Goodbye)*, were more ballad-oriented, presaging the style of the million-selling mid-1970s Buddah hits like *Midnight Train To Georgia* and *Best Thing That Ever Happened To Me*, which eventually boosted the group to superstardom. Knight, like her contemporaries Patti LaBelle and Aretha Franklin, is one of the great soul divas, and her Motown recordings have only gained in stature over the years.

Discographical Details

133 Anthology
Gladys Knight and the Pips
Motown MOTD 2-792
Every Beat Of My Heart/Letter Full Of Tears/Giving Up/Just Walk In My Shoes/ Take Me In Your Arms And Love Me/Everybody Needs Love/I Heard It Through The Grapevine/The End Of Our Road/It Should Have Been Me/I Wish It Would Rain/ Didn't You Know (You'd Have To Cry Sometime)/The Nitty Gritty/Friendship Train/The Tracks Of My Tears/You Need Love Like I Do (Don't You?)/Every Little Bit Hurts/If I Were Your Woman/I Don't Want To Do Wrong/Make Me The Woman You Go Home To/Help Me Make It Through The Night/For Once In My Life/Neither One Of Us (Wants To Be The First To Say Goodbye)/Daddy Could Swear, I Declare

(vi) Other Sides Of Detroit

As we have noted, Detroit in the "glory years" of the 1960s was not all Motown. The most important of the non-Motown labels during this period included Robert West's Lupine/Flick/Contour operations, which produced the harder soul of the Falcons, and Ollie McLaughlin's Karen/Carla/Moira complex, which came up with a polished, pop sound providing a real alternative to the Motown Sound. In contrast, there were Ed Wingate's Golden World, Ric–Tic, and Wingate labels, which whenever possible used moonlighting Hitsville session men to back up the likes of Edwin Starr, J. J. Barnes, and others. It should also be noted that some of the Motown sessionmen and producers (including Joe Hunter and Herbie Williams), under the rubric of "Pied Piper Productions," produced a steady stream of releases by such artists as Willie Kendrick, the Metros, and Lorraine Chandler which came out on the major RCA label – sadly, these have not been reissued on albums. Coming into the end of the 1960s, important Detroit operations included H–D–H's post-Motown Invictus/Hot Wax group and Armen Boladian's Westbound label, which launched George Clinton's Parliament/Funkadelic "thang" onto the world.

The two **Detroit Gold** albums, considered together as one entry, effectively sum up the story of the late Ollie McLaughlin's Karen/Carla/Moira labels complex. In an almost 15-year run, McLaughlin successfully established an alternative to the then-dominant Motown sound, and left behind a legacy of music that still both demands and rewards close listening today. McLaughlin, together with his brother Maxie, started out promoting shows in the Michigan area by such performers as Count Basie, Cootie Williams, the Ravens, the Flamingos, and others in the late 1940s and early 1950s. He broke into radio broadcasting on WHRV in Ann Arbor in 1954, one of the first black deejays in the area. Dubbing himself "Scooby Doo" (at one time his "Scooby Doo" fan club was said to have 25,000 members) and playing a mixture of Top 40 and jazz, he quickly became involved in record production, as two concerts he promoted at the Masonic Temple in Ann Arbor, by the Chet Baker Quartet and Dave Brubeck, were recorded by him and released by the Hollywood-based Pacific Jazz label, including Brubeck's hit album **Jazz Goes To College**.

McLaughlin inaugurated further involvement in the local music scene when he discovered and co-managed the late Del Shannon in 1960. When *Runaway* raced up the charts and made Shannon a star, McLaughlin left the radio business, established his own McLaughlin Publishing Company, and looked after Shannon's business affairs. One of his first signings to his new Karen/Moira/Carla complex (named for his daughters) was Barbara Lewis, who proved to be his biggest hitmaker. The soft and sensual *Hello Stranger* was picked up nationally by Atlantic Records, and in short order it was number 1 R & B and number 3 pop. This both launched Lewis's career, which eventually spanned ten national hits (much of her later recording taking place in New York and Chicago), and cemented McLaughlin's relationship with Atlantic, which was to prove crucial in the future success of such artists as Deon Jackson and the Capitols.

Detroit Gold Vol. 1 provides a general overview of the McLaughlin labels, with hits from Barbara Lewis and Deon Jackson, whose *Love Makes The World Go 'Round* shows him to be a convincing stylist in the Smokey Robinson groove, and then looks at some of the company's fine, if lesser-known, singers. Outstanding tracks include the throaty Belita Woods and big-voiced Jimmy "Soul" Clark. In yet another example of the close, almost incestuous relationships between many of the Detroit labels and producers, Woods and Clark benefited from the production and songwriting expertise of Richard "Popcorn" Wylie, a veteran of the Motown and Ric-Tic organizations. Wylie's own, very Motownish *Rosemary What Happened* – sounding like the Funk Brothers band moonlighting from Hitsville, and supposedly inspired by the horror film "Rosemary's Baby" – became a firm favorite on England's Northern soul circuit in the 1970s, where he still performs. Clark later recorded for the Soul Hawk and Cotillion labels.

Then there's the always delicious Betty Lavette, a long serving veteran of the Detroit music scene who had first notched the bestseller charts in 1962 with *My Man He's A Lovin' Man*, produced by Johnnie Mae Matthews and placed with Atlantic. Lavette's discography is quite extensive, taking in everything from early Detroit sides and the deepest Memphis Soul (her *He Made A Woman Out Of Me* – originally on Silver Fox – is an essential buy) and on to recent dance/disco efforts. Matthews's Northern label had been among the first to record the embryonic Temptations (as the Distants), and is also credited with having first discovered Mary Wells (aged 14) and longtime producer/writer/performer Richard "Popcorn" Wylie. The Firestones had previously been the "second" Falcons group (led by Carlis "Sonny" Monroe), and their 1968 tracks are solid dancers.

Vol. 2 is less consistent, but more focused, with no fewer than six tracks by the wonderful Jimmy Delphs. Discovered singing lead for a Toledo-based group called Pendulum, Delphs was signed as a solo artist and debuted with *Almost*. He had some of the wailing power of the Four Tops' Levi Stubbs and was given the bigger productions typical of later 1960s Detroit, complete with strings, horns, and background singers wailing over crashing rhythm sections. Throughout, Delphs displays a convincing emotional involvement. Although *Don't Sign The Papers Baby* was his biggest hit (number 29 R & B in the summer of 1968), this collection, by making available six of his best tracks never previously released on album, makes a strong case for him as one of McLaughlin's finest singers. On *Mrs Percy* he rocks with the gospel fervor of a Wilson Pickett. Some of McLaughlin's 1970s productions have also been included, and while the Percy and Them track now seems a little dullish, the Compacts' *That's How My World Began* is a little gem of soft, sophisticated, mid-decade soul. The Volumes, who had previously had a hit in 1962 with *I Love You* for Chex Records, cut the infectious *Ain't Gonna Give You Up* for McLaughlin in 1971, although it went unissued until the release of this album.

The Capitols' *We Got A Thing That's In The Groove* and *Cool Jerk* (covered in England by the legendary theatrical mod-rock band Creation) provide the hit power on **Vol. 2**, while the funky beats and instrumental breaks of the Fabulous Counts are being sampled to this day by rap performers. It is notable that only rarely did McLaughlin and his producers go for an out-and-out Motown sound (unlike Ed Wingate's Golden World/Ric-Tic group), and on this album only some of the Delphs tracks and the Gambrells' *You Better Move* chase the Hitsville sound and feel (the Gambrells had sung backup for Deon Jackson). The Johnnie Mae Matthews track is a big production effort with strings and chorus – curious, as she is better known as a blues-based performer. Blue-eyed soulster Matt Lucas, better known in country-and-western and rock circles for hits like *I'm Movin' On* and work with country-bopper Narvel Felts, delivers a novelty redeemed by some funky guitar and band-work (his other Karen release, *Baby You Better Go-Go*, is also a popular dance item). Together, these collections prove that there was a viable local alternative to the 1960s Motown sound. Ollie McLaughlin passed away on February 19, 1984, aged 58.

Edwin Starr (b. Charles Edwin Hatcher, January 21, 1942, in Nashville, Tennessee), Ric-Tic's most successful performer in the mid-1960s, may be best known to pop fans for his 1970 chart-topping million-seller, *War*. But that is only the tip of the iceberg in a career as singer and songwriter that has spanned three decades. Raised in Cleveland, Ohio, he first got on record with his teenage doo-wop group the Futuretones (*Roll On/I Know* on Tress). After army service in Germany (where he wrote *Oh How Happy*, which became a number 12 pop hit in 1966 for the Shades Of Blue), he fronted the Bill "Honky Tonk" Doggett band before signing with the Ric-Tic label in 1965. Starr's early Ric-Tic material had a strong Motown sound, courtesy of the moon-lighting Funk Brothers band. Earl Van Dyke recalled that Berry Gordy fined them $1,000 apiece for playing on Starr's *Agent Double-O Soul*, a Top 10 R & B and number 21 pop hit in 1965; Wingate was more than happy to cover their fines. Smaller hits followed with *Back Street, Stop Her On Sight (SOS)*, and *Headline News*, records which are still popular today on the Northern soul circuit. Starr also provided the uncredited lead vocal on the Holidays' 1966 Top 10 R & B hit *I'll Love You Forever* and co-wrote (with J. J. Barnes) *Baby What'cha Got (For Me)* for Darrell Banks. Not just a tough, soulful vocalist, Starr is also an excellent writer (on this collection, eight tracks are his, including the Ric-Tic hits as well as *25 Miles, Who's Right Or Wrong, There You Go*, and *Time*).

Starr was touring England in 1967 when Wingate sold his Golden World/Ric-Tic complex to Gordy. Starr told *Soul Survivor*: "I went away a Ric-Tic artist and returned a Motown one. They didn't want to recognize me as an artist because I was a soul artist . . . they didn't think I had crossover potential." Like many of the transplanted Ric-Tic artists (J. J. Barnes, the Fantastic Four), Starr had to struggle for recognition at Motown. The company initially rejected *25 Miles*, but Starr's faith in his song was vindicated when it went to number 6 in the pop charts in 1969, paving the way for his biggest hit, *War*. This Norman Whitfield–Barrett Strong song, originally tucked away on the Temptations' **Psychedelic Shack** album, sold over three million singles for Starr and was taken way up the charts worldwide when revived in 1984 by shock-rock troupers Frankie Goes To Hollywood, while Bruce Springsteen's "live" recording reached the number 8 position in 1986. Starr's follow-ups (*Stop The War Now, Funky Music Sho Nuff Turns Me On*, and *There You Go*) were less successful, but he was making some excellent recordings. The old Miracles' ballad *Way Over There* becomes a stomping rocker in his hands, while *Gonna Keep On Tryin' Till I Win Your Love* was also cut by Marvin Gaye, the Temptations, and Jimmy Ruffin. *Take Me Clear From Here* is a fine effort in Gaye's *Heard It Through The Grapevine* groove. Starr also had the opportunity to do soundtrack work for the film "Hell Up In Harlem." He signed with Granite Records in 1976 (*Abyssinia Jones*), and came back strong on 20th Century in the late 1970s with the disco-soul styled *Contact* and *H.A.P.P.Y Radio*. Later he recorded for the Hippodrome and Avatar labels. Starr continues to be extremely popular in England, where he has lived for the past several years. All of his Ric-Tic material was collected on the album **Soul Master**, while the **War And Peace** set on Gordy and **Happy Radio** on 20th Century are also worth hunting for.

Discographical Details

134 Detroit Gold Vol. 1
Various Artists
Solid Smoke SS 8021 (LP)

Barbara Lewis: *Hello Stranger*; Jimmy "Soul" Clark: *If I Only Knew/Take A Little Time To Tell Her*; Belita Woods: *My Magic Corner/You Do Your Thing/That's When I'll Stop Loving You*; The Firestones: *Buy Now And Pay Later/I Just Can't Wait*; The Compacts: *Why Can't It Be/That's How My World Began*; Deon

Jackson: *Love Makes The World Go 'Round/Ooh Baby*; Betty Lavette: *Hey Love*; The Four Pros: *The Reason Why*; Richard "Popcorn" Wylie: *Rosemary What Happened*

Detroit Gold Vol. 2
Various Artists
Solid Smoke SS 8022 (LP)

The Capitols: *Cool Jerk/ We Got A Thing That's In The Groove*; Jimmy Delphs: *Almost/Am I Losing You/Feels Like Summer's Comin' On/Don't Sign the Papers [Baby]/Mrs Percy/I've Been Fooled Before*; The Fabulous Counts: *Jan Jan/It's A Man's, Man's, Man's World*; Percy and Them: *Sing A Sad Song*; The Volumes: *Ain't Gonna Give You Up*; The Gambrells: *You Better Move*; Johnnie Mae Matthews: *Worried About You*; Matt Lucas: *M-C Twine*

135 The Hits Of Edwin Starr – 20 Greatest Motown Hits
Edwin Starr
Tamla Motown WL 72429 (UK) (LP)

Stop Her On Sight (SOS)/25 Miles/Headline News/Agent Double-O Soul/Back Street/ I Want My Baby Back/Funky Music Sho Nuff Turns Me On/Soul Master/You've Got My Soul On Fire/Who's Right Or Wrong/War/Stop The War Now/Way Over There/ Take Me Clear From Here/Cloud Nine/There You Go/Gonna Keep On Tryin' Till I Win Your Love/Time/My Weakness Is You/Harlem

Basic Recordings

Detroit Soul Roots
136 Motor City Memories, Vol. 1
Various Artists
Motor City MC 1001 (LP)

The Serenaders: *Gates Of Gold*; The Five Js: *My Darling*; The Montclairs: *Golden Angel*; The Laredos: *Now The Parting Begins*; Ty Hunter and the Voice Masters: *Memories*; The Satintones: *Tomorrow And Always/Motor City*; Nolan Strong and the Diablos: *Someday You'll Want Me To Want You*; Lamont Anthony and the Voice Masters: *I Didn't Know*; Cornell Blakley and Johnson Brothers: *Promise To Be True*; The Distants: *Come On*; The Majestics: *Hard Times*; The Five Quails: *Get To School On Time*; The Tornados: *Genie In The Jug*

Motor City Memories, Vol. 2
Various Artists
Motor City MC 1002 (LP)

The Five Scalders: *Girl Friend*; The Falcons: *Just For Your Love*; The Creations: *This Is Our Night*; Ty Hunter and the Voice Masters: *Lonely Baby*; The Satintones: *I Know How It Feels*; The Martiniques: *Tonight Is Just Another Night*; The Seminoles: *It Takes A Lot*; The Voice Masters: *Needed (For Lovers Only)*; The Deans: *Oh Little Star*; The Five Quails: *Been A Long Time*; The Five Dollars: *I Will Wait*; The Downbeats: *Your Baby's Back*; David Ruffin and Voice Masters: *I'm In Love*

Motor City Memories, Vol. 3
Various Artists
Motor City MC 1003 (LP)
The Royal Jokers: *I Don't Like You That Much*; The Five Emeralds: *Let Me Take You Out Tonight*; The Serenaders: *Love Me Now*; The Sierras: *Stormy Weather*; The Four Imperials: *My Girl*; The Fresandos: *I Mean Really*; The Satintones: *Going To The Hop/My Beloved*; The Fascinators: *My Beauty, My Own*; Cornell Blakley and the Johnson Brothers: *Don't Touch The Moon*; The Five Scalders: *Willow Blues*; The Metronomes: *My Dearest Darling*; Ty Hunter and Voice Masters: *Everytime*; The Flints: *Why Did You Go*

Although these three albums are blatant bootlegs – plain covers with no liner notes – here is early Detroit R & B history in a heavy dose, with extremely rare sides from such Motown-associated labels as Anna, Harvey, and Tri-Phi, very early Motown obscurities by the Satintones, Creations, and Downbeats, rare cuts from early Gordy associate Roquel "Billy" Davis's Check-Mate label, a few stray items from Devora Brown's Fortune label by Nolan Strong and the Diablos, the Montclairs, and the Five Dollars, plus fine doo-wop tracks from such otherwise hopelessly obscure Detroit labels as Drummond, Teen Life, Chant, and Star-X. Crucial items collected here include early vocals by such future Motowners as Lamont Anthony (Lamont Dozier), Ty Hunter and the Voice Masters (who later evolved into the Originals of *Baby I'm For Real* fame), the Distants (soon to become the Temptations), as well as future Tempts' lead singer David Ruffin. The Satintones' delightfully ragged *Motor City* and *Going To The Hop* were among the earliest Tamla/Motown releases. Their *Tomorrow And Always* (an answer to the Shirelles' hit *Will You Still Love Me Tomorrow*) is perhaps their rarest release, having been almost instantly withdrawn following a copyright infringement lawsuit. The Five Scalders' 1956 *Girl Friend* offers lead vocals by Sir Mack Rice, pre-Falcons. Considering their origin, these albums have better-than-acceptable sound quality – transferred from original 45s and 78s – and make a useful supplement to the Robert West–Lupine–Relic reissue series, while offering much important material that has never otherwise been available on albums.

137 Mind Over Matter
Nolan Strong and the Diablos
Fortune 8015 (LP)
Mind Over Matter/The Masquerade Is Over/Welcome (Baby To My Heart)/Ali Coochie/Everything They Said Came True/Harriette, It's You/You Are Love/Are You Sincere/Can't We Talk It Over/I Really Love You/Village Of Love/(You're Not Goodlooking) You're Presentable

If Nolan Strong (b. January 22, 1934, in Scottsboro, Alabama, died February 21, 1977) and the Diablos (Quentin Eubanks, Willie Hunter, Jimmy Strong, and Bob Edwards) had recorded nothing more than *The Wind, Adios My Desert Love*, and *Mind Over Matter* they would still sit among the all-time top ten R & B vocal groups. Fortunately their decade-long (1954–64) legacy for Detroit's legendary Fortune label is both extensive and easily available (though only on LP). Stories of sessions being cut in dirt-floored back rooms, with sax players stepping over frying burgers to blow their solos into the studio's one microphone, have only added to their mystique. Strong's skyscraping falsetto was hugely influential on the young Smokey Robinson, whose first test recording was a version of *Adios My Desert Love*. The group's intricate harmonies and Edward's raw but graceful guitar-work produced the most ethereal of doo-wop stylings, inspired by Sonny Til and the Orioles and by Clyde McPhatter's gospel-drenched work with the Dominoes and the Drifters. These stylings were both tender (*The Wind* and the much-recorded standard *The Masquerade Is Over* – Marvin Gaye, who cut this as the lead track of his debut album **The Soulful Moods Of Marvin Gaye**, must surely have been listening) and tough (*Welcome (Baby To My Heart)*). Also produced were the influential early soul sounds of *Can't We Talk It Over* and *Mind Over Matter*. Berry Gordy, who in his early days had tried to place some of his songs with Fortune, and was never slow to recognize a good tune, even covered *Mind Over Matter* with the Temptations in their pre-hitmaking days.

But in contrast to Motown's polished sound, Fortune's recordings reflect the delightful crudeness of many pre-Motown Detroit labels. *You Are Love* is a Strong ballad solo performance, written and cut by label-owner Devora Brown in less than an hour (Brown: "I sang it to Nolan, he went right into the studio, sang it once and that was it – I was lucky I had the piano player there!"). *I Really Love You*, with its Jackie Wilson-style vocal swoops, sounds straight from the Robert West–Lupine–Falcons canon. Four albums by Strong and the Diablos are available (on vinyl only) in addition to this set: **Fortune Of Hits** (includes *The Wind*), **Fortune Of Hits, Vol. 2** (includes *Adios My Desert Love*), **From The Beginning To Now**, and **Daddy Rock**. Warning: these records are not for those whose listening criteria include super-clean digital sound quality. Additional warning: listening to Nolan Strong can be habit-forming!

138   Switched On Blues

Various Artists

Motown MOTD 5463

Sammy Ward: *What Makes You Love Him/Bread Winner/Part Time Love/Someday Pretty Baby*; Gino Parks: *For This I Thank You/Same Thing (Will Happen To You)/ That's No Lie*; Stevie Wonder: *I Call It Pretty Music But The Old People Call It The Blues, Pt 2*; Mabel (sic) John: *(I Guess There's) No Love*; Amos Milburn: *My Daily Prayer*

This is a most interesting look at the "other" side of Motown. In the early 1960s, Berry Gordy put out a number of hard-core blues releases, basically for local sales and quick cash. Artists included the heavily Ray Charles-influenced Sammy Ward, the lighter Gino Parks, Mable John (sister of Detroit superstar Little Willie John), and the then-faded boogie pianist/vocalist Amos Milburn (his earlier hits included *Chicken Shack Boogie* and *Bad Bad Whiskey*), who even had a now extremely rare album release **The Return Of The Blues Boss**. This set was originally released in 1968 to capitalize on the perceived "blues boom" of the era – that same year, Motown's Rare Earth subsidiary also issued an album licensed from EMI (UK) called **Blues Helping** by Love Sculpture, featuring a young Dave Edmunds on guitar. Star of the show here is Stevie Wonder, with one of his first cuts ever, *I Call It Pretty Music*. Wonder is featured on harmonica and sings out the title line at intervals in his pre-adolescent squeak. Sammy Ward's *Part Time Love* shares some root feel with Bennie McCain's *I Don't Want No Part Time Love* on Lupine, while Mable John sounds much like her brother on her track (an alternate version, lacking the string overdubs of the original Tamla single). John subsequently migrated to Memphis, where she achieved success as a singer (*Your Good Thing Is About To End*), and more recently has been a songwriter for Ray Charles. Parks later recorded for Golden World. Ward has recently recorded for Ian Levine's Motorcity label. Milburn died 1980 in Houston, Texas.

139 The Soul Of Detroit

Various Artists

Relic 7034

Mack Rice: *Baby I'm Coming Home*; The Conquerors: *Since You've Been Gone/ Lover's Celebration*; The Rivals: *Love Me*; Charles Amos: *Thunder In My Heart*; Gene Martin and the Primettes: *Lonely Nights*; Eddie Floyd: *Lonely/People Gonna Talk About You*; Betty Lavette: *You Killed The Love*; Joe Stubbs: *Hey Hey/ What's My Destiny*; The Majestics: *Hard Times*; Don Revel and the Primettes: *Return Of Stagger Lee*; Al Garner: *I'll Get Along Without You*; The Minor Chords: *Let Her Go Now*

Baby I'm Coming Home was ex-Falcons singer Mack Rice's best side for Lupine, his vocal equal parts Jackie Wilson and Ray Charles, helped by a really dynamic arrangement. Other Falcons members heard here include Eddie Floyd, with the ethereal ballad *Lonely* (with organ and girl group), and Joe Stubbs with the dramatic *What's My Destiny*. The group also sings backup on Betty Lavette's mid-paced, bluesy *You Killed The Love*. Gene Martin does his Jackie Wilson imitation, with the Primettes (later the Supremes) contributing the shrill vocal backups on *Lonely Nights*, a song also cut by the Falcons and closely modeled on Wilson's hit *Lonely Teardrops*. Charles Amos's previously unreleased *Thunder In My Heart* and Benny McCain's *Don't Want No Part Time Love* (backed by the Ohio Untouchables, with Robert Ward's stirring Magnatone vibrato guitar) are tortured soul balladry of the highest order. Listening to these recordings today (mostly from master tape, although some were dubbed from records), it is obvious that by 1965 time had passed Lupine owner Robert West by – his style remained cruder, rawer, and closer to the roots than contemporary productions by Motown, Ollie McLaughlin's Karen/Carla sides, or even the sounds from Stax and other Southern studios – but this does not diminish the pleasure in listening to these sides today.

140 The Detroit Girl Groups

Various Artists

Relic 7017

The Primettes: *Tears Of Sorrow/Pretty Baby*; The Kittens: *He's My Guy/I Love You So* (two versions); The La Dolls: *I'll Be Back/Sick Spell*; Ruby and her Swinging Rocks: *It's Been A Long Time/I Cried A Tear Over You*; Clara Hardy: *Touch Of Love*; The Corvells: *He's So Fine/Baby Sitting*; The Clevers: *Love Me Now*: The Taylor Tones: *Too Young To Love/My Heart Went Zing*; The Conquerors: *Dutchess Conquers Duke*; The Satin Angels: *Town Sensation/Pity Me*

The highlights of this collection are of course the first (1960) recordings by the Supremes (then a quartet) under the name the Primettes. *Tears Of Sorrow* borrows some feel from the Drifters' *There Goes My Baby*, while the use of flute suggests some influence from Berry Gordy's early Marv Johnson productions. Diana Ross's voice is distinctive enough, but it was several years and a lot of training before *Where Did Our Love Go*. Mary Wilson sings lead on the flip side *Pretty Baby*. Most of the other groups here were one-shot efforts – one suspects they ended up right back on the same street corners they had begun harmonizing on. The main problem is that only rarely did they have a really good song to work with, and most of these sides saw little success even locally. The Corvells provided an "answer" to the Falcons' hit and took a novelty approach, probably drawn from real life, on its flip *Baby Sitting*, while the Conquerors likewise answered Gene Chandler's smash *Duke Of Earl*. The Kittens' tracks were produced by West's nephew Eddie Floyd (then with the Falcons) and their acappella version of *I Love You So* suggests that with work they might have achieved some success. These early 1960s recordings were a far cry from the polished East Coast "girl-group" sounds of the Shirelles, the Chiffons, and the Orlons that were then burning up the charts, being altogether rougher and rawer, but they provide insight into the ferment and experimentation of early 1960s Detroit that was to soon blossom into the Motown sound.

141 I Love You: Golden Classics
The Volumes

Collectables COL-5032

Angel/Roly Poly/You Put A Spell On Me/I Wanna Be Your Man/Miss Silhouette/ Dreams/Bells/County Jail/I Love You/Come Back Into My Heart

Eddie Union (lead), Elijah Davis, Larry Wright, Joe Truvillion, and Ernest Newman (all from Detroit) formed the Volumes in 1960, singing at the same round of house parties and teen clubs that had launched such contemporaries on the Motown label as the Miracles, the Supremes, and the Temptations. In 1962, they signed with Willie Ewing's new Chex label, and broke into the upper reaches of the charts with the quick-beat *I Love You*, a record that, like much of the Detroit output of the period, combined doo-wop harmonies with a soulful lead. Producer Richard "Popcorn" Wylie, later to work with the Motown, Ric-Tic, and Karen organizations, laid a sparse track behind them, keeping the focus on displaying their good harmony work (some tracks here are a cappella). Other strong tracks include the thumping *County Jail*, and the hit follow-up, *Come Back Into My Heart*. Although they never achieved another hit, the group went on to record for Jubilee, Old Town, American Arts, Twirl, Impact, and Inferno, and even as late as 1971 recorded for Ollie McLaughlin. The Chex label also produced sides by the Majestics (who later evolved into Motown's Elgins), the Bohemians, Othea George, and Tony and the Techniques, which are collected on **The Best Of Chex**, released by Relic Records.

Early Motown Hitmakers

142 The Best Of Marv Johnson: You Got What It Takes
Marv Johnson

United Artists–EMI E2-98895

Come To Me/Whisper/I'm Coming Home/You Got What It Takes/Don't Leave Me/I Love The Way You Love/Let Me Love You/Ain't Gonna Be That Way/All The Love I've Got/(You've Got To) Move Two Mountains/Happy Days/Baby, Baby/Merry-Go-Round/Tell Me That You Love Me/How Can We Tell Him/I've Got A Notion/Oh Mary/Easier Said Than Done/Magic Mirror/Keep Tellin' Yourself/Another Tear Falls/ Congratulations, You've Hurt Me Again/The Man Who Don't Believe In Love/That's All I Want

Marv Johnson (b. October 15, 1938, in Detroit, Michigan) was Hitsville's first star. Although the recordings included here, spanning 1959–64, were released through the major United Artists label, they were the first Berry Gordy productions to crack the national charts', and are the roots of the Motown sound. Johnson had gained early experience with a vocal group, the Junior Serenaders, and first recorded in 1958 for Robert West's Kudo label (*Once Upon A Time* and *My Baby-O* are included on Relic's **The Best Of Lupine**.

Johnson met Berry Gordy in early 1959 while working as a clerk in a local record store, and the first results of their collaboration were *Come To Me* and *Whisper*. Firmly in the Jackie Wilson groove, with a sparse production over a jerky, bass-led beat, Johnson's high tenor was backed by a vocal group styled the Rayber Voices, which included Brian Holland, Robert Bateman, Gwen Murray, and Raynoma Liles (Gordy's wife). The very first record released on Gordy's Tamla label and quickly licensed to United Artists, *Come To Me* made the Top 30 and reached number 6 in the R & B charts in May of 1959. Johnson even headlined the first "Gordy Star Attractions" shows (predecessor of the barnstorming Motown Revues) alongside the Miracles, Eddie Holland, and Mable John. *I'm Coming Home, You Got What It Takes* (the first Gordy production to hit the pop Top 10), *(You've Got To) Move Two Mountains*, and, biggest of all, *I Love The Way You Love* (number 9 in April 1960) continued Johnson's hit streak. *Move Two Mountains* showed Gordy moving beyond the Jackie Wilson- and Drifters-influenced sounds of the earlier hits, with a crisp beat anchored by burping baritone sax and polished chorus backup. The Eddie Holland song *Merry-Go-Round* featured a flute-based "circus" motif later used on the Miracles' smash hit *Tears Of A Clown*, while *I'm Coming Home* introduced vibes alongside the flute and baritone over a cha-cha beat. Unfortunately for Johnson, as Motown grew he found himself, as he put it, caught between two camps, without strong support from either.

This carefully compiled set includes a judicious selection of Johnson's later (1962–4) New York recordings. *Keep Tellin' Yourself* mines the Chuck Jackson *Any Day Now* groove nicely, and the Bacharach–David *Another Tear Falls* similarly would have made a good song for Dionne Warwick. But the prize of these late sessions comes from soul avatar Bert Berns – *Congratulations* is close in feel to Solomon Burke's classic *Cry To Me* (the song's author Joy Byers had in fact penned *I Said I Was Sorry* and *Go On Back To Him* for Burke).

Johnson eventually signed directly with Motown in 1965, but his earlier success was not revived despite cutting a handful of more than respectable sides (*I Miss You Baby (How I Miss You)* and *I'll Pick A Rose For My Rose* – the latter a Top 10 hit in England in 1969).

143 Do You Love Me (Now That I Can Dance)
The Contours

Motown MODT 5415

Do You Love Me/Just A Little Misunderstanding/Shake Sherrie/Can You Do It/Don't Let Her Be Your Baby/First I Look At The Purse/Whole Lotta Woman/Can You Jerk Like Me/It's So Hard Being A Loser/You Get Ugly

The immortal musical question, "Do you love me, now that I can dance?" blasted out of a million teenage radios in October 1962 as the Contours (Billy Gordon on lead, Joe Billingslea, Sylvester Potts, Hubert Johnson, and Hugh Davis on guitar) twisted and shouted their way into musical history. The song was the first million-seller on the Gordy Records label (the second, Martha and the Vandellas' *(Love Is Like A) Heat Wave* came almost a year later), and the first and biggest of the Contours' eight chart records, in a career which continues to this day. The Contours had already unsuccessfully auditioned for Robert West's Lupine operation, and saw two releases for Motown before *Do You Love Me*. Berry Gordy had originally written the song as a take-off of the Isley Brothers' *Twist And Shout*, and first tried to cut it with the Temptations. From the shimmering opening guitar riff to Gordon's gospel squall and the gimmick false fade-out ending, this record was sheer perfection (note that the version on this set is an alternate take with a slightly different vocal to the original single). This set, although retaining the front cover art of the original **Do You Love Me** album, effectively compiles all of their chart hits except the minor (and atypical) ballad *That Day When She Needed Me*. The group was as renowned for their dancing as for their dance-grooved records.

In their seven years with Motown, the Contours worked with almost every combination of writing/producing talent the label had to offer, including Smokey Robinson (*First I Look At The Purse*), Clarence Paul – the man behind Little Stevie Wonder's hits – and Mickey Stevenson (the Northern soul floorshaker *Just A Little Misunderstanding*, with lead vocals by ex-Falcon Joe Stubbs), while William Weatherspoon and James Dean (the team behind Jimmy Ruffin's *What Becomes Of The Brokenhearted*) contributed *It's So Hard Being A Loser*, with lead vocal by future Temptations lead singer Dennis Edwards. The Contours' material provided successful fodder for a number of revivals. *Do You Love Me* was covered by British beat groups Faron's Flamingos (who also took a shot at *Shake Sherrie*), Brian Poole and the Tremeloes, and the Dave Clark Five (who took the song to number 11 in the US Hot 100 in May 1964), and more recently by the late punk rocker Johnny Thunders (and the Heartbreakers). *First I Look At The Purse* became a staple for the J. Geils Band, while Grand Funk Railroad revived *Can You Do It*.

144   Greatest Hits
Marvelettes
Motown MODT 5180

Don't Mess With Bill/Please Mr Postman/Playboy/Beechwood 4-5789/You're My Remedy/Locking Up My Heart/As Long As I Know He's Mine/Too Many Fish In The Sea/Danger Heartbreak Dead Ahead/Strange I Know/Twistin' Postman

The Marvelettes featured two leads, Gladys Horton and Wanda Young, and were completed by Katherine Anderson, Juanita Cowart, and Georgeanna Dobbins. They were formed in 1960 at Inkster High School (Inkster is a Detroit suburb). Their first release, *Please Mr Postman* with Horton on lead, was an archetypal "girl-group" sound with a funky cha-cha groove (Marvin Gaye played the drums). It became a million-seller, topping the pop and R & B charts in late 1961, and inspired a cover version by the Beatles. Following on with additional "girl-group" hits in (the inevitable) *Twistin' Postman*, *Playboy*, and *Beechwood 4-5789*, their bouncy sound gradually became more sophisticated. Horton was the main lead singer on their earlier records, trading off with Young on tracks like *Locking Up My Heart* (1963) and *Too Many Fish In The Sea* (1964). A greater reliance on the smoother-voiced Young as lead also contributed to the more polished sound of *Danger Heartbreak Dead Ahead* and the sublime Smokey Robinson production *Don't Mess With Bill* (both 1965). Dogged by personnel changes, by the mid-1960s they had been eclipsed by the Supremes, although Smokey supplied them with one last Top 20 hit in 1968, *The Hunter Gets Captured By The Game*. Buffed to a high gloss in the studio (their now rare 1963 **Live On Stage** album has some of the most ragged harmonies ever heard on a Motown record), their delightfully innocent sound still holds up today. The Young Disciples' recent club hit, *Apparently Nothing*, was closely based on the group's *Here I Am Baby*.

145   Greatest Hits
Martha and the Vandellas
Motown MODT 5204

Dancing In The Street/(Love Is Like A) Heat Wave/Quicksand/Nowhere To Run/Come And Get These Memories/Live Wire/You've Been In Love Too Long/In My

Lonely Room/Love (Makes Me Do Foolish Things)/A Love Like Yours (Don't Come Knocking Everyday)/Wild One/My Baby Loves Me

Martha and the Vandellas, featuring lead Martha Reeves (b. July 18, 1941, Alabama, raised in Detroit), Rosalind Ashford, and Annette Sterling, represented the gritty side of Motown that too often has been overlooked. They originated in the early 1960s as a quartet with one Gloria Williams as lead singer, and were first known as the Del-Phis, recording for Check-Mate and doing session work behind Mike Hanks and J. J. Barnes. They first recorded for Motown as the Vels, after which Williams dropped out, and provided the churchy backup vocals for Marvin Gaye's first hit *Stubborn Kind Of Fellow*. Gaye later repaid the favor, co-writing their biggest hit, the immortal *Dancing In The Street* (1964), and playing piano on the session. Their other Top 10 hits were also rockers exploiting the explosive Reeves voice – *(Love Is Like A) Heat Wave* (1963), *Quicksand* (1963), *I'm Ready For Love* (1966), and *Jimmy Mack* (1967). Reeves was also strong on the torchy blues ballads *Love (Makes Me Do Foolish Things)* and *My Baby Loves Me*. The latter remains a big favorite in the African American community, which finds its mid-tempo groove perfect for steppin' (the white community remains unresponsive to mid-tempo tunes).

Like Motown's other early girl group the Marvelettes, the Vandellas, dogged by company politics and personnel changes, were eclipsed by the Supremes. Leaving Motown in 1972, Reeves has since recorded as a solo artist for various labels, sadly without recapturing her earlier success. The **Heatwave** and **Dance Party** albums (available coupled on one CD) are nice additions to a more detailed collection.

They Also Served – Motown's Second-Level Performers

146 **(60's) Greatest Hits And Rare Classics**
Isley Brothers
Motown MODT 5483

Twist And Shout/This Old Heart Of Mine (Is Weak For You)/There's No Love Left/Take Some Time Out For Love/Who Could Ever Doubt My Love/I Guess I'll Always Love You/I Hear A Symphony/Nowhere To Run/Just Ain't Enough Love/Got To Have You Back/Behind A Painted Smile/Put Yourself In My Place/It's Out Of The Question/Take Me In Your Arms (Rock Me A Little While)/Why When Love Is Gone/Little Miss Sweetness/All Because I Love You/Tell Me It's Just A Rumour Baby/My Love Is Your Love (Forever)/That's The Way Love Is/One Too Many Heartaches/It's Your Thing

Twist And Shout is the original 1962 Wand recording, while *It's Your Thing* was the Brothers' first hit on their own T-Neck label in 1969 – these tracks are presumably included to fatten up the "hits" quota. The Isleys (brothers Ronald on lead, Rudolph, and O'Kelly, from Cincinnati, Ohio), unlike most Motown performers of the 1960s, were already experienced performers, with successful tenures on such big labels as RCA, United Artists, Atlantic, and Wand, had worked with top producers including Leiber and Stoller, Bert Berns, and Hugo and Luigi, and had achieved hard-rocking hits like *Shout* (1959) and *Twist And Shout* (1962) before they signed with Motown in 1966. *This Old Heart Of Mine (Is Weak For You)*, a classic H–D–H song and production, gave them their biggest hit since *Twist And Shout* of four years earlier, but their 1966–8 association was not entirely a happy one. Their first-time-out success stirred up jealousy of these new jacks among the established Motown acts, and despite

some fine material supplied by H–D–H, Harvey Fuqua, Smokey Robinson, Ivy
Jo Hunter, and Norman Whitfield, their other hits – *I Guess I'll Always Love You,
Got To Have You Back*, and *Take Me In Your Arms (Rock Me A Little While)*, the
last a pulsating revival of Kim Weston's 1965 hit, subsequently taken well up the
charts in 1975 by the Doobie Brothers – did not maintain their initial
momentum, nor was the group able to develop a strong relationship with
consistent production support. Good non-hit material here includes *Behind A
Painted Smile* (with rock guitarisms presaging their 1970s **3+3**/*Who's That Lady*
era), and the powerful reworkings of *Nowhere To Run* and *I Hear A Symphony*.

The raw-edged funk sound of *It's Your Thing* kicked off a revived hit streak for
the Isleys which continued through the 1970s and on to the 1990s. When Rod
Stewart chose to revive *This Old Heart* in 1991 he did it right, drafting in Ronald
Isley to sing a duet with him. The result was an elegant record and video, and
notice (as if such was needed) that Ronald Isley was and is one of the great voices
of soul.

147 Irresistible
Tammi Terrell

Motown MOTD 5231

*I Can't Believe You Love Me/That's What Boys Are Made For/Come On And See
Me/What A Good Man He Is/Tears At The End Of A Love Affair/This Old Heart Of
Mine (Is Weak For You)/He's The One I Love/Can't Stop Now (Love Is Calling)/
Just Too Much To Hope For/Hold Me Oh My Darling/I Can't Go On Without You*

For most soul and pop fans, Terrell's fame and reputation rest solely on her
classic series of duets with Marvin Gaye, beginning with *Ain't No Mountain High
Enough*. Even Funk Brothers bandleader Earl Van Dyke recalls these recordings
as among his very favorites in all his years of service in the Hitsville studios. But
there was far more to this woman's talents than (merely) as adjunct to some of
the greatest recordings Gaye ever made. Terrell (b. Tammy Montgomery, 1946,
in Philadelphia, Pennsylvania) had first recorded under producer Luther Dixon
for New York's Scepter/Wand set-up at age 15, toured with James Brown (who
recorded *I Cried* for his Try Me label), and cut *If I Would Marry You* with master
producer Bert Berns, all before signing with Motown in 1965. Her first Motown
recordings were solo sides produced by Harvey Fuqua and Johnny Bristol,
including *I Can't Believe You Love Me, Come On And See Me*, and Fuqua's old
Spinners' hit *That's What Boys (Girls) Are Made For*. Terrell was not a wailer or
shouter. Rather, she had an intoxicatingly sensuous quality, equally effective on
up-tempo numbers (listen to the way she rocks *This Old Heart Of Mine* or how
she interjects "Oh yeah!" in *He's The One I Love*) and ballads like *That's What
Boys Are Made For*, while on the mid-paced *Just Too Much To Hope For* she
creates a devastating feeling of loss with her little hesitations and changes of
tempo – this is *soul*. Also of note is the fine male vocal group harmony backup on
many of her sides – possibly the Spinners, as most of both theirs and Terrell's
sessions were produced by Fuqua. Tammi Terrell died, after several brain
operations, on March 16, 1970, aged only 24. Her mentor James Brown called
her death "a tragedy on a par with Otis Redding's."

148 Greatest Hits
Junior Walker and the All Stars

Motown MODT 5208

*Shotgun/What Does It Take (To Win Your Love)/How Sweet It Is (To Be Loved By
You)/(I'm A) Road Runner/Come See About Me/Hip City/Home Cooking/Money*

(That's What I Want)/Shake And Fingerpop/Shoot Your Shot/Pucker Up Buttercup/ Cleo's Mood

Junior Walker (b. Autry DeWalt, Jr, 1942, Blytheville, Arkansas) was inspired by such big-toned jazz tenormen as Illinois Jacquet, Arnett Cobb, and Buddy Tate. By the early 1960s Walker and his band (Vic Thomas on organ, Willie Woods on guitar, and James Greaves on drums) were working the Midwestern club circuits, playing hard roadhouse jazz and the R & B of the day, and had even cut an obscure 45 for legendary Detroit producer Joe Von Battle. Signed to Harvey Fuqua's Harvey Records label in 1962, they cut three singles (one track, *Cleo's Mood*, later became a Top 50 hit when reissued by Motown in 1966) and other material which made up the **Soul Session** album. After switching over to Motown along with the rest of Fuqua's roster, Walker unleashed his best-known hits – *Shotgun, (I'm A) Road Runner, Shake And Fingerpop* – which exemplified his style, all raw, hard-rocking rhythm fronted by his searing sax and gravelly vocals. In the late 1960s he scored further hits with more ballad-oriented titles such as *What Does It Take (To Win Your Love)* – a real Harvey/Tri-Phi family reunion with producer/writers Fuqua and Johnny Bristol, plus the Spinners on background vocals – and his reading of the Guess Who's *These Eyes*. In 1981 his blasting sax was featured on Foreigner's smash hit *Urgent*. Walker and his band (with some changed personnel, of course) are still rocking the house everywhere they play. All of Walker's classic 1960s albums, such as **Shotgun** and **Roadrunner** (available on CDs either separately or packaged on one disc) and the out-of-print **Home Cookin'** and **Soul Session**, are worth picking up – prime slabs of mid-1960s Detroit funk.

149 Greatest Hits And Rare Classics
Brenda Holloway

Motown MOTD 5485
Every Little Bit Hurts/Who's Loving You/When I'm Gone/Just Look What You've Done/You've Made Me So Very Happy/Hurt A Little Everyday/Starting The Hurt All Over Again/How Many Times Did You Mean It/Operator/I'll Always Love You/ Unchained Melody/I'll Be Available/I've Been Good To You/Where Were You/You Can Cry On My Shoulder/A Favor For A Girl (With A Love Sick Heart)/I've Got To Find It/Together Till The End Of Time

Brenda Holloway (b. June 21, 1946, in Atascadero, California) in 1964 was Motown's first West Coast signing. Her debut single *Every Little Bit Hurts* (written and produced by Ed Cobb, a former member of the Four Preps, who went on to write and produce the punk-rock classic *Dirty Water* for the Standells), was the first Motown hit to be produced on the West Coast, reaching the charts (number 13 pop) two months before the Supremes' *Where Did Our Love Go*, and was later revived by H–D–H for Laura Lee's Hot Wax album, **The Two Sides Of Laura Lee**. The British release of Holloway's single gained her a spot on the Beatles' 1965 US tour (including an appearance at Shea Stadium). She enjoyed half-a-dozen Top 100 entries, including *When I'm Gone*, written and produced by Smokey Robinson (and later revived by ex-Pointer Sister Bonnie Pointer for her 1979 Motown debut solo album **Bonnie Pointer**), and the original version of *You've Made Me So Very Happy* (written by Brenda, her sister Patrice – with whom she had recorded pre-Motown for Era – Berry Gordy, and producer Frank Wilson). Her soft and sweet rendition barely made the Top 40, but in 1969 Blood, Sweat and Tears' psychedelicized version went all the way to number 2, selling two million singles. Holloway's strong, gospel-rich vocals could range from the wailing *Starting The Hurt All Over Again* to the tender but tough *How Many Times Did You Mean It*. The young Stevie Winwood, that most tasteful of British blue-eyed soulboys, clearly paid close attention to Holloway, cutting versions of both *Every Little Bit Hurts* and *Together Til The End Of Time* with the Spencer Davis Group. *Unchained Melody*, first established in the R & B field in the 1950s by Roy Hamilton and taken from Holloway's sole original album release – she also cut *Embraceable You* – is a superb big ballad performance, standing comparison with contemporary soul treatments by Al Green and Walter Jackson. If Holloway had done a few duets with Marvin Gaye, who also loved to sing standards, who knows to what heights she might have climbed? Instead, she eventually returned to the church after marrying a minister. The world of soul music is poorer for her departure, but this collection preserves some of the gems she left behind.

150   Greatest Hits And Rare Classics
Kim Weston

Motown MOTD 5486

It Takes Two (with Marvin Gaye)/*Take Me In Your Arms (Rock Me A Little While)*/ *Helpless/Do Like I Do/Teach Me Tonight* (with Marvin Gaye)/*I'm Still Loving You/ A Little More Love/It Should Have Been Me/Love Me All The Way/Looking For The Right Guy/What Good Am I Without You* (with Marvin Gaye)/*A Love Like Yours (Don't Come Knocking Everyday)/Another Train Coming/Feel Alright Tonight/Baby (Don't You Leave Me)* (with Marvin Gaye)/*I'll Never See My Love Again/A Thrill A Moment/Just Loving You/Don't Compare Me With Her/Go Ahead And Laugh*

Although Kim Weston (b. 1939, in Detroit) is best known for her hit duets with Marvin Gaye *It Takes Two* (1967) and *What Good Am I Without You* (1964), she also had the original hit version of the much-revived rocker *Take Me In Your Arms* (the Isley Brothers, Tammi Terrell, the Doobie Brothers), and introduced (after leaving Motown) *Lift Ev'ry Voice And Sing*, which quickly became the unofficial "black national anthem." Weston was married to Motown A & R head William "Mickey" Stevenson, but curiously this seemed to hold back her career rather than advancing it, as she never saw an album release in her own name during her tenure with the label. She certainly did get some fine songs, tailored to her strong, bluesy voice. *It Should Have Been Me*, originally consigned to the B side of her first single *Love Me All The Way*, was successfully revived in 1968 by Gladys Knight and the Pips, and much later by Adeva. The Four Tops did a beautiful job with *Helpless*, while its B side, *A Love Like Yours*, saw cuts by Martha and the Vandellas and by Tina Turner (the latter produced by Phil Spector). Weston sounds very comfortable and playful with Gaye in their duet on *Teach Me Tonight* (Joe Williams with Count Basie, Dinah Washington, and James Ray of *If You Gotta Make A Fool Of Somebody* fame head the list of R & B versions of this standard tune). *Just Loving You*, a production number with the polished feel of a standard, provides a taste of Weston's jazzy ballad style, a sound toward which her post-Motown releases for MGM and Volt veered with songs like *The Impossible Dream*. Of late, Weston has been much involved in community service in Detroit.

151   Here Comes The Judge
Shorty Long

Soul SS 709 (LP)

Here Comes The Judge/Night Fo' Last (instrumental)/*Function At The Junction/ Don't Mess With My Weekend/Ain't No Justice/Devil With The Blue Dress/Night Fo' Last* (vocal)/*Stranded In The Jungle/Here Comes Fat Albert/Sing What You Wanna/ Another Hurt Like This/People Sure Act Funny*

Aptly nicknamed "Shorty" as he stood only 5 feet 1 inch, Long (b. Frederick Long, May 20, 1940, in Birmingham, Alabama), along with fellow Harvey/Tri-Phi alumnus Junior Walker, made some of the rawest, funkiest, most fun records of Motown's "Golden Era." Funk Brothers' bandleader Earl Van Dyke fondly recalled in Don Waller's *The Motown Story* how Shorty would come into sessions declaring, "Today we ain't playin' nuthin' but funk. If you don't feel funky, take a drink of this," then reaching into his pocket for a bottle. Writer/producer Sylvia Moy (who co-penned his valedictory *I Had A Dream*) concurred, "Shorty was a mess, a real comedian." This well sums up Long's best-remembered music – rollicking, good-time R & B. After three early singles for Tri-Phi, Long's first Motown release was *Devil With The Blue Dress* (which inaugurated the Soul label). While not a big hit for him, it was soon taken into the Top 5 by Mitch Ryder and the Detroit Wheels, the Motor City's finest white rockers, and later became an incendiary staple of Bruce Springsteen's live shows. Long's own Top 10 success came in 1968 with the rocking novelty *Here Comes The Judge* (inspired by a then-popular routine on the TV show "Laugh-In," although its roots went back to the early black vaudeville comedian Pigmeat Markham). *Here Comes The Judge* headlined this, his debut album. Ranging from rocking originals like *Function At The Junction* (which inspired a popular black dance) and the anthemic *Don't Mess With My Weekend*, to his uproarious version of the Cadets/Jayhawks 1950s classic *Stranded In The Jungle*, this album captures the good humor, tough bandwork, fun, and funk that Long made seem so spontaneous, but which actually masked years of experience. Long had a serious side too, which came out more on his second, also worthwhile album **The Prime Of Shorty Long**. Posthumously released in 1969 (Long drowned in the Detroit River while fishing on June 29, 1969, aged only 29), the album featured his Martin Luther King-influenced *I Had A Dream* and his take (including a fine trumpet solo) of Procol Harum's hit *A Whiter Shade Of Pale*. This album may be a little more arranged, and a little less fun (though his version of Fats Domino's *Blue Monday* is great), but it makes a nice addition to a more detailed collection. What Long might have gone on to achieve must, sadly, remain mere speculation. Picture Shorty leaping around on stage in a silver jumpsuit and six-inch platform heels, throwing down his brand of funk while brandishing a strap-on keyboard synthesizer – roll over Rick James and tell George Clinton the news!

152   The Best Of The Spinners
The Spinners

Motown MODT 5199

Together We Can Make Such Sweet Music/It's A Shame/I've Got To Find Myself A Brand New Baby/I'll Always Love You/We'll Have It Made/Bad Bad Weather (Till You Come Home)/My Whole World Ended (The Moment You Left Me)/Truly Yours/Sweet Thing/O-o-h Child

The Spinners achieved their greatest success subsequent to these sides, for Atlantic Records under Thom Bell's Philadelphia-based production. However, there is much to savor in their mid-1960s Motown recordings. The basic quartet of Bobbie Smith, Henry Fambrough, Billy Henderson, and Pervis Jackson had been singing together in their native Detroit since the late 1950s, and the group had in fact hit the Top 30 in 1961 with *That's What Girls Are Made For* on Harvey Fuqua's Tri-Phi label – at this time, only the Miracles and Mary Wells had had big hits for Motown. When Gordy absorbed Fuqua's operation, the Spinners, along with Junior Walker and the All Stars and Shorty Long, went over to Motown. The Spinners enjoyed modest success on Motown, with the archetypal pounding dancers *I'll Always Love You* (1965), *Truly Yours* (1966), and *We'll Have It Made* (1971). Their biggest success came in 1970 with the Top 15 hit *It's*

A Shame (written and produced by Stevie Wonder), with new member G.C. Cameron taking the lead vocal. The song was successfully revived in 1990, incorporating a fat sample of the original recording, by rap star Monie Love. The group's Motown discography contains some other gems, such as the sublime *What More Could A Boy Ask For* (which went unreleased until its appearance on the **From The Vaults** collection) and Smokey Robinson's bluesy *Like A Good Man Should*. Clearly the talent was there during their Motown years, but the group was mostly overshadowed by the label's established star roster, and it took the changeover to Atlantic and the crucial additions of Philippe Wynne as lead singer and Thom Bell as producer to boost them to superstar status in the 1970s.

153 From The Vaults
Various Artists
Motown M5-190V1 (LP)

The Temptations: *Nobody But You*; The Supremes: *Take Me Where You Go*; The Monitors: *Cry*; Marvin Gaye: *Sweeter As The Days Go By*; The Marvelettes: *I Should Have Known Better*; The Spinners: *What More Could A Boy Ask For*; The Miracles: *It's Fantastic*; Mary Wells: *Drop In The Bucket*; Gladys Knight and the Pips: *The Lonely Heart And Lonely Eyes of Lonely Me*; Martha and the Vandellas: *Undecided Lover*

For many years prior to the release of this album, rumours had circulated about the unreleased material in the Motown vaults. This collection, drawn from the 1962–6 period, is no mere rag-bag of cutting-room leftovers, but a testament to both the depth of the vaults and the very high standards of Motown's "Golden Era." It is delightful from beginning to end, with a more than usually raunchy Mary Wells on *Drop In The Bucket*, a superbly emotional Gladys Knight performance of *Lonely Heart*, and Eddie Kendricks's firm, choirboy lead on the early *Nobody But You* setting the table. Then there is a typically excellent Miracles up-tempo groover, *It's Fantastic*. Miracle-man Smokey Robinson outdoes himself in a rare 1965 production for the Supremes, *Take Me Where You Go*, with an ingratiatingly clear and cute vocal by Diana Ross (classic Smokey couplet: "In the desert where it's hot, or in the North Pole where it's not"). Marvin Gaye's *Sweeter As The Days Go By* is in the *Ain't That Peculiar* vein, with that rambling rhythm that makes Gaye's 1966 hits such driving soul masterpieces, these in particular being a big influence on David Bowie and Lou Reed. A different version, by the song's producer/writer Frank Wilson, was issued (in England only) in 1979, having been originally scheduled for 1966 release on the Soul label. *Sweeter* was also cut in 1966 by Motown's blue-eyed soulgirl Chris Clark. That the Spinners' marvelous dancer *What More Could A Boy Ask For* was never released illustrates how thoroughly they were pushed into the background during their Motown years; it more than stands comparison with anything they cut for the label. *Undecided Lover* is a very early (1962) Norman Whitfield production, while the Monitors' 1964 track *Cry* is in the then-popular Four Seasons style, complete with skyscraping falsetto and bass voice cut-ins, and actually predates their original 1965 VIP releases. It was through the efforts of the late Motown expert Tom de Pierro that this album was assembled, and in retrospect we should all be grateful. A much-delayed follow-up set, **Never-Before-Released Masters From Motown's Brightest Stars: The 1960s** reached back even further for Mary Wells's 1961 effort *The Day Will Come*, and also marked the only appearance on album of the Temptations' (originally masquerading as the Pirates) 1962 cut of Nolan Strong and the Diablos' *Mind Over Matter*.

Soul From The Other Side – Non-Motown From The Glory Years

154 Ric-Tic Relics
Various Artists

Motown STML 11232 (UK) (LP)

J. J. Barnes: *Real Humdinger/Day Tripper/Please Let Me In/Ain't Gonna Do It/Say It*; Edwin Starr: *Harlem/Agent O-O-Soul* (instrumental)/*Stop Her On Sight (SOS)/Back Street*; The San Remo Golden Strings: *Hungry For Love/Festival Time*; Al Kent: *You Gotta Pay The Price/Ooh Pretty Lady*; Laura Lee: *To Win Your Heart*; The Fantastic Four: *Can't Stop Looking For My Baby*; The Mark II Trio: *G'wan (Go On)*

After Berry Gordy took over Ed Wingate's Ric-Tic/Golden World operations, the Ric-Tic material remained very popular in England, especially with the Northern soul all-nighter crowd – perhaps the precursors of the Techno/House/Ecstasy-fueled "raves" of recent years. This album has remained in strong demand since its release. There is the mellow, Marvin Gaye-styled J. J. Barnes with his happy soul hit *Real Humdinger* (1966), the George Clinton-produced cover of the Beatles' *Day Tripper*, and the smooth sound of his self-penned (with Don Davis) *Say It*. Edwin Starr's *Stop Her On Sight* (1966) and *Agent O-O-Soul* (instrumental, 1965) still retain their power to fill dance floors after over 25 years (the vocal version of *Agent O-O-Soul*, available on Starr's own album, is the best James Bond/secret agent take-off next to Jamo Thomas's crazed *I Spy (For The FBI)*). Then there is the cruise-control grooving of the San Remo Golden Strings (actually the Motown session band moonlighting), the Jackie Wilson-influenced Al Kent (also known as Al Hamilton, who recorded a few years earlier for Robert West's Lupine/Flick complex), Laura Lee, of future *Women's Love Rights* fame, with the tough soul sound of *To Win Your Heart* (Lee recalls that both Edwin Starr and J. J. Barnes attended the session to lend encouragement), the Fantastic Four . . . you get the idea. This album is an essential buy.

155 Best Of The Fantastic Four
The Fantastic Four

Motown MOTD 5464

I Love You Madly/The Whole World Is A Stage/You Gave Me Something (And Everything's Alright)/I've Got To Have You/To Share Your Love/Goddess Of Love/Can't Stop Looking For My Baby/As Long As I Live (I Live For You)/Man In Love/Romeo And Juliet's "I Don't Want To Live Without You (Play)"/Just The Lonely

James Epps, Jr (lead), Joe Pruitt, Ralph Pruitt, and Wallace "Toby" Childs first got together at Detroit's Eastern High School. They signed with Ric-Tic in 1966 and their first record, *Can't Stop Looking For My Baby*, with its Temptations-influenced sound, could have rolled right off the Motown assembly line – hardly surprising as label boss Ed Wingate used moonlighting Hitsville sessionmen whenever possible. The Four notched the R & B charts with half a dozen releases between 1966 and 1968, from *The Whole World Is A Stage* through to *I Love You Madly*. Their distinctive vocal sound was also heard backing up the likes of Edwin Starr (*Stop Her On Sight*) and J. J. Barnes (*Real Humdinger*). The ballad *To Share Your Love* was in fact Bobby Bland's *Share Your Love With Me*, which was also taken to the top of the R & B charts in 1969 by Aretha Franklin. All tracks here are taken from the original Ric-Tic masters, acquired by Motown in 1968. After several uneventful years with Motown, which saw only a handful of little-heard releases, the group's career (with Cleveland Horne, a longtime associate of the group and former solo artist on "Popcorn" Wylie's Soul Hawk label, replacing Childs) took an upswing in the 1970s with such successful singles as *If You Need Me, Call Me, I'm Falling In Love, Alvin Stone, Meet Me At The Hideaway*, and *I've Got To Have Your Love* on Armen Boladian's Westbound label.

156   Darrell Banks Is Here!
Darrell Banks

Atco SD 33-216 (LP)

Here Come The Tears/I've Got That Feeling/I'm Gonna Hang My Head And Cry/ Look Into The Eyes Of A Fool/Our Love (Is In The Pocket)/Open The Door To Your Heart/Angel Baby (Don't You Ever Leave Me)/Somebody Somewhere (Needs You)/ Baby What'cha Got (For Me)/You Better Go

June 1966 saw the release of the song for which Darrell Banks (b. Darrell Eubanks, 1938, in Buffalo, New York) will be remembered: *Open The Door To Your Heart*, which achieved number 2 R & B and Top 30 pop-chart status. Having sung gospel and worked with the late soulman Donnie Elbert, he was discovered in a Detroit club appearance and signed to Don Davis and LeBaron Taylor's Solid Hitbound/Revilot operation. *Open The Door To Your Heart* is a self-defining classic song and performance, leaving cover versions as just that – covers. Even the great Jackie Wilson could not improve on it. Other top-quality tracks here include the dance groovers *Our Love (Is In The Pocket)*, *Angel Baby*, and *Somebody Somewhere*, all modeled on the classic Motown canon, which are still played today at Northern soul all-nighters. *Our Love* was co-written by George Clinton, whose group the Parliaments were also recording for Solid Hitbound/Revilot, and was cut for the label as well by J. J. Barnes, who, together with Edwin Starr, wrote *Baby What'cha Got For Me*. *Angel Baby* (by Sylvia Moy and Hank Cosby) had first been cut by Stevie Wonder, while *Somebody Somewhere* was penned by Motown producer Frank Wilson, who later created the Four Tops' classic album **Still Waters Run Deep**. *Somebody Somewhere* proved only a small success as a follow-up, and in 1969 Banks switched over to the Stax/ Volt group, where his second album, **Here To Stay**, yielded a couple of singles in a rather unsuitable hybrid Detroit/Memphis style. Banks was shot to death by an off-duty police officer in Detroit in March 1970, in the course of an alleged assault on a woman friend.

157   Don Davis Presents The Sound Of Detroit – J. J. Barnes, Steve Mancha, Darrell Banks
J. J. Barnes, Steve Mancha, and Darrell Banks

Ace CDSXD 061 (UK)

Rare stamps: J. J. Barnes: *Baby, Please Come Back Home/Chains Of Love/Now That I Got You Back/Easy Living/Sweet Sherry*; Steve Mancha: *Don't Make Me A Storyteller/A Love Like Yours/Keep The Faith/I Don't Wanna Lose You/Hate Yourself In The Morning/Just Keep On Loving Me*

Here To Stay: Darrell Banks: *Just Because Your Love Has Gone/Forgive Me/Only The Strong Survive/Don't Know What To Do/When A Man Loves A Woman/We'll Get Over/Beautiful Feeling/I Could Never Hate Her/Never Alone/No One Blinder (Than A Man Who Won't See)/My Love Is Strictly Reserved*

This is a reissue of the long sought-after Barnes–Mancha **Rare Stamps** album on Volt, issued when Detroit producer Don Davis joined Stax, bringing along many of his Groovesville masters, coupled with Darrell Banks's **Here To Stay** album. Detroit native Barnes had a long career, beginning in 1962 with releases on the Mickay's label, then Ring, then Ric-Tic (he is represented with tracks on the **Ric-Tic Memories** album), and getting a hit with the infectious *Real Humdinger* – number 18 R & B in 1966. Barnes was switched over to Motown along with the rest of the Ric-Tic roster. Although he cut many tracks, he never saw a single release, supposedly because he sounded too much like Marvin Gaye, and his tracks on this album, cut after his departure from Motown in 1967, certainly bear this out. Unencumbered by ancient business politics, we can now enjoy some bedrock soul sounds. *Sweet Sherry,* a much-bootlegged Northern soul dance raver, has some vintage blaring baritone sax in the classic style by Mike Terry, a longtime Hitsville sessionman who became a solid producer (Garland Green, Maxine Brown). *Baby, Please Come Back Home,* which achieved Top 10 R & B status for Groovesville in mid-1967, beats the Marvin Gaye blindfold test. Barnes noted in *Soul Survivor* that the recording of *Easy Living* credited to him here was actually sung by Steve Mancha. Mancha's voice has slightly more grit, but either way it is a lovely mid-tempo groover.

Mancha was also a veteran of the Detroit scene. His most notable tracks here are the heartbreakers *Don't Make A Storyteller* and *I Don't Wanna Lose You,* and *Just Keep On Loving Me,* a strong dancer that became a Top 20 R & B hit for bluesman Bobby Bland in 1970 (again produced by Don Davis). Mancha later settled down as co-lead singer (with Joe Stubbs) of 100 Proof Aged In Soul.

Darrell Banks had made his reputation with *Open The Door To Your Heart* in 1966. His Revilot tracks, collected on **Darrell Banks Is Here!,** oozed confidence and attitude, but on his 1969 Volt sides he mostly just sounds lost in the sauce, and this material has never been very highly rated. Buy this set for the Barnes and Mancha **Rare Stamps** tracks.

H–D–H Post-Motown – The Hot Wax/Invictus Years

158   Greatest Hits

Laura Lee

H–D–H/Fantasy 3903

Rip Off/Women's Love Rights/Love And Liberty/Her Picture Matches Mine/Two Lonely Pillows/You've Got To Save Me/I Can't Hold On Much Longer/Crumbs Off The Table/Since I Fell For You/Wedlock Is A Padlock/I'll Catch You When You Fall/ If You Can Beat Me Rockin' (You Can Have My Chair)/If I'm Good Enough To Love (I'm Good Enough to Marry)

The tough, independent women performers of today owe a strong debt to Laura Lee (b. Laura Newton, 1945, in Chicago, Illinois), who paved the way with such women's liberationist anthems as *Rip Off, Wedlock Is A Padlock, Love And Liberty,* and of course the song with which she will be forever associated, *Women's Love Rights.* Easily the toughest and raunchiest of the Hot Wax ladies, Laura Lee started by singing gospel in Detroit, recording several albums with the Meditation Singers for the HOB and Gospel labels owned by Carmen Murphy (HOB had some years earlier issued the early Berry Gordy production *I Need You* by Herman Griffin, supposedly the very first song published by Jobete Music). Switching over to secular material, Laura Lee made her debut on Ed Wingate's Ric-Tic label with *To Win Your Heart,* then recorded extensively for Chess, mostly in Muscle Shoals, Alabama. Her hits included the hard-core soul of *Dirty Man* and *Uptight Good Man* (both 1967). After two singles for Atlantic's Cotillion imprint she signed with Hot Wax in 1970, starting off with a bang with the stinging *Wedlock Is A Padlock.* With material penned by such ex-Motown stalwarts as William Weatherspoon, Richard "Popcorn" Wylie, and the H–D–H new jacks Greg Perry and Ron Dunbar, as well as H–D–H themselves, the style was set: Laura's powerful vocalizing and tough, streetwise lyrics, crystallized with driving drums and bass, strong piano, and guitar-work topped with dominant horns and vocal choruses. Lee could also deliver a ballad such as the old Buddy and Ella Johnson standard *Since I Fell For You*, on which she improvised a biting rap introduction. After her Hot Wax years, Lee recorded for Fantasy and Ariola Records, and has since returned to gospel.

159 Greatest Hits
Freda Payne

H–D–H/Fantasy 3905

Band Of Gold/The Unhooked Generation/Deeper And Deeper/Two Wrongs Don't Make A Right/You Brought The Joy/Through The Memory Of My Mind/Bring The Boys Home/Cherish What Is Dear To You (While It's Near To You)/I'm Not Getting Any Better/The Road We Didn't Take/I Shall Not Be Moved

Indelibly associated with her number 1 hit of 1970 *Band Of Gold*, a classic tale of wedding-night frustration, Freda Payne (b. September 19, 1945, in Detroit) originally intended to pursue a career in jazz, working in New York with the bands of Quincy Jones, Duke Ellington, Lionel Hampton, and Count Basie. In 1969 old schoolfriend Eddie Holland, perhaps viewing the ultra-glamorous Payne as his new Diana Ross (Payne's sister Scherrie actually served as a post-Ross Supreme in the 1970s), persuaded her to switch to R & B for his post-Motown Hot Wax/Invictus set-up. Payne was at her best on the bright, up-tempo numbers crafted for her by the likes of Ron Dunbar, General Johnson, William Weatherspoon, and Holland–Dozier–Holland themselves, with *Cherish*, *Deeper*, *Joy*, and *I Shall Not Be Moved* being sterling examples. A more bittersweet feeling surfaces on the mid-tempo melodrama *Memory*, and *The Road* provides a ballad for change of pace. But Payne reaches her peak on *Bring The Boys Home*, a chilling, commanding performance. Post-H–D–H recordings for Capitol and ABC are nice but less essential.

Payne makes an interesting contrast with her H–D–H label-mate Laura Lee: while the impudent but submissive Payne lay in her lonely room hoping her man would "come walking through that door and love me like you tried before," the altogether more gritty and streetwise Lee would have told her: "Wedlock is a padlock, honey, when you're married to a no-good man, so stand up and fight for your love rights!"

160 Greatest Hits
Honey Cone

H–D–H/Fantasy 3902

Want Ads/Stick Up/One Monkey Don't Stop No Show/The Day I Found Myself/Take Me With You/Woman Can't Live By Bread Alone/When Will It End/While You're Out Looking For Sugar/Girls It Ain't Easy/Sitting On A Time Bomb (Waiting For The Hurt To Come)/Innocent Till Proven Guilty/Ace In The Hole/The Truth Will Come Out/If I Can't Fly

Honey Cone (Edna Wright on lead, Shellie Clark, and Carolyn Willis) was formed when Andy Williams and Burt Bacharach brought these three experienced, West Coast session singers together to sing backup on a television special. Wright is the sister of Darlene Love (of Phil Spector fame) and, like her, has a big, gospel-trained voice. The group was one of the first signings to H–D–

H's Invictus/Hot Wax operation, making their debut with the Top 30 R & B hit *While You're Out Looking For Sugar*. From the start, the Honey Cone were presented as tough, impudent women – not girls – reaching a peak with their 1971 number 1 million-seller, *Want Ads*. Wright sings that for her new lover "experience in love preferred but will accept a young trainee:" this attitude is continued on their other hits such as *Stick Up, Girls It Ain't Easy*, and *One Monkey Don't Stop No Show*. Even a softer-edged song like *The Day I Found Myself* has a sting in it: "The day I lost you was the day I found myself." This album includes all of their hits, and a few oddities like the psychedelicized period piece *When Will It End*. The group's members were active and successful in Los Angeles in the early 1990s doing commercials and session work, although, as Wright, talking to Paul Williams, observed, "if we'd had hits at the beginning of the 1980s instead of the 1970s we would all be filthy rich right now."

161 Greatest Hits

100 Proof Aged In Soul

H–D–H/Fantasy HDH 3904

Somebody's Been Sleeping In My Bed/One Man's Leftovers (Is Another Man's Feast)/ 90 Day Freeze/ Everything Good Is Bad/Not Enough Love To Satisfy/Nothing Sweeter Than Love/Too Many Cooks (Spoil The Soup)/Driveway/Love Is Sweeter/Since You've Been Gone/Don't Scratch Where It Don't Itch/I'd Rather Fight Than Switch

100 Proof Aged In Soul was built around co-lead singers Joe Stubbs and Steve Mancha. Stubbs (brother of Four Tops' lead Levi) had previously sung lead (*You're So Fine*) with the Falcons in the late 1950s and had had some solo releases on Robert West's Lupine label in the mid-1960s. Co-lead singer Steve Mancha (b. Clyde Wilson) had also been around the Detroit scene for years, had written *For Better Or Worse* for Wilson Pickett, and recorded in the late 1960s for Don Davis's Groovesville label. When H–D–H set up their Hot Wax label they obviously saw this group as their new Four Tops (much as Freda Payne was their new Diana Ross), with the added bonus of Mancha's smoother, Marvin Gaye-influenced style added to a volatile mix. The rocking *Too Many Cooks* nudged the pop and R & B charts in late 1969, and paved the way for their million-seller *Somebody's Been Sleeping In My Bed* (written by Hot Wax producers Greg Perry and Angelo Bond, together with General Johnson of H–D–H's biggest group, Chairmen of the Board). They specialized in blunt, knowing tales of the sexual lives of adults (*One Man's Leftovers, Don't Scratch*), but could also purvey some extremely smooth and mellow sounds, as in *Love Is Sweeter*. Backup singer/ guitarist Ron Bykowski went on to join George Clinton's P-Funk Mob.

162 Greatest Hits

Chairmen Of The Board

H–D–H/Fantasy HDH 3901

Give Me Just A Little More Time/(You've Got Me) Dangling On A String/ Everything's Tuesday/Patches/Pay To The Piper/Bless You/Chairmen Of The Board/ Hanging On To A Memory/Try On My Love For Size/Men Are Getting Scarce/ Everybody's Got A Song To Sing/Let Me Down Easy/Finders Keepers/Bravo, Hooray/ Let's Have Some Fun

Chairmen of the Board (General Norman Johnson on lead, Danny Woods, Eddie Curtis, and Harrison Kennedy) were made distinctive by the high tenor voice of General Johnson. Former lead singer of the Showmen (*It Will Stand*), his overwrought warble sparked the up-tempo *Give Me Just A Little More Time*

(1970), the first million-seller for Invictus. Johnson was also a fine songwriter, having part-penned Freda Payne's *Bring The Boys Home* as well as Clarence Carter's hit *Patches* – included here is the melodramatic original. The group seldom strayed far from the Motown sound on their other hits, like *Pay To The Piper* and *Everything's Tuesday*, but their last hit, *Finders Keepers* (1973), is solid funk. General Johnson in the early 1990s was active on the Carolinas' beach-music scene, recording for the Surf Side label.

163   Rhenium
Parliament

Demon/HDH HDH CD008 (UK)

Breakdown/I Call My Baby Pussycat/Put Love In Your Life/Little Ole Country Boy/ Moonshine Heather/Oh Lord, Why Lord – Prayer/Red Hot Mama/My Automobile/ Nothing Before Me But Thang/Funky Woman/Livin' The Life/Come In Out Of The Rain/The Silent Boatman

This 1990 release is of recordings of George Clinton's Parliament group made while at Holland–Dozier–Holland's Invictus label, from 1970 to 1972. It includes the **Osmium** album he did in 1970, now a collector's item, plus three single sides that came out around the same time – *Breakdown, Red Hot Mama*, and *Come In Out Of The Rain*. This early funk-styled music never received the recognition it deserved, but years later it is evident that all the same elements present in these recordings are the same by which Clinton later achieved massive success with his Parliament/Funkadelic recording empire. One can hear heavy metal, jazz, funk, country, and soul group balladeering, even classical influences. Plus, there are the bizarre lyrics that so typified his later work. That Clinton could not connect with the public with these recordings shows how much he was ahead of his time.

The Soul Goes On – Recent Detroit Productions

164   Heavy Love
Dee Edwards

Cotillion SD 5212 (LP)

Don't Sit Down/Stranger On The Shore/Put The World On Hold/Long Long Time/ Loving You Is All I Want To Do/I Wanna Be Your Woman/Heavy Love/No Love No World

Dee Edwards (b. 1942, in Alabama) had seen a dozen singles released since 1962, mostly on local Detroit labels including Tuba, D-Town, and Bumpshop, and had even recorded on RCA before cutting her first album, with husband Floyd Jones as producer and the assistance of such former Motown sessionmen as Johnny Griffith (piano), Eddie Willis (guitar), and Uriel Jones (drums). Edwards excels both on the up-tempo items *Don't Sit Down, Loving You Is All I Want To Do*, and *Heavy Love* (written by longtime Motowner Barrett Strong), and on the ballads *I Wanna Be Your Woman* (by Edwards) and the old Acker Bilk standard *Stranger On The Shore*. Edwards followed this up with a much-inferior, disco-oriented album produced by Michael Zager, **Two Hearts Are Better Than One**, and since then it has been back to local Detroit singles releases.

165   Person To Person
Ortheia Barnes

Michigan Satellite MSR 508107 (LP)

Drive Me To Love/Touched/Green-Eyed Monster/Doin' The Do/I'll Give/Life (Ain't Complicated)/I Know Your Love Will See Me Through (In The Storm)/Person To Person

Ortheia Barnes (from Detroit, Michigan), an intense, gospel-inspired singer who has recorded for various small Detroit labels since 1962, had to wait nearly 25 years for her first album, on ex-Motown producer/writer Sylvia Moy's Michigan Satellite label. The younger sister of Northern soul legend J. J. Barnes, she shares some of his mellow, Marvin Gaye-touched style, reaching a peak on the smooth *Touched* and the driving *I'll Give*. Although poorly distributed (the same fate that befalls most modern Detroit soul productions), this album can and should be obtained directly from MSR.

Chicago 5

Robert Pruter

In the early 1990s, with the United States recording industry concentrated in New York, Nashville, and Los Angeles, it is hard to imagine Chicago was once a major center for the production and recording of soul music. But during the 1960s and 1970s, Chicago-style soul music was produced by such large homegrown labels as Vee Jay, Chess, Curtom, and Mercury, and such major labels as Columbia (through its OKeh subsidiary) and ABC–Paramount set up offices in the city and courted the city's African American talent. There were numerous lesser lights, many mere mom-and-pop operations, that also helped fuel the city's soul explosion – Brainstorm, Formal, Cortland/Witch, Nike/Tip Top, St Lawrence/Satellite, Giant, Four Brothers, One-derful – a veritable laundry list of names.

Many of the world's major soul acts, such as Jerry Butler, the Impressions, Gene Chandler, the Chi-lites, and the Dells, called Chicago their home. At one time, as many as one-third of all the records played on the city's black radio stations were locally produced, and, internationally, Chicago was putting as many records into the charts as such soul factories as Detroit, Memphis, and New York.

Michigan Avenue, just south of Chicago's downtown, was the city's "Record Row" and the center of its flourishing music scene. There the offices of Chess, Vee Jay, One-derful, ABC–Paramount, Constellation, and a host of record distributors were located. The distribution firms and the local radio stations, principally WVON, worked in symbiotic fashion to contribute immeasurably to the growth of the local record industry.

The first Chicago company to experience great success in the emerging soul market was Vee Jay, founded in 1953 by Vivian and James Bracken. For most of its history, as the largest black-owned record label before Motown, the company was headed by Ewart Abner, Jr. By the time the 1960s arrived, Vee Jay had become one of the nation's largest independents, and the company's creative department, under the direction of Calvin Carter, was in a strong position to make its presence felt in soul music. Some observers claim that Chicago's first soul record had indeed come out of Vee Jay – *For Your Precious Love* (1958) by Jerry Butler and the Impressions. The company was so impressed with Butler's soulful baritone that within months Carter split the young singer from the group and promoted him as a single artist. He went on to become one of Chicago's biggest hitmakers. Other successful Vee Jay recording artists were Dee Clark, Betty Everett, Fred Hughes, and Gene Chandler.

Abner left Vee Jay in 1963 and formed Constellation, taking with him Gene Chandler and Dee Clark. Chandler thrived on his new label but Clark struggled along with a host of other artists. Constellation could not survive on Chandler hits alone and went under in 1966. In the empty offices of Constellation, Bill "Bunky" Sheppard, who had worked with the Sheppards and Dukays at Vee Jay and Gene Chandler at Constellation, set up the small Bunky label, which recorded the Esquires.

OKeh was Columbia's longtime, independently distributed R & B subsidiary. By the early 1960s, however, the label was practically moribund, and in 1962 Columbia hired Carl Davis to serve as producer and A & R director of the label, based on his success with Gene Chandler's *Duke Of Earl*. He brought his own team of musicians and arrangers (principally Johnny Pate and Riley Hampton) and, most importantly, writer Curtis Mayfield. Within a year Davis had rejuvenated OKeh. The most successful OKeh artist was Major Lance, for whom Davis employed a deep brass sound to enhance Lance's reedy vocals. Davis also discovered Billy Butler, brother of Jerry Butler, and recorded the artist with his neighborhood friends in a vocal group, the Enchanters. Another OKeh artist was Detroit native Walter Jackson, the master of the love ballad.

After a dispute with Columbia executive Len Levy, Davis left OKeh in late 1965. Following several years of futile attempts to maintain the label, Columbia shut it down in 1970.

When the 1960s began, Chess Records, owned by Leonard and Phil Chess, had a group of bluesmen (such as Muddy Waters and Howlin' Wolf) and rock-and-rollers (most notably Chuck Berry and Bo Diddley). The company could hardly be said to have been ready for the coming soul era. But the Chess brothers adapted by bringing in from Detroit Roquel "Billy" Davis as A & R head and by beefing up their in-house production, arranging, and writing staff. During the 1960s Chess sustained itself with both hard soul acts (Etta James, Sugar Pie DeSanto, and Little Milton) and soft soul acts (Dells, Fontella Bass, the Radiants, and Billy Stewart). By the late 1960s Chess was producing few hits, except for the

Dells with producer Don Davis in Detroit. The in-house production team lost its touch and gradually drifted away from the company. Chess folded in 1975.

ABC–Paramount was based in New York, but in 1961 signed the Mayfield-led Impressions, which resulted in its signing a number of other Chicago acts too. By the early 1960s Mayfield had fully developed as a songwriter, and the Impressions had a hit with their very first ABC release, *Gypsy Woman* (1961). In the years after that, the group delivered hit after hit for the company with producer Johnny Pate. Mayfield also had considerable success recording acts for his own labels – Mayfield and Windy C – and got hits with the Fascinations and the Five Stairsteps. ABC had one other significant Chicago-based act, the Marvelows, who were produced by Johnny Pate.

A harder side of Chicago soul was provided by George Leaner in his One-derful operations. He specialized in Southern-style hard soul, best exemplified by Otis Clay, McKinley Mitchell, Harold Burrage, Johnny Sayles, the Sharpees, and the Five Du-Tones. The act that had the most hits for Leaner, much to his dismay, was an all-brother dance team from St Louis, Alvin Cash and the Crawlers, who chanted their way through a bevy of funky dance records, notably *Twine Time* (1964).

Leaner did not monopolize Chicago's hard-soul market. Syl Johnson, who developed as an artist in the city's blues community, had hits continuously on Twinight Records from 1967 to 1972 with funky, aggressive songs distinguished mostly by his sharp piercing vocals, and Bright Star/Four Brothers had hits in the hard-soul vein with blues harmonica-player Junior Wells, as well as with Johnny Moore and Ricky Allen.

For the 1970s the story of Chicago soul was basically that of Carl Davis and his productions at Brunswick. Outstanding releases early in Davis's tenure at Brunswick, before the 1970s had even arrived, were the Artistics, Gene Chandler, Jackie Wilson, and Barbara Acklin. During the next decade Davis was unable to achieve much success for these artists, but two acts – Tyrone Davis and the Chi-lites – became international superstars while at Brunswick.

Chicago's one major label, Mercury, which was founded in the city in 1945, was during the 1960s less than diligent in recording the city's soul talent, but in the 1970s woke up and signed a spate of Chicago acts, mainly Gene Chandler and Jerry Butler.

Curtis Mayfield's Curtom label was also active in the 1970s, recording the Impressions, the Natural Four, Leroy Hutson, Linda Clifford, and at least a dozen other acts besides Mayfield himself. But aside from Mayfield's own solo work, notably his **Superfly** soundtrack from 1972, there was very little that was truly distinguished about the company's output.

Essential Recordings

(i) The Vee Jay Balladeers

Jerry Butler's rich, warm baritone was put to great use on a spate of Vee Jay ballad hits, which perfectly epitomized the Chicago style of light and subtle soul during the early and mid-1960s. Butler was born in Sunflower, Mississippi, on December 8, 1939, but when he was three years of age he went with his parents to Chicago. Butler struggled at first, scoring some minor hits – *Lost*, *Rainbow Valley*, and *A Lonely Soldier* – in the two years after his separation from the Impressions. These songs were somewhat in the pop mode and had the same kind of fluffy arrangements as Atlantic was putting out on its R & B artists at the time. A flute, tinkling piano, chirpy girl chorus, syrupy strings, and bouncy rhythm did not work that well with Butler's forceful vocal approach. The songs were good, but producer Calvin Carter was saddling them with ill-advised production.

In 1960 Butler began working with Curtis Mayfield, who replaced Phil Upchurch as his guitarist on the road. The Impressions were somewhat moribund at this time, and Mayfield started touring, writing, and recording with Butler. Their first collaboration was *He Will Break Your Heart*, Butler's first number 1 R & B record and a Top 20 pop-charter. Its pop success was ironic, because the record eschews the pop arrangements of Butler's earlier discs and has a blacker, tauter sound. It is set to a Brazilian baiao rhythm, which had great popularity in the early 1960s, especially on records recorded in New York City.

During 1961 Butler sustained his recording career with two other fine collaborations with Mayfield, *Find Another Girl* and *I'm A Telling You*. Mayfield then left Butler to take leadership of a newly revived Impressions group. Butler recorded a thoroughly pop song, Henry Mancini and Johnny Mercer's *Moon River*, which was both an R & B hit and a crossover hit in late 1961. Since the late 1960s, when rock critics began evaluating Jerry Butler, based on his tremendous success recording for Gamble and Huff in Philadelphia for Mercury, *Moon River* has been used ignorantly and mindlessly to condemn the singer's Vee Jay output as pop fluff. That this charge is absurb is evident upon hearing the following tracks, not to mention most of the preceding ones.

The year 1962 was weak for Butler in recording terms. The one bright star was the Burt Bacharach and Hal David song, *Make It Easy On Yourself*. Another equally good Bacharach–David song, *Message To Martha*, was inexcusably kept in the can until it surfaced on a greatest hits collection several years later. Dionne

Warwick, who built her career on Bacharach–David songs, got sizable hits with both of those songs several years later.

Butler came out with a number of fine records in 1963, but did not have a hit again until he put out the sublime Mayfield ballad, *Need To Belong*. The song is one of his most soulful, and solidly brought Butler into the soul era.

Butler's best year with Vee Jay was 1964. The hauntingly soulful *Giving Up On Love* was a big hit for him in the spring, and the summer produced the best double-sided record of his career, with two ballads – *I Stand Accused* (written by his brother Billy) and *I Don't Want To Hear Anymore* (one of Randy Newman's earliest and best songs). Butler was also compatibly teamed up with stablemate Betty Everett for a series of successful duets, notably *Let It Be Me*, which can be found on Charly's Everett collection.

The years 1965 and 1966 were wasted for Butler. Vee Jay was in financial trouble and the in-house creative staff was breaking down. Vee Jay seemed unable to match Butler with good songs. In desperation, the company had Butler record a remake of *For Your Precious Love*, which is not bad and even nudged into the charts in 1966, just before Vee Jay went bankrupt.

Gene Chandler's one claim to rock-and-roll fame is *Duke Of Earl* (1962); but as a soul star Chandler was a giant, having had more than 25 national pop hits during the 1960s and 1970s. His artistry rests in his voice; though in a technical sense somewhat limited in range and lacking in resonance and tone quality (and a bit flat), it has a personality and clarity of expression that are magnificent. This timbre, as musicologists would call his vocal coloration and intonations, is often hard for the uninitiated to grasp; they do not hear all the nuances and subtleties that separate soul music from pop, but Chandler sings lyrically uncomplicated songs that are highly sophisticated in their manner of expression. Some might want to call it a folk expression, in that his style is an unconscious art form shaped by the experiences and non-esthetic concerns of African American youth on the streets of his home town of Chicago. To know Chandler and understand his music is to truly appreciate what the "soul" is in soul music.

Chandler (b. Eugene Dixon, July 6, 1937, in Chicago) came out of the vocal harmony, or doo-wop, tradition of the 1950s, when the cities were alive with the sounds of harmonizing street-corner ensembles all in vigorous competition with one another. Chandler thus first made his mark as lead singer of the Dukays, a group that began singing doo-wop, but by the time they got on record in 1961 soul was making its influences felt and the group was singing something in between. In *Girl Is A Devil* (not included here) and *Nite Owl* the Dukays made the national charts in 1961 with a transitional music that bridged the doo-wop and soul eras. The songs were forcefully and aggressively sung with gospel passion, but with doo-wop stylings still intact. Perhaps the penultimate transitional hit for the Dukays was the *Duke Of Earl* (1962).

The *Duke Of Earl* was indeed recorded by the Dukays, but through a marketing decision, based on a switch of record companies from Nat to Vee Jay, the name of the artist was changed to "Gene Chandler," the name Dixon chose to record under. The song was composed by members of the group with songwriter Bernice Williams. The obvious appeal of the song is the haunting chant of "Duke Duke Duke, Duke of Earl, Duke Duke, Duke of Earl, Duke Duke, Duke of Earl," and that is what made the record a memorable rock-and-roll hit; but what made it a great proto-soul record was the magnificent stylings of Chandler, especially on the bridge where he sings in falsetto. Other Dukays recordings that were successes on this collection are *The Big Lie* and *Festival Of Love*.

With the success of *Duke Of Earl*, a number 1 hit in the country in both R & B and pop charts, Vee Jay rushed out an album, which naturally contained many of Chandler's Dukays recordings and a few new Chandler solo efforts, but as was the custom of the day most of the cuts were covers of then popular tunes. This Charly collection contains several of these, namely *Stand By Me* (the Ben E. King hit), *Daddy's Home* (Shep and the Limelights), *I Wake Up Crying* (Chuck Jackson), and *Turn On Your Love Light* (Bobby Bland). As well as these quick covers hold up today, their inclusion is unfortunate, since they displace a number of later Chandler hits on Constellation and far superior recordings that belong in the collection.

Chandler failed to sustain his rock-and-roll success with follow-up hits. The public saw through the contrived sound-alike *Walk On With The Duke*, and records after that did not achieve much. By the end of 1962, however, Chandler found his niche as an up-and-coming soul star when *Tear For Tear* found a place on the R & B stations' playlists. The record has a sparkling bounce to it, but because of its mid-tempo it did not have a chance for rock-and-roll crossover. Soul fans understood it, however. The record was followed with a respectable answer song to Mary Wells's *You Beat Me To The Punch*, called *You Threw A Lucky Punch*. It was the flip to this record, *Rainbow*, a ballad written by Curtis Mayfield, that sealed Chandler's relationship with the soul audience.

Rainbow is a deep-soul ballad, somewhat out of character for Chandler, but the singer saw the song as a perfect vehicle to establish his soul credentials and pushed the record everywhere he went, and soon the deejays flipped *You Threw A Lucky Punch* to make *Rainbow* the bigger R & B hit. The song is sometimes difficult for less-than-devoted soul fans to appreciate, because it sounds so stark and painful. And Chandler sings flatter than usual.

Man's Temptation (1963) is another Mayfield composition that was a hit for Chandler, and with it the classic Chandler treatment is established – mellow, soulful, and intense, but not gut-wrenching as in his *Rainbow* performance.

Chandler moved to Constellation in the fall of 1963, but his first release, *It's No Good For Me*, was a flop. Listening to this appealing dramatic ballad, one can see why it did not sell. The arrangement probably sounded dated to the emerging soul audience in 1963. After the next release also failed, Sheppard brought in Carl Davis, who was at OKeh at the time, to save the situation. Davis from then on was producing Chandler surreptitiously, and his next production for Chandler, Mayfield's *Think Nothing About It*, is a gem. It proved to be a modest hit, though, in early 1964. The next record, *A Song Called Soul*, is a Mayfield up-tempo number somewhat in the mode of Major Lance's *Um Um Um Um Um Um*. Had Lance done it, perhaps it would have been a hit.

The remainder of 1964 proved far more fruitful for Chandler, when he came out with a succession of stunning ballads. The first of these, *Just Be True*, a Mayfield composition naturally, was his biggest hit since *Duke Of Earl*, and established Chandler as a soul superstar. He followed with another big hit, the splendid Billy Butler song *Bless Our Love*, which inexcusably is not included in this collection. *What Now*, Chandler's third Top 10 hit in a row, is another Mayfield composition that is somewhat derivative from the two previous hits, but is solid nonetheless.

Chandler's Constellation years were truly his golden era, as it seemed every release proved to be either a blockbuster commercial hit or an artistic triumph. The year 1965 was no less successful than 1964, with five records in the charts, three included here: *You Can't Hurt Me No More* is a remake of the Opals' local hit from a year earlier, and features a magnificent wall-of-sound orchestral backing. *Nothing Can Stop Me* is a delightful up-tempo anthem of positive thinking. *(Gonna Be) Good Times* is a fabulous sound of summer, capturing the atmosphere of the streets in Chicago in the mid-1960s. The omissions are *Rainbow 65*, a splendid live recording from Chandler at the Regal Theater in Chicago, and *Here Come The Tears*, a Gerald Sims ballad that Chandler achingly and superbly emoted at his best.

For most of 1966, Chandler had little success in the national charts, but he was nonetheless coming out with good records, including two marvelous mid-tempo numbers, *Bet You Never Thought* and *(I'm Just A) Fool For You*. Both records were played frequently in Chicago, but not much in other parts of the country, which may explain why they are not included in this collection. One more Chandler record in 1966 made the local charts, *I Can Take Care Of Myself*, but it was not an inspiring disc. Constellation was rapidly running down both creatively and in terms of marketing, and by the summer of 1966, the label had closed its doors. Chandler continued his productive ways on two other Chicago labels, Brunswick and Checker, with Carl Davis producing for both.

Discographical Details

66   Soul Workshop
Jerry Butler

Charly R & B 54 (UK)

For Your Precious Love/Sweet Was The Wine/He Will Break Your Heart/Find Another Girl/I'm A Telling You/Aware Of Love/Moon River/I'm The One Who Loves You/Make It Easy On Yourself/You Can Run (But You Can't Hide)/Whatever You Want/Message To Martha/Where's The Girl/Need To Belong/Giving Up On Love/I've Been Trying/I Don't Want To Hear Anymore/I Stand Accused/I Can't Stand To See You Cry/Nobody Needs Your Love/Just For You/For Your Precious Love (remake)

67   Stand By Me
Gene Chandler

Charly R & B 55 (UK)

Duke Of Earl/The Big Lie/Nite Owl/Festival Of Love/Stand By Me/Daddy's Home/I Wake Up Crying/Turn On Your Love Light/Tear For Tear/You Threw A Lucky Punch/Rainbow/Check Yourself/Baby That's Love/Man's Temptation/It's No Good For Me/Think Nothing About It/A Song Called Soul/Just Be True/What Now/You Can't Hurt Me No More/Nothing Can Stop Me/(Gonna Be) Good Times

(ii) The Chicago Sound Of OKeh

The most successful artist in this collection is Major Lance (b. April 4, 1941, in Chicago). Aside from the Curtis Mayfield-led Impressions, he was the largest-selling artist from Chicago in the years in the mid-1960s, when he was on OKeh. His thin but interestingly forceful vocals were perfectly showcased by producer Carl Davis, and the result was a series of sparkling dance records that virtually defined the more energetic side of the "Chicago Sound," as OKeh then marketed Davis productions. For Lance, he employed a deep, rich brass sound, perhaps the brassiest in the country. Especially prominent was the use of the bass trombone and its characteristic bleating riffing. Compiler Joe McEwen wisely concentrates on selecting Lance's best without regard to hit status, and the result is eight simply indispensable tracks.

The first tune Lance recorded for Davis is a Mayfield tune, *Delilah*, which was no bigger than a minor hit in 1962. Nonetheless, it is a marvelous tune with the patented Chicago lope and Johnny Pate's piano-led arrangement, which perfectly showcases Lance's vocals. Pate had not yet developed the bass trombone-dominated brass arrangements for Lance.

That came in the summer of 1963 with Lance's immense *Monkey Time* hit. The Mayfield song not only launched Lance's career but established OKeh as a force in the emerging soul market. Two more Mayfield hits followed. In the fall there was the delightful *Hey Little Girl*, with its deep brass sound and its monkey beat and theme, and in the winter, *Um Um Um Um Um Um*, the second biggest hit of Lance's career. With Lance at this peak, OKeh released an album called **Um Um Um Um Um Um: The Best Of Major Lance**, and it was further subtitled, "The great songs of Curtis Mayfield." It is one of the most outstanding albums of Chicago soul ever produced and therefore in this chapter's "Basic Recordings" section despite its age. McEwen includes two numbers from that LP, *You'll Want Me Back* and *Think Nothing About It*. The latter came out on a single, but it is very rare, apparently withdrawn by OKeh because Gene Chandler had come out with a version on Constellation.

Breaking the string of Mayfield songs was *The Matador*, written by Lance, Carl Davis, and Billy Butler, and it easily kept the run of Lance hits alive during early 1964. Lance's next record, *It Ain't No Use/Girls* (neither side included here), was a double-sided hit during the summer. Although both are fine Mayfield tunes and rank among Lance's strongest efforts, they did not do as well in the charts as his previous efforts. Lance bounced back with another big Mayfield record, *Rhythm*; although it echoes previous efforts, the formula is so winning that the record raced up the charts in the early fall.

Lance continued his string of chart records with OKeh through 1968, notably with three 1965 hits not included in this collection – *Sometimes I Wonder, Come See*, and *Ain't It A Shame*. The last of these was also the last Lance chart record written by Mayfield, and without the remarkable songwriting talents of his neighborhood friend, Lance's career went into decline.

One of the most compelling acts on OKeh was Billy Butler (b. June 7, 1945, in Chicago) and the Enchanters. The lead vocalist and songwriter of the group is the younger brother of Jerry Butler. Although Billy's substantive body of Curtis Mayfield-styled work is not as well known as that of his brother and other Chicago artists, it ranks with the best. Butler specialized in bright, vigorous, and highly melodic songs, but he is equally at home with mid-tempo and ballad material. On all his songs, his controlled and slightly gospelly vocals lend just enough intensity to give the songs that rich, soulful feeling. Unfortunately McEwen could only find room for four Butler sides.

Found True Love, a collaboration by Butler and Mayfield, was released in late summer of 1963, and sold well enough to establish the name of the group in the Midwest. Of all the group's songs, it best reflects the close-harmony, 1950s doo-wop tradition, probably because it had more voices than most of the later records (five in all). On the group's next record, the spirited *Gotta Get Away*, the group was reduced to three – Butler, Errol Batts and Jesse Tillman. This record too was a regional hit, and the string of regional successes continued during 1964 with the splendid, mid-tempo *Can't Live Without Her* and the faster and more frenetic *Nevertheless* (neither included here).

The group's biggest and last hit was another Mayfield composition, *I Can't Work No Longer* (1965), a rousing number in the *Chain Gang* tradition. Mayfield revived this song for his **Short Eyes** soundtrack of the prison movie of the same name from 1977, calling it *Need Someone To Love*. The Enchanters broke up shortly after *I Can't Work No Longer* left the charts. OKeh released one last record by the group under Butler's name alone, *(You Make Me Think) You Ain't Ready*, a Mayfield song that had the punch of a Major Lance record. It did not get into the charts.

Butler got a solo national hit in 1966 with the energetic *Right Track*, which unfortunately is not included in this collection. Shortly afterwards, Davis took Butler with him to Brunswick, but unlike the Artistics, who went on to bigger success at Brunswick, Butler failed to get anything going. As a retrospective of Billy Butler's career, **OKeh Soul** is obviously inadequate. Besides the earlier mentioned omissions, others are *I'm Just A Man*, *Tomorrow Is Another Day*, and *You Ain't Ready*.

Walter Jackson (b. March 19, 1938, in Pensacola, Florida) is an interpreter of song, especially the love ballad, and at OKeh he helped marvelously to define the Chicago Sound of soul. His husky baritone is in the mode of such sophisticated pop luminaries as Arthur Prysock and Billy Eckstine, but it has been put to superb use on R & B song and ballads with an R & B flavor. The end result is obviously a brand of pop soul, but Jackson is far more adult and subtle than the pop-soul Motown artists. The six songs chosen to represent the singer are a perfect selection.

Jackson was discovered in 1962 by Carl Davis, singing in a Detroit nightclub, and the producer brought him to Chicago to record. The first three singles – released on OKeh's parent label, Columbia – were below par. But in early 1964 Jackson released a superb double-sided single on OKeh, *That's What Mama Say/ What Would You Do*. The A side is an evocative, mid-tempo answer to Jan Bradley's *Mama Didn't Lie*, and the flip is a simply lovely ballad. It was not the change of labels that resulted in the sudden improvement in quality in the material; it was the songwriting talents of Curtis Mayfield. Although neither side got into the charts, Mayfield was able to get Jackson his first hit later in 1964 with *It's All Over*. The flip, *Lee Cross* (not included here), was originally recorded by Aretha Franklin, but Jackson was able to get it played widely. More Davis-produced national hits followed in quick succession: the wistful *Suddenly I'm All Alone* (1965), the magnificent *Welcome Home* (1965), and the sophisticated *Funny (Not Much)* (1966). Only *Welcome Home* has found its way into this collection.

Davis departed at the end of 1965, but Jackson continued his hitmaking ways with new producer Ted Cooper. Although the sessions took place in New York, Cooper kept perfectly to the Chicago-style sound established by Davis, by using the same Chicago musicians and arrangers. The first Cooper-produced release, in 1966, featured two rousing numbers, *It's An Uphill Climb (To The Bottom)*, backed by a wonderful remake of the old Gene Chandler hit, *Tear For Tear*. Only the former made the national charts, but in Chicago both sides were well played. Other strong Cooper-produced hits came in quick succession: *After You There Can Be Nothing* (1966), *A Corner In The Sun* (1966), and one of his biggest, the hauntingly beautiful *Speak Her Name* (1967). *My Ship Is Coming In* (1967), a powerful remake of the Jimmy Radcliffe hit from 1965, never made the charts. Unfortunately, of the Cooper-produced sides only this song and *It's An Uphill Climb (To The Bottom)* are on this CD.

My Ship Is Coming In ended a remarkable three-year period for Jackson, in which he, with his producers, created a formidable and enduring body of music that easily ranks with the best soul music of the day. Then the good songs stopped coming, and Jackson did not return to the charts until he joined up with Carl Davis on Chi-Sound again in 1976. Jackson died in 1983.

The weakest parts of **OKeh Soul** are the last six cuts by the Opals, the Artistics, and the Vibrations. For the Opals (led by the emotive voice of Rose Addison) a better inclusion would have been *You Can't Hurt Me No More*, a truly majestic Mayfield composition, instead of the teen-beat *Does It Matter*. Possible other inclusions could have been *Restless Days* and *I'm So Afraid*. Two other delightful teen-girl sound OKeh records from this period were the Kavettes' *You Broke Your Promise* and Marlina Mars's *Just Another Dance*.

The Vibrations, except for *Sloop Dance* and *Watusi Time*, neither of which is included here, worked in an altogether different vein than Chicago artists, and could have easily been omitted in favor of more Butler and Jackson. The Artistics' three Detroit-style songs are the best of their recordings, so the listener gets a good selection there. The group's full OKeh output is discussed in the "Basic Recordings" section.

From the foregoing, it should be obvious that **OKeh Soul**, despite its essential nature, is inadequate in representing the label's soul output during the 1960s. In 1987 Columbia released two LP greatest-hits collections on Walter Jackson and Major

Lance, and if they had been on CD, they would have been included in this survey.

Discographical Details

68   OKeh Soul
Various Artists

CBS Special Products A 37321
Major Lance: *Delilah/The Monkey Time/Um Um Um Um Um Um/Hey Little Girl/ You'll Want Me Back/Think Nothing About It/The Matador/Rhythm*; Billy Butler and the Enchanters: *Found True Love/(You Make Me Think) You Ain't Ready/ Gotta Get Away/I Can't Work No Longer*; Walter Jackson: *Welcome Home/That's What Mama Say/What Would You Do/My Ship Is Coming In/It's An Uphill Climb (To The Bottom)/It's All Over*; The Opals: *Does It Matter*; The Artistics: *Patty Cake/Get My Hands On Some Lovin'/This Heart Of Mine*; The Vibrations: *Misty/ Forgive And Forget*

(iii) Chess Shouters And Smoothies

Etta James was Chess's first soul star. The singer had initially made a name for herself at the age of 17 with the early rock-and-roll hit *Wallflower* (a.k.a. *Roll With Me Henry* – see chapter 1), in 1955, but when she joined Chess in 1959 she had been unsuccessful for several years, commercially though not artistically. Her career at Chess was one of ups and downs, but she was prolifically recorded by the company and she had innumerable hits, showcasing her biting, intense vocals. She best represents Chess's hard-soul output.

James's first work at Chess was as a duo with Harvey Fuqua, who was in the process of disengaging from the Moonglows to get into A & R work and producing. As Etta and Harvey, the duo had a fine double-sided hit in 1960, *My Heart Cries/If I Can't Have You* (which unfortunately are not on this collection). These songs looked back to the rhythm-and-blues era rather than forward to the soul era. The future would come with James's work as a solo artist.

With James, Chess launched it new era of recording soul with a beefed-up production, arranging, and writing staff. James's output during her first several years at the company was primarily string-laden ballads, many of them old standards. The healthy tension generated between the pop-like arrangements of Riley Hampton and the gospel-blues vocals of James produced an early type of soul heavy on melodrama. From 1960 through 1962 most of her songs were of this type, and most were Top 10 hits in the R & B market. James became a major soul artist.

James's first solo hit, *All I Could Do Was Cry* (1960), was brought from Detroit by Billy Davis, and it helped facilitate his entry into the Chess organization as A & R man/producer the following year. James quickly followed with an excellent Paul Gayton tune, *My Dearest Darling* (1960), a remake of a Glenn Miller song, *At Last* (1961), and a remake of a Wayne King song, *Trust In Me* (1961). All the above songs appeared on James's first Chess album, **At Last** (1960), which also included a great remake of *A Sunday Kind Of Love* (1961). The album was an explosive debut.

James in 1961 came out with her **Second Time Around** album, which, though filled with delights, yielded only two hits, a Billy Davis bluesy original, *Don't Cry Baby* (1961), not included in this collection, and another standard remake, *Fool That I Am* (1961). James's third Chess album, **Etta James** (1962), unleashed a new, incendiary artist with a raw, shouting style as featured on the hit single from the LP, *Something's Got A Hold On Me* (1962). Another LP track, and the flip to the single, was a magnificent ballad from the pens of Burt Bacharach and Bob Hilliard, *Waiting For Charlie To Come Home*. James closed the year with two more melodramatic ballads, *Stop The Wedding* and *Would It Make Any Difference To You* (the latter not included), and a blues, *Next Door To The Blues*. An album of standard ballads, **Etta James Sings For Lovers**, also made its appearance and got a good reception.

By 1963, with the emergence of soul as the predominant R & B style, James's records became harder and more aggressive as blaring horns replaced strings and the beat became heavier and more insistent. Launching her in this phase were *Two Sides (To Every Story)* (1963) (not included here), *Pushover* (1963), and *Baby, What You Want Me To Do* (1964). The last was a remake of a Jimmy Reed blues that was recorded live at the New Era Club in Nashville, Tennessee. The entire set was released in 1964 as **Etta James Rocks The House**.

After 1963, James's hits became more sporadic. She was fighting a drug habit, and for that reason the company's commitment to her career was perhaps not all it could have been. She did come up with two minor hard-soul hits in 1964, *Loving You More Every Day* and *Mellow Fellow* (neither included in this set), which were taken from her worthy **Queen Of Soul** album. Virtually nothing was released on James during 1965–6, while she was trying to get her personal life into shape; there was only a duet with Chess stablemate Sugar Pie DeSanto. In 1968, Chess, whose house production system had lost steam, sent James to Muscle Shoals, Alabama, and the result was a rejuvenation of her career. Four songs in this collection – *Tell Mama*, *I'd Rather Go Blind*, *Steal Away*, and *Security* – are from her Muscle Shoals work, which is discussed in chapter 6.

The Telstar collection, poorly illustrated and devoid of liner notes, could have been a lot better package by 1990s standards.

But it is the most solid and complete collection available. An ideal collection would be a two-CD box set, which is large enough to make available all the great songs whose absence was lamented above. James deserves a kind of collection that is on a par with those of Chess's famous bluesmen or rock-and-rollers.

The Dells were Chess's biggest hitmakers in the soft-soul vein. They began in 1953, singing impassioned doo-wops under the corner street-lamps in their hometown of Harvey, Illinois, and during the 1950s with Johnny Funches as lead they had a hit with the classic *Oh What A Nite*. The group broke up in 1958, and when they came together again in 1960, without Funches, they brought in ex-Flamingos falsetto tenor Johnny Carter, a move that had a tremendous impact on their sound. Raspy-voiced baritone Marvin Junior sang the principal lead, reflecting the greater forcefulness of soul, but more often than not Carter would come in with a sweet-sounding answering lead. Tenor Verne Allison, baritone Mickey McGill, and bass Chuck Barksdale created the basic harmony for the chorus, but Carter often joined in to add an outstanding edge on the top. The Dells worked brilliantly to create a diversity of sounds, usually with frequent and technically precise switch-offs on the leads and the choruses. This ability was matched by very few groups.

Although obviously loaded with talent, the Dells did not burst into the 1960s. They had a minor hit in 1961 on Chess's Argo label, *The (Bossa Nova) Bird* (not included here), and after a return to their 1950s label, Vee Jay, they got another minor hit in 1965 with *Stay In My Corner*, written by Barrett Strong and Wade Flemons (both recording artists in their own right).

In 1966 the Dells signed with Chess, where the company placed them on the Cadet label (a successor to Argo). They got a little success with two Billy Davis productions, *Thinking About You* and *Run For Cover*, that got the group some notices and modest national chart success. The latter is included here, but both are rousing, up-tempo numbers that reflect well on the group.

Davis and arranger Phil Wright were the golden team that put out most of Chess's soul hits in the 1960s, but in 1967 the Dells ended up with a new producing team, songwriter Bobby Miller and arranger Charles Stepney. It was a magical marriage, and the Dells were explosively successful as hitmakers during the late 1960s and early 1970s.

The first success the Dells had with Miller and Stepney was a richly harmonized ballad, *O-O-I Love You* (1967). Surprisingly, the tremendous jump, *There Is*, was relegated to the B side; but after it started getting played heavily in Philadelphia, Chess put out a separate release of the song, and it became the Dells' first pop smash. *Wear It On Our Face*, a rousing, up-tempo number in the same vein as *There Is*, continued the Dells' hit streak. The group magnificently brings the listener into the song by humming the opening lick and following with a vocal "whoo whoo" riff in the repeat of the same lick. Chess then released the Dells' marvelous **There Is** album, their all-time best, a perfect blend of doo-wop with the triumphant sound of soul.

The song that put the Dells into the big time was a remarkable remake of *Stay In My Corner* (1968), which became the Dells' first number 1 R & B hit and first Top 10 pop hit. Barksdale explains how the remake came about: "We brought up redoing the song to Stepney. The song was quite long so Charles suggested we cut it down. We said no, stating that we preferred to stay with the long version, which was the exact same way we were singing it in concerts. We ended up recording *Stay In My Corner* in its entirety, six minutes and ten seconds long."

A long-overlooked gem in the Dells' *oeuvre* is *Love Is So Simple*, which got lost as the ballad-flip of *Stay In My Corner*. The song features a rich, thick harmony that makes the listener melt. The song is typical in showing every aspect of the Dells' richly creative approach, from the use of Barksdale's magnificent bass to fill holes and provide flavorings to the separation of the harmony on the talking bridge part.

The Dells could hardly have been expected to top the success of the **There Is** album, which contained six chart hits, but **Always Together** and its title song were respectable efforts. *Always Together* (1968) epitomizes the Dells' genuine group approach, with the Junior–Carter switch-off leads that segue into the splendid harmonized choruses. The song has been adopted by the group as their signature song for their long career with just one change in personnel. Two other nice cuts from the LP that were hits for the Dells in 1969 were *Does Anybody Know I'm Here* and *I Can't Do Enough* (neither included in this set).

Miller and Stepney continued their commercially winning ways with the **Love Is Blue** album from 1969. It contained only one new song, but produced some strong singles. The first, *I Can Sing A Rainbow-Love Is Blue*, a medley, raced up the charts in the spring. The album and single were undeniable successes, but some critics (including this one) feel that these were not the best recordings of the Dells. Almost every song on the **Love Is Blue** LP was given an overblown and inflated arrangement, to milk the most drama possible from each song, featuring pretentious breaks to allow Junior to shout his lyrics declaratively over the thunderous background.

One bright spot on the LP was the Dells' 1969 remake of their 1956 hit, *Oh What A Night* (now spelled correctly). It was the group's only other number 1 record besides *Stay In My Corner*. Normally when artists attempt re-recordings of their old hits the magic is not there, but *Oh What A Night* works, helped immeasurably by Barksdale's opening recitation. Among the patented Dells tricks featured in the song is the technique whereby Junior holds the note and Carter pushes off it for a great contrast. Another album cut, *Sitting On The Dock Of The Bay*, followed on the charts – the Otis Redding hit dreadfully speeded up, Dells style. Another cut from the LP, *Glory Of Love*, got a belated release and entered the lower reaches of the soul charts in 1971. (Thankfully, neither of these numbers appears on this collection.)

At the end of 1969, the Dells came out with perhaps their second-best Miller–Stepney album collaboration, **Like It Is, Like It Was**, one side containing new, strong material and the other remakes of doo-wop oldies. The first single from the LP was a double-sided hit – a smooth new Miller ballad, *Open Up My Heart*, and a remake of an oldie, *Nadine*. *Open Up My Heart*, included here in the long album version, is most serene, and the arpeggio guitar work gives it a nice lyrical feel. I find it tremendously boring. *Nadine*, which rode its coat-tails, was originally done for Chess records in 1954 by the Coronets. The Dells retain the flavor of the original, especially in the use of Carter's floating tenor, so redolent of the age of doo-wop, yet update the song marvelously for the soul market. Another successful single from the LP was a superb McGill neo-doowop, *Oh What A Day* (not included here).

Chess was failing fast during the early 1970s, but the one act that kept the company alive was the Dells. The year 1971 saw the Dells enter a new phase of their career with the first Chess album without the services of Bobby Miller, **Freedom Means**. Produced and arranged by Charles Stepney, the album yielded one outstanding single, *The Love We Had (Stays On My Mind)*, an engaging ballad that proved to be the Dells' biggest hit in two years. The song came from Jerry Butler's Writers Workshop and was from the pens of Terry Callier and Al Wade.

Stepney was failing to produce hits with the Dells, and the new president of the company, Marv Schlacter, had lost faith in the producer. He sent the Dells to Detroit in 1973 to record under producer Don Davis, who had developed a good track record with Johnnie Taylor and such Detroit-based acts as J. J. Barnes, Steve Mancha, and the Dramatics. Davis found the magic groove; the Dells' career was rejuvenated, notably with the million-selling *Give Your Baby A Standing Ovation* (1973). Davis most effectively uses an ersatz live approach with MC introduction and crowd noises to give the feeling of a live concert.

Later in the year, the Dells came out with their first all-Davis produced album, called simply **The Dells**, which yielded two fine hits, *My Pretending Days Are Over* and *I Miss You*. *My Pretending Days Are Over* (1973) is one of the group's great overlooked ballads. It contains terrific lyrics that effectively use the metaphor of an actor to explain the love relationship. *I Miss You* (1973) is one of the best examples using Junior's gruff baritone to create a sweat-drenched, sexy atmosphere.

One of the best of the Davis-produced hits is *I Wish It Was Me You Loved* (1974), featuring a more subdued, almost tender, lead by Junior, who as always is answered beautifully in chorus by the rest of the Dells. *Learning To Love You Was Easy* (1974) is a refreshingly different, hard-driving number in which Junior performs with great elan. The fine, mid-tempo flip, *Bring Back The Love Of Yesterday*, also got into the charts, but is not included here. Despite the R & B chart success of these singles, they achieved nothing on the pop charts. By 1974 soul was fading as a force in the pop market, and the Dells were no longer crossover hitmakers.

Discographical Details

169   The Best Of Etta James
Etta James
Telstar 3505
I'd Rather Go Blind/At Last/Stop The Wedding/Tell Mama (Tell Daddy)/Dance With Me Henry/Something's Got A Hold On Me/Trust In Me/All I Could Do Was Cry/Steal Away/Pushover/Fool That I Am/Security/My Dearest Darling/Baby, What You Want Me To Do/A Sunday Kind Of Love/Spoonful (duet with Harvey Fuqua)/Waiting For Charlie To Come Home/Next Door To The Blues

170   On Their Corner: The Best Of The Dells
The Dells
Chess/MCA CHD-9333
Oh What A Night/Wear It On Our Face/Love Is So Simple/I Can Sing A Rainbow – Love Is Blue/O-O-I Love You/There Is/Nadine/The Love We Had (Stays On My Mind)/Run For Cover/Stay In My Corner/Give Your Baby A Standing Ovation/Always Together/Open Up My Heart/I Miss You/Since I Found You/My Pretending Days Are Over/Learning To Love You Was Easy/I Wish It Was Me You Loved

(iv) Curtis Mayfield and the Impressions

The Impressions are among the giants of the soul era and belong in everybody's essential soul collection. Following their initial huge success on Vee Jay with *For Your Precious Love* in 1958, the group drifted after losing their lead, Jerry Butler. But in 1961 Curtis Mayfield gathered the group together and went to New York to record their first record for ABC–Paramount Records, *Gypsy Woman*. At this time the group consisted of (besides Mayfield) Sam Gooden, Fred Cash, and brothers Arthur and Richard Brooks. Mayfield wrote a light, delicate song to match his high-tenor lead and the subdued chorusing by the rest of the group. The use of castanets and muted instrumental support gives the song a dreamlike, fantasy flavor. *Gypsy Woman* became a big hit in 1961 and launched the Impressions on a long and illustrious career.

The light, airy *Grow Closer Together* and the jaunty *Little Young Lover* were modest chart successes in 1962. *Never Let Me Go*, the old Johnny Ace hit, was the outstanding flip to the latter, in which the Impressions use neo-doo-wop harmonies to create a flavorful rendition. *Minstrel And Queen* is another feathery-light fantasy in the same vein as *Gypsy Woman*, and a sizable hit in 1962. *I'm The One Who Loves You* is another solid effort, but upon its release in 1963 it failed to enter the charts anywhere. It was the last release in which the Brooks brothers were a part of the Impressions; they left before the end of 1963.

The new three-man Impressions returned to Chicago and in January, 1963, recorded their first session there with arranger and producer Johnny Pate. The best product of the session was the moody ballad, *Sad Sad Girl And Boy*. Although recorded in the same light, airy style as their earlier hits, the song shows something rather different in vocal approach. No longer are the rest of the Impressions quietly echoing in a subdued chorus to Mayfield's lead; they now show a stronger presence with interjections and call-and-response patters. It was a modest hit in the spring of 1963.

An August, 1963, session yielded the first single to define the classic style of the 1960s Impressions. The single was *It's All Right*, on which Pate lifts the energy level considerably, adding blaring horns and a more forceful, percussive bottom. The vocal style of the three is now fully developed, the lead switching off from among the three and the two others singing in harmony with the lead on the end phrases. The record was a number 1 soul hit in late 1963 and undoubtedly brought the Impressions firmly into the soul era.

The three-part switch-off lead of the Impressions was a fresh, new sound in rhythm and blues, but it was not new to African American music, as Mayfield relates: "there was nothing original about it if you ever sang gospel. In gospel, you knew how to be a good singer, not only to sing lead but to be able to incorporate oneself into the blend of the group too. And sometimes everyone comes out and sings in harmony a portion of the lead part. It was something totally different during those times. It made us as a three-man group stronger than we were as a five-man group."

The Impressions became a major act with a series of hit singles from two albums released during 1964. From the exceedingly weak **The Never Ending Impressions** album came only one hit, but a scrumptious ballad, *I'm So Proud*. The other album, **Keep**

On Pushing, was stronger, featuring a nice, loping, mid-tempo number, *Talking About My Baby*; a rousing number with intimations of black pride, *Keep On Pushing*; and a spiritualized folk song, *Amen*. The last, not a Mayfield original, is undoubtedly the most tiresome hit the Impressions ever recorded. As well, the **Keep On Pushing** album yielded the excellent ballad *I've Been Trying*, which was also recorded by Jerry Butler with notable success.

Continuing their splendid hit streak, the Impressions opened 1965 with their best album, **People Get Ready**. Its most outstanding cut was the title track, with its heavy, gospel-style imagery and feel. Other 1965 hits from the album were *You Must Believe Me* and *Woman's Got Soul*. The album is the Impressions' all-time best, and thus merits an extended discussion in the "Basic Recordings" section.

The year 1965 produced two more outstanding singles: *Meeting Over Yonder*, a churchy number that stands as a terrific example of the way Pate uses horns for percussion, and *You've Been Cheatin'*, featuring a propulsive drive made famous by Motown but thoroughly Chicagoan in sound. The ballad flip, *Man Oh Man*, ranks as a great undiscovered Impressions' masterpiece.

The years 1966–7 were somewhat quiet for the Impressions; **Ridin' High** was the one album from 1966 and it was less than a stellar achievement. It consisted of mostly Mayfield songs that had earlier been done by other artists. The group's one big hit during the year is the rousing *Can't Satisfy*. It has the same impelling drive as a Motown record, and no wonder: it borrows heavily from the Isley Brothers' Motown hit, *This Old Heart Of Mine*. Mayfield eventually had to settle with Motown and give the publishing of *Can't Satisfy* to the Detroit company.

The Fabulous Impressions, from early 1967, continued the Impressions' artistic slide, yielding only mediocre singles. The year was salvaged by the single *We're A Winner*. It is a driving song with a funky beat that evokes the spirit of the times, as African Americans inspired by the civil rights movement were asserting themselves as equal human beings in American society. The album, **We're A Winner**, did not contain much, however, producing one other hit, the fine ballad *I Loved And I Lost*.

The Impressions had one other hit single on ABC in 1968, their last for the label, *We're Rolling On*, which directly apes *We're A Winner*, but with less inspiration.

After the summer of 1968, the Impressions moved to Mayfield's own label, Curtom, and continued their winning ways with three big single hits, *This Is My Country*, *Choice Of Colors*, and *Check Out Your Mind*. The last, with its aggressive funk sound, intimated Curtis Mayfield's future direction as a solo artist. In 1970 he left the group.

Curtis Mayfield is rightly recognized as the preeminent talent and one of the principal architects of Chicago's soul-music industry, both for his membership in the Impressions and for his producing, songwriting, and entrepreneurial gifts. Thus, when he left the Impressions to establish himself as a solo artist in 1970, he was expected by many observers to become a superstar. It did not happen, and his solo career was decidedly mixed artistically. His thin, high-tenor vocals have been faulted for lacking punch, his jarring rhythms for being unfocused, his lyrics for being wordy and pretentious, and his songs for lacking melodic meat. Yet some of the very best black popular music of the 1970s came from Mayfield, who was one of the creative leaders in establishing a new contemporary style of rhythm and blues, one with a militant, harder edge. Mayfield's style may best be described as rumbling funk, in which he sings his didactic lyrics of social commentary over an instrumental accompaniment of wah-wah guitar, heavy bass lines, swirling strings, and blaring horns.

Mayfield's first solo album release was **Curtis**, from late 1970, and it got a sympathetic reception from rock critics who were strongly interested in singer-songwriters and found his work as a member of a vocal group too alien. The big hit single in the United States from it was *(Don't Worry) If There's A Hell Below, We're All Going To Go*, which, with its thunderous bass opening and some girl reciting commentary on the Book of Revelation, sounded truly apocalyptic. In the United Kingdom, another cut, *Move On Up*, was the hit single. The song is something of a transitional work for Mayfield, making use of funky percussion but also using traditional horn charts and choruses as he had during his Impressions years.

The next album, **Curtis Live**, from 1971, was intended to introduce Mayfield's new, contemporary style in a nightclub setting. The LP is a terrific showcase for rumbling funk, in which the heavy bass line, magnified by a live recording, contributes immensely to the ominous, militant tone of the music. Mayfield's third album, **Roots** (1971), yielded three hit singles, *Get Down*, *We Got To Have Peace*, and *Beautiful Brother Of Mine* (the last included here), a prime example of Mayfield's threatening-sounding rumbling funk sound, even if the lyrics are overly didactic.

Superfly, the soundtrack of the movie of the same name, established Mayfield as a major artist of the 1970s, and ranks as his all-time best. It produced two hit singles, *Freddie's Dead* and *Superfly*, and a strong album cut, *Pusherman*. The album is included in the "Basic Recordings" section, where the reader can find some extended comments.

Mayfield's **Back To The World** (1973) was the follow-up to **Superfly**, and the carry-over from the latter made **Back To The**

World a gold record. It is not strong, however. The rumbling funk had evolved into something closer to meandering funk. But the album produced three hit singles – *Future Shock, If I Were Only A Child Again*, and *Can't Say Nothing*. And this collection, to its credit, does not include the songs. Likewise with the *Kung Fu* and *Sweet Exorcist* hit singles from the album **Sweet Exorcist** (1974), and the *Mother's Son* hit from the album **Got To Find A Way**; the collection wisely omits these dated, meandering funk numbers.

On Warner Brothers in 1975 Mayfield released **There's No Place Like America Today**, which unhappily sustained the artist's downward creative slide. The saving grace is the outstanding single it produced, *So In Love*, which has a brass-style accompaniment reminiscent of 1960s soul. It proved to be his biggest hit in two years, but it did not cross over, for by the mid-1970s the pop audience had largely abandoned soul music.

Mayfield's next album, **Give Get Take And Have**, was likewise uninteresting, yet as with the previous album it yielded a truly exceptional single, *Only You Babe*, Mayfield's last Top 10 hit. The ballad possesses a recognizable and appealing melody and manages to showcase Mayfield's difficult-to-record thin vocals especially well. **Never Say You Can't Survive** (1977) also produced only one respectable single, *Show Me Love*, which did little in the charts, however, and is not included here.

Mayfield in his previous three albums certainly demonstrated he was still capable of writing solid, memorable songs, but not the same number of them as in earlier years. The record business required that he keep churning out albums every year whether he had enough songs to fill an album or not. Mayfield obviously did not, yet many of his best songs during this time, ironically, went to other artists on the label, notably on movie soundtracks.

The one other soundtrack besides **Superfly** featuring Mayfield was **Short Eyes** (1977). The film from which it was scored was several steps above the usual black action films of the period, having been based on Miguel Pinero's award-winning prison stage drama from 1974. The soundtrack yielded a sharp-selling single, *Do Do Wop Is Strong In Here*. It was edited from the LP's long version, which is included here. After 1977, Mayfield continued to produce occasional hit records, but the albums remained weak.

In 1990, Mayfield was the victim of a terrible stage accident in which a lighting tower fell on him, permanently paralysing this great talent from the neck down. The prospect that this great recording artist will ever be able to create again appears exceedingly slim.

Perhaps no compiler of a Mayfield collection will appease every critic. **The Anthology** provides the best overview of Mayfield's remarkable career. Readers interested in Mayfield's work after 1977 are advised to try several of his releases on his Curtom label distributed by Atlantic-based Ichiban, notably a greatest hits collection called **Of All Time**.

Discographical Details

171 The Anthology
Curtis Mayfield and the Impressions

MCA D2 10664 (2-disc set)

Impressions: *Gypsy Woman/Grow Closer Together/Never Let Me Go/Little Young Lover/Minstrel And Queen/I'm The One Who Loves You/Sad Sad Girl And Boy/It's All Right/Talking About My Baby/I'm So Proud/Keep On Pushing/You Must Believe Me/See The Real Me/Amen/I've Been Trying/People Get Ready/Hard To Believe/Woman's Got Soul/Meeting Over Yonder/You've Been Cheatin'/Man Oh Man/I Need You/Can't Satisfy/We're A Winner/We're Rolling On (Pt 1)/I Loved And I Lost/Fool For You/This Is My Country/Choice Of Colors/Check Out Your Mind*; Curtis Mayfield: *(Don't Worry) If There's A Hell Below, We're All Going To Go/ Move On Up/The Makings Of You/Beautiful Brother Of Mine/Freddie's Dead/Superfly/ Pusherman/So In Love/Only You Babe/Do Do Wop Is Strong In Here*

(v) The First Family of Soul

Before there was the Jackson Five – Michael, Jackie, Tito, Marlon, and Jermaine – there was the Five Stairsteps – Clarence Jr, James, Dennis, Kenneth, and Alohe – four sons and a daughter of Clarence Sr (Papa Burke) and Betty Burke of Chicago. The Five Stairsteps were solid R & B stars as chart regulars from 1966 to 1971, and before Motown's Jackson Five came to prominence were known as the "first family of soul." The group consisted of high- and middle-schoolers, and its members were groomed by Papa Burke from the time they were in diapers. In 1965 a chance meeting with the Impressions' Fred Cash resulted in the Five Stairsteps being signed to Curtis Mayfield's small Windy C label. Their first album, **The Five Stairsteps** (1966), which yielded five chart singles, was one of the most impressive debuts of the soul era.

For the group's first single, *You Waited Too Long* was paired with *Don't Waste Your Time*. The A side is a slow ballad written by the Burkes and the flip is a gently up-tempo number written by Mayfield. With Mayfield's sympathetic production, Clarence Jr's wonderful dry lead, and the group's harmonies providing an understated eloquence and soulfulness without sounding mannered and overly pretty, the result is like much of Chicago soul – engagingly subtle rather than obvious in appeal. Both sides were big hits in Chicago, but only the ballad side got into the national charts (which still does not justify the omission of *Don't Waste Your Time* in this Sequel collection).

The Five Stairsteps followed in 1966 with three outstanding ballad hits from their first album – *World Of Fantasy, Come Back,* and *Danger! She's A Stranger*. The flip to the last song, *Behind Curtains*, was widely played as well, and was actually something from Mayfield's back catalog, having been recorded in 1963 by teen soprano Jan Bradley. Yet another hit from the first album was the fine remake of the Miracles' 1964 hit, *Oooh Baby Baby* (1967).

In late 1967 the distributor for Windy C, Cameo/Parkway of Philadelphia, was collapsing, and the Five Stairsteps were forced to find a new home. An executive at Cameo/Parkway, Neil Bogart, found a position at newly formed Buddah and took the Five Stairsteps with him. The group's second album and first for Buddah, **Our Family Portrait**, yielded two chart singles in 1968, the fine Burke composition *Something's Missing*, and a cover of the 1960 Jimmy Charles ballad, *A Million To One*, neither of which can be found on **Comeback**.

Before 1968 was out, however, Curtis Mayfield had set up Curtom Records with distribution by Buddah, and the Five Stairsteps rejoined the legendary talent. Their stint at Curtom was just as brief, with one album to their credit, **Love's Happening**. Four remarkable singles were taken from the album, though – *Don't Change Your Love, Stay Close To Me, Baby Make Me Feel So Good*, and *We Must Be In Love*. The best of them was the rousing, up-tempo *Stay Close To Me*, which surprisingly did not get into the charts. The album also contained some remakes of earlier Impressions songs, namely *Little Young Lover* and *I'm The One Who Loves You*, which are pleasant enough but which do not improve on the originals.

The Five Stairsteps ended their Chicago years in 1970 and began recording for Buddah again under producer Stan Vincent in New York. With Vincent they got their first million-seller, the splendid *O-o-h Child*, which was the group's only real crossover hit. The song has become a perennial on oldie radio stations, which by playing only this song have deprived their audience of a great body of Five Stairsteps music.

In 1971 the Five Stairsteps moved to New Jersey, and Alohe dropped out to attend college. Under the name "Stairsteps" the group had two more hits, *I Love You – Stop* (1972), a weak, imitative, Jackson-Five-type song, and, following a three-year breakup, the uninteresting *From Me To You* (1975), recorded on George Harrison's Dark Horse label (not included here). Much of the later Buddah material was decidedly below par, so it is dismaying to see so many of the later songs on this collection. The addition of some early Windy C songs from the first album is regrettable – notably, besides *Don't Waste Your Time, The Touch Of You, You Don't Love Me*, and *Playgirl's Love*. Still, **Comeback** contains at least 16 memorable songs that fully encompass the Five Stairsteps' career, more than enough to develop a warm appreciation for the first "first family of soul."

Discographical Details

172   Comeback: The Best Of The Five Stairsteps
The Five Stairsteps
Sequel NEX CD 114 (UK)
You Waited Too Long/World Of Fantasy/Comeback (sic)/*Danger! She's A Stranger/*
Behind Curtains/Ooo[h] Baby Baby/Under The Spell Of Your Love/Don't Change
Your Love/Baby Make Me Feel So Good/We Must Be In Love/Loves Happening/Stay
Close To Me/Little Young Lover/I'm The One Who Loves You/O-o-h Child/Dear
Prudence/Because I Love You/Didn't It Look So Easy/I Love You – Stop/Peace Is
Gonna Come/I Feel A Song In My Heart Again/Easy Way/Hush Child/Snow/Look
Out

(vi) Urban Funky Soul from Brother Syl

Syl Johnson (b. Syl Thompson, July 1, 1936, in Holly Springs, Mississippi) is the brother of bluesmen Jimmy Johnson and Mac Thompson, and began his career playing behind such notables as Shakey Jake, Elmore James, and Billy Boy Arnold. He has a strong, sharp, and piercing voice that can really etch a song into one's consciousness. He almost unconsciously projects a deep, contradictory, bittersweet feeling; he seems as though he is crying even when he sings a joyful rouser. His lyrics are functional and sometimes awkward, but more often they are exactly right. As with most soul, one should not closely examine attitudes, feelings, and thoughts as expressed in lyrics, but rather concentrate on the nuances and subtleties of the music and vocal delivery, and that is where Johnson is a master.

This collection, on the P-Vine label from Japan, comes from Johnson's years on Twinight (1967–71), before he began recording in Memphis on Hi for producer Willie Mitchell (see chapter 6). Johnson's Hi output was consistently higher in quality than his Twinight work, but the looseness of production at Twinight allowed Johnson to sing with more abandon and funkiness. Whereas the Hi records evoke the spirit of a well-meshed studio system, the Twinight records seem to evoke more the spirit of life – they sound as though they came out of the mean urban streets of Chicago. Johnson feels that his best work was on Twinight, and listening to *Come On Sock It To Me*, *Dresses Too Short*, *Is It Because I'm Black*, *Concrete Reservation*, and *One Way Ticket To Nowhere* makes this a compelling argument.

Come On Sock It To Me (1967), written by Johnson and Joshie Jo Armstead, made Johnson a national star. From the opening infectious guitar riff, through Johnson's wailing vocals, to the chunk-chunk beat, the record has all the ingredients of a powerful hit. The record is quintessential hard soul without a whisper of pop to it, and thus had not a chance of crossover success. It sold furiously in the African American community, though. *Different*

Strokes (1967) was a strong follow-up commercially, but as with many follow-ups, it is something of a sound-alike. But the song is done at a slower, funkier tempo, and is effective because of it. *Dresses Too Short* (1968) is a sharply etched, funky, up-tempo tune that introduces for the first time the talents of Memphis producer Willie Mitchell. Although produced and recorded in Memphis, the song was written by Johnson and another Chicago songwriter, Carl Smith.

Johnson had a hit with one of his finest efforts in 1969, *Is It Because I'm Black*. In this superbly arranged and produced song by Twinight's studio group, the Pieces of Peace, Johnson's plaintive vocals evoke the moodiness of this lamentation over the struggle of being black. The song, however, suggests pride rather than defeatism. *Concrete Reservation* (1970), written and produced by Jimmy Jones, was a successful follow-up, in which Johnson sings a laundry list of ghetto problems.

The singer returned to a lighter vein with a rousing, horn-driven number written by Jack Daniels and Johnny Moore called *One Way Ticket To Nowhere* (1970). It was the same song that Tyrone Davis had a hit with a year later, and as good as Johnson's version is, Davis's had the arrangement that more fully realized the song. *Get Ready* (1971) was Johnson's next chart record. It was a remake of the Temptations' 1966 hit, but Johnson makes the record his own with one of his grittiest and funkiest vocal performances. This was the singer's last hit on Twinight. But his next Twinight record was *Annie Got Hot Pants Power*, and it would have been nice if this collection could have found room for this piece of supreme silliness.

Despite the worth of Syl Johnson's work on Twinight, it is exceedingly hard to obtain. He made two albums on Twinight, **Dresses Too Short** and **Is It Because I'm Black**, but both are long out of print. In 1979 P-Vine came out with an album of previously unissued Twinight material called **Goodie Goodie Good Times**, but it is a purchase for completists only. The CD from P-Vine is well worth a soul consumer's search, and one hopes that some day a United States company will see fit to reissue Johnson on Twinight.

Discographical Details

173   Chicago Twinight Soul

Syl Johnson

P-Vine PCD 2157 (Jap)

Dresses Too Short/I Can Take Care Of Business/Try Me/Come On Sock It To Me/ Different Strokes/I'll Take Those Skinny Legs/I Feel An Urge/Take Me Back/Take Care Of Homework/Going To The Shack/I Resign/Get Ready/Is It Because I'm Black/ Concrete Reservation/Right On/One Way Ticket To Nowhere/Thank You Baby

(vii) Uptown And Down-home At Brunswick

The Chi-lites exploded onto the soul scene in 1969, at the very beginning of the early 1970s vocal/dance group renaissance, when such ensembles as the Delfonics, the Stylistics, and the Moments, as well as the Chi-lites, achieved great crossover popularity and significantly shaped the popular music of the era with a soft kind of uptown soul that emphasized high-tenor leads. Chicago for more than a decade had been turning out soft-soul vocal groups with high-tenor leads, and it was only natural that the city would produce such a group as the Chi-lites who could compete with other soft-soul groups who were mostly East Coast-based. This Kent collection contains the cream of the Chi-lites' output recorded on the Brunswick label from 1969 to 1976.

Eugene Record was the Chi-lites' lead and their creative force as songwriter, producer, and all-round instrumentalist. His ballads featured strong, pretty melodies sung with a high-tenor, soulful edge, and Record projected an appealing persona, vulnerable and forlorn. In his up-tempo hits, however, he presented a vivid, contrasting image of black militancy in proto-funk instrumental settings, and as such represented the trend incorporating African American social concerns into the lyrics and irregular rhythms in the music.

Marshall Thompson was the group's baritone, but his role was that of the Chi-lites' spokesman and leader. Robert "Squirrel" Lester, as second tenor, and Creadal "Red" Jones, as bass, rounded out this remarkable group.

The origins of the Chi-lites go back to the era of doo-wop in the late 1950s, when rhythm-and-blues ensembles warbled rock-and-roll tunes with exaggerated barbershop harmonies. All of the Chi-lites were high-schoolers then, and they were motivated to join groups after listening to such locals as the El Dorados, the Danderliers, and the Moroccos. Eventually, after several years of doo-wopping on street corners and in talent shows, the future Chi-lites joined to form a group around 1961.

The Chi-lites then struggled for a decade before their first national hit in 1969, *Give It Away*, a delightful, mid-tempo ballad Record had co-written with Carl Davis. The song, a Top 10 hit on the R & B charts, established the Chi-lites' name with the soul audience. The vocals on this one rest mainly on the shoulders of Record, who produces flavorful singing while the rest of the group mainly chants "give it away" in support. The richly textured harmonies that characterized so many Chi-lites' records are not yet evident.

The group sustained their name with *Let Me Be The Man My Daddy Was* (1969), another terrific Record ballad that proved its worth by becoming a substantial soul hit. With its graceful lope and elegant softness, the song is one of the great unheralded Chi-lites efforts. Here, the harmonies in chorus are strong, making for a genuine group sound on the record.

24 Hours Of Sadness (1970) continued the Chi-lites' string of R & B hits with a change of pace. It is a peppy, up-tempo number which, although featuring greater aggression in execution, is thoroughly in the soft-soul mode. The group soon broke out of that mode with a number of militant, proto-funk numbers.

The group's second album, **I Like Your Lovin'**, was released in 1970. The ballad material was not up to par, and the two songs released as singles, *I Like Your Lovin'* and *Are You My Woman? (Tell Me So)*, present the Chi-lites in a proto-funk, up-tempo mode that does not stand the test of time. If the style sounds vaguely familiar, conjure if you will the Temptations' "psychedelic soul" period, which seems to have made a big impact on Eugene Record at the time.

The year 1971 was the breakthrough one for the Chi-lites. They had already established themselves in the soul market but they were still unknown in the popular market. **Give More Power To The People**, the first million-selling album for the group, changed all that and launched the Chi-lites as international entertainers. The first two singles from the album, *(For God's Sake) Give More Power To The People* and *We Are Neighbors* (not included here), introduced the theme of black assertiveness and were strong R & B hits.

Have You Seen Her, the beautiful, haunting ballad from the album, zoomed to the top of the charts and brought the Chi-lites their first crossover success. Another superb number from the album was *I Want To Pay You Back (For Loving Me)*; perhaps because it was only a modest hit, the song is not included on this collection. Most critics pay little attention to harmonized choruses, which is not only their failing but their loss, for on these two songs the choruses are central to their great appeal. Their sublime atmospherics should directly be attributed to the group's rich, perfectly realized harmonies, further enhanced at the top of the blend by Record's falsetto tenor.

By 1972, the Chi-lites could do no wrong. Their album that year, **A Lonely Man**, produced another spate of hits. Standing out above all is *Oh Girl*, one of the Chi-lites' most memorable ballads, and a number 1 R & B and pop record. Opening with the mournful sound of a harmonica, this sad lament has Record sounding at his most hurt and alone. The next hit from the album was *The Coldest Days Of My Life* (1972), which thoroughly encapsulates the Record lachrymose ballad style – so monumental it is baroque. Amid swirling strings accompanying the chirping of birds and the sound of lightly blowing wind, in comes the forlorn voice of Record singing about the "coldest day of my life."

Halfway through this eight-minute epic the sound-effect wind gets more blustery and Record sounds like the saddest man on the planet – great stuff.

We Need Order (1972) was the Chi-lites' last hit in their proto-funk style. Perhaps, by this time, Record had gotten the Temptations' *Psychedelic Shack* out of his system. With *A Letter To Myself* in 1973 the Chi-lites return to their well-established ballad style. It is a great song, but observers were beginning to mutter that Record had dipped into the well once too often for his formula.

Fortunately, Record was beginning to get lyrics from a country-music deejay from Kentucky, Stan McKenny, who inspired him with a new burst of compositional creativity, notably with *Homely Girl*. This 1974 soul hit is a wistful ballad about a plain-Jane schoolgirl who blossoms beautifully upon reaching adulthood. The ethereal harmonies are still patented Chi-lites, but it is a fresh ballad sound and a long underrated classic.

I Found Sunshine (1973) is perky and upbeat and shows lingering traces of the Chi-lites' proto-funk phase when a very prominent guitar twangs noticeably, in the absence of the horns that make their presence felt on most Chi-lites' records. *Stoned Out Of My Mind* (1973) is a good example of the Chi-lites' forceful, up-tempo material once the group got the funk out of their system.

In 1974 the Chi-lites got the last Top 10 hit of their career with *Toby*, from the great **Toby** album. One of Record's and Acklin's best collaborations, this pensive ballad tends to be overlooked. It builds pathos by relating the death of a longtime love interest going back to childhood, Toby. When Record sings "it was a sad day when Toby went away" within the rich soup of swirling string arrangements, he makes one feel the pain. One quibble with the song might be the spare use of group chorusing on the song; it is virtually a Record solo. The lush flip, *That's How Long*, also got into the charts, and one misses its inclusion here.

There Will Never Be Any Peace (Until God Is Seated At The Conference Table) (1974) was another terrific hit from the **Toby** album. Chi-lites fans in the United States sometimes are not aware of the international impact that American music has on the rest of the world, but in 1975 when there was conflict between the Greeks and Turks on Cyprus the radio station played this song over and over the airwaves. (I guess "God" never made his appearance, since Cyprus remains bitterly divided between two armed camps.) The Chi-lites, in fact, on many of these later releases sold far better overseas than in the States.

Toby produced two more mid-1970s hits, the uptempo *You Got To Be The One* (not included here) and a ballad *It's Time For Love*. The latter adds a new feature to the Chi-Lites by having Marshall

Thompson, with his handsome low-register voice, sing an alternate lead to Record's falsetto, and the contrast is most effective. One wishes they had employed the alternate leads more often in their career. *You Don't Have To Go* (1976) is a mid-tempo workout that was disparaged at the time as a concession to disco, but in retrospect it really lights up this set and shows the irrationality of criticism of disco.

The Chi-lites undoubtedly created an enduring body of music, but surprisingly at the time it was not deemed so by the self-proclaimed experts of pop music criticism, who unfortunately were still mooning over the past glories of soul rather than listening to the marvelous sounds coming out of their radios. The Chi-lites, with Eugene Record as their creative force, were one magnificent group, whose impassioned, florid music still resonated in popular music years later.

Chicago recording artist Tyrone Davis was one of the brightest stars in the 1970s galaxy of soul artists and scored hit after hit for the Dakar label, consistently selling at least 250,000 on his singles. Yet Davis remains fairly obscure to white America, at least compared to such leading 1970s crossover stars as Al Green, Teddy Pendergrass, and Donna Summer. Perhaps Davis's down-home music was too alien to the white, middle-class youth who constituted the bulk of the popular music audience. He sang in a slightly softer version of an urban soul-blues style pioneered in Chicago by his fellow soulsters Otis Clay, Johnny Sayles, and Harold Burrage. His vocals range from energetic shouting to the most subtle of soft whispering, but mostly he sang in a relaxed, cool, confessional style to a gentle lope. The subject matter of his songs – domestic discord and reconciliation, infidelity, and friends who cannot be trusted – reflected his black, adult, working-class constituency and, as with the blues artists of an earlier era, Davis's most loyal following came from that audience.

By 1966, Davis (b. May 4, 1938, in Greenville, Mississippi) was recording songs on the small, local Four Brothers label. After a few more struggling years, Davis was signed to Dakar in 1968. *Can I Change My Mind*, the first Davis release, serves as the archetypal record establishing the singer's confessional style, in which he presents the persona of a vulnerable and contrite lover. If his lyrics make Davis sound lacking in confidence, the brassy Willie Henderson production and arrangements certainly do not. The fat, impudent brass section provides a nice counterpoint to the blues-based lope of the rhythm track, and the tight, swinging playing of the Chicago musicians helps immeasurably to contribute to one of the most exhilarating sounds of soul music, which Davis recapitulated on record after record during the 1970s.

The next four singles for Davis were poor, futile attempts to recapture the successful formula of *Can I Change My Mind*. Surprisingly, one of them, *Is It Something You Got* (1969), was a Top 5 hit. Davis found real success in 1970 with *Turn Back The Hands Of Time*, which was his second million-seller and his only other pop success after *Can I Change My Mind*. Written by Daniels and Moore, produced by Henderson, and arranged by Washington, the song is something of a signature tune for Davis. Why this record and not so many of his others crossed over is one of the mysteries of the record business. *I Keep Coming Back*, the ballad flip to *Turn Back The Hands Of Time*, presents Davis at his most contrite and abject. His eschewing the usual macho stance of so many of his soul contemporaries made him a target of a lot of good-natured ribbing from MCs ("Tyrone, why are you always pleading with your women?").

Following on the heels of *Turn Back The Hands Of Time*, the team of Daniels and Moore came up with a winner in *I'll Be Right Here* (1970). The song breaks tempo often, changing from mid-tempo to up-tempo and back again throughout, with also a change back and forth from brass to strings support, techniques that work effectively to showcase Davis's vocals when he must talk-sing his lyrics at points of slower tempo and strings backing. The singer followed on the charts with *Let Me Back In* (1970). Written by fellow Chicago soul singer Cash McCall, the song allows Davis to milk his vulnerable, contrite persona to the hilt. Here he is standing outside the door knocking to be let in, and he has to state his case in the most abject manner – the man is practically groveling.

With *Could I Forget You*, from 1971, the composing talents of Leo Graham are introduced. The record does not have the crisp drive that characterized his later hits, but it does have its charms and was appealing enough to become a top hit for Davis. *One-Way Ticket* (1971) was a remake of a hit from a year earlier by fellow Chicago soulster Syl Johnson, but the way Davis sings it, the song sounds as though it was composed with Davis in mind – perhaps because it was written by the same team, Johnny Moore and Jack Daniels, that had given Davis *Turn Back The Hands Of Time*. By 1971 producer Henderson was assisted by arranger Tom Washington in crafting Davis's records, and the pair proved to be the perfect team for the singer, giving him hit after hit.

The rousing *You Keep Me Holding On* (1971) followed *One-Way Ticket* on the charts, and was another marvelous song from the pens of Daniels and Moore. The record is quintessential Tyrone Davis, his voice reaching out to his female followers in semi-sung pleading amid great brassy flourishes.

Davis got one of his biggest hits in 1972 with *I Had It All The Time*, which opens with a refrain from *Is It Something You Got*, then goes into a sentimental, banal recitation (surprisingly appealing), in which Davis pleads successfully with his girl over the phone to come back to him. The song was one of the earliest contributions by songwriter Richard Parker, who provided many more marvelous compositions for Davis. Davis finished 1972 with two modest hits not included in this collection, *Was I Just A Fool*, one of his abject ballads, and *If You Had A Change In Mind*, a pensive, mid-tempo workout that he often used in his concerts to change the mood.

Davis exploded onto the charts in 1973 with the magnificent *Without You In My Life*. It is one of the great unheralded songs in the extensive Davis *oeuvre*, and one of Henderson's finest productions. On black radio it was played like the national anthem. With its splendid drive, it is a perfect demonstration of how an R & B tune can rock without degenerating into histrionic soul shouting ("oversouling," as Atlantic Records executive Jerry Wexler was fond of saying). Enjoy the sharp riffing of the brass, which further pushes the hard-pumping rhythm section from start to finish. An excellent flip with a pumping beat, *How Can I Forget*, was widely played as well.

Dakar kept Davis in the charts in 1973 with *There It Is*, a masterful demonstration of the use of horns to carry a record, beginning with an introduction, over half a minute long, of blaring horns to generate the excitement before Davis comes in on the vocals. The song, another Leo Graham opus, features the arrangements of James Mack and Willie Henderson. Graham and Mack would be the architects of Davis's late 1970s hits on Dakar and Columbia.

Davis entered 1974 with a mid-tempo ballad from Leo Graham, *I Wish It Was Me*, which provided a change in style from the driving sort of tunes that Davis had been having hits with. If Davis fans thought he was going soft on them, there was no need to worry, because his next hit, *What Goes Up (Must Come Down)* (1974), of all the records from the Dakar factory, ranks as Davis's most magnificently hard-driving production, courtesy of Leo Graham and Richard Parker. Unfortunately, this collection omits the song. The flip, *There Must Be An Answer Somewhere*, is also a great driving number. Davis closed 1974 with two more chart entries, a dreadful ballad, *Happiness Is Being With You*, and a flashy spirited number, *I Can't Make It Without You* (neither included here).

With his next hit, *Homewreckers* (1975), Davis reverts to a bluesier and more down-home manner, departing a little from his mid-1970s approach. The creative team was slightly different, the song having been written by Southern-style singer Sam Dees and produced by Carl Davis and Otis Leavill.

A Woman Needs To Be Loved got into the charts in 1975, but it was recorded back in 1968 and was the intended A side of the *Can I Change My Mind* release. The deejays ignored the side back in 1968, but not in 1975, which was some sort of vindication for Carl Davis, who believed in the record and thought it would have been Tyrone's vehicle to stardom. One can see why; on this masterful, blues-based song Davis's vocals are at their most powerful, and during the 1970s his performance of the song was *the* highlight of his concerts.

In 1975 Davis got his third number 1 hit with *Turning Point*, which by rights should have been a million-seller. It was written and produced by Leo Graham, who by this time had taken full command of Davis's career. The song, with its relaxed lope, has become something of a standard in many Chicago blues bands, which find the down-home number most complementary to their usual blues material.

So Good (To Be Home With You) (1976) is Davis's biggest ballad hit on Brunswick and he used it often in concert to slow things down and to "talk to the ladies," who would then go into their squealing mode as Davis did his rap. By this time in his career, Davis was wearing his shirt opened to his navel and his neck was weighed down with so much gold his chest sparkled like Fort Knox. His concerts were featuring more ballads and less of his driving ravers, and obviously Davis was beginning to believe he was the best thing for womanhood since God made Adam.

Davis's last hit for Dakar was *Ever Lovin' Girl*, which hit the charts after the singer had switched to Columbia Records. It effectively prevented Davis from getting a hit from one of his Columbia releases, as the deejays preferred the Dakar song. It would have been nice to have had this song on the collection.

Tyrone Davis is still recording and still packing them in the clubs, but he is no longer the major star of yesteryear. He comes out with an album every year or so, most recently on Ichiban, and each contains one or two gems that remind the listener of his golden era at Dakar. His most loyal audience remains working-class, African American women. Some time ago at the Chicago blues fest Davis performed on the main stage, dismaying the white, middle-class blues aficionados, who dismissed him as a "black Tom Jones" and sat on their hands. On the other hand, throngs of black women, as well as this writer, were leaping out of their seats, waving their hands, and enjoying the show immensely.

Discographical Details

174 The Best Of The Chi-lites

The Chi-lites

Kent CDKEN 911 (UK)

Give It Away/Let Me Be The Man My Daddy Was/24 Hours Of Sadness/I Like Your Lovin' (Do You Like Mine)/Are You My Woman? (Tell Me So)/(For God's Sake) Give More Power To The People/Have You Seen Her/Oh Girl/The Coldest Days Of My Life (Pt 1)/We Need Order/A Letter To Myself/Stoned Out Of My Mind/I Found Sunshine/Homely Girl/Too Good To Be Forgotten/There Will Never Be Any Peace (Until God Is Seated At The Conference Table)/Toby/It's Time For Love/You Don't Have To Go

175 Greatest Hits
Tyrone Davis
Rhino R2 70533

Can I Change My Mind/A Woman Needs To Be Loved/Is It Something You Got/Turn Back The Hands Of Time/I Keep Coming Back/I'll Be Right Here/Let Me Back In/ Could I Forget You/One-Way Ticket/You Keep Me Holding On/I Had It All The Time/Without You In My Life/There It Is/I Wish It Was Me/Homewreckers/So Good (To Be Home With You)/Turning Point

Basic Recordings

Vee Jay Artists

176 Raindrops
Dee Clark
Charly R & B 69 (UK)

I Just Can't Help Myself (with the Kool Gents)/When I Call On You (with the Kool Gents)/Just Like A Fool (with the Kool Gents)/Seven Nights/Why Don't You Come Home/24 Boyfriends/Oh Little Girl (with the Upsetters)/Wondering (with the Upsetters)/Nobody But You/Blues Get Off My Shoulder/Just Keep It Up/Hey Little Girl/Your Friends/Raindrops/You're Telling Our Secrets/Walk Away From Me/You Are Like The Wind/Drums In My Heart/Bring Back My Heart/Fever/I'm A Soldier Boy/Shook Up Over You

There is no album that adequately represents Dee Clark (b. Delecta Clark, November 7, 1938, in Blytheville, Arkansas), one of the most successful rhythm-and-blues/rock-and-roll artists ever to come out of Chicago. **Raindrops**, in its overview of Clark's career on Vee Jay, most laudably includes his best recordings as lead of the doo-wop group the Kool Gents, 1955–6, and as a solo artist on Vee Jay, 1957–63. Missing, however, is his marvelous mid-1960s Constellation output, when he had hits with *Come Closer* (1964), *Warm Summer Breezes* (1964), *Heartbreak* (1964), and *TCB* (1965). This collection shows three aspects of Clark, as a rhythm-and-blues artist recording with the Kool Gents (notably on *I Just Can't Help Myself*), as a rock-and-roll artist (notably on *Nobody But You* and *Hey Little Girl*), and as a proto-soul stylist (notably on *Raindrops* and *Your Friends*). Clark's warm, lilting tenor needs just the right kind of material to be effective, and sometimes the wrong song disables him, as on *How About That*, a surprising Top 10 hit, but as with any greatest hits collection, it belongs on the album. Charly thus delivers the time-frame for this marvelous artist who died in 1990.

77 The Real Thing
Betty Everett

Charly R & B 56 (UK)

You're No good/Chained To Your Love/It's In His Kiss (The Shoop Shoop Song)/ Hands Off/It Hurts To Be In Love/Hound Dog/Until You Were Gone/I Need You So/I Can't Hear You/Let It Be Me (with Jerry Butler)/Love Is Strange (with Jerry Butler)/I Can't Stand It (with Jerry Butler)/The Way You Do The Things You Do (with Jerry Butler)/Getting Mighty Crowded/Chained To A Memory/I'm Gonna Be Ready/The Real Thing/No Place To Hide/Too Hot To Hold/Trouble Over The Weekend/The Shoe Won't Fit

Berry Everett (b. November 23, 1939, in Greenwood, Mississippi) for a time in the 1960s was one of the hottest female vocalists in the soul field. Her bittersweet voice was equally at home with blues, soul, Tin Pan Alley standards, and rock-and-roll, and the result was a number of memorable songs for several Chicago-based companies, most notably Vee Jay from 1963 to 1966. Everett's hits have been remade by several pop artists, some with excellent versions, but the originals nonetheless have never been surpassed. Her first hit, *You're No Good* (1963), was a superb hit for Linda Ronstadt in 1974, but only Everett's declarative and evocative vocals truly capture the flavor of the song. Her biggest hit, *It's In His Kiss (The Shoop Shoop Song)*, was remade by Kate Taylor in 1977 in a good but not great effort and by Cher in 1991 in a dreadful version, so one can appreciate all the better how Everett's soaring vocals bring out the proper exuberance in the song. Other top-notch songs from this collection include the long underappreciated *Getting Mighty Crowded* (1965) and a duet with Jerry Butler, *Let It Be Me* (1964). A regrettable omission is the Everett and Butler remake of Charlie Chaplin's *Smile* (1965), especially considering the dubious value of some of the other selections in the collection.

78 Island Of Love: Golden Classics
The Sheppards

Collectables CD-5078

Island Of Love/Never Felt Like This Way Before/Loving You/Elevator Operator/ Meant To Be/I'm Not Wanted/Feel Like Lovin'/Glitter In Your Eyes/Queen Of Hearts/Forgotten/Tragic/Come To Me/It's Crazy/So In Need For Love/Every Now And Then/Just When I Needed You Most/Just Like You/Pretend You're Still Mine

Along with the Impressions, the Daylighters, the Radiants, and the Dells, the Sheppards rank foremost of the groups that established Chicago as a soul-music mecca. The group featured two first-rate leads – Millard Edwards, who worked the smooth ballads, and Murrie Eskridge, who worked the more sweat-drenched, soulful songs. Members O.C. Perkins and guitarist Kermit Chandler wrote most of the best material. Jimmy Allen and James Dennis Isaac rounded out this remarkable group. The cuts here date from 1959 to 1963 and were recorded for Bill Sheppard's Apex label and for Vee Jay. They draw much of their character from earlier doo-wop, yet they incorporate instrumentation and vocal stylings that in later years informed soul music. In their best songs, namely *Island Of Love*, *I'm Not Wanted*, *Never Felt Like This Way Before*, *Tragic*, and *Glitter In Your Eyes*, the Sheppards show the ability to meld effectively the obvious romanticism and moon-June-spoon lyricism of doo-wop with the passion and energy of soul. As such, the Sheppards are a perfect example of a transitional soul group.

OKeh Artists

179 Um Um Um Um Um Um: The Best Of Major Lance
Major Lance

OKeh OKS 12106 (LP)

Um Um Um Um Um Um/Hey Little Girl/Gypsy Woman/Gotta Right To Cry/Little Miss Love/That's What Mama Say/The Monkey Time/It's All Right/Mama Didn't Know/Think Nothing About It/You'll Want Me Back/I'm The One

The **Um Um Um Um Um Um** album encapsulates only about six months of Lance's recording career, July 1963 to January 1964, and only three hits are on the album – *Monkey Time*, *Hey Little Girl*, and *Um Um Um Um Um Um* – but no fan of Chicago soul should miss this long-neglected album. Producer Carl Davis manages to produce an aggressive sound that evoked the urban streets, yet paradoxically is light, melodic, and nuanced, and the reason rests in songwriter Curtis Mayfield, who wrote every one of the selections. Among the songs are three superbly done remakes – the Impressions' *Gypsy Woman* and *It's All Right*, and Gene Chandler's *Think Nothing About It* – and two spin-offs from Jan Bradley's *Mama Didn't Lie* – *Mama Didn't Know* and *That's What Mama Say*. This is one of the most splendid OKeh albums ever produced.

180 Be Ever Wonderful
Ted Taylor

OKeh OKS 12104 (LP)

Be Ever Wonderful/Can't Take No More/Close Your Eyes/That's Life I Guess/I'll Release You/Pretending Love/You Give Me Nothing To Go On/Him Instead Of Me/Don't Lie/St James Infirmary/You Must Have Been Meant For Me/This Love Of Mine

Ted Taylor (b. February 16, 1934, in Okmulgee, Oklahoma) was not a Chicago artist, but from Los Angeles. He was, however, one of Carl Davis's first producing projects and he did a magnificent job, most notably on the **Be Ever Wonderful** album, Taylor's first (and one of the lost treasures of Chicago soul). Taylor's soaring bittersweet tenor is, if anything, soulful, and one of the most captivating in African American music. *Be Ever Wonderful* was a remake of Taylor's hit for Duke in 1960, but this is given a full-bodied orchestration that superbly enhances Taylor's soulful emoting on the ballad. Other outstanding tracks include another ballad, *This Love Of Mine*, and the most incredible version of *St James Infirmary* ever put on wax. Taylor's soaring vocals must be heard on the hard soul knockouts *You Give Me Nothing To Go On*, *Can't Take No More*, and *Don't Lie*, all sung with a gut-wrenching feeling that is thoroughly evocative of the mean streets of the urban ghetto.

181 Get My Hands On Some Lovin'
The Artistics

OKeh OKS 14119 (LP)

Get My Hands On Some Lovin'/I'll Leave It Up To You/Patty Cake/So Much Love In My Heart/I'll Come Running/This Heart Of Mine/What'll I Do/Loveland/I Need Your Love/In Another Man's Arms

The Artistics are best known for their hits recorded under producer Carl Davis for Brunswick, but perhaps their most solid LP collection is **Get My Hands On**

Some Lovin'. The group was only a minor act on OKeh and their record is undoubtedly rare, but it is well worth searching out in record collector auction lists. Davis recorded the Artistics on OKeh with the idea of imitating the sound of Motown, and one of the group's early hits was a cover of a Marvin Gaye LP cut, *Get My Hands On Some Lovin'*. The Artistics' first record, *I Need Your Love*, featured Robert Dobyne as lead, backed by Larry Johnson (first tenor), Jesse Bolian (second tenor), and Aaron Floyd (baritone-bass). Dobyne was replaced by Marvin Smith, and the group then had hits with the aforementioned *Get My Hands On Some Lovin'* and *This Heart Of Mine*. Other top-notch numbers include *I'll Come Running* and *So Much Love In My Heart*.

182   The Right Track
Billy Butler and the Enchanters

Edsel ED 147 (UK) (LP)
Right Track/Can't Live Without Her/Found True Love/My Heart Is Hurtin'/I'm Just A Man/Boston Monkey/Tomorrow Is Another Day/Lady Love/(I've Got A Feeling) You're Gonna Be Sorry/I Can't Work No Longer/Nevertheless/My Sweet Woman/You Won't Let Me Forget It/Gotta Get Away/(You Make Me Think) You Ain't Ready/ Does It Matter

The four tracks on the **OKeh Soul** collection in the "Essential Recordings" section were insufficient to properly represent Billy Butler, hence the inclusion of **The Right Track** as a basic which has enough of the "right tracks" to show how gloriously engaging Billy Butler was as a Chi-town artist. Butler – as with another Carl Davis-produced act, Major Lance – made his name mainly with bright, vigorous, and highly melodic songs, notably *Found True Love* (1963), *Gotta Get Away* (1964), *Nevertheless* (1964), *I Can't Work No Longer* (1965), and *Right Track* (1966). *Found True Love*, unfortunately, is the demo version of the song, which notes-writer Clive Anderson describes as "thin." The released version was emphatically not "thin." Butler and his group were equally at home with more reflective, mid-tempo, and ballad material, as evidenced by such sublime tracks as *I'm Just A Man* (1964), *Can't Live Without Her* (1964), and *Tomorrow Is Another Day* (1965). On all the material Butler's controlled and slightly gospelly lead vocals lend just enough intensity to give the songs that rich, R & B feeling. This is something numberless rock critics have never understood about soul – that you do not need a lot of energy or drive to be soulful. With 16 cuts, including two previously unreleased gems (*Does It Matter* and *You Won't Let Me Forget It*), this album is easily basic for any serious soul fan.

Chess Artists

183   Best Of Chess Rhythm And Blues
Various Artists

CD Chess 1006 (UK)
The Moonglows: *Please Send Me Someone To Love*; The Miracles: *Bad Girl*; Jimmy McCracklin: *The Walk*; The Corsairs: *Smokey Places*; The Vibrations: *The Watusi*; Sugar Pie DeSanto: *I Want To Know/Soulful Dress*; Etta James: *Something's Got A Hold On Me/Tell Mama*; Clarence "Frogman" Henry: *But I Do*; Bobby Moore and the Rhythm Aces: *Searching For My Love*; Jan Bradley: *Mama Didn't Lie*; Billy Stewart: *I Do Love You/Summertime*; Little Milton: *We're Gonna Make It/If Walls Could Talk*; Tony Clarke: *The Entertainer*; Mitty Collier: *I Had A Talk With My Man Last Night*; The Radiants: *Voice Your Choice*; The

Dells: *Stay In My Corner*; Laura Lee: *Dirty Old Man* (sic); Fontella Bass: *Rescue Me*; The Ramsey Lewis Trio: *The "In" Crowd*; Jackie Ross: *Selfish One*

This is basically a collection of some Chess hits from the soul years, and a few comments are in order for those artists not covered elsewhere. The Vibrations' *The Watusi* is one of the better dance records of the period, even if producer Ralph Bass did take the tune from Hank Ballard's *Let's Go Let's Go Let's Go*. Jan Bradley's *Mama Didn't Lie* set the standard for many later Chicago records featuring young soprano girl singers; one of these was Jackie Ross's classic *Selfish One*, using as an opening an old vaudeville fanfare. Tony Clarke had only one hit, *The Entertainer*, but it remains an oldie station standard to this day. The Radiants created a spirited and highly melodic, yet sophisticated form of soul. Their best work was done when the group consisted of a trio – Maurice McAlister, Leonard Caston, Jr, and Wallace Sampson – which used marvelous switch-off lead-work to create durable hits in *Voice Your Choice* and *It Ain't No Big Thing* (the latter sadly not included here). *I Had A Talk With My Man Last Night*, beautifully rendered by Mitty Collier's great contralto voice, is a perfect example of a secularized gospel tune (being derived from James Cleveland's *I Had A Talk With God Last Night*). The Ramsey Lewis Trio turned from supper-club jazz to making R & B instrumentals, and none was better than *The "In" Crowd*.

184   Rescued: The Very Best Of Fontella Bass
Fontella Bass

Chess/MCA CHCD 9335

Rescue Me/You'll Never Know (sic)/*Don't Mess Up A Good Thing* (with Bobby McClure)/*Soul Of A Man/Sweet Lovin' Daddy/Recovery/Since I Fell For You/You're Gonna Miss Me* (with Bobby McClure)/*I Surrender/Free At Last/Baby What You Want Me To Do* (with Bobby McClure)/*Joy Of Love/I Can't Rest/Oh No Not My Baby/Don't Jump* (with Bobby McClure)/*Leave It In The Hands Of Love*

With its riveting bass-line introduction that magnificently layers on instruments, with Fontella Bass's great soprano lead, and with the electrifying call-and-response chorusing, *Rescue Me* is a terrific example of the Chess studio system operating at its best under producer Billy Davis. Bass (b. July 3, 1940, in St Louis) was the daughter of famed gospel singer Martha Bass, and her name recognition rests solely on that one crossover hit. But as this collection amply demonstrates, she is a tremendous singer whose catalog of songs is more substantial than one might have imagined. Two songs produced by St Louis bandleader Oliver Sain, *Soul Of A Man* and *You'll Never Ever Know*, are Southern-style, secularized gospel ballads that most assuredly deserved to become hits, but were buried as flips. The zestful duets with fellow St Louisian Bobby McClure, *Don't Mess Up A Good Thing* and *You're Gonna Miss Me*, were both substantial R & B hits, deservedly so, and introduced Bass to the public. After *Rescue Me*, Chess sustained her name with sound-alike songs with similar themes, *Recovery* and *Surrender* notably. They were mild R & B hits that do not hold up well.

185   Down In The Basement – The Chess Years
Sugar Pie DeSanto

Chess/MCA CHD 9275

In The Basement, Pt 1 (duet with Etta James)/*I Want To Know/Mama Didn't Raise No Fool/Maybe You'll Be There/Do I Make Myself Clear* (duet with Etta James)/*Ask*

*Me/Use What You Got/Can't Let You Go/Soulful Dress/Going Back To Where I
Belong/She's Got Everything/Slip-In Mules*

Sugar Pie DeSanto (b. Umpeylia Marsema Balinton, October 16, 1935, in New
York City) was a little 4-feet-11-inch bundle with a big contralto voice. She had
only a few hits with Chess, but they are powerfully sung and gripping songs and
most typify Chess's approach to hard soul, with stinging blues guitar and full-
blown instrumental accompaniment well arranged.. The atmospheric but
somewhat thin *I Want To Know* was actually recorded in Oakland and picked
up by Chess to become DeSanto's first hit in 1961. Her first successful Chicago
recording was *Slip-In Mules* (1964), an answer record to Tommy Tucker's
monster blues hit, *Hi-Heel Sneakers*. She followed with a fine Maurice McAlister
(of the Radiants) song, *Soulful Dress*, with its excellent flip, *Use What You Got*.
Both sides exemplify DeSanto at her aggressive best, shouting out her sexual
prowess over a stinging blues guitar. Though one misses one of her few chart
hits, *Go Go Power*, making this collection most worthwhile is *In The Basement*, an
intense duet with Etta James.

186   Sings Big Blues/We're Gonna Make It
Little Milton
Chess/MCA CHD 5906

Sings Big Blues: *Feel So Bad/Reconsider, Baby/Stormy Monday/Woke Up This
Morning/Hard Luck Blues/Please, Please, Please/Sweet Sixteen/Fever/Sneakin'
Around/Don't Deceive Me/Have Mercy, Baby/Part Time Love*
We're Gonna Make It: *We're Gonna Make It/You're Welcome To The Club/I'm
Gonna Move To The Outskirts Of Town/Blues In The Night/Country Style/Who's
Cheating Who/Blind Man/Can't Hold Back The Tears/Believe In Me/Stand By Me/
Life Is Like That/Ain't No Big Deal On You*

Little Milton (b. Milton Campbell, September 7, 1934, in Inverness,
Mississippi) came to Chess in 1961 as a respected St Louis blues artist and
left the company ten years later as an average soul performer. The company
originally paid attention to Little Milton's blues roots and built his reputation as
a soul-blues stylist along the lines of Bobby Bland's gospelized blues vocal
stylings and B.B. King's guitar stylings. The result was a whole spate of hits,
notably *Blind Man*, *We're Gonna Make It*, *Who's Cheating Who*, and *Feel So Bad*,
which captured the very essence of 1960s soul-blues. These hits are included on
the two classic albums reissued on one CD. **We're Gonna Make It** (1965) was
produced by Billy Davis and **Sings Big Blues** (1966) was produced by Gene
Barge. In later years, Chess recorded Milton on more pure soul songs, in which
Milton's blues guitar was rarely heard and Milton seemed out of his element.

187   One More Time
Billy Stewart
Chess/MCA CHD 6027

*Billy's Blues, Pt 2/Fat Boy/Reap What You Sow/Sugar And Spice/Strange Feeling/
Count Me Out/I Do Love You/Keep Lovin'/Sitting In The Park/Love Me/
Summertime/How Nice It Is/Because I Love You/Every Day I Have The Blues/
Secret Love/Cross My Heart/One More Time/Golly Golly Gee/Tell Me The Truth/I'm
In Love (Oh, Yes I Am)*

The Washington, DC, native Billy Stewart (b. March 24, 1937) was nicknamed
"motormouth" for his unique style of vocalizing (a stuttering, rapid-fire

explosion of words). **One More Time** includes every one of his unforgettable
local and national hits before his death in 1970, as well as more than a few total
failures. The best-known inclusions are Stewart's speeded-up remakes of old
standards, *Summertime* and *Secret Love*, but these were recorded in 1966, later in
his career, when his style had become formulized, calculated, and exaggerated.
The best songs are the ballads from 1962 to 1965, when Stewart wrote and sang
such classics as *I Do Love You, Sitting In The Park*, and *Strange Feeling*. It is nice
to see the local Chicago up-tempo hit, *Count Me Out*, included. In these songs
the "doubling of words," as Stewart characterized his style, was most tasteful and
effective. The songs are beautiful, romantic, and slightly wistful, and received
wonderfully sympathetic arrangements by Chess's house production system. The
result was some of the best and most original soul to come out of Chicago in the
1960s.

Soft-Soul Artists of the 1960s

188 People Get Ready

The Impressions

ABC–Paramount ABC 505 (LP)

*Woman's Got Soul/Emotions/Sometimes I Wonder/We're In Love/Just Another Dance/
Can't Work No Longer/People Get Ready/I've Found That I've Lost/Hard To Believe/
See The Real Me/Get Up And Move/You Must Believe Me*

The **People Get Ready** (1965) album has always been considered the
Impressions' best collection during their ABC years, 1961–8. Mayfield in 1965
had peaked as the creative force behind the Impressions, and Johnny Pate had
come up with probably the most sublime arrangements of his long association
with the group. That only three songs from the collection hit the charts – *People
Get Ready, Woman's Got Soul*, and *You Must Believe Me* – means that those are
usually the only three that appear on reissue CDs while the remaining nine are
lost to posterity. Some of the songs had been done earlier for OKeh artists,
namely *Just Another Dance* (Marlina Mars), *Can't Work No Longer* (Billy Butler
and the Enchanters), and *Sometimes I Wonder* (Major Lance), but these are all
excellent versions. Pate's arranging touches are an absolute delight – notably, the
brassy introduction and riffing on *See The Real Me*, the pizzicato work on *Hard To
Believe*, and the bow-string work on *I've Found That I've Lost*. Pate was brilliant at
providing Mayfield's high-tenor leads and the group's feather-light harmonies
with exactly the right musical settings. This is the most beautiful album of
Chicago soul music ever produced.

189 Chi-Town Showdown

The Esquires and the Marvelows

Solid Smoke SS-8017 (LP)

The Esquires: *Get On Up/No Doubt About It/You've Got The Power/I Know I Can/I
Don't Know/Part Angel/And Get Away;* The Marvelows: *I Do/In The Morning/My
Heart/A Friend/I've Got My Eyes On You/I'm Without A Girl*

The Esquires and the Marvelows are both fine representatives of the soft side to
Chicago soul. Both groups traced their origins back to doo-wop and both thus
provided a fine, 1950s-style group harmony flavor to their brand of soul. The
Esquires (brothers Gilbert and Alvis Moorer, Shawn Taylor, Sam Pace, and Mill
Edwards) came from Milwaukee but had to go to Chicago to record. Their
records on Bunky and later Wand, as produced by Bill "Bunky" Sheppard and

arranged by Tom Washington, were bright, bouncy, and eminently pop-like soul. As a result they achieved great crossover success with *Get On Up* and *And Get Away* in 1967, but their career was sustained with such soul chart hits as *You've Got The Power* and *I Don't Know*.

The Marvelows came out of the suburb of Chicago Heights and consisted of Melvin Mason, Willie Stephenson, Johnny Paden, Frank Paden, and Jesse Smith (later replaced by Andrew Thomas). Their records on ABC Paramount were produced and arranged by Johnny Pate. The Marvelows' first hit, *I Do* (1965), was later remade by the J. Geils Band and represents the Marvelows at their most aggressive. But it was on ballads that the group especially sparkled, notably *I'm Without A Girl* and *In The Morning*. The Esquires and the Marvelows are valued not only because they were fine groups who sang fine songs, but because they helped to sustain the tradition of genuine vocal harmony. This album serves as a terrific document of that tradition in soul music.

190 Jealous Kind Of Fellow
Garland Green

Uni 73073 (LP)

Jealous Kind Of Fellow/Girl I Love You/Mr Misery/All She Did (Was Wave Goodbye At Me)/I Can't Believe You Quit Me/Don't Think That I'm A Violent Guy/Ain't That Good Enough/Forty Days And Nights/Love Now, Pay Later/You Played On A Player/Angel Baby

Garland Green (b. June 24, 1942, in Dunleath, Mississippi) has one of the most appealing voices in soul music, a distinctive baritone that has a pleading quality with a blues feel, much in the same vein as his fellow Chicagoan soulster, Tyrone Davis. Green sang soft soul with a hard-soul sensibility. These sides were produced by independent record entrepreneur and songwriter Joshie Jo Armstead. The first release was put out on her Gamma label and later releases were leased to Uni. The album's best-known songs – *Girl I Love You* (1967), *Jealous Kind Of Fellow* (1969), and *Don't Think That I'm A Violent Guy* (1969) – superbly epitomize the mid-tempo approach to soul music, which is especially characteristic of Chicago records. Surprisingly, the songs were recorded in Detroit and arranged by Detroiter Mike Terry (but because the producer and singer were based in Chicago we opted for flexibility and placed the LP in this chapter).

191 Casanova (Your Playing Days Are Over)
Ruby Andrews

Collectables CD-5201

Casanova (Your Playing Days Are Over)/Everybody Saw You/Help Yourself Lover/I Guess That Don't Make Me A Loser/Gotta Break Away/You Made A Believer Out Of Me/Casanova 70/Can You Get Away/You Can Run, But You Can't Hide/Uh! Uh! Boy, That's A No No/Since I Found Out/Tit For Tat

This album by Ruby Andrews (b. Ruby Stackhouse, March 12, 1947, in Hollandale, Mississippi) is another breaker of chapter rules, with most of the songs having been recorded in Detroit and Memphis; but the singer, producer, and record company were all located in Chicago. Andrews is one of the finest stylists in soul music, having an equal ability to sing soft melodic songs and hard-driving, beat-laden ones. When she sings shouting-style, it is done with total control and a full, clear tone, yet with all the power and force the song demands. The CD is essentially Andrews's **Everybody Saw You** LP from 1970 with the addition of her big hit *Casanova (Your Playing Days Are Over)*. Why Collectables did not just make a best-of collection is a mystery, so one laments the absence of *The Love I Need, You Ole Boo Boo You*, and *Hound Dog*. Her main producers/writers were Fred Bridges, Robert Eaton, and Richard Knight, the Brothers Of Soul group who had a hit in 1968 with *I Guess That Don't Make Me A Loser*, remade here by Andrews. This is not a definitive collection of Andrews, but one worth obtaining.

192   There'll Come A Time
Betty Everett

Uni 73048 (LP)

You're Falling In Love/Better Tomorrow Than Today/Maybe/1900 Yesterday/Sugar/I Need A Change/I Can't Say No To You/Hold On/There'll Come A Time/Take Me/Is There A Chance For Me/The Same Old Me

Produced by Leo Austell, Archie Russell, and Hillery Johnson, **There'll Come A Time** was something of a comeback for Everett after her career went slack following the collapse of her label, Vee Jay, in 1966. The hit single of the same name was from the pens of Eugene Record and Floyd Smith, and they wrote for Everett a perfect tune, wistful, sad, and just right for her bittersweet vocals. She sounds so marvelous one wishes she had recorded more ballads during her career. *I Can't Say No To You*, which also got into the charts, has a nice, dramatic interaction between Everett and the choruses that really makes the song. *1900 Yesterday*, written by Johnny Cameron, has great hooks, an engaging melody, and a riveting, string-heavy arrangement – all the ingredients for a hit – yet it never got into the charts. Instead, an Hawaiian bar band, Liz Damon's Orient Express, took the song up the pop charts in 1970. Everett never recorded anything better afterwards and retired from the business in 1980, possibly lamenting the success of Liz Damon.

193   With Love From The Lovelites
The Lovelites

Uni 73081 (LP)

Oh My Love/This Love Is Real/You've Hurt Me Now/How Can I Tell My Mom And Dad/I'm In Love/Gotta Let You Go/Who You Gonna Hurt Now/Certain Kind Of Lover/I Love You (Yes I Do)/I Don't Want To Cry/I've Got Love/Shy Boy

The critical establishment (and there *is* a critical establishment) would not have a clue about this record. It has no screamers, no fast, pounding beats, no instrumental virtuosos; in short, none of their usual yardsticks by which the establishment determines what is good in soul music. Instead, there are the incredibly emotive voice and songwriting talents of Patti Hamilton wonderfully backed by Joni Berlmon and Dell McDaniel. Producer Clarence Johnson and arranger Johnny Cameron give the Lovelites a bright-sounding and delicate instrumental support that work marvelously with the largely mid-tempo tunes, an approach thoroughly Chicagoan in conception. *How Can I Tell My Mom And Dad* (1969) was the group's only national hit, but *Oh My Love, This Love Is Real*, and *You've Hurt Me Now* merit all the attention the hit got. In 1971 the Lovelites had another national hit with *My Conscience* (unfortunately, not included here) and then broke up in 1973. This album is a real treasure.

Hard-Soul Artists of the 1960s

194 12 Great Songs
McKinley "Soul" Mitchell

P-Vine Special PLP 9008 (Jap) (LP)
The Town I Live In/I've Been Wrong/Reckless Lover/Tell It Like It Is/I Think You're
The Girl/Hand Full Of Sorrow/I'm So Glad/Don't You Know That's Love/All Of A
Sudden/Stop Crying Over You/Darling That's What You Said/A Bit Of Soul

McKinley Mitchell (b. December 25, 1934, in Jackson, Mississippi) in the early
1960s was one of the most popular nightclub performers in Chicago and was a
distinctive rhythm-and-blues stylist of the first rank. On first hearing his vocals
are thin and raspy and his tendency to talk the lyrics rather than sing them seems
to diminish his authority over the songs; but a second hearing is called for. And
one then finds his voice and approach are so undeniably "soulful" and riveting
that one cannot deny the artistry involved. Mitchell's first release for One-derful,
The Town I Live In (1962), is most remarkable. Showing years of gospel
experience, Mitchell sings exceedingly raw, but it is a lyrical, enchanting song,
urban yet urbane. The King Kolax arrangements add much to the atmosphere
with blaring horns, pulsating organ, and jangling guitar. Other fine songs are *I'm
So Glad, A Bit Of Soul, Tell It Like It Is*, and the bluesy *All Of A Sudden*, but they
failed to find an audience and Mitchell left One-derful in 1964. In 1976 the
singer returned to the South and began recording regional hits, notably *The End
Of The Rainbow*. Mitchell died January 18, 1986.

195 The Pioneer Of Chicago Soul
Harold Burrage

P-Vine Special PLP 9003 (Jap) (LP)
I'm In Love/Take Me Now/That's A Friend/Faith/More Power To You/You Mean
The World To Me/Hang My Head And Cry/Mr Window/Got To Find A Way/I'm
Alright/How You Fix Your Mouth/You Make Me So Happy

Harold Burrage (b. March 30, 1931, in Chicago) was an experienced recording
artist when he joined One-derful in 1962, having recorded as early as 1950 for
Decca and in the late 1950s for Cobra. Thus, he served as a kind of mentor to
Otis Clay and other One-derful artists, and seemed to deserve the title "Pioneer
of Chicago Soul." Only Chicago could have produced a Harold Burrage, with a
powerful, deep baritone somewhat reminiscent of Solomon Burke that does not
have the "Southern" flavor typical of most hard soul. The record is a mixed bag.
There is Burrage's one hit – an excellent, hard-pounding number from 1965,
Got To Find A Way – and then two pale imitations in *More Power To You* and *You
Make Me So Happy*. There are two tepid country-and-western-styled tunes in
Faith and *Mr Window*, and then there are marvelous unreleased numbers such as
the powerful *I'm In Love*, the rolling *Hang My Head And Cry*, and the talking
blues *That's A Friend*. Despite its weaknesses, the album will grow in appeal on
repeated play. Burrage died November 25, 1966.

196 Soul On Fire
Johnny Sayles and Andrew Tibbs

P-Vine Special PLP 9007 (Jap) (LP)
Johnny Sayles: You Did Me Wrong (Take 1)/Don't Turn Your Back On Me/I Got A
Whole Lots Of Loving/I'm Satisfied/Tell Me Where I Stand/Got You On My Mind/

You Told A Lie/The Girl I Love/You Did Me Wrong (Take 2); Andrew Tibbs: *Stone Hearted Woman/Woman's Love/I Made A Mistake*

Johnny Sayles (b. February 9, 1937, in Winnsboro, Texas) never attained the level of success of his compatriot deep-soulsters – Tyrone Davis, Otis Clay, and McKinley Mitchell – but nonetheless he left an indelible mark with truly exceptional recordings. *Don't Turn Your Back On Me* is an exceedingly aggressive, upbeat number with Sayles's screaming vocals providing an intensity that made the record a Southern hit. *You Told A Lie* is a fine example of a blues performed in a soul style. *You Did Me Wrong* and *Got You On My Mind* are an outstanding pair of moody ballads, whose horn blues riffing rivals the great brass treatments on Bobby Bland's legendary *Your Friends*. The above four songs, released on the One-derful subsidiary label Mar-V-lus in 1963, plus the previously unreleased sides, constitute the most uncompromisingly raw soul treatments ever performed on record in the 1960s, the hardest of hard soul. Andrew Tibbs is best known as the first recording artist for Leonard and Phil Chess, in 1947, and here he performs a set of appealing blues, his last recordings.

197   The Beginning: Got To Find A Way
Otis Clay

P-Vine PCP 2195 (Jap)
Got To Find A Way/Wrapped Up In Her Love/I Don't Know What I Do/Cry Cry Cry/A Flame In Your Heart/Tired Of Falling In And Out Of Love/I Paid The Price/ I'm Satisfied/I Testify/It's Easier Said Than Done/I Lost Someone/Funny Life/This Love Of Mine/Nothing To Look Forward To/Come My Dear/That's How It Is/Must I Keep On Waiting/Don't Pass Me By/That'll Get You What You Want

Otis Clay (b. February 11, 1942, in Waxhaw, Mississippi) has a style of deep soul that owes a great debt to Chicago's blues milieu; and, like its often-indistinguishable counterpart, Southern soul (Otis Redding, Percy Sledge, et al.), it has that black church element, gospel. Clay sang gospel for some 15 years before he took up secular music, in 1965, and the singer's raw vocals project a breathtaking intensity of emotion and a religiosity that can only come from a long gospel experience. This collection contains the best material Clay recorded for George Leaner's One-derful label from 1965 to 1968. Highlights include his biggest One-derful hit, *That's How It Is*; a fine remake of Harold Burrage's *Got To Find A Way*; a local Chicago sensation, *Tired Of Falling In And Out Of Love*; and two secularized gospel songs, *I'm Satisfied* and *I Testify*. A revelation is the number of fine previously unreleased titles, some of them, notably *Cry Cry Cry* and *Come My Dear*, far better than some of the released sides. Later Clay recorded for Memphis-based Hi records and in the 1980s he made a couple of well-received live recordings in Japan, but his early recordings should be the starting point for anybody who is looking for the best in Northern deep soul.

198   You're Tuff Enough
Junior Wells

Blue Rock/Mercury SRB 64002 (LP)
You're Tuff Enough/It's All Soul/Gonna Cramp Your Style/Where Did I Go Wrong?/ That'll Hold Me/Sweet Darling Think It Over/Up In Heah/You're The One/You Ought To Quit That/Messing With The Kid/The Hippies Are Trying/Junior's Groove

The squalling harmonica-blowing and gritty, spunky blues singing of famed bluesman Junior Wells (b. Amos Blackmore, December 9, 1934, in Memphis) has always epitomized Chicago bar-band blues. In 1966, after recording straight blues for some 13 years, Wells joined the Bright Star label owned by Willie Barney and producer Jack Daniels, and started recording soul-style blues. To many purist blues fans, Daniels's work with Wells was considered nothing but soul music and was rejected. In the African American community, Wells, most happily, started getting hits, notably *Up In Heah* (1966) and *You're Tuff Enough* (1968). By the standards of the mid-1960s the Bright Star sides were genuinely down-home, and for Wells to come out with records directed to blacks featuring harmonica-blowing was extraordinary. The Monk Higgins horn arrangements were superb in updating Wells yet staying true to the esthetic considerations of the black, working-class audience. In 1968 Daniels took Wells and his Bright Star masters with him to Mercury's Blue Rock label. **You're Tuff Enough** was released to try to reach the album-buying rock audience, hence the awful *The Hippies Are Trying*. This album is a splendid early example of the soul-blues style that became much more common in later years.

Brunswick Artists

199 Chicago Soul: The Legendary Brunswick/Dakar Hits
Various Artists

Epic PE2 39895 (2-LP set)

Barbara Acklin: *Love Makes A Woman/Just Ain't No Love/Am I The Same Girl/I'll Bake Me A Man*; The Artistics: *I'm Gonna Miss You/Girl I Need You*; Young–Holt Unlimited: *Soulful Strut*; The Young–Holt Trio: *Wack Wack*; Willie Henderson: *Funky Chicken*; The Lost Generation: *Sly Slick And Wicked/Talking The Teenage Language*; Tyrone Davis: *Home Wrecker* (sic)/*One-Way Ticket To Nowhere*; The Chi-lites: *I Like Your Lovin'/Let Me Be The Man My Daddy Was/Give It Away/I Wanna Pay You Back*; Gene Chandler: *Fool For You/Good Times/The Girl Don't Care/Here Come The Tears/There Goes The Lover/Show Me*

That this wonderful collection of Brunswick and Dakar hits from the late 1960s and early 1970s is not available on CD is almost criminal. It represents the apex of Carl Davis's production work at the company. The Artistics are featured with their two big hits from 1966–7. The songs came from the group's first Brunswick album, which was so good I was tempted to list it as a basic. Barbara Acklin (b. February 28, 1943, in Chicago) is represented by her two great hits, *Love Makes A Woman* and *Just Ain't No Love*, where her pretty soprano voice is put to great use on some really punchy numbers. *Am I The Same Girl* is interesting because it served as the source for the big instrumental hit *Soulful Strut* for Young–Holt Unlimited. Davis took Acklin's voice off the track and substituted a fine Floyd Morris piano track. Neither drummer Red Holt nor bassist Eldee Young was on the disc, but the pair, along with pianist Hysear Don Walker, were on their big hit, *Wack Wack*, from 1966, when Latin soul was all the rage. (Holt and Young, incidentally, were the other two-thirds of the Ramsey Lewis Trio up to 1966.) Willie Henderson's *Funky Chicken*, basically an imitation Rufus Thomas number, met the needs of dancers in 1970, but does not hold up well.

The Lost Generation (Lowrell Simon, Fred Simon, Jesse Dean, and Larry Brownlee) is a sorely underrated group, whose style was built on Lowrell Simon's dry lead contrasting with sweet chorusing. Their two biggest hits here well represent their talents. The Gene Chandler numbers contain three great songs that he recorded for Constellation and three terrific sides recorded for Brunswick. This taste of Chandler whets one's appetite for a complete collection of this magnificent singer's Brunswick hits. The best previous collection is Chandler's fabulous **The Girl Don't Care** LP from 1967, and if this collection had not existed that would have been listed as a basic. **Chicago Soul** omits only Otis Leavill from the Brunswick/Dakar stable, but otherwise is a superb collection.

200 Higher And Higher: 18 Soul Sensations

Jackie Wilson

Kent CDKEN 901 (UK)

(Your Love Keeps Lifting Me) Higher And Higher/I Get The Sweetest Feeling/I've Lost You/I Don't Want To Lose You/The Who Who Song/Nothing But Blue Skies/ Soul Galore/Uptight (Everything's Alright)/Whispers (Gettin' Louder)/You Got Me Walking/Let This Be A Letter (To My Baby)/Because Of You/What'cha Gonna Do About Love/This Love Is Real (I Can Feel Those Vibrations)/Since You Showed Me How To Be Happy/You Brought About A Change In Me/I'm The One To Do It/ Nobody But You

Jackie Wilson's early recordings are covered in chapter 1, so this CD covers his soul years, recording largely in Chicago with producer Carl Davis. Brunswick, recording Wilson in New York, only fitfully moved into the soul era. He got some soul-idiom songs into the lower reaches of the charts, which was not the level of success Brunswick was used to, and *Soul Galore* (1965), the title cut for his last LP cut in New York, did not even enter the charts. In 1966 Brunswick executive Nat Tarnopol made an alliance with Carl Davis to produce Wilson in Chicago, and the first result is one of the finest and biggest recordings of Wilson's career, *Whispers (Gettin' Louder)*. While this classic song does not get played on the pop oldies stations, their black counterparts, which appreciate mid-tempo tunes, have made it a programming staple. *I Don't Want To Lose You* (1967) likewise has a nice, mid-tempo lope and sustained the singer's Chicago success.

(Your Love Keeps Lifting Me) Higher And Higher (1967) is the one Wilson song that everybody knows, since it is played incessantly on radio, is heard on TV ads, and pops up in movies; and not to be a curmudgeon I have to admit it is his greatest song. Davis brought in the famed Motown rhythm section, anchored by the legendary bassist James Jamerson, to give the song its terrific drive; but no one could beat the Brunswick horn section at this time, and the horns raise the excitement level considerably. *Since You Showed Me How To Be Happy* (1967) works the same groove but remains only a pleasant song. *I Get The Sweetest Feeling* (1968) is a vast improvement and Wilson rides the Chi-town mid-tempo with verve and zest. *You Got Me Walking* (1972), from the pen of Eugene Record, is one of the great overlooked treasures of the Wilson catalog, and *This Love Is Real* (1970) was Wilson's last Top 10 hit, but does not hold up well. Wilson's soul years in Chicago were obviously not an unalloyed success, but still should not be ignored.

Artists of the 1970s and 1980s

201 Superfly

Curtis Mayfield

Curtom CUR 2002 CD

Little Child Runnin' Wild/Pusherman/Freddie's Dead/Junkie Chase (instrumental)/ *Give Me Your Love (Love Song)/Eddie You Should Know Better/No Thing On Me (Cocaine Song)/Think* (instrumental)/*Superfly*

Superfly, the soundtrack of the black action film of the same name from 1972, is easily Mayfield's most notable achievement as a solo artist. The artist and his band also appeared in this movie about a drug pusher, playing in a nightclub the pusher frequented. Praise for the album has been almost universal, as Mayfield's jagged guitar lines seem just right for conveying the nervous energy of the black urban ghetto and the pusher's milieu. In the numbers that stand out, *Freddie's Dead*, *Pusherman*, and *Superfly*, the lack of melody serves as a strength, allowing the rhythms to shine and resonate. Mayfield's vocals sympathetically come across more relaxed and cool than thin. The album, with huge sales in the white community, made Mayfield for a time a crossover artist.

202   Leaving Me: Their Golden Classics
The Independents

Collectables CD 5245

Leaving Me/I Found Love On A Rainy Day/The First Time We Met/I Just Want To Be There/It's All Over/Let This Be A Lesson To You/No Wind, No Rain/Just As Long As You Need Me (Pts 1 & 2)/Baby I've Been Missing You/Couldn't Hear Nobody Say (I Love You Like I Do)/Arise And Shine (Let's Get It On)

The style of the Independents (Chuck Jackson, Helen Curry, Maurice Jackson, and Eric Thomas) was distinctive. Practically all their songs were soft ballads in which the lead vocalists, usually Chuck Jackson and Helen Curry, trade leads in the gospel manner. The vocals are heavily melismatic but in a very quiet, soft style, and are perfectly set off by beautifully harmonized choruses. This approach is best realized in their million-seller *Leaving Me*, but *Baby I've Been Missing You* and *Let This Be A Lesson To You* are most delicious as well. The Independents came together only after their first hit, *Just As Long As You Need Me* (1972), was in the charts. This was recorded by the independent songwriting/producing team of Chuck Jackson and Marvin Yancy Jr, as a demo, but it got a regular release and the name "Independents" was put on the label. The group broke up in 1974 when Jackson and Yancy wanted to concentrate their energies on a new talent, Natalie Cole.

203   Love And Touch
Tyrone Davis

Columbia 34268 (LP)

Give It Up (Turn It Loose)/Close To You/Why Is It So Hard (To Say You're Sorry)/You're Too Much/Put Your Trust In Me/Givin' Myself To You/Wrong Doers/Beware, Beware

Love And Touch came out in 1976 and was the first album Tyrone Davis recorded for Columbia after leaving Brunswick. Conventional soul music was fading fast as disco, funk, and new sounds began taking over the black charts, and the album was Davis's last full-bodied soul work before those influences began making themselves felt. The subject matter is classic Davis, dealing with his usual areas of domestic discord and reconciliation (*Why Is It So Hard*), infidelity (*Wrong Doers*), and friends who cannot be trusted (*Beware Beware*). Compared to his earlier Brunswick albums, there are more ballads, which Davis sings with great elan, but unfortunately being a ladies' man went to his head. Too many of his subsequent albums were excessively ballad-heavy. The up-tempo numbers remain Davis's basics, and on *Put Your Trust In Me* there's the famed brassy flourishes and relaxed, swinging rhythm that make for an outstanding number. The hit single from the album, *Give It Up (Turn It Loose)*, consists of no more than a repeated musical phrase over an insistent but appealing drum riff, but Davis, whose vocals soar, swoop, slide, and pause at all the right moments, transforms the song. Phrases are turned over again and again so that every subtlety, every nuance is wrung out, savored and enjoyed, making for soul singing at its very best. **Love And Touch** is one of the great underrated, if not overlooked, soul albums of 1976.

204 Ms Fine Brown Frame
Syl Johnson

P-Vine PCD-1257 (Jap)

Ms Fine Brown Frame/Keep On Loving Me/They Can't See Your Good Side/Groove Me/Sweet Thing/You Don't Have To Go/Foxy Brown

This Japanese reissue of a Boardwalk LP from 1982 (with one change in the selection) is an amazing album, because it incorporates two seemingly incompatible styles – blues and disco – and makes it work marvelously. After hard-soul stylist Syl Johnson returned to his blues roots with the single *Brings Out The Blues In Me* and an album of the same name, he continued to try to create a new kind of syncretic music that was both rootsy and contemporary. **Ms Fine Brown Frame**, with production help from General Crook, is the happy result. The title cut was Johnson's last hit record, and it not only meshes blues and disco but also incorporates a rhythmic rap. *Keep On Loving Me* is a remake of *Brings Out The Blues In Me* and significantly improves on it. The down-home guitar-work and the harmonica-blowing from James Cotton provide a feeling that somehow turns a seeming disco record into a genuine blues. (Incidentally, the song is heavily based on the Rolling Stones' *Miss You.*) *You Don't Have To Go*, the old Jimmy Reed blues, is also tasty.

205 Soul Man: Live In Japan
Otis Clay

Bullseye Blues BB9513

Hard Working Woman/Here I Am (Come And Take Me)/Love Don't Love Nobody/A Nickel And A Nail/Precious Precious/Holding On To A Dying Love/His Precious Love/Love And Happiness

There is no listening experience that can short one's emotional circuits as much as a tight, driving soul band vamping with great verve and feeling. Vamping – that is, improvising the music – is a great tradition in black music, and is especially characteristic of jazz and gospel. When a soul band vamps, the rhythm section will break down to a few chord changes from the chorus or verse and repeat them endlessly while the brass adds embellishment and the vocalist jams the song.

Soul Man, recorded in Japan in 1983, is one of the great vamp albums of soul music. In a marriage made in heaven, Clay took with him to Japan the great Hi Records rhythm section, the backing band for Al Green consisting of the Hodge brothers – Charles, Leroy, and Teenie – and Howard Grimes. With Clay's own expert Chicago Horns and keyboardist, the results are simply spectacular. The opening track, *Hard Working Woman*, was a Clay hit for Hi in 1970, and this new, pumping version is full of energy. The band plays with the intimate familiarity one would expect on two Al Green remakes – *Here I Am (Come And Take Me)* and *Love And Happiness*. On the latter, after the body of the song the rhythm shifts into a hard-pounding overdrive and there are eight minutes of the most mind-blowing vamp this listener has ever heard. *A Nickel And A Nail*, the

O.V. Wright Hi hit from 1971, is particularly outstanding. The rhythm section lay down such a pumping sound that the original studio version sounds almost constipated. Virtually every song on the album is enhanced with a vamp, and Clay's sense of how to embellish is supremely tasteful and represents the most subtle of instincts in the art of soul singing. This sense is the highest art in African American music.

The South: Tennessee, Alabama, Georgia, Virginia, Carolinas

Bill Dahl

C all it what you will – Southern soul, deep soul, the Stax sound – some of the most emotionally gripping rhythm and blues of the 1960s and 1970s emanated from Memphis, Tennessee, and Muscle Shoals, Alabama. Characterized by sizzling horn charts, churning grooves, and a legion of super-charged, gospel-drenched vocalists, the Southern soul sound was a fascinating hybrid of styles then prevalent in the region.

Blues was certainly a factor in the development of the Southern soul sound – when Stax house band Booker T. and the MGs backed Albert King on his ground-breaking series of recordings in the mid-to-late 1960s, the quartet was so in tune with the idiom that they instantly were transformed into a world-class blues combo. But there was a great deal more to the approach.

The melismatic vocal deliveries of Wilson Pickett, Otis Redding, and Sam and Dave display a profound gospel influence in the way they work themselves into a fervor, and many of the leading artists in the Southern soul style (Johnnie Taylor, O.V. Wright, Aretha Franklin) graduated to the secular arena directly from the church.

The influence of country music was more of a primary factor on the Southern soul front than anywhere else. That should not be too surprising, since many of the leading labels' founders (Jim Stewart at Stax, Rick Hall at Fame, and Quinton Claunch of Goldwax, for example) boasted a strong background in hillbilly music. The moralistic tone of a great many Southern soul ballads was also a direct throwback to traditional country themes. Several important soul vocalists, especially those recording in Nashville (notably Joe Tex and Joe Simon), happily embraced country-rooted material and adapted Music Row compositions to their own style.

Most of the area's major recording studios developed their own house bands, a convenience that gave Stax records a slightly different drive than those cut in Muscle Shoals or Nashville. Formed in 1960 by banker and ex-country fiddler Jim Stewart and his sister Estelle Axton, and initially known as Satellite Records, Memphis-based Stax and its Volt subsidiary were blessed practically from the outset with the presence of Booker T. and the MGs, highly innovative session players who scored numerous instrumental hits of their own in addition to backing virtually every act on the voluminous Stax roster.

Leader Booker T. Jones's main instrument was organ, but he handled everything from baritone sax and tuba to lead guitar during his tenure at the firm. Steve Cropper's slashing licks and succinct chording set a lofty standard for Southern soul guitarists, and he was a prolific source of material as well. Drummer Al Jackson, Jr's stick-work was spare and elegant – he never overplayed or rolled when it was not necessary; and bassist Donald "Duck" Dunn (from 1964 on) laid down a rock-solid bottom. Trumpeter Wayne Jackson and tenor saxist Andrew Love formed the core of the Memphis Horns, whose precise blowing was another integral factor in the Stax sound.

Over in Muscle Shoals, it was often impossible to tell the players without having a scorecard; but the turnover never seemed to hinder founder Rick Hall, who built his Fame studio in 1962 and initially leased his productions to various labels. Hall produced his first hit, Arthur Alexander's *You Better Move On*, in 1962 and leased it to Dot. Hall inaugurated his own Fame logo in 1964 and emerged with Jimmy Hughes's pleading blues ballad *Steal Away*, a tremendously influential Southern soul smash.

While the Fame label was initially distributed by Vee Jay and later by Atlantic, Hall's productions also appeared regularly on Atlantic and Chess, the latter label reaping success with Bobby Moore and the Rhythm Aces' *Searching For My Love* in 1966, and memorable Hall-produced 45s by Irma Thomas, Laura Lee, and the duo of Maurice and Mac.

Upon opening his studio, Hall installed the first of several rhythm sections to work with his artists, and when that group left, he simply recruited a new batch. Hall had an ear for young talent, and each new aggregation seemed to perform as well as the preceding one, although the best-known crew – guitarist Jimmy Johnson, keyboardist Spooner Oldham, bassist David Hood, and drummer Roger Hawkins – epitomized the vital Muscle Shoals sound. With Barry Beckett replacing Oldham, the band gave Fame some fierce competition when they split to open their own Muscle Shoals Sound studio in 1969.

Although less prolific than Stax and Fame, Memphis-based Goldwax Records was responsible for some exceptionally intense Southern soul. Formed in 1964 by Quinton Claunch and Doc Russell, and also distributed at first by Vee Jay before joining up with Bell Records, Goldwax issued O.V. Wright's blistering debut, *That's How Strong My Love Is*, but the firm's principal artists were the incomparable James Carr, gritty vocalists Spencer Wiggins and Percy Milem, and the Ovations, whose lead singer, Louis Williams, possessed a delivery that uncannily recalled Sam Cooke's.

Goldwax often utilized many of the same session players (guitarist Reggie Young, bassists Mike Leech and Tommy Cogbill, keyboardists Bobby Wood and Bobby Emmons, and drummer Gene Chrisman) that later played on numerous hits for producer Chips Moman at his American Studio, and Moman engineered many Goldwax dates.

Memphis and Muscle Shoals were not the only southeastern soul capitals. Nashville boasted heady representation in the R & B charts, and important records also emerged during the 1960s from Atlanta, Georgia, Norfolk, Virginia, and the Carolinas (home of "beach music").

Essential Recordings

(i) Memphis: Stax–Volt – Otis Redding, Wilson Pickett, Sam and Dave

When Otis Redding (b. September 9, 1941, in Dawson, Georgia) visited the Stax studios for the first time in October, 1962, no one could possibly have guessed that he would eventually prove the label's most important artist. Although he had already waxed a handful of derivative singles for the tiny Confederate and Finer Arts labels, Redding was on hand ostensibly as little more than an observer. But when attempts to elicit a hit from his Macon, Georgia, cohorts Johnny Jenkins and the Pinetoppers proved futile, Redding was ready with the tremulous ballad *These Arms Of Mine*, and the song proved a respectable R & B hit when issued on Volt.

Redding's early singles were largely aching ballads. *Pain In My Heart* (his adaptation of the Irma Thomas hit *Ruler Of My Heart*), *Something Is Worrying Me*, and the tortured *That's What My Heart Needs* established Redding as an emotionally intense vocalist with a vulnerable edge. The singer scored his first three hefty hits in 1965: the driving *Mr Pitiful*, a heartbroken *I've Been Loving You Too Long (To Stop Now)* (co-written by Chicago soul singer Jerry Butler), and the searing original reading of *Respect*. Another 1965 hit, *I Can't Turn You Loose*, sported a powerhouse, mid-tempo groove and pile-driving brass; in concert, Redding insisted on singing it at a ridiculously feverish tempo.

A gifted composer, Redding wrote many of his best slow songs himself, but his biggest 1966–7 sellers were up-tempo items that stemmed from outside sources – his chaotic rendition of the Rolling Stones' *Satisfaction* and a brilliant arrangement of the pop standard *Try A Little Tenderness* that opens very slowly, shifts to a rhumba, and then accelerates at full throttle.

The charming *Fa-Fa-Fa-Fa-Fa (Sad Song)* is anything but downcast, Redding's uplifting vocal darting around a sturdy horn line that made it stand out in 1966. Pairing the king of Memphis soul with its resident queen was a natural development, and though hardly earthshaking, Redding's duets with Carla Thomas, *Tramp* and *Knock On Wood*, were both major chart items in 1967.

Redding scored his biggest seller shortly after he perished in a Wisconsin plane crash on December 10, 1967, along with much of his promising young backing band, the Bar-Kays. The introspective *(Sittin' On) The Dock Of The Bay*, recorded only three days before the tragedy, was a distinct departure with its wistful pop overtones, and it soared to the peak of the R & B and pop lists shortly after his death.

The prolific Redding left behind enough first-class material for three more complete albums, and unlike many such ventures, the posthumous singles *The Happy Song (Dum-Dum-De-De-De-Dum-Dum)*, *Hard To Handle*, and *I've Got Dreams To Remember* added substantially to his legacy.

Unlike Redding, Wilson Pickett (b. March 18, 1941, in Prattville, Alabama) had already enjoyed a fair amount of success, both as lead singer of the Detroit-based Falcons and on his own with Lloyd Price's Double L logo in New York, before he ever set foot inside Stax in May, 1965. There was one other major difference between the two: while Redding was contracted directly to Jim Stewart's company, Pickett journeyed to Memphis accompanied by his boss, Atlantic Records' Jerry Wexler, who was concerned about Pickett's lack of success with slickly produced New York sessions that failed to properly showcase the leather-lunged screamer. Since Atlantic distributed Stax, it benefited everyone to pair Pickett with the funky grooves of the MGs.

At first, the strategy worked magnificently. Pickett and Cropper co-wrote the incendiary *In The Midnight Hour* (Wexler choreographed the song's slightly-behind-the-beat tempo by dancing the Jerk on the studio floor), and it proved the singer's first number 1 R & B hit. Pickett encored with the enticing *Don't Fight It* and a loping *634-5789 (Soulsville, USA)*, another soul chart-topper, in early 1966. But after three sizzling sessions at Stax, the politics of the set-up turned sour, so Pickett switched to Muscle Shoals and immediately cut his third number 1 R & B hit, a supercharged revival of Chris Kenner's *Land Of 1000 Dances*, with Pickett screaming like a banshee over Charles Chalmers's King Curtis-influenced sax and Roger Hawkins's dynamic drum rolls.

Pickett "the Wicked One" scored repeatedly from 1966 to 1968 with revivals of recent soul songs that deserved a higher profile: Sir Mack Rice's *Mustang Sally*, Dyke and the Blazers' *Funky Broadway*, and Roger Collins's *She's Looking Good*. Pickett's versions were often better than the originals, in no small part due to the fine Muscle Shoals and Memphis bands that backed him.

Ex-Valentinos lead singer Bobby Womack contributed some of Pickett's best late 1960s originals and added delicate lead guitar to the atypically tender *I'm In Love*, cut at Chips Moman's American Studio during a momentary return to Memphis. Womack also co-wrote the unsubtle *I'm A Midnight Mover* with Pickett.

But things began to unravel artistically, as Pickett was reduced to gutturally wailing raucous covers of rock hits – the Beatles' *Hey Jude* and, most improbably, the fictional Archies' *Sugar Sugar* (ironically, the more palatable of the two). Far more appealing is the blasting 1969 original *A Man And A Half*, an eloquent testimonial to the Wicked Pickett's cocky image. As the decade turned, Pickett moved once again – this time to Philadelphia, where producers Kenny Gamble and Leon Huff rejuvenated his sound with *Don't Let The Green Grass Fool You* and *Get Me Back On Time, Engine Number 9*. He finally left Atlantic in 1973 and rapidly faded as a hitmaking force.

Aptly billed as "Double Dynamite," Sam and Dave summoned up the unrestrained glee of a sanctified Sunday morning Baptist prayer meeting with their non-stop call-and-response routine and slick showmanship. Miami-based Sam Moore (b. October 12, 1935, in Miami) and Dave Prater (b. May 9, 1936, in Ocilla, Georgia) were already seasoned studio veterans, having appeared on Alston, on Marlin, and quite effectively on Roulette without a great deal of commercial success prior to signing with Stax in 1965.

The Stax brass immediately paired the newcomers with another talented duo, writer/producers Isaac Hayes and David Porter, who steadily churned out exceptional material to match the kinetic energy level of their charges. After laying the groundwork with the bubbling *I Take What I Want*, Sam and Dave burst onto the R & B charts in late 1965 with the rapturous *You Don't Know Like I Know*, the song's complex structure anchored by the rock-solid MGs.

Hayes and Porter effortlessly turned out hits for Sam and Dave through the mid-1960s, and the pair returned the favor by injecting each song with a supercharged zeal, Moore usually prevailing as lead but switching off to Prater with engaging ease. *Hold On, I'm Comin'*, their first number 1 R & B smash in 1966, is a particularly hard-driving piece, full of savage seventh chords punctuated by short horn bursts and Jackson's eminently sparse backbeat.

The pair testified sensuously on *You Got Me Hummin'*, sweetly caressed the tender *When Something Is Wrong With My Baby*, and paid homage to Sam Cooke with a delicious revival of his *Soothe Me* before capturing the collective consciousness of the nation in 1967 with the anthemic *Soul Man*, a glorious celebration of the entire genre that gave them their second number 1 R & B hit and their biggest pop seller.

I Thank You/Wrap It Up was an exceptionally potent coupling in 1968, but the pair's career was derailed later that year when Atlantic assumed their contract after a disagreement with Stax. Despite the label change, Sam and Dave persevered, emerging with the wonderful 1968 outing *You Don't Know What You Mean To Me*, a Steve Cropper–Eddie Floyd composition as good as anything the pair had done, and the incendiary *Soul Sister, Brown Sugar*.

By 1970, the dynamic duo was floundering commercially despite some deserving releases, and sojourns to Muscle Shoals and Miami failed to rekindle the fire. The pair eventually parted ways amid much acrimony and bizarre accusations, and Prater died in an auto accident in 1988.

Discographical Details

206 The Otis Redding Story
Otis Redding

Atlantic 7 81762-2 (3-disc set)

These Arms Of Mine/That's What My Heart Needs/Mary's Little Lamb/Pain In My Heart/Something Is Worrying Me/Security/Come To Me/Your One And Only Man/ Chained And Bound/That's How Strong My Love Is/Mr Pitiful/Keep Your Arms Around Me/For Your Precious Love/A Woman, A Lover, A Friend/Home In Your Heart/I've Been Loving You Too Long (To Stop Now)/A Change Is Gonna Come/ Shake/Rock Me Baby/Respect/You Don't Miss Your Water/Satisfaction/Ole Man Trouble/Down In The Valley/I Can't Turn You Loose/Just One More Day/Papa's Got A Brand New Bag/Good To Me/Cigarettes And Coffee/Chain Gang/My Lover's Prayer/It's Growing/Fa-Fa-Fa-Fa-Fa (Sad Song)/I'm Sick Y'All/Sweet Lorene/Try A Little Tenderness/Day Tripper/Ton Of Joy/Hawg For You/Stay In School/You Left The Water Running/The Happy Song (Dum-Dum-De-De-De-Dum-Dum)/Hard To Handle/Amen/I've Got Dreams To Remember/Champagne And Wine/Direct Me/ Merry Christmas Baby/White Christmas/Love Man/Free Me/Look At That Girl/The Match Game/Tell The Truth/(Sittin' On) The Dock Of The Bay/Tramp (with Carla Thomas)/*Knock On Wood* (with Carla Thomas)/*Lovey Dovey* (with Carla Thomas)/*New Year's Resolution* (with Carla Thomas)/*Ooh Carla, Ooh Otis* (with Carla Thomas)

207 A Man And A Half: The Best Of Wilson Pickett
Wilson Pickett

Rhino 70287

Falcons: *I Found A Love;*Wilson Pickett: *Let Me Be Your Boy/If You Need Me/It's Too Late/I'm Gonna Cry/Come Home Baby/In The Midnight Hour/Don't Fight It/*

I'm Not Tired/That's A Man's Way/634-5789 (Soulsville USA)/Ninety-Nine And A Half (Won't Do)/Land Of 1000 Dances/Mustang Sally/Three Time Loser/Everybody Needs Somebody To Love/Soul Dance Number Three/You Can't Stand Alone/Funky Broadway/I'm In Love/Stag-O-Lee/Jealous Love/I've Come A Long Way/In The Midnight Hour (live)/I'm A Midnight Mover/I Found A True Love/She's Looking Good/A Man And A Half/Hey Jude/Mini-Skirt Minnie/Toe Hold/Hey Joe/You Keep Me Hangin' On/She Said Yes/Cole, Cooke And Redding/Sugar Sugar/Get Me Back On Time, Engine Number 9/Don't Let The Green Grass Fool You/Don't Knock My Love (Pt 1)/Call My Name, I'll Be There/Fire And Water/(Your Love Has Brought Me) A Mighty Long Way/Funk Factory/Funky Broadway (live)

208 The Best Of Sam And Dave
Sam and Dave
Atlantic 7 81279-2

A Place Nobody Can Find/Goodnight Baby/I Take What I Want/Sweet Home/You Don't Know Like I Know/Hold On, I'm Comin'/Said I Wasn't Gonna Tell Nobody/ You Got Me Hummin'/When Something Is Wrong With My Baby/Small Portion Of Your Love/Soothe Me/Soul Man/May I Baby/I Thank You/Wrap It Up/Still Is The Night/You Don't Know What You Mean To Me/This Is Your World/Can't You Find Another Way (Of Doing It)/Soul Sister, Brown Sugar/Come On In

(ii) Memphis: Stax/Volt – The Other Artists

Not all of the artists on the illustrious Stax/Volt roster achieved the same exalted level of commercial acceptance as Redding or Sam and Dave, although an examination of the massive nine-disc boxed set **The Complete Stax/Volt Singles: 1959–1968** proves that many of them merited a higher profile. Its 244 selections demonstrate how consistent the label's output remained throughout Atlantic's association with the firm, thanks to the yeoman contributions of Booker T. and the MGs, a talented in-house production staff, and an endless supply of exceptional material and talented vocalists.

The father-and-daughter team of Rufus and Carla Thomas acted as the catalyst for Jim Stewart's entry into the R & B world. Their 1960 duet *'Cause I Love You* was issued when the label was still known as Satellite, and both Thomas generations scored influential solo hits (though Carla's utterly innocent 1960 smash *Gee Whiz* and subsequent releases into 1965 were issued on Atlantic instead of Stax).

Rufus (b. March 26, 1917, in Cayce, Mississippi) carved out a niche for himself with a series of canine dance rave-ups – *The Dog, Walking The Dog, Can Your Monkey Do The Dog* – that were far removed from his blues roots and marked him as the firm's resident dancemaster into the early 1970s, when his high-stepping output challenged James Brown's claim on the collective feet of black youth.

An enduring Stax tradition of punchy instrumentals was firmly established in 1961 with the Mar-Keys' *Last Night*, with Smoochy Smith's two-fisted keyboards rolling over a twistable, brass-driven beat. For that memorable debut, the band also featured Steve Cropper (b. October 21, 1942, in Ozark Mountains, Missouri) on keyboards, not guitar, and Wayne Jackson on trumpet; during the mid-1960s, the revived Mar-Keys name served as a convenient showcase for instrumental releases by various permutations of the MGs (for Memphis Group), the Memphis Horns, and session players.

When it came to hit instrumentals, Booker T. and the MGs had few peers. The self-contained quartet led by keyboardist Booker T. Jones (b. November 12, 1944, in Memphis) made a spectacular debut with *Green Onions*, which leaped to the top of the R & B charts in 1962, blending Booker T.'s bubbling organ and Cropper's slashing guitar with a deceptively simple, minor-key bass line. The MGs never got too complex or jazzy, sticking with savage licks played over devastating grooves, and by the mid-1960s, their reputation rested on catchy melodies such as *Boot-Leg* and *Hip Hug-Her*.

The most overlooked important artist during the early years of Stax had to be vocalist William Bell (b. William Yarborough, July 16, 1939, in Memphis), whose plaintive *You Don't Miss Your Water* barely grazed the pop lists in 1961. Bell's warm, assured style was well suited to the Southern soul ballad genre, and a steady string of worthy 45s during the early 1960s – *Any Other Way, Somebody Mentioned Your Name, I'll Show You* – spotlighted his deep-hued delivery. Bell later contributed one of the most heartfelt homages in the wake of Otis Redding's tragic death, *A Tribute To A King*.

Vocal groups were few and far between on the Southern soul front, but Stax boasted one of the tightest aggregations around in the Mad Lads (John Gary Williams, Julius Green, William Brown, and Robert Phillips). The group's Volt output centered on smoothly harmonized ballads, despite making their debut in late 1964 with an untypical novelty item, *The Sidewalk Surf*. Later efforts such as *Don't Have To Shop Around, I Want A Girl*, and *Patch My Heart* better showcase their polished harmonies. Only the Astors, whose *Candy* was a solid seller in 1965, and latecomers Ollie and the Nightingales mounted any real challenge to the group's status as the top Stax group.

Carla Thomas was not the only contender for Stax soul-queen honors. Spunky Wendy Rene, sultry Ruby Johnson, and blues belter Mable John all turned out exceptional efforts during too-brief stints on the imprint. John, the sister of the legendary Little Willie John, introduced the David Porter–Isaac Hayes classic *Your*

Good Thing (Is About To End), while Rene's *Bar-B-Q* is a delectable ode to down-home cooking.

With so much talent strolling daily through the doors of the former movie palace that housed Stax headquarters, a few excellent artists were bound to get lost in the shuffle. Chicagoan Eddie Purrell's lone 1967 single *The Spoiler* is a thundering rocker in the best Redding mode that deserved a happier fate, and Sir Mack Rice, Oscar Mack, Prince Conley, Gorgeous George, and former Huey "Piano" Smith and the Clowns' frontman Bobby Marchan were all there long enough to leave an obscure gem or two behind.

Discographical Details

209 The Complete Stax/Volt Singles: 1959–1968
Various Artists

Atlantic 7 82218-2 (9-disc set)

The Veltones: *Fool In Love*; Carla and Rufus: *'Cause I Love You/That's Really Some Good/Night Time Is The Right Time/When You Move You Lose/Birds And Bees*; Carla Thomas: *Gee Whiz/(Mama. Mama) Wish Me Good Luck/I Kinda Think He Does/I'll Bring It Home To You/What A Fool I've Been/Gee Whiz It's Christmas/I've Got No Time To Lose/A Woman's Love/How Do You Quit (Someone You Love)/Stop! Look What You're Doin'/Comfort Me/Let Me Be Good To You/B-A-B-Y/All I Want For Christmas Is You/Something Good (Is Going To Happen To You)/When Tomorrow Comes/I'll Always Have Faith In You/Pick Up The Pieces/A Dime A Dozen*; The Chips: *You Make Me Feel Good*; The Mar-Keys: *Last Night/ Morning After/About Noon/Foxy/Pop-Eye Stroll/Whot's Happenin'!/Sack-O-Woe/Bo-Time/Bush Bash/Banana Juice/Grab This Thing (Pt 1)/Philly Dog*; Rufus and Friend: *I Didn't Believe*; Prince Conley: *I'm Going Home*; Barbara Stephens: *The Life I Live/Wait A Minute/That's The Way It Is With Me*; The Triumphs: *Burnt Biscuits*; William Bell: *You Don't Miss Your Water/Formula Of Love/Any Other Way/I Told You So/Just As I Thought/Somebody Mentioned Your Name/I'll Show You/Who Will It Be Tomorrow/Crying All By Myself/Share What You Got (But Keep What You Need)/Marching Off To War/Never Like This Before/Everybody Loves A Winner/Eloise (Hang On In There)/Everyday Will Be Like A Holiday/A Tribute To A King/Every Man Oughta Have A Woman*; Macy Skipper: *Goofin' Off*; Nick Charles: *Sunday Jealous/The Three Dogwoods*; The Tonettes: *No Tears/Teardrop Sea*; The Canes: *Why Should I Suffer With The Blues*; The Del-Rios: *Just Across The Street/There's A Love*; Rufus Thomas: *Can't Ever Let You Go/The Dog/ Walking The Dog/Can Your Monkey Do The Dog/Somebody Stole My Dog/Jump Back/Little Sally Walker/Willy Nilly/The World Is Round/Sister's Got A Boyfriend/ Sophisticated Sissy/Down Ta My House/The Memphis Train/I Think I Made A Boo Boo*; Booker T. and the MGs: *Green Onions/Behave Yourself/Jelly Bread/Home Grown/Chinese Checkers/Mo' Onions/Soul Dressing/Can't Be Still/Boot-Leg/Outrage/ Be My Lady/My Sweet Potato/Booker Loo/Jingle Bells/Hip Hug-Her/Groovin'/Slim Jenkins' Place/Winter Snow*; Otis Redding: *These Arms Of Mine/That's What My Heart Needs/Pain In My Heart/Come To Me/Don't Leave Me This Way/Security/ That's How Strong My Love Is/Mr Pitiful/I've Been Loving You Too Long (To Stop Now)/I'm Depending On You/Respect/I Can't Turn You Loose/Just One More Day/ Satisfaction/My Lover's Prayer/Fa-Fa-Fa-Fa-Fa (Sad Song)/Try A Little Tender-ness/I Love You More Than Words Can Say/Shake/Glory Of Love/(Sittin' On) The Dock Of The Bay/The Happy Song (Dum-Dum)*; Deanie Parker and the Valadors: *My Imaginary Guy*; Eddie Kirk: *The Hawg, Pt 1/Them Bones*; Oscar Mack: *Don't*

Be Afraid Of Love/Dream Girl; Cheryl and Pam Johnson: *That's My Guy*; Bobby Marchan: *What Can I Do/You Won't Do Right*; The Astors: *What Can It Be/Candy/In The Twilight Zone/Daddy Didn't Tell Me*; Billy and the King Bees: *Bango*; Floyd Newman: *Frog Stomp*; The Drapels: *Wondering (When My Love Is Coming Home)/Young Man*; Deanie Parker: *Each Step I Take*; The Van-Dells: *The Honey Dripper*; Eddie Jefferson: *I Don't Want You Anymore*; The Cobras: *Restless*; Barbara and the Browns: *Big Party/In My Heart/My Lover*; Dorothy Williams: *Closer To My Baby*; Wendy Rene: *After Laughter (Comes Tears)/Bar-B-Q/Give You What I Got*; Ivory Joe Hunter: *I Can't Explain How It Happened*; Fleets: *Please Return To Me*; Johnny Jenkins: *Spunky*; The Mad Lads: *The Sidewalk Surf/Don't Have To Shop Around/I Want Someone/Sugar Sugar/I Want A Girl/Patch My Heart/I Don't Want To Lose Your Love/My Inspiration/Whatever Hurts You*; The Baracudas: *Yank Me (Doodle)*; The Del-Rays: *Don't Let Her Be Your Baby*; David Porter: *Can't See You When I Want To*; The Admirals: *Got You On My Mind*; Gorgeous George: *Biggest Fool In Town*; Sam and Dave: *A Place Nobody Can Find/Goodnight Baby/I Take What I Want/You Don't Know Like I Know/Hold On I'm Comin'/Said I Wasn't Gonna Tell Nobody/You Got Me Hummin'/When Something Is Wrong With My Baby/Soothe Me/I Can't Stand Up/Soul Man/I Thank You/Wrap It Up*; The Premiers: *Make It Me*; Sir Isaac and the Do-Dads: *Blue Groove*; Johnnie Taylor: *I Had A Dream/I've Got To Love Somebody's Baby/Little Bluebird/Toe Hold/Ain't That Loving You (For More Reasons Than One)/You Can't Get Away From It/Somebody's Sleeping In My Bed/Next Time/I Ain't Particular*; Eddie Floyd: *Things Get Better/Knock On Wood/Raise Your Hand/Don't Rock The Boat/Love Is A Doggone Good Thing/On A Saturday Night/Big Bird*; Ruby Johnson: *I'll Run Your Hurt Away/Come To Me My Darling/When My Loves Comes Down/If I Ever Needed Love (I Sure Do Need It Now)*; The Four Shells: *Hot Dog*; Albert King: *Laundromat Blues/Oh, Pretty Woman/Crosscut Saw/Born Under A Bad Sign/Cold Feet/(I Love) Lucy*; Mable John: *Your Good Thing (Is About To End)/You're Taking Up Another Man's Place/Same Time Same Place/I'm A Big Girl Now/Wait You Dog/Don't Hit Me No More/Able Mable*; The Charmels: *Please Uncle Sam (Send Back My Man)/I'll Gladly Take You Back/As Long As I've Got You*; Bobby Wilson: *Let Me Down Slow*; Sir Mack Rice: *Mini-Skirt Minnie/Love Sickness*; Eddie Purrell: *The Spoiler*; Otis and Carla: *Tramp/Knock On Wood/Lovey Dovey*; The Bar-Kays: *Soul Finger/Knucklehead/Give Everybody Some/A Hard Day's Night*; Jeanne and the Darlings: *How Can You Mistreat The One You Love/Soul Girl/What Will Later On Be Like/Hang Me Now*; C.L. Blast: *I'm Glad To Do It/Double Up*; Judy Clay: *You Can't Run Away From Your Heart*; Johnny Daye: *What'll I Do For Satisfaction*; The Memphis Nomads: *Don't Pass Your Judgement*; Ollie and the Nightingales: *I Got A Sure Thing*; Derek Martin: *Soul Power*; Linda Lyndell: *Bring Your Love Back To Me*

(iii) Memphis – Other Labels

Double or triple the emotional intensity of Otis Redding and you have the devastating sonic impact of James Carr (b. June 13, 1942, in Memphis), whose tortured vocal delivery apparently mirrored a troubled offstage existence. Carr was the most impressive artist on the roster of Goldwax Records, a relatively small Memphis label that consistently issued incendiary soul efforts during the 1960s. Like fellow Memphis-based powerhouse O.V. Wright, another gospel refugee who made his debut on Goldwax, Carr was a protégé of songwriter Roosevelt Jamison, who wrote his bluesy 1964 debut, *You Don't Want Me.*

O.B. McClinton, who later became a rare commodity indeed –
a black country singer – wrote Carr's initial smash in 1966. Carr
delivered the searing *You've Got My Mind Messed Up* at a truly
intimidating level of intensity, with Reggie Young's ringing guitar
sharply echoing the singer's mournful cries. McClinton wrote
several more deep soul classics for Carr, notably the spine-chilling
Lovable Girl and *She's Better Than You* and the churchy *A Man
Needs A Woman*, a 1968 hit that contains a batch of especially
imaginative metaphors.

At his best, especially on the romping, brass-powered *Pouring
Water On A Drowning Man* and the stunning (and often-covered)
Chips Moman–Dan Penn ballad *The Dark End Of The Street*,
Carr's utterly overwhelming delivery is definitive of the entire
genre. When the singer attempts a rave-up dance number such as
Coming Back To Me Baby or *That's What I Want To Know*, the
results are often disappointing: Carr's emotionally devastating
delivery is best displayed on tear-stained ballads.

During the late 1960s, label-owners/producers Quinton
Claunch and Rudolph "Doc" Russell emphasized the country
side of Carr's sound with a comparatively mellow reading of
Harlan Howard's *Life Turned Her That Way*, even adding steel
guitar to a faithful cover of Joe Simon's *My Adorable One*. But by
1969, Carr's unpredictable behavior scuttled his career, after he
scored his last hit with a revival of the Bee Gees' *To Love
Somebody*. In the early 1990s returned to the revived Goldwax and
cut an exceptional new collection, **Take Me To The Limit**, that
found his talent happily intact after a long layoff. (Since Carr's
indispensable performances are evenly spread between the two
Vivid discs, they are considered as one entry for review purposes.)

During the early 1970s, producer Willie Mitchell assembled his
own self-contained soul empire at Hi Records, another highly
successful Memphis imprint. Hi had been in existence since 1957
and initially focused primarily on rockabilly, with a pronounced
emphasis on generic instrumentals.

Trumpeter Mitchell's own punchy combo waxed numerous
instrumental albums for Hi through the 1960s, and he eventually
assembled a young rhythm section around the Hodges brothers
(Mabon, nicknamed "Teenie," on guitar, Charles on organ, and
Leroy on bass) and drummer Howard Grimes that was every bit as
distinctive and well meshed as the MGs (whose own drummer, Al
Jackson Jr, was alternate anchor of the Hi rhythm section).

Mitchell's most successful acquisition was Al Green (b. April
13, 1946, in Forest City, Arkansas), who epitomized the gradual
softening of the Memphis soul sound in the early 1970s. Green's
vulnerably sensual vocal delivery stood in stark contrast to the
raspy cries of Pickett, although Green exhibited definite echoes of

Cooke and Redding on his earlier efforts, which included a major 1967 hit for Hot Wire, the hypnotic *Back Up Train*.

In 1971, Green and Mitchell concocted *Tired Of Being Alone*, following a period of experimentation that included a solid-selling and considerably more lowdown remake of the Temptations' *I Can't Get Next To You*. Utilizing some of the most complex chord progressions of the era, Green rode the very pinnacle of the soul charts for the next four years, with no fewer than six number 1 R & B hits. *Let's Stay Together*, the biggest of them all in late 1971, found Green passionately pleading for another chance over a hypnotic rhythm track and muted horns. Aiming directly for "the ladies" (overwhelmingly his constituency), Green moaned *I'm Still In Love With You*, *You Ought To Be With Me*, and *Call Me (Come Back Home)*, while the chunky *Here I Am (Come And Take Me)* and *Let's Get Married* ventured a little closer to the traditional Memphis soul sound.

Although they inexplicably were not issued as singles at the time, *Love And Happiness* (taken from one of his most consistent albums, 1972's **I'm Still In Love With You**) and Green's original *Take Me To The River* (from the 1974 **Explores Your Mind** LP) rank among the singer's very best works. Both co-written by Green and guitarist Teenie Hodges, they emphasize Green's vast creativity as a composer. Even unlikely cover choices such as the Bee Gees' *How Can You Mend A Broken Heart* and Kris Kristofferson's country chestnut *For The Good Times* benefit from Green's lilting delivery and subtle support from Hi's resident rhythm masters (though hardly rating with the singer's own material).

In 1977, Green left Mitchell, and his unprecedented hitmaking streak soon ran its course (*Belle* was his last major R & B chart appearance that year). Three years later, Green turned his back on commercial show business, establishing his own church in Memphis and successfully confining his activities to the gospel field.

Discographical Details

210 You Got My Mind Messed Up

James Carr

Vivid VGCD 002 (Jap)

She's Better Than You/You Don't Want Me/You've Got My Mind Messed Up/That's What I Want To Know/Love Attack/Coming Back To Me Baby/Forgetting You/ Pouring Water On A Drowning Man/Lovable Girl/These Ain't Raindrops/To Love Somebody/Who's Been Warming My Oven/Please Your Woman/I Don't Want To Be Hurt Anymore/I'm Going For Myself/The Dark End Of The Street/Let It Happen/My Adorable One/Everybody Needs Somebody/Row Row Your Boat/What The World Needs Now Is Love/I've Gotta Go

A Man Needs A Woman
James Carr
Vivid VGCD 005 (Jap)
*A Man Needs A Woman/Stronger Than Love/A Losing Game/I'm A Fool For You/
Can't Help Myself/Gonna Send You Back To Georgia/More Love/You Didn't Know
It But You Had Me/A Woman Is A Man's Best Friend/Sowed Love And Reaped A
Heartache/What Can I Call My Own/Lifetime Of A Man/Your Love Made A "U"
Turn/You Gotta Have Soul/Love Attack/Pouring Water On A Drowning Man/Life
Turned Her That Way/A Message To Young Lovers/That's The Way Love Turned
Out For Me/Freedom Train/Hold On*

211 Compact Command Performances
Al Green
Motown MOTD-6111
*Tired Of Being Alone/Call Me (Come Back Home)/I'm Still In Love With You/Here I
Am (Come And Take Me)/How Can You Mend A Broken Heart/Let's Stay Together/
I Can't Get Next To You/You Ought To Be With Me/Look What You've Done For
Me/Let's Get Married/Love And Happiness/Take Me To The River/For The Good
Times/Livin' For You*

(iv) Muscle Shoals

The first Muscle Shoals production to register at number 1 on
both the pop and R & B charts was not even cut in the fabled town
proper, but in nearby Sheffield, Alabama. Its creator, Percy Sledge
(b. November 15, 1940, in Leighton, Alabama), was a local
product seemingly born to pour his heart and soul into the deeply
affecting *When A Man Loves A Woman*, and the wrenching ballad
proved a creative and commercial benchmark for the thriving
Southern soul genre.

Amazingly, the 1966 masterpiece represented Sledge's debut on
wax. Borrowing Rick Hall's first-rate rhythm section, including
guitarist Jimmy Johnson, bassist Junior Lowe, and drummer
Roger Hawkins, neophyte producers Quin Ivy and Marlin Greene
somehow emerged from their primitive studio with a genuine
classic. The track's ethereal mix and Sledge's moving, high-
pitched wail combined to create an unforgettable million-seller.

Sledge specialized in ballads throughout his tenure on Atlantic
(of the 20 tracks on **The Ultimate Collection**, only two – *Put A
Little Lovin' On Me* and Bobby Womack's *Baby Help Me* – are up-
tempo), and a legion of local songwriters supported him. The
prolific Dan Penn and Spooner Oldham contributed two of
Sledge's best outings, the agonized *It Tears Me Up* and the
touching *Out Of Left Field*. Another pair of respected area
tunesmiths, Eddie Hinton and Donnie Fritts, handed the singer
You're All Around Me, and Sledge responded with a remarkable
performance that communicates an intense sense of hopeless
isolation (buoyed by a gospel-drenched female choir).

Warm And Tender Love, a glistening showcase for Sledge's choirboy-level vocal purity, was a remake of an obscure single penned by Harlem entrepreneur Bobby Robinson, while *Take Time To Know Her*, a well-crafted tale of matrimonial deceit, was Sledge's last major hit in early 1968. Even when Sledge covers the most innocent of songs, an overwhelming feeling of heartbreak prevails. His *Love Me Tender* is an aching plea for affection light years removed from Elvis Presley's effortless crooning, and a revival of *Just Out Of Reach* drips more desperation than Solomon Burke's classy, uptown rendition. Sledge's impassioned versions of *The Dark End Of The Street* and *You're Pouring Water On A Drowning Man* rival James Carr's intense readings. Sledge remained in the charts through 1969, but was heard from infrequently after that.

Although she recorded a grand total of one complete song and part of a second at Rick Hall's Fame facilities, Aretha Franklin nevertheless belongs squarely within the Muscle Shoals section. Atlantic Records producer Jerry Wexler repeatedly brought the nucleus of Hall's resident rhythm section to New York for Franklin's seminal 1967–9 sessions, a time-frame that neatly corresponds to her coronation as the Queen of Soul.

Most importantly, Franklin brought her own incomparable gospel-fired voice and rock-ribbed, direct-from-the-pulpit piano to the proceedings. Born on March 25, 1942, Franklin developed her soaring vocal delivery by observing the royalty of gospel music pass through her father's famous church in Detroit, and she made her debut on wax in 1956 with a handful of primitively recorded live gospel tracks. Legendary Columbia Records producer John Hammond introduced her to the secular world in 1960, and for the next seven years, Franklin recorded in an occasionally bewildering variety of styles for the company – jazzy blues, string-laden sentimentality, Broadway show tunes, and some very underrated uptown soul among them. When Wexler signed Franklin to Atlantic in 1967, he was determined to emphasize her sanctified roots in an R & B setting, bringing her to Muscle Shoals in January, 1967.

Wexler's strategy paid off magnificently when Franklin cut the unrestrained and spine-chilling *I Never Loved A Man (The Way I Love You)*, her first number 1 R & B smash. Spooner Oldham's electric piano kicks off the mesmerizing track, which steadily builds to a sensuous climax. But after rhythm tracks for the Dan Penn–Chips Moman-penned flip, *Do Right Woman – Do Right Man*, had been laid down, an argument in the studio brought the session to a grinding halt.

Faced with this problem, Wexler simply imported the Muscle Shoals rhythm section to New York and resumed work on Franklin's first album, which also included her anthemic take-off

of Otis Redding's *Respect*. Franklin added her own signature
touches to the song's framework, defiantly spelling out the title in
a non-negotiable demand, while King Curtis contributed a wailing
tenor-sax solo that helped Franklin's remake eclipse the original
by entering both the pop and R & B charts. The single's passionate
flip, *Dr Feelgood*, reaffirmed Franklin's mastery of the blues idiom,
her crashing piano pushing a vocal alternately sweet and
impudent.

Every Franklin 45 released by Atlantic during 1967–8 raced to
the uppermost reaches of both charts, from the inviting, mid-
tempo *Baby, I Love You* and roaring *Chain Of Fools* to a high-
flying *(Sweet, Sweet Baby) Since You've Been Gone* and the
romping *Think*, another sisterly call to arms that opens with
Franklin's gospel-drenched 88s and brilliantly spotlights her
heavenly voice. The Muscle Shoals sound apparently traveled
well – the grooves on the relentless *The House That Jack Built* and
a powerful revival of Don Covay's *See-Saw* were as right as
anything coming directly out of Fame.

Franklin's late 1960s output was not limited strictly to hard-
edged soul. *(You Make Me Feel Like) A Natural Woman*, written
by Wexler and Brill Building veterans Carole King and Gerry
Goffin, is pure pop, and the majestic *Ain't No Way*, contributed by
Aretha's sister Carolyn (who often added backing vocals along
with their sister Erma), is a bravura ballad reminiscent of
Franklin's Columbia days. As she had with *Respect*, Franklins
usurped *I Say A Little Prayer* from its originator (Dionne
Warwick), her breathtaking vocal transforming the Burt Bacharach–Hal David pop tune into yet another R & B masterpiece.

Wexler was convinced that Miami could thrive as another R & B
recording mecca, so after two additional huge hits – a remake of
the Band's *The Weight* (Duane Allman providing stinging slide
guitar) and a smooth cover of Bobby Bland's *Share Your Love
With Me* – the Muscle Shoals/New York hybrid phase of
Franklin's career came to a close (although the Fame session
crew made a trip to Miami for Franklin's sugary *Call Me* and a
pointless rehash of the Beatles' *Eleanor Rigby*). Except for three
1969 covers, the last half of Rhino/Atlantic's exhaustive four-disc
Franklin boxed set examines her post-Muscle Shoals output
exclusively (her up-tempo 1970 Miami treatment of Ben E. King's
Don't Play That Song (You Lied) absolutely soars).

Boasting a low-pitched bluesy growl and the sexiest groan this
side of Conway Twitty, Clarence Carter (b. 1936, in Montgomery, Alabama) sounded like no one else in Muscle Shoals – or in
the entire Southern soul pantheon, for that matter.

Blind from the age of one, Carter took up guitar at 11 and soon
teamed up with another sightless musician, pianist Calvin Scott.
As Clarence and Calvin, the duo recorded for Fairlane, Duke

(billed as the C & C Boys), and Atco through the early-to-mid-1960s before an auto accident broke up the act. Carter started on Rick Hall's own Fame label in 1966 as a solo, cutting a handful of solid singles (including the original *Tell Daddy*, which evolved into *Tell Mama* in Etta James's capable hands). Carter's Muscle Shoals output began to appear on Atlantic in 1968, and his fortunes rose markedly.

With the release of *Slip Away*, Carter had his first huge hit. Atmospherically capturing the urgency of forbidden love with his impassioned vocal, *Slip Away* was a terrific piece of production by Hall, the singer framed by a catchy rhythm guitar riff, tasty horns, and accurate bass. *Too Weak To Fight* was a perfect follow-up, similar enough to *Slip Away* to reinforce Carter's ribald persona without being derivative. Hall and his charge wisely stayed down in the alley for the sizzling *Snatching It Back* and the amusing *I Smell A Rat*, and Carter was also responsible for the most lascivious Christmas song of the millennium with *Back Door Santa*, St Nick's customary jolly message supplanted by Carter's evil chuckle.

From 1968 to 1970, Carter could do little wrong, writing the warm *I Can't Leave Your Love Alone* with prolific Muscle Shoals tunesmith George Jackson and delivering the lascivious *Doin' Our Thing* totally credibly. Strangely, Carter's treatment of James Carr's *The Dark End Of The Street* is a disappointment, marred by a ponderous spoken introduction and a dreary dirge tempo.

In 1970, Hall handed Carter an overlooked album track by Chairmen of the Board called *Patches*. The maudlin narrative tale of death, destruction, and redemption was clearly a change of pace from Carter's usual leering output, but his faithful treatment proved his biggest pop-seller. Reverting to Hall's revived Fame logo in 1972, Carter made a number of solid recordings before breaking away from Hall's guidance to make three mid-1970s albums for ABC (the last two cut at Carter's own Atlanta studio). With no need to beat around the lyrical bush any longer, Carter's contemporary output is usually licentious (and frequently hilarious).

Discographical Details

212 The Ultimate Collection – When A Man Loves A Woman
Percy Sledge

Atlantic 7 80212-2

When A Man Loves A Woman/It Tears Me Up/Take Time To Know Her/My Special Prayer/Baby Help Me/It's All Wrong But It's Alright/You're All Around Me/The Dark End Of The Street/Warm And Tender Love/Love Me Tender/Out Of Left Field/Come Softly To Me/What Am I Living For/You're Pouring Water On A Drowning Man/Just Out Of Reach (Of My Two Empty Arms)/Cover Me/Sudden Stop/That's How Strong My Love Is/You Really Got A Hold On Me/Put A Little Lovin' On Me

213   Queen Of Soul: The Atlantic Recordings
Aretha Franklin

Rhino/Atlantic R2 71063 (4-disc set)
I Never Loved A Man (The Way I Love You)/Do Right Woman – Do Right Man/
Save Me/Respect/Baby, Baby, Baby/Dr Feelgood/(You Make Me Feel Like) A
Natural Woman/Soul Serenade/Drown In My Own Tears/Chain Of Fools/Baby, I
Love You/Ain't Nobody (Gonna Turn Me Around)/(Sweet, Sweet Baby) Since
You've Been Gone/You Are My Sunshine/Going Down Slow/Never Let Me Go/I
Wonder/Prove It/Good Times/Come Back Baby/A Change/You're A Sweet, Sweet
Man/Good To Me As I Am To You/People Get Ready/Ain't No Way/Think/See-Saw/
The House That Jack Built/Night Time Is The Right Time/I Say A Little Prayer/You
Send Me/My Song/I Take What I Want/I Can't See Myself Leaving You/Night Life
(live version)/Today I Sing The Blues/Pitiful/Tracks Of My Tears/River's Invitation/
Share Your Love With Me/It Ain't Fair/Sit Down And Cry/Honest I Do/The Weight/
When The Battle Is Over/Eleanor Rigby/One Way Ticket/Call Me/Pullin'/Son Of A
Preacher Man/Try Matty's/The Thrill Is Gone/Dark End Of The Street/You And Me/
Let It Be/Spirit In The Dark/Why I Sing The Blues/Don't Play That Song/Young,
Gifted And Black/Border Song (Holy Moses)/A Brand New Me/You're All I Need To
Get By/Spanish Harlem/Rock Steady/Oh Me Oh My (I'm A Fool For You Baby)/
Day Dreaming/All The King's Horses/Bridge Over Troubled Water/Angel/Spirit In
The Dark (with Ray Charles)/How I Got Over/So Swell When You're Well/Master
Of Eyes (The Deepness Of Your Eyes)/Somewhere/I'm In Love/Ain't Nothing Like
The Real Thing/Until You Come Back To Me (That's What I'm Gonna Do)/Every
Natural Thing/Without Love/With Everything I Feel In Me/Mr DJ (5 For The DJ)/
Look Into Your Heart/Sparkle/Rock With Me/Break It To Me Gently/Something He
Can Feel

214   Snatching It Back: The Best Of Clarence Carter
Clarence Carter

Rhino/Atlantic 70286
Step By Step/I Stayed Away Too Long/Tell Daddy/The Road Of Love/I Can't See
Myself/Looking For A Fox/Slip Away/Back Door Santa/That Old Time Feeling/Too
Weak To Fight/I'd Rather Go Blind/Making Love (At The Dark End Of The Street)/
Snatching It Back/Soul Deep/I Smell A Rat/Doin' Our Thing/The Feeling Is Right/I
Can't Leave Your Love Alone/Patches/It's All In Your Mind/Slipped, Tripped And
Fell In Love

(v) Nashville

Joe Tex (b. Joseph Arrington, Jr, August 8, 1933, in Rogers, Texas) was already a seasoned veteran of nearly a decade's experience in the studio when he traveled to Muscle Shoals for the first time in 1964. And for the first time his sincere brand of secular sermonizing vaulted him into the soul charts. Once he got there, he hovered around the uppermost reaches for the next seven years despite nomadically recording in all three major soul centers – Nashville, Memphis, and Muscle Shoals.

Tex exhibited a chameleon-like quality early in his career. He recorded rocking R & B for King, beginning in 1955, and accurately imitated Little Richard and the Coasters for Ace in New Orleans a few years later, with little commercial feedback. In

1961, Tex joined up in Nashville with country-music publisher/ producer Buddy Killen, who produced three years' worth of workmanlike Tex singles for Killen's own Dial label to another round of resounding indifference.

Just when Tex was poised to give up the partnership, he journeyed down to Muscle Shoals with his own band in tow and cut the gospel-influenced ballad *Hold What You've Got*, alternately singing and preaching his plea for old-fashioned faithfulness. It catapulted Tex into soul stardom in early 1965, and his sermonizing became an enduring trademark.

No matter where Tex recorded – Nashville, Muscle Shoals, or, in the case of many of his late 1960s hits, Chips Moman's American Studio in Memphis – his homespun humor ran true under Killen's expert direction. His second hit, the clever *You Got What It Takes*, sported a lascivious hook and a relaxed groove, while a catchy break riff bowed on an acoustic bass distinguished the 1966 mid-tempo *I've Got To Do A Little Bit Better*. Both of Tex's exultant 1965 number 1 R & B smashes, *I Want To (Do Everything For You)* and *A Sweet Woman Like You*, rode on top of chugging bass lines and slashing rhythm guitar licks, his vocals sometimes attractively double-tracked.

The hard-charging brassy rockers *S.Y.S.L.J.F.M. (The Letter Song)* and *Show Me* represent some of Tex's most uncompromising up-tempo efforts from the mid-1960s, but his novelty leanings emerge fully on the hilarious, ersatz-live *Skinny Legs And All*, a late 1967 hit. Tex's last R & B number 1, the grunting *I Gotcha*, is in the same teasing mode, with strutting horns pushing Tex's vocal. After briefly cashing in on the disco uproar, Tex died of a heart attack in 1982.

Discographical Details

215   The Best Of Joe Tex
Joe Tex

Rhino/Atlantic R2 70191

Hold What You've Got/S.Y.S.L.J.F.M. (The Letter Song)/One Monkey Don't Stop No Show/I Believe I'm Gonna Make It/Papa Was Too/The Love You Save (May Be Your Own)/I've Got To Do A Little Bit Better/Buying A Book/Show Me/You're Right, Ray Charles/You Got What It Takes/Don't Make Your Children Pay/Grandma Mary/Anything You Wanna Know/Skinny Legs And All/A Sweet Woman Like You/I Want To (Do Everything For You)/I Gotcha

Basic Recordings

Memphis – 1960s

216   Soul Dressing
Booker T. and the MGs

Atlantic 7 82337-2

Soul Dressing/Tic-Tac-Toe/Big Train/Jellybread/Aw'Mercy/Outrage/Night Owl Walk/Chinese Checkers/Home Grown/Mercy Mercy/Plum Nellie/Can't Be Still

Even though there's no major hit of the order of *Green Onions* or *Hip Hug-Her* on it, **Soul Dressing** captures the unparalleled Stax house band at their most persuasive. Unlike many of their 1960s albums, there is only one non-original (a sleek reworking of Don Covay's *Mercy Mercy*), and pumping Memphis grooves permeate every track.

Cut from 1962 to 1964, most of the album features original bassist Lewis Steinberg instead of successor Duck Dunn, but the principals are otherwise in place – Booker T. Jones's bubbling organ (on *Chinese Checkers*, he doubles on electric piano and trombone), Steve Cropper on slashing guitar, and Al Jackson Jr, pounding out the backbeat. Cropper is particularly well served, stretching out on *Jellybread* and the ominous *Plum Nellie*, while the quartet settles into some mellow, jazz-laced blues on *Night Owl Walk* and produces a cool, minor-key groove on the title track. The incendiary interplay between the foursome on the imaginative rocker *Outrage* is genuinely exciting, befitting a band that spent the majority of its waking hours in the studio.

217   Knock On Wood
Eddie Floyd

Atlantic 7 80283-2

Knock On Wood/Something You Got/But It's Alright/I Stand Accused/If You Gotta Make A Fool Of Somebody/I Don't Want To Cry/Raise Your Hand/Got To Make A Comeback/634-5789/I've Just Been Feeling Bad/High Heel Sneakers/Warm And Tender Love

Despite its load of eight covers (ironic, considering his vaunted reputation as a writer), the album **Knock On Wood** by Eddie Floyd (b. June 25, 1935, in Montgomery, Alabama) ranks as one of the most propulsive sets ever cut at Stax. A founding member of the Detroit-based Falcons before Stax newcomer Al Bell brought him in from Washington, DC, Floyd's reliability as a vocalist is underscored by a shimmering revival of Chuck Jackson's *I Don't Want To Cry* and a driving *634-5789* (co-written by Floyd and Steve Cropper) that betters Wilson Pickett's hit version. The MGs and Memphis Horns contribute fresh, innovative arrangements to Chris Kenner's *Something You Got* and a torrid remake of Tommy Tucker's *High Heel Sneakers*.

Originally intended for Otis Redding, the R & B chart-topper *Knock On Wood* is an all-time Memphis classic. Al Jackson's pounding snare-drum defines the simmering groove here, while Duck Dunn's rock-solid bass anchors the infectious call-and-response *Raise Your Hand*. Floyd is not incompetent as a balladeer either – witness the gorgeous originals *I've Just Been Feeling Bad* and *Got To Make A Comeback*, with Steve Cropper's vibrato-enriched guitar winding around Floyd's intimate vocals.

218   See-Saw
Don Covay

Atlantic 8120 (LP)

*See-Saw/The Boomerang/Everything Gonna Be Everything/Fat Man/Precious You/
Iron Out The Rough Spots/Please Do Something/I Never Get Enough Of Your Love/
The Usual Place/A Woman's Love/Sookie Sookie/Mercy, Mercy*

Don Covay (b. March, 1938, in Orangeburg, South Carolina) had been in the
music business for some years by the time he arrived in Memphis. He sang doo-
wop in the mid-1950s in Washington, DC, with the Rainbows, imitated Little
Richard on Atlantic, and enjoyed limited success as a dance specialist before
signing with Rosemart and having a hit in 1964 with his innovative, mid-tempo
Mercy, Mercy, which sported prominent rhythm guitar and an imaginative chord
progression.

When Atlantic shipped Covay off to very briefly record at Stax in 1965, he
responded with some of his most incendiary work. The hit title track drives on
top of churchy piano and Duck Dunn's beefy bass, the singer's vocals answered
by a raspy, falsetto voice that was a Covay trademark. The insistent *Iron Out The
Rough Spots* (penned by Steve Cropper, Booker T., and David Porter) and *I
Never Get Enough Of Your Love* boast gliding, mid-tempo grooves, Cropper's
slashing chords adding color. Like many of Covay's melodies, the simple dance
number *Sookie Sookie* fared better commercially in a cover by Steppenwolf, but
the original's MGs-powered groove is a distinct improvement on the lightweight
feel of several others here that were cut elsewhere.

219   The Best Of Willie Mitchell
Willie Mitchell

Hi 2 SHL 32068/9 (LP)

*Soul Serenade/Papa's Got A Brand New Bag/Mercy Mercy Mercy/Bum Daddy/
Barefootin'/Have You Ever Had The Blues/Grazing In The Grass/Strawberry Soul/
Misty/Buster Browne/20-75/Sunrise Serenade/Searching For My Love/The Horse/
Woodchopper's Ball/Slippin' And Slidin'/Bad Eye/Everything's Gonna Be Alright/
That Driving Beat/The Crawl*

From 1961 on, trumpeter/producer Willie Mitchell (b. 1928, in Ashland,
Mississippi) turned out instrumentals for Hi that were permeated by Memphis
funk. He adopted a relaxed stance on *Sunrise Serenade* in 1962, but his first real
hit in 1964, *20-75*, was a charging, horn-powered workout that rivaled the
excitement of anything Stax could muster.

Utilizing a pool of tenor-sax talent that included his brother James, Andrew
Love, and Charles Chalmers, Mitchell proved that he could accurately duplicate
the sounds of the MGs (*Woodchopper's Ball*) and Motown saxman Junior Walker
(*That Driving Beat* and *Everything's Gonna Be Alright*, the set's only vocals). But it
was not until he personally groomed a young rhythm section revolving around
three brothers – guitarist Teenie Hodges and his siblings Charles on organ and
Leroy on bass – and veteran drummer Howard Grimes that Mitchell developed
his unique sound. He scored his biggest instrumental hit on a cover of the King
Curtis classic *Soul Serenade* in 1968, but his greatest triumphs came as mentor to
Hi's stable of talented vocalists.

220 Chronicle: The 20 Greatest Hits
Johnnie Taylor

Stax FCD-60-006

Who's Making Love/Take Care Of Your Homework/Testify (I Wonna)/I Could Never Be President/Love Bones/Steal Away/I Am Somebody (Pt 1)/Jody's Got Your Girl And Gone/I Don't Want To Lose You/Hijackin' Love/Standing In For Jody/Doing My Own Thing (Pt 1)/Stop Doggin' Me/I Believe In You (You Believe In Me)/Cheaper To Keep Her/We're Getting Careless With Our Love/I've Been Born Again/It's September/Try Me Tonight/Just Keep On Lovin' Me (with Carla Thomas)

Johnnie Taylor (b. May 5, 1938, in Crawfordsville, Arkansas) bridged the stylistic gap between the aggressive Stax sound of the 1960s and the firm's slicker, more heavily produced approach of the early 1970s. A Sam Cooke protégé who replaced his idol in the Soul Stirrers and made his secular debut on Cooke's SAR imprint in 1961, Taylor joined Stax in 1966. His initial output there consisted mostly of succulent, blues-drenched efforts. But the gritty vocalist altered his approach and found soul success in 1968 with a blistering alert to unfaithful lovers, *Who's Making Love*, that topped the R & B charts. The thought-provoking song set the tone for a string of Taylor smashes, notably *Take Care Of Your Homework*, *Love Bones*, and *Jody's Got Your Girl And Gone*, a number 1 R & B hit that inspired a raft of *Jody* sequels by various imitators as well as Taylor himself.

Under the knowledgeable guidance of Detroit-trained producer Don Davis, Taylor mellowed as the 1970s wore on, giving Jimmy Hughes's Muscle Shoals classic *Steal Away* a gripping, minor-key treatment, while his smooth *I Believe In You (You Believe In Me)* espouses a reassuring message of trust and intimacy. The cynical *Cheaper To Keep Her* was a rare up-tempo offering by 1973, gliding over a jazzy, walking bass line, and only 1974's slashing, Southern rock-influenced *I've Been Born Again* recalled his earlier, brash sound. Taylor remained with Stax through 1975, then moved to Columbia and went platinum with the hideous *Disco Lady*.

221 Echoes Of Yesteryear Vol. 1
Various Artists

Goldwax GW-5004-CD

O.V. Wright: *That's How Strong My Love Is*; James Carr: *My Adorable One/What Can I Call My Own*; The Ovations: *It's Wonderful To Be In Love/Pretty Little Angel/I'll Be True*; Willie Hightower: *Caught In The Middle/Too Many Irons In The Fire*; Percy Milem: *He Cried Baby, Baby/Call On Me*; Ollie Nightingale: *Disco Granny/I'm In Love*

Owned by Quinton Claunch and Doc Russell and distributed by New York-based Bell Records, the Goldwax imprint issued some of the most overtly gospel-influenced Memphis soul of the 1960s. This worthwhile if slightly inconsistent compilation spotlights four of the top artists gracing the Goldwax stable, although the pair of obscure Carr efforts are more country-oriented than usual.

Ovations' lead Louis Williams could reproduce Sam Cooke's mellifluous vocal delivery perfectly, and the lilting *It's Wonderful To Be In Love*, a solid seller in 1965, sounds amazingly like Cooke in a Memphis setting (a tantalizing fantasy). O.V. Wright's searing *That's How Strong My Love Is* was his secular debut in 1964, and a regional success despite competition from Otis Redding's cover, while Percy Milem's pair, especially the moving *He Cried Baby, Baby*, are similarly impressive. Underrated Willie Hightower's contributions apparently stem from a later period and rank as decent deep soul, but ex-Stax artist Ollie Nightingale's *Disco Granny* may well be the worst thing Muscle Shoals tunesmith George Jackson ever committed to paper.

Memphis – Early 1970s

222 Chronicle: Their Greatest Stax Hits
Rufus and Carla Thomas

Stax SCD-4124-2

Rufus Thomas: *Do The Funky Chicken/Sixty Minute Man/The Preacher And The Bear/(Do The) Push And Pull (Pts 1 & 2)/The World Is Round/The Breakdown (Pts 1 & 2)/Do The Funky Penguin*; Carla Thomas: *Where Do I Go/I've Fallen In Love/I Like What You're Doing (To Me)/Guide Me Well/You've Got A Cushion To Fall On/ Sugar*

After a few years of gross neglect from R & B record buyers, Rufus Thomas came back strong in 1970 as the genre's oldest reigning dancemaster. The ebullient singer employed a pumping Memphis bass line and impudent horns on his initial comeback, the sizzling raver *Do The Funky Chicken*, and retained the formula for a sweaty series of double-sided dance workouts – *(Do The) Push And Pull, The Breakdown*, and *Do The Funky Penguin*. Not everything was aimed solely at the steppers – *The World Is Round* is funky but meatier, while his update of the Phil Harris warhorse *The Preacher And The Bear* and a panting cover of the Dominoes' *Sixty Minute Man* hint at Thomas's vaudeville origins.

Daughter Carla wasn't as successful during the same era, although her last major seller from 1969, the uplifting *I Like What You're Doing (To Me)*, is typically captivating. Once she has plowed through the seemingly endless monolog introduction of *Guide Me Well*, it develops into a solid bluesy outing, but *I've Fallen In Love* and *Where Do I Go* are awash in strings and pop-styled brass in a too-obvious gambit to propel her toward mainstream stardom.

223 The Best Of William Bell
William Bell

Stax SCD-8541-2

I Forgot To Be Your Lover/Born Under A Bad Sign/My Kind Of Girl/Lonely Soldier/ Save Us/A Penny For Your Thoughts/My Whole World Is Falling Down/All For The Love Of A Woman/'Til My Back Ain't Got No Bone/I'll Be Home/A Smile Can't Hide (A Broken Heart)/Gettin' What You Want (Losin' What You Got)/Private Number (with Judy Clay)/*My Baby Specializes* (with Judy Clay)

One of the most consistent performers at Stax from 1961 on but inexplicably enjoying only limited commercial success, William Bell finally began to climb the soul charts on a regular basis in 1968. Booker T. Jones produced Bell's breakthrough hit, the remorseful *I Forgot To Be Your Lover*, deftly utilizing muted strings and horns to frame the singer's urgent delivery. The follow-up, *My Kind Of Girl*, is a churning, mid-tempo track boasting attractive vocal harmonies.

Jones also produced Bell's engaging duet that same year with Judy Clay, *Private Number*, resulting in another sizable seller. Isaac Hayes and David Porter wrote and produced an encore Bell–Clay duet, *My Baby Specializes*, in a hard-charging style reminiscent of Sam and Dave's dynamic output. Many of Bell's slicker, early 1970s Stax outings are certainly credible if not quite as compelling as earlier efforts, although a delicious, up-tempo *I'll Be Home*, written by Eddie

Floyd, and the steamy *Gettin' What You Want (Losin' What You Got)*, are classy efforts.

224   The Best Of The Staple Singers
The Staple Singers

Stax 60-007

Heavy Makes You Happy (Sha-Na-Boom-Boom)/You've Got To Earn It/Love Is Plentiful/This World/(Sittin' On) The Dock Of The Bay/The Weight/Respect Yourself/ We'll Get Over/I'll Take You There/Oh La De Da/Be What You Are/This Old Town (People In This Town)/If You're Ready (Come Go With Me)/Touch A Hand (Make A Friend)/My Main Man/City In The Sky

Already venerated figures with 15 years on the gospel circuit when they signed with Stax in 1968 and veered off in a secular direction, Chicago's Staple Singers enjoyed sustained R & B and pop success from 1970 on by retaining their customary positive outlook, albeit without direct religious references, and adopting a subtly funky beat to energize it.

Although Stax vice-president Al Bell produced the group's major hits, many of the Staples' rhythm tracks were done in Muscle Shoals. The luminous Mack Rice–Luther Ingram composition *Respect Yourself* (1971), *I'll Take You There* (number 1 R & B and pop in 1972), and *If You're Ready (Come Go With Me)* (number 1 R & B in 1973) showcase the sensuous yet soothing lead vocals of Mavis Staples, supported by the rich, gospel-rooted vocal harmonies of her father, eminently tasteful guitarist Roebuck "Pop" Staples, and her sisters Cleotha and Yvonne (the latter replacing her brother Pervis shortly after the quartet began recording for Stax). The Staples' unabashedly joyous, socially relevant style made them one of the top soul groups of the 1970s, and they remain a family musical institution.

225   Chronicle: Greatest Hits
The Emotions

Stax SCD-4121

So I Can Love You/The Best Part Of A Love Affair/Stealin' Love/When Tomorrow Comes/Heart Association/You Make Me Want To Love You/Show Me How/My Honey And Me/I Could Never Be Happy/From Toys To Boys/Runnin' Back (And Forth)/Put A Little Love Away/Baby, I'm Through/Shouting Out Love

Stax also raided the Windy City for the Emotions, who stormed into the upper reaches of the R & B playlists in 1969 with their immensely appealing *So I Can Love You* on Volt. Like the Staples, the Emotions hail from a gospel background, and lead singer Wanda Hutchinson and her sisters Sheila and Jeannette had no problem adapting their seductive vocal blend to the Stax approach.

Sheila Hutchinson wrote *So I Can Love You*, a silky song with spare but immaculate production by Isaac Hayes and David Porter that strongly emphasizes an insistent organ riff. Occasionally their work echoes other regional genres – *Stealin' Love*, a Hayes–Porter work all the way, sounds a little like vintage Motown with its pounding rhythm, and the strident *From Toys To Boys* might have been better suited to Detroit's Honey Cone. But many of these 1969–74 tracks qualify as soft, sinuous Memphis soul – a hybrid just growing popular at the time – and the trio's youthful, floating vocal harmonies are a delicious breath of fresh air.

226 Chronicle
Soul Children

Stax SCD-4120-2

Give 'Em Love/I'll Understand/Tighten Up My Thang/The Sweeter He Is/Hold On, I'm Coming/Hearsay/Don't Take My Kindness For Weakness/It Ain't Always What You Do (It's Who You Let See You Do It)/Love Is A Hurtin' Thing/I'll Be The Other Woman/Love Makes It Right/Can't Give Up A Good Thing

Personally assembled by producers Isaac Hayes and David Porter, the two-male (Norm West and John Colbert), two-female (Anita Louis and Shelbra Bennett) Soul Children were one of the brightest new developments of the early 1970s at Stax. Eschewing the customary practice of primarily featuring one singer, the quartet shared the lead with exciting spontaneity during the course of a song.

Give 'Em Love, the group's 1968 debut on the R & B lists, is a hard-driving Hayes–Porter piece in the best Stax tradition, with punchy horns and a propulsive drive, and *Hearsay*, a big 1972 R & B hit penned by Colbert and West, boasts a raw-edged lead vocal and a relentless groove that harks back to the label's heyday. Emphasizing their collective gospel roots, the group emote with a searing edge on the mid-tempo *Don't Take My Kindness For Weakness* and the ballads *I'll Understand* and *The Sweeter He Is*, the last of these another huge soul hit in 1969. *Can't Give Up A Good Thing*, the last track here, is a disco artifact from 1978 and clashes with the rest of the disc. Colbert found solo fame during the mid-1980s, billed as J. Blackfoot.

227 I Like The Feeling
Luther Ingram

Urgent! URG 4119

(If Loving You Is Wrong) I Don't Want To Be Right/I Can't Stop/Always/Let's Steal Away To The Hideaway/Get To Me/Sweet Inspiration/I'll Just Call You Honey/Help Me Love/I Remember/I'll Be Your Shelter (In Time Of Storm)/You Got To Give Love To Get Love/Missing You/Oh Baby You Can Depend On Me/I'm Trying To Sing A Message To You/I Like The Feeling

When producer Johnny Baylor brought his tiny KoKo label into the Stax fold in 1968, its principal asset was a promising singer named Luther Ingram. By 1972, thanks to the million-selling *(If Loving You Is Wrong) I Don't Want To Be Right*, Ingram had escaped obscurity forever.

Ingram (b. November 30, 1944, in Jackson, Tennessee) leaped to stardom as an intimate soul crooner with an obvious Sam Cooke influence. With the Muscle Shoals rhythm section providing evocative, bluesy backing, the 1972 number 1 R & B hit, written by Homer Banks, Raymond Jackson, and Carl Hampton, is a steamy tale of cheating and its emotional consequences. The set contains many of Ingram's notable R & B chart items, including *I'll Be Your Shelter (In Time Of Storm)* and a Cooke-influenced *Always*, although his hit reading of *Ain't That Loving You (For More Reasons Than One)*, first recorded by Stax heavyweight Johnnie Taylor, and the chunky *My Honey And Me* are inexplicably absent. The disc follows Ingram's career into 1978 with *Get To Me*, long after the demise of Stax.

228 The Soul Of O.V. Wright
O.V. Wright

MCA MCAD-10670

You're Gonna Make Me Cry/I'd Rather Be (Blind, Crippled And Crazy)/When You Took Your Love From Me/I'm Gonna Forget About You/Everybody Knows (The River Song)/Don't Let My Baby Ride/I Don't Want To Sit Down/I Was Born All Over/Ace Of Spade/Eight Men, Four Women/A Nickel And A Nail/Heartaches – Heartaches/Drowning On Dry Land/Monkey Dog/He's My Son (Just The Same)/I've Been Searching/Motherless Child/I'm Going Home (To Live With God)

After Goldwax issued O.V. Wright's (b. September 10, 1939, in Leno, Tennessee) secular debut single in 1964, Duke label boss Don Robey reclaimed this ex-lead singer of the Sunset Travelers gospel group and began recording Wright on Houston-based Duke's Back Beat subsidiary. Although the 1965 ballad smash *You're Gonna Make Me Cry* is gorgeous, Wright did not hit his full stride until he and Memphis producer Willie Mitchell crystallized as a team.

Mitchell's rhythm section laid down a bluesy base to showcase Wright's emotionally charged, gospel-soaked vocals, and the singer had a hit with the doomy, minor-key *Eight Men, Four Women* and the intense *Heartaches – Heartaches* in 1967, before the unrestrained, strutting, horn-powered *Ace Of Spade* three years later. Wright sounds perilously close to losing emotional control on his best efforts, notably the grinding, minor-key *A Nickel And A Nail* from 1971. Mitchell fashioned churning, mid-tempo grooves for the 1973 hit *I'd Rather Be (Blind, Crippled And Crazy)* and the rolling *I'm Gonna Forget About You*, while Wright's *Drowning On Dry Land* boasts a far more imaginative arrangement than Albert King's celebrated version. Wright regularly scaled the lower reaches of the R & B charts until his death on November 16, 1980.

229 Ann Peebles' Greatest Hits
Ann Peebles

Hi CD 100 (UK)

99 Pounds/Walk Away/Give Me Some Credit/Heartaches, Heartaches/Somebody's On Your Case/I Still Love You/Part Time Love/Generation Gap Between Us/Slipped, Tripped And Fell In Love/Trouble, Heartaches And Sadness/I Feel Like Breaking Up Somebody's Home/I Pity The Fool/Do I Need You/One Way Street/I Can't Stand The Rain/Beware/A Love Vibration/Doctor Love Power/It Was Jealousy/Being Here With You/I'm Gonna Tear Your Playhouse Down/When I'm In Your Arms/A Good Day For Lovin'/Come To Mama/Old Man With Young Ideas/If This Is Heaven

Ann Peebles (b. April 27, 1947, in East St Louis, Illinois) sang with a bristling intensity that belied her tiny frame. She joined Hi in 1968, and as one of the first artists to fully benefit from Mitchell's mature production techniques, Peebles sounds utterly assured from the outset on a sizzling 1969 rendition of Little Johnny Taylor's tough blues *Part Time Love* that proved her first important R & B seller. Peebles's *I Feel Like Breaking Up Somebody's Home* remains the definitive version, despite heavy competition from Albert King and Denise LaSalle.

Peebles's most enthralling work, much of it co-written by the singer and her husband, fellow Hi artist Donald Bryant, blends a strong blues base with seductive Memphis soul. The determined *I'm Gonna Tear Your Playhouse Down* flows over a classy, string-drenched chart, and the heart-rending *I Can't Stand The Rain*, her biggest seller from 1973, stands as a delicious masterpiece of subtle production, the Hodges brothers concocting a steadily simmering groove behind Peebles's impassioned vocal. *Come To Mama*, from 1975, is a coy, up-tempo invitation to sample Peebles's charms, propelled by extra-heavy percussion from Howard Grimes.

230 That's How It Is
Otis Clay

Hi CD 110 (UK)

Trying To Live My Life Without You/I Die A Little Each Day/Holding On To A Dying Love/I Can't Make It Alone/You Can't Keep Running From My Love/Let Me Be The One/Brand New Thing/Precious, Precious/I Didn't Know The Meaning Of Pain/That's How It Is/Too Many Hands/I Love You, I Need You/Pussy Footing Around/Too Much Mystery/I Can't Take It/Home Is Where The Heart Is/I've Got To Find A Way (To Get You Back)/Slow And Easy/House Ain't A Home (Without A Woman)/Keep On Loving Me/Born To Be With You

Producer Willie Mitchell imported Otis Clay (b. February 11, 1942, in Waxhaw, Mississippi) from the Windy City, where he was already a regional attraction after recording some fine deep soul for One-derful during the mid-1960s. In 1968, Clay inaugurated Atlantic's Cotillion subsidiary by journeying to Muscle Shoals to collaborate with producer Rick Hall on a searing revival of the Sir Douglas Quintet's *She's About A Mover.*

Mitchell first produced Clay during his Cotillion phase, but their partnership really crystallized when the singer signed with Hi in 1971. Utilizing Mitchell's house rhythm section, Clay's gospel-fortified delivery was perfect for the regretful, mid-tempo *Trying To Live My Life Without You,* his biggest R & B hit in late 1972, as well as the very similar *I Didn't Know The Meaning Of Pain,* and an elegant *Precious, Precious* that nearly eclipses Jackie Moore's original. Both of Clay's Hi albums are included in their entirety; his 1977 encore LP suffers from the occasional disco cliché, although a cover of O.V. Wright's *I Can't Take It* is remarkably intense, full of the cool, rhythmic surges that characterize Mitchell's best productions. Clay's uplifting 1973 hit *If I Could Reach Out* is unfortunately absent.

231 Music To My Ears
Syl Johnson

Hi CD 117 (UK)

Back For A Taste Of Your Love/We Did It/I'm Yours/Don't Do It/I Hear The Love Chimes/Anyway The Wind Blows/The Love You Left Behind/I Want To Take You Home/Feelin' Frisky/Let Yourself Go/Wind, Blow Her Back My Way/You Don't Know Me/I Hate I Walked Away/Watch What You Do To Me/Diamond In The Rough/I Only Have Love/Bustin' Up Or Bustin' Out/Stuck In Chicago/Keeping Down Confusion/'Bout To Make Me Leave Home/Take Me To The River/Music To My Ears/Steppin' Out/It Ain't Easy/That's Just My Luck

This selected compilation of Syl Johnson's three 1973–5 Hi albums spotlights another important cog in Willie Mitchell's hitmaking machine. Like Clay, Johnson (b. Syl Thompson, July 1, 1936, in Holly Springs, Mississippi) was a veteran Chicago recruit (see chapter 5), having already had seven R & B chart entries for the Twilight and Twinight labels prior to signing with Hi in 1972 and having a hit with *The Love You Left Behind.*

Johnson's engaging vocal style is airier than Clay's and more in tune with Al Green's floating delivery, emphasized on introspective material such as *Anyway The Wind Blows* and *Wind, Blow Her Back My Way.* Mitchell impeccably layers his punchy horns, strings, and guitarist Teenie Hodges's subtle octave runs on the up-tempo *Back For A Taste Of Your Love,* and the producer's insistence on the importance of the groove kicks along the playful *I Want To Take You Home* and *Let Yourself Go.* It is all but forgotten now that Johnson enjoyed the first hit with label-mate Al Green's *Take Me To The River* in 1975, and his concept of the tune is bluesier than its composer's, the singer incorporating a brief harmonica solo in the introduction.

232   On The Loose/Trapped By A Thing Called Love
Denise LaSalle

Westbound CDSEWD 018 (UK)

On The Loose: *A Man Size[d] Job/What It Takes To Get A Good Woman (That's What It's Gonna Take To Keep Her)/Harper Valley PTA/What Am I Doing Wrong/ Breaking Up Somebody's Home/There Ain't Enough Hate Around (To Make Me Turn Around)/Your Man And Your Best Friend/Lean On Me/Making A Good Thing Better/I'm Over You/I'm Satisfied*
Trapped By A Thing Called Love: *Trapped By A Thing Called Love/Now Run And Tell That/Heartbreaker Of The Year/Goody Goody Getter/Catch Me If You Can/ Hung Up Strung Out/Do Me Right/The Deeper I Go/You'll Lose A Good Thing/Keep It Coming/It's Too Late*

Chicagoan Denise LaSalle (b. July 16, 1939, in LeFlore County, Mississippi) made her earliest 45s on Billy "The Kid" Emerson's Tarpon logo in the mid-1960s. But it was not until the early 1970s, when she recorded a series of earthy releases with Willie Mitchell's Hi rhythm section, that she established herself as a decidedly non-demure soul belter, and as a hitmaker.

The two LaSalle albums that comprise this disc were originally issued on the Westbound label, where she scored a number 1 R & B hit in 1971 with the simmering *Trapped By A Thing Called Love*. LaSalle wrote much of the exceptional album that followed herself, and her strutting compositions slide into the relaxed Memphis groove snugly, especially *Keep It Coming* and her encore smash, *Now Run And Tell That*.

On the Loose, LaSalle's second Westbound LP, is by comparison a mild disappointment, with superfluous covers of *Harper Valley PTA* and *Lean On Me* detracting from the swaggering power of her own brassy, ribald *A Man Sized Job* and *Your Man And Your Best Friend*, precursors to her later output for Malaco.

Muscle Shoals

233   The Greatest
Arthur Alexander

Ace CDCHD 922 (UK)

Anna (Go To Him)/You're The Reason/Soldier Of Love/I Hang My Head And Cry/ You Don't Care/Dream Girl/Call Me Lonesome/After You/Where Have You Been/A Shot Of Rhythm And Blues/Don't You Know It/You Better Move On/All I Need Is You/Detroit City/Keep Her Guessing/Go Home Girl/In The Middle Of It All/Whole Lot Of Trouble/Without A Song/I Wonder Where You Are Tonight/Black Night

If it had not been for an ex-bellhop named Arthur Alexander (b. May 10, 1940, in Florence, Alabama), Rick Hall's Fame Studio might have never flourished at all. Ironically, Hall only produced Alexander's initial hit before the singer was snatched away by Nashville-based Dot Records producer Noel Ball.

For a novice producer, Hall instinctively brought out the best in Alexander's quavering baritone on that memorable 1962 hit *You Better Move On*, sparingly arranging the track with acoustic guitar, prominent high-hat cymbals, and ghostly backing vocals. Alexander lobbied for *A Shot Of Rhythm And Blues* on the upbeat flip, but there were often strong country overtones to his Dot output, notably here on *You're The Reason* and *Detroit City*. Ball got a number of strong performances from Alexander, especially the heartbroken *Anna (Go To Him)* and the Barry Mann–Cynthia Weil uptown ballad *Where Have You Been*, both hits in 1962. A few years later, Alexander popped up on the Sound Stage 7 label, and in 1972 cut a Tommy Cogbill–produced comeback album for Warner Brothers that included his superior treatment of the Elvis Presley smash *Burning Love*.

234 Why Not Tonight?
Jimmy Hughes

Atco 33-209 (LP)

Why Not Tonight/I'm A Man Of Action/I Worship The Ground You Walk On/ Neighbor, Neighbor/It Was Nice/Slippin' Around With You/Midnight Affair/It's A Good Thing/I'm The Loving Physician/I Stand Accused

Unlike Alexander, Jimmy Hughes stayed with Fame long enough to compile an impressive legacy. Utilizing his pleading, high-pitched tenor to the utmost effect, the Florence, Alabama, product handed Hall his second hit production in 1964 when his intense blues ballad *Steal Away* inaugurated Hall's own Fame logo.

Unfortunately, *Steal Away* is not included on **Why Not Tonight?** (Hall having switched allegiance from Vee Jay to Atlantic), but this sterling 1967 collection boasts some of the toughest cheating songs in the deep-soul pantheon. Fabled Texas entrepreneur Huey Meaux wrote the pounding *Neighbor, Neighbor*, powered by relentless brass and drums, but most of the highlights involve illicit affairs or the promise thereof – notably the spine-chilling *Why Not Tonight*, *Midnight Affair*, and Dan Penn and Spooner Oldham's *Slippin' Around With You*. That prolific songwriting duo also contributed the devotional *I Worship The Ground You Walk On*, while Hughes, no incompetent himself as a composer (he wrote *Steal Away*), came up with the lowdown *It Was Nice*. Hughes went to Volt for one album in 1969.

235 Sweet Soul Music
Arthur Conley

Warner/Pioneer 20P2-2384 (Jap)

Sweet Soul Music/Take Me (Just As I Am)/Who's Foolin' Who/There's A Place For Us/I Can't Stop (No, No, No)/Wholesale Love/I'm A Lonely Stranger/I'm Gonna Forget About You/Let Nothing Separate Us/Where You Lead Me

Arthur Conley (b. January 4, 1946, in Atlanta) could almost as accurately be listed under Memphis soul, since he recorded his debut single at Stax and half of his last Atco album at Chips Moman's American Studio. But much of this debut album was done in Muscle Shoals, as was his encore set, **Shake, Rattle And Roll**.

Otis Redding discovered Conley in Baltimore in 1965, adopting him as his protégé and producing Conley's first 45, the haunting *I'm A Lonely Stranger*, for his fledgling Jotis label. Redding cut Conley's follow-up tracks in Muscle Shoals, and Hall's Fame label issued the pleading ballad *Take Me (Just As I Am)* and the pumping *I Can't Stop (No, No, No)*. Conley's vocal approach variously suggests both his mentor and Sam Cooke, and he had a huge hit for Atco in early 1967 with the celebratory *Sweet Soul Music*, modeled on Cooke's *Yeah Man*. With its shrill trumpet section, churning groove, and lyrical bows to a legion of soul luminaries, it was a great success in both the pop and R & B charts. Three more Atco albums followed, **Soul Directions** spotlighting his 1968 hit *Funky Street* and the Redding-produced *Hear Say*.

258   The South

236   The Best of James and Bobby Purify: Do It Right!
Bobby and James Purify

Arista ALB-6-8392 (LP)

I'm Your Puppet/Wish You Didn't Have To Go/You Left The Water Running/Blame Me (Don't Blame My Heart)/So Many Reasons/I've Got Everything I Need (I've Got You)/Shake A Tail Feather/Let Love Come Between Us/I Take What I Want/I Don't Want To Have To Wait/Soothe Me/I Don't Know What It Is You Got

Duos were everywhere on the soul scene in 1966, and James and Bobby Purify briefly became Muscle Shoals's answer to Sam and Dave, with the widespread success of their melodic, mid-tempo *I'm Your Puppet*, a giant R & B and pop hit. Their name suggested that they were brothers, but in fact James (b. May 12, 1944, in Pensacola, Florida) and Bobby (b. Robert Lee Dickey, September 2, 1939, in Tallahassee, Florida) were cousins.

Independent producer Papa Don Schroeder brought the pair to Fame, where they prospered on the house band's reliable grooves and a steady diet of solid material from Dan Penn and Spooner Oldham, who wrote the rocking *Wish You Didn't Have To Go* and the extremely popular cover item *You Left The Water Running*, in addition to *I'm Your Puppet*. Schroeder placed his productions on New York-based Bell Records. The Purifys come out second best on the Sam and Dave covers included here, but their own joyous 1967 hit *Let Love Come Between Us* and a revival of the Five Du-Tones' *Shake A Tail Feather* (from a Memphis session at American) crackle with exciting harmony. When his cousin defected in the late 1960s, James went solo for a while before recruiting a new Bobby and making a last chart appearance in 1974.

237   Tell Mama
Etta James

MCA/Chess CHD-9269

Tell Mama/I'd Rather Go Blind/Watch Dog/The Love Of My Man/I'm Gonna Take What He's Got/The Same Rope/Security/Steal Away/My Mother-In-Law/Don't Lose Your Good Thing/It Hurts Me So Much/Just A Little Bit

After spending more than a decade turning out a spate of R & B hits on the West Coast for Modern and in Chicago for the Chess subsidiaries Argo and Cadet, Chess dispatched Etta James (b. Jamesetta Hawkins, January 25, 1938, in Los Angeles) to Rick Hall's Fame Studios in 1967 and were rewarded with a stunning album that stands as a classic of the idiom.

Kicking off with the hit title track – an irresistible combination of blasting horns, a piledriving bass line, and her roughly seductive vocal – James then slows down radically for *I'd Rather Go Blind*, a thin-sounding organ and wordless backing vocals floating ethereally behind James's devastating delivery. Those opening salvos are hard to follow, although *Watch Dog* comes close with its searing, up-tempo feel. Prolific Atlantic vocalist/composer Don Covay wrote the powerful *I'm Gonna Take What He's Got*, while *The Same Rope* strikes a rolling groove, with churchy piano and a vocal group prominent. Unfortunately, James's association with Muscle Shoals was short-lived, and subsequent Cadet sessions reverted to other parts of the country.

238   Womack Winners: The Best Of Bobby Womack 1967–1975
Bobby Womack

Charly R & B 154 (UK)

Broadway Walk/Somebody Special/What Is This?/I'm A Midnight Mover/How I Miss You Baby/More Than I Can Stand/Communication/That's The Way I Feel About Cha/If You Don't Want My Love, Give It Back/I Can Understand It/Woman's Gotta Have It/Harry Hippie/Across 110th Street/Nobody Wants You When You're Down And Out/I'm Through Trying To Prove My Love To You/Lookin' For A Love/I Don't Wanna Be Hurt By Ya Love Again/You're Welcome, Stop On By/I Don't Know (What The World Is Coming To)/If You Want My Love, Put Something Down On It/ Check It Out/It's All Over Now/Where There's A Will, There's A Way/Daylight

Bobby Womack defies easy categorization, having cut hits in both Memphis and Muscle Shoals. As the Valentinos' gospel-soaked lead, Womack (b. March 4, 1944, in Cleveland, Ohio) recorded *Lookin' For A Love* in 1962 and *It's All Over Now* in 1964 on Sam Cooke's SAR label in Los Angeles, before earning a reputation as a writer and guitarist at Chips Moman's American studio in Memphis (where this CD begins). American's crew backed Womack on his early solo hits for Minit, including *How I Miss You Baby* (1969) and *More Than I Can Stand* (1970), the singer adopting a gritty, intimate delivery far distant from the usual Memphis fare.

Womack fully developed his unique, relaxed approach during the early 1970s on United Artists, scoring giant R & B hits with *That's The Way I Feel About Cha* in 1971, and with *Woman's Gotta Have It* and the humanistic *Harry Hippie* the next year. Womack recorded many of his top-sellers in Muscle Shoals, including the funky *You're Welcome, Stop On By*, and an infectious, R & B-chart-topping update of *Lookin' For A Love* in 1974.

239 Sweet Soul Music: Voices From The Shadows
Various Artists

Sire/Warner Bros/Blue Horizon 9 26731-2

Percy Sledge: *True Love Travels On A Gravel Road*; O.V. Wright: *Nickel And A Nail*; Aretha Franklin: *My Song*; George Perkins and the Silver Stars: *Crying In The Streets*; Laura Lee: *Separation Line*; The Soul Brothers Six: *Some Kind Of Wonderful*; Arthur Alexander: *Rainbow Road*; Otis Clay: *She's About A Mover*; The Invincibles: *Heart Full Of Love*; James Carr: *Hold On (To What We've Got)*; Eddy Giles: *Losing Boy*; The Enchanters: *I Paid For The Party*; Solomon Burke: *I Stayed Away Too Long*; Judy Clay: *Greatest Love*; Don Covay and the Good Timers: *It's In The Wind*

Although not exclusively limited to Southern soul, this intended aural companion to Peter Guralnick's groundbreaking book *Sweet Soul Music* boasts several obscure, deep-soul masterpieces not available elsewhere, and even Aretha Franklin's 1968 reading of Johnny Ace's *My Song* is reasonably rare.

Chicagoan Otis Clay launched Atlantic's Cotillion subsidiary the same year with his blistering, brass-powered remake of the Sir Douglas Quintet's *She's About A Mover*, produced by Rick Hall in Muscle Shoals, while James Carr's track was cut in 1971. Eddy Giles's marvelously atmospheric *Losing Boy* was issued on the tiny, Jewel-distributed Murco logo in 1966, and O.V. Wright's *Nickel And A Nail* is an acknowledged classic of the genre, a 1972 Willie Mitchell production featuring a tortured vocal and the surging power of Hi's resident rhythm section. Solomon Burke, Don Covay, and Percy Sledge are all represented with overlooked gems, and although the Soul Brothers Six from Rochester, New York, do not fit into the Southern soul idiom, their intense vocal harmonies on *Some Kind Of Wonderful* are as gospel-soaked as 1960s soul gets.

Nashville

240 Lookin' Back (The Best Of 1966–1970)
Joe Simon

Charly R & B CD 144 (UK)
The Chokin' Kind/My Special Prayer/No Sad Songs/San Francisco Is A Lonely Town/
Message From Maria/Lookin' Back/Baby, Don't Be Looking In My Mind/Teenager's
Prayer/Nine Pound Streel/(You Keep Me) Hangin' On/Put Your Trust In Me
(Depend On Me)/It's Hard To Get Along/Misty Blue/Farther On Down The Road/
Yours Love/That's The Way I Want Our Love/Moonwalk Pts 1 & 2/Rainbow Road/
Silver Spoons And Coffee Cups/In The Ghetto/I Got A Whole Lot Of Lovin'/Don't Let
Me Lose The Feeling/I'm Too Far Gone (To Turn Around)/(Sittin' On) The Dock Of
The Bay

Hardly an R & B metropolis like Memphis, country-oriented Nashville still
turned out its share of deep soul during the mid-to-late 1960s, much of it
produced by popular WLAC deejay John Richbourg for his Sound Stage 7 label.
Many of Richbourg's session players were refugees from Music Row, often
imparting a definite country influence to his productions.

   Joe Simon (b. September 2, 1943, in Simmesport, Louisiana) had already
done exceptional work at his Bay Area home base and in Muscle Shoals (with his
1965 R & B chart debut on Vee Jay, *Let's Do It Over*) prior to joining Sound
Stage 7 in 1966. Simon's deep, slightly pinched baritone boasted an intimate
resonance, and his moving *My Special Prayer, Nine Pound Steel*, and *(You Keep*
Me) Hangin' On are an intriguing hybrid of soul and country. Country tunesmith
Harlan Howard wrote Simon's 1969 mid-tempo, R & B chart-topper *The*
Chokin' Kind, its insistent bass line and punchy brass perfectly complementing
Simon's resigned vocal. The singer was also capable of an occasional searing
raver, notably *No Sad Songs* and *Put Your Trust In Me (Depend On Me)*.

241 The Sound Stage Seven Story
Various Artists

Charly R & B CD 191 (UK)
Roscoe Shelton: *Easy Going Fellow/Strain On My Heart/I Know Your Heart Has*
Been Broken; Earl Gaines: *Hymn No. 5/I'll Take Care Of You*; Ann Sexton: *I'm*
His Wife You're Just A Friend/You're Gonna Miss Me; Sam Baker: *I Love You/*
Sometimes You Have To Cry/Just A Glance Away; Charles Smith: *The Only Time*
You Say You Love Me; Joe Simon: *(You Keep Me) Hangin' On/The Chokin' Kind*;
Geater Davis: *A Whole Lot Of Man/Your Heart Is So Cold*; Ella Washington: *All*
The Time/He Called Me Baby; Lattimore Brown: *I'm Not Through Loving You*;
Bobby King: *What Made You Change Your Mind/Let Me Come On Home*; Brief
Encounter: *Human*; Willie Hobbs: *Judge Of Hearts*; Moody Scott: *We've Got To*
Save It/A Woman's Touch; The Cashmeres: *Ooh I Love You*

This generous compilation highlights Richbourg's Sound Stage 7 (SS7) activities
from 1965–70 while under the aegis of Monument Records, as well as his
independent revival of the label during the 1970s. There are quite a few gems
among the later efforts, including Ann Sexton's lowdown *You're Gonna Miss Me*,
Willie Hobbs's strong *Judge Of Hearts*, and both bluesy tracks by the Bobby
Bland-influenced Geater Davis.

On the earlier material, Ella Washington, Richbourg's top female soul belter, takes the Joe Simon country route to great advantage with her 1969 rendition of Harlan Howard's *He Called Me Baby*, while the vastly underrated "Sir" Lattimore Brown contributes the heartfelt *I'm Not Through Loving You*. Richbourg produced Nashville native Roscoe Shelton's 1965 hit *Strain On My Heart* for the Sims label, and the big-voiced Shelton returned with *Easy Going Fellow* a year later on SS7. Charles Smith and rough-edged Bobby King also turn in impressive deep-soul items. This set confirms that Sound Stage 7 issued a great many exceptional if obscure records during its existence.

Other Regional Centers: Atlanta

242   The Tams' 15 Greatest Hits
The Tams

Ripete MSD 35190

What Kind Of Fool (Do You Think I Am)/Hey Girl Don't Bother Me/I've Been Hurt/ You Lied To Your Daddy/Laugh It Off/Riding For A Fall/Silly Little Girl/Untie Me/ Get Away/Breaking Up/Shelter/It's Better To Have Loved A Little/Why Did My Little Girl Cry/You Might As Well Forget Him/Be Young, Be Foolish, Be Happy

Fronted by rough-voiced Joseph Pope, the Tams, whose other members were Charles Pope, Robert Smith, Floyd Ashton, and Horace Key, were the most important soul act to record in Atlanta during the 1960s. Three of the vocal group's initial hits for ABC–Paramount, however, were done in Muscle Shoals with Rick Hall producing. Among them was the quintet's biggest pop-seller in 1963, the atmospheric *What Kind Of Fool (Do You Think I Am)* (a sparkling outing with attractive interplay between Pope, bass singer Robert Smith, and a prominent flute that became a trademark) and the follow-up *You Lied To Your Daddy*. *Untie Me*, the group's first hit for Arlen in 1962, is represented by an inferior remake.

Later Tams efforts cut in Atlanta mined the talents of a select group of local tunesmiths, notably Ray Whitley (who wrote the quintet's 1964 hit *Hey Girl Don't Bother Me* and their original version of *I've Been Hurt*) and Joe South, producer of the Tams' last smash for ABC in 1968, the buoyant *Be Young, Be Foolish, Be Happy*, and writer of the reassuring *It's Better To Have Loved A Little*. With their bouncy tempos and bright harmonies, the Tams remain favorites on the beach-music scene.

Other Regional Centers: Norfolk, Virginia

243   The Best Of Gary U.S. Bonds
Gary U.S. Bonds

Rhino R2 70971

New Orleans/Take Me Back To New Orleans/Quarter To Three/No More Homework/ School Is Out/School Is In/Dear Lady Twist/Twist, Twist Senora/Havin' So Much Fun/Do The Bumpsie/Perdido (Pts 1 & 2)/Seven Day Weekend/Soul Food/Copy Cat/I Wanta Holler (But The Town's Too Small)/Lover's Moon/Not Me/Where Did The Naughty Little Girl Go

During the early 1960s, what little R & B recording activity existed in Norfolk, Virginia, centered on one location: the headquarters of producer Frank Guida's tiny Legrand Records. Somehow Guida, who displayed a lifelong fascination with West Indian folk songs and calypso rhythms, managed to wring a pseudo-live, joyous atmosphere from his primitive studio set-up.

By far Guida's most talented and consistent artist was Gary U.S. Bonds (b. Gary Anderson, June 6, 1939, in Jacksonville, Florida). His rousing 1960 debut, *New Orleans*, was propelled by Nabs Shields's booming bass drum and a raucous brass line, with Bonds's double-tracked singing answered by a forceful male vocal group. A series of equally successful dance-oriented follow-ups, notably his biggest hit from the next year, *Quarter To Three*, also showcased the wailing tenor sax of Gene "Daddy G." Barge, whose day-job as a teacher inspired Bonds's string of educational treatises: *School Is Out*, the inevitable *School Is In*, and *No More Homework*. At his best, as on the irresistible rockers *Havin' So Much Fun* and *Where Did The Naughty Little Girl Go*, Bonds concocted some of the most uninhibited R & B of the highly disposable twist era, and even the belated 1966 sequel *Take Me Back To New Orleans* pounds its message home unmercifully.

244   The Best Of Jimmy Soul
Jimmy Soul

Rhino R2 70527

If You Wanna Be Happy/Treat 'Em Tough/Take Me To Los Angeles/My Baby Loves To Bowl/Go 'Way Christina/She's Alright/My Girl – She Sure Can Cook/I Know Why Dreamers Cry/Guess Things Happen That Way/Twistin' Matilda (And The Channel)/When Matilda Comes Back/Food Of Love/Change Partners/Hands Off/A Woman Is Smarter In Every Kind[a] Way/One Million Tears/I Hate You Baby/ Church Street In The Summertime

Bonds's only real rival for commercial viability in Guida's self-contained Norfolk empire was Jimmy Soul (b. James McCleese, August 24, 1942, in Weldon, North Carolina). Recording for Legrand's fledgling SPQR subsidiary, the energetic vocalist memorably capitalized on Guida's long-standing Caribbean fixation when his calypso-based *If You Wanna Be Happy* topped the pop charts in 1963. Soul seemed doomed to inherit Bonds's cast-offs – the singer's first hit in 1962, *Twistin' Matilda*, had filtered down to him in precisely such a manner, and even *If You Wanna Be Happy* had been rejected by Bonds (who may have been understandably shy of the style after enduring the embarrassment of his dreadful **Twist Up Calypso** album).

Soul's subsequent attempts to recreate the success of his number 1 hit with derivative West Indian ditties, such as *Treat 'Em Tough* and *A Woman Is Smarter In Every Kinda Way*, and with trivial novelty songs never restored him to the charts, but the engaging Bonds sound-alikes *Church Street In The Summertime* and *She's Alright* crackle with a vibrant urgency that proves Guida was really the chief architect of the Norfolk sound, infusing as much of his own musical sensibilities into his productions as either vocalist (for both better and worse). McCleese died on June 25, 1988.

Other Regional Centers: Carolinas

245   Stay – The Best of Maurice Williams And The Zodiacs
Maurice Williams and the Zodiacs

Relic 7004

Stay/Do You Believe/We're Lovers/I Remember/Always/The Winds/I Love You Baby/ Do I/Come Along/Someday/Dearest Baby/High Blood Pressure/Running Around/Little Mama/But Not For Me/Please/The Nearness Of You/Come And Get It/It's Alright/So Fine/I Got A Woman/Here I Stand

When people dance to "beach music" down in the Carolinas, the Beach Boys are nowhere in sight. The region's indigenous beach-music scene centers on vintage, up-beat R & B and soul, and South Carolina's Maurice Williams and the Zodiacs remain local favorites.

Prior to forming the Zodiacs, Williams led another vocal group, the Gladiolas, whose 1957 hit for Excello, *Little Darlin'* soared up the charts via a sentimental, sanitized pop cover by the Diamonds. In 1960, the reformed Zodiacs signed with Herald Records in New York and cut the catchy and extremely concise *Stay* (just over a minute and a half long), a number 1 pop hit. Williams's lighthearted lead vocal and the swirling backing (notably Henry Gaston's falsetto answering lead) suggest doo-wop roots, but there is a gospel tinge to much of Williams's early 1960s Herald output, and the less commercially successful *I Remember, Come Along,* and *Come And Get It* contain a similarly pleasing mix of vocal group harmonies and quirky rhythmic patterns. Williams later cut the original *May I,* another beach-music perennial after Bill Deal and the Rhondels revived it in 1969.

The South: Louisiana, Texas, Florida, Mississippi

7

Jeff Hannusch

As its title suggests, this chapter covers a lot of geography, and necessarily a wide range of soul styles. The Deep South has naturally always been a hotbed for soul and blues, obviously because it boasts America's largest population of African Americans, the major supporters and creators of soul music.

An R & B incubator, Louisiana naturally became a soul-music capital when the direction of African American music shifted that way in the 1960s. Soul music in New Orleans can be traced back to 1960, when Allen Toussaint began producing records for the Minit label. Toussaint's productions were rooted in the R & B sound that was heard in New Orleans during the 1950s, but he brought it up-to-date by adding a unique, freewheeling, festive approach to his arrangements. The heyday for early New Orleans soul was 1960–3, when artists such as Ernie K-Doe, Chris Kenner, Irma Thomas, and Benny Spellman helped the city rule the charts. The city's musical fortunes took a turn for the worse after the Beatles struck in the mid-1960s, but the New Orleans sound stayed in the charts – though to a lesser degree – via hits by Lee Dorsey, Robert Parker, and Aaron Neville. The early 1970s introduced an even more contemporary New Orleans sound – a sound that put the Meters in the charts. Some New Orleans artists, namely Jean Knight and King Floyd, achieved chart success recording in a new southern recording center, Jackson, Mississippi.

In the early 1990s the Neville Brothers are the most visible link to the city's soul tradition. While their latest records are rap-pop-rock odysseys into oblivion, on their live shows they often reach back for that great sound that made them famous. Besides obtaining several of the recordings discussed here, the best way to hear a lot of this great music is to visit the New Orleans Jazz and Heritage Festival in the spring.

Southern and northern Louisiana have also been important soul centers at various times. The best southern Louisiana soul, "Bayou soul," was influenced by New Orleans and to a lesser degree Cajun music. Recorded exclusively on small labels, Bayou soul never caught on nationally – outside of Cookie and the Cupcakes – but locally it was popular for two decades.

The northern Louisiana soul center was found in Shreveport, where Stan Lewis operated a distribution company and the Jewel, Paula, and Ronn labels. In many ways Lewis continued to carry the torch passed on from the famed Chicago-based indies, Vee Jay and Chess, as he was the only record man still issuing a steady flow of blues, gospel, and soul records into the 1970s. Two notable artists in his stable included Little Johnny Taylor and Ted Taylor. Lewis's releases did not follow any one style, as he leased sessions from producers in Chicago, New Orleans, and Muscle Shoals, in addition to cutting his own material in Shreveport. Other Shreveport labels that had minor success were Whit, owned by Lionel Whitfield, whose main artist was Bobby Powell, and Alarm, whose main artist was Ted Taylor.

Another soul hotbed – particularly in the 1980s – is Jackson, Mississippi. It is the home of Malaco Records, the label that became successful by appealing to black, middle-aged record buyers who were being ignored by the major labels. All Malaco productions are done in-house, employing staff musicians. While their production can be unoriginal and stiff on occasion, their bank of songwriters keeps coming up with fine material. In the early 1990s they were the busiest soul-blues-gospel label, with the most enviable roster of talent performing such music, namely Bobby Bland, Little Milton, Denise LaSalle, and Johnnie Taylor. Jackson also spawned another outfit in the 1980s, the La Jam/ Retta's complex of labels, owned by record distributor James Bennett. His principal artist was Bobby Rush.

The major purveyor of Florida soul, dubbed "sunshine state soul," was Miami's Henry Stone, who owned a myriad of labels that were grouped under the T.K. Records banner. For a short time in the early 1970s, Miami rivaled Detroit and Memphis as the center of the soul music industry, with such artists as Betty Wright, Latimore, George McCrae, Gwen McCrae, and K.C. and the Sunshine Band. For the most part, T.K. releases were instantly recognizable as possessing a bright, pop sound, often with a hint of reggae in their arrangements. As commercial as this sound was, unfortunately the disco boom of the mid-1970s killed it as it did many other soul styles.

The compact disc boom, sad to say, has not completely caught up with the soul-music tradition. As a result a number of essential and basic albums that are recommended here exist only on vinyl.

While this fact may displease audiophiles, true soul aficionados know they can never throw away their turntables.

Essential Recordings

(i) New Orleans

The early sound of New Orleans soul was almost exclusively heard on the Minit and Instant labels. The man responsible for that sound was the ubiquitous Allen Toussaint, who not only produced and played on the sessions, but also wrote most of the material. While a number of collections include several Instant and Minit classics, the best concentration of this New Orleans output is heard on **It Will Stand**.

In terms of history, Minit Records came before Instant, having been formed in 1960. Co-owned by New Orleans record man Joe Banashak, the label had a distribution deal with Los Angeles-based Imperial Records, the major purveyor of New Orleans R & B during the 1950s. Minit signed up the lion's share of young New Orleans talent and parlayed it, via Toussaint, into a fair amount of chart success.

Despite several national hits, after one year Banashak grew dissatisfied with the agreement with Imperial and went into a partnership with another label, Valiant. The new label's name was soon changed (appropriately) to Instant, however, when it was found that a Valiant label already existed in California. Instant's early sessions were also put into the hands of Toussaint, who continued to write and produce for both Minit and Instant.

Jessie Hill's raucous *Ooh Poo Pah Doo* (1960) was Minit's first national success. Initially, the song was a popular Mardi Gras record around New Orleans, but its surging R & B beat eventually infected the entire country.

Considered by many music fans to be New Orleans's premier vocalist, Aaron Neville got his start on Minit Records. His first R & B chart appearance was in 1960, when the deadly *Over You* was released. *Let's Live* was a local success that became a prototype for the ornate, melisma-heavy ballad style that became his trademark.

Aaron's brother, Art, scored one of the biggest local records of all time with *All These Things* on Instant. Although Neville's version never got into the charts, several covers of the song have, notably by a Louisiana rock-and-roll group, the Uniques, in 1966. It remains a popular prom and juke-box song around the state. Minit's lone female alumna was the talented Irma Thomas. *It's Raining* missed the national charts but it remains one of her most popular songs when she performs. Another local success was *Ruler*

Of My Heart, a song that inspired Otis Redding's first hit, *Pain In My Heart*.

The Showmen were almost illicit for Minit as they were from Norfolk, Virginia, and not New Orleans. Their biggest record, *It Will Stand* (1964), hit the charts twice and remains a standard on oldies radio. One of their more obscure sides was *Country Fool*, which actually owes more to R & B than true soul. Ernie K-Doe topped the charts in 1961 for Minit with the unforgettable *Mother-In-Law*. The song could not avoid being a hit. "People that normally didn't buy records bought *Mother-In-Law* because it was a novelty," recalled Joe Banashak. "It shot to the top so fast, we really couldn't savor it at the time." A constant source of great singles, K-Doe also got a good local hit with *I Cried My Last Tear*.

One of K-Doe's label-mates was Benny Spellman (who provided the bass voice on *Mother-In-Law*), and he accounted for several fine sides but only one national record. It was a double-side hit, *Lipstick Traces* and *Fortune Teller*. Diamond Joe's *Moanin' And Screamin'*, a release on Minit, is considered the label's rarest single and is worth a listen.

Chris Kenner was a vocalist and songwriter whose career had many peaks and valleys. His first success was *I Like It Like That* (1961) on Instant, which was also produced by Toussaint and reached number 2 in the pop chart. (The record spawned the Popeye dance, which was more popular than the Twist in New Orleans.) After a series of local hits, including *Something You Got*, Kenner got back into the national spotlight with *Land Of 1000 Dances*, in 1963. While Kenner's version was only in the charts briefly, the covers it inspired, notably by Wilson Pickett and by Cannibal and the Headhunters, became million-sellers.

Two of Instant's biggest local hits were provided by a street hustler, Raymond Lewis, who accounted for *I'm Gonna Put Some Hurt On You*, and by Eskew Reeder's organ instrumental, *Green Door*. Reeder was better known as Esquerita, the artist who was Little Richard's prime influence. A resident of New Orleans briefly during the early 1960s, Reeder cut several great sides on Instant.

It Will Stand also includes two Instant sides that were exceptions in that they were not produced by Allen Toussaint. *Coo Coo Over You* was recorded by the Hueys, a group led by the 1950s rock-and-roll legend, Huey "Piano" Smith. It was a big local hit. Even bigger was Skip Easterling's *I'm Your Hoochie Coochie Man*, from 1971. A blue-eyed soul brother, Easterling is unknown outside the Crescent City, but his record was a huge hit on black New Orleans radio in the early 1970s.

Veterans of the New Orleans record business, the Neville Brothers (Cyril, Aaron, Charles, and Art) had all forged individual careers before uniting in 1977. Somewhat of a Crescent City supergroup, the Nevilles by the 1990s had emerged as the city's most famous group. The best sampling of their individual careers – and their work as a group – is contained on **Treacherous: A History Of The Neville Brothers**.

The oldest of the brothers, Art, has had the longest and most checkered career. He got his professional start as the pianist with the Hawkettes, who were a popular R & B vocal ensemble around New Orleans in the 1950s. The group only made one record, *Mardi Gras Mambo*, a local hit in 1955 on the Chicago-based Chess label. It has since and rightly become a Carnival standard. Art Neville's solo career got started in 1958 on the Specialty label through the intercession of his friend Larry Williams, who also recorded for the Hollywood-based company. Both *Cha Dooky Doo* and *Zing, Zing* are great examples of New Orleans rock-and-roll. Later he recorded for Instant his sublime ballad, *All These Things*, mentioned earlier. By the mid-1960s, Art had gone on to form the Meters and a decade later joined his family to make up the Neville Brothers.

The Nevilles' main singer is of course Aaron Neville, whose career stretches back to 1960 when he auditioned for Minit. Two Aaron Neville songs that are included on both **Treacherous** and **It Will Stand** are *Over You* and *Let's Live*, but obviously they deserve inclusion on any concise Neville Brothers collection. However, two other Minit classics are found on **Treacherous**, the churning *Waiting At The Station* and *Wrong Number*. Like all Minit sides, Neville's singles were produced and written by Toussaint.

Aaron Neville's penultimate ballad, *Tell It Like It Is*, most naturally included here, is his calling card. Made for Parlo in 1966, it was the number 2 record in the country that summer. *Where Is My Baby* (1968) is a similar ballad, which, unlike *Tell It Like It Is*, was produced by Toussaint. So too was *Hercules* (1973), which sported a strutting, more contemporary sound. Two other excellent Aaron ballads are also on display, the countryish *The Greatest Love* (1977) and *I Love Her Too* (1980), from the 1980 **Heart Beat** soundtrack.

Two songs that predate the formation of the Neville Brothers by only a year, and in many ways served as the incubator for the group, are *Brother John* and *Meet De Boys On The Battlefront*. Both tracks are credited to the Wild Tchoupitoulas, a Mardi Gras "Indian tribe" led by the Nevilles' uncle, George Landry. Basically traditional street songs sung by Indian-costumed groups at Mardi Gras, the tracks feature Landry, the existing Nevilles, and the Meters, who provide the rhythm section. These tracks are highlights of this collection.

The remaining nine tracks are taken from various Neville Brothers' LPs recorded between 1978 and 1985. The 1978 tracks, *Dancing Jones, Washable Ink,* and *Arianne*, come from their first, self-titled LP recorded for Capitol. The ballad, *Arianne*, is especially satisfying as Aaron's voice has rarely been more emotive.

Initially, the Neville Brothers had difficulty staying with one label because their sales lagged well behind major label expectations. They did not record again until 1981, when A & M financed **Fiyo On The Bayou**. *Hey Pocky Way, Fiyo On The Bayou*, and *Sitting Here In Limbo*, included here, originally saw the light of day on that A & M release. While the tracks are not bad, producer Joel Dorn seemed more intent on recreating the mid-1970s Meters sound than documenting the then-current Neville Brothers sound. Much more satisfying are the live tracks, *Fever* and *Fear, Hate, Envy, Jealousy*, which originally were released on the **Nevillization** LP in 1985. The LP was released on the independent Black Top label, and in many ways was somewhat of a comeback LP for the group, because at the time they had no success in finding a major-label recording contract. **Nevillization** eventually did so well that it did attract major-label interest. In the early 1990s the Neville Brothers were signed to A & M and enjoyed the status of pop gods.

New Orleans's premier funk group, the Meters (bassist George Porter, guitarist Leo Nocentelli, drummer Zigaboo Modeliste, and keyboardist Art Neville) were very much the city's answer to Memphis's Booker T. and the MGs. Like the MGs, the Meters were an instrumental group (initially anyway), cut numerous sessions as backing musicians, and had several successes on the R & B charts. The Meters first made a real impact in 1969 when they had five singles in the R & B charts. The group had begun as Art Neville and the Neville Sounds, had been around New Orleans since the mid-1960s playing clubs, and began doing session work for Allen Toussaint after he discovered them in a French Quarter nightclub. Aware of the contemporary sound the group boasted, Toussaint used them on various sessions backing other artists, notably Lee Dorsey, Aaron Neville, and Betty Harris.

The Meters' solo success began by accident in 1969 as they found themselves with extra studio time after completing a session. They used the time to cut four concise instrumentals, which Marshall Sehorn, Toussaint's business partner, then tried to sell in New York. After being shown the door more than once, Sehorn made a deal with the fast-fading Jubilee Records, who realized they had nothing to lose and agreed to release the session – thus keeping themselves in business a few more years. Jubilee placed the group on their Josie subsidiary.

The initial Meters' single, *Sophisticated Cissy*, became an instant hit in New Orleans as it satisfied dancers eager to do the Cissy, a dance that was very popular in the city at the time. So too did the answer, *Cissy Strut*. Both records danced their way to the Top 10 in the R & B charts in 1969 and established the Meters as a national act. When the year ended, the Meters had three more singles – *Ease Back, Dry Spell,* and *Look-Ka Py Py* – that made the R & B charts. The group was later honored as the top R & B instrumental group by the trade publication *Record World.*

The year 1970 was almost as successful with three chart entries, namely *Chicken Strut, Hand Clapping Song,* and *A Message From The Meters,* all included in this Charly collection, **Struttin'**. All three made the Top 30, but the Meters were losing steam at Josie. Their only two chart records, *Stretch Your Rubber Band* and *Doodle Oop,* went to numbers 42 and 47 on the national R & B chart respectively, and are not included here.

It is easy to see why the Meters were so popular at the time. Their style was a blend of catchy rhythms, bouncy off-beats, and simple funk. In fact, some scribes have dubbed them America's first funk band. While this may or may not be true, the group influenced numerous 1970s funk groups, including James Brown, Funkadelic/Parliament, and Sly Stone.

Despite being just a four-piece group and recording in a period that predated for the most part modern sound enhancement, the Meters had a remarkably full sound. The Meters' rhythm section was responsible for this trait. In soul brogue, Zigaboo Modeliste is "one bad drummer." Like most great New Orleans drummers, Modeliste played on every beat rather than on every second beat. However, he was also able to embellish his playing with off-handed snare-drum and cymbal rolls, playing in between the beat when called upon. Modeliste's partner, George Porter, was a pioneer funk bassist. His quirky bass lines were often the highlight of the Meters' sides and provided the springboard for Art Neville's wandering organ and Leo Nocentelli's scratchy guitar.

The Meters continued to work as session musicians in New Orleans between tours and their own recordings, notably backing Robert Palmer and Paul McCartney on LPs. In the early 1970s they moved to Reprise/Warner Brothers Records, a move that heralded a different approach. Not only were horns and extra keyboards added, but Art's brother Cyril was taken on as a full-time vocalist. Several great LPs were recorded in the 1970s, notably **Rejuvenation, Cabbage Alley,** and **Fire On The Bayou** (the last of which is reviewed in the "Basic Recordings" section).

Touring with Dr John and the Rolling Stones helped bring their sound to new audiences, but the group was constantly frustrated by lagging record sales and a lack of hits. The Meters ceased to exist in 1977, when Cyril and Art headed off to form the Neville Brothers. In the early 1990s the Meters occasionally reunite but new recordings have not materialized. In terms of Meters reissues, Rounder in the United States has collected three volumes of Josie material released as **Jam, Look-Ka Py Py**, and **Good Old Funky Music**, but none of them can match the Charly collection.

A constant source of fine recordings, Johnny Adams (b. January 5, 1932, in New Orleans) may well be the city's most recorded soul artist. Originally a gospel singer, Adams served choirs and quartets before switching to R & B. In 1959, he worked by day as a landscapist and was singing at night with Bessie Griffin's Soul Consolers. At the time he was living in the same apartment building as songwriter Dorothy LaBostrie. The composer had interested Ric Records owner Joe Ruffino in a ballad she wrote called *I Won't Cry*, but they had no one to sing it. However, that changed after LaBostrie overhead Adams singing a spiritual one evening while he was in the bathtub.

Initially against singing secular songs, Adams resisted the approach, but he was eventually worn down by LaBostrie and signed with Ric. *I Won't Cry*, a most spectacular ballad, became the first of several strong local sellers, but it was the Mac Rebennack (Dr John) composition, *Losing Battle*, which became Adams's first national chart record. Both these Ric sides are found on **Reconsider Me**, the best collection of Adams's early work.

However, the bulk of this set was recorded between 1968 and 1974, after he was on the New Orleans Watch label and later the Nashville-based SSS label. While at Watch, Adams cut the old country standard, *Release Me* (backed with *You Made A New Man Out Of Me*), and it topped the New Orleans charts and sparked the interest of SSS. The Nashville company bought the master and his contract, and also placed *Release Me* high in the charts in 1968. (It had earlier been remade by another R & B singer, Esther Phillips, who took the song to the top in 1962.)

Once Adams signed with SSS, he began recording in Nashville and was backed by excellent country musicians, giving him a unique sound. The title track, *Reconsider Me* (1968), is a glorious example, in which on this basically country song Adams's soaring falsetto gives the performance a unique feel. The song got into both the pop and the R & B charts.

After the success of *Reconsider Me* and *Release Me*, the Adams–SSS formula was set: give him a country song or a ballad and a good country band, and expect a soul hit. It did not always work but it accounted for some great records. On the ballad side Adams excels on *Real Live Hurting Man, Lonely Man*, and especially *I Want To Walk Through This Life With You*. Adams was capable of jumping instantly to a higher octave and his effectively placed falsetto became his signature and a primary attraction of his records.

Occasionally, Adams was given inferior material – *I Don't Worry Myself* and *Georgia Morning Dew* – but primarily this CD contains nothing but spectacular music. Hits that missed on SSS include *Too Much Pride*, *In A Moment Of Weakness*, and the extraordinary *Something Worth Leaving For*, the last of which was recorded in Florida.

This collection includes a handful of undated tracks that seem to have been recorded in the late 1970s, well after Adams's relationship with SSS had terminated. At the time Adams was cutting singles for Hep Me, a New Orleans label that had ties with Marshall Sehorn. Since Sehorn leased material to Charly regularly in the 1980s, it is reasonably safe to assume these previously unreleased sides came from him. The tracks in question – *Let Me Be Myself*, *Down By The River*, *You Can Depend On Me*, and *I Have No One* – show Adams in fine form, but unfortunately dreadful mixes mar their effectiveness.

In the 1980s, Adams signed with the Rounder label, based in Cambridge, Massachusetts. The best of his Rounder albums are **From The Heart** (reviewed in the "Basic Recordings" section), **The Real Me**, and **Room With A View Of The Blues**. While he still remains a favorite in New Orleans, Adams has found new popularity on the East and West coasts as well as in Japan and Europe as a result of his Rounder affiliation.

For three decades, Irma Thomas (b. Irma Lee, February 18, 1941, in Ponchatoula, Louisiana) has been referred to as "the Soul Queen of New Orleans," a richly deserved appellation. During that time she managed to wax an impressive string of excellent New Orleans soul records that have only grown in stature over the years. While her recording dossier is large and enviable, her best recordings were made in the early 1960s when she was contracted to Minit and Imperial. Most of these recordings for these labels are available on **Time Is On My Side: The Best Of Irma Thomas**.

No stranger to adversity, Thomas was already a teenage mother when her career got started. In 1959 she was waitressing at a club where Tommy Ridgely and the Untouchables were a regular attraction. Thomas talked Ridgely into letting her sing a song with the band during their warm-up. Ridgely liked what he heard, but Irma's boss did not appreciate her neglecting her duties, and fired her. Quick to help out, Ridgely hired Thomas to open his shows and introduced her to his recording patron, Joe Ruffino, owner of the Ric and Ron labels.

Thomas had a big local (and small national) hit with her first offering, *Don't Mess With My Man* (1960), which was very blues slanted. She left Ruffino after just one other single and, through Allen Toussaint's intercession, signed with Minit in 1961. Thomas's association with Toussaint produced some memorable New Orleans music but no national hits. Toussaint had two formulas for recording Thomas: a pop ballad style or an up-tempo, second-line New Orleans style. On **Time Is On My Side**, the emphasis is on the ballads. If the collection has a weakness, it is that it does not contain strutting classics like *I Did My Part* and *Somebody Told Me*. Also strangely missing is her wonderful ballad, *Cry On*.

Of the Minit songs the collection does contain, *Girl Needs Boy* and *It's Too Soon To Know*, both from 1961, boast complicated pop arrangements without a distinct New Orleans sound. Much more satisfying is the simple *It's Raining* (1962), Thomas's most popular New Orleans record. Oddly, *Gone* is also included, a song virtually identical to *It's Raining*. Two other Minit songs are included, the pop-style *Two Winters Long* (1962) and the devilish *Ruler Of My Heart* (1963). The latter proved not only Thomas's last Minit single, but the last single released on the label.

When Minit was absorbed by Imperial in 1964, Thomas was transferred to the new label, on which she had her greatest commercial success. In 1964 she produced four chart records, namely *Wish Someone Would Care, Anyone Who Knows What Love Is, Times Have Changed*, and *He's My Guy*. The production process of her Imperial sessions in Los Angeles was far more painstaking than that of her Minit sides. Produced by Eddie Ray and arranged by H.B. Barnum, Thomas was surrounded by orchestras, overdubs, vocal groups, and even kettle drums. The combination was for the most part satisfying, particularly the title track, where Thomas really steps out.

One might not think that LA musicians could get much of a New Orleans sound, but listen to *Breakaway*, the fabulous flip to *Wish Someone Would Care*: it all but personifies the second-line sound. Of all Thomas's Imperial singles, the biggest hit in her home town was *Breakaway*. The title track, *Time Is On My Side*, is most worthy of discussion. It was the flip to *Anyone Who Knows What Love Is*, and was covered by the Rolling Stones and turned into a Top 10 hit despite theirs being an inferior version. Justifiably resentful over the British group's success with the song, Thomas rarely performs the song on live dates. (It is a good thing Thomas has no animus towards folk-rock singer Tracy Nelson, because she would not have a repertoire to sing: Nelson in the course of her career remade eight of Thomas's songs.)

Wish Someone Would Care proved to be Thomas's biggest hit, and Imperial came out with an album of the same name. After 1964, Thomas unaccountably could not squeeze back into the charts with subsequent Imperial singles. Most of these more obscure classics in this collection come from her second, woefully overlooked Imperial album, **Take A Look**. Although none of the singles from the album found success with the public, the songs are solid, as evidenced by the inclusions on this CD: *Some Things You Never Get Used To, Times Have Changed, It's Starting To Get To Me Now*, and *Take A Look*. The last song was produced by Toussaint near the end of Thomas's Imperial tenure. One misses her utterly sublime *Wait, Wait, Wait* from this period.

Thomas left Imperial in 1966, signed with Chess the following year, and had a sizable hit with Otis Redding's *Good To Me* – tit-for-tat considering he confiscated *Ruler Of My Heart* for his *Pain In My Heart*. With club-work around the New Orleans area at a minimum, Thomas moved to Los Angeles in 1969, where she worked in a department store and continued to record for Fungus, Canyon, and Roker, but with little success. She returned to the Crescent City in the mid-1970s, scoring a mild disco hit with *Safe With Me* in 1979. Recordings on several small labels followed and local club-work became bountiful. After signing with Rounder in the mid-1980s, Thomas got her recording career on track once again. In the 1990s she was reaping the fruits of her labors with national tours and engagements in Europe.

Without a doubt the best representation of the recorded output of Lee Dorsey (b. Irving Lee Dorsey, December 4, 1926, in New Orleans) is **Great Googa Mooga**. Dubbed "Mr TNT" by the trade papers, Dorsey was the Crescent City's most commercially successful soul artist during the mid-1960s. He scored 10 chart singles between 1961 and 1970, including five Top 10 entries. Dorsey grew up in the musically fertile Ninth Ward of New Orleans, and was a boyhood friend of Fats Domino. Dorsey sang with kids in his neighborhood and even developed an appreciation for country music via the Grand Ole Opry. His family moved to Portland, Oregon, when he was 10, which was obviously a cultural shock for the young New Orleansian. He served in the navy during World War II, and when he returned to America he developed into a successful featherweight prize-fighter.

Tiring of the fight business, in 1955 Dorsey returned to the city where he was born. He worked by day as a body and fender man and frequented clubs like the Dew Drop to see live music at weekends. As he related, "I liked to sing to make work go easier." One day in 1957, Reynauld Richard, a record producer and songwriter, brought his car into the shop where Dorsey worked. Upon hearing him sing, Richard asked him if he wanted to make a record. With nothing to lose, Dorsey went to the studio that very night and cut *Rock Pretty Baby*, which was released on Rex. While the single did not set the world on fire, Richard saw enough promise in it to get Dorsey back in the studio a month later, when he cut *Lottie Mo*. It was released on Valiant.

A landmark single as far as Dorsey's career was concerned, *Lottie Mo* was leased to ABC, and its subsequent national success earned him a place on Dick Clark's "American Bandstand" show. It also began a long association with the New Orleans soul producer Allen Toussaint. Dorsey switched to the New York-based Fury in 1961 after being courted by their promotion man, Marshall Sehorn. Dorsey cut the nursery rhyme-like *Ya Ya*, which surprisingly made it to number 1 in the R & B charts. He had one other chart record on Fury, *Do-Re-Me* (1962), but not long after he returned to New Orleans and picked up where he left off – banging dents out of fenders.

Dorsey was in the spotlight in 1965 after Toussaint and Sehorn dragged him from under a car and got him back in the studio. Dorsey cut *Ride Your Pony* (1965), one of the greatest soul records of all time. Released on the Amy subsidiary of New York-based Bell, the record, which peaked at number 7 R & B, began an impressive string of hits.

The combination of Dorsey, Toussaint, Sehorn, and the Meters as the rhythm section proved to be lethal. The follow-up to *Ride My Pony*, the bluesy *Get Out Of My Life, Woman* (1965), proved to be an even bigger hit, peaking at number 5. The unforgettable *Working In The Coal Mine* (1966) also soared to number 5 and other hits followed, including *Holy Cow* (1966), *Go-Go Girl* (1967), and the fabulous *Everything I Do Gonh Be Funky* (1969), the last a spectacular presentation of the New Orleans soul–funk sound.

Toussaint's skills as writer and producer may well have peaked on Dorsey's recordings. Not only was Dorsey's material simple and superior, the arrangements were inventive but attractively simple. Even Coca-Cola employed Toussaint and Dorsey to produce a radio jingle that later became *My Old Car*, a song included in this package. Other solid Amy tracks include *Four Corners, Who's Gonna Help Brother Get Further,* and *Can You Hear Me?* – flip sides and LP tracks that screamed for attention but failed to get into the charts.

Dorsey moved on to Polydor in 1970 when he waxed **Yes We Can**, an otherwise obscure LP that accounted for only one mild hit, the title track. With the Meters in tow, Dorsey recorded *Riverboat; Tears, Tears And More Tears; O Me-O, My-O*; and *Sneakin' Sally Through The Alley* – all fabulous examples of New Orleans soul.

Dorsey's chart success was all behind him by 1970, because black radio moved away from his style and because Toussaint got wrapped up in his own solo career and in producing national acts for major labels. His last recording outing occurred in 1978 when ABC released the super-contemporary **Night People** album. It contained plenty of great songs but outside of New Orleans it had little impact (the title track scraped the bottom of the charts).

Dorsey became a major player in the history of soul and New Orleans music, having cut several original and happy-go-lucky tracks listeners will remember for years. His death in 1986 left the world with one fewer great "soul artist."

Discographical Details

246 It Will Stand
Various Artists

Charly 99 (UK)

Jessie Hill: *Ooh Poo Pa Doo*; Aaron Neville: *Over You/Let's Live*; Ernie K-Doe: *Mother-In-Law/I Cried My Last Tear*; Chris Kenner: *I Like It Like That/Land Of 1,000 Dances/Something You Got*; Diamond Joe: *Moanin' And Screamin'*; The Showmen: *It Will Stand/Country Fool*; Skip Easterling: *I'm Your Hoochie Coochie Man*; The Hueys: *Coo Coo Over You*; Irma Thomas: *Ruler Of My Heart/It's Raining*; Eskew Reeder: *Green Door*; Benny Spellman: *Lipstick Traces/Fortune Teller*; Art Neville: *All These Things*; Raymond Lewis: *I'm Gonna Put Some Hurt On You*

247 Treacherous: A History Of The Neville Brothers 1955–1985
The Neville Brothers

Rhino 71494

The Hawkettes: *Mardi Gras Mambo*; Art Neville: *Cha Dooky Do/Zing, Zing/All These Things*; Aaron Neville: *Over You/Let's Live/Waiting At The Station/Wrong Number/Tell It Like It Is/Where Is My Baby/Hercules/The Greatest Love/I Love Her Too*; Cyril Neville: *Gossip*; The Wild Tchoupitoulas: *Brother John/Meet De Boys On The Battlefront*; The Neville Brothers: *Dancing Jones/Arianne/Washable Ink/ Hey Pocky Way/Sitting Here In Limbo/Fiyo On The Bayou/Fever/Fear, Hate, Envy, Jealousy/Amazing Grace – Down By The Riverside – Amen* (medley)

248 Struttin'
The Meters

Charly 63 (UK)

Look-Ka Py Py/Cissy Strut/Ease Back/Chicken Strut/A Message From The Meters/ Tipple Toes/Sophisticated Cissy/Here Comes The Meter Man/Ride Your Pony/Dry Spell/Hand Clapping Song/Liver Splash/Same Old Thing/Schorns Farm/Yeah Your Right/9 Till 5/Pungee/Rigor Mortis/Little Old Money Maker

249 Reconsider Me
Johnny Adams

Charly 89 (UK)

I Won't Cry/A Losing Battle/Release Me/You Made A New Man Out Of Me/ Reconsider Me/If I Could Just See You One More Time/I Can't Be All That Bad/In A Moment Of Weakness/Proud Woman/Real Live Hurting Man/Georgia Morning Dew/ Living On Your Love/Lonely Man/Too Much Pride/I Want To Walk Through This Life With You/Down By The River/I Don't Worry Myself/I Have No One/South Side Of Soul Street/Something Worth Leaving For/You Can Depend On Me/Let Me Be Myself

250 Time Is On My Side: The Best Of Irma Thomas
Irma Thomas

EMI 97988

Girl Needs Boy/It's Too Soon To Know/Gone/It's Raining/Two Winters Long/Ruler Of My Heart/While The City Sleeps/Wish Someone Would Care/Breakaway/Time Is On

My Side/Anyone Who Knows What Love Is/True, True Love/Think Again/Long After Tonight/Times Have Changed/He's My Guy/Maybe/I'm Gonna Cry Till My Tears Run Dry/The Hurt's All Gone/Live Again/Some Things You Never Get Used To/It's Starting To Get To Me Now/Take A Look

251   Great Googa Mooga
Lee Dorsey

Charly 3 (UK)

Lottie Mo/Ya Ya/Do-Re-Me/Hoodlum Joe/You're Breaking Me Up/Messed Around/ Ay-La-Ay/Great Googa Mooga/People Sure Act Funny/Ride Your Pony/Can You Hear Me?/Get Out Of My Life, Woman/Confusion/Working In The Coal Mine/Holy Cow/My Old Car/Go-Go Girl/Love Lots Of Lovin'/Four Corners/A Lover Was Born/ Everything I Do Gonh Be Funky/Give It Up/Candy Yam/What You Want/Yes We Can/O Me-O, My-O/Sneakin' Sally Through The Alley/Tears, Tears And More Tears/Occapella/Riverboat/Who's Gonna Help Brother Get Further/A Place Where We Can Be Free/Freedom For The Stallion/If She Won't/When Can I Come Home?/On Your Way Down/Lonely Avenue/Can I Be The One?/Night People/Soul Mine

(ii) Texas

The primary purveyor of Texas soul during the 1960s was the Duke/Peacock/Backbeat group of labels owned by the Houston entrepreneur Don Robey (Robey had been in the record business since the late 1940s, and by the mid-1950s he was the kingpin in Texas as far as blues and gospel records were concerned). A shrewd businessman, Robey was able to continue his success on the black charts in the 1960s by introducing soul arrangements to his established artists, and by adding younger soul artists to his roster. While not all of his records were memorable – there were several duds along the way – many were unique. Robey used several different writers and arrangers to keep things interesting.

Many great Duke soul sides are contained on **Houston's Deep Throat Rhythm And Blues**, a Japanese collection that contains some great Texas soul. The set gets started with Al "TNT" Braggs's curiously effective *So Used To Having You Around*. Braggs (b. May 23, 1938, in Dallas, Texas) had recorded excellent singles in the early 1960s, a period when he served as the warm-up act for Bobby Bland. This track, however, comes from a decade later and features a near-New Orleans sound, and its appeal is the quirky tempo changes and of course Braggs's inimitable vocals. This man obviously deserves his own CD.

The best-known Texas artist here is Joe Hinton, who accounts for *How Long Can I Last, Lots of Love*, and *I'm Watching And Waiting*. The Hinton sides are surprising and enjoyable, as he is heard outside of the ballad style which typified his more popular records, such as *Funny* (the Willie Nelson song). Joe Scott arranged and produced these masterpieces, recorded in 1967. *How Long Can I Last* is very much in the Texas blues shuffle style while *Lots Of Love* is danceable, up-tempo soul at its finest. His final track, *I'm Watching And Waiting*, is straight blues on which Hinton puts his patented falsetto to good use.

Gene Allison (b. August 29, 1934, in Nashville), who had some great R & B records on Vee Jay during the late 1950s, was with Duke briefly in the early 1960s. Possessing a light, bouncy voice, he handles pop-style soul/ballads like *Walking In The Park* and *Which Way To Turn* very well. *Am I The One* is taken at a quicker pace but suffers slightly from a rather obtrusive vocal backup group.

A familiar name in the Duke catalog was Buddy Ace (b. Jimmy Lee Land, 1936, in Jasper, Texas). Ace was a Robey-inspired pseudonym that was used as a semi-tribute to the late Johnny Ace, his big hitmaker in the 1950s. Buddy Ace had several fine singles in the 1960s. While *Counting On You* is a pop-style throwaway, *It's Gonna Be Me* is Texas soul at its best, with flashy horn arrangements, crisp drumming, and a strutting bass line.

Another familiar name, Ernie K-Doe – who signed with Duke after his Minit tenure – is represented by *The Boomerang*, a song which owes more to James Brown's style than to New Orleans's. This song, obviously aimed at the dance market, can only be labeled frantic soul. The ballad, *Mr Lonesome*, is a poor representative of K-Doe's talent as well.

Robey had several females in his stable of artists and two excellent ones are included here – Luvenia Lewis (b. in Lufkin, Texas) and Helen Wilson. Lewis's emotive soul ballad, *So Many Times*, is simple but hard hitting. The arrangement to *Nobody's Gonna Take My Man* is curiously similar to Joe Jones's *You Talk Too Much*, but far more impudent. Helen Wilson's *Do What You Did Yesterday* is a romping, organ-led shuffle which captures the early Texas soul style quite well.

Oscar Perry, who was better known as a songwriter, contributes *Poor Me*, a rather odd song which borrows heavily from the Drifters' hit *Save The Last Dance For Me*. Henry Moore's *Did You Miss Me* is nothing more than a demo and did not really deserve inclusion when other great Duke tracks could have taken its place. Much better is Harold Hopkins's *Bad Understanding*, a good soul-blues performance. Robey sold his Duke catalog to ABC in the early 1970s and it has since been assumed by MCA.

Bobby Bland (b. January 27, 1930, in Rosemark, Tennessee) was quite certainly the brightest star in the Duke/Peacock/Backbeat constellation. Representing the veritable essence of the soul-blues style, Bobby Bland achieved a level of commercial success during the 1960s that was surpassed only by Ray Charles and James Brown. No less than 26 of these successes are contained on **The Voice: Duke Recordings, 1959–1969.**

Bland's sound from this period was aptly described by Peter Guralnick in *Lost Highway*:

> Bobby was like another member of the band, and it's no accident that the sound built around him included sophisticated big-band arrangements, intricate instrumental voicings, and brass squalls to match Bobby's gargled vocal interpolations – dramatic orchestral flourishes in sharp contrast to the warmth, intimacy, and projected vulnerability of Bobby's singing voice. The guitar was always of crucial importance in the formula . . . but it was the horns that carried the sound.

The man credited with creating this sound was Bland's bandleader and Duke arranger Joe Scott. Scott painstakingly dressed Bland with complicated but melodic arrangements, with a lot of brassy punch. Many of the songs presented on **The Voice** had to be re-recorded as many as 40 times until they were right. But right they were, as the stunning performances on this set so eloquently testifies.

The set's opening track, *Who Will The Next Fool Be* (1962), very much sets the tone of the release. Originally a country hit for Charlie Rich, Bland and Scott made this song their own with smokey vocals and busy R & B arrangements. It proved to be one of Bland's biggest records.

While Bland primarily interpreted slow soul–blues ballads much later in his career, in the early 1960s he was presented with some excellent blues shuffles. The best of these are *Ain't That Lovin' You* (1962), *Ain't Doing Too Bad* (1964), *Back In The Same Old Bag* (1966), and *Good Time Charlie* (1966), the last thankfully appearing in album form for the first time. On these particular numbers he recalls the sound Texas made famous a decade earlier. Horns – as stated, a cornerstone of Bland's sound – also are used to good effect on the gospel-tinged *Turn On Your Love Light* (1961), *Yield Not To Temptation* (1962), and *These Hands (Small But Mighty)* (1965). Never far from the sound of the sanctified chapel, Bland's delivery made even his bluesier records palatable to the soul and even the pop buyer.

One of the landmark tracks from Bland's career was *Two Steps From The Blues*, the title track from the ultimate Bobby Bland album. The arrangements are simple in comparison to many of his other performances, but Bland's message and delivery are particularly effective. That album also contained the haunting *I'll Take Care Of You* (1959), *I Pity The Fool* (1961), and the masterpiece *Cry, Cry, Cry* (1961), all which are reissued on **The Voice**.

Bland especially excels on mid-tempo and ballad soul tunes, such as *Call On Me* (1963) and *Share Your Love With Me* (1964), both included here, but the omission of the classic *That's The Way Love Is* (1963) is almost criminal. Other egregious omissions were his hits *Lead Me On* (a great gospel-blues from 1960), *Poverty* (a lightweight yet engaging 1966 number), and *If You Can Read My Mind* (a sublime 1966 ballad). Instead, the collection includes such lesser tracks as *Blue Moon* and *Shoes*. Admittedly, Bland's catalogue is so rich with great songs that a critic can easily find twenty other numbers that deserve representation. Not only does **The Voice** belong in every soul and blues collection but I guarantee that it will be played often.

Discographical Details

252   Houston's Deep Throat Rhythm And Blues
Various Artists

P-Vine 2515 (Jap)

Al "TNT" Braggs: *So Used To Having You Around*; Oscar Perry: *Poor Me*; Gene Allison: *Walking In The Park/Which Way To Turn/Am I The One*; Luvenia Lewis: *So Many Times/Nobody's Gonna Take My Man*; Ernie K-Doe: *The Boomerang/Mr Lonesome*; Buddy Ace: *Counting On You/It's Gonna Be Me*; Helen Wilson: *Do What You Did Yesterday*; Joe Hinton: *How Long Can I Last/Lots Of Love/I'm Watching And Waiting*; Henry Moore: *Did You Miss Me*; Harold Hopkins: *Bad Understanding*

253   The Voice: Duke Recordings, 1959–1969
Bobby Bland

Ace 323 (UK)

Who Will The Next Fool Be/I Pity The Fool/Don't Cry No More/Ain't That Loving You/I'm Not Ashamed/Cry, Cry, Cry/I'll Take Care Of You/Call On Me/Blue Moon/Turn On Your Love Light/Stormy Monday/Two Steps From The Blues/Ain't Nothing You Can Do/Ain't Doing Too Bad/Sometimes You Got To Try A Little/Ain't No Telling/Yield Not To Temptation/I'm Too Far Gone To Turn Around/These Hands (Small But Mighty)/Good Time Charlie/Ask Me About Nothing (But The Blues)/Share Your Love With Me/That Did It/Shoes/Back In The Same Old Bag/Chains Of Love

(iii) Florida

While Miami, Florida, will never compare with Detroit, Memphis, or Philadelphia as a consistent soul music center, a very danceable, durable and energetic brand of music evolved there during the 1970s. During that decade a steady flow of hits poured out of Miami that not only made the R & B charts, but also consistently crossed over into the pop charts as well.

Most Sunshine State soul appeared on T.K. Productions Inc., a group of labels that included T.K., Alston, Glades, Cat, Marlin, Drive, and Stone Dog, and was owned by the legendary black music impresario Henry Stone. He doubled as the owner of Tone

Distributors, the largest supplier of black records in Florida and the southeast. In the 1950s, he produced sessions for Chess, King, and Modern, co-owned Federal and Deluxe for a short time, and owned the Rockin' and Dade labels outright. However, Stone did not achieve huge success until the early 1970s upon the foundation of T.K. Obviously, **Get Down Tonight: The Best Of T.K. Records** contains Stone's most memorable successes and presents most of his roster of soul artists.

Ironically T.K. had several white artists who mined the soul field, most notably K.C. and the Sunshine Band, whose nucleus consisted of H.W. Casey and Rich Finch, two white kids fresh out of high school. Casey, an assistant studio engineer, and Finch, a bassist, became songwriting partners and together produced several hits of their own for other T.K. acts. Their sound was heavily influenced by an indigenous music across the waters in the nearby Bahamas called Junkernoo. Their attractively simple *Get Down Tonight* (1975) was the first of four singles to reach number 1 in the pop markets, and *I'm Your Boogie Man* (1977) was the last. These songs at the time were dismissed as mindless disco by mindless critics, but hold up marvelously years later.

Another white artist with his thumb on the pulse of black music was Peter Brown (b. July 11, 1953, in Blue Island, Illinois). A native of the Chicago suburbs, Brown built a home studio, recorded himself playing all the instruments, and sent the takes to T.K. *Do You Wanna Get Funky With Me* was one of the tapes and it topped the R & B charts in 1977. Brown's other successes, *Dance With Me* (1978) and *Crank It Up* (1979), are here too.

T.K. also had success with Foxy, a Miami prom/disco band. The band consisted of Ish Ledesma (lead vocals, guitar), Richie Puente (clarinet, percussion), Arnold Pasiero (bass), Charlie Murciano (keyboards), and Joe Galdo (drums), and reflected the greater influence of Latin music on late 1970s R & B. Verging on disco, *Get Off* (1978) was another chart topper, and *Hot Number* (1979) did nearly as well.

One of the first national disco hits was provided by T.K. when in 1974 George McCrae (b. October 19, 1944, in West Palm Beach, Florida) scored with *Rock Your Baby*. Not to be outdone, George's wife, Gwen (b. December 21, 1943, in Pensacola, Florida), had a hit the following year with her own *Rockin' Chair*. Disco gold was produced by Anita Ward (b. December 20, 1957, in Memphis), a Southern soul stylist who performed *Ring My Bell* (1979) with a metronomic beat arrangement that is the veritable essence of disco.

T.K.'s most successful female artist turned out to be Betty Wright, whose *Tonight's The Night* was a hit twice, once as the 1974 studio version and then as a 1978 live version. This appealingly melodic song about a girl losing her virginity is now a staple in the repertoires of many female Southern soul stylists. The original A side to the studio version was the rousing *Shoorah! Shoorah!*, which was unfairly overlooked in the United States. In Europe, however, it became a big hit.

One of T.K.'s early successes came from Timmy Thomas (b. November 13, 1944, in Evansville, Indiana), who contributed the memorable *Why Can't We Live Together* (1972), which was echoed by Rodney King twenty years later when he tried to quiet a race riot that was taking place in LA supposedly on his behalf. The record, T.K.'s first gold disc, is a haunting, slow-burning groove, consisting of nothing more than Thomas's voice, his organ, and a drum machine.

Benny Latimore brought a strong blues flavor to contemporary soul music during the 1970s. *Keep The Home Fire Burnin'* (1975) was one of the best examples of his style. Two of T.K.'s regular studio musicians had brief moments in the sun during the company's heyday: guitarist Little Beaver (b. Willie Hale, August 15, 1945, in Forest City, Arkansas) entered the charts with *Party Down* (1974) and Jimmy "Bo" Horne did the same the following year with *Gimme Some*.

T.K. also had limited success with two previously established artists who were in Miami briefly. Ronnie Spector provided a reasonable version of *It's A Heartache*, but more memorable was James Brown's *Rapp Payback* (1980), one of his last soul-funk excursions before he disappeared from the charts.

Unfortunately for T.K., after 1980 they lost their touch – eaten by the disco bear they helped to conceive. Their records became overproduced as they shunned the simple soul sounds that had been their original calling card. The change in direction led to artistic and commercial disaster, as well as eventual bankruptcy.

Discographical Details

254   Get Down Tonight: The Best Of T.K. Records
Various Artists

Rhino 71003

Peter Brown: *Crank It Up/Dance With Me/Do You Want To Get Funky With Me*; Timmy Thomas: *Why Can't We Live Together*; George McCrae: *Rock Your Baby*; Gwen McCrae: *Rockin' Chair*; K.C. and the Sunshine Band: *Get Down Tonight/ I'm Your Boogie Man*; Betty Wright: *Tonight's The Night/Shoorah! Shoorah!*; Little Beaver: *Party Down*; Foxy: *Get Off/Hot Number*; Ronnie Spector: *It's A Heartache*; James Brown: *Rapp Payback*; Jimmy "Bo" Horne: *Gimme Some*; Anita Ward: *Ring My Bell*; Latimore: *Keep The Home Fire Burnin'*

(iv) Mississippi

The modern Mississippi soul and blues sound was – and still is – kept alive on the Jackson-based Malaco label. The company surprised many observers by reviving the soul and blues sounds in the 1980s, proving that there was still such a thing as a middle-aged African American record buyer. Malaco had a fairly simple formula for success: they signed proven blues and soul artists once they were dropped by major labels and put them back in familiar recording surroundings. This was what they did with Bobby Bland, Denise LaSalle, Little Milton, Shirley Brown, Johnnie Taylor, and Latimore, which revived their careers.

However, the artist that got Malaco on the map in the first place was the otherwise obscure Z.Z. Hill, who cut the landmark **Down Home** (1981), the artist's second album for the label. An unprecedented success that spent more than a year on the R & B charts, the album established Malaco as a modern-day blues and soul empire.

While many listeners will file **Down Home** in the blues section of their collection – an obvious place for it because of the title track – several of the tracks take the soul road. The album was produced by Malaco co-owners Tommy Couch and Wolf Stephenson, two men who went through hundreds of songs before picking the final tracks. Using their usual integrated group of studio musicians, the producers added a contemporary touch to even the straight blues arrangements. The album's centerpiece, *Down Home Blues*, had been found on an old demo tape that had been submitted to the Muscle Shoals Studio a decade earlier. Penned by the prolific George Jackson, the song's lyrics naturally appealed to blues listeners, but its appeal went far beyond.

Another excellent Jackson blues composition, *Cheating In The Next Room*, is also included, as is the cover of Little Johnny Taylor's *Everybody Knows About My Good Thing*. Not a hard blues singer, Hill used a smooth approach tailor-made for soul-blues ballads like *Love Me* and *When Can We Do This Again*. On the up-tempo side, Hill does a great job with *When It Rains It Pours* and the humorous Swamp Dogg composition, *Right Arm For Your Love*.

Initially, Malaco decided not to issue any singles from **Down Home**, in order to force record buyers to purchase the entire album. The ploy worked and even radio stations not prone to play soul-blues discovered what a great album this was. Hill was for a long time deemed a journeyman performer, having recorded for decades in California without any remarkable success (see chapter 8 for a review of this output). After the release of **Down Home**, however, Hill's popularity grew to the point where he rivaled such established artists as B.B. King, Bobby Bland, Johnnie Taylor, and Tyrone Davis. Excellent new recordings followed, but unfortunately Hill's premature death in 1984 robbed the blues and soul world of yet another great artist.

Discographical Details

255   Down Home

Z.Z. Hill

Malaco 7406

Down Home Blues/Cheating In The Next Room/Everybody Knows About My Good Thing/Love Me/That Means So Much To Me/When Can We Do This Again/Right Arm For Your Love/When It Rains It Pours/Woman Don't Go Astray/Givin' It Up For Your Love

Basic Recordings

New Orleans

256   Sehorn's Soul Farm

Various Artists

Charly 1032 (UK) (LP)

Warren Lee: *Star Revue/Climb The Ladder*; Willie Harper: *Why You Want To Do It/That's What You Need*; John Williams: *Blues, Tears And Sorrow*; Benny Spellman: *Sinner Girl*; Eldridge Holmes: *Love Affair*; Joe Hayworth: *Let's Make It*; Curley Moore: *Get Lowdown/Don't Pity Me*; Aaron Neville: *Hercules/Struttin' On Sunday*; Sonny Fisher: *Love, This Is Sonny*; Earl King: *All My Love*; Diamond Joe: *Gossip, Gossip*; Ernie K-Doe: *Hotcha Mama*

Except for K-Doe, Spellman, and Neville, most of the artists presented here never have made a name for themselves outside of New Orleans. Nevertheless, these Toussaint-produced sides include some of his best production work. Recorded in the late 1960s and early 1970s, these sides flaunt a simpler New Orleans soul sound, probably because Toussaint had to turn this stuff out quickly. Listen to Warren Lee and Willie Harper and ask yourself why these songs were not hits.

257   The Allen Toussaint Collection

Allen Toussaint

Reprise 26459-2

From A Whisper To A Scream/What Is Success/Am I Expecting Too Much/On Your Way Down/Soul Sister/Country John/Last Train/Southern Nights/What Do You Want The Girl To Do?/You Will Not Lose/Night People/Lover Of Love/Motion/Viva La Money/Happiness/With You In Mind

Although Toussaint (b. January 14, 1938, in New Orleans) is best known for playing behind and producing other artists, his own work is quite impressive, even though he never got any national hits. This CD collects his best-known sides from four different albums recorded between 1969 and 1978. Many of these songs were hits for other artists, hence their inclusion. Unfortunately, some of Toussaint's better solo sides, notably *Sweet Touch Of Love* (1969), are not found here.

258 Burn! K-Doe, Burn!
Ernie K-Doe

Charly 21 (UK)

Mother-In-Law/Mother-In-Law (alternate take)/*Talkin' Out Of My Head/Make You Love Me/Reaping What I Sow/Hurry Up And Know It/Waiting At The Station/ Love You The Best/Te-Ta-Te-Ta-Ta/A Certain Girl/Easier Said Than Done/T'Ain't It The Truth/The Fight/There's A Will There's A Way/Baby, Since I Met You/Wanted $10,000 Reward/I Cried My Last Tear/Hello My Lover/Real Man/Be Sweet/Loving You/Beating Like A Tom Tom/Penny Worth Of Happiness/Get Out Of My House*

A most important New Orleans artist, K-Doe (b. Ernest Kador, February 22, 1936, in New Orleans) was very much influenced by the gospel quartet style. With producer Allen Toussaint he cut several spectacular singles on the Minit label. Of course, the best known is his number 1 hit from 1961, *Mother-In-Law*, but *A Certain Girl*, *T'Ain't It The Truth*, and *I Cried My Last Tear* truly embody the commercial New Orleans sound even better. The only other chart record K-Doe got on Minit was *Te-Ta-Te-Ta-Ta*, from 1961, but he did score in the late 1960s with two singles on the Houston-based Duke label. This collection just missed the "Essential Recordings" list.

259 Fire On The Bayou
The Meters

Reprise 2228 (LP)

Out In The Country/Fire On The Bayou/Love Slip Up On Ya/Talkin' 'Bout New Orleans/They All Ask'd About You/Can You Do Without?/Liar/You're A Friend Of Mine/Middle Of The Road/Running Fast/Mardi Gras Mambo

This album comes from the Meters' second period, when they signed with Warner Brothers in the early 1970s and added Cyril Neville on vocals. All of the Meters' five Warner Brothers LPs were excellent and are worth hunting down, but this one is perhaps the best. It was one of the funkiest soul records ever to come out of New Orleans. The Meters could not sell enough records to stay viable, however, and broke up in 1977, the Neville brothers graduating to the Neville Brothers group. Despite leaving a legacy of terrific music, the Meters on Warner Brothers, because of legalities, unfortunately have yet to be reissued on CD. It is to be hoped that this will be rectified soon.

260 The Wild Tchoupitoulas
The Wild Tchoupitoulas

Mango CD 9908

Brother John/Meet De Boys On The Battlefront/Indians, Here They Come/Hey Pokey A-Way/Indian Red/Big Chief Got A Golden Crown/Hey Mama/Hey, Hey

This is a very interesting and important CD that was first released in 1976. The Wild Tchoupitoulas are one of several black Mardi Gras "Indian tribes" that mask on Carnival Day. Their traditional songs have been heard on the streets of New Orleans for a century. The Big Chief of the Wild Tchoupitoulas was George Landry, who was an uncle of the Neville brothers. Obviously, their blood relationship led to this fine release. On the album several of the traditional Indian songs are backed by the Meters and 11 of the Neville brothers help on vocals. The combination is lethal.

261   Barefootin': Golden Classics
Robert Parker

Collectables CD 5163

*Barefootin'/Let's Go Baby (Where The Action Is)/A Little Bit Of Something/Sneakin'
Sally Through The Alley/Better Luck In The Summertime/You See Me/Give Me The
Country Side Of Life/Get Right On Down/Get Ta' Steppin'/The Hiccup/Hot 'n' Cold/
Skinny Dippin'/I Like What You Do To Me/Disco Doctor*

Robert Parker (b. October 14, 1930, in New Orleans) is of course best known for
his danceable chart smash from 1966, *Barefootin'*. Parker was a veteran artist,
having been a saxophonist in Professor Longhair's band back in the late 1940s.
Thus, he was predisposed to combine the older New Orleans R & B sound with
the funkier contemporary soul sound of the 1960s, and the result is very
appealing. He was no hit champion, however; only the title track entered the
national charts. This collection includes several excellent danceable tracks,
including *The Hiccup* and *Sneakin' Sally Through The Alley*.

262   I Like It Like That
Chris Kenner

Charly 230 (UK)

*I Like It Like That/Anybody Here Seen My Baby?/Shoo-Rah/Johnny Little/Gonna
Getcha Baby/Never Reach Perfection/Something You Got/That's My Girl/Land Of
1,000 Dances/She Can Dance/Come Back And See/How Far/Time All Night
Rambler/Packing Up/I Found Peace*

Perhaps better known as a tunesmith, Chris Kenner (b. December 25, 1929, in
New Orleans), provided a spate of hits for other recording artists, notably *Land
Of 1,000 Dances* for Cannibal and the Headhunters and Wilson Pickett, *I Like It
Like That* for the Dave Clark Five, and *Something You Got* for Alvin Robinson.
But with production assistance from Allen Toussaint, Kenner with his
serviceable but hypnotic vocals managed to get hits with his original versions
first with *I Like It Like That* (1961) and *Land Of 1,000 Dances* (1963). Kenner's
sound suffered somewhat after he stopped working with Toussaint, and a couple
of tracks from this later period are included. After a stint in prison, Kenner died
in 1977.

263   Some Folks Don't Understand It
The Showmen

Charly 226 (UK)

*It Will Stand/Country Fool/This Misery/The Wrong Girl/Fate Planned It This Way/
For You My Darling/Valley Of Love/The Owl Sees You/Swish Fish/I'm Coming
Home/Strange Girl/I Love You, Can't You See/Let Her Feel It In Your Kiss/True Fine
Mama/39-21-40 Shape/It Will Stand (alternate take)/The Owl Sees You (alternate
take)/For You My Darling (alternate take)/Skinny McGinney/I'll Go On Loving You*

This is proto-soul. The Showmen (Norman Johnson, Leslie Johnson, Milton
Wells, and Gene and Dorsey Knight) were a group from Norfolk, Virginia, that
auditioned for and signed with the New Orleans Minit label. Produced by Allen
Toussaint, the Showmen produced a sound that was a blend of 1950s doo-wop
and 1960s Crescent City soul. Their biggest record, *It Will Stand*, has rightfully
become an anthem on oldies stations and their *39-21-40 Shape* a staple of the

Carolinas' "beach-music" scene. Norman Johnson, whose dry lead vocals so distinguished the group, later formed Chairmen of the Board in Detroit.

264   Back In The Saddle
Betty Harris

Charly 1002 (UK) (LP)

Ride Your Pony/Show It/What A Sad Feeling/Take Care Of Your Love/I'm Gonna Get Ya/Nearer To You/What'd I Do Wrong/Trouble With My Lover/Twelve Red Roses/I'm Evil Tonight/Cry To Me/I'll Be A Liar/There's A Break In The Road/All I Want Is You/I Can't Stand It Much Longer/Mean Man

A Florida artist who recorded in New Orleans, Harris (b. 1943, in Orlando) had a legitimate hit twice with the remake of Solomon Burke's *Cry To Me* – in 1963 and 1969 – and a minor hit with *Nearer To You* (1967). Toussaint produced these mid-1960s sides with the Meters' backing on which Harris cried and moaned about her relationships. A few weak tracks are included here – Harris's voice occasionally strays out of tune – but *Trouble With My Lover* and *Ride Your Pony* (a remake of Lee Dorsey's 1965 hit) make this package definitely worth obtaining.

265   Street Parade
Earl King

Charly 232 (UK)

Street Parade/You Make Me Feel Good/Some People Are/Fallin'/A Mother's Love/ Mama And Papa/Medieval Days/This Is What I Call Living/Do The Grind/A Part Of Me/Love Look Out For Me/Street Parade (Pt 2)

Many listeners consider Earl King (b. February 7, 1934, in New Orleans) a blues artist solely, but this 1972 effort contains some extra-funky modern soul. The witty lyrics and inventive arrangements here are really superb, as King is at his best on originals like *You Make Me Feel Good* and *This Is What I Call Living*. The title track has become a Carnival standard in New Orleans.

266   Brimful of Soul
Charles Brimmer

Charly 1123 (UK) (LP)

I Love Her/Dedicating My Love To You/With You In Mind/My Sweet Thing/That's How Strong My Love Is/I Want To Be Your Bread Winner/Play Something Sweet/ Don't Break My Heart/We've Only Just Begun/You're Man's Gonna Be In Trouble

Charles Brimmer (b. October 10, 1948, in New Orleans) might well be considered New Orleans's answer to O.V. Wright. A definite deep-soul stylist, Brimmer had several local hits in the early 1970s on the Hep Me label and only got national attention with *God Bless Our Love* on the Chelsea label in the late 1970s. Some songs on this collection are rather weak – and Brimmer's spectacular adaptation of *Afflicted* is absent – but for the most part this is an excellent representation of his work on Hep Me. The Allen Toussaint touch is also felt here.

267 The New Rules
Irma Thomas

Rounder 2046

The New Rules/Gonna Cry 'Till My Tears Run Dry/I Needed Somebody/Good Things Don't Come Easy/The Love Of My Man/One More Time/Thinking Of You/The Wind Beneath My Wings/I Gave You Everything/Yours Until Tomorrow

Tremendously popular in her home town, Irma Thomas with **The New Rules** documents the modern New Orleans soul sound – and the current Irma Thomas sound – better than any other. Although there are a couple of throwaway tracks, the title track and *Gonna Cry 'Till My Tears Run Dry* are superb.

268 From The Heart
Johnny Adams

Rounder 2044

I Feel Like Breaking Up Somebody's Home/Why Do I/Laughin' And Clownin'/If I Ever Had A Good Thing/Scared Knees/From The Heart/Your Love Is So Doggone Good/We Don't See Eye To Eye/Roadblock/Teach Me To Forget

Perhaps the most talented vocalist to come out of New Orleans, Johnny Adams has rarely cut a record that is much less than spectacular. Of course, this is no exception – especially the wonderful title track. This is a satisfying mix of blues and deep soul recorded in 1984, with Adams especially effective on the slow ballads, notably the title track.

269 Wolf At The Door
Walter Washington

Rounder 2098

Hello Stranger/Is It Something You've Got/I Had It All The Time/It Doesn't Really Matter/Heatin' It Up/Tailspin/At Night In The City/Don't Say Goodbye

Walter Washington (b. 1943, in New Orleans) is one of those artists who walk the line between blues and soul. A longtime sideman – he plays guitar – Washington paid his dues with such New Orleans notables as Lee Dorsey, Johnny Adams, and Irma Thomas. In the mid-1980s he began forging a solo career via his recordings on Rounder. Washington does not really display any New Orleans influences; rather he combines several styles to achieve his own sound. His two earlier Rounder efforts were slanted more towards blues, but this one takes the most soulful approach.

Louisiana

270 In Time
Bobby Powell

P-Vine 2156 (Jap)

Our Love/C.C. Rider/That Little Girl Of Mine/Never Look Back/Straighten Up And Fly Right/In Time/It's Getting Late In The Evening/Do Something For Yourself/Hold My Hand/I'm Gonna Leave You/I'm Not Gonna Cry Over Spilled Milk/Who Is Your

Lover/Cry To Me/Your Cheating Heart/Baby Don't Do It/The Bells/Funky Broadway '69/A Hard Day's Night/Into My Own Thing/Red Sails In The Sunset

A gospel-influenced, Baton Rouge soul artist, Bobby Powell achieved huge success when *C.C. Rider*, a remake of a 1920s blues standard, was a hit in 1965. He got another hit with the marvelous deep-soul original *Do Something For Yourself* (1966), and broke into the charts again in 1971 with a lowdown remake of Baby Washington's *The Bells*. Powell brought an incredible depth to his vocals and he ranks as one of the great unheralded talents from the South, as evidenced by the remarkable *I'm Gonna Leave You*. Supported by stinging blues guitar and a shouting gospel chorus, the release ranks as one of the funkiest, most down-home soul records of all time. There are many remakes in Powell's catalog, but listening once to *Cry To Me*, a revival of the Solomon Burke hit, convinces that Powell is an original artist who brings his own artistic sense to all his songs. These recordings originally appeared on Whit, a Baton Rouge label owned by producer Lionel Whitfield. Powell's later work on Hep Me is also worth listening to, but these Whit tracks are the genuine article, not to be missed. In the 1990s Powell functions as the ultimate opening act in Baton Rouge: whoever comes into town, he gets the opening gig.

271 Nobody But You
Little Bob and the Lollipops

La Louisianne 113 (LP)

Nobody But You/Just Got To Forget You/Agent Double-O Soul/All These Things/Out Of Sight/With These Hands/My Heart's On Fire/Life Can Be So Lonely/Song For My Father/My Girl/Cry, Cry, Cry

This one is Bayou soul. Little Bob (b. Camille Bob, November 7, 1937, in Arnaudville, Louisiana) and the Lollipops were the premier soul band in Lafayette, Louisiana, in the 1960s. With plenty of local hits they stayed busy working lounges and University of Southern Louisiana fraternity functions. Their best-known number, *I Got Loaded* (unfortunately not included here), has been covered by Robert Cray and Los Lobos. While half of this LP consists of remakes, Bob's melodic, south Louisiana approach to them is unique and refreshing.

272 Taylor Made
Ted Taylor

Paula CD 337

It's A Funky Situation/Something Strange Is Going On In My House/Houston Town/Who's Doing It To Who/Call The House Doctor/This Is A Troubled World/Papa' Gonna Make Love/How's Your Love Life Baby/Only The Lonely Knows/Sweet Lovin' Pair/Can't Take No More

With a dramatic falsetto, Ted Taylor (b. Austin Taylor, February 16, 1934, in Okmulgee, Oklahoma) has had a following in R & B circles since 1958, when he put out *Days Are Dark* for Ebb, and in 1960, when he had a hit with *Be Ever Wonderful* for Duke. He continued a remarkable output that merged blues, soul shouters, and romantic ballads into a distinctive body of music with such labels as Top Rank, Gold Eagle, Dade, Apt, Warwick, OKeh, and others. (His OKeh sides are covered in chapter 5.) These blues and soul sides were recorded in the early 1970s when Taylor was with the Shreveport, Louisiana, Ronn label, and rank as the most satisfying of his career. This is a straight reissue of Taylor's 1970

LP, but includes two of his chart singles, *Something Strange Is Going On In My House* and *How's Your Love Life Baby*. One hopes that Paula will get around to reissuing their two other LPs by this important if underrated artist, a reissue album of his early work, **Shades Of Blue**, and a 1969 album, **You Can Dig It**. Taylor died in a car wreck in 1987.

273   Everybody Knows About My Good Thing/Open House At My House
Little Johnny Taylor

P-Vine 2522 (Jap)

Everybody Knows About My Good Thing: *Baby Get Hip To Yourself/How Are You Fixed For Love/How Can A Broke Man Survive/Keep On Keeping On/ Everybody Knows About My Good Thing (Pts 1 & 2)/There's Something On Your Mind/You've Got The Love I Need/It's My Fault Darling/Make Love To Me Baby/ Sweet Soul Woman*
Open House At My House: *Open House At My House (Pts 1 & 2)/You're Not The Only One Baby/My Special Rose/1,000 Miles Away/I Can't Stop Loving You/ What Would I Do/You're Saving Your Best Lovin' For Me/As Long As I Don't See You/Strange Bed With A Bad Head/I'll Make It Worth Your While*

Ostensibly a blues singer, Little Johnny Taylor (b. Johnny Young, February 11, 1943, in Memphis) was quite popular in soul markets in the early 1970s during his tenure with Stan Lewis's Ronn label. This CD contains two straight reissues of his two important Ronn LPs, which contain all his biggest hits on the label: *Everybody Knows About My Good Thing* (1971), *It's My Fault Darling* (1972), *Open House At My House* (1972), *I'll Make It Worth Your While* (1973), and *You're Saving Your Best Lovin' For Me* (1974). Taylor launched the soul–blues nexus with *Part Time Love* in 1963 on Galaxy (his work for that label appears in chapter 8) and has become a mainstay on Southern radio. Even in the early 1990s he maintains a strong following in the South.

Texas

274 You'll Lose A Good Thing
Barbara Lynn

Jamie/Sound of the Fifties GTCD 002 (Neth)

Second Fiddle Girl/Give Me A Break/Dina And Petrina/Lonely Heartaches/You Don't Sleep At Night/I'm Sorry I Met You/You'll Lose A Good Thing/Heartbreaking Years/ Teen Age Blues/What I Need Is Love/You Don't Have To Go/Letter to Mommy And Daddy/You're Gonna Need Me/It's Better To Have It/Dedicate The Blues To Me/Oh! Baby (We Got A Good Thing Goin')/Unfair/(I Cried At) Laura's Wedding

A Texas artist who recorded in New Orleans, Barbara Lynn (b. Barbara Lynn Ozen, January 16, 1942, in Beaumont, Texas) successfully combined both areas' soul styles in the 1960s. Besides the title track and *Second Fiddle Girl*, both hits for Lynn in 1962, this well-paced album includes all the tracks from her 1962 Jamie album, plus later hits for the label. These include *You're Gonna Need Me* (1963), *(I Cried At) Laura's Wedding* (1963), *Oh! Baby (We Got A Good Thing Goin')* (1964), which the Rolling Stones covered, and *It's Better To Have It* (1965). Although some of her titles have a teen appeal approach, Barbara Lynn, who plays guitar and composes, had a maturity in her voice and presentation that holds up well. Her later recordings on Tribe (*You Left The Water Running*),

Atlantic (*This Is The Thanks I Get* and *(Until Then) I'll Suffer*), Jetstream, and Antones are also recommended.

275 Takin' Care Of Business
Bobby Patterson

Kent 911 (UK)
Till You Give In/You Just Got To Understand/What's Your Problem Baby/If I Didn't Have You/Long Ago/Soul Is Our Music/Let Them Talk/Sock Some Lovin' At Me/I'm Leroy I'll Take Her/Broadway Ain't Funky No More/I Met My Match/Don't Treat Me So Mean/The Good Old Days/Busy, Busy Bee/Sweet Taste Of Love/TCB Or TYA/What A Wonderful Night For Love/My Thing Is Your Thing/Keeping It In The Family/My Baby's Coming Back To Me/Guess Who/The Knock Out Power Of Love/The Trial Of Mary McGuire/If A Man Ever Loved A Woman/You Taught Me To Love/I'm In Love With You/Married Lady/If I Didn't Know Better/Who Wants To Fall In Love

A journeyman soul singer, Bobby Patterson (b. March 13, 1944, in Dallas) was an enjoyable and amazingly prolific recording artist during the 1960s. He had one moderate-size R & B hit with *TCB Or TYA* in 1969 on Jetstar, and these other tracks first saw the light of day on Abnak or Jetstar. Patterson is at his best on up-tempo or novelty material. The singer was active in the business as an independent record promoter in the South during the early 1990s.

276 Joe Hinton
Joe Hinton

Duke 91 (LP)
Funny/A Kid Named Joe/If It Ain't One Thing It's Another/Be Ever Wonderful/The Whole Town's Talking/There Ought To Be A Law/Don't Tell Her The Truth/I'm Waiting/Now I'm Satisfied/Got You On My Mind/Baby, Please

A splendid vocalist who often employed the gospel falsetto, Joe Hinton (b. 1929) was an underrated, versatile Texas soulster whose trademark was jumping octaves. He did it most dramatically on his big hit, an R & B version of Willie Nelson's *Funny* (1964), on which his voice went into the stratosphere on the last note. He scored several other hits for Duke's subsidiary label Backbeat, notably *You Know It Ain't Right* (1963), but none unfortunately is included here. Hinton died from a rare skin disease August 13, 1968.

Mississippi

277 King Floyd
King Floyd

Cotillion 9047 (LP)
Groove Me/Let Us Be/Woman Don't Go Astray/Baby Let Me Kiss You/Messing Up My Mind/It's Wonderful/So Glad That I Found You/Don't Leave Me Lonely/Day In The Life Of A Fool/What Our Love Needs

It's hard to believe that there is not a CD by King Floyd (b. February 13, 1945, in New Orleans) currently available. Of his four magnificent albums, this ranks as number 1 because it includes the hits *Groove Me* (1970), *Baby Let Me Kiss You* (1971), and *Woman Don't Go Astray* (1972). A New Orleans artist, Floyd recorded these sides in Jackson, Mississippi, with (ironically) country session musicians. All his sides were released on Chimneyville, an early label in the Malaco complex. Floyd was an artist who had the potential to rival Al Green, but his career was wiped out by the disco boom.

278 Mr Big Stuff
Jean Knight

Stax 8554

Mr Big Stuff/A Little Bit Of Something/Don't Talk About Jody/Think It Over/Take Him/You City Slicker/Why I Keep Living These Memories/Call Me Your Fool If You Want To/One Way Ticket To Nowhere/Your Six-Bit Change/Do Me/Helping Man/ Carry On/Save The Last Kiss For Me/Pick Up The Pieces/You Think You're Hot Stuff

The 1971 title track, recorded at Malaco and leased to Stax, is of course Jean Knight's calling card. Like Floyd, Knight (b. June 26, 1943, in New Orleans) was a New Orleans-based artist who recorded in Jackson, Mississippi. Knight excels on the impudent, up-tempo material which dominates this collection. Her later hits on Stax, *You Think You're Hot Stuff* (1971) and *Carry On* (1972), are included, but not *You Got The Papers* (1981) and *My Toot Toot* (1985), which were recorded for other labels.

279 McKinley Mitchell
McKinley Mitchell

Chimneyville 203 (LP)

Open House At My House/You're So Fine/The Town I Live In/Same Old Dream/You Know I've Tried/Run To Love/Dream Lover/The End Of The Rainbow/Mr Music Man/Follow The Wind

McKinley Mitchell (b. December 25, 1934, in Jackson, Mississippi) was a soul-blues stylist with several great singles dating back to the early 1960s. His popularity was confined to the deep South and Chicago, where he started with *The Town I Live In* in 1962. (His Chicago output is covered in chapter 5.) A Southern hit recorded in Chicago, *Trouble Blues*, returned him to the South in 1976, and he signed with Malaco's Chimneyville subsidiary. He immediately had a hit with *The End Of The Rainbow* and the company put out this debut album. Although occasionally overburdened with strings, Mitchell's mellow voice always saves the day. *The Town I Live In* is an inferior remake, but his remake of Bobby Darin's *Dream Lover* is outstanding. Mitchell died in 1986, after recording a lesser album for another Jackson, Mississippi, company, Retta's.

280 Misty Blue
Dorothy Moore

Malaco 6351

The Only Time You Ever Say You Love Me/Dark End Of The Street/Funny How Time Slips Away/Misty Blue/Enough Woman (Left To Be Your Lady)/I Don't Want To Be With Nobody But You/Ain't That A Mother's Luck/Too Much Love/It's So Good

Dorothy Moore (b. 1946, in Jackson, Mississippi) started in the music business as a member of the Poppies. However, at the time of her 1975 smash, *Misty Blue*, she was working as a Malaco receptionist and background singer. While this is essentially a two-hit package – the title cut and a splendid version of Willie

Nelson's *Funny How Time Slips Away* (1976) – it is a good representation of Malaco's mid-1970s sound.

281 Right Place, Right Time
Denise LaSalle

Malaco 7417
Right Place, Right Time/He's Not Available/Treat Your Man Like A Baby/Good Man Gone Bad/Boogie Man/Your Husband Is Cheating On Us/Why Does It Feel So Right/Keep Your Pants On/Bump And Grind/Love School

Denise LaSalle (b. Denise Craig, July 16, 1939, in LeFlore County, Mississippi) was very much Malaco's female counterpart of Z.Z. Hill. An impudent songwriter and vocalist, she created songs that especially appealed to women, as she was rather fond of putting "no good men" in their place. This 1984 album, her second for Malaco, represents the best of her output for the label. Like many great artists, LaSalle has not changed her style appreciably since the beginning of her career, in Chicago decades ago. Her great 1970s output, recorded in Memphis and released on the Detroit-based Westbound label, is reviewed in chapter 6.

282 A Man Can Give It
Bobby Rush

La Jam 0005 (LP)
A Man Can Give It/Ain't That Good Lovin'/Bad Mother For Ya/I Am Tired/Hurt Me So Bad/Nine Below Zero/Hoy Hoy/Playin' Me Crazy

A journeyman performer with a lengthy résumé of minor hits, Bobby Rush (b. Emmett Ellis, Jr, November 10, 1940, in Homer, Louisiana) has constantly walked the line between blues and soul. During the 1980s – after moving down to Jackson, Mississippi, from his longtime home in Chicago – he cut several enjoyable albums on the Jackson-based La Jam label. He had several regional hits on La Jam, notably *Sue* (1982), but no national success. This 1988 album is his best. (Rush, before moving to the South, recorded an album in Philadelphia for Kenny Gamble and Leon Huff that was as down-home as anything he did for La Jam. See the review in chapter 3.) Rush has become a busy trouper on the Southern circuit and has continued to record into the 1990s.

Florida

283 The Best Of Betty Wright
Betty Wright

Rhino/Atlantic R2 71085
Clean Up Woman/I'm Gettin' Tired Baby/It's Hard To Stop (Doing Something When It's Good To You)/Outside Woman/He's Bad Bad Bad/Baby Sitter/Ooola La/Pure Love/Let Me Be Your Lovemaker/When We Get Together Again/Girls Can't Do What The Guys Do/Slip And Do It/Cryin' In My Sleep/Secretary/Where Is The Love/Tonight Is The Night, Pt 1 (Rap)/Shoorah! Shoorah!/You Can't See For Lookin'/Is It You Girl/Lovin' Is Really My Game

The Miami soul queen, Betty Wright (b. December 21, 1953, in Miami) has enjoyed a long and successful run of hit records dating back to 1968, when at the age of 15 she recorded *Girls Can't Do What The Guys Do* for the T.K. subsidiary

Alston. *Clean Up Woman* (1971) was her first major single, and her only million-seller, and it is contained here along with all her hits, notably *Baby Sitter* (1972), *Let Me Be Your Lovemaker* (1973), *Secretary* (1974), and *Shoorah! Shoorah!* (1974). Aside from *Tonight's The Night, Pt 1 (Rap)* (1978), which is a live remake of her 1974 studio recording, most of her Alston late 1970s material is less interesting disco-styled soul. But this is mostly vibrant, exhilarating music, made before she had to change her style to suit the disco market. In the late 1980s and early 1990s, Wright was back in the charts with an odd series of singles – *Pain, More Pain,* and *Too Much Pain,* on Profile.

284   Best Of Latimore
Latimore

Sequel 166 (UK)

Stormy Monday/Ain't Nothing You Can Do/Snap Your Fingers/Let's Straighten It Out/Keep The Home Fires Burning/There's A Red Neck In The Soul Band/It Ain't Where You Been/Somethin' 'Bout 'Cha/Sweet Vibrations/I Get Lifted/Dig A Little Deeper/Long Distant Love

Singer/keyboardist Benny Latimore (b. September 7, 1939, in Charleston, Tennessee) brought a strong blues flavor to contemporary soul in the 1970s, recording for the T.K. subsidiary Glades. He had several hits during the decade, including the number one R & B hit *Let's Straighten It Out* (1974), *Keep The Home Fires Burning* (1975), and an exuberant paean to his white keyboardist, *There's A Red Neck In The Soul Band* (1975). This collection contains his best sides from the five LPs he waxed for Glades, although *Qualified Man* (1976) and the spectacular *Discoed To Death* (1979) are missing. Unfortunately, like other Sequel releases, the sound quality of this one is not exactly state-of-the-art.

285   Cornelius Brothers and Sister Rose
Cornelius Brothers and Sister Rose

United Artists UAS-5568 (LP)

Too Late To Turn Back Now/I'm So Glad (To Be Loved By You)/Let Me Down Easy/Don't Ever Be Lonely (A Poor Little Fool Like Me)/Gonna Be Sweet For You/I'm Never Gonna Be Alone Anymore/Good Loving Don't Come Easy/Treat Her Like A Lady/Just Ain't No Love (Like A Lady's)/Lift Your Love Higher/Let's Stay Together

Carter, Eddie, and Rose Cornelius (Cornelius Brothers and Sister Rose) were a Florida act that came from a family that included 15 siblings, all of whom could play and sing. One, Billie Jo, was added to the group in 1973. This spectacular debut album features two million-sellers, *Treat Her Like A Lady* (1971) and *Too Late To Turn Back Now,* both of which remain stables on oldies radio, as well as many other top-notch songs written by Eddie Cornelius. The group was recorded in Miami and, unlike most of their Southern counterparts, featured not a deep-soul sound but one that was pop-style, perky, and melodic, sounding as though it could have come out of New York or Chicago. When Carter Cornelius joined a Black Hebrew sect in 1976 the group broke up, having never matched their first album.

West Coast   8

Randal C. Hill

During the rapid growth of the independent record industry in California during the 1950s, only a handful of small West Coast-based labels (chiefly in LA) managed to create national hits. In 1954, the tiny Dootone outfit sold a million copies of *Earth Angel* by the Penguins. Two years later came somewhat lesser national hit singles on Flip (*A Casual Look*, by the Six Teens) and RPM (*Eddie My Love* by the Teen Queens). In 1957, record fans were purchasing shiny new 7-inch discs on Ebb (*Buzz-Buzz-Buzz* by the Hollywood Flames), Keen (*You Send Me* by Sam Cooke), and Aladdin (*Little Bitty Pretty One* by Thurston Harris). Such independents as Class (*Rockin' Robin* by Bobby Day), Demon (*Western Movies* by the Olympics), and Del-Fi (*Donna/La Bamba* by Ritchie Valens) had success the following year. The year 1959 saw no big winners by LA R & B artists, with the exception of black bongo-player Preston Epps, who made the Top 15 with a blistering pop instrumental, *Bongo Rock*, on the newly formed Original Sound label.

The California independents continued to see a great deal of success in the early 1960s, mostly with a style now called neo-doo-wop. It was LA deejay Art Laboe who launched a series of reissue albums on his Original Sound label and who helped create the neo-doo-wop phenomenon. The nation's disc jockeys began playing cuts from his albums and made such songs as the Penguins' *Earth Angel* hits once again. Companies (many from LA) also began making new records that were a recreation of the doo-wop style. Original Sound even pitched in with the Penguins' *Memories Of El Monte*, which was produced by a then-unknown Frank Zappa. Bob Keane's Del Fi/Donna complex produced a host of neo-doo-wop hits, most notably Little Caesar and the Romans' *Those Oldies But Goodies (Remind Me Of You)*, Ron Holden's *Love You So* and the Pentagons' *To Be Loved (Forever)*. Other neo-doo-wop labels included Arvee (*Big Boy Pete* by the

Olympics and *Peanut Butter* by the Marathons), Eldo (*Image Of A Girl* by the Safaris and *Lost Love* by H. B. Barnum), and Milestone (*Diamonds And Pearls* by the Paradons and *Lover's Island* by the Blue Jays).

Contributing immensely to the neo-doo-wop phenomenon were the "low-rider" hits coming out of LA's sprawling Hispanic community on the east side of the city. Such artists as Rene and Ray (*Queen Of My Heart*), the Romancers (*My Heart Cries*), and the Salas Brothers (*Darling*) enjoyed popularity with large numbers of Chicanos and Chicanas.

But neo-doo-wop was a transitional form, and soul music was making itself felt by 1963 with records emerging from strong independents in both LA and the Bay Area, nearly 400 miles to the north. In Los Angeles, the biggest independent was Lew Chudd's Imperial/Minit outfit, which Chudd founded in 1948. The company drew on both West Coast and New Orleans talent. LA-based soul artists in Chudd's stable included Jimmy McCracklin (*Think*), the O'Jays (*Lonely Drifter*), Leon Haywood (*She's With Her Other Love*), Young Hearts (*I've Got Love For My Baby*), and Jimmy Holiday (*Baby I Love You*). Liberty eventually absorbed Chudd's labels, but before that the company had success on its own with such artists as Gene McDaniels (*Hundred Pounds Of Clay*) and the Rivingtons (*Papa-Oom-Mow-Mow*).

Like Lew Chudd, the Bihari Brothers – Jules, Joe, and Lester – had been in LA since the 1940s, making records on a number of labels (Modern, RPM, and Kent). The Biharis' biggest success came in the 1950s, with bluesmen B.B. King and Lowell Fulsom. They were able to maintain both artists' careers into the 1960s with brassy urban blues that worked well in the soul market (King with *Rock Me Baby* and Fulsom with *Tramp*). Other Bihari artists that had soul-market hits were Z.Z. Hill (*You Were Wrong*), Mary Love (*Move A Little Closer*), Ike and Tina Turner (*Good Bye, So Long*), and the Ikettes (*I'm So Thankful*).

Two of the most interesting independent labels in LA were SAR and its Derby subsidiary, which were formed by soul artist Sam Cooke and his manager J.W. Alexander. Unlike some of the other independents, SAR knew instinctively what the "new" soul music was – secularized gospel – and the label released some of the most exciting of the early soul records. The label's artists included the Valentinos (*Lookin' For A Love* and *It's All Over Now*), the Sims Twins (*Soothe Me*), and Mel Carter (*When A Boy Falls In Love*).

Phil Spector (New York-born but LA-bred) teamed up with his business partner, Lester Sill, to form Philles Records in 1961. The following year, Spector was recording both his New York girl groups and homegrown LA talent at Gold Star studios, which saw the advent of his "wall-of-sound" productions. Notable acts in

Spector's operation, from 1961 to 1966, included the Ronettes and the Crystals from New York, and Darlene Love, Bob B. Soxx and the Blue Jeans, the Righteous Brothers, and Ike and Tina Turner from LA.

Smaller LA independents included Mirwood, which had hits with Jackie Lee (*The Duck*) and the Olympics (*Baby, Do The Philly Dog*); Marc, which did well with Bob and Earl (*Harlem Shuffle*); Double Shot, which enjoyed winners with Brenton Wood (*Gimme Little Sign*) and the Bagdads (*Bring Back Those Doo-Wops*); Crusader, which featured Dobie Gray (*The "In" Crowd*); Mustang/Bronco, whose roster included Felice Taylor (*It May Be Winter Outside (But In My Heart It's Spring)*); Audio Arts, which had a hit with the Incredibles (*I'll Make It Easy*); and Upfront, which did well with Gloria Jones (*Heartbeat*). Jones, incidentally, later moved to the United Kingdom and became something of a cult soul sensation.

The Dore label, formed by Lew Bedell in 1958, made an impact in the soul market with the Whispers (*Take A Lesson From The Teacher*) and the Superbs (*Baby Baby All The Time*). Rock-and-roll hitmaker Johnny Rivers began the Soul City label, which had hits with Al Wilson (*The Snake*) and many successful releases by the Fifth Dimension. Original Sound recorded a few artists during the soul era, most notably Dyke and the Blazers (*Funky Broadway*). Motown producer Mickey Stevenson preceded Motown's move to the West Coast when in 1968 he left Berry Gordy and set up Venture Records in LA. Stevenson created a few hits, the most successful being by the Ballads (*God Bless Our Love*).

In San Francisco was Fantasy/Galaxy, founded in 1951, which was the recording home of Little Johnny Taylor (*Part Time Love*), the Blackbyrds (*Walking In Rhythm*), and Johnny "Guitar" Watson (*I Don't Want To Be A Lone Ranger*). Also in the Bay Area, Ron Carson, with his considerably smaller Soul Clock label, recorded the Whispers (*Seems Like I Gotta Do Wrong*).

Several major labels made their headquarters in LA, namely MGM, Capitol, Warner Brothers, and MCA. The output in the soul market by these majors was at first minimal and offered little competition to the city's independents. MGM's efforts went almost unnoticed, with Spyder Turner's *Stand By Me* (1966) being one of the label's few soul hits. Capitol's attempts to place singles on the soul charts initially featured work done by their jazz artists, namely Nancy Wilson (*How Glad I Am*), Cannonball Adderly (*Mercy, Mercy, Mercy*), and Lou Rawls (*Love Is A Hurtin' Thing*). Later, Capitol recorded the first album by the integrated Checkmates and earned modest hits with Patti Drew. In the 1970s and 1980s, as majors took over most of the soul market, Capitol had regular hits by the Tavares, Natalie Cole, Tina Turner, and many others.

Up to the mid-1960s, Warner Brothers was not a factor in black music; but, as the label grew, so did its commitment to the soul market. Warner Brothers began the Loma label in 1964. On Loma (as well as on the Warner Brothers imprint itself), the company released 1960s hits with the Olympics (*Good Lovin'*), the Apollas (*All Sold Out*), the Marvellos (*We Go Together*), the Invincibles (*Can't Win*), Lorraine Ellison (*Heart Be Still*), and Linda Jones (*Hypnotized*). Loma was discontinued in 1968, as Warner Brothers decided not to "ghettoize" its black acts on a separate label. During the 1970s and 1980s, the company had big hits in both the pop and soul markets with Chaka Khan, Larry Graham, Ashford and Simpson, and Prince.

MCA was the successor label to the long-established Decca Records. Though based in New York, Decca got a few West Coast-produced hits with Leon Haywood; for the most part, though, its soul efforts proved meager. In the late 1960s, MCA, through its Uni/Revue complex under Russ Regan, began mining California's soul talent, earning a winner with *The Midnight Hour* by the Mirettes (actually the Ikettes). By the 1970s, with all the labels consolidated under the MCA imprint, the company hit its stride and earned hits in the black market with such luminaries as Klique, New Edition, and Stephanie Mills. In 1979, MCA took over ABC Records – a company that began in New York but moved to LA in 1970 – and inherited the Four Tops, B.B. King, and Bobby Bland.

LA independents continued to be a factor in the 1970s and 1980s, most notably 20th Century Fox (also under Russ Regan, who had moved from MCA), which was begun in New York in 1958 but by the early 1970s had relocated to the West Coast. Its biggest artist was Barry White, but the label also had hits with Leon Haywood (*I Want'a Do Something Freaky To You*), Stephanie Mills (*Never Knew Love Like This Before*), and Carl Carlton (*She's A Bad Mama Jamma*). Clarence Avant's Sussex label was highly successful with Bill Withers and Creative Source. Herb Alpert and Jerry Moss, heading A & M Records, did well in the soul market with Quincy Jones, LTD, and Jeffrey Osborne. Dick Griffey's outfit, Solar (an acronym for The Sound Of Los Angeles Records), had a long string of hits with Lakeside, Carrie Lucas, Whispers, Midnight Star, and Dynasty.

In the early 1970s, Motown moved its base of operations to the West Coast, establishing its offices in Hollywood and using California studios to capture the works of Diana Ross, the Commodores, Eddie Kendricks, the Jackson Five, Stevie Wonder, Marvin Gaye, Rick James, and Teena Marie.

Of the many albums released by these and other West Coast artists, a select few rise above the commonplace to establish themselves as truly essential in terms of importance in connection with the evolution of R & B to soul. Most of these works are readily available on CD or cassette, but a few are out of print, having long ago been assigned space in bargain-priced "cutout bins." Such rarities (which sometimes now command hefty prices) are worth seeking out if one wishes to have a complete collection of the works of California artists who contributed to an important musical style that, in more refined terms, lives on with today's recording stars.

Essential Recordings

(i) Soul Pioneers

Ray Charles and Sam Cooke are the titans of early soul. In the pantheon of artists who first contributed to the evolution of soul, Charles and Cooke both stand head and shoulders above all others who, knowingly or unknowingly, contributed to a major stylistic change. Both singers fused gospel with pop from different perspectives, and both reached worldwide, mainstream audiences.

Ray Charles (b. Ray Charles Robinson on 23 September, 1930, in Albany, Georgia) joined Atlantic Records in 1952 and made the R & B charts consistently between 1954 and 1959, recording such classics as *I've Got A Woman* (1955) and *Drown In My Own Tears* (1956). His breakout in the pop market came with the million-selling *What'd I Say* (1959), the splendid fusion of fervid gospel and steamy, primitive rock 'n' roll that became the forerunner of modern soul music. (The Atlantic years of Ray Charles are covered in chapter one.) This essay will discuss his output on ABC-Paramount, a label he joined late in 1959.

uh huh: His Greatest Hits takes Charles's career from his last hit on Atlantic, *What'd I Say*, in 1959, to his great rendition of *America The Beautiful*, in 1976, on his own Crossover label. Between these numbers this collection contains 34 other chart records made for ABC-Paramount and five other outstanding numbers such as his classic duet with jazz stylist Betty Carter on *Baby It's Cold Outside* and his gently rocking remake of the ancient *Careless Love*. The peculiar title of the collection comes from Ray Charles's use of the expression, "uh huh." in Pepsi Cola commercials from 1992, which because it constitutes Charles's only claim to fame for many young people, unfortunately, has been appropriated to sell this collection.

Charles's ABC years were the years of his greatest commercial success, which began shortly before he moved his base of operations from New York to California. (He recorded exclusively in Los Angeles after 1962.) At his RPM International Studio and United Studios Charles redid mellow standards, created jazzy instrumentals, worked R & B grooves, and created a new blend of country and western with soul. Notable among his early ABC hits were *Georgia On My Mind* (1960), a gently soulful remake of the Hoagy Carmichael standard, featuring a strong male group and supported with mellow strings and cocktail-lounge piano, *One Mint Julep* (1961), an instrumental (except for Charles mumbling "just a little bit o' soda") that is dominated by strong horns and Charles's effective organ playing, and *Hit The Road Jack* (1961), a Percy Mayfield-composed rock 'n' roll number that kept Charles in the teen market.

I Can't Stop Loving You (1962), a remake of the Don Gibson hit from 1958, marked Charles's entry into country-and-western music. As he had earlier blended gospel with R & B, so he now mixed elements of gospel and R & B with country, the result being plaintive and imaginative works that could rightfully be tagged country-soul. He mined this vein in two remarkable albums, **Modern Sounds In Country And Western Music**, volumes one and two, and in frequent remakes of country hits until the late 1960s. The voices behind Charles are now too often that of a choir rather than background vocalists, and the orchestral strings are generally heavy but sweet. The flip of *I Can't Stop Loving You* was *Born To Lose*, a 1944 country number that is arguably the most soulful of all of Ray Charles's country-styled songs. It too is set before a strong, choir-like musical curtain with a string-section supplement. On another country standard, *You Are My Sunshine*, Charles sounds on the verge of tears in the most soul-styled of his country hits. *Take These Chains From My Heart* (1963), a remake of a Hank Williams hit from 1953, remains one of the all-time biggest Charles hits.

Charles returned to a more R & B style in early 1963 with *Don't Set Me Free*, which includes a blazing, squealing sax and strong blatting horns. (The unnamed female co-lead actually comes across as somewhat more soulful than Ray Charles on this particular hit!) *Busted*, in late 1963, was the Genius at play and one of his biggest crossover hits. *Let's Go Get Stoned* and *I Don't Need No Doctor* – both from 1966 – came from the collective pens of New York songwriters Nicholas Ashford, Valarie Simpson, and Joshie Jo Armstead, and along with *I Chose To Sing The Blues*, also from 1966, represents Charles's greatest connectiveness with the soul audience.

Perhaps Charles's most notable remake was his steaming live version of Eddie Cantor's *Makin' Whoopee*, which he effectively revived and modernized in 1965, twenty-six years after it first hit the charts. Buck Owens's *Crying Time* (1966) and *Here We Go Again* (1967) returned Charles to remakes of country songs, and both proved immensely successful. In the latter part of his career, however, Charles mined the Beatles to get hits, namely *Yesterday* (1967) and *Eleanor Rigby* (1968), which are not all that interesting.

More preferable would have been the inclusion of *Understanding*, the flip to *Eleanor Rigby*.

Few soul artists have been able to take the national anthem or other patriotic tunes and make their soul versions acceptable to mainstream America, but Charles's remarkable rendition of *America The Beautiful* is the happy exception and has become something of a standard since its release in 1976, when it barely scraped the bottom of the charts. It is a great closer for this collection.

The importance of Ray Charles has never been in question, although too many music historians concentrate too heavily on his Atlantic period. **uh huh: His Greatest Hits** provides the corrective and gives Brother Ray's fans a chance to fully appreciate the years when he reached a huge and widely diversified audience, not just appreciative R & B fans.

Sam Cooke (b. January 22, 1931, in Clarksdale, Mississippi) was one of the great voices of the second half of this century (see chapter 1 for his early work). He influenced a wide and diverse array of recording artists from Marvin Gaye to Mick Jagger, Otis Redding to Rod Stewart, Al Green to Bob Marley. Cooke grew up in Chicago as one of eight children born to a minister. By age six, he was singing in his father's church. He recruited a brother and two sisters for a gospel group, the Singing Children, a few years later. After a while, Cooke and a brother joined another gospel aggregation called the Highway QCs. Moving to LA in the early 1950s, the perfectly articulating Cooke eventually took over the lead spot of the highly successful gospel group the Soul Stirrers, replacing popular vocalist Rebert H. Harris, who was retiring. For six years, Cooke traveled the country and recorded, often utilizing a smooth, rising-and-falling yodel that would later become his pop trademark. In 1956, "Bumps" Blackwell, the A & R man for LA-based Specialty (the Soul Stirrers' label), recorded the confident Cooke singing original secular material, much to the chagrin of Specialty owner Art Rupe. Blackwell later took Cooke to LA producer Bob Keane, who had just begun the Keen label. Unlike Rupe, Keane was eager to make inroads into the pop market with Cooke.

Beginning with *You Send Me* (1957), Cooke created eight Top 40 songs for Keen before being wooed to RCA in 1960 for a $100,000 advance. (A ninth Keen hit, *Wonderful World*, appeared after Cooke was established at the larger label.) RCA had few black artists on its roster and few contacts in the burgeoning R & B market, but Cooke successfully built a bridge between the black and white cultures, making 27 chart singles in five years. He also began his own record labels (SAR/Derby), a music-publishing concern (Kags Music), and a management firm. Cooke's life ended violently when, on December 11, 1964, he picked up a young woman at a party and checked into the seedy Polaris Motel on Figueroa Street in Los Angeles. According to legend, Cooke was showering when his new companion fled with most of Cooke's clothes. Bursting into the office in a rage, Cooke insisted that the female desk clerk was part of a ruse to set him up. Moments later, the terrified clerk fatally shot Cooke. He died six weeks before his thirty-fourth birthday.

The Man And His Music contains 21 of Cooke's 43 charting pop singles, each of which he wrote or co-wrote. Many notable tunes are missing, but this offering does include two of Cooke's Soul Stirrers recordings, as well as some outstanding RCA album tracks. Of his two gospel tracks here, *That's Heaven To Me* stands as a mid-1950s forerunner of his pop style; change the words and you have Cooke emoting a secular love ballad. He burst onto the pop scene when *You Send Me* rocketed to number 1 in 1957 and stayed in the charts for half a year. Within weeks, Specialty re-released Cooke's *I'll Come Running Back To You.* Keen countered with a re-release of its own, *(I Love You) For Sentimental Reasons* (not included). The version of *Win Your Love For Me* (1958) here is not the full-bodied, Latin-flavored Keen original but a weak remake. *Everybody Likes To Cha Cha Cha* (1959) is one of Cooke's few forgettable early tracks – not bad, just not outstanding. Far more important are the teen classics *Only Sixteen* (1959) and *Wonderful World* (1960). Both represent Cooke at his youthful best, delivering adolescent-oriented fluff that holds up surprisingly well to this day.

At RCA in 1960, Cooke first recorded the forgotten but nonetheless excellent *Teenage Sonata* (not included). *Chain Gang* (1960) became his second-biggest hit ever, reaching number 2. The song sets an absurd scene, but Cooke's convincing vocals make us believe that we really *are* bearing witness to warbling convicts lamenting their ignominious, wretched lives. The melancholy *Sad Mood* from the same year has strong blues idioms and phrasings. *Cupid* (1961) is another excellent teen-oriented work. (Both *Chain Gang* and *Cupid* feature the Sims Twins, who had their own minor hit, the Cooke-composed *Soothe Me*, on Cooke's SAR label.) *Twistin' The Night Away* (1962) does not quite ring true; it not only lacks a heavy twist beat, but one finds it hard to imagine this dignified entertainer actually *doing* such a dance. The slightly more believable *Having A Party* later that year continued the "good-time" spirit of *Twistin' The Night Away.* Its flip side, *Bring It On Home To Me*, is actually more important, as it features a then-unknown Lou Rawls backing Cooke in a call-and-response delivery set before a laconic piano figure straight out of the black church. *Nothing Can Change This Love* (1962) is a gospelly, slowed-down version of *You Send Me.* The flip, *Somebody Have Mercy*, comes across as a "standard Sam Cooke song."

Moving deeper into the soul era in 1963 with *Another Saturday Night* (1963), Cooke laments his lack of luck with the opposite sex (hardly true) in this warm, lighthearted number. *Good News* (1964) is an upbeat tune that surprisingly includes a banjo, but Cooke sounds ultimately unconvincing. That same year, *Good Times*, potentially musical cotton-candy, was rescued by Cooke's soulful and restrained phrasing. One of the best tracks of his 1964 releases is the unappreciated *That's Where It's At*, which drew heavily on *Bring It On Home To Me*. *Shake*, released posthumously early in 1965, became Cooke's fifth and final Top 10 song and is little more than polite, cocktail-lounge rock-and-roll. It is the flip side that is one of his finest efforts: *A Change Is Gonna Come* was Cooke's return to gospel, yet it is also full-blown early soul. The lyrics rank among his finest ever ("It's been too hard livin' but I'm afraid to die"). *A Change Is Gonna Come* is laden with shimmering strings and muted horns and anchored by a dirge-like drumbeat that drives the singer's weary-sounding voice slowly but relentlessly forward. Sam Cooke ranks among the most important black artists of the late 1950s and early 1960s; **The Man And His Music** bears eloquent testimony to that.

Discographical Details

286 uh huh: His Greatest Hits
Ray Charles
DCC D2 33079–2 (2-disc set)
What'd I Say, Parts 1 & 2/Georgia On My Mind/Hardheaded Hannah/Ruby/Sticks And Stones/Them That Got/One Mint Julep/Hit The Road Jack/Unchain My Heart/Hide Nor Hair/Baby, It's Cold Outside/At The Club/I Can't Stop Loving You/Born To Lose/Careless Love/You Don't Know Me/You Are My Sunshine/Your Cheating Heart/Don't Set Me Free/Take These Chains From My Heart/No One/Busted/Without Love (There Is Nothing)/That Lucky Old Sun/My Heart Cries For You/Baby Don't You Cry/Smack Dab In The Middle/Makin' Whoopee, Pts. 1 & 2/I'm A Fool To Care/Crying Time/Let's Go Get Stoned/Together Again/I Chose To Sing The Blues/I Don't Need No Doctor/Here We Go Again/In The Heat Of The Night/Yesterday/Eleanor Rigby/If You Were Mine/Don't Change On Me/America The Beautiful

287 The Man And His Music
Sam Cooke
RCA PCD1-7127 (2-disc set)
Touch The Hem Of His Garment/That's Heaven To Me/I'll Come Running Back To You/You Send Me/Win Your Love For Me/Just For You/Chain Gang/When A Boy Falls In Love/Only Sixteen/Wonderful World/Cupid/Nothing Can Change This Love/Rome Wasn't Built In A Day/Love Will Find A Way/Everybody Likes To Cha Cha Cha/Another Saturday Night/Meet Me At Mary's Place/Having A Party/Good Times/Twistin' The Night Away/Shake/Somebody Have Mercy/Sad Mood/Ain't That Good News/Bring It On Home To Me/Soothe Me/That's Where It's At/A Change Is Gonna Come

(ii) Latino Soul

Many of the recordings by Mexican-American LA artists were R &
B-styled (or at least R & B-influenced) numbers that served to
feed the stream of LA soul music later, especially since the vocal
approach on many Chicano records featured a dreamy, soulful
sound. (These local hits had no real discernible gospel influences.)
The "Eastside sound" was, on one hand, the raucous, fiery,
metallic hard rock of the Thee Midniters, wailing and screaming
their way through *Whittier Boulevard*; and on the other, Lil' Julian
Herrera intoning a plodding, soulful, and nasal *Lonely, Lonely
Nights*, a song that doubtlessly lit untold adolescent fires on many
junior-high gymnasium floors on Friday nights.

With the lone exception of Ritchie Valens (who actually hailed
from the San Fernando Valley, several miles northwest of east
LA), no Eastside acts ever broke into the national Top 10. The
Premiers had a fluke hit, *Farmer John*, which reached number 19,
and Cannibal and the Headhunters made number 30 with *Land
Of 1,000 Dances*. The remaining Eastside recording artists
included on **The History Of Latino Rock: Vol. 1 – 1956–
1965: The Eastside Sound** sold only well enough to reach the
lower slots on the charts or failed to sell well enough to reach a
national audience at all. To be sure, young East LA Hispanics did
embrace the "big-ticket" R & B songs – *Earth Angel, In The Still
Of The Nite* – as well as ballads by local black singers (Tony
Allen's *Nite Owl*, for example) or the integrated Jaguars (*The Way
You Look Tonight, Thinking Of You*). For the most part, though,
members of the "low-rider culture" seemed more interested in
cruising in tuck-and-roll-upholstered, wildly hued, lowered-to-
the-pavement autos and attending concerts rather than purchasing
large quantities of discs. Every weekend, enthusiastic and loyal
Chicanos and Chicanas, eager to see and hear their favorite
performers, would fill such venues as the El Monte Legion
Stadium in El Monte, the Rainbow Gardens in Pomona, and the
Golden Gate Theater and Kennedy Hall in East Los Angeles.
Such performance outlets would often find the likes of the
Romancers and the Velveteens – both are included here – as well
as the better-known Johnny Otis or the Jaguars. The zenith of the
Eastside sound materialized in 1964 and 1965 – the British
invasion notwithstanding – and it was during this two-year
period that some of the best and most commercially viable work
emerged. The music, thick and greasy, was often light on
substance and quality but heavy on emotion and soulful
delivery. It was, in a word, wonderful.

**The History of Latino Rock: Vol. 1 – 1956–1965: The
Eastside Sound** features the grandfather of Hispanic rock,
Ritchie Valens (b. Richard Valenzuela on May 13, 1941, in Los

Angeles). He composed *Donna* (1958) for girfriend Donna Ludwig and put a blistering, pre-heavy-metal-rock version of a traditional Mexican wedding song, *La Bamba*, on the flip. Two years before Valens made the scene, though, Lil' Julian Herrera became the first full-fledged Eastside rock star. Replete with a plinking piano, gently honking sax, and one-note background vocals, Herrera's *Lonely, Lonely Nights*, which he co-wrote with Johnny Otis, was a splendid "grinder" (a slow, sensual R & B ballad to which closely dancing couples could grind their hips together). Chan Romero's screamer of *Hippy Hippy Shake* (1959) was adopted by the British group the Swinging Blue Jeans years after Romero had stopped recording in southern California and returned home to Billings, Montana. (The good-looking lad never entered the charts but did become a favorite among East LA teens for a while.) The enigmatic Velveteens recorded *You've Broken My Heart* in 1960. The song is highly reminscent of the Six Teens' *A Casual Look* and Rosie and the Originals' *Angel Baby*. Lead singer Terry Bonilla does a creditable job on her original composition. The Romancers, frequent headliners at the Rainbow Gardens, covered Etta (James) and Harvey (Fuqua)'s 1960 R & B ballad, *My Heart Cries*. The Romancers were smooth and professional in their vocal delivery, but their instrumentation is unfortunately amateurish and ragged. Rene and Ray (Paul Valenzuela and Ray Quiniones), both former Velveteens, got into the national charts in 1962 with their smooth, self-penned *Queen Of My Heart*.

Steve and Rudy Salas – the Salas Brothers – were only in their early teens when they remade Johnny and Joe's haunting *Darling* around 1963. This simple but sweetly soulful tune garnered a great deal of airplay on LA's East Side but got little attention elsewhere. The Salas Brothers later performed as members of the Jaguars and El Chicano before forming the septet Tierra, which had a Top 20 smash in 1980 with *Together*. The Premiers (Larry Perez, John Perez, George Delgado, Phil Ruiz, Joe Urzua, and Frank Zuniga) hailed from San Gabriel and had a hit with the Don and Dewey screamer *Farmer John* (1964). The song was recorded in a Hollywood studio packed with friends and family members clapping and shouting to give it a "live" feel.

Little is known of the minor-league Blendells; their one-off *La La La La La* (1964) was a remake of a pre-success Stevie Wonder tune. There is an odd spoken introduction out in front of an Indian tom-tom on *La La La La La*, as well as a wah-wah trumpet that adds aural spice to the track. Ronnie and the Pomona Casuals' *I Want To Do The Jerk* is a noisy throwaway, while the remake of Ben E. King's *I (Who Have Nothing)* by Lil' Ray (Ray Jiminez) is actually more dramatic and emotional than the soul star's original.

Thee Midniters (Willie Garcia, Danny Lamont, Romeo Prado, Larry Rendon, and Benny Savallos) enjoyed great popularity in east LA. Lead singer Garcia possessed an incredible, soaring voice (listen to it on *That's All*). Thee Midniters' clarion call to cruising, *Whittier Boulevard* (1965), was named for the primary place to drive "low and slow" in east LA during the 1950s and 1960s. Punctuated by screams of "Arriba! Arriba!," *Whittier Boulevard* features a piercing guitar coupled with a locomotive-drive organ. Cannibal and the Headhunters (Frank Garcia, Bob Jarramillo, Joe Jarramillo, and Richard Lopez) caused such a sensation in 1965 with their version of Chris Kenner's soul hit, *Land Of 1,000 Dances*, that they were asked to open the show for the Beatles when the Fab Four appeared in LA that year. Supposedly the chanted "na-na-na-na-na" by lead vocalist Garcia came about by accident when he became so immersed in the rhythm that he temporarily forgot the words. Or so the legend goes.

The History Of Latino Rock: Vol. 1 – 1956–1965: The Eastside Sound is an essential for students of LA R & B and soul. This album offers proof positive that not everything musically valid in the world of early LA music came out of the South-Central-area churches several miles – and a totally different culture – away.

Discographical Details

288   The History of Latino Rock: Vol. 1 – 1956–1965: The Eastside Sound

Various Artists

Zyanya RNLP 061 (LP)

Ritchie Valens: *La Bamba/Donna*; Chan Romero: *Hippy Hippy Shake*; Lil' Julian Herrera: *Lonely, Lonely Nights*; The Blendells: *La La La La La*; Thee Midniters: *That's All/Whittier Boulevard*; Rene and Ray: *Queen Of My Heart*; Ronnie and the Pomona Casuals: *I Want To Do The Jerk*; The Salas Brothers: *Darling (Please Bring Your Love)*; Lil' Ray: *I (Who Have Nothing)*; The Premiers: *Farmer John*; The Romancers: *My Heart Cries*; The Carlos Brothers: *Tonight*; The Velveteens: *You've Broken My Heart*; Cannibal and the Headhunters: *Land Of 1,000 Dances*

(iii) Spector Soul

Phil Spector (b. December 25, 1940, in New York) moved from the Bronx to LA at the age of 12. Later, within a decade, he changed the course of popular record production and raised the level of soul-rock sophistication. In doing so, Spector gave music fans some of the best-produced and most enduring three-minute musical melodramas ever offered up over the AM airwaves. Spector's thundering, Wagnerian approach to music, which brought a soaring architecture to his works, caused music historians later to dub his productions the "wall of sound," although the impish Spector claimed only that he recorded "little symphonies for the kids." When Spector made Gold Star Studios (at the corner of Santa Monica and Vine in Hollywood) his primary producing arena in 1962, traditional recording concerns (costs for the musicians, studio time, etc.) were tossed out. A typical Spector "wall-of-sound" production might include three or four pianos, several guitars and multiple drum-kits, in addition to castanets, timpani, and tambourines, all of which might be overdubbed several times.

Spector began his career in 1958, when he formed the Teddy Bears by recruiting Fairfax High School classmates Marshall Lieb and Annette Kleinbard (later known as Carol Connors, the co-composer of *Hey Little Cobra* and *Rocky*). Before long, Spector took his friends to Gold Star and had them tape an original Spector ditty called *Don't You Worry My Pretty Pet*. With 10 minutes left on the studio clock, the singing trio laid down a B side, *To Know Him Is To Love Him*. (Spector had taken the title from his father's tombstone, which in part read "To Have Known Him Is To Have Loved Him.") The 17-year-old high-school senior found he had produced a million-seller when his flip-side throwaway on the LA-based Dore label shot to number 1 nationally. Between 1960 and 1961, the budding musical genius produced hits for other artists, mostly recording in New York. He then joined forces with fellow record producer Lester Sill to form the label Philles (Phil plus Les).

Spector's first big girl group was the black Brooklyn ensemble called the Crystals, for whom Spector created a half-dozen Top 20 singles within 20 months. A year later, he was successful again with a black LA trio, Bob B. Soxx and the Blue Jeans. He took gospel-trained Darlene Love – she and her own group, the Blossoms, sometimes recorded as the Crystals – and made her a minor-league solo star in 1963. Later that year, Spector began recording another New York-based girl group, the Ronettes. After creating five Top 40 Ronettes hits, Spector turned his interests to the Righteous Brothers and scored four Top 10 hits for the blue-eyed soulsters.

By now, though, changing musical tastes were slowly rendering his "wall of sound" archaic. By 1966, Phil Spector was no longer a valid force in rock music; Ike and Tina Turner, for whom Philles was their fifth recording home, failed to sell many copies (at least in America) of *River Deep, Mountain High*, a song Spector considered his masterpiece. Philles folded late in 1966, and Phil Spector chose to spend most of the next two decades behind tightly drawn curtains at his luxurious Hollywood mansion. He emerged from self-imposed seclusion in 1991 to (reluctantly) give interviews to accompany the release of his long-awaited, multi-box CD set.

Phil Spector: Back To Mono (1958–1969) features the highlights of a brilliant musical career and includes Spector's classic 1963 Christmas album. Following his success with the Teddy Bears, Spector produced Ray Peterson's heavily stringed, Dunes-label remake of Joe Turner's 1956 hit *Corrine, Corrina*, giving Peterson a Top 10 hit in 1960. The next month, Spector helped produce Atco artist Ben E. King's haunting *Spanish Harlem*. (The uncredited Drifters sang in the background.) In the summer of 1961, Spector took a Yuma, Arizona, construction worker named Curtis Lee, added vocal backing by the Halos (*Nag*), and created another Dunes winner, *Pretty Little Angel Eyes*. San Francisco's Paris Sisters (Priscilla, Albeth, and Sherrel) laboriously breathed life into the Gregmark label's *I Love How You Love Me* (later reprised by Bobby Vinton). That single reached the Top 5 in 1961.

Later that year, with his Philles label now in place, Spector unleashed New York's Crystals (Barbara Alston, La La Brooks, Dee Dee Kinnibrew, Mary Thomas, and Priscilla Wright). With Alston on lead, the first two Crystals hits, recorded in New York, were the dirge-like *There's No Other (Like My Baby)* (1961) and the Latin-flavored *Uptown* (1962), a magnificent song by Barry Mann and Cynthia Weil that perfectly evokes the gritty, urban street scene of Spanish Harlem.

Moving his recording base to Gold Star in 1962, Spector produced ersatz "Crystals" records using gospel-throated Darlene Love, and had big hits with the Love-led *He's A Rebel* (1962) and *He's Sure The Boy I Love* (1962). The real Crystals then returned – featuring La La Brooks in the lead – with two outstanding productions: *Da Doo Ron Ron* (1963) and *Then He Kissed Me* (1963), in which the minimalist lyrics by Jeff Barry and Ellie Greenwich served only to enhance the aural stew. (The "da doo ron ron" vocal riff was originally only meant as a filler until lyrics could be written later.) The remaining Crystals tracks range from merely good to superb, especially the unappreciated *Little Boy* (1964), killed apparently by the British Invasion.

Near the close of 1962, Bob B. Soxx and the Blue Jeans (Darlene Love, Fanita James, and Bobby Sheen) had a hit with *Zip-A-Dee-Doo-Dah*, a crunching, somewhat bizarre remake of a 1948 Oscar-winning song from the Disney film "Song Of The South." Darlene Love (b. Darlene Wright, 1938, in Los Angeles), who had sung with the Blossoms since her days at LA's Fremont High School, sometimes recorded with her group as the Crystals, sometimes as part of the Blue Jeans, and sometimes as a solo singer. Her gospel voice appealed to Spector, and he used the versatile Love on many of his sessions. Besides recording a pre-Dixie-Cups version of *Chapel Of Love*, she made the plaintive and forceful *(Today I Met) The Boy I'm Gonna Marry* (1963). With that, Love reached the Top 40. She fared even better with her second hit, the urgent *Wait Til' My Bobby Gets Home* (1963). Later releases by her did not sell as well, although some of Love's Philles tracks are unquestionably first rate, especially *Strange Love* and *Stumble And Fall.*

The enigmatic Alley Cats (Billy Storm, Chester Pipkin, Ed Walls, and Bryce Caulfield) were given their one moment in the sun with their 1963 hit, the catchy (albeit juvenile) *Puddin' N' Tain.* Spector then seemed to lose interest in recording the quartet.

A Puerto Rican group, the Ronettes (Veronica "Ronnie" Bennett, Estelle Bennett, and Nedra Talley) became worldwide stars in 1963 under Spector's demanding tutelage, which brought Ronnie Bennett's Frankie Lymon-style voice to full flower with Spector's production gloss. The by-now wealthy and powerful producer became immediately smitten with Ronnie (b. August 10, 1943, in New York) and concentrated for the next year-and-a-half on writing (in collaboration first with Barry Greenwich and later with Vince Poncia Jr, and Pete Andreoli) and producing for what he considered his greatest "find." (Ronnie eventually became Spector's second wife.) Phil Spector, at his zenith by 1963, gave burnished depth to some of the finest and most enduring rock-soul tunes ever with such Ronettes classics as *Be My Baby* (1963), *Baby, I Love You* (1963), *(The Best Part Of) Breakin' Up* (1964), *Do I Love You* (1964), and *Walking In The Rain* (1964). These discs rank as some of the most flawlessly crafted tunes made during the rock era. *Paradise*, obviously lifted melodically from *Walking In The Rain*, is a superlative, uplifting, teen-dream ballad replete with every element that characterized Spector's best works. (But where is the Ronettes' magnificent *I Can Hear Music* from 1966?).

By the end of 1964, Spector had "retired" Ronnie – against her will – from the studio and now concentrated on the Righteous Brothers (Bill Medley and Bobby Hatfield). Smoothing – and drowning – out their raw, R & B-honed edges, Spector created such overblown but resonant "blue-eyed soul" odes as *You've Lost That Lovin' Feelin'* (1964), *Just Once In My Life* (1965), *Unchained Melody* (1965), and *Ebb Tide* (1965).

When Ike and Tina Turner became Philles artists, Spector promised them their biggest career hit ever with *River Deep, Mountain High* (1966). While the screaming, pounding, all-stops-pulled-out musical treasure did reach number 3 in England, it barely dented America's Top 100, stalling at only number 88. Now, to Spector, it was mostly over. He closed down Philles and walked away from it all for three years. He returned to the studio in 1969 to produce a fine, socially conscious single by an integrated Fort Wayne, Indiana, quintet called Sonny Charles and the Checkmates (Bobby Stevens, Harvey Trees, Bill Van Buskirk, and Marvin Smith). Their *Black Pearl* reached the Top 15.

During the later 1960s, the innocence of the Crystals and the Ronettes gave way to a time of musical experimentation, and the magic of Phil Spector gradually faded from public prominence. With **Back to Mono (1958–1969)**, though, his flawless recordings can once again be appreciated. Hopefully they will show younger generations just how magnificent a studio artist Phil Spector once was, and just how well he painted timeless musical canvases for music fans three decades ago.

Discographical Details

289 Phil Spector: Back to Mono (1958–1969)
Various Artists

ABKCO 7118–2 (4-disc set)

The Teddy Bears: *To Know Him Is To Love Him*; Ray Peterson: *Corinne, Corrina*; Ben E. King: *Spanish Harlem*; Curtis Lee: *Pretty Little Angel Eyes/Under The Moon Of Love*; Gene Pitney: *Every Breath I Take*; The Paris Sisters: *I Love How You Love Me*; The Crystals: *There's No Other (Like My Baby)/Uptown/He Hit Me (And It Felt Like A Kiss)/He's A Rebel/He's Sure The Boy I Love/Da Doo Ron Ron/Heartbreaker/All Grown Up/Then He Kissed Me/Girls Can Tell/Little Boy/Santa Claus Is Coming To Town/Rudolph The Red-Nosed Reindeer/Parade Of The Wooden Soliders*; Bob B. Soxx and the Blue Jeans: *Zip-A-Dee-Doo-Dah/Why Do Lovers Break Each Others Hearts?/Not Too Young To Get Married/The Bells Of St Mary's/ Here Comes Santa Claus*; The Alley Cats: *Puddin' N' Tain*; Darlene Love: *Chapel Of Love/(Today I Met) The Boy I'm Gonna Marry/Wait Til' My Bobby Gets Home/ A Fine, Fine Boy/Strange Love/Stumble And Fall/A Long Way To Be Happy/White Christmas/Marshmallow World/Winter Love/Christmas Baby (Please Come Home)*; Veronica: *Why Don't They Let Us Fall In Love/So Young*; The Ronettes: *Be My Baby/Baby, I Love You/I Wonder/(The Best Part Of) Breakin' Up/Soldier Boy Of Mine/When I Saw You/Do I Love You/Keep On Dancing/You Baby/Woman In Love (With You)/Walking In The Rain/Born To Be Together/Is This What I Get For Loving You?/Paradise/I Wish I Never Saw The Sunshine/You Came, You Saw, You Conquered/Frosty The Snowman/Sleigh Ride/I Saw Mommy Kissing Santa Claus*; The Treasures: *Hold Me Tight*; The Righteous Brothers: *You've Lost That Lovin' Feelin'/Just Once In My Life/Unchained Melody/I Love You (For Sentimental Reasons)/Ebb Tide*; The Modern Folk Quartet: *This Could Be The Night*; Ike and Tina Turner: *River Deep, Mountain High/I'll Never Need More Than This/A Love Like This (Don't Come Knockin' Everyday)/Save The Last Dance For Me*; Sonny Charles and the Checkmates: *Black Pearl/Love Is All I Have To Give*; Phil Spector and Artists: *Silent Night*

(iv) Vocal Groups

Both the O'Jays and the Four Tops recorded important soul songs in LA. The O'Jays first recorded for two small Midwestern labels before moving to California to begin a four-year tenure with Imperial. The O'Jays' Imperial waxings are simply some of the best LA vocal-group offerings to come out of the early-to-mid-1960s. The Four Tops enjoyed incredible years of success at

Motown, where they cut their best-remembered songs, all of which were recorded within the parameters of a rigid pop-soul formula. After departing from Motown, the hitmaking quartet continued to put out dynamic, high-quality works for the LA-based Dunhill label, and a few of these songs rank as the most intense and important works ever committed to wax by the Four Tops.

Do not be fooled by the currently available Philadelphia International Records (PIR) CD of **Collectors Items** by the O'Jays; the *real* collector's tracks – all Imperial cuts except one – are to be found on the obscure, long-out-of-print United Artists album called **Greatest Hits**. No doubt UA (which had absorbed Imperial years before) rush-released this 13-track LP immediately following the success of the O'Jays' *Back Stabbers* single on PIR in 1972. Predictably, the UA package quickly went to the cutout bins – and that is a shame, as it contains some truly excellent material. The roots of the O'Jays can be traced to Canton, Ohio, where high-school friends Eddie Levert and Walter Williams joined forces to sing gospel music in 1958. They later added three neighborhood friends (William Powell, Bob Massey, and Bill Isles), became the Triumphs, and started singing mellow R & B. The Triumphs eventually signed with a small label called Wayco. Following one failed release, they joined up with Cleveland deejay Eddie O'Jay, who helped steer them to a contract on the King label. When the King singles went nowhere, O'Jay found himself offering up sympathy, encouragement, and guidance in large doses to the often-discouraged performers; in return, they altered their name to the O'Jays as a gesture of appreciation. But their luck was soon to change. When the O'Jays went to LA, they recorded four chart hits. They later made sides for Bell, Saru, and Neptune. But it was not until the 1970s that they made such real winners as *Back Stabbers, Love Train, I Love Music,* and *Used Ta Be My Girl*, all on Philadelphia International and all done under the aegis of the slick and successful Gamble–Huff production/ writing team.

LA producer H.B. Barnum had signed the group in 1962 to his Little Star label, recording *Crack Up Laughing* (1963), a superb neo-doo-wop. When the song started to be successful, Barnum took the O'Jays to Imperial, for whom he worked. The O'Jays' first hit on Imperial, *Lonely Drifter* (1963), later became one of the great "lost" singles of the early soul era. The song opens with crashing waves, then eases slowly into a smoothly building vocal backdrop anchored by a muted, slowly rolling bass voice offering haunting "bom-*boms*." Next comes the strong, sure tenor lead of Eddie Levert, whose voice soars majestically above all else on this ballad of yearning emotions and heartbreak. (The lyrics place Levert at the beach, where he is gazing out to sea and pining for his lost love.) Barnum's great orchestration is highlighted by a superlative string section. *Lonely Drifter* inexplicably went only to number 93 in the charts.

The fine but poorly selling follow-up, *Stand Tall* (1964), rocks with a staccato, mid-tempo energy from start to finish. It is one of the best tracks here. *Oh, How You Hurt Me* (1964) ranks close to *Lonely Drifter* in quality. The listener once more finds Levert's tight tenor rising majestically above lilting horns and a sweet, doo-wop background.

The O'Jays later reworked the Benny Spellman chestnut *Lipstick Traces (On A Cigarette)* (1965). As done by the O'Jays, this song is insipid and falls far short of the excellent Spellman version on Minit. The O'Jays' version outsold Spellman's, though, and the song gave them their only Top 50 hit prior to 1972. The flip was a much better number called *Think It Over Baby*, which is reminiscent of the mid-1960s works of pop purveyors Jay and the Americans. *Let It All Out* went only into the 1965 R & B charts, reaching number 28. It is not included here. *I've Cried My Last Tear* (1965) is loping and boring and understandably barely earned airplay. But its flip, *Whip It On Me Baby*, is a great, mid-tempo tune that sounds once more like a product of Jay and the Americans. (Barnum must have been an avid pop fan.) *Stand In For Love* (1966) is reminiscent of *Lonely Drifter*, with a strong vocal background and a catchy, horn-section background. *Working On Your Case* (1967) is an interesting, upbeat piece. *How Does It Feel, I'll Never Forget You*, and *Hold On* are decent works but not outstanding.

Collectors of 1960s soul should have a place at or near the top of their lists for **Greatest Hits**, a package of O'Jays songs that never were hits but should have been.

The tenure of the Four Tops (Levi Stubbs, Abdul "Duke" Fakir, Lawrence Payton, and Renaldo "Obie" Benson) at Detroit's Motown label, 1963–72, was by far the most successful of the quartet's extensive and highly successful recording career. By 1972, though, the Four Tops were losing momentum. Two years had passed since they had released a Top 40 Motown hit song. Dunhill Records' aggressive and creative production and writing team of Dennis Lambert and Brian Potter approached the Four Tops with a pair of demos which had been created especially for them. When the singers heard *Keeper Of The Castle* and *Ain't No Woman (Like The One I Got)*, they knew the songs would be perfect for lead singer Stubbs's rough-hewn vocals.

Their maiden Dunhill disc was *Keeper Of The Castle* (1972), an upbeat – and very Motownish – song that explored socially conscious themes ("There's a lot of us been pushed around/Red and yellow, black and white and brown"). On Dunhill, as on Motown, Stubbs's dramatic, piercing voice featured a perfect ratio of abandon and restraint, and he delivered the goods with unrelenting intensity and all passions unleashed. *Ain't No Woman (Like The One I Got)* (1973) was a slick, sweet, smooth work fueled in part by a strong and confident background. *Are You Man Enough* (1973), whose melody line seemed directly lifted from the O'Jays' *Back stabbers,* was featured in the black exploitation film "Shaft In Africa." By the time Dunhill released the Four Tops' fourth single, though, momentum was once more slowing for them. *Sweet Understanding Love* (1973) proved to be cheerful but forgettable, most likely due to the fact that the song had been based too closely on *Are You Man Enough.* Next came *Just Can't Get You Out Of My Mind* (1974), which was pleasant but lacked a commanding melody line. *One Chain Don't Make No Prison* later in the year included a heavy rhythm section and some deft horn-work running throughout a strong production. The song received extensive airplay but missed even the Top 40 charts. *Midnight Flower* (1974) was a standard Four Tops song, and by now the public seemed to be tiring of a sound that was apparently repeating itself. *Seven Lonely Nights* (1975) marked a return to the Four Tops' Motown style with a loping (and, again, highly familiar) approach. *We All Gotta Stick Together* (1975) and *Catfish* (1976) were less than satisfactory, the latter a futile stab at disco – definitely not the foursome's forte. Still, it is worth expending some energy to seek out **Greatest Hits: 1972–1976** in order to experience one of pop-soul music's most dynamic and most polished recording groups ever.

Discographical Details

290 Greatest Hits
The O'Jays

United Artists UAS-5655 (LP)

Lonely Drifter/Oh, How You Hurt Me/Whip It On Me Baby/How Does It Feel/I'll Never Forget You/Lipstick Traces (On A Cigarette)/Stand Tall/I've Cried My Last Tear/Think It Over Baby/Working On Your Case/Hold On/Crack Up Laughing/Stand In For Love

291 Greatest Hits: 1972–1976
The Four Tops

MCAD-27019

Ain't No Woman (Like The One I Got)/Are You Man Enough/Seven Lonely Nights/ Catfish/One Chain Don't Make No Prison/Keeper Of The Castle/Midnight Flower/ Sweet Understanding Love/I Just Can't Get You Out Of My Mind/We All Gotta Stick Together

(v) Supper-club Soul

Two artists of note – Lou Rawls and Bill Withers – found success with mainstream audiences by performing songs suitable for small club audiences, with material often delivered in a somewhat flat fashion yet presented with deep, soulful feeling at the same time. Rawls's material was obviously intended for traditional (that is, spare) cocktail-lounge instrumentation, while Withers's choice of songs called for him to perch on a bar stool and strum an acoustic guitar. In either case, these artists' songs often drew heavily on gospel and blues, as well as standard pop. Both Rawls and Withers possess rich and full voices, and each enjoyed great crossover success during their salad days (with Rawls, the 1960s and 1970s; with Withers, the 1970s and 1980s).

Lou Rawls (b. December 1, 1935, in Chicago) sang in much the same manner as his mentor, Sam Cooke. Rawls came to maturity on Chicago's mean and gritty South Side, where he learned the ways of the street during the week but found his way to church on Sundays, where he excelled in gospel singing. Rawls finished high school in 1953 and soon headed to LA. He began singing with a noted gospel aggregation called the Pilgrim Travelers, who recorded for Specialty, the same label that had Cooke's Soul Stirrers. At 21, Rawls joined the army. Two years later, he joined forces with Cooke and toured with him as a background singer. On one tour, Rawls nearly lost his life: he and Cooke were motoring to a gig when they were involved in a grinding auto crash. Cooke was barely injured, but Rawls was (briefly) pronounced dead at the scene. Rawls spent five days in a coma before awakening to begin a long and arduous recovery. When the Pilgrim Travelers disbanded in 1959, Rawls turned his talents to the secular and began performing blues music in LA nightclubs. He did some acting – he had a small running part on the hit TV show "77 Sunset Strip" – but was always more interested in vocalizing.

After recording for the tiny LA labels Shar-Dee and Candix (the latter being the first recording home of the Beach Boys), Rawls was hired by Sam Cooke to back him on the bluesy, gospel-drenched 1962 RCA single *Bring It On Home To Me*. No large-scale airplay was earned by Rawls until he landed a minor Capitol hit of his own with *Three O'Clock In The Morning* (1965). He followed that with a smash, the soul-styled *Love Is A Hurtin' Thing*, a year later. Between 1965 and 1970, he placed 11 singles and 13 albums in the charts. A switch to MGM in 1971 provided Rawls with a lone but important winner, *A Natural Man* (1971), which earned him the prestigious Grammy award. Five years later, Rawls cut his biggest song ever, *You'll Never Find Another Love Like Mine* (not included here). He had hits consistently in the R & B lists throughout the remainder of the 1970s and well into the next decade. Rawls, the singer with the smiling voice, became a spokesperson for Budweiser beer, which brought him to a whole new audience. He earned his final gold LP (his fourth, in addition to one platinum) in 1977 with the Budweiser-ad-influenced **When You Hear Lou, You've Heard It All**.

There is not a bad track on Rawls' **Greatest Hits** CD: only *On A Clear Day (You Can See Forever)* and *A Fool Such As I* would rate as less than excellent. Rawls began his hit streak in 1965 with a reworking of the 1921 pop standard *Three O'Clock In The Morning*. He offers up this song in the form of a somewhat dreamy sing-a-long, his deep voice rising and falling in a smooth and confident vibrato while the subdued instrumentation gently urges everything along. *Love Is A Hurtin' Thing* (1966) features slightly muffled horns coming in and out of a basically very simple song, melodically and instrumentally. Rawls's voice sounds slightly tortured here, as befits the lyrics. *Dead End Street* (1967) begins with a live, Rawls-composed monologue that he lays out in a delightful jive rap before a most appreciative audience. (He describes some of the street characters he came to know well on Chicago's South Side.) The song itself comes wrapped around a smokey, bluesy shuffle – Rawls sounds as if he is genuinely having a good time.

Isaac Hayes co-composed Rawls's *Your Good Thing (Is About To End)* (1968), a song that also features spare instrumentation. It is plodding and gritty, the perfect nightclub song, and Rawls's smooth voice rises and falls with precision across its lyric lines. *A Natural Man* (1971) is far and away the best track on **Greatest Hits**. This million-seller is one socially conscious work that is without the vitriol normally found in "protest" songs (*à la* Sly and the Family Stone). *A Natural Man* is more a celebration of humanity – with all its inequities and imperfections – than an evaluation of the rights and wrongs of society. The *South Side Blues* monologue (taken from **Lou Rawls Live!**) is another clever, Rawls-written piece. The work segues smoothly into his soulful and gently growling, half-spoken, half-sung version of *Tobacco Road*. *What Now My Love*, a French tune that had been a 1966 hit for Sonny and Cher and also for Herb Alpert and the Tijuana Brass, is given an upbeat treatment with a punchy, 1950s-style staccato sax playing out behind Rawls. (The song becomes somewhat of a horn blowout as it drives relentlessly to its conclusion.) Mention *Georgia On My Mind* and you think of the Ray Charles version from 1960: co-composed by Hoagy Carmichael in 1931, it is given a vocal twist here by Rawls that is more reminiscent of Louis Armstrong than Charles. *A Fool Such As I* (done as a hit in the 1950s by both Hank Snow and Elvis Presley) is only a pleasant, string-laden filler. **Greatest Hits** really fills the bill for Rawls fans. It is highly recommended.

Bill Withers (b. July 4, 1938, in Slab Fork, West Virginia) did not seek a career in music until he was nearly 30. The youngest of six children, he dropped out of high school at 15 and soon joined the navy. During his nine-year military tenure, Withers worked tirelessly at correcting a lifelong stuttering problem. He later delivered milk and worked as a mechanic, all the while dabbling in songwriting in his spare time. He eventually moved to LA when he was 29 and began installing toilet seats in Boeing 747s. Withers was inspired to enter the music business after seeing Lou Rawls in a nightclub. He taught himself to play an acoustic guitar and then spent $2,500 recording demos of his original songs. Nobody showed interest. In 1970, he met veteran Memphis sessionman Booker T. Jones (*Green Onions, Hang 'Em High, Time Is Tight*), who was impressed with the talented factory worker and took him under his creative wing. Withers signed with Clarence Avant's Sussex label.

Withers's first album, a Jones production which featured Stephen Stills on lead guitar, was **Just As I Am**. Its highlight was *Ain't No Sunshine*, which landed near the top of the charts and won a Grammy; the follow-up, *Grandma's Hands*, sold rather poorly. Withers's second album, **Still Bill**, became a million-seller and included both *Lean On Me* and *Use Me*. (It was only after these successes that Withers left his factory job.) After two more Sussex albums – including a Carnegie Hall concert disc – and ongoing legal hassles, Withers moved to the Columbia label in 1975. But five Columbia LPs never allowed him to recapture his early momentum. His best song with Columbia was *Lovely Day*. He returned briefly to the spotlight when he sang lead on Grover Washington Jr's million-selling single *Just The Two Of Us* in 1981, on the Elektra label.

Withers wrote or co-wrote nine of the ten tracks on **Greatest Hits**; only *Soul Shadows* is not his. He also produced or co-produced six of the songs here. Most of his output can be classified as folk-soul, with the inventive artist bringing such an art form to a solidly middle-class audience. *Ain't No Sunshine* (1971) is a simple work featuring his acoustic guitar and thick, sweet strings. The folk-flavored *Grandma's Hands* is Withers's slow, plodding reminiscence of childhood. The song is both emotional (in his delivery) and unique (it is a little-covered subject in contemporary soul music). *Grandma's Hands* simply was not commercial and comes off sounding like what it probably was meant to be: an album track. Withers's gospelly *Lean On Me* topped the charts in 1972. Here the preacher-like singer is both urgent and believable, emoting before a gentle, churchy piano, whose music rises and falls smoothly as it carries him along. The song could easily be a hymn with a change of lyrics. *Use Me* (1972), his third Top 5 single, was an odd, chugging ditty with spare instrumentation (percussion, guitar, and horns). Withers's vocals here are both snappy and sophisticated. *Lovely Day* (1977) features subdued strings, horns, and piano out in front of a male backup that repeats the phrase "lovely day" throughout the song. Withers gives *Lovely Day* a (purposely) flat reading, in the vein of a supper-club standard. Four years later came *Just The Two Of Us*, a song done with Grover Washington that was Withers's "comeback" work. It had a more complex production than any of Withers's Sussex works and incorporates a wailing, sweet sax as well as catchy Latin influences.

Non-hit tracks on **Greatest Hits** include *Spend The Night*, a superb song that moves smoothly with a thumping percussion, muted, click-clack Latin instrumentation, and a lilting piano figure. Withers's lyrics hold our interest throughout the song, and we find he is not (contrary to the way the title sounds) looking for a one-night stand, when he proclaims "I want to spend the night with you . . . forever." *Soul Shadows* begins with melodic guitar runs and horn stings that punch their way into the fabric of the song as it progresses. It is a supper-club-style filler and, ultimately, somewhat uninteresting. *Who Is He, What Is He To You?* was obviously structured along the lines of *Use Me*. It is slower, less commercial, and rather poorly produced: a jangling tambourine running throughout the song proves to be merely annoying. A much better version of the song produced a soul hit for fellow Sussex artists Creative Source in 1974. *Hello Like Before*, though, begins with a seductive guitar; then strings fade in, foglike, to create a stark, somber, haunting mood on what turns out to be one of the album's most listenable tracks. **Greatest Hits** is well worth owning and pays homage to a talented artist whose fame was – unfortunately – fleeting.

Discographical Details

292 Greatest Hits
Lou Rawls

Curb D2-77380

A Natural Man/Love Is A Hurtin' Thing/Your Good Thing (Is About To End)/Dead End Street/On A Clear Day (You Can See Forever)/Three O'Clock In The Morning/South Side Blues (monologue)/*Tobacco Road/What Now My Love/Georgia On My Mind/A Fool Such As I*

293 Greatest Hits
Bill Withers

Columbia CK 37199

Just The Two Of Us/Use Me/Ain't No Sunshine/Lovely Day/I Want To Spend The Night/Soul Shadows/Lean On Me/Grandma's Hands/Hello Like Before/Who Is He, What Is He To You?

(vi) Soul-Rock

Sly and the Family Stone and Ike and Tina Turner, were essentially both black rock-and-roll acts, but they approached their music from a very different perspective. Sly and the Family Stone blended soul-infused psychedelia with abstract (and sometimes bizarre) experimentation in their music, while Ike and Tina Turner took a more straight-ahead tack, mixing bar-band rock with raw R & B wrapped around Tina's gospel shouts that often stretched her vocal histrionics to the limit.

Enthusiastic voices and blaring instruments vie for dominance on the records of Sly and the Family Stone (Sylvester "Stone" Stewart, Rose "Stone" Stewart, Freddie "Stone" Stewart, Larry Graham, Cynthia Robinson, Jerry Martini, and Gregg Enrico). The septet consisted of black and white men and women; as often as not, the women played instruments while the men sang. Their work featured musical bits and pieces – scraps, actually – of cacophonous R & B songs melded with close-knit rock. Sly's material – "psychedelic soul" – came at a time of musical turbulence and experimentation that dominated the late-1960s, creative, West Coast music scene.

By age four, Sly Stone (b. Sylvester Stewart, March 15, 1944, in Dallas, Texas) was singing in a gospel group in his home town. His parents eventually relocated to the working-class town of Vallejo, a few miles away from San Francisco. Stone, a scrappy street kid replete with self-confidence, was inspired by a high-school music course he took during the early 1960s. He formed a vocal aggregation called the Viscanes and later worked for San Francisco deejay Tom Donahue, who headed Autumn Records. Stone became a deejay himself on one of the Bay Area's black stations, but his eccentricities eventually led to his dismissal. (He sometimes interrupted commercials and often spent an inordinate amount of time exhorting listeners to call in with dedications.) He produced Autumn singles for Bobby Freeman, the Beau Brummels, and the Mojo Men in the mid-1960s. In 1966, Stone organized a club band he called the Stoners. He put together the Family Stone a year later. The outfit consisted of Stone, a brother, a sister, a cousin (Graham), and three Bay Area musician friends.

Anthology features every Sly and the Family Stone chart single that Epic released between early 1968 and mid-1973. (Stone wrote and produced each track here.) First into the charts was *Dance To The Music*, an enduring musical work featuring bleating horns and jangling tambourines in concert with a party atmosphere. There are numerous clap-along instrumental breaks on the song, and a warm bass voice counterpoints Sly's throaty, well-stretched falsetto lead. The forgettable (and poorly charting) two-sided single of *Life/M'Lady* followed; listeners obviously felt both sides were poor copies of *Dance To The Music*. All was salvaged, though, by the release of *Everyday People* (1968), a socially conscious masterpiece that encouraged Stone's fans to examine attitudes of brotherhood and acceptance. "Different strokes for different folks" found its way into the late-1960s lexicon via *Everyday People*, which featured the funk-chant flip of *Sing A Simple Song*. (Though it was a somewhat mediocre song, the style dominant on this emerged years later in the early work of the Commodores.)

One of the best **Anthology** tracks is *Stand!* (1969). It's a timely and well-structured peace–love–brotherhood anthem ("Stand for the things you know are right") and includes some blatantly inflammatory lyric lines that strongly urged people to take a (hostile?) stand against the negative forces of society. The song features a strong, chugging rhythm and powerful vocal/instrumental progressions, as well as an outstanding (albeit incendiary) flip side, *I Want To Take You Higher*, later one of the high points of "Woodstock," the film of the watershed concert from 1969. *I Want To Take You Higher* really stretches out – it runs for 5 minutes 22 seconds – and is nearly free-form in its execution. The production is busy and loud and includes enthusiastic, slam-bang Sly Stone lead vocals. *Hot Fun In The Summertime* (1969) brought a change of pace; it is slower, more subdued, and drenched in strings – a wonderful "feel-good" song in the mode of the Rascals' *Groovin'*. Now an anachronism, *Thank you Falettinme Be Mice Elf Agin* is a slinky, simple dance track that stumbled and jerked its way to the top of the charts early in 1970. In the middle of the year, a re-released *I Want To Take You Higher* became a Top 40 hit. Sly did not have another hit for 18 months, when he reached the top again with *Family Affair* (1971), a superb song which is often incorrectly identified as being about the Woodstock Festival. The somewhat forgettable 1972 songs *Runnin' Away* and *(You Caught Me) Smilin'*, as well as *If You Want Me To Stay* (1973), finish up the long hit list for Sly and the Family Stone. (A 1974 Top 40 single, *Time for Livin'*, is not included in this package.)

Ike Turner (b. November 5, 1931, in Clarksdale, Mississippi) came from the same Southern town as Sam Cooke. By age 10, Turner had mastered the piano and by his mid-teens had formed a band. He moved to Memphis, started a new group, and became a talent scout for the LA-based Modern label. At age 19, Turner created what is often considered the first rock-and-roll song, *Rocket 88* (1951), which was sung by Turner's band vocalist, Jackie Brenston. (The R & B chart-topper was the first to incorporate three basic rock-and-roll instruments – sax, piano, and guitar – into an R & B "jump" tune.)

Turner moved to East St Louis in the late 1950s and teamed up with Tina (b. Annie Mae Bullock, November 26, 1939, in Nutbush, Tennessee). Tina, who spent her childhood singing gospel in church and listening to R & B radio at home, moved to St Louis at age 16. She attended high school there and later found work as a hospital nurse's aide. She began going to a hot spot in East St Louis called the Club Manhattan, which was presided over by Ike Turner and his Kings of Rhythm band. Tina got on stage one night (because of a dare from her sister) and offered the world its first glimpse of her vocal prowess and flamboyant sexuality. She and Ike eventually married, and Ike, always the astute business-man, later built an entire show around his extrovert spouse. The successful Ike and Tina Turner Revue featured nine musicians and three scantily clad background singers, the Ikettes. After touring and recording for many years, Ike and Tina Turner split up in 1976, with Tina accusing Ike of years of wife-beating. Tina enjoyed a sensational solo career a decade later, while Ike often languished in prison on various drug charges.

Proud Mary includes 15 of the 23 Ike and Tina Turner tracks that became hits over a 16-year period. The duo began its successful career in 1960 with the ragged and raw screamer *A Fool In Love*, which had been intended for Ike's band vocalist, who failed to show up at the studio in a St Louis suburb that day. It and follow-ups appeared on the New York-based Sue label. *I Idolize You* (1960), a loping shuffle that utilized call-and-response, was the next Sue hit, and a forerunner of Ray Charles's *Unchain My Heart* a year later. *It's Gonna Work Out Fine* (1961), recorded in New York City, became the duo's first across-the-board hit. Ike hired Mickey "Guitar" Baker to do Ike's spoken lines while Sylvia Robinson played guitar. (Mickey and Sylvia had recorded *Love Is Strange* five years earlier.) As before, Tina's voice is all sandpapery soul and sexiness. *Poor Fool* was released after Ike and Tina had left the Sue label and were preparing to move to California. The tune was obviously gleaned from *It's Gonna Work Out Fine*, and Tina is in all her wailing glory here. *Tra La La La La*, an old St Louis master, was belatedly released in 1962. It features a funky, detuned piano as well as a muted trumpet.

After the Turners moved to Los Angeles in 1962, they made several records for Kent, only one of which got into the charts; unfortunately, *I Can't Believe What You Say (For Seeing What You Do)* (1964) is not to be found on this disc. Two years later came the explosive *River Deep, Mountain High*. The version here is a 1973 Ike and Tina Turner Revue album track and therefore lacks the dynamics of the original Phil Spector production.

In 1970, Ike and Tina Turner signed with the Minit label and rejuvenated their career with a series of fabulous soul-rock confections, combining the gospel soul of black vocalizing with the drive of a rock beat. The first Turner soul-rock product, *Come Together* (1970), was a compelling and dramatic remake of the Beatles song from a year earlier. The version here, with slightly skewed lyrics and altered guitar chords, followed the Fab Four's as it was fading. Two months later, the duo was on Minit's parent label, Liberty, and earning airplay with another remake, *I Want To Take You Higher* (Sly and the Family Stone's hit). Southern-style R & B horns dominate, and there are even keyboards producing a haunting wah-wah sound on this track. Next came Ike and Tina's biggest career song. Recorded in a small Florida studio while the Revue was touring, *Proud Mary* (1971) had been a live-show staple since Creedance Clearwater Revival had struck gold with it two years earlier. Following an extended, teasing, spoken introduction by Tina ("We never do *anything* nice and easy . . ."), *Proud Mary* becomes the closest thing to vocal mayhem on vinyl. Tina Turner's shrieked vocals overpower those of the high-energy Ikettes and even dominate a jack-hammer drum and crying, rapid-fire guitar backdrop.

After *Proud Mary*, it was mostly downhill for Ike and Tina. A moderate-sized hit followed; *Ooh Poo Pah Doo* (1971) recreates Jesse Hill's 1960 hit and features a cogent, classically based piano lead-in. *Up In Heah* (1972) is a failed effort that mistakenly combines Tina's gospel shouts with Ike's overly fuzzed guitar set amid a country-style arrangement. Tina wrote *Up In Heah*, as well as 1973's *Nutbush City Limits* (Ike and Tina's third-biggest career single) and *Sexy Ida* (1974). *Nutbush* was Tina's toe-tapping ode to her Southern youth, while *Ida* is a forgettable bar-band track. *Baby – Get It On* (1975), the last Ike and Tina Turner effort to earn any airplay, is a commendable work and is one of the few Turner-team songs to feature Ike sharing lead vocals with Tina. For fans of unpolished and exciting soul-rock, **Proud Mary** easily fills the bill.

Discographical Details

294 **Anthology**
Sly and the Family Stone
Epic EGK37071 (2-disc set)
Dance To The Music/M'Lady/Life/Fun/Sing A Simple Song/Everyday People/Stand!/I Want To Take You Higher/Don't Call Me Nigger, Whitey/You Can Make It If You Try/Hot Fun In The Summertime/Thank You (Falettinme Be Mice Elf Agin)/ Everybody Is A Star/Family Affair/Runnin' Away/(You Caught Me) Smilin'/Thank You For Taking Me To Africa/Babies Makin' Babies/If You Want Me To Stay/Que Sera Sera (Whatever Will Be, Will Be)

295　Proud Mary: Legendary Masters
Ike and Tina Turner

EMI/Sue E2-7-95846-2

A Fool In Love/I Idolize You/I'm Jealous/It's Gonna Work Out Fine/Poor Fool/Tra La La La La/You Should'a Treated Me Right/Come Together/Honky Tonk Women/I Want To Take You Higher/Workin' Together/Proud Mary/Funkier Than A Mosquita's Tweeter/Ooh Poo Pah Doo/I'm Yours (Use Me Anyway You Wanna)/ Up In Heah/River Deep, Mountain High/Nutbush City Limits/Sweet Rhode Island Red/Sexy Ida, Pt 1/Sexy Ida, Pt 2/Baby – Get It On/Acid Queen

Basic Recordings

296　The Official Record Album Of The Olympics
The Olympics

Rhino RNC-207

Baby Do The Philly Dog/Big Boy Pete/The Bounce/Dance By The Light Of The Moon/Dooley/Good Lovin'/(Baby) Hully Gully/Little Pedro/Mine Exclusively/Peanut Butter/Private Eye/Shimmy Like Kate/Western Movies/Workin' Hard

This noteworthy package takes the Olympics (Walter Ward, Eddie Lewis, Charles Fizer, and Walter Hammond) through their eight chart years on five labels and includes the original (some would say better) version of *Good Lovin'*. A minor hit that was successfully covered by New York's Young Rascals nearly a year after the Olympics' release on Loma (a Warner Brothers subsidiary, begun in order to move Warners into the burgeoning soul field), the Olympics' original never received the airplay it deserved. The quartet had begun as Coasters imitators at Los Angeles's Centennial High School in 1956. Led by Walter Ward, they had a big hit with their first release, *Western Movies*, in 1958. The Olympics later recorded some of the happiest and silliest records of the early 1960s (*Big Boy Pete, Shimmy Like Kate*). Those songs, as well as the little-remembered releases on the Tri Disc and Mirwood labels, are given their due here.

297　The Del-Fi and Donna Story
Various Artists

Ace CHCHD 313 (2-disc set) (UK)

Chan Romero: *Hippy Hippy Shake/I Don't Care Now/I Want Some More/My Little Ruby*; Ritchie Valens: *That's My Little Suzie/Fast Freight* (as Arvee Allens)/*La Bamba*; Ron Holden: *My Babe/Love You So/Everything's Gonna Be Alright*; The Shadows: *Jungle Fever/Under Stars Of Love*; The Addirisi Brothers: *Gonna See My Baby/Cherrystone/Back To The Old Salt Mine*; Johnny Crawford: *Rumours/Proud*; The Carlos Brothers: *Little Cupid*; Dick Dale: *Marie*; Rene Hall: *The Untouchables*; The Fantastics: *Blabbermouth*; Johnny Flamingo: *Is It A Dream*; Larry Bright: *When I Did The Mashed Potato*; The Hawks: *A Little More Wine, My Dear*; The Pentagons: *To Be Loved (Forever)*; Ronnie and the Pomona Casuals: *Please, Please, Please*; The Lively Ones: *Misirlou*; The Sentinals: *Big Surf*; David Gates: *The Okie Surfer*; Bruce Johnson: *The Original Surfer Stomp*; The Surfettes: *KRLA Jingle*

Former bandleader Bob Keane began his own label, Keen, in 1957 and produced the first million-seller (*You Send Me*) for gospel singer turned pop

vocalist Sam Cooke. After conflicts with his business partner, Keane later formed
Del-Fi Records and discovered 17-year-old Richard Valenzuela, who became
known to the world as Ritchie Valens. (The name of the Donna label came from
the success of Del-Fi's biggest single, *Donna*, a ballad Valens penned to girlfriend
Donna Ludwig.) Valens set the stage for Keane to record a spate of records by
artists from East LA's sprawling Chicano community. Of the Latino artists on
this compilation, rocker Chan Romero gets four tracks, more than any other
singer. He is best known to record collectors for his original 1959 screamer of
Hippy Hippy Shake, a song which the Beatles performed often during their
scuffling Liverpool days, and which became a worldwide hit in 1964 for
England's Swinging Blue Jeans. Another Romero track, *I Don't Care Now*, is a
fine, R & B-style ballad. There are a number of chart hits here but more
interesting, perhaps, are the misses: the Shadows' *Under Stars Of Love* is a great,
slow, East-LA "grinder"; *Is It A Dream*, by southern California's unappreciated
Johnny Flamingo, is an arresting R & B tune akin to Tony Allen's LA classic *Nite
Owl*; the Fantastics' *Blabbermouth* recalls the best of the Coasters' late-1950s
period. Students of the Los Angeles sound of the late 1950s and early 1960s will
do well to acquire this worthwhile and lovingly assembled double album.

298 My Answer
Jimmy McCracklin
Imperial 9306 (LP)

*My Answer/Beulah/Every Night, Every Day/Believe In Me/I Don't Care/I Did
Wrong/Think/Steppin' Up In Class/Someone/Let's Do It All/Just Got To Know/
Farewell*

This collection gathers nearly all the hits Jimmy McCracklin made for the Art-
Tone and Imperial labels from 1961 to 1966, when the bluesman was
experiencing success in the soul market. McCracklin (b. August 13, 1921, in
St Louis) began his recording career in 1945 making country blues for Globe
Records in Oakland. After stints with many of the LA companies – Modern,
Aladdin, Swingtime, and Hollywood – he earned his first chart hit with *The Walk*
on the Checker label in 1958. Over the years, McCracklin's music became more
uptown, and by the mid-1960s he was making records that the black community
still called blues, but which the white community considered soul – we will call it
soul-blues. There was a later greatest-hits collection, but **My Answer** (1966) is
notable for its inclusion of *Just Got To Know*, *Every Night, Every Day*, and
Think – and, thankfully, unlike the greatest-hits collection, it does not include
These Boots Were Made For Walking, McCracklin's remake of the Nancy Sinatra
smash. It also would have been nice to have had the rocker *Club Savoy* included,
as well as the blues hit *Shame, Shame, Shame*; however, even the greatest-hits
collection does not include them.

299 Anthology (1962–1974)
The Righteous Brothers
Rhino R271488 (2-disc set)

*There She Goes (She's Walking Away)(by the Paramours)/Little Latin Lupe Lu/My
Babe/Ko Ko Joe/Try To Find Another Man/I Just Want To Make Love To You/This
Little Girl Of Mine/Bring Your Love To Me/You Can Have Her/Justine/Georgia On
My Mind/You've Lost That Lovin' Feelin'/Just Once In My Life/See That Girl/
Unchained Melody/Hung On You/Ebb Tide/(You're My) Soul And Inspiration/Stand
By/He/Go Ahead And Cry/The White Cliffs Of Dover/On This Side Of Goodbye/A
Man Without A Dream/Melancholy Music Man/Stranded In The Middle Of Noplace/*

Hang Ups (Bobby Hatfield)/*Can't Make It Alone* (Bill Medley)/*Brown Eyed Woman* (Bill Medley)/*Rock And Roll Heaven*/*Give It To The People*/*Dream On*

In pre-Spector days, Bill Medley and Bobby Hatfield (both of whom were born in southern California in 1940) cut a few tracks as the Paramours on the Smash label in 1961. A name change resulted when black bar patrons at Orange County bars began voicing their approval of Bill and Bobby's stage shows with exulting cries of "That's *righteous*, brothers!" The duo later signed with the LA-based Moonglow label and reworked such chestnuts as *Ko Ko Joe* and *Justine*, originally done by seminal Los Angeles R & B shouters Don and Dewey. (The Brothers once borrowed shamelessly from Don and Dewey, right down to their comic stage act.) The Moonglow discs brought the duo their first fame on the R & B charts and undoubtedly shocked more than a few black radio programmers later, when the Righteous Brothers became "Shindig" television show regulars and turned out to be white! The blue-eyed soulsters came to the attention of Phil Spector, and the famed producer proved to be the quintessential cleric in his wedding of the Righteous Brothers' soulful voices (Hatfield's confident tenor being anchored by Medley's thundering bass) to his Wagnerian-style wall of sound. One bonus to this collection: it include's the pair's solo hits, too.

300   The Liberty Years
The Rivingtons

Liberty CDP-7-95204-2

Papa-Oom-Mow-Mow/*Deep Water*/*Kickapoo Joy Juice*/*My Reward*/*Mama-Oom-Mow-Mow (The Bird)*/*Waiting*/*Love Pill*/*Long Tall Sally*/*Unchain My Heart*/*You Are My Sunshine*/*Happy Jack*/*Slippin' And Slidin'*/*Old Time Love*/*Have Mercy, Mercy Baby*/*Standing In The Love Line*/*The Bird's The Word*/*I'm Losing My Grip*/*The Shaky Bird, Pt 1*/*The Shaky Bird, Pt 2*/*Cherry*/*Little Sally Walker*/*The Weejee Walk*/*Fairy Tales*

The Rivingtons (Carl White, Al Frazier, Sonny Harris, and Rocky Wilson Jr) reached the pop charts only twice. The four veteran artists scored first in 1962 with *Papa-Oom-Mow-Mow*, a highly charged, pounding, energetic bit of dance-based silliness. Early in 1963, the group did moderately well in the charts once more with *The Bird's The Word*. This classic novelty single became the basis for the Trashmen's million-selling *Surfer Bird*. (Liberty successfully sued later.) But it is the Rivingtons' commercial failures that make this disc worthwhile. *Papa-Oom-Mow-Mow* was followed by *Kickapoo Joy Juice*, which featured more good-time foolishness amid squeaky trumpet stings and the same Marcels-style rolling bass. The *Kickapoo Joy Juice* flip, *My Reward*, is simply one of the greatest, most mellifluous love songs of the early rock-and-soul era. While badly skewed grammatically ("caressing you delightly," "All this and you is my reward"), the song features dense background harmony supporting Carl White's superlative and sweet tenor, as well as a heavily stringed bridge that soars majestically. (There is a nice spoken bridge, too.) Another desirable track is *Cherry*, an R & B-ballad send-up which is highlighted by an hilarious spoken bridge ("Cherry, honey, baby, sugar darling," "Give you a little time to grow up and everything"). Other worthwhile cuts are *Waiting, Love Pill, Slippin' And Slidin'*, and *Standing In The Love Line*. The Rivingtons lasted from 1953 to 1973, recording under half a dozen names and on 22 labels. This collection represents, arguably, their finest hour.

301   The Galaxy Years
Little Johnny Taylor

Ace CDCHD 967 (UK)

You'll Need Another Favor/What You Need Is a Ball/Part Time Love/Somewhere Down The Line/Since I Found A New Love/My Heart Is Filled With Pain/First Class Love/If You Love Me (Like You Say)/You Win, I Lose/Nightingale Melody/I Smell Trouble/True Love/For Your Precious Love/I've Never Had A Woman Like You Before/Somebody's Got To Pay/Help Yourself/One More Chance/Please Come Home For Christmas/All I Want Is You/Zig Zag Lightning/The Things That I Used To Do/Big Blue Diamonds/I Know You Hear Me Calling/Driving Wheel/Sometimey Woman/Double Or Nothing

Little Johnny Taylor (b. Johnny Young, February 11, 1943, in Memphis) came to recording prominence behind a highly charged, wailing gospel delivery featuring a confident, falsetto vibrato out in front of discreet guitar fills and moaning horns. Taylor's biggest Galaxy hit was *Part Time Love* (1963), one of the most splendid early examples of gospel-infused blues to ever come over the airwaves. Taylor and his family relocated in the Los Angeles area when he was very young, and there he was performing R & B hits in LA clubs by his late teens. He also sang in two gospel groups, the Mighty Clouds of Joy and the Stars of Bethel. It was the latter experience that was the primary contribution to Taylor's stirring vocal intensity. He recorded for the Ronn label in the early 1970s and cut the hit *Everybody Knows About My Good Thing*. Taylor's Ronn efforts, though, showed that his voice had lost some of its lilting gospel edge by then. It is his earlier (and superior) Galaxy work that is presented on this exemplary CD.

302   The Downhome Soul Of Z.Z. Hill
Z.Z. Hill

Kent CDKEN 099 (UK)

Baby I'm Sorry/I Need Someone (To Love Me)/Have Mercy Someone/The Kind Of Love I Want/Hey Little Girl/I Found Love/No More Doggin'/You Can't Hide A Heartache/That's It/Happiness Is All I Need/Everybody Has To Cry/Nothing Can Change This Love/Set Your Sights Higher/Steal Away/You're Gonna Need My Lovin'/You're Gonna Make Me Cry/Oh Darling/If I Could Do It All Over/You Don't Love Me/You Won't Hurt No More/What More/You Got What I Need

Z.Z. Hill (b. Arzell Hill, September 24, 1941, in Naples, Texas) is one of the foundation artists for the Southern-styled soul-blues phenomenon. Hill began singing in black Dallas clubs in the late 1950s and started recording a few years later. From 1964 through 1972, Los Angeles-based Kent released 18 singles and three LPs. His work on the label featured a somewhat lazy funk beat, hard-punching horns, a bluesy guitar, and a cocktail-lounge piano. He emotes in a smooth and relaxed voice, his vibrato full yet soulfully high and nasal. Hill composed most of his material, but at times the influence of his mentors is a little too overt (Sam Cooke's *Somebody Have Mercy* is the obvious basis for Hill's *Have Mercy Someone*). Best tracks: *Happiness Is All I Need, You Don't Love Me, If I Could Do It All Over, That's It, I Need Someone (To Love Me)* (the last of these recorded in 1964 but his biggest hit for Kent in 1971). Before Hill died in 1984, he had established himself as a giant in soul-blues with what has become the most famous song in the genre, *Downhome Blues*, for the Malaco label. A complete Z.Z. Hill collection includes both the Malaco and Kent output.

303   Soul Shots Vol. 2: Sweet Soul
Various Artists

Rhino RNLCS70038 (LP)

The Esquires: *Get On Up*; Leon Haywood: *It's Got To Be Mellow*; Deon Jackson: *Love Makes The World Go Round*; Bobby Hebb: *Sunny*; The Intruders: *Cowboys To Girls*; Brenton Wood: *Gimmie Little Sign/The Oogum Boogum Song*; Sonny Charles and the Checkmates: *Black Pearl*; Dobie Gray: *The "In" Crowd*; The Joe Jeffrey Group: *My Pledge Of Love*; Mel and Tim: *Backfield In Motion*; Clifford Curry: *She Shot A Hole In My Soul*; The Larks: *The Jerk*; Larry Williams and Johnny Watson: *Mercy, Mercy, Mercy*

This 14-track sampler features the biggest singles by Brenton Wood and Sonny Charles and the Checkmates (both discussed elsewhere in this chapter), as well as works by Dobie Gray, Leon Haywood, the Larks, and Larry Williams and Johnny Watson. Leon Haywood (b. February 11, 1942, in Houston) moved to Los Angeles after high school and joined up with R & B pioneer Big Jay McNeely. Haywood's first Decca Records hit, *It's Got To Be Mellow* (from 1967), was an airy, mid-tempo, Chicago-styled offering. Later he had a hit with *I Want'a Do Something Freaky To You* (1975) and *Don't Push It Don't Force It* (1980) on the LA-based 20th Century label. The Larks had begun – with different personnel – in 1953 as Don Julian and the Meadowlarks. After failing completely on RPM in 1954, the group found success a year later with *Heaven And Paradise* on Dootone. Julian then played LA clubs until finding his biggest success in 1964 with the strong-harmony, highly danceable *The Jerk* on Money Records. *Mercy, Mercy, Mercy* features the combined efforts of a pair of 1950s legends. New Orleans-born singer/songwriter/pianist Larry Williams cut three hits in 1957, then dropped off the charts for a decade until the appearance of the horn-drenched *Mercy, Mercy, Mercy*; guitar virtuoso Watson came from Houston and first recorded as Young John Watson before becoming Guitar Johnny Watson in the mid-1950s. The soulful *Mercy, Mercy, Mercy* was covered by the Buckinghams as a pop hit three months after the Williams–Watson original. The name Dobie Gray (b. Leonard Ainsworth, July 26, 1942, in Brookshire, Texas) usually conjures up *Drift Away*, his million-selling country-soul work made in Nashville in 1973. Eight years prior to that, though, Gray recorded *The "In" Crowd*. Supplemented by stinging trumpets and a tasty (if subdued) doo-wop background, this playful paean to the disco high-life gave Gray his first taste of real recording success.

304   Tramp/Soul
Lowell Fulsom

Ace CDCHD 339 (2-disc set) (UK)

Tramp: *Tramp/I'm Sinking/Get Your Game Up Tight/Back Door Key/Two Way Wishing/Lonely Day/Black Nights/Year Of 29/No Hard Feelings/Hustlers Game/Goin' Home/Pico*

Soul: *Black Nights/Talkin' Woman/Shattered Dreams/Sitting Here Thinking/Little Angel/Change Your Ways/Blues Around Midnight/Everytime It Rains/Just One More Time/Ask At Any Door In Town/Too Many Drivers/My Aching Back*

Fulsom was born of black and American Indian descent in 1921 in Tulsa, Oklahoma, and spent much of his adolescence working in country string bands as Tulsa Red. In the late 1930s, he was overseas in the military. Fulsom settled in California's East Bay area after the service and began singing blues and gospel, although eventually he became a full-time blues singer/guitarist. Fulsom eventually moved south to Los Angeles. He began recording in 1946 and had hits on several labels – Big Town, Down Town, Downbeat, Swingtime, and Checker – before joining up with Kent in Los Angeles in 1964. By then in his mid-40s, he found renewed inspiration and creativity at Kent and reached his musical maturity, recording songs from 1965 to 1967 that involved soul-blues of the most extreme emotions: loneliness, sorrow, fear, anger, and unrequited love. His Kent tracks include a fine, spare rhythm section featuring two guitars, piano, bass, and drums, with horns filling out a few of the cuts. **Soul** (1965) is a solid achievement and helps explain why *Black Nights* and other selections were staples on black radio. **Tramp** (1967) is less solid but features the smash title track that Otis Redding and Carla Thomas later reprised.

305 Make Me Yours
Bettye Swann

Golden Classics Collectables CD 5177

Make Me Yours/Fall In Love With Me/Don't Look Back/Don't Wait Too Long/Don't Take My Mind/I Can't Stop Loving You/I Think I'm Falling In Love/You Gave Me Love/The Heartache Is Gone/I Will Not Cry/What Is My Life Coming To?/A Change Is Gonna Come

This exemplary CD captures Swann's earlier (and less polished) period for Money Records – she later recorded for Capitol and Atlantic – and includes her debut hit *Don't Wait Too Long* (penned by Carolyn Franklin, the late youngest sister of Aretha). Swann's Motownish, chart-topping *Make Me Yours* and *Fall In Love With Me* are included here, also. Bettye Swann (b. Betty Jean Champion, October 24, 1944, in Shreveport, Louisiana) grew to adolescence singing in church and at social gatherings. She and her family moved to the Golden State in the late 1950s. At 20, Swann began her five-year stint on the Los Angeles-based Money label, which was owned by the widow of legendary record man John Dolphin. The mid-tempo and teen-girl sound of Swann's music typified mid-1960s soul – and was the kind that did not cross over much. **Make Me Yours** is not a bad place to start to familiarize oneself with this music.

306 Heart And Soul
The Incredibles

Audio Arts AAS 7000 (LP)

Heart And Soul/For Sentimental Reasons/Lost Without You/Standing Here Crying/I'll Make It Easy/Miss Treatment/Without A Word/All Of A Sudden/Another Dirty Deal/There's Nothing Else To Say Baby

The Incredibles' two soul-chart hits well defined the relaxed Los Angeles soul scene of the mid-1960s. Three of their four members met while students at LA's Jefferson High. Formed in 1963, the quartet (Cal Waymon, Carl Gilbert, Jean Smith, and Alda Denise Edwards – listed on the LP as Denise Erwin) first reached a vast audience on the Audio Arts label in the fall of 1966 with their gently stirring *I'll Make It Easy*, a song reminiscent of the Dells' 1956 classic of *Oh What A Nite*. This was followed by a smooth, string-and-horn-dominated rewaxing of the Hoagy Carmichael standard *Heart And Soul*. Other infectious Incredibles tracks here are *For Sentimental Reasons*, *Lost Without You*, and *Another Dirty Deal*. Some music fans will no doubt consider this LP disposable; the hard-core soul fan/collector of vocal groups, though, will undoubtedly feel otherwise and diligently seek out this hard-to-find and long-out-of-print disc.

307   So Sharp!
Dyke and the Blazers
CDKEND 004 (UK)

So Sharp/Don't Bug Me/Funky Broadway, Pt 1/Funky Broadway, Pt 2/Shotgun Slim/City Dump/My Sisters And My Brothers/Funky Walk, Pt 1/Funky Walk, Pt 2/ Uhh, Pt 1/Uhh, Pt 2/It's Your Thing/You Are My Sunshine/Broadway Combination/ Stuff/Funky Bull, Pt 1/Funky Bull, Pt 2/Let A Woman Be A Woman – Let A Man Be A Man/We Got More Soul/The Wobble/Uhh (edit)/*The Wrong House/Runaway People/I'm So All Alone*

Wilson Pickett's 1967 smash *Funky Broadway* had first been recorded a year earlier by Dyke and the Blazers. Dyke (b. Arlester Christian, 1943, in Buffalo, New York) began his career singing background and playing bass guitar for the Blazers, the O'Jays' road band. When the struggling O'Jays could not afford the band's bus fare back to Buffalo, the Blazers stayed where they were: in Phoenix, Arizona. Dyke soon moved to center stage while working local clubs. He later created an original song (and accompanying dance) dubbed the *Funky Broadway*. Recorded in Phoenix in 1966, *Funky Broadway* was released to good local airplay on the small Artco label and soon found national success on Original Sound. For four years, Dyke and the Blazers – recording in both Phoenix and Los Angeles – did well with Dyke's sandpapery, bar-band vocals in front of raw, punchy, James Brown-style horns and bluesy guitar, most notably on *We Got More Soul* and *Let A Woman Be A Woman – Let A Man Be A Man* (both from 1969). The life of Arlester Christian ended violently in 1971 when he was shot to death by a deranged gunman in Phoenix.

308   Lou Rawls Live!
Lou Rawls
Capitol T 2459 (LP)

Stormy Monday/Southside Blues (monologue)/*Tobacco Road/St James Infirmary/ The Shadow Of Your Smile/I'd Rather Drink Muddy Water/Goin' To Chicago Blues/ In The Evening When The Sun Goes Down/The Girl From Ipanema/I Got It Bad And That Ain't Good/Street Corner Hustler's Blues* (monologue)/*World Of Trouble*

This was his biggest album – it reached number 4 in the charts, earning a gold disc – and perfectly captures who Lou Rawls was: the quintessential saloon singer, confident, polished, and offering perfectly phrased lyrics with the utmost in controlled emotion. Rawls is obviously right at home in what sounds to be an intimate venue. He is backed by a tight group of veteran musicians (Herb Ellis on guitar, Tommy Strode on piano, James Bond on bass, and Earl Palmer on drums) who never overpower the songmaster. Rawls's material runs the gamut from blues to toned-down rock to pop to easy-going standards by such stellar composers as Count Basie and Duke Ellington. Be assured, though, that Rawls does not eschew true soul: he is at his best here with T-Bone Walker's *Stormy Monday* and his (original) monologs *Southside Blues* and *Street Corner Hustler's Blues*, the latter of which sounds much like an early form of rap (really!). This LP bears repeated listenings; strangely enough, it is also out of print.

309   Anthology (1967–1973)
The Fifth Dimension
Rhino RNDC 71104

Another Day, Another Heartache/Aquarius – Let The Sunshine In/California My Way/California Soul/Carpet Man/Everything's Been Changed/Girls' Song/Go Where You Wanna Go/(Last Night) I Didn't Get To Sleep At All/If I Could Reach You/ Learn How To Fly/Love's Lines, Angles And Rhymes/Never My Love/One Less Bell To Answer/Paper Cup/Puppet Man/Save The Country/Stoned Soul Picnic/Sweet Blindness/Together Let's Find Love/Up–Up And Away

From the late 1960s through the early 1970s, the Fifth Dimension (Marilyn McCoo, Florence LaRue, Billy Davis, Jr, Lamont McLemore, and Ron Townson) honed their ultra-tight harmonies to perfection and earned 29 slots in the charts. (Six singles and eight LPs won gold awards.) They began as the Hi-Fis and cut their road teeth with Ray Charles's revue; later, two Hi-Fis members formed the highly successful Friends of Distinction. With new personnel, the Hi-Fis metamorphosed into the Versatiles. A signing with Johnny Rivers's fledgling Soul City label brought with it a directive from Rivers for a name change. (Johnny proclaimed the name "too old-fashioned.") The new appellation was soon provided by member Ron Townson and his wife. The Fifth Dimension stumbled on their first outing (*I'll Be Lovin' You Forever*) but had a real success with a polished reworking of the Mamas and Papas' *Go Where You Wanna Go.* Then came *Up–Up And Away* and a garnering of no less than four Grammys. Drawing on some of the most adroit tunesmiths of the day (Jimmy Webb, Laura Nyro, Neil Sedaka), the Fifth Dimesion became synonymous with well-crafted AM radio pop-soul: light, melodic, and, as **Anthology (1967–1973)** shows, surprisingly enduring.

310 Brenton Wood's 18 Best
Brenton Wood
Original Sound OSCD – 8886

Gimmie Little Sign/Oogum Boogum Song/Baby You've Got It/I Think You've Got Your Fools Mixed Up/Great Big Bundle Of Love/I'm The One Who Knows/Lovey Dovey Kind Of Love/Can You Dig It/Whoop It On Me/Take A Chance/Catch You On The Rebound/Me And You/I Like The Way You Love Me/Darlin'/Where Were You/Two Time Loser/Sad Little Songs/Good Night Baby

Brenton Wood (b. Alfred Smith, July 26, 1941, in Shreveport, Louisiana) moved to California at age two and spent his formative years in the seedy LA port city of San Pedro. As a teenager, he warbled with a neighborhood group called Little Freddy and the Rockets. Wood, a triple-threat vocalist/songwriter/pianist, later formed an outfit he dubbed the Quotations. Eventually, he auditioned solo for a number of local labels as Brenton Wood, his stage name being taken from the fashionable LA suburb of Brentwood. Double Shot Records, fresh from a national hit with the Count Five's *Psychotic Reaction,* signed Woods, and he had a hit with his maiden effort, the playful *Oogum Boogum Song* – a nonsensical, falsetto-fueled ditty which was little more, lyrically, than a cataloging of the day's fashion trends: high-heeled boots, miniskirts, sloppy shirts, bell-bottom pants, oversize earrings, and trench coats. This was followed by Woods's chugging *Gimmie Little Sign,* a Top 10 success featuring the cheapest-sounding organ heard this side of ? and the Mysterians' *96 Tears.*

311 Planets Of Life
The Whispers
Soul Clock 22001 (LP)

You Must Be Doing All Right/Seems Like I Gotta Do Wrong/Planets Of Life/They're Going To Hear From Me/Sing Of Songs/I Can Remember/Needle In A Haystack/ Creation Of Love/I'm The One/You Make Me So Very Happy

The minuscule Soul Clock label became the Whispers' second recording home after a brief stint on the Dore label, where they scored with the soul-doo-wop classic *I Was Born When You Kissed Me* (1966). Soul Clock allowed the quintet (Gordy Harmon, Walter and Wallace Scott, Marcus Hutson, and Nicholas Caldwell) an opportunity to make their album debut with the long-out-of-print but highly laudable **Planets Of Life**. Here one finds the R & B hit *Seems Like I Gotta Do Wrong* (1969) as well as nine other Whispers tracks that well represent the southern Californian soulsters a decade before major crossover success (with *And The Beat Goes On*). Understatement is the key theme on **Planets Of Life**: with the exceptions of two mid-tempo tunes (*They're Going To Hear From Me* and *I Can Remember*), all the tracks here move smoothly and calmly, yet feature a kind of gentle urgency fueling the lead vocals. There are pleasant, unexpected touches (the flute on *Seems Like I Gotta Do Wrong*, the gentle organ on *Sing Of Songs*) popping up between the unobtrusive guitars and muted horns that play out behind the songs. One misses the terrific first single on Soul Clock, the neo-doo-wop *Great Day*, but virtually all of the Whispers' Temptations-style offerings here sound as fresh today as they did a score of years ago. Try to find this vinyl winner if you can.

312   Viva! El Chicano: Their Very Best
El Chicano

MCAD-25197

Viva Tirado/The Latin One/Brown-Eyed Girl/Cantaloupe Island/El Cayuco/Tell Her She's Lovely/Quiet Village/Ahora Si/Pyramid (Of Love And Friends)/Mas Zacato

El Chicano began as a southern California Latin-rhythm quartet in the mid-1960s under the name of the VIPs (which included Jerry Salas, Mickey Lespron, Robert Espinosa, Fred Sanchez, and Andre Baeza), but failed to earn recognition until they changed their name. They signed with the tiny Gordo label in Los Angeles early in 1970 and soon saw their chugging, shuffling *Viva Tirada* hit the national pop and R & B charts after the larger Kapp label had acquired the master. (El Chicano's success was no doubt aided by the rise in popularity several months earlier of the commercial Latin music of the Bay Area's Santana group.) Looking to follow the momentum of *Viva Tirada*, El Chicano went awry when they redid old rock hits (by the Beatles, the Archies, and Van Morrison) with a Latin beat. After MCA absorbed the Kapp label, El Chicano managed just one more hit, the ultra-cool *Tell Her She's Lovely*, before fading from the music scene.

313   Anthology
Diana Ross

Motown 3746360492 (2-disc set)

Reach Out And Touch (Somebody's Hand)/Ain't No Mountain High Enough/ Remember Me/Reach Out I'll Be There/Surrender/I'm Still Waiting/Good Morning Heartache/Touch Me In The Morning/You're A Special Part Of Me (with Marvin Gaye)*/My Mistake (Was To Love You)* (with Marvin Gaye)*/Sleepin'/Sorry Doesn't Always Make It Right/Theme From Mahogany (Do You Know Where You're Going To)/I Thought It Took A Little Time (But Today I Fell In Love)/One Love In My Lifetime/Baby I Love Your Way/Young Mothers/Brown Baby – Save The Children/*

Love Hangover/Gettin' Ready For Love/Your Love Is So Good For Me/You Got It/ Top Of The World/Lovin' Livin' Givin'/What You Gave Me/The Boss/It's My House/Upside Down/I'm Coming Out/It's My Turn/One More Chance/Crying My Heart Out For You/My Old Piano/My Man (Mon Homme)/Endless Love (with Lionel Ritchie)/*Imagine/Too Shy To Say*

As the lead singer of the Supremes, when her cooing voice was all things tender and light (yet emoting about subjects most womanly), Diana Ross (b. Diane Ross, March 26, 1944, in Detroit) took her Motown hitmaking-machine group into the record books as the first rock-era female group to cut 12 number 1 singles. She went solo in 1970 (right after *Someday We'll Be Together*) and, with her career being carefully controlled by Motown head Berry Gordy, Jr, retained her commercial momentum with numerous well-crafted discs that consistently made the upper reaches of the charts. On her own, Ross had understandably outgrown her Supremes-era innocence but continued to deliver quality Motown material with her trademark breathy confidence. The gushy Ross persona is sometimes rather hard to take, but overlook that and there are some really fine tunes in this 38-song package of her Motown hits.

Berry first got Ross high in the charts with a series of Nicholas Ashford and Valerie Simpson songs, *Reach Out And Touch (Somebody's Hand)* (1970), *Ain't No Mountain High Enough* (1970), and *Remember Me* (1971). After Ashford and Simpson left to start their own recording career, Berry recruited pop songwriter Michael Masser from Chicago. His songs, which included *Touch Me In The Morning* (1973) and *Theme From Mahogany (Do You Know Where You're Going To)* (1975), moved Ross to the pinnacle of show-business success as a name star with Middle America. She also managed to retain ties to her original soul audience with the magnificent disco hit *Upside Down* (1980). Motown had made Ross such a giant talent that the company could not afford to renew her contract in 1981; as a result, the singer moved to RCA, where she gradually dissipated her career. (Masser went on to write songs for Whitney Houston.)

314 The Time Has Come
The Chambers Brothers
Columbia CK 9522

All Strung Out Over You/People Get Ready/I Can't Stand It/Romeo And Juliet/In The Midnight Hour/So Tired/Uptown/Please Don't Leave Me/What The World Needs Now Is Love/Time Has Come Today

The highlight of this CD is, of course, the Chambers Brothers' lone big hit, *Time Has Come Today*, quite possibly the best – and most unusual – example of a psychedelic soul song ever to be played frequently on the air. The Chambers Brothers (George, Willie, Lester, and Joe) grew up as sharecroppers' sons in Flora, Mississippi, and sang at the local Baptist church. In time, they formed a gospel quartet in Los Angeles, and began their recording career in 1965, singing an interesting folk–soul–blues blend for the tiny Vault label. Within a few years, they were rocking hard on the East Coast, a white drummer slamming out a jackhammer rhythm behind them. The diverse Chambers Brothers even drew rave reviews at the 1965 Newport Folk Festival. By the late 1960s, they were equally at home in psychedelic rock and in soul venues. This is a reissue of their 1971 LP **The Time Has Come.**

315 Eddie Kendricks . . . At His Best
Eddie Kendricks
Motown 37463548122

Keep On Truckin'/He's A Friend/Skippin' Work Today/Girl You Need A Change Of Mind, Pt 1/Shoeshine Boy/Boogie Down/Intimate Friends/Just My Imagination (Running Away With Me)/Can I/It's So Hard For Me To Say Goodbye

Eddie Kendricks (b. December 17, 1939, in Union Springs, Alabama) sang both lead and high harmony on over 20 Temptations hits between 1963 and 1971. He was raised in Birmingham, Alabama, where, like so many future soul artists, he grew up singing emotional gospel music and raw, gritty R & B. After leaving high school, Kendricks and his boyhood friend Paul Williams moved to Cleveland, Ohio, where they recruited some other singers (also with a gospel background) and formed the Cavaliers. They, in turn, moved to Detroit in 1959 and began going by the name of the Primes. Before long, they merged with another R & B vocal group, the Distants, and called themselves the Elgins: Berry Gordy, Jr, later rechristened the act the Temptations. Kendricks sang lead vocal on the Temptations' breakthrough hit, their seventh single, *The Way You Do The Things You Do*. He announced his solo move in 1971 with an album entitled **All By Myself**, which he recorded in Los Angeles. On his own, Kendricks scored half-a-dozen Tamla hits in his inimitable "sweet" style before making the falsetto-topped crossover smash *Keep On Truckin'* in 1973, followed by nine Top 10 R & B hits. Not all his hits are included here (such as *One Tear* and *Happy*), but this CD strikes a better balance than if the collection had included too many similar-sounding tunes. Kendricks died in 1992.

316   Billy Preston! The Best
Billy Preston

A & M CD – 3205

Fancy Lady/Get Back/Girl/God Loves You/I'm Really Gonna Miss You/Nothing From Nothing/Outa-Space/Space Race/Will It Go Round in Circles/You Are So Beautiful

From 1972 to 1974, Billy Preston (b. September 9, 1946, in Houston) rode the crest of the charts (four Top 5 hit singles) with his trademark "locomotive" creations – simplistic, upbeat, and catchy. Preston, who had been singing gospel at church by age three, had led his own R & B vocal group at LA's Dorsey High and knocked everyone out with his skills on the piano and organ. At 16, he toured England as a piano player for Little Richard. While overseas, on a gospel tour that evolved into a full-blown rock-and-roll forum, Preston met Sam Cooke, who later signed the confident and talented youngster for his debut LP, *16-Year-Old Soul*. Preston became a regular on the briefly popular rock-and-roll TV show "Shindig." He was given a credit on the label of the Beatles' *Get Back*, played on a number of Sly and the Family Stone hits, and worked on the Concert for Bangladesh. Preston recorded for a number of labels before he became a hitmaker on A & M. His happy and hard-driving *Outa-Space* won a Grammy as Best Pop Instrumental; he also composed Joe Cocker's classic *You Are So Beautiful*, which is featured here.

317   Blame It On Love And All The Great Hits
Smokey Robinson

Motown MOTD – 5401

Blame It On Love (with Barbara Mitchell)/*Just Like You/Don't Play Another Love Song/Tell Me Tomorrow/Being With You/Crusin'/If You Wanna Make Love (Come 'Round Here)/Just A Touch Away/Baby Come Close/Let Me Be The Clock*

In the early 1970s, Motown moved its corporate headquarters from Detroit to Hollywood, and one-time Miracles leader Smokey Robinson (b. William Robinson, February 19, 1940, in Detroit) became a Motown vice-president in 1972 at age 32. He also established himself as a solo artist and wrote, produced, and sang an impressive number of ultra-smooth and well-crafted love songs. The man with the velvet tenor voice and the infallible pen did not fail to please his longtime fans – the Miracles had been Motown's first successful group a dozen years earlier – with such offerings as *Baby Come Close* and *Cruisin'* (the only 1970s songs featured on this CD), as well as *Let Me Be The Clock*, *Being With You*, and *Tell Me Tomorrow*. Robinson's voice here lacks some of the barely controlled urgency found on his early-to-mid-1960s Miracles recordings, but the Grand Old Man of Motown is still in fine voice nonetheless on this collection from one of America's premier rock-and-soul-era tunesmiths.

318   Barry White's Greatest Hits, Vol. 1
Barry White
Casablanca 822782-2

What Am I Gonna Do With You?/You're The First, The Last, My Everything/Can't Get Enough Of Your Love, Babe/Honey Please, Can't Ya See/Love Serenade/Never, Never Gonna Give Ya Up/I'm Gonna Love You Just A Little More, Baby/I've Found Someone/I've Got So Much To Give/I'm Standing In The Shadows Of Love

Barry White (b. September 12, 1944, in Galveston, Texas) came to music at an early age. In 1952, when he was eight, White made his gospel debut in a church; within two years, he had become church organist and a part-time choir director. The White family moved to racially mixed east Los Angeles during the mid-1950s. Later, 11-year-old Barry played the piano on Jesse Belvin's 1956 classic *Goodnight My Love*. In 1960 he began playing piano and singing in an R & B group called the Upfronts, who cut six failed singles for the minuscule Lummtone label. He arranged Bob and Earl's *Harlem Shuffle* in 1963 and continued paying his dues as a producer/arranger/songwriter/singer/conductor for such labels as Atlantic, Downey, Veep, and Mustang/Bronco. The portly artist – White weighed nearly 300 pounds – became a 20th Century Fox solo artist in 1973 and made the first of half-a-dozen million-selling singles with *I'm Gonna Love You Just A Little More, Baby*. His rumbling, smokey, bedroom voice, a slow disco backbeat, plus lush and heavily stringed musical arrangements – as well as the steamiest of lyrics – helped make Barry White a best-selling (if highly unlikely) sex symbol. This collection covers his hits only from 1973 to 1975, but only *It's Ecstasy When You Lay Down Next To Me* (from 1977) would add anything.

319   Greatest Hits
The Commodores
Motown MODC – 912

Brick House/Easy/Fancy Dancer/Just To Be Close To You/Machine Gun/Slippery When Wet/Sweet Love/This Is Your Life/Three Times A Lady/Too Hot Ta Trot

Lionel Ritchie (b. June 20, 1949, in Tuskegee, Alabama) grew up on the campus of Tuskegee Institute and began college there in 1967. As a freshman, the musically eclectic Ritchie became a member of the Jays, a funky, boogaloo party band on campus, whose influences ranged from Sly and the Family Stone to the Bar-Kays. After graduation, the Jays found employment as the opening act for Motown's Jackson Five. The Alabama sextet wanted to record but so resisted the

Motown formula that they were not offered a contract for two years. Motown executives in Los Angeles later signed the group as the Commodores, a name chosen at random from a dictionary. **Machine Gun** (1974) became the debut album by the Commodores (Ritchie, William King, Thomas McClary, Milan Williams, Ronald LaPread, and Walter Orange) and featured the title track – an instrumental – as the first hit. On the Commodores' first three LPs, the sound was dominated by a thumping funk that actually leaned toward a kind of black heavy metal. Later works featured Lionel Ritchie taking the Commodores into sweet pop smoothness – some would say melodic blandness – and much greater crossover appeal. The group hit its commercial stride with the simply titled **Commodores** (1977), which included both the dreamy *Easy* and the chugging, feet-moving *Brick House*.

320   The Natalie Cole Collection
Natalie Cole

Capitol CDP 7-466192

I've Got Love On My Mind/This Will Be (An Everlasting Love)/Our Love/I Can't Say No/Sophisticated Lady (She's A Different Lady)/Inseparable/I'm Catching Hell (Living Here Alone)/Party Lights/Mr Melody/Stand By/Gimmie Some Time/Someone That I Used To Love/Nothin' But A Fool/You Were Right Girl/Your Lonely Heart

Natalie Cole (b. February 6, 1950, in Los Angeles) burst onto the mid-1970s pop and soul scene with a commanding voice, top-quality arrangements, and a surname that commanded respect. She earned hit after hit before fading from the music scene due to drug and personal problems. When she won seven *Unforgettable* Grammys in 1992 for her "duets" with her late father, Nat "King" Cole, Natalie Cole re-established herself as a superstar. This collection of her earliest Capitol works (recorded in Chicago and Los Angeles) shows Cole at her youthful best, brimming with confidence and belting out tunes that showed her ability to shift from one style to another with fluidity. She grew up under the musical spell of Aretha Franklin (to whom she was often compared early on), Stevie Wonder, and Sly Stone. Cole earned a college degree from the University of Massachusetts while working as a singing waitress and later became an opening act for both Jerry Butler and the Stylistics. In 1975, she was signed to Capitol by Larkin Arnold, the same Capitol executive who had signed a Capitol contract for her father 32 years earlier.

321   Music Speaks Louder Than Words
Candi Staton

Warner Brothers BS 3040 (LP)

Nights On Broadway/You Are/A Dreamer Of A Dream/Music Speaks Louder Than Words/Cotton Candi/Listen To The Music/When You Want Love/One More Chance On Love/Main Thing/Before Then The Next Teardrop Falls

Candi Staton (b. Hanceville, Albama) began her career in the South recording for Rick Hall's Fame Studios at Muscle Shoals. For Hall, she recorded most of her biggest hits on the Fame label from 1969 to 1973. (The albums **I'm Just A Prisoner** (1969) and **Stand By Your Man** (1970) are worth searching out.) After moving to Warner Brothers, Hall recorded Staton on one more album, **Candi,** and one more big hit, *As Long As He Takes Care Of Home*. But Warner Brothers apparently decided to make Staton more contemporary with the new disco sounds and started recording her in Los Angeles in 1975. Perhaps the obvious choice for a basic would have been the Dave Crawford-produced **Young**

Hearts Run Free, which produced the number 1 title single in 1976, but this reviewer opts for the Bob Monaco-produced **Music Speaks Louder Than Words**, which produced in 1977 the more modest hits *Nights On Broadway* (a Bee Gees remake) and *Listen To The Music* (a Doobie Brothers remake). Monaco seemed to draw from Staton's remarkable voice a sublimity and pathos that her other producers never could. Hall and Crawford got the biggest hits, but Monaco got an artistic triumph. This was the last Staton album not "done in" by the excesses of disco.

322 Greatest Hits
Rose Royce
Whitfield 3457-2

Car Wash/Do Your Dance/First Come, First Serve/I Wanna Get Next To You/I Wonder Where You Are Tonight/I'm Going Down/I'm In Love (And I Love The Feeling)/Is It Love You're After?/It Makes You Feel Like Dancin'/Love Don't Live Here Anymore/Ooh Boy/Pop Your Fingers/Wishing On A Star/You're A Winner

Former Motown mastermind Norman Whitfield had the routine of a real car wash in mind when he created *Car Wash*, a 1976 hit single now relegated to the slag heap of disco oldies. The song and a soundtrack of the same name were written for the movie "Car Wash" (1976). Whitfield structures the song first on the initial rinsing process (musically, percussion, drums, and hand-claps), followed by the brushing (bass, guitar), then the final rinse (funky horns rising to a crescendo that segues into a sledgehammer beat integral to dance tracks of that time). Rose Royce had been started by Whitfield as the Temptations' road band; in time, the eight male musicians were joined by female lead Gwen Dickey, who brought the group to prominence with Whitfield's assistance. The gold-selling **Car Wash** soundtrack also included *I Wanna Get Next To You* and *I'm Going Down*. Rose Royce enjoyed a decade of commercial soul success, although only the Whitfield years (1977–81) are included here. They are the most important, anyway.

323 Shalamar's Greatest Hits
Shalamar
Columbia ZK75308

The Second Time Around/Take That To The Bank/Make That Move/This Is For The Lover In You/Dancing In The Sheets/A Night To Remember/Full Of Fire/Games/Right In The Socket/Uptown Festival (Motown Medley)

Shalamar, black teen idols of the late 1970s and early 1980s, belted out a long string of perfectly crafted dance ditties that earned them over a dozen slots on the Top 30 R & B charts – every track in this fine CD collection was a hit single. Shalamar made its first recordings on Don Cornelius's Soul Train label (named, of course, for the popular TV dance show). The original Shalamar outfit consisted of several LA session singers brought together by Dick Griffey, a friend of Cornelius and a southern California concert promoter. When Shalamar's 1977 debut disc *Motown Medley* became a sudden big success, Griffey began the Solar label posthaste and tagged Jeffrey Daniels and Jody Watley (one-time "Soul Train" dancers) and Gerald Brown (later replaced by Howard Hewett) as the "new" Shalamar. Beginning with *Take That To The Bank*, Shalamar ran up an impressive list of catchy Solar hits, although *Dancing In The Sheets*, from the popular teen dance flick "Footloose," appeared on Columbia.

324 Anthology
Patrice Rushen

Elektra ELK 60465-4

All We Need/Feels So Real (Won't Let Go)/Forget Me Nots/Givin' It Up Is Givin'
Up/Hang It Up/Haven't You Heard/High In Me/Look Up/Number One/Remind Me/
When I Found You

The enigmatic Patrice Rushen (b. September 30, 1954, in Los Angeles) came
onto the R & B scene offering a light, breezy, jazz-oriented alternative to the
thumping disco beat that was filling the airwaves during the late 1970s.
Growing up in a professional and musically eclectic LA family, she was placed
in a special USC children's music program at the tender age of three. Rushen
began her recording career with two LPs of original jazz instrumentals for
Fantasy; on her third effort, she added her lilting, breathy voice to the tracks,
but as before, her album did not sell. She turned to session work for both jazz
and R & B artists before finally getting a minor hit for herself, *Haven't You*
Heard, in 1980. Her biggest success came two years later with the Top 30 single
Forget Me Nots. As always, Rushen offered up a fresh voice that was full of hope
for good relationships and fulfilling lives together. She has been overlooked by a
great many people, which is a shame. **Anthology** gives the collector a chance to
get to know one of LA's better artists of the recent past.

325 Greatest Hits
Teena Marie

Epic EK 48652

Lovergirl/Work It/Ooo La La La/If I Were A Bell/Dear Lover/Here's Looking At You/
Call Me (I Got Yo Number) (featuring Rick James)/*Cassanova Brown/My Dear Mr*
Gaye/Out On A Limb

Teena Marie (b. Mary Christine Brockert, 1957, in Santa Monica, California) is
a white torch singer with impressive soul credentials. She grew up in a racially
mixed neighborhood in Venice, a decaying beach town near Los Angeles.
Though her white school-friends embraced Top 40 rock, Marie preferred R & B,
which was a favorite among her black neighbors. She had fronted several local R
& B bands in and around Venice by her mid-teens and, lying about her age, later
sang in black LA clubs. Armed with a five-song demo tape, she was signed to
Motown after earning her high-school diploma. Marie recorded nine Motown
chart singles with the aid of funk producer Rick James. A switch to Epic in 1983
brought Teena her first Top 10 crossover hit with *Lovergirl* the following year. On
this CD, Marie (an accomplished guitarist and keyboard player) wrote, arranged,
and produced every track, with the exception of *Out On A Limb*, which she wrote
and produced. Even though much of her Epic work lacks the hard, somewhat
unpolished edge of her early Motown singles, **Greatest Hits** offers collectors of
the 1980s soul-pop sound a chance to hear a really good artist who can sing both
convincingly sultry ballads and gritty up-tempo tunes with equal flair and
confidence.

Great Britain and the European Continent

9

Geoff Brown

To many, the phrase "British and European 'soul' music" is a
virtual contradiction in terms. How could a music which
springs almost entirely from African American expressions of
emotion have any base in or find common ground with the Old
World? The historical experience and the contemporary realities
of the cultures have been and remain so markedly different.

Quite simply, African American music – jazz, soul, blues,
rhythm and blues – took such a fundamental grip on the creative
minds of generations of Europeans, particularly Britons, because
it communicated excitement, passion and joy, pain, desperation,
and despair so immediately and thoroughly. Its universality is a
measure of its power. African American music in all its forms has
arguably become the United States' greatest contribution to world
culture in the twentieth century, greater, because more subliminally pervasive, than its other totems of cultural colonization like
Hollywood and Mickey Mouse, Coca-Cola and McDonalds.

To begin, it is essential to provide a brief resumé of how the
music crossed the Atlantic and prospered to such an extent that it
has been the biggest single stylistic influence on the development
of popular music in Great Britain since World War II. First came
the jazz of the 1940s and 1950s, awareness spreading when
thousands of American servicemen arrived in Europe midway
through the war. Later in the 1950s came rock-and-roll, whose
great black stars – Chuck Berry, Little Richard, Fats Domino –
made a demonstrably more lasting contribution than headline
grabbers like Bill Haley.

In the early 1960s, a younger generation of Britons found new
heroes. They were, in droves, attempting to imitate the country
blues of the Deep South – Robert Johnson and his antecedents,
John Lee Hooker and his contemporaries – and the later, virile
urban blues of Chicago, personified by the likes of Howlin' Wolf
and Muddy Waters. Of the rock stars who survived from the

1960s, 50 per cent (the Rolling Stones, Eric Clapton, Fleetwood Mac, etc.) cut their teeth this way. The other 50 percent (Paul McCartney, Rod Stewart, Elton John, etc.), although cogniscent of the blues, rhythm and blues, and rock-and-roll, more often found more fertile fields of influence in soul. Of all Europeans, Van Morrison synthesized this range of influences better than anyone. The influence continues still – on Paul Young, George Michael, Lisa Stansfield, and countless others.

Seaports such as Liverpool, Belfast, Cardiff, Bristol, Manchester, and London (indeed, the whole Thames estuary) landed merchant seamen who brought in 45s by fresh, unique-sounding singers and groups on then-exotic labels like Stax, Motown, Atlantic, and King. Other great conduits of the sounds remained: there were American servicemen on US bases all over Britain and Europe, especially (the then West) Germany; Radio Luxemburg, the Continent-based station, reflected the mood of the postwar, baby-boom kids coming of age in the 1960s; and a few British deejays had travelled to the States, and some American deejays came to Britain.

When some of the black American servicemen stationed in Europe began singing with local musicians, cross-cultural cross-pollination began, made more exotic by the increasing number of Caribbean musicians who entered Britain with the first great influx of immigrants in the 1950s. But it took several generations before the "soul" singing of Britons (and other Europeans, already at a disadvantage because they lacked the common language with America) could be realistically compared with the genuine American article.

The British experience was so far removed from that of the African American that no matter how much they loved the music, they did not have a learning process, like singing in a stomping, Baptist choir, to turn to. So it took years of awkward but diligent, hopeful, earnest, well-meaning imitation. Of course, African American music revolutionized British popular music, and lit the fuse of what later exploded into a hugely profitable and dominant industry. But it was some generations before British soul came of age with a real, home-grown sound and spirit of its own. Only, in fact, since the 1980s have singers emerged who do not sound thin and weedy beside their vocal role models.

Essential Recordings

(i) Flamingo and Marquee, Rik Tik and Ram Jam

The first British blues boom, in which competent jazz and folk players coached younger boys like Mick Jagger, Brian Jones, and

Keith Richards, reached its apogee in 1966 when the John Mayall
Bluesbreakers, featuring Eric Clapton, recorded the emphatic
musical statement of the UK guitar-based blues-band style.
Concurrently, a vogue for a more sophisticated lineup with
horns had developed. Preeminent among these seven- and eight-
piece bands were Georgie Fame and the Blue Flames, Zoot
Money and his Big Roll Band, Herbie Goins and the Night-
timers, Jimmy James and the Vagabonds, Ronnie Jones and the
Blue Jays, and Geno Washington and the Ram Jam Band.

Although many recorded likable enough albums, and Fame, for
one, recorded several hit singles, none was perhaps quite so
evocative as Geno's **Hand Clappin'-Foot Stompin'-Funky
Butt-Live!** album of 1966, which was in the charts for 42 weeks.
By comparison with Fame's jazz-based All Stars and Money's Big
Roll Band, the Ram Jam Band were a brash lot, and Washington,
a former American GI and gymnastics instructor, was brasher still.
But Geno – whose name was chanted throughout his shows in a
manner with which British soccer crowds were familiar – had
boundless enthusiasm and energy. Through this, coupled with his
innate ability to communicate with his audience, Geno made them
feel part of this big, loud, blasting, soul-music experience, and
they embraced it with all the frantic zeal of new converts.

There was scarcely any original music in his sets and he picked
none but the best-known tunes to cover. Otis Redding, Wilson
Pickett, Sam and Dave, Rufus Thomas, Junior Walker, and Stevie
Wonder were among the singers whose hits he blusters through in
this boisterous, rough-hewn live set. Washington's limitations are
perhaps best expressed in his reading of the CODs' *Michael*, a
small British hit for him as a single. Geno's throaty, gravelly rasp,
as though he is on the forty-ninth gig of a 50-day tour (which in all
probability he was), is not well suited to the comparatively delicate
melody and light beat.

In 1975, describing his arrival on the UK scene with the benefit
of a decade's hindsight, Geno, talking to the *New Musical Express*,
was fittingly modest. "I had no real experience. I used to go and
watch Charlie and Inez Foxx who were on tour then. I took
Charlie's movements, combined them with Inez's kind of
personality and it worked; next month I was a star." It was a
brief shining. Soon flower power made these groups redundant at
best, ludicrous at worst. But which music lasted better and has
been less of a fad? There is no contest, because the music of
African Americans is the fountain to which British-based
musicians most often return when their own music needs
refreshment.

Washington continued to get work, profitably touring South
America in the 1970s, being feted in Dexy's Midnight Runners'
hit, *Geno*, touring Britain in a stage musical celebration of 1960s

soul in 1991, and gigging still in 1992. Others of the era often surfaced as superstars: the jazz roots of Georgie Fame's drummer Mitch Mitchell created sparks with the seminal Jimi Hendrix Experience; session guitarist and solo artist Albert Lee first emerged with Chris Farlowe and the Thunderbirds; and Police guitarist Andy Summers hailed from Zoot Money's band.

Discographical Details

326   Hand Clappin'-Foot Stompin'-Funky Butt Live!
Geno Washington and the Ram Jam Band

Pye NSPL 18618 (UK) (LP)

Philly Dog/Ride Your Pony/Up Tight (Everything's Alright)/(I'm A) Road Runner/ Hold On (I'm Comin')/Don't Fight It/Land Of A Thousand Dances/Respect/Willy Nilly/Get Down With It/Michael/Que Sera Sera/You Don't Know (Like I Know)

(ii) It's Like A Heatwave

If we are to be judged by the company we keep then Rod Temperton, formerly of Heatwave, is probably the best British soul songwriter of all time. The classy hits he has written place him far above any other British writer working in the soul mine. Here are a few nuggets: *Off The Wall, Thriller, Rock With You* (Michael Jackson); *Love X Love, Give Me The Night* (George Benson); *Razzamatazz, Somethin' Special*, co-writer on *The Dude, Back On The Block* (Quincy Jones); co-writer on all but two of the tracks on Brothers Johnson's **Stomp!!**; plus smaller sellers for, among others, Aretha Franklin, Patti Austin, and Rufus. Most of those cuts were produced by Jones, who regarded Temperton as one of the outstanding songwriters of the 1980s.

Born in Cleethorpes, on the east coast of England – not a hotbed of soul music – Temperton was a drummer turned keyboard-player whose career as the archetypal hack musician was becalmed. Aged 24, he was scuffling a living on the German club circuit and living in Worms when he answered an advertisement in a London-based newspaper which put him in touch with American singer Johnny Wilder, from Dayton, Ohio, who was living 20 miles away in Heidelberg. Temperton joined Heatwave and at last found an outlet for his songs.

Heatwave was an astonishing United Nations of a band, the Anglo-Afro-American lineup being completed by a Spanish bassist resident in Switzerland and a Czech drummer. Because Wilder did not want to use horns, Temperton had to write vocal arrangements to give his music the depth of sound he wanted. This gave a richness to hugely catchy melodies which flitted and skittered on top of crisp rhythms. He was, recall, a drummer first, so his keyboard-playing and thus composing style were initially heavily percussive. By using Barry Blue, an out-and-out pop producer best known for grinning, chart-busting, teenybop material and cute, winsome ditties with a songstress/co-writer named Lynsey de Paul, Heatwave's label ensured maximum commercial returns.

Wilder himself was no mean songwriter – the ballad *Mind-Blowing Decisions* was his – but that was the only track out of the dozen on Heatwave's 1982 hits collection **Power Cuts** not penned by Temperton. In fact, Rod's songs were the difference between Heatwave and the spate of Brit-soul and Brit-funk acts (Light of the World, Hi Tension, Freeez, and others heard on **Slipstream** – see the "Basic Recordings" section) burgeoning in the late 1970s disco scene in Europe. Be it in *Boogie Nights*, the compelling dance track that first alerted producer Quincy Jones to Temperton's talent, or in the creamy ballad *Always And Forever*, the composer's grasp of the current musical and lyrical vernacular of black American sounds is completely persuasive.

Discographical Details

27 Power Cuts: All Their Hottest Hits
Heatwave
Epic 468921-2 (UK)
Boogie Nights/Jitterbuggin'/Too Hot To Handle/Look After Love/The Big Guns/The Groove Line/Mind-Blowing Decisions/Always And Forever/Posin' Till Closin'/Razzle Dazzle/Lettin' It Loose/Gangsters Of The Groove

(iii) Here Comes Summer

In 1970 LaDonna Gaines (b. December 31, 1948, in Boston, Massachusetts) arrived in Munich after touring Europe in "Hair." Marriage had made her Mrs Donna Sommer. Meanwhile, to the west, vast Parisian clubs known as discotheques were blasting out thumping dance music. Their appeal spread to Germany, Italy, and elsewhere on the Continent, and to the States. In Munich, Sommer met producers/writers Giorgio Moroder, an Italian bassist busily investigating the synthesizer, and Pete Bellotte, a former guitarist with a less-than-successful British beat band, the Sinners. Remarkably, these three ostensibly moderate talents dominated the disco scene in the mid-1970s.

In the States, Isaac Hayes had already broken the three- and four-minute barrier by which black artists' album tracks and singles had long seemed bound, and Gloria Gaynor's version of the 1971 Jackson Five hit *Never Can Say Goodbye* (MGM, 1974) defined the early disco sound. But the giant maw of a night of dancing in the strobe-lit disco required bigger feasts. Moroder/Bellotte created 15-minute-plus tracks. Simple melodies and even simpler lyrics were cooed and breathed by Donna and teased out as though stretching unto infinity, all driven by a locomotive electronic beat propelled as much by the throb of the synthesizer as by the rhythm laid down by the drummer. "Soul" it was not, though it was populist art of a type Andy Warhol appreciated. But what it certainly was was an astute, clear-eyed, and well-crafted appreciation of a new market, and it sold accordingly.

The orgasmic moaning of the now renamed Summer on 1975's *Love To Love You Baby* (GTO; Casablanca in the USA) predictably offended some church elders and the BBC, which never hurts sales, and the discotheques played it and the dancers bought it, and pretty soon it was impossible to buy a 45 under 10 minutes long. I exaggerate, of course, but the impact was considerable. Rhythms took on a synthetic pulse which echo to this day. The late 1980s and early 1990s acid house and janglier techno sounds are rooted, subliminally but clearly so, in the later Moroder–Bellotte productions of Donna Summer.

Her best album as a cohesive piece of work is **I Remember Yesterday** (GTO/Casablanca, 1977), and the **Greatest Hits Of Donna Summer** (GTO, 1977) is the best summation of her work within the limited disco style; but the set which gives the best idea of her full range and what she attempted to do as she broke free of disco is a greatest hits collection, **On The Radio** (1979). It does not have the great thumping *Love's Unkind* and the tracks are a little short, but it contains her best vocal performances (sung ones, that is).

There were, of course, several other German disco producers whose time coincided with Moroder–Bellotte's success. Michael Kunze put together three girls as Silver Convention and had several hits on Magnet (UK), the best known of which was *Fly Robin Fly*. But Frank Farian was more successful in purely commercial terms for Hansa–Atlantic. Taking material – bits of arrangements or songs wholesale – from several decades and several continents, rather in the manner of a mad professor experimenting in a laboratory, Farian constructed trite and kitsch hits for Boney M (*Rivers Of Babylon, Rasputin*, and *Hooray Hooray, It's A Holiday*) and for Eruption (*I Can't Stand The Rain*) – best left alone.

Discographical Details

328   On The Radio: Greatest Hits Vols 1 and 2
Donna Summer

Casablanca 822558-2

On The Radio/Love To Love You Baby/Try Me, I Know We Can Make It/I Feel Love/Our Love/I Remember Yesterday/I Love You/Heaven Knows/Last Dance/

MacArthur Park/Hot Stuff/Bad Girls/Dim All The Lights/Sunset People/No More Tears (Enough Is Enough)/On The Radio (Long Version)

(iv) Missing Linx Found

The 1960s soul boom referred to earlier was partly fueled by black American GIs singing with white British musicians. In the 1950s, thousands of Caribbean nationals were encouraged to emigrate to Britain to work in the public services and industry of a country attempting to recover from World War II. The musicians among them tended towards jazz, calypso, bluebeat (a catch-all title named after a label started in Britain to satisfy the tastes of Caribbean immigrants living there), ska, and later reggae, although in the 1960s West Indians Jimmy James and the Vagabonds were Geno's great rivals. Nonetheless, if one saw a black British musician at any time through the 1970s it was almost inevitably in a reggae band or, much later, an African group.

For a time, soul became unfashionable in Britain outside of the fanatical base which always existed. That changed with the mature Motown albums of Marvin Gaye (**What's Goin' On** in 1971 and **Let's Get It On** in 1973) and Stevie Wonder (**Music Of My Mind** in 1972, **Talking Book** and **Innervisions** both in 1973, etc.). By the time the immigrants of the 1950s were supplanted by second and third generations, reggae itself was beginning to wane, and in the late 1970s its great mentor Bob Marley was looking to Africa for fresh musical input and inspiration.

Then Anglo-Caribbeans found a voice in the mainstream of popular music – quite suddenly, as it now seems, but in fact as the product of gradual progress. Although they were by no means the first, David Grant and Sketch, known as Linx, certainly produced the best records of the early 1980s. Londoners Grant, from Hackney, and Peter "Sketch" Martin, from Silvertown, began writing together in the late 1970s, pressed 1,000 copies of You're Lying and sold it through a specialist soul-record shop, and eventually signed with Chrysalis, a label not known for its understanding of black music. But catchy pop-soul songs, considerably and consistently more varied and attractive than those of their UK contemporaries, and bright production (with keyboard player Bob Carter co-producing) made the 1981 debut album, **Intuition**, a hit on both sides of the Atlantic. Like many other writers whose debut album contains the results of several years' accumulation, Linx were not able to sustain that level of composing. Grant has continued a solo career and in 1985 had a fairly successful duet with Jaki Graham on a remake of the Detroit Spinners' hit, Could It Be I'm Falling In Love.

Discographical Details

329 Intuition

Linx

Chrysalis CHR 1332 (UK)
Wonder What You're Doing Now/I Won't Forget/Intuition/There's Love/Rise And Shine/Throw Away The Key/Together We Can Shine/Count On Me/You're Lying/Don't Get In My Way

(v) Soul II Soul

The most recent benchmark set in British and European "soul" is the achievement of Jazzie B and the conglomeration of talents – deejays, singers, programmers, MCs, dancers, models – known as Soul II Soul. They (or it) evolved from a mobile sound system led by B, a.k.a. Beresford Romeo, which gained great popularity in London clubs from the middle of the 1980s onwards, expanding from a base in the Finsbury Park area of north London to become a substantial mini-industry which included shops and hit records. By the time their first records were released, Soul II Soul the sound system already had an enormous following, a ready-made market just waiting for the records.

The first album, called **Club Classics Vol. 1** in Britain, but renamed **Keep On Movin'** for North American consumption (after its first hit single), featured thunderous, bass-driven dance rhythms and some remarkably assured and mature vocals, notably by Caron Wheeler. But it was the no-nonsense productions which made the record's statement, and that was that advanced studio technology in the wrong hands is the enemy of soul. Records had become overproduced. Soul II Soul stripped them down to basics but did not ignore the tunes, the grooves.

In most respects, the artistic and fiscal aspirations of black Britons involved in the indigenous "soul" scene during the previous two decades came together in Jazzie B's group. The watchwords were fun, pride, and good tracks. Several careers were launched and considerable financial benefits gained, over which the artists kept as much control as anyone could in a venal industry. In Jazzie B the group had a "face" whose lack of shyness regarding publicity and whose understanding of how to work it provided both a focal point and a perfect sales pitch. Aged 26 when Soul II Soul had its first big international year (1989), B was quick with the quotable quote and the sellable slogan – "A happy face, a thumpin' bass, for a lovin' race" – and he had an image, the Funki Dred look – long dreadlocks tied up so that they sprouted from the top of his head – that set him apart from the many faceless purveyors of dance music in the late 1980s.

Discographical Details

330 Keep On Movin'
Soul II Soul

791267-2 Virgin Records America

Keep On Movin'/Fairplay/Holdin' On/Feeling Free/African Dance/Dance/Feel Free/ Happiness/Back To Life/Jazzie's Groove

Basic Recordings

331 Walking On Sunshine: The Very Best Of Eddy Grant
Eddy Grant

Parlophone CDP 7925622 (UK)

I Don't Wanna Dance/Gimme Hope Jo'anna/Electric Avenue/Living On The Frontline/Do You Feel My Love/Till I Can't Take No More/Walking On Sunshine/ Baby Come Back/Romancing The Stone/Can't Get Enough Of You/Harmless Piece Of Fun/Put A Hold On It

332 The Very Best Of Hot Chocolate
Hot Chocolate

EMI CDP 7463752 (UK)

It Started With A Kiss/So You Win Again/I Gave You My Heart (Didn't I)/No Doubt About It/Brother Louie/Tears On The Telephone/Chances/You Could've Been A Lady/Every One's A Winner/Girl Crazy/You Sexy Thing/I'll Put You Together Again/ Are You Getting Enough Happiness/Emma/What Kind Of Boy Are You Looking For (Girl)?/Heaven In The Back Seat Of My Cadillac/Disco Queen/Heartache No 9

Grant and Hot Chocolate's Erroll Brown are two somewhat extraordinary individualists whose successful careers have spanned decades and styles with equal distinction. Born in Guyana in 1948, Grant led the Equals, one of the first British inter-racial groups. The energetic, if trite, *Baby Come Back*, a number 1 hit in Britain in 1965 and a big hit in the USA, was followed by two other Grant-written hits, but in 1971 serious illness forced him to quit the group.

Meanwhile, Errol Brown, from Jamaica, formed a much underrated pop-writing team with Trinidadian Tony Wilson in the late 1960s. In 1970, they started recording as Hot Chocolate. Wilson left the group but Brown's later UK hits with them, such as *You Sexy Thing*, *Brother Louie*, and *Disco Queen*, crossed over to the American rhythm-and-blues charts as "soul" definitions broke down in the disco boom of the mid-1970s.

Grant had re-established himself as a producer/writer by the middle of the 1970s with his own label, Ice, and with new hits blending Caribbean roots and African influences with contemporary pop and funk stylings. By the end of the 1970s he was a solo star with **Living On The Front Line**, a success consolidated by 1982's **Killer On The Rampage**, which included *I Don't Wanna Dance* and *Electric Avenue*, a hit in the USA. At the moment, London-born Seal, sounding not unlike a young black Steve Winwood, seems set to adopt their mantle, though he is a far less confident live performer.

333   Greatest Hits
Billy Ocean

Jive BOCD1 (UK)

When The Going Gets Tough, The Tough Get Going/Licence To Chill/Caribbean Queen Calypso/There'll Be Sad Songs (To Make You Cry)/Loverboy/Suddenly/Get Outta My Dreams, Get Into My Car/Love Zone/Here's To You/I Sleep Much Better In Someone Else's Bed/The Colour Of Love/Calypso Crazy/Mystery Lady

Like Grant and Brown, Billy Ocean came from the West Indies (b. Leslie Sebastian Charles, January 21, 1950, in Trinidad). He was raised in London and enjoyed a career spanning more than one era of black British pop, but was patently more of a soul singer in that his phrasing, tone, and inflections were drawn from American models. In the late 1970s, he had a run of solid, thumping pop hits on GTO, starting with *Love Really Hurts Without You* and ending with *Red Light Spells Danger*. In the 1980s he moved to the Jive label and achieved even greater success with strong, confident singing on US chart-toppers such as *Caribbean Queen*, *When The Going Gets Tough* (used in and greatly helped by the film "The Jewel Of The Nile"), and *Get Outta My Dreams, Get Into My Car*.

334   Blue Eyed Soul
Biddu

Epic EPC80836 (UK) (LP)

Blue Eyed Soul/Black Magic Man/Aranjuez Mon Amour/Hot-Ice/Northern Dancer/ Summer Of "42"/Couldn't We Be Friends (Song For Su)/Exodus/You Don't Stand A Chance If You Can't Dance

Born in Bangalore, southern India, Biddu emigrated to Britain aged 21 and became an improbable if brief king of the poppier end of 1970s disco. He produced Carl Douglas's massive if sickly *Kung Fu Fighting* and two hits for Tina Charles (*I Love To Love*, and *Love Me Like A Lover*), and gave Jimmy James (see the section above on Geno Washington) his first hit in 11 years of recording. Also, he became something of a poor Brit cousin to Barry White with this album's mixture of swooping strings and disco beat.

335   A Golden Hour Of The Real Thing
Real Thing

Knight–PRT KGHCD 153 (UK)

Can't Get By Without You/Why, Oh Why (Oh Why)/Keep An Eye On Your Best Friend/Loving You Like A Dream/Flash/Young And Foolish/Topsy Turvy/You'll Never Know What You're Missing/You To Me Are Everything/Love Is Such A Wonderful Thing/Plastic Man/Lightning Strikes Again/I Wish You Well/Liverpool Medley: Liverpool 8, Children Of The Ghetto, Stanhope Street, Hallelujah Man

Real Thing (Chris Amoo, Ray Lake, Dave Smith, and Kenny Davis) hailed from Toxteth, Liverpool 8, the city's ghetto. Years of cabaret work ended in 1976 when they had pop hits and were joined by Chris Amoo's brother, Eddie, a veteran of the Chants, almost the only black group in the Merseybeat boom. Their best vinyl work was **4 From 8**, which explained their background while retaining an inherent pop appeal.

336 Pick Up The Pieces: The Best Of Average White Band

The Average White Band

Rhino/Atlantic R2 71054

Pick Up The Pieces/Person To Person/Got The Love/You Got It/Work To Do/Cut The Cake/If I Ever Lose This Heaven/School Boy Crush/Queen Of My Soul/Cloudy (live version)/*The Love Of Your Own/Soul Searching/I'm The One* (live version)/*Get It Up* (with Ben E. King)/*Your Love Is A Miracle/When Will You Be Mine/Let's Go 'Round Again/For You, For Love*

This excellent Scottish band, more often than not called simply AWB, played tight and light funk as well as any, and in bassist Alan Gorris and guitarist Hamish Stuart had two outstanding singers (other members: guitarist Onnie McIntyre, saxophonist Malcolm Duncan, keyboard-player Roger Ball, and drummer Robbie McIntosh, replaced upon his death in 1974 by Steve Ferrone). Here is all their best material, recorded on Atlantic from 1974 to 1979 and on Arista in 1980. The most notable cuts are *Pick Up The Pieces* and *Cut The Cake*. The collection also includes one of their outstanding cuts with Ben E. King, *Get It Up*, but the listener must search out the AWB/King collaboration, **Benny And Us** (Atlantic, 1977), to hear the gloriously incandescent *A Star In The Ghetto*.

337 Unreal

Bloodstone

Decca SKL 5156 (UK) (LP)

Outside Woman/What Did You Do To Me? Pts 1 & 2/Unreal/Everybody Needs Love/Something/Keep Our Own Thing Together/Let Me Ride/The Traffic Cop (Dance)/Moulded Oldies: Hound Dog, Searchin' So Fine

Because the States was awash with good vocal groups, many went uncherished in their own land and sought solace in Europe, as did Bloodstone, from Kansas City via Los Angeles, after rave reviews as support to Al Green on his 1972 tour. The group (Charles McCormick, Willis Draffen, Charles Love, Henry Williams, and Roger Durham) was fortunate in meeting Mike Vernon, a sympathetic UK producer steeped in black American music, who had produced many strong, blues-based albums. With a clutch of good UK session players (including keyboard-player Pete Wingfield, later of Olympic Runners and a solo hitmaker in his own right with *Eighteen With A Bullet*), Vernon provided fine sweet-soul settings for the 1973 USA Top Ten hit, *Natural High*, and this album's *Outside Woman*. On their return to US recording they never rediscovered the feeling, despite group member Charles McCormick's ability to write strong material. Sometimes, the grass really is greener on the other side.

338 Round Trip

Light Of The World

Ensign ENVY14 (UK) (LP)

Time/London Town/I Shot The Sheriff/I'm So Happy/More Of Myself/Visualise Yourself (And Your Mind)/Painted Lady/Pete's Crusade/I Walk The Streets Alone/Something For Nothing

Londoners LOTW were the first of the new wave of young black British funk bands to make an impact in the late 1970s. Alas, they lacked the sort of individual vocalist and ingenious writers who raise, say, a proficient American funk band out of the ordinary. But in Britain their breakthrough was a watershed for young black British musicians. They splintered into bands such as Beggar and Co and, particularly good, Incognito. This set, their second, includes the hit *London Town*.

339 Ji
Junior Giscombe
Mercury PHCR 1095 (Jap)

Mama Used To Say/Love Dies/Too Late/Is This Love/Let Me Know/Down Down/I Can't Help It/Darling You (Don't You Know)

Produced by Linx's Bob Carter, Giscombe's ebullient Brit-soul singing on the Stevie Wonder-styled *Mama Used To Say* was a UK hit and a number 2 US soul hit, and enabled him to become the first black Briton to appear on "Soul Train." Another hit, *Too Late*, also came from this LP, but Junior struggled, somewhat mysteriously, to follow up the success.

340 Level Best
Level 42
Polydor 841399-2 (UK)

Running In The Family/The Sun Goes Down/Something About You/Tracie/Starchild/ It's Over/Hot Water/Take Care Of Yourself/Heaven In My Hands/Children Say/Love Games/The Chinese Way/Leaving Me Now/Lessons In Love/Micro Kid/Take A Look/ To Be With You Again/The Chant Has Begun

Although later hits sold in greater quantities and they crossed over in a big way, Level 42 laid the foundations in 1981 with an eponymous Mike Vernon-produced, Brit-funk album which incuded *Love Games* and *Starchild*, both included here in this best-of collection. Dominated by bassist Mark King, Level 42's music became the epitome of commercial jazz-funk, British-style, its strong sense of rock enabling the group to sell worldwide.

341 Slipstream: The Best of British Jazz Funk
Various Artists
Beggars Banquet BEGA31 (UK) (2 LPs)

Light Of The World: *London Town*; UK Players: *Girl*; Shakatak: *Feels Like The Right Time*; Central Line: *You Know You Can Do It*; Morrissey Mullen: *Slipstream*; Hipnosis: *Shaping Up*; Freeez: *Southern Freeez*; Level 42: *Turn It On*; Inversions: *Locomoto*; Multivizion: *WTLDLTW*; Cayenne: *Roberto Who* (instrumental); Incognito: *Incognito*

This is a 1981 collection of a dozen tracks by most of the best bands of the period. Light funk content is predominant; the "jazz" quotient is negligible, Morrissey Mullen's title track aside. It is a varied and balanced selection which certainly ought to persuade the discerning listener to further investigate Shakatak, represented by the jauntily catchy *Feels Like The Right Time*, Incognito, and the aforementioned Morrissey Mullen. But a second double set a year later showed just how thin was the spread of talent.

342 Gold
Imagination
R & B/PRT RBLP 1006 (UK) (LP)

Flashback/Music And Lights/Body Talk/Changes/Looking At Midnight/Just An Illusion/Burnin' Up/In And Out Of Love/New Dimension/In The Heat Of The Night

Knowingly produced by Tony Swain and Steve Jolley, Imagination (vocalist Leee John, keyboard-player Ashley Ingram, and drummer Errol Kennedy) made convincing pop-soul records such as *Flashback* and *Body Talk*. Their surprisingly accomplished lead singer, Leee John, has taken his nice tone and good control to become one of Arthur Blake's Backbeat Disciples.

343 Luxury Of Life
Five Star
Tent/RCA PD70735 (UK)
Love Take Over/All Fall Down/Let Me Be The One/System Addict/Hide And Seek/ RSVP/Now I'm In Control/Say Goodbye/Crazy Winners

The "Jackson Five" of Romford, Essex, the Pearson family proved that a sure-fire way to success for aspiring British pop-soul acts was to mimic the most popular sounds from the USA. In Deniece Pearson, they had a good lead vocalist who could pass muster for not only Michael Jackson, but also Mary Davis of the SOS Band and the Howard Hewett–Jody Watley mix of Shalamar. Dad Buster, a musician who emigrated from Jamaica in the 1950s, managed them and signed them to his Tent label. **Luxury**, their debut album of 1985, had five hit singles. Things have never been quite so good since.

344 Look How Long
Loose Ends
Ten DIXCD94 (UK)
Look How Long/Don't You Ever (Try To Change Me)/Time Is Ticking/Love's Got Me/Don't Be A Fool/Cheap Talk/Love Controversy Pt 1/Try My Love/Hold Tight/I Don't Need Love/Symptoms Of Love

345 The Chimes
The Chimes
CBS 466481-2 (UK)
Love So Tender/Heaven/True Love/1-2-3/Underestimate/Love Comes To Mind/Don't Make Me Wait/Stronger Together/I Still Haven't Found What I'm Looking For/Stay/ I Still Haven't Found What I'm Looking For (Street Mix)/Heaven (Physical Mix)

346 Intervention
Lavine Hudson
Virgin V2529 (UK)
Intervention/Flesh Of My Flesh/Celebrate Salvation/Create In Me/Can't You See/ Material World/Learning How To Love/Prodigal Boy/Home/Does Jesus Care

347 UK Blak
Caron Wheeler
RCA PD 74751 (UK)

UK Blak/ Livin' In The Light (The Remix)/Blue (Is The Colour Of Pain)/No Regrets/ This Is Mine/Don't Quit/Never Lonely/Song For You/Somewhere/Enchanted/Proud/ Kama Yo

From the second half of the 1980s, there was a glorious flowering in Britain of young women singers, both in bands with men and as solo singers. Cases in point are, first, Carl McIntosh's Loose Ends. Commercially popular since 1985, by the time **Look How Long** was recorded in 1990 Carl had lost founding members Jayne Eugene and Steve Nichol and was using various singers like Linda Carriere and Sunay Suleyman. It is the tracks on which they sing or duet on that are the successes. Second, the focus of the Chimes is Pauline Henry's strong, impressive voice, which gives life to the synthetic sheen of the group's productions. Their eponymous album, including an adventurous soul reading of U2's *I Still Haven't Found What I'm Looking For* and a gorgeous first single, *Heaven*, was one of the best debuts of 1990. And then there is Lavine Hudson on **Intervention**. If the notion of a British soul singer once seemed odd, the thought of a UK gospel singer was positively outlandish; but Hudson, born and raised in south London, is as sanctified as any rumpus-raising, God-fearing, Baptist belter. Great power, splendid control, marvelous range – her voice has them all. Given better material and production she would be quite unbeatable, as would UK pop-gospel singer Mica Paris. Finally, Caron Wheeler, a graduate of a large number of sessions, including importantly some for Soul II Soul, was nothing if not ambitious in attempting **UK Blak**, an album that told the story of the arrival of West Indian imr.ligrants in Britain and their life there so far. It is a strong record whose aims and enterprise recall the scope of the pioneering works of Marvin Gaye and Stevie Wonder at the beginning of the 1970s.

348   Roads To Freedom
Young Disciples

Talkin' Loud 510 097-2 (UK)

Get Yourself Together, Pts 1 & 2/Apparently Nothin' (Soul River)/Funky Yeh Funki (Mek It)/Talkin' What I Feel/All I Have (In Dub)/Move On/As We Come (To Be)/ Step Right On (Dub)/Freedom Suite (i) Freedom, (ii) Wanting, (iii) To Be Free/ Young Disciples Theme

This release is a fine representative of a long, long line of febrile collaborations between black Americans (singer Carleen Anderson is the daughter of Vicki Anderson and Bobby Byrd, stalwarts both of many a James Brown band and record) and white Europeans, and it is one of several fine UK soul records put out by the Talkin' Loud label. The grooves are tight and spare, but it is Anderson's powerful voice that makes the record.

349   Dreamland
Black Box

deConstruction/BMG PD 74572 (UK)

Everybody Everybody/I Don't Know Anybody Else/Open Your Eyes/Fantasy/Dream-land/Ride On Time/Hold On/Ghost Box/Strike It Up

By no means as stylish as an Armani jacket or a Ferrari sports car, Italian dance music nonetheless usually takes the right style decisions – in short, keep the rhythm and arrangements simple and get a good, powerful and loud black voice out there in front where everyone can hear it. It is then hardly necessary to concern oneself with the tune. This was first perfected by Mauro Malavasi and

Jaques Fred Petrus, who constructed tracks in Bologna and sent them to New York, where Luther Vandross added his luster to *Searching* and *The Glow Of Love*, and Change had hits with them. Members of that operation lent their experience to Black Box, who are joined by Loleatta Holloway on the coruscating, if deafening, *Ride On Time*. Throughout **Dreamland**, Black Box reveal little knowledge of light and shade – they just provide a thumping beat and let the girl holler.

350   Paul Johnson
Paul Johnson

CBS 450640 2 (UK)

When Loves Comes Calling/Fear Of Falling/New Love/Every Kinda People/Intimate Friends/Burnin'/Heaven Is 10 Zillion Light Years Away/Are We Strong Enough/Half A World Away

Here, lastly, is the unquenchable, ineffable ability of the great ones to slip through the net. Johnson is a young British singer who came up through gospel with a breathtaking voice – soaringly so at the top of a big range – and in the middle of the 1980s dance boom released this "singer's" album with brave versions of Eddie Kendricks, Stevie Wonder, and Robert Palmer songs. It got great reviews and no sales, but the huge potential in his quite wonderful voice is palpable. It remains painfully unfulfilled by a patchy, nervous-going-on-desperate follow-up and subsequent drift from the spotlight.

Funk and Later Trends   10

Geoff Brown

This chapter covers some 25 years and the whole of the United States. The regionalization which informed the soul music described in previous chapters has now collapsed, by and large. With a few exceptions (Malaco, Ichiban), local independent record labels have disappeared and production has become concentrated in New York and Los Angeles. Moreover, "soul" as a style has splintered. Some off-shoots – like hip-hop and rap – are clearly new and vital forms of expression. Others seem to be the invention of record-company marketing departments and/or a compliant media anxious to be first with the latest "new thing." The breakdown of the old world of soul has been fully documented in Nelson George's *The Death of Rhythm and Blues.* So, what is this thing called funk?

"The music on the 1-and-3, the downbeat, in anticipation:" thus James Brown, "inventor" of funk as we know it in this chapter. Funk is a rhythm. The emphasis in each four-four bar is placed not on the second and fourth beats – the upbeats, the snare-drum beats – but on the first and third beats, the downbeats, the bass-drum beats. In his autobiography *The Godfather of Soul,* Brown describes his schooling of William "Bootsy" Collins, then bass player in the Pacesetters, who were about to become Brown's band. "When I met [Bootsy] he was playing a lot of bass – the ifs, the ands, and the buts. I got him to see the importance of the *one* in funk . . . I got him to key in on the dynamic parts of the one instead of playing all around it. Then he could do all his other stuff in the right places – *after* the one." All his other stuff, by the way, is the creation, with drummer, guitarist, and keyboard player, of a coruscating riot of polyrhythms.

George Clinton, Brown's most consistent funk disciple, raised "on the one" to a fine art. For instance, in *Give Up The Funk (Tear The Roof Off The Sucker)* the whole weight of his music falls purposefully and with a deafening, hip-twitching thud onto the first beat of the bar. The effect is to move the music's emphasis from the feet to the groin. And in strict musical terms, that is all there really is to know about funk. But now, a pause for some etymology.

Funk has come a long way. In the late seventeenth century, it used to mean strong-smelling tobacco smoke and probably came from the Flemish word *fonck*. In the early eighteenth century, if you had the funk you stank with fear. By the middle of the century, to be in a funk simply meant you were in a state of fear and/or cowardice: the stink was optional. In the twentieth century, to old Etonians, Harrovians, and the like, to funk something would be to make a mess of it, usually through fear. But funk continued to mean smelly and was appropriated by African Americans, as in funky socks, funky drawers. Then musicians took the word over to describe their dirtiest, earthiest playing. Of course, the fact that funk is but a letter away from the Anglo-Saxon for fornication was hugely in its favor – rock-and-roll and jazz are descriptions of music *and* copulation. And listening to the tough and urgent or slow and steamy, grinding funk of James Brown, George Clinton, or the Ohio Players at its lubricious best, it is often patently obvious that this is a soundtrack to something other than a vertical good time.

Meanwhile, back in soul music in the 1970s, nobody wanted to be left out. With a will, artists set about adapting funk to their own particular talents and needs. Jazz-funk, street-funk, and the funk suffix generally became a sought-after commercial accessory. Then disco, which is dealt with in chapter 9, enervated funk's polyrhythms and syncopations, supplanting them with a leaden, four-on-the-floor stomp as white acts invaded the rhythm-and-blues black charts in numbers for the first time.

Amoeba-like, funk reproduced itself in other forms. House in Chicago and go-go in Washington were street-level extemporizations on the funk formula. Also, there was rap. The spread of drum machines and other technical ephemera made the "democratization" of music a reality and also made for a greater percentage of genuinely ghastly records. Anyone could make a record and now they did not even need to sing; cussin' and hollerin' would do. After a while, this palled and melody entered rap. And, not before time, so did women. The sexism of early rap had long appalled and alienated potential customers. Interestingly, when asked to offer an opinion about the violence and sexism in rap during an interview on the British TV program "The Word," rock singer Sinead O'Connor demanded to know why she was not being asked about the violence and sexism in rock. Was it just because rappers were black? The question hardly needs answering, does it?

Although rap and hip-hop, music for the masses by the masses, rediscovered melody by the end of the 1980s, there had always been a parallel market for classy soul singers like Luther Vandross. Even his acolytes did very nicely banging away at increasingly formularized big ballads.

By the start of the 1990s one could postulate a sort of big bang theory of the evolution of soul. After funk, African American music expanded and exploded, the pieces settling into categories, though whether this was a natural process or a marketing convenience is debatable. These categories defined African American music in terms of a series of syntheses of styles (pop-soul, pop-gospel, rock-soul) or as a mild variation on a soulless dance music theme in which electronic bleeps and blips and a dull thudding four-four rhythm attempted to (1) generate artificial excitement and (2) camouflage the lack of a tune or a good singer to carry it. Remakes of classics of the 1960s and 1970s proliferated; polyrhythms meshed frantically, obliterating "the one" on which all funk should be based. The nemesis of rap and techno-dance records came in the shape of one hundred and one litigants, like James Brown and Jocelyn Brown, who were keen to know why parts of *their* records had been borrowed ("sampled"), usually without permission or payment, by producers and artists singularly lacking the natural talent to sing or play an instrument.

As I write, the prognosis set out in Nelson George's book has proven to be despairingly accurate. He hoped for a new birth of African American musical culture. White rock music can teach soul music very little other than in terms of packaging and marketing – and in one other respect. Whenever white rock musicians need revitalizing they return to African American music – blues, rhythm and blues, soul, jazz – and draw nourishment from it. A few great ones (Stevie Wonder, Prince) apart, African Americans in popular music appear reluctant to do this. They are always pushing on to the next phase; the past is dead. (The sampling one hears on records is rarely creative. Jazz musicians quote from one tune during a solo in another; here, though, the well-known riff seems to be used primarily for marketing purposes.) A pause for reflection about where they have come from and what that next phase might be could be no bad thing.

Essential Recordings

(i) Funk Genesis

In the beginning, there was James Brown (b. May 3, 1928, in Barnwell, South Carolina). From "Mr Dynamite" through "the

Hardest Working Man in Showbusiness," "Soul Brother Number One," and "the Godfather of Soul" to "the Minister of New Super Heavy Funk," Brown has earned every syllable of every soubriquet (though perhaps the last one is slightly hyperbolic). But great self-esteem is part of the man's character, and the character informed the music. Without such a confident, assertive, and dominant personality it is unlikely that Brown would have survived to see his thirtieth birthday, let alone grab control of his recording career at King Records and change the sound of black music in the 1960s.

Brown's career until the end of the 1950s is covered in chapter 1. In the early part of the 1960s, he remained in the vanguard of black music, stretching its rhythmic and emotional parameters, despite Syd Nathan, the doubting owner of King Records. *I'll Go Crazy* and *Think* (both 1960) were fiery numbers, the horn section scarcely able to catch its breath. *Night Train* (1962) is only slightly less frenetic, with Brown himself on drums. His ballads, like 1963's *Prisoner Of Love*, featured heart-wrenching performances. That year too, King released **Live At The Apollo**, the seminal on-stage album. Nathan's reluctance to release that album fueled Brown's dissatisfaction and, after moonlighting on Smash, recording *Out Of Sight* (1964) and *I Got You* (1965) (whose jerky arrangements and tight rhythm predicted later funk explorations), Brown's negotiations with Mercury failed and he returned, with a considerably stronger hand, to King.

With full artistic control, Brown recorded *Papa's Got A Brand New Bag* in February, 1965. It took no more than an hour but it fundamentally changed soul music and for the rest of the decade his contemporaries were scurrying to catch up. *Brand New Bag* was quite unlike anything else at the time – the scratched guitar licks of Jimmy Nolen, the clipped riffs of the horn section marshaled by Maceo Parker, the furious pace steadfastly set by drummer Melvin Parker (actually, the tape speed was increased on the final master), and Brown's aggressively enthusiastic singing (drawing on the call-and-response of gospel) meshed into a single swirling vortex of rhythm. Funk was born.

As in the late 1950s, when Brown's *Try Me* tapped into a specifically black market immune to the dulling influence of white rock-and-roll, so many of Brown's tougher recordings of the mid-1960s, such as *Ain't That A Groove, Pts 1 and 2* and *Money Won't Change You, Pts 1 and 2*, appealed primarily to the same market. The dulling effect of "crossover" was far distant, but on **Star Time** the *Pts 1 and 2* are presented as a cohesive whole. The effect of hearing Brown's grooves, previously fractured by the time limitations of the 45-r.p.m. single, is staggering, if only for the profoundly locomotive drive of the precision-engineering rhythm section.

Brown's "new bag" would also lead into sociopolitics (*Don't Be A Dropout, Say It Loud – I'm Black And I'm Proud, King Heroin*), predating rap by at least a decade, and to new dance grooves. Before most had absorbed the changes of *New Bag*, Brown cut *Cold Sweat*, a blistering 1967 track, which tightened the funk further. And in 1970, when his road band quit, he hired a young King Records band, the Pacesetters (see the introduction to this chapter), who would again invigorate his music. *Get Up (I Feel Like Being A) Sex Machine, Super Bad, Pts 1 & 2, Talkin' Loud & Sayin' Nothing, Get Up Get Into It and Get Involved*, and *Soul Power* all came from this fertile meeting of generations.

Others would later add sophistications but here is the root and stem of funk. Brown struggled to find a niche in disco, and had drug problems and a spell in jail. But his early recodings, like 1969's *Funky Drummer*, have been sampled *ad infinitum*, his 1960s stage shows formed a blueprint for soul revues, and every male soul, funk, rap, hip-hop, and dance-music artist owes him a big debt.

Discographical Details

351 Star Time

James Brown

Polydor 849 108-2 (4-disc set)

Please Please Please/Why Do You Do Me/Try Me/Tell Me What I Did Wrong/ Bewildered/Good Good Lovin'/I'll Go Crazy/I Know It's True/(Do The) Mashed Potatoes, Pt 1/Think/Baby, You're Right/Lost Someone/Night Train/I've Got Money/I Don't Mind (live)/*Prisoner Of Love/Devil's Den/Out Of The Blue/Out Of Sight/Grits/ Maybe The Last Time/It's A Man's World/I Got You/Papa's Got A Brand New Bag, Pts 1, 2 & 3/Papa's Got A Brand New Bag, Pt 1/I Got You (I Feel Good)/Ain't That A Groove/It's A Man's Man's Man's World/Money Won't Change You/Don't Be A Dropout/Bring It Up (Hipster's Avenue)/Let Yourself Go/Cold Sweat/Get It Together/I Can't Stand Myself (When You Touch Me), Pt 1/I Got The Feelin'/Licking Stick- Licking Stick/Say It Loud – I'm Black And I'm Proud, Pt 1/There Was A Time* (live)/*Give It Up Or Turnit A Loose/I Don't Want Nobody To Give Me Nothing (Open Up The Door I'll Get It Myself)/Mother Popcorn/Funky Drummer/Get Up (I Feel Like Being A) Sex Machine/Super Bad, Pts 1 & 2/Talkin' Loud And Sayin' Nothing/Get Up, Get Into It And Get Involved/Soul Power, Pts 1 & 2/Brother Rapp – Ain't It Funky Now* (live)/*Hot Pants, Pt 1/I'm A Greedy Man, Pt 1/Make It Funky, Pt 1/It's A New Day* (live)/*I Got Ants In My Pants/King Heroin/There It Is, Pt 1/Public Enemy No. 1, Pt 1/Get On The Good Foot/I Got A Bag Of My Own/ Doing It To Death/The Payback/Papa Don't Take No Mess, Pt 1/Stoned To The Bone, Pt 1/My Thang/Funky President (People It's Bad)/Hot (I Need To Be Loved, Loved, Loved)/Get Up Offa That Thing (Release The Pressure)/Body Heat, Pt 1/It's Too Funky In Here/Rapp Payback (Where Iz Moses), Pt 1/Unity, Pt 1* (with Afrika Bambaataa)

(ii) Sly: Slick and Wicked

Musically innovative, politically and culturally provocative, and a fundamental conjuror of good, good-time sounds with a kick in their lyrics, Sly Stone (b. Sylvester Stewart, March 15, 1944, in Dallas, Texas) was a former deejay and record producer – notable hit acts included Bobby Freeman and the Beau Brummels – who changed not only the face of funk but its body as well.

In the late 1960s, Sly's work was a combustible mixture of hard-driving funk rhythms, strong ensemble playing, and exultant singing, a joyful noise which illustrated the mixed-sex, multiracial unity of the band and captured the mood of the times (see chapter 8). Their *I Wanna Take You Higher* was no idle promise.

Then, in 1971, after wild acclaim by the white rock crowd at Woodstock in 1969, came **There's A Riot Goin' On**, a veritable "Citizen Kane" of an album whose scope comprehensively wrong-footed critics and, indeed, an entire industry. Yet **Riot**, unlike Orson Welles's movie, remains undervalued as a pivotal piece of work in the development of a form, *pace* Greil Marcus's illuminating essay on Sly in *Mystery Train*.

The album had been presaged by 1970's *Thank You Falettinme Be Mice Elf Agin*, which tempered the free-spirited nature of earlier hits with a more measured and more sombre mood, initiated by the unsteadily tumbling funk and Sly's brooding, almost schizophrenic vocal delivery. **Riot** moved this on, and more.

Funk that was once a boiling ferment became a darker, bubbling cauldron. The positive optimism of his previous work remains on the surface but one does not have to dip very far beneath it to find an extremely discouraging reality of black experience. The picture Sly presents is the total antithesis of almost all of his previous, upbeat work. The love-power and racial harmony that seemed so implicit in the philosophy of the late 1960s is revealed as a sham having little or no long-term impact on, meaning for, or relevance to African Americans.

Drugs shuffle and stumble through the record. In fact, they compounded Sly's later creative inertia; after the more upbeat **Fresh** (1973) and patchy **Small Talk** (1974), Sly's decline was rapid and, despite rescue attempts by many of the artists he influenced (notably George Clinton) has remained apparently irreversible. But no one using funk can claim to stand outside the influence of Sly Stone and his **Riot** which, at its essence, is a genuinely great *blues* album in a funk framework.

Discographical Details

352 There's A Riot Goin' On
Sly and the Family Stone
Edsel ED CD 165 (UK)
Luv n' Haight/Just Like A Baby/Poet/Family Affair/Africa Talks To You "The Asphalt Jungle"/There's A Riot Goin' On/Brave And Strong/(You Caught Me) Smilin'/Time/Spaced Cowboy/Runnin' Away/Thank You For Talkin' To Me Africa

(iii) It is a Parliafunkadelicment Thang!

To rephrase a well-known saying, "if George Clinton did not exist, you would *not* be able to invent him." Originally leader of an orthodox vocal group, the Parliaments, who had one big hit (*I Wanna (Testify)* on Revilot, 1967), Clinton (b. July 22, 1940, in Kannapolis, North Carolina – though, typically, reference books also place his birth in Blainfield, Ohio, and New York City) totally altered course in the late 1960s. He plugged into the funk of James Brown, into the black rock of Jimi Hendrix, and into the synthesis of those two styles with pop which Sly Stone had achieved. He added not only a bundle of adventurous images, consisting of a wildly off-the-wall mixture of street consciousness and sci-fi mythology, comic-book and cartoon characters, but also conversational philosophizing and a movable feast of similarly imaginative musicians who were able to interpret and add to the outpourings of his febrile mind. Not surprisingly, his career has been punctuated by brushes with despairing representatives of the many record labels to which his several outfits were signed.

First in Clinton's post-Parliaments career came mind-bent Funkadelic. Their early albums for Westbound – such as **Free Your Mind And Your Ass Will Follow** (1970), **Maggot Brain** (1971), and **America Eats Its Young** (1972) – mixed screaming, post-Hendrix, rock-guitar solos with thumpingly emphatic drumming behind some challenging (if occasionally nonsensical and incoherent) lyrics. The lyrics became more comprehensible as one learned the vocabulary – indeed, later Clinton works sometimes included a glossary of terms.

Before **America**, Clinton had added a younger rhythm section to Funkadelic, including William "Bootsy" Collins (bass), Phelps Collins (guitar), and Frank Waddy (drums), who had previously added youthful vigor to James Brown's band. With old hands Bernie Worrell (keyboards), Eddie Hazel and Gary Shider (guitars), and Tyrone Lampkin (drums), they formed a formidable, hard-playing, funk big band.

A dispute with Westbound pushed Clinton to reactivate Parliament, whom he signed to newly formed Casablanca. Their brand of funk, while reinforcing the required rhythmic imperative, gradually became more melodically accessible by dispensing with the long guitar solos, adding discreet but razor-sharp horn arrangements, building lyrics around catch phrases and chants ("get up for the downstroke," "tear the roof off the sucker," "shit, goddam, get offa your ass and jam," and so forth), and creating a story line and cast of characters like nothing to be found elsewhere in contemporary music. Three studio albums between 1975 and 1977 – **Mothership Connection, The Clones Of Dr Funkenstein**, and **Funkentelechy vs The Placebo Syndrome** – and the double **Parliament Live**, commemorating an extraordinarily spectacular, exhaustingly long P-funk tour, form a substantial body of work. The **Uncut: The Bomb** collection picks plums from the broad time-scale of P-funk, as his style was known.

With Parliament established, Clinton's empire, which he dubbed the Parliafunkadelicment Thang, now concentrated its musical and marketing efforts on revitalizing Funkadelic. Signed to Warner Brothers and mindful of the commercial lessons learned in Parliament, Clinton, Shider, and Walter "Junie" Morrison wrote *One Nation Under A Groove*, a blend of funk manifesto and anthem. Like the single, the album presents a more cogent Funkadelic while remaining fairly true to Clinton's aware, acute sloganizing ("think! It ain't illegal yet!") and previous, somewhat anarchic recordings. *Who Says A Funk Band Can't Play Rock?!* (the answer is MTV for one), for instance, turned the "can whites play blues" question on its head, tacitly made the point that rock via rock-and-roll is an extension of black music anyway, and actually posed a question Funkadelic had answered years before.

Although later Funkadelic albums had the by-now standard external trappings – vivid language and wacky visuals – they were musically less satisfying. Clinton's Uncle Jam label was not a glittering success, and his solo albums were patchy; but in 1989, aptly signed to Paisley Park, the label founded by Brown's, Sly's, and Clinton's funk successor Prince, George Clinton recorded **The Cinderella Story**, an underrated record.

In addition to Clinton's recordings, many of his Parliafunkadelicment troupe wrote and/or recorded, and he put together girl groups like Parlet and the Brides Of Funkenstein. But the most successful offshoot, commercially and artistically, was Bootsy's Rubber Band, fronted by bassist Bootsy Collins (b. 26 October, 1951, in Cincinnati, Ohio). Here was superficial silliness, kiddies' stories and punning gone mad and underpinned by gutsy funk, with the Horny Horns, a section led by Fred Wesley (trombone) and Maceo Parker (tenor and alto) and lured from James Brown, and a splendidly comic leader who seems to have learned the English language from Yogi Bear and other cartoon characters. **Ahh . . . The Name Is Bootsy, Baby!** exudes innocence and innuendo in the same breath, nursery-rhyme lyrics and schoolyard humor set to a rhythm track that moves hip and groin – subversive stuff, really.

Discographical Details

353   One Nation Under A Groove
Funkadelic

Warner Bros K56539 (LP)

One Nation Under A Groove/Groovallegiance/Who Says A Funk Band Can't Play Rock?!/Promentalshitbackwashpsychosis Enema Squad (The Doodoo Chasers)/Into You/Cholly (Funk Getting Ready To Roll!)/Lunchmeataphobia (Think! It Ain't Illegal Yet!)/PE Squad/Doodoo Chasers ("Going All The Way Off") (instrumental version)/Maggot Brain

354   Uncut Funk . . . The Bomb: Parliament's Greatest Hits
Parliament

Casablanca 842620-2

P Funk (Wants To Get Funked Up)/Give Up The Roof (Tear The Roof Off The Sucker)/Up For The Down Stroke/Chocolate City/The Big Bang Theory/Flashlight/Gloryhallastoopid (Pin The Tale On The Funky)/Aqua Boogie (a Psychoalphadiscobetabioaquadoloop)

355   Ahh . . . The Name Is Bootsy, Baby!
Bootsy's Rubber Band

Warner Bros 3629 (Jap)

Ahh . . . The Name Is Bootsy, Baby/The Pinocchio Theory/Rubber Duckie/Preview Side Too/What's A Telephone Bill?/Munchies For Your Love/Can't Stay Away/Reprise: We Want Bootsy

(iv) Keeping It In The Family

Or as an imaginary Isley song might be titled, *A Life In The Funk Lane, Pts 1 & 2.* Ronald (b. May 21, 1941), O'Kelly (b. December 25, 1937), and Rudolph (b. April 1, 1939) Isley from Cincinnati, Ohio, recorded some of the most exciting sides of the early, earthy, gospel-based soul; sounds like *Shout, Twist And Shout* and *Nobody But Me.* Then, at the end of the 1960s, they signed to Motown's Tamla label, where they again recorded vibrant, commercial, ecstatic music such as *This Old Heart Of Mine (Is Weak For You), I Guess I'll Always Love You,* and *Behind A Painted Smile.*

But at the end of the decade, as Sly Stone developed a dynamic "band" funk extending the boundaries of black and dance music, the Isleys, realizing they would never be a top priority at Berry Gordy's Motown family, looked to family of their own to facilitate a canny adjustment to the fast-changing scene. They brought in younger brothers Ernie (lead guitar) and Marvin (bass) and cousin Chris Jasper (keyboards) to give a weightier bottom to their music.

The vigorous, cutting vocal performances of Ronald mellowed; the younger musicians compensated through the energy and heft of Ernie's Hendrix-styled guitar (Jimi had been an Isleys sideman in the mid-1960s) and the Sly-slanted funk foundations laid by Marvin and Chris Jasper, aided considerably by the electronic music programming of Malcolm Cecil and Robert Margouleff, who also contributed to some of Stevie Wonder's best work.

At first, they cleverly mixed original songs with some of the more obviously attractive white-rock melodies – 1972's **Brother, Brother, Brother**, on their T-Neck label, included three Carole King songs rubbing shoulders with their own *Work To Do* and *Pop That Thang*. The success of the younger Isleys' induction was acknowledged in the title of **3 + 3 Featuring That Lady**, by which time the Isleys' choice of songs had veered even deeper into soft-rock country, teasing out unexpected passions in the lyrics. Their own writing combined love ballads with material addressing social and political issues on increasingly lengthy tracks divided into *"Pts 1 & 2,"* a technique derived from long funk vamps in the studio, parts of which were then edited for release. James Brown was *the* past master of it.

After **Live It Up** (1974), the Isleys concentrated on their own material, a direction which peaked with 1977's **Go For Your Guns**, wherein hard funk, sociopolitics, and love music combined in the most succinct statement yet of Isleyness. Nothing they recorded subsequently, despite good moments, is quite so sustained an achievement. The younger members split away, O'Kelly died in 1986, and Ronald recorded the solo album the music industry had been predicting for two decades.

Discographical Details

356 Go For Your Guns
Isley Brothers
Epic ZK 34432
The Pride, Pts 1 & 2/Footsteps In The Dark, Pts 1 & 2/Tell Me When You Need It Again, Pts 1 & 2/Climbin' Up The Ladder, Pts 1 & 2/Voyage to Atlantis/Livin' In The Life/Go For Your Guns

(v) The Wonder Of It

The music of Stevie Wonder's youth – if in musical terms he ever was young, which must be open to doubt – has been dealt with in chapter 4. The later work, over which he exercised immeasurably more creative autonomy, not unnaturally also provides us with a clearer, more accurate reflection of the scope of his talent as a writer, musician, singer, and producer.

When he turned 21 in 1971, Wonder was able to (1) gain control of the considerable royalties accrued during his teenage years, (2) get a lawyer and renegotiate a more favorable contract with Motown, and (3) break from the mold which the label had fashioned for him. The combination of these factors, allied to Wonder's considerably inquiring mind into matters musical, social, and political, *and* an ear for a commercial melody, led to the recording of a sequence of albums in the early 1970s which is still hard to fault for inventiveness and accessibility.

Starting with 1972's **Music Of My Mind**, on which he worked with synthesizer programmers Malcolm Cecil and Robert Margouleff, Wonder began to explore adult themes – world and American politics, social and racial issues – couching them all in attractive musical packages. It was an extraordinary outburst of creativity as **Talking Book** (1972), **Innervisions** (1973), and **Fulfillingness' First Finale** (1974) followed in quick succession. A near-fatal car crash in the summer of 1973 briefly interrupted the flow, but in retrospect merely highlighted how much material Wonder had put in the bank by then.

By 1976 Wonder had signed a generous new Motown contract as, as was only fitting, cut a generous new album, **Songs In The Key Of Life**, which was followed in 1980 by **Hotter Than July**, an exuberant collection which obliterated the memory of the failed, instrumental experiment of **Journey Through The Secret Life Of Plants** (1979). **Musiquarium** is a digest of these years, whisking us from the hard-funk commentaries of *Superstition, Living For The City*, and *Front Line*, through the love themes of *You Are The Sunshine Of My Life, Superwoman*, and *Ribbon In The Sky*, to exultant blasts like *Sir Duke* (his tribute to Ellington), *I Wish*, and *Higher Ground*. This is like no other fish tank you will ever come across.

Discographical Details

357 Stevie Wonder's Original Musiquarium 1
Stevie Wonder
Tamla TCD061113TD
Superstition/You Haven't Done Nothin'/Living For The City/Front Line/Superwoman (Where Were You When I Needed You)/Send One Your Love/You Are The Sunshine Of My Life/Ribbon In The Sky/Higher Ground/Sir Duke/Master Blaster (Jammin')/Boogie On Reggae Woman/That Girl/I Wish/Isn't She Lovely/Do I Do

(vi) Tres Chic

When disco of the late 1970s is discussed, it is traditional to throw brickbats at ridiculous groups like Village People and mourn the desperate lengths to which good soul singers went to get themselves a dance hit. And then there was Chic. No hollow name, the band oozed class both as musicians – the leaders Nile Rodgers (guitar; b. September, 19, 1952, in New York) and Bernard Edwards (bass; b. October 31, 1952, in Greenville, North Carolina) formed a rhythm section with drummer Tony Thompson which in its way was as adventurous and influential as James Brown – and as an image. Contrasting with the garish garb of the majority of disco acts, Chic donned smarter clothes, eventually graduating to classic-cut suits and *à la mode* casuals. But it was the music, not the image, which first and foremost made Chic's bag of tricks so different.

At bottom was the rhythmic mesh. Thompson's heavy, four-square drumming, Edwards's nimble bass lines, and Rodgers's chorded guitar phrases were frequently imitated but never duplicated, just like Jimmy Nolen's chicken-scratch patterns for James Brown in the 1960s. They hired Alfa Anderson and Luci Martin, singers whose reliable voices gave the dance cuts a no-frills topping, while breathier delivery added a wash of vocal color to the ballads. And they had clear, crisp production of the simply constructed Rodgers–Edwards originals, which graduated from the sophisticated dance chants of *Dance, Dance, Dance (Yowsah, Yowsah, Yowsah)* (1977) and *Le Freak* (1978) to danceable ballads like *I Want Your Love* (1979) and *My Forbidden Lover* (1979) – a style which clearly provided an early model for producers/writers Jimmy Jam and Terry Lewis, while even later the guitar riff and vocal refrain of *Good Times* (1979) were much sampled.

Their success soon brought demands to work with others, and the mix on **Freak Out** of Chic tracks with cuts that Rodgers and Edwards fashioned for Sister Sledge – particularly three 1979 hits, *He's The Greatest Dancer, Lost In Music,* and *We Are Family* – provides eminently durable examples of their work outside Chic. Indeed, the calls on their time proved damaging to Chic, and after the 1979 album **Risque** their output stagnated as their best work went into other artists' records, notably **Diana**, a 1980 album which remains one of Diana Ross's best solo works. After working singly with top rock acts like Madonna, Rod Stewart, Robert Palmer, and David Bowie, among many others, Rodgers and Edwards got together again as Chic in 1992 to record **Chicism**, an excellent comeback.

Discographical Details

358 **Freak Out**

Chic and Sister Sledge

Telstar TCD2319 (UK)

Chic: *Le Freak/I Want Your Love/Everybody Dance/My Forbidden Lover/Good Times/Dance, Dance, Dance (Yowsah, Yowsah, Yowsah)/My Feet Keep Dancing/*

Jack Le Freak (edit); Sister Sledge: *He's The Greatest Dancer/We Are Family* (remix)/*Thinking Of You/All American Girls/Lost In Music* (remix)/*Frankie/Mama Never Told Me/Got To Love Somebody*

(vii) Jacko

During 1982–3 that part of the world which buys records was gripped by a sort of collective mania – everyone had to have a copy of Michael Jackson's **Thriller**, otherwise they would be unable to join in normal conversation. Since then, the tabloid interest in the private life, physical transformations, and exotic menagerie of Wacko Jacko, as they dubbed him, has tended to obliterate discussion of his music, which in the light of **Bad** (1987) and **Dangerous** (1992) is perhaps a good thing. What the success of **Thriller** *definitely* meant was the subsequent undervaluing of its predecessor, **Off The Wall**, made in 1979 and in most ways a superior work.

Although during his time at Motown Jackson had recorded solo albums, he had little control over them. By the time he came to work with Quincy Jones on **Off The Wall** (they had earlier collaborated on the soundtrack for "The Wiz," a dreadful remake of "The Wizard Of Oz" which crunched Diana Ross's film career into reverse gear), Jackson was also writing, performing, and producing, with his brothers, two albums between which **Wall** was sandwiched. It is clear that he is the dominant creative force behind the other two albums, **Destiny** and **Triumph**. The shortcomings on them are expunged by Jones's sympathetic production on **Wall**, and Jackson succeeds with the blend of fierce, post-disco music (*Don't Stop 'Til You Get Enough, Working Day And Night, Burn This Disco Out*), slightly slower, easily flowing dance tunes (*Rock With You, Off The Wall, Get On The Floor*), and delightful ballads, like his achingly touching performance of Tom Bahler's *She's Out Of My Life* and the involvingly joyful *It's The Falling In Love*.

Here, the music has a natural flow and feel, conveying to the listener the sense of freedom and fun Jackson was experiencing. Its follow-up, the massive **Thriller**, seems by contrast a coldly calculating attempt to appeal to every market, cover all bases, and satisfy every possible consumer aspiration. One can almost *touch* the thinking behind each admittedly ingenious track. It became the blueprint for recording company marketing departments – "Do me a **Thriller**," became the demand of the 1980s, in much the same way that "Do me a **Sergeant Pepper** or *Tracks Of My Tears*" or "Get me a Dylan" were the call-signs of the 1960s. If they had listened to the music instead of looking at the balance sheet, they would have used **Off The Wall** as the master-plan. Jackson tried to keep things fresh by switching co-producers, using

Teddy Riley, king of new jack swing (see Bobby Brown in the "Basic Recordings" section) on **Dangerous**.

Discographical Details

359 Off The Wall
Michael Jackson

Epic EPC 83468
Don't Stop 'Til You Get Enough/Rock With You/Working Day And Night/Get On The Floor/Off The Wall/Girlfriend/She's Out Of My Life/I Can't Help It/It's The Falling In Love/Burn This Disco Out

(viii) Going To A-nother A Go-Go

Much of the appeal of funk is its groove. Once you are locked into it, the groove will take you anywhere you want to go. One can make a few adjustments to allay boredom, an accentuation here and there, but the beat goes on, like a seamless highway stretching way off up the gentle slope there to the horizon. There have been many variations on the theme of funk, of course, and many names for the variations. Chuck Brown (b. 1936, in North Carolina) thought of one in Washington, DC, in the late 1970s. He called the hard, insistently thudding grooves he and his Soul Searchers laid down for the DC dance marathons "go-go."

Brown's life story has a familiar ring to it – he was a hustler, and a thief, he did a stretch in jail, he boxed, he did odd jobs, and he sang. His rough, aggressive voice resounds with the struggle implicit in every hour of every day of that life. Singing, of course, brought redemption of sorts. With his band, the Soul Searchers, Brown evolved a style as demanding on its audiences' reserves of energy as it was on his band's stamina. The songs, or grooves, lasted 20 minutes or more, each one melding into the next until the end of the set. The beat would go-go on and on, never faltering, a mantric, metronomic, superheavy, funk rhythm track above which Brown would bark raps confidently, croon standards jazzily, and refer to gospel, blues, and cartoon ditties. All human life was there – everything *and* the kitchen sink. Although Brown made no bones about the Soul Searchers' function – they were a dance band, pure and simple – go-go certainly kept its audiences' minds, as well as their bodies, fully engaged.

After hits on Clarence Avant's Sussex label in the first half of the 1970s, the Soul Searchers, though still a hugely popular live draw, were without a recording deal for four years until Source signed them towards the end of the decade – and were immediately repaid by the 1978 hit *Bustin' Loose*, which really got go-go going. It was a hit seven years later in Britain, after Brown had broken through in 1984 with *We Need Some Money*.

The emphatic, unending, and unbending concentration on the groove implicit in go-go marks it as the link between funk and the myriad of dance-music styles which followed at various tempi – house and all of its sub-divisions, variations on the hip-hop theme, and on and on.

Discographical Details

360 **Another Way To Go?**
Chuck Brown and the Soul Searchers
Rhythm Attack RT 501-2
It Don't Mean A Thing/Midnight Sun/Moody's Mood/Wood Woodpecker/Here We Go Again/Harlem Nocturne/The Message/Run Joe/Stormy Monday/Family Affair/Do That Stuff/Go-Go Drug Free/Be Bumpin' Fresh

(ix) Small is Beautiful

The success of George Clinton's Parliafunkadelicment conglomeration and bands like Ohio Players, Earth Wind And Fire, and Larry Blackmon's Cameo led to a proliferation of large aggregations whose personnel were so numerous it was a major achievement in stage management that they did not continuously bump into each other. Although many of the self-contained funk bands at first thrived in the disco boom, demand for their services gradually declined, and finding gainful employment for up to a dozen musicians became arduous for group leaders. In addition to the pressures of economies of scale, changes in style and advances in sound technology meant that big horn sections were suddenly less than fashionable.

Cameo leader Larry Blackmon (b. May 24, 1956, in New York) was one of the first to successfully address the problem. At the start of the 1980s he reassessed Cameo and began ruthlessly pruning the 12-piece until there were just three left (Blackmon, Nathan Leftenant, and Tomi Jenkins). By doing so, he naturally changed the sound too. Always a tight funk band, the music, without losing its punch, became leaner and crisper. Although other bands, like Earth Wind And Fire, tried similar contraction, none fared half as well as Blackmon's trio.

Previously known for scorching funk dance tracks and lush ballads, Blackmon now gave Cameo a lighter touch which greatly enhanced their pop appeal. His quirky vocal delivery became part conversational, part conspiratorial, an altogether *unusual* sound – quite unique. Instrumentally, Cameo relied on the harder, metallic sounds of synthesized programs. Blackmon had formed his Atlanta Artists label and in 1983 *She's Strange* inaugurated the new, whittled-down, souped-up sound. But 1985's **Single Life** most fully defined Cameo mark II. A year later, **Word Up!**

brought further success, and it is certainly worth hearing; but almost everything Blackmon has tried since then has sounded lackluster and lacking in new ideas. The Club label edition of **Single Life** includes *She's Strange* as a bonus track.

Discographical Details

361 Single Life
Cameo
Club/Polygram 824 546-2 (UK)
Attack Me With Your Love/Single Life/I've Got Your Image/A Goodbye/She's Strange/I'll Never Look For Love/Urban Warrior/Little Boys – Dangerous Toys

(x) Crown Prince

Prince Nelson Rogers (b. June 7, 1960, in Minneapolis, Minnesota) is arguably by a considerable distance the most interesting writer, producer, and musician to have emerged in the past 15 years. Certainly nobody's work is awaited with such anticipation, and listened to with such care and admiration by his peers. His work has provided the standard against which all others are judged. As his music evolved, Prince pulled together most if not all of the contemporary popular styles – jazz, rock, gospel, blues, rhythm and blues, soul, and pop – and created a body of work not bettered in that time. Musically authoritative, his early writing was sexually highly charged. His lyrics have continued to be never less than challenging. If the scope of his work were not enough, critics were also confronted in the early part of his career with a somewhat androgynous image, fine in the white rock and pop markets but alien to the macho African American marketplace. His voice is not a particularly powerful tool but he has an ear for interesting phrasing that gets the maximum from his naturally gentle tone.

It says much for the volume and consistency of his writing and recording that two double albums stand as his best work. His 1982 album **1999** was a funky party on the eve of the apocalypse; but five years later, **Sign O' The Times** proved he had grown musically, and the sheer breadth of his work – from fiery rock to hard funk to lush ballads to perky pop – marks him as the 1980s and 1990s equivalent of Duke Ellington. In terms of vision and influence, he is simply that important.

In Minneapolis, he formed his own label, Paisley Park, and a mighty army of acts, from former band members Wendy and Lisa to the Time (whence came Morris Day and the Jimmy Jam–Terry Lewis production team), and elder artists like Mavis Staples and George Clinton either sprang from his sphere of influence or joined the label. He put together magnificent stage shows, too.

Discographical Details

362 Sign O' The Times
Prince

Paisley Park 7599 25577-2

Sign O' The Times/Play In The Sunshine/Housequake/The Ballad Of Dorothy Parker/ It/Starfish And Coffee/Slow Love/Hot Thing/Forever In My Life/U Got The Look/If I Was Your Girlfriend/Strange Relationship/I Could Never Take The Place Of Your Man/The Cross/It's Gonna Be A Beautiful Night/Adore

(xi) Luther's Lead

At the start of the 1980s, the black music scene had become exceptionally fragmented and most of the directions taken were leading away from the traditional vocal forms of "soul." Disco and the various dance sounds that followed relied increasingly on hard and shiny tones produced by electronic programming; rap, which was clearly no place for a good singer, was establishing itself as the hip noise from the streets. Vocalists, *per se*, were redundant. And then came Luther Vandross (b. April 20, 1951, in New York).

A busy session singer throughout the 1970s, Vandross built a reputation as a vocal arranger, which brought him work on David Bowie's **Young Americans** album and tour. He was also hired by the Italian producers of Change to add vocals to *Searching* and *The Glow Of Love*. Their success gave Vandross the chance to record under his own name, and in 1981 **Never Too Much** announced the return of the soul balladeer. With phrasing and taste acquired, according to Vandross, through a passion for the singing of women vocalists like Dionne Warwick and Diana Ross, with a fine tone, good range, and quite outstanding control, Vandross was simply head and shoulders above the competition – not that there was much of it left at that decade's start.

His distinctive arrangements and sympathetic performances of carefully selected cover versions – Warwick's *A House Is Not A Home*, Stevie Wonder's *Creepin'*, and The Temptations' *Since I Lost My Baby*, among others – claimed each song as his, while his own writing, often with longtime band members Marcus Miller (bass) or Nat Adderley Jr (keyboards), ranged from sophisticated ballads to fun dance tunes.

Critical acclaim of his first album opened the door for an army of sensitive male soul balladeers (Freddie Jackson and Alexander O'Neal in the vanguard), and even the rap labels, like Def Jam, re-evaluated by signing young and quite classy singers like Oran "Juice" Jones and Chuck Stanley. But Vandross's subsequent sets, such as **Forever, For Always, For Love** (1982), **Busy Body** (1983), and **The Night I Fell In Love** (1985), kept him comfortably ahead of the competition. By identifying and filling a niche in the soul market, Vandross formed the latest link in a chain of innovative and influential soul balladeers stretching back to Sam Cooke. The "love man" list goes on: Marvin Gaye – Al Green – Teddy Pendergrass – Luther Vandross. Bids for the next link remain open.

Discographical Details

363 The Best Of Luther Vandross: The Best Of Love

Luther Vandross

Epic 465801-2

Searching/The Glow Of Love/Never Too Much/If This World Were Mine/A House Is Not A Home/Bad Boy – Having A Party/Since I Lost My Baby/Promise Me/'Til My Baby Comes Home/If Only For One Night – Creepin'/Superstar – Until You Come Back To Me/Stop To Love/So Amazing/There's Nothing Better Than Love/Give Me The Reason/Any Love/I Really Didn't Mean It/Love Won't Let Me Wait/Treat You Right/Here And Now

(xii) Baker's Breakthrough

For every great male soul singer in the 1960s there was a woman every bit as popular and as good. But in the 1970s, their influence and ability to build lasting careers rarely fulfilled early promise. Not that one would call Stephanie Mills, Melba Moore, Phyllis Hyman, Angela Bofill, Patti Austin, or Randy Crawford, among others, "failures." But patchy material and production and ill-advised career moves frequently surrendered real artistic progress in favor of brief, voguish popularity. Culpable were the welter of superficial disco recordings, in which the voice was not the focus, and self-contained, male-dominated funk bands, a market in which only the all-women Klymaxx had any success (though bands like Rufus and Rose Royce were fronted by women singers).

And then there was Chapter 8 – not a vastly successful band, but they had a good writer/producer in Michael J. Powell, who kept in touch with one of the group's former singers, Anita Baker. Signed to Otis Smith's small but select Beverly Glen label, Baker cut a solo debut, **The Songstress** (1983), remarkable for its lack of concession to much else that was contemporary. It was a singer's album full of singer's songs, brimful of potential.

After several years spent extricating herself from the label, Baker signed to Elektra, which allowed her control as executive producer. With Powell, she immediately, or so it seemed, confirmed her potential with **Rapture** (1986). It is an album of carefully chosen songs and sensitively performed arrangements all in the service of the voice. On **Rapture**, this magnificent instrument combined a rich, warm tone, the sensual phrasing of a jazz singer, the confidence and free-spirited adventure of a gospel singer, and the commercial ear of a chart-oriented soul-ballad singer. Much of the album's success comes from the obvious pleasure Baker gets from her own voice. She quite genuinely *delights* in singing and you can hear it in every note.

Her follow-up, **Giving You The Best That I Got** (1988), again with Powell as producer, was less successful, her selection of material more fallible. **Rapture**, however, alerted record companies to a big gap in the market, and of the women ballad singers who have filled the void three are worth hearing. Oleta Adams most closely resembles Baker, and her **Circle Of One** (1990) is a lovely album; **Dianne Reeves** (1987) heralds a singer with roots deeper in jazz; and Regina Belle's voice on **All By Myself** (1987) comes from a more soulful home base.

Discographical Details

364 Rapture
Anita Baker
Elektra 960 444-2
Sweet Love/You Bring Me Joy/Caught Up In The Rapture/Been So Long/Mystery/No One In The World/Same Ole Love/Watch Your Step

(xiii) Rap To Basics

Rap, as Quincy Jones observed, is the only real new development in African American culture in the past two decades. Street-bred in the late 1970s, it became the underground music of the 1980s. It sold far more records through small indie labels than the charts suggested, and the major labels eventually succumbed to what they had imagined would be a passing fashion by buying up the labels or scouting and signing their own rap acts. Early pioneers like Kurtis Blow, Grandmaster Flash and The Furious Five, and Afrika Bambaataa kept the beats hard and strong and attempted to inject a degree of melodic modulation into their raps.

They were succeeded by ever more aggressive, noisily macho, gold-draped rapping crews such as Public Enemy, NWA, Big Daddy Kane, Ice-T, Ice Cube, Run-DMC, and LL Cool J. They were usually supported by scratchers, mixers, or deejays, who essentially performed much the same function. This was to provide "borrowed" beats – samples – from vinyl classics; which usually meant lifting a James Brown lick, uncredited and unaudited.

The random, unfocused anger in the raps often meant that they degenerated into incoherent rants which cried out for the ordered and logical arguments of Malcolm X, the Black Panthers, and the rappers' other sources of inspiration. But the best of them managed to harness their fury and, eschewing the absurb sexism in raps that dealt with emotional relationships, helped rap to properly voice the concerns of African Americans: lack of jobs, money, food, good housing, and equality of opportunity, and the tyranny of drugs.

It is hard to recommend just one album when there have been whole books devoted to rap, hip-hop, house, and the many other dance forms of the late 1980s, but deejay Eric B. and rapper Rakim catch the mood of rap without entirely dispensing with melody or a sense of humor. While MC Hammer had the biggest crossover hits, Louis Eric Barrier (a.k.a. Eric B., b. in Queens, New York) and William Griffin (a.k.a. Rakim, b. 1968, in Brooklyn) created one of the most listenable and involving rap records with 1986's **Paid In Full**. Rakim, nephew of the great rock-and-roll singer Ruth Brown, and Eric B., a guitarist and trumpeter, approached rap with a musical sensibility.

Although as a style rap is still in its infancy, the earliest records already seem dated in a way that, say, Motown or Stax sounds, which had catchy melodies and good singers, do not.

Discographical Details

365 Paid In Full

Eric B. and Rakim

4th & Broadway 162 444005 2

I Ain't No Joke/Eric B. Is On The Cut/My Melody/I Know You Got Soul/Move The Crowd/Paid In Full/As The Rhythm Goes On/Chinese Arithmetic/Eric B. Is President/ Extended Beat

Basic Recordings

366 Live At The Apollo Vol. 2

James Brown

Polydor 823001-2

Introduction/Think/I Want To Be Around/Thanks/That's Life/Kansas City/Let Yourself Go/There Was A Time/I Feel All Right/Cold Sweat/It May Be The Last Time/I Got You (I Feel Good)/Prisoner Of Love/Out Of Sight/Try Me/Bring It Up/It's A Man's Man's Man's World/Lost Someone (medley)/*Please Please Please*

Although already thoroughly represented in this book, one more James Brown in-performance recording demands inclusion in any examination of funk, but we will keep it brief. By the time the Godfather went into the famous Harlem theater for his second live recording, in June, 1967, his funk style had crystallized into a tougher, blacker, prouder sound. The band was, in the vernacular, "really cookin'"; the excitement crackles in the grooves. One single side of the original double LP which preceded the CD includes what is arguably his finest live performance committed to tape, as he powers from *Let Yourself Go* into *There Was A Time* and, via a brief, linking *I Feel All Right*, into a mesmerizing *Cold Sweat*, none of which should be missed.

367   The Best Of Isaac Hayes
Isaac Hayes

Stax FCD 60-002

Never Can Say Goodbye/The Look Of Love/The Theme From "The Men"/Joy/Let's Stay Together/Ike's Mood/By The Time I Get To Phoenix

Until 1969, Isaac Hayes (b. August 6, 1938, in Covington, Texas) had been best known as a writer of Stax hits, mostly co-written with David Porter. Then he used spare studio time to record long, lushly orchestrated, but rhythmically forceful tracks over which he crooned in a deep, dark growl. **Hot Buttered Soul** (1969) set a benchmark for 1970s soul and heralded the big productions of Barry White. Two years later, Hayes wrote the Oscar-winning soundtrack to "Shaft," but soon after, Stax's impending bankruptcy sent Hayes's career into a tailspin from which it never wholly recovered. This collection, although oddly partial, features enough of his trademarks to satisfy the curious.

368   Gold
Ohio Players

Mercury 824 461-2

Feel The Beat (Everybody Disco)/Love Rollercoaster/I Want To Be Free/Fopp/Far East Mississippi/Skin Tight/Fire/Sweet Sticky Thing/Jive Turkey, Pt 1/Only A Child Can Love/Who'd She Coo?

Leroy "Sugar" Bonner has one of the most distinctive voices in any of the big aggregations which dominated the late 1960s and early 1970s funk scene. The prime earthy funk of the Players – formerly backing band to Wilson Pickett's Falcons – couched lyrics dripping with sexual innuendo (thanks to Bonner's lubricious tone) in thumping, danceable rhythms, as in *Fire* (1974), *Skin Tight* (1974), and *Sweet Sticky Thing* (1975). The down-and-dirty message was unsubtly hammered home by album sleeves at first featuring leather, domination, and bondage images, replaced later by, among other things, hoses, horses, honey pots, and hair dryers, all modeled by virtually naked women.

369   Twice As Kool
Kool and the Gang

De-Lite PROLP-2

Ladies' Night/Big Fun/Celebration/Take It To The Top/Summer Madness/Open Sesame/Steppin' Out/Night People/Street Kids/Ooh La, La, La (Let's Go Disco Dancin')/Get Down On It/Funky Stuff/Hollywood Swinging/Jones Vs Jones/Too Hot/Take My Heart (You Can Have It If You Want It)/Hangin' Out

Originally sharp, jazz-based practitioners of street-funk with a bristling horn section and no-nonsense rhythm players, bassist Robert "Kool" Bell and his Gang necessarily reinvented themselves after realizing the limitations of their chant-based vocals – *Funky Stuff* (1973) and *Hollywood Swinging* (1974). It would be nice, however, to have available a larger collection that could include some more of the chanting hits, notably *Jungle Boogie* (1973), *Higher Plane* (1974), and *Spirit Of The Boogie*. At the end of the 1970s, they hired singer James "JT" Taylor, who could carry a tune, and with co-producer Eumir Deodata completely refashioned their style, with a greater emphasis on pop melodies and using lighter, though still danceable, rhythms. Street-funk forsook chants for tunes, notably *Ladies Night* (1979), *Celebration* (1980), and *Joanna* (1983). The latter style dominates this hits collection.

370 Now Do-U-Wanta Dance
Graham Central Station
Warner Bros BS 3041

Happ-E-2-C-U-A-Gin/Now Do-U-Wanta Dance/Last Train/Love And Happiness/ Earthquake/Crazy Chicken/Stomped Beat-Up And Whooped/Lead Me On/Saving My Love For You/Have Faith In Me

Bassist Larry Graham (b. August 14, 1946, in Beaumont, Texas) was the only graduate of Sly's pioneering Family Stone school of funk to make anything other than a session musician of himself. Possessed of a deep, dark, rich voice and hard-driving band, Graham had recorded four albums before this thumping, riotous party-piece of work in 1977. The Station's jaunty style put the funk back into funky. The first seven tracks give an enormous blast of adrenalin funk; but Larry later found God and the funk became rather apologetic.

371 I Am
Earth, Wind And Fire
CBS 86084-2

In The Stone/Can't Let Go/After The Love Is Gone/Let Your Feelings Show/Boogie Wonderland/Star/Wait/Rock That!/You And I

Led by Maurice White, former drummer with jazz group the Ramsey Lewis Trio, Earth, Wind and Fire, a Chicago band transplanted to California, raised early 1970s, horn-heavy, earthy, street-funk to a stylish high with a blistering horn section, crisp and tight rhythm players, and enormous vocal breadth, courtesy of White and Philip Bailey. Hits collections exist, but White's superb musicians, in line with 1970s rock bands, conceived albums as entities and not sets of disparate songs. Their 1979 **I Am** contains their most consistent writing and playing. If sequenced in almost any other order, the tracks would not work so well. Here is cohesive thought and planning. Here also is more of White's mystical interest in Egyptology and other spooky stuff.

372 IV
Gap Band
Total Experience MERS 6

Early In The Morning/Season's No Reason To Change/Lonely Like Me/Outstanding/ Stay With Me/You Dropped A Bomb On Me/I Can't Get Over You/Talkin' Back

After Earth, Wind and Fire's Egyptology, here we have Roman numerals. Several funk bands evinced an obsession with them, notably Brooklyn's Brass Construction and Oklahoma's Gap Band, formed by Charlie, Ronnie, and Robert Wilson of Tulsa. By now, street-funk had lost all connection with jazz and looked to rock, pop, and a synthesis of contemporary sounds. Lead singer Charlie sounds not unlike Stevie Wonder, particularly at the top of his range. Gap had already had solid hits – *Burn Rubber On Me (Why You Wanna Hurt Me)* (1980), *I Don't Believe You Want To Get Up And Dance (Oop!)*, a.k.a. *Oops! Upside Your Head* (1981) – when **IV**, from 1982, defined their now much-covered and sampled mix of funk, pop, dance, and rock-ballads.

373   Golden Classics Featuring Movin'
Brass Construction

Collectables Col–5239

Movin'/Right Place/The Message (Inspiration)/What's On Your Mind (Expression)/ Never Had A Girl/Changin'/Ha Cha Cha (Funktion)/Can You See The Light/Party Line/Walkin' By The River/Help Yourself/L-O-V-E-U

In the Mid-1970s, producer Jeff Lane had the touch. His main protege was Randy Muller, whose 9-member band Brass Construction recorded strong, heavy funk with jazz, reggae, and calypso feels befitting the nonet's roots in Guyana, Trinidad, and Jamaica. Muller had spent some time in a steel band in the West Indies. This collection covers Construction's biggest hits for the United Artists label, notably *Movin'* and *Changin'* from 1976. The songs were from the band's eponymous debut album, which was a hit first in Britain, and is their most cohesive and consistent work, the concision of the song titles matching the locked-tight playing. Notable later hits in this package are *Ha Cha Cha (Funktion)* (1977), *L-O-V-E-U* (1978), and *Can You See The Light* (1982). Muller also produced soul veteran Garnet Mimms and funk band Skyy and worked with rap acts.

374   Express — Golden Classics
B.T. Express

Collectables Col – 5190

Express/If It Don't Turn You On (You Oughta To Leave It Alone)/Once You Get It/ Everything Good To You (Ain't Always Good For You)/Metal Telepathy/Do It ('Til You're Satisfied)/Do You Like It/That's What I Want For You Baby/This House Is Smokin'/Peace Pipe/Give It What You Got/Close To You

B.T. Express was another discovery of producer Jeff Lane. The group was formed in Brooklyn in 1972 as the King Davis House Rockers, and the name evolved to Madison Street Express, to Brooklyn Trucking Express, to the concise B.T. Express. Members were Bill Risbrook (sax), Carlos Ward (flute), Michael Jones (keyboards), Richard Thompson (guitar and vocals), Louis Risbrook (bass, organ, and vocals), Dennis Rowe (percussion), and Leslie Ming (drums). This collection covers their best work for Scepter and Roadshow during 1974-6, notably their giant hits *Do It ('Til You're Satisfied)*, *Express*, and *Give It What You Got*.

375   Fatback's Greatest Hits
The Fatback Band

Spring 33-6745 (LP)

Wicky Wacky/Yum Yum (Gimme Some)/(Are You Ready) Do The Bus Stop/Spanish Hustle/The Booty/I Like Girls/Backstrokin'/Is This The Failure?/The Girl Is Fine (So Fine)/I Found Lovin'

Funk is a fat sound and it is only right and proper that one of its most reliable and prolific practitioners in the 1970s should have been the Fatback Band. An East Coast sextet grounded by the profoundly solid drumming of leader Bill Curtis, they produced a consistent series of hits and showed a remarkable capacity to go with the flow of dance crazes. Initially locked in to street funk (*Street Dance* and *Nija Walk (Street Walk)*, both 1973), their albums revealed a band first incorporating jazzier phrasing into street-funk (1974's **Keep On Steppin'** and

1975's **Yum Yum**) before biting the bullet and moving into full-time disco with tracks like *(Are You Ready) Do The Bus Stop, Spanish Hustle*, and *Party Time* (all 1975), and *Double Dutch, Spank The Baby*, and *Duke Walk* (all 1977), the last four unfortunately not on this collection.

376   Best Of Johnny "Guitar" Watson
Johnny Guitar Watson

DJM 825364-2 (Ger)

Gangster Of Love/Booty Ooty/Ain't That A Bitch/Love Jones/What the Hell Is This?/ It's About The Dollar Bill/Ain't Movin'/I Need It/A Real Mother For Ya/Strung Out

A Texan blues guitarist, Watson (b. February 3, 1935, in Houston) boasted a long and varied career beginning in the early 1950s before venturing into funky waters in the 1970s. He first signed with Fantasy and cut the excellent **I Don't Want To Be A Lone Stranger**, which included the 1975 hit *I Don't Want To Be A Lone Stranger*. Next, and somewhat extraordinarily, he signed to Dick James's British DJM label and wrote, arranged and produced the more determinedly commercial **Ain't That A Bitch** album, from which *I Need It* and *Superman Lover* were 1976 hits. A second successful DJM album, **A Real Mutha For Ya**, consolidated his position, producing the Top 5 hit, *A Real Mother For Ya* in 1977. After more than two decades as a recording artist, funk had finally made Watson a star. His last successful album was **Love Jones**, which produced the 1980 title hit single. By 1984, Watson was off the charts and a one-time star.

377   Street Songs
Rick James

Gordy G8 1002M1

Give It To Me Baby/Ghetto Life/Make Love To Me/Mr Policeman/Super Freak/Fire And Desire/Call Me Up/Below The Funk (Pass The J)

This is an example of Motown as a reactive rather than active label. Rick James (b. James Johnson, February 1, 1952, in Buffalo) was signed in 1978 to give the label a much-needed foothold in the raunchier funk market. He did not disappoint them with hits like *Mary Jane* (1978) and *You And I* (1978) from his debut album. But this, his fifth set – like the rest it is written, arranged, and produced by James – presented a wilder, wider, lustier, tougher picture of the ghetto. The raunchy, life-on-the-road epic *Super Freak* (1981) was so accurate that mega-successful rapper MC Hammer sampled it for his hit *You Can't Touch This*. James recorded several more sets of his self-styled punk-funk but was never as pointed and punchy or more salacious. He was a blend of Bootsy, minus the cartoon humor, with the Ohio Players' "Sugar" Bonner on Spanish fly, and a lot more besides.

378   Rags To Rufus
Rufus featuring Chaka Khan

MCA MCAD 31365

You Got The Love/I Got The Right Street/Walkin' In The Sun/Rags To Rufus/Swing Down Chariot/Sideways/Ain't Nothin' But A Maybe/Tell Me Something Good/Look Through My Eyes/In Love We Grow/Smokin' Room

When she exploded on the scene with the accomplished Rufus, Chaka Khan (b. Yvette Marie Stevens, March 23, 1953, in Great Lakes Naval Training Center,

Illinois) sounded like Aretha's soul child, a testifying blues shouter of a singer with a lower register that dripped honey. She fronted Rufus for five years, during which time hits like *Tell Me Something Good* (1974), written for her by Stevie Wonder, established her talent. Although she subsequently made some interesting if patchy solo albums – **What Cha Gonna Do For Me** (Warner Brothers, 1981) being the pick – arguably her freshest work was done on this 1974 set.

379 Caught Up
Millie Jackson
Southbound CDSEW 003 (UK)

If Loving You Is Wrong I Don't Want To Be Right/The Rap/If Loving You Is Wrong I Don't Want To Be Right (reprise)/All I Want Is A Fighting Chance/I'm Tired Of Hiding/It's All Over But The Shouting/It's Easy Going/I'm Through Trying To Prove My Love To You/Summer (The First Time)

Long before "rap" signified an African American street style, it referred to a spoken preamble or interlude in a soul ballad, and Millie Jackson (b. July 15, 1944, in Thompson, Georgia) was the mother of them. Using rap sparingly but to great effect on a three-album sequence – the one here from 1974, plus **Still Caught Up** (1975) and **Free And In Love** (1976) – Jackson told a convincing story of a three-way love affair, a staple of the Southern soul diet. It is recounted in coruscating, emotion-wringing performances from the points of view of both mistress and wife. Latterly, Jackson has become known for cursing and cussing her way through shows, much like a "rap" artist.

380 Look Out For No. 1
Brothers Johnson
A & M AMLH 64567

I'll Be Good To You/Thunder Thumbs And Lightnin' Licks/Get The Funk Out Ma Face/Tomorrow/Free And Single/Come Together/Land Of Ladies/Dancin' And Prancin'/The Devil

Los Angeles-born child prodigies, the Johnson Brothers George (guitar; b. May 17, 1953) and Louis (bass; b. April 13, 1955) became part of Quincy Jones's team, recording his **Mellow Madness** (1975) album before releasing this skilled debut a year later. As one would expect from a Jones "discovery" (they had actually been around for years), the funk is light on its feet and melodic on the ear. The brothers' writing and instrumental strength were always more impressive than their singing, which was not merely delicate but genuinely fragile. Nonetheless, their early work had energy and spark which, sadly, was spent rather quickly.

381 The Best Of War . . . And More
War
Avenue R2 70072

Livin' In The Red/Low Rider/The Cisco Kid/Slippin' Into Darkness/Me And Baby Brother/Galaxy/Spill The Wine/All Day Music/Can't We Be Friends?/Summer/City Country City/Whose Cadillac Is That?/Low Rider (remix)

War's street-funk was heavily spiced with Latin percussion and most usually taken at a gentle, insistent, mid-tempo lope, as though they were ready to sit in the groove all night, which on stage they often seemed to. A genuine band, in that none of the players seemed exceptional but everyone knew their strengths and wrote for and played to them accordingly, War's best tracks came in a rush in the early 1970s with *All Day Music, Slippin' Into Darkness,* and *Baby Brother* (all 1971), and *The Cisco Kid* and *The World Is A Ghetto* (1972), the last of these not included here. After the 1973 album **Deliver The Word**, only *Low Rider* was genuinely memorable.

382 Headhunters
Herbie Hancock
CBS CK 32731
Chameleon/Watermelon Man/Sly/Vein Melter

A gifted pianist who came to prominence with the Miles Davis Quintet in the 1960s, Hancock pioneered jazz-funk with this 1973 set. Drummer Harvey Mason's rearrangement of Hancock's standard *Watermelon Man* placed the emphasis firmly on Paul Jackson's bass, boosted by extra bottom from the leader's keyboards. Jazz purists were, of course, appalled, crying "sell-out!" But **Headhunter's** commercial success started a stampede of jazz stars into funk and rock formats. Hancock shrewdly balanced new and old styles. The former led him into, horror of horrors, *singing*, with his voice artificially enhanced with a vocoder, on the 1978 pop hit *I Thought It Was You* and *You Bet Your Love* a year later.

383 Native New Yorker–Golden Classics
Odyssey
Collectables Col-8500
Native New Yorker (12" version)/*Weekend Lover* (12" version)/*Don't Tell Me, Tell Her/Going Back To My Roots/Inside Out* (12" version)/*Together* (12" version)/*Easy Come, Easy Go–Hold De Mota Down* (12" version)/*I Got The Melody/Hold On To Love*

By the late 1970s, the rougher edges of funk were being smoothed by disco writers, producers, and singers. Sylvester, produced by doo-wop and Motown veteran Harvey Fuqua, epitomized the gay scene's input with his hits *Dance (Disco Heat)* (1978) and *(You Make Me Feel) Mighty Real* (1979), while Odyssey and producer/writer Sandy Linzer opted for a more cosmopolitan sound to render sophisticated-sounding disco hits. The appeal of Odyssey relies largely on the leads of Louise and Lillian Lopez, whose engaging vocals helped make the delicious *Native New Yorker* a Big Apple Anthem in 1977. Other hits include *Weekend Lover* (1978) and *Inside Out* (1982), the latter their last chart hit. An unfortunate omission is the delightful ballad *If You're Lookin' For A Way Out*.

384 Street Life
The Crusaders
MCA MCF 3008
Street Life/My Lady/Rodeo Drive (High Steppin')/Carnival Of The Night/The Hustler/Night Faces

We have frequently referred to the influence of jazz on the development of funk. In the late 1970s jazz musicians cashed in their chips, as Miles Davis, Herbie Hancock, Chick Corea, and many others cut commercial dance records. Stix

Hooper's implacable drumming gave the Crusaders (formerly the Jazz Crusaders) a better start than most, laying a funky, down-home backbeat behind the lyrical playing of Joe Sample (piano) and saxophonist Wilton Felder. By 1979 the appeal of wordless songs had reached its limit. They found an exquisite, warm voice in Randy Crawford, and *Street Life* became a sizable hit, which benefited both parties. Hear, too, Crawford's **Now We May Begin** (Warner Bros, 1980), produced by the Crusaders and including her beautiful ballad singing on *One Day I'll Fly Away*.

385   Live In New Orleans
Maze featuring Frankie Beverly

Capitol SKBK 12156 (UK)

You/Changing Times/Joy And Pain/Happy Feelin's/Southern Girl/Look At California/ Feel That You're Feelin'/The Look In Your Eyes/Running Away/Before I Let Go/We Need Love To Live/Reason

Maze was arguably the last of the self-contained bands to exercise autonomy over material and production before outfits became a producer's tool or marketing department's invention. Nonetheless, the band came to symbolize one man's dream. Though they were from Philadelphia, Frankie Beverly's best writing and Maze's best playing was Los Angeles cool. Relaxed almost to the point of being spaced out, Maze were funky but gently so, sunny and supremely optimistic, with Beverly's light, hoarse, but honeyed voice the focus. This first live set includes most of the best material from **Maze Featuring Frankie Beverly, Golden Time Of Day, Inspiration** and **Joy And Pain**, their early studio albums.

386   The Best Of Gil Scott-Heron
Gil Scott-Heron

Arista 206 618 620 (UK)

The Revolution Will Not Be Televised/The Bottle/Winter In America/Johannesburg/ Ain't No Such Thing As Superman/Re-Ron/Shut 'Um Down/Angel Dust/"B" Movie

Long before rap, artists like the Last Poets and Gil Scott-Heron (b. April 1, 1949, in Chicago) were addressing political and social issues head-on or in thinly veiled metaphors or satires. Scott-Heron did so the more musically, making assimilation of the message, delivered in a rich and casual drawl, much simpler. Apartheid, drugs, and nuclear energy are among the targets accurately and ruthlessly savaged here. But perhaps *Winter In America, Ain't No Such Thing As Superman*, and *The Revolution Will Not Be Televised*, which dissect the very soul of America, make the deepest cuts.

387   Just The Way You Like It
SOS Band

Tabu FZ 39332

No One's Gonna Love You/Weekend Girl/Just The Way You Like It/Break Up/ Feeling/I Don't Want Nobody Else/Body Break

Fueled by producer-dominated disco, studio technicians held sway in the 1980s. They had done so at Motown in the 1960s and at Philadelphia International in the early 1970s, but now most artists had less personality or individuality. The best Motown producers and writers had also been good singers or musicians. So it was in the 1980s when Jimmy Jam and Terry Lewis, formerly of Minneapolis's

The Time, formed Flyte Tyme Productions and wrote and/or produced a series of seamless ballads and punchy dance songs for Janet Jackson, Alexander O'Neal, and others. But the finest vehicle they had was the voice of SOS's Mary Davis, at its best here. As with Motown, few acts fared well away from the Jam–Lewis factory.

388   Don't Be Cruel
Bobby Brown
MCA DMCF 3425

Cruel Prelude/Don't Be Cruel/My Prerogative/Roni/Rock Wit'cha/Every Little Step/I'll Be Good To You/Take It Slow/All Day All Night/I Really Love You Girl/Cruel Reprise

After Jimmy Jam and Terry Lewis, one of the hottest producing teams was Babyface and LA. Their acts regularly competed on the charts with those of producer Teddy Riley, the originator of New Jack Swing (a 1990s cocktail of funk and hip-hop, with rhythm predominant). It was Riley's production of Keith Sweat's *Make It Last Forever* that served as a blueprint for the new jack swing style, and Sweat is clearly a better singer than Brown, but Babyface and LA, in their production of the former teen idol from the New Edition, have apparently lifted the crown from Riley as the king of new jack swing. Brown possesses the energy and determination that trembles on every swinging beat of LA and Babyface's production here. Also, investigate Riley's group, Guy, on **Guy, The Future**.

389   It's Your Night
James Ingram
Qwest 92-3970-2

Party Animal/Yah Mo Be There/She Loves Me (The Best That I Can Be)/Try Your Love Again/Whatever We Imagine/One More Rhythm/There's No Easy Way/It's Your Night/How Do You Keep The Music Playing?

Back in what might be termed soul's mainstream, the current of gospel, one of the fonts of African American music, had never been far from the surface, and it bubbled up vigorously in the 1980s. Soon, every album on the black or rhythm-and-blues chart was dedicated to the Almighty and had, so it seemed, at least one obligatory gospel cut. The obligation was best fulfilled by James Ingram's *Ya Mo Be There* (1983), an uplifting, splendidly sung duet with Michael McDonald, late of the Doobie Brothers. The rest of the recording is a summation of where "soul" was then "at" – classy production and playing, a few thumping, quite funky dance tracks, and a ballad from a forgettable movie soundtrack (on Ingram's album, the last track is the theme from "Best Friends," a Burt Reynolds–Goldie Hawn weepie). So all bases are covered, all markets happy. Ingram had the voice to carry it off. Not everyone did.

390   Introducing The Winans
The Winans
Light LS 5792 (LP)

The Question Is/Self/Are We Really Doing Your Will/I Know Someone/Goodness, Mercy And Grace/Fallow Ground/How Good It Feels To Be Loved/Flyin' Away/Restoration

The re-emergence of gospel as a visible component of African American music also meant that unswerving young gospel acts found it easier to get rhythm-and-blues hits. They broadened the instrumentation used and adopted more sophisticated production techniques without diluting the strength of their message or, more importantly, the power and exuberance of their singing. Later, wooed by major labels, the Winans (brothers Michael, Ronald, Marvin, and Carvin, from Detroit, Michigan) got even lusher production values. These smoothed the edges a fraction too round, but there is no denying their emphatic, joyful, vocal conviction, best heard in Marvin Winans's uplifting leads. Eventually, the entire Winans family became a gospel-music factory, with sister Vicki and both parents also releasing a batch of albums.

391   Rapped Uptight
Various Artists
Sugarhill SHLD 1001 (2 LPs)
Grandmaster Flash and the Furious Five: *The Message*; The Mean Machine: *Disco Dream*; Trouble Funk: *Hey Fellas*; Sylvia: *It's Good to Be The Queen*; Candi Staton: *The Sunshine Of Our Love*; Sequence: *Simon Says*; The Sugarhill Gang: *Rapper's Delight/Apache*; The Funky Four: *Do You Want To Rock (Before I Let Go)*; The Crash Crew: *We Want To Rock*; The Treacherous Three with special guest Philippe Wynne: *Whip It*; Wayne and Charlie (The Rapping Dummy): *Check It Out*

For the reasons outlined in the introduction to this chapter, rap had difficulty selling itself, but Sugarhill is where it made a first and lasting impression. Formed by Sylvia Robinson from the embers of All Platinum, which had been successful in the 1970s disco years, Sugarhill was home to rap pioneers Grandmaster Flash and the Furious Five and the more musically productive Trouble Funk. Flash, on *The Message*, gave rap credentials of social awareness; Trouble Funk's *Hey Fellas* gave notice of the more common macho stance, here yet to reach puberty. It is an album that catches a style in its innocence, before Public Enemy, NWA, and various flavors of Ice came on the scene.

392   Never Underestimate The Power Of A Woman
Klymaxx
Solar S-21 (LP)
All Fired Up/I Wish You Would (Tell Me Something Good)/I Want To Love You Tonight/You're The Greatest/Never Underestimate The Power Of A Woman/The Beat Of My Heart (Is For You)/No Words/Can't Let Love Just Pass Me By

Self-contained funk bands are a singularly male-dominated clique, but in 1981 Solar signed Klymaxx, an all-women octet formed in Los Angeles by drummer Bernadette Cooper. Although **Never Underestimate**, their debut album produced by Otis Stokes and Stephen Shockley of Lakeside (another Solar funk band) did little to further feminism, its solid funk marked the group as more than a novelty act. A second set, **Girls Will Be Girls** (1982), was Jimmy Jam and Terry Lewis's first project outside The Time. When Klymaxx switched labels to Constellation their own writing prospered. Their biggest hit, *The Men All Pause* (Klymaxx's puns were not subtle), from the album **Meeting In The Girls Room**, was a watershed. Cooper, a promising producer, and bassist Joyce "Fenderella" Irby made solo LPs.

393   Music From The Motion Picture Soundtrack "New Jack City"

Various Artists

Giant–Reprise 7599-24409-2

Ice-T: *New Jack Hustler (Nino's Theme)*; Christopher Williams: *I'm Dreamin'*; Guy: *New Jack City*; Johnny Gill: *I'm Still Waiting*; Keith Sweat: *(There You Go) Tellin' Me No Again*; Danny Madden: *Facts Of Life*; Troop-Levert: *For The Love Of Money – Living For The City* (medley); Color Me Badd: *I Wanna Sex You Up*; Essence: *Lyrics 2 The Rhythm*; F.S. Effect: *Get It Together (Black Is A Force)*; 2 Live Crew: *In The Dust*

In the early 1970s, many major African American artists wrote and recorded soundtracks for violent, ghetto-based films known as black exploitation movies – Curtis Mayfield for "Superfly," Marvin Gaye for "Trouble Man," James Brown for "Black Caesar" and "Slaughter's Big Rip Off," and Isaac Hayes for "Shaft" and "Truck Turner" among them. Usually, the films did not deserve the often excellent music. In 1977, the Bee Gees' soundtrack for the disco movie "Saturday Night Fever" sold millions, and ever since soundtracks have been regarded as "A Good Thing" to be on. Also, a star-studded soundtrack will bolster the revenue of a bad (as in dreadful) movie. In the late 1980s, after several successful movies by director Spike Lee, came "Black Exploitation 2: The Sequel," or in other words another rash of crime-related movies featuring drugs, violence, and African American actors. The difference this time was that they were also written and directed by African Americans. Soundtracks were important and on "New Jack City" one hears new jack swing (Keith Sweat, Guy, and Johnny Gill), contemporary pop-soul (Color Me Badd), and rap (Ice-T, who starred in the movie). Other soundtracks to hear are "Juice," "Boyz 'n The Hood," and Stevie Wonder's sounds for Spike Lee's "Jungle Fever."

394   3 Feet High And Rising

De La Soul

Big Life–Tommy Boy DLSMC1

Intro/The Magic Number/Change In Speak/Cool Breeze On The Rocks/Can U Keep A Secret/Jenifa Taught Me (Derwin's Revenge)/Ghetto Thang/Transmitting Live From Mars/Eye Know/Take It Off/A Little Bit Of Soap/Tread Water/Say No Go/Do As De La Does/Plug Tunin' (Last Chance To Comprehend)/De La Orgee/Buddy/Description/ Me Myself And I/This Is A Recording 4 Living In A Fulltime Era (LIFE)/I Can Do Anything (Delacratic)/DAISY Age/Plug Tunin' (original 12" version)/*Potholes In My Lawn*

Towards the end of the 1980s, there emerged several younger rap groups who were keen to inject a sense of fun and humor into their work and to wear clothes other than black, hooded sweaters. By far the most successful at this was the Prince Paul-produced trio De La Soul, though perhaps others wore clothes better. They used words and rhythm much as George Clinton did (even their names – Posdnuos, Trugoy the Dove, and Mace – seem not unlike his inventions), but one can hear the influence of Afrika Bambaataa and Public Enemy. After ten years, rap had an audible history. (Note that I have recommended the cassette version because, for the correct "attitood," this music should only be listened to on a Walkman.)

395   Beats, Rhymes And Basslines: The Best Of RAP
Various Artists

4th & Broadway 515 384-2

P. M. Dawn: *Set Adrift On A Memory Bliss*; Eric B. and Rakim: *Paid In Full* (edited version); De La Soul: *Say No Go*; Queen Latifah and De La Soul: *Mamma Gave Birth To The Soul Children*; The Dream Warriors: *My Definition Of A Boombastic Jazz Style* (radio mix); Monie Love featuring True Image: *It's A Shame (My Sister)*; DJ Jazzy Jeff and Fresh Prince: *Summertime*; Heavy D and the Boyz: *Now That We Found Love*; Public Enemy: *Rebel Without A Pause*; Beastie Boys: *(You Gotta) Fight For Your Right (To Party)*; NWA: *Express Yourself*; MC Hammer: *U Can't Touch This*; Salt 'N' Pepa: *Push It* (US remix); The Rebel MC and Double Trouble: *Street Tuff* (radio mix); Tone Loc: *Funky Cold Medina*; The Cookie Crew: *Got To Keep On* (remix)

Having fulminated like Luddites upon the lack of creativity implicit in sampling, we must now backtrack, on tiptoe, because of course in the right hands samples *can* be used artistically (for want of a better word), just as cover versions occasionally reveal a new facet of a melody or lyric. This varied and largely listenable collection offers pieces from many of the more important rap acts of the late 1980s and early 1990s, sequenced to give eight "smoove" cuts – Dawn, De La Soul, etc. – and eight "ruff" ones. Play this CD and spot the sample. Songwriters spliced into action include Quincy Jones, Hall and Oates, Stevie Wonder, Rick James, Spandau Ballet, and Gamble and Huff. Someone has got good ears. You must, of course, skip the Beastie Boys track.

Recommended Reading

General Histories and Ethnomusicological Studies

Betrock, Alan. *Girl Groups: the story of a sound*. New York: Delilah Books, 1982.

Booth, Stanley. *Rythm Oil: a journey through the music of the American South*. New York: Pantheon Books, 1992.

Chambers, Iain. *Urban Rhythms: pop music and popular culture*. New York: St Martin's Press, 1985.

Dannen, Fredric. *Hit Men: power brokers and fast money inside the music business*. New York: Times Books/Random House, 1990.

Dawson, Jim, and Propes, Steve. *What Was The First Rock 'N' Roll Record?*. Boston: Faber and Faber, 1992.

DeCurtis, Anthony, and Henke, James, with George-Warren, Holly (eds). Original editor, Miller, Jim. *The Rolling Stone Illustrated History of Rock and Roll*. Second revision. New York: Random House, 1992.

Garland, Phyl. *The Sound of Soul*. Chicago: Henry Regnery Company, 1969.

Garr, Gillian G. *She's A Rebel: the history of women in rock and roll*. Seattle, WA: Seal Press, 1992.

George, Nelson. *The Death of Rhythm and Blues*. New York: Pantheon Books, 1988.

Gillett, Charlie. *The Sound of the City*. Revised and enlarged. New York: Pantheon Books, 1983.

Greig, Charlotte. *Will You Still Love Me Tomorrow?: girl groups from the 50s on . . . .* London: Virago Press, 1989.

Haralambos, Michael. *Right On: from blues to soul in black America*. London: Eddison Press, 1974.

Hirshey, Gerri. *Nowhere to Run: the story of soul music*. New York: Times Books, 1984.

Hoare, Ian, Anderson, Clive, Cummings, Tony, and Frith, Simon. *The Soul Book*. New York: Delta Books, 1976.

Jackson, John. *Big Beat Heat: Alan Freed and the early days of rock and roll*. New York: Schirmer Books, 1991.

Keil, Charles. *Urban Blues*. With new afterword. Chicago: University of Chicago Press, 1991.

Kinder, Bob. *The Best of the First: the early days of rock and roll*. Chicago: Adams Press, 1986.

Marcus, Greil. *Mystery Train: images of America in rock 'n' roll music*. Third revised edition. New York: Obelisk/Dutton, 1990.

McCutcheon, Lynn Ellis. *Rhythm and Blues*. Arlington, VA: Beatty, 1971.

Roberts, John Storm. *The Latin Tinge: the impact of Latin American music on the United States*. New York: Oxford University Press, 1979.

Shaw, Arnold. *The World of Soul: black America's contribution to the pop music scene*. New York: Cowles Book Co., 1970.

Shaw, Arnold. *Honkers and Shouters: the golden years of rhythm and blues*. New York: Macmillan, 1978.

Toop, David. *Rap Attack 2: African rap to global hip hop*. London: Serpent's Tail, 1992.

Biographical Encyclopedias and Other Reference Works

Albert, George, and Hoffmann, Frank. *The Cashbox Black Contemporary Singles Charts, 1960–1984*. Metuchen, NJ: Scarecrow Press, 1986.

Albert, George, and Hoffman, Frank. *The Cashbox Black Contemporary Album Charts, 1975–1987*. Metuchen, NJ: Scarecrow Press, 1989.

Bonds, Ray (ed.). *The Illustrated Encyclopedia of Black Music*. New York: Harmony Books [1983].

Clarke, Donald (ed.). *Penguin Encyclopedia of Popular Music*. London: Viking, 1989.

Gambaccini, Paul, Rice, Tim, and Rice, Jonathan. *British Hit Singles*. New York: Billboard Books, 1991.

Gregory, Hugh. *Soul Music A–Z*. London: Blandford/Cassell, 1992.

Hardy, Phil and Laing, Dave. *The Faber Companion to 20th-Century Popular Music*. London: Faber and Faber, 1990.

Jancik, Wayne. *The Billboard Book of One-Hit Wonders*. New York: Billboard Books, 1990.

Nelson, Havelock, and Gonzales, Michael A. *Bring The Noise: a guide to rap music and hip-hop*. New York: Harmony Books, 1991.

Nite, Norm N. *Rock On: the illustrated encyclopedia of rock n' roll, vol. 1*. Updated edition. New York: Harper & Row, 1982.

Nite, Norm N., with Newman, Ralph M. *Rock On: the illustrated encyclopedia of rock n' roll, vol. 2*. New York: Harper & Row, 1984.

Nite, Norm N., with Crespo, Charles. *Rock On: the illustrated encyclopedia of rock n' roll, vol. 3*. New York: Harper & Row, 1985.

Stambler, Irwin. *The Encyclopedia of Pop Rock and Soul*. Revised edition. New York: St Martin's Press, 1989.

Tee, Ralph. *Who's Who in Soul Music*. London: Weidenfeld & Nicolson, 1991.

Tosches, Nick. *Unsung Heroes of Rock 'N' Roll: the birth of rock in the wild years before Elvis*. Revised edition. New York: Harmony Books, 1991.

Whitburn, Joel. *Joel Whitburn's Top R & B Singles 1942–1988*. Menomonee Falls, WI: Record Research, Inc., 1988.

Regional and Label Studies

Bane, Michael. *White Boy Singin' The Blues*. Reissue of 1982 printing with new introduction. New York: DaCapo Press, 1992.

Benjaminson, Peter. *The Story Of Motown*. New York: Grove Press, 1979.

Berry, Jason, Foose, Jonathan, and Jones, Tad. *Up From The Cradle of Jazz: New Orleans music since World War II*. Athens, GA: University of Georgia Press, 1986.

Bianco, David. *Heat Wave: the Motown fact book*. Ann Arbor, MI: Pierian Press, 1988.

Bowmen, Rob. Liner notes, *The Complete Stax/Volt Singles: 1959–1968*. Atlantic 82218-2, 1991.

Broven, John. *Walking to New Orleans: the story of New Orleans rhythm and blues*. Bexhill-on-Sea, Sussex: Blues Unlimited, 1974. Republished as *Rhythm and Blues in New Orleans*, Gretna, LA: Pelican, 1978.

Broven, John. *South to Louisiana*. Gretna, LA: Pelican, 1983.

Cummings, Tony. *The Sound of Philadelphia*. London: Eyre Methuen, 1975.

Davis, Sharon. *Motown: the history*. Enfield, CT: Guinness Books, 1988.

Finnis, Rob. *The Phil Spector Story*. London: Rockon, 1975.

Gart, Galen, and Ames, Roy C., with contributions from Funk, Ray, Bowman, Rob, and Booth, David. *Duke/Peacock Records: an illustrated history with discography*. Milford, NH: Big Nickel Publications, 1990.

George, Nelson. *Where Did Our Love Go?: the rise and fall of the Motown sound*. New York: St Martin's Press, 1985.

Gillett, Charlie. *Making Tracks*. New York: E.P. Dutton, 1974.

Groia, Phil. *They All Sang on the Corner*. West Hempstead, NY: Phillie Dee Enterprises, 1983.

Guralnick, Peter. *Lost Highway: journeys and arrivals of American musicians*. New York: Vintage, 1982.

Guralnick, Peter. *Sweet Soul Music*. New York: Harper & Row, 1986.

Hannusch, Jeff. *I Hear You Knocking: the sound of New Orleans rhythm and blues*. Ville Platte, LA: Swallow, 1985.

Hoskyns, Barney. *Say It One More Time for the Broken Hearted*. Glasgow: Fontana/Collins, 1987.

Lahr, John (introduction), and Palmer, Robert (text). *Baby, That Was Rock and Roll: the legendary Leiber and Stoller*. New York: Harcourt Brace Jovanovich, 1978.

Lepri, Paul. *The New Haven Sound: 1946–1976*. New Haven, CT: privately published, 1977.

Loza, Steven. *Barrio Rhythm: Mexican American Music in Los Angeles*. Urbana, IL: University of Illinois Press, 1993.

Pruter, Robert. *Chicago Soul*. Urbana, IL: University of Illinois Press, 1991.

Ribowsky, Mark. *He's A Rebel: the truth about Phil Spector – rock and roll's legendary madman*. New York: E.P. Dutton, 1989.

Rowe, Mike. *Chicago Breakdown*. London: Eddison Press, 1973. Republished as *Chicago Blues: the city and the music*. New York: DaCapo Press, 1981.

Singleton, Raynoma Gordy, with Brown, Bryan and Eichler, Mim. *Berry, Me, and Motown*. Chicago: Contemporary Books, 1990.

Taraborrelli, J. Randy. *Motown*. Garden City, NY: Doubleday, 1986.

Wade, Dorothy, and Picardie, Justine. *Music Man: Ahmet Ertegun, Atlantic Records, and the triumph of rock 'n' roll*. New York: W.W. Norton & Co., 1990.

Waller, Don. *The Motown Story*. New York: Charles Scribner's Sons, 1985.

Williams, Richard. *Out of His Head: the sound of Phil Spector*. New York: Outerbridge & Lazard, Inc., 1972.

Biographies

Bego, Mark. *Aretha Franklin: the queen of soul*. New York: St Martin's Press, 1989.

Brown, James, with Tucker, Bruce. *James Brown: the godfather of soul*. New York, Macmillan, 1986.

Charles, Ray, and Ritz, David. *Brother Ray: Ray Charles' own story*. New York: The Dial Press, 1978.

Escott, Colin. *Clyde McPhatter: a biographical essay*. Vollersode, West Germany: Bear Family, 1987.

Hill, Dave. *Prince: a pop life*. New York: Harmony Books, 1989.

Licks, Dr. *Standing in the Shadows of Motown: the life and music of legendary bassist James Jamerson*. Milwaukee: Hal Leonard Publishing Corp., 1989.

Marsh, Dave. *Trapped: Michael Jackson and the crossover dream*. New York: Bantam Books, 1985.

McEwen, Joe. *Sam Cooke: the man who invented soul*. New York: Sire Books, 1977.

Miller, Bill. *The Drifters*. New York: Collier Books, 1971.

Miller, Bill. *The Coasters*. London: W.H. Allen & Co., 1975.

Mills, Bart. *T*I*N*A*. New York: Warner Books, Inc., 1985.

Ritz, David. *Divided Soul: the life of Marvin Gaye*. New York: McGraw-Hill, 1985.

Robinson, Smokey, with Ritz, David. *Smokey: inside my life*. New York: McGraw-Hill, 1989.

Rose, Cynthia. *Living in America: the soul saga of James Brown*. London: Serpent's Tail, 1990.

Spector, Ronnie, with Walden, Vince. *Be My Baby*. New York: Harmony Books, 1990.

Swenson, John. *Stevie Wonder*. New York: Harper & Row, 1986.

Taraborrelli, J. Randy. *Call Her Miss Ross: the unauthorized biography of Diana Ross*. New York: Birch Lane Press, 1989.

Taraborrelli, J. Randy. *Michael Jackson: the madness and the magic*. New York: Birch Lane Press, 1991.

Turner, Tina, with Loder, Kurt. *I Tina: my life story*. New York: William Morrow and Co., 1986.

Warner, Jay. *The Billboard Book of American Singing Groups: A History 1940–1990*. New York: Watson-Guptill Publications.

White, Charles. *The Life and Times of Little Richard: the quasar of rock*. New York: Harmony Books, 1984.

Williams, Otis, with Romanowski, Patricia. *Temptations*. New York: G. P. Putnam's Sons, 1988.

Wilson, Mary, and Romanowski, Patricia. *Dreamgirl: my life as a Supreme*. New York: St Martin's Press, 1986.

Wilson, Mary, and Romanowski, Patricia. *Supreme Faith: someday we'll be together*. New York: HarperCollins, 1990.

Wynn, Ron. *Tina: the Tina Turner story*. New York: Collier Books, 1985.

Glossary

Words in **bold type** within an entry refer readers to other entries.

A & R, an abbreviation for "artists and repertoire," which refers to a department or position at a record company. The A & R director at a record company is responsible for finding recording artists and other talent for the label and for finding song material. During the soul era, the A & R director for companies that recorded soul usually also served as producer and would suggest the tone of the arrangements. The A & R director could be considered the taste-maker of the label.

Acid house, a British-European development from **house** music. The music is stripped to the bone, leaving not so much finished songs as **grooves**. Interspersed in the music are odd vocal **samples** and various electronic beeps and noises. Acid house departed from most dance music, which shows soul-music influences, by exhibiting strong rock and electric-guitar influences. The style emerged at the turn of the 1990s.

Album, a term from the 1940s when a record company would release a set of 78s in the form of an album (a booklet enclosing sleeves for each disc). When the long play $33\frac{1}{3}$ record became the standard release at the beginning of the 1950s, the release with a standard 12 tracks was called an album. The compact disc now contains many more tracks and may also be called an album if it contains more than three or four songs.

Answer song, a song written to cash in on the popularity of a **hit** record. Usually it uses the same melody and is a reply to the previous record, as when Gene Chandler replied to Mary Wells's *You Beat Me To The Punch* with *You Threw A Lucky Punch*.

A side, the side of a **single** promoted by a record company as a potential **hit**. A company will often send **deejays** promotional copies with the A side on both sides. *See also* **B side**.

Backbeat, ordinarily in most **pop** music the weak beats of a four-beat measure, but in soul music the backbeats tend to be emphasized.

Ballad, in popular music, a slow-tempo song dealing with romance or love.

Bass line, in popular music, a term used to describe the playing of the **rhythm section** of a band, especially the bass guitar.

Beach music, the term that arose in the college fraternities in the Carolinas in the late 1940s to describe the **rhythm-and-blues** music they would listen and dance to on the juke-boxes in the dance clubs along the beaches. During the soul era, many soul hits were described in the Carolinas as "beach-music" hits.

Bluebeat, a synonym for ska, named after a particular label in Great Britain that featured many ska artists. *See* **ska**.

Blue-eyed soul, a term developed during the soul era by African American **deejays** for music they played by white acts that exhibited authentic soul styling. Blue-eyed soul hits included the Righteous Brothers' *Little Latin Lupe Lu*, the Rascals' *Groovin'*, and the Soul Survivors' *Expressway To Your Heart*.

Boogie, a term that comes from the piano style called **boogie-woogie**, but refers to an up-tempo, boogie-woogie beat as adopted in band settings.

Boogie-woogie, an eight-to-the-bar piano style, in which the left hand plays a repeated phrase while the right hand plays the melody. Boogie-woogie was a popular style during the 1940s and was rarely evident during the soul era.

Bottom, in popular music, the bass rhythm part of the song, especially the bass drum and the bass guitar.

Break, a term of jazz origin that refers to the place in a performance where a largely unaccompanied instrumental soloist plays for a few measures, usually an **improvisation**.

Break beat, in popular music, the part of the song that contains a repetitious instrumental dominated by drums, usually embellished by rhythmic **riffs** by the brass or keyboards. It comes in as the melody or vocal stops. Some break beats were released separately on a record. The 45 Kings' *The 900 Number* is a classic example of a break-beat record.

Bridge, in popular music, the part of the song two-thirds the way through that involves a change in rhythm and key for eight measures, before returning to the original rhythm and key.

B side, the side of a **single** not considered strong enough by the company to be promoted as a potential **hit**. Also called the flip side. Sometimes, the company is confounded when the B side becomes the one that succeeds.

Call-and-response, a feature in African American music, especially gospel and soul, in which the lead vocalist sings a line and is answered or repeated by the chorus. Many records of the soul era feature lead and choruses using call-and-response.

Calypso, a lilting, syncopated music developed in Trinidad and Tobago.

Can, a way of saying that a recording is unreleased. It is said to be "in the can."

Chalypso, in popular music, a dance record that combines the feel and the beat of a calypso and a cha-cha.

Chart, refers to the lists of bestselling and most popular records. Also refers to the musical score or written arrangement.

Chestnut, a synonym for an old **standard** or evergreen.

Chitlin' circuit, the live entertainment theaters in the major northern cities of the United States that served the African American community. The most famous ones during the soul era were the Apollo in Harlem, the Howard in Washington, DC, the Royal in Baltimore, the Uptown in Philadelphia, the Fox in Detroit, and the Regal in Chicago. "Chitlin" comes from "chitterlings," a dish of pig intestines that is popular with African Americans in the South.

Close harmony, a style of vocal music in which the individual notes of a chord are near each other. Many soul vocal groups exhibited close harmony in their singing.

Combo, a term of jazz origin that refers to ensembles smaller than a full orchestra and ranging in size from a trio to an octet.

Cover record, a record released shortly after the original version to garner sales from interest in the song. Covers were common in the pre-rock-and-roll era, when the song was often more important than the artist. The cover record developed a less benign reputation in the early days of rock-and-roll when many white artists covered **rhythm-and-blues** records to reap rewards in the **pop** market that were unavailable to the R & B performers. A song recorded years after the original version is more correctly called a "remake" and not a cover.

Crossover, a record intended for one market, usually a **rhythm-and-blues** or country-and-western hit, that achieves success in another market, usually the **pop** market. The record is said to have crossed over from one **chart** to another. Pop records can also cross over to rhythm-and-blues or country-and-western charts, but it is rare.

Cut, an old term meaning **track** or take from a recording tape or a selection on an **album.** It is a survival from the days when a record **master** was made by a needle cutting grooves on a metal disc.

Deejay, or **DJ,** an abbreviation for "disc jockey," a person who plays records over the air or in clubs.

Deep soul, *see* **hard soul.**

Demo, an abbreviation for "demonstration record," used to audition a song or recording artist. Sometimes a record company will release the original demo rather than re-record the song, because they find the demo performance cannot be improved on. Some singers had their recording careers begun with a demo that went into regular release.

Disco, a style of **rhythm-and-blues** music that emerged at the end of the soul era and emphasized a steady dance beat. The word is derived from "discotheque," a term of French origin for dance club.

DJ, *see* **deejay.**

Doo-wop, a style of vocal harmony popular in the 1950s among **rhythm-and-blues** groups, in which nonsense syllables, prominent bass and falsetto, and an exaggerated lead often characterize the vocal arrangement.

Down-home, an African American expression for music that sounds primitive and earthy. "Down home" originally referred to the South, where the ethnic roots of the music were found. In soul music, it is used much as a synonym for **hard soul** or deep soul.

Drive, refers to strong, propulsive playing.

Drum machine, a synthesizer in which a player uses a keyboard to make electronically produced drum sounds. The keyboard player can create new drum sounds or produce **sampled** drum sounds available in the drum machine.

Dusties, an African American term for old **hit** records. The records are thought to have gathered dust. In the 1980s some big city markets saw the emergence of dusties radio stations that specialized in playing primarily soul music of the 1960s and 1970s. *See also* **oldie.**

Easy listening, a music trade paper term for middle-of-the-road music, or **MOR.**

88s, an old music-business term for the piano, after its 88 keys.

Evergreen, an old **standard,** once a **hit** but now part of the repertoire of popular music.

Falsetto, a high-pitched voice, usually that of a male whose voice is pitched so high he sounds like a woman. Falsetto was especially common in soul music, particularly in male vocal groups.

Fanfare, a flourish of trumpets often used to introduce an entertainer. Some soul records featured fanfares in the opening bars to immediately grab the listener. A notable fanfare, which had its origin in vaudeville, appeared on both Jackie Ross's *Selfish One* and Edwin Starr's *Stop Her On Sight*.

Flip, *see* **B side.**

Floating tenor, a term used in **doo-wop** harmony in which the highest-pitched voice, usually a **falsetto,** can be heard weaving in and out of the vocal mix, as though it is "floating" above it.

Fusion, usually refers to a hybrid of jazz and rock, but can also refer to hybrids of soul and jazz and of soul and rock.

Fuzztone, a blurring guitar sound especially popular in rock music. It can be created by using an electronic device called a fuzzbox or by creating distortion.

Garage, a style of dance music that combines Philadelphia soul with **house.** The lyrics are important and tend to have a spiritual or uplifting quality. The music has a heavy, throbbing bass and exuberant, "hot" vocals. Garage was developed in a Greenwich Village dance club called the Paradise Garage during the early 1980s. At first the **deejays** played records from Philadelphia International Records, the preeminent purveyor of Philadelphia soul, and also from the Prelude and West End labels in New York. Then "garage" records started being made specifically to fit that sound.

Gig, a performer's job at a club, theater, or other venue.

Girl groups, an early 1960s development that generally involved African American, Hispanic, and "black-sounding" white girl groups. The girl-group sound, considered strident for the time, married the vocal textures of black teen vocals with the approaches of **pop**-style rock-and-roll. Girl groups were among the primary purveyors of songs from the **Tin Pan Alley** composers located on Broadway, notably in the Brill Building.

Go-go, a heavily percussive music featuring lots of horns and heavy beats. It tends to emphasize a continuous flow from song to song by connecting them with percussion work. The style was developed in Washington, DC, and largely came from the funk style of James Brown.

Gold record, a music-industry term for a **single** or an **album** that sold a million copies or an album that sold 500,000 copies. Those numbers are no longer officially the standard to achieve gold, but it is the standard that the public largely knows. *See also* **platinum record**.

Groove, in popular music, when all of a band's musicians are locked into one rhythmic **drive** that virtually defines the feel of the song.

Hard soul, a type of music that relies on a raw delivery and makes heavy use of **melisma** and screaming. Vocals are shouted rather than smoothly delivered. Hard soul tends to draw more on gospel and blues than its counterpart, **soft soul**. Hard soul can also be called deep soul, **down-home** soul, or Southern soul (the last designation because much of the music was developed in the South).

Head arrangement, an arrangement created by sessionmen in the studio without the use of printed music.

Hip-hop, originally a synonym for **rap**, the term has evolved to encapsulate an entire rap-related culture, involving dance, dress styles, partying, and a state of mind called "attitude."

Hit, a record that goes high on the **charts** either nationally or locally.

Hook, a musical phrase that is so memorable and appealing to the listener that it "hooks" him or her to the song. Songwriters and producers often try to strengthen their creations by purposely adding hooks.

Hot jazz, a synonym for traditional jazz, which is distinguished from modern jazz. Before the advent of bebop and other modern forms, the term "hot jazz" was often used in contradistinction to "sweet jazz," which was considered more commercial and refined than hot jazz.

House, a style of African American music derived from **disco**. House diminishes the orchestration to focus on the rhythm and the beat. Firmly based on black dance music, it was originated by a club **deejay**, Frankie Knuckles, at the Warehouse in Chicago. Variations of house developed in other US cities and Europe, notably hip-house, deep-house, **acid house**, **techno**, and **garage**.

Improvisation, most commonly found in jazz, but also found in soul music, especially in funk bands. During the soul era, in live concerts, the vocalist might improvise a closing of the set to rouse the crowd by exhortations and **call-and-response** routines. Few soul recordings feature improvisation, but they can be found in some live concert recordings. *See also* **vamp**.

Independent, or **indie**, a generally small record company that does not own its own pressing plants or distribution branches. An independent must rely on either independent operators or a **major** label to press, distribute, and market its records. During the soul era, most independent labels relied on independent distributors and pressing plants. Most soul records in the 1960s and early 1970s were produced by independent labels.

Indie, *see* **independent**.

Jump, in popular music, a rousing, up-tempo, **rhythm-and-blues** song. In the early days of rhythm and blues a **single** record featured a jump side and a **ballad** side.

Latino soul, soul music created by Mexican-Americans centered in Los Angeles, or East LA. Much of the music consists of slow ballads with a melancholy feel in the same manner as some of the **pop** music of Mexico.

Latin soul, a mid-1960s hybrid of soul music and Cuban-styled up-tempo dance music. It originated in the Cuban and Puerto Rican communities of the Bronx and East Harlem in New York City. Latin soul records featured exuberant brassy accompaniment and English as well as Spanish lyrics. The bugalú (English: boogaloo) dance was associated with Latin soul, and the two terms were often used interchangeably.

Lick, a term originally used in jazz for a rhythmic or melodic phrase that is distinctive to a certain musician, usually while **improvising**.

Liner notes, in its broad meaning all information that appears on the back of an **album**, such as facts on songs, performers, producers, arrangers, as well as any commentary on the recording artist. In its narrow meaning, "liner notes" refers to the commentary itself. During the 1950s most albums contained brief commentary, usually a lot of words saying nothing written by a marketing person for the purpose of encouraging the consumer to purchase the album. By the mid-1960s the use of liner notes commentary had died out on most popular music albums. In the 1980s liner notes commentary was revived for reissue packages, in which detailed biographical and historical essays were considered an essential element for selling the package.

Lowdown, a term used to describe music that is primitive and earthy.

Low-rider music, refers to a body of **doo-wop** and **soft-soul** music that has particular appeal to Mexican-Americans. The songs are most often **ballads** and mid-tempo songs, often with a melancholy feel. Soul records, especially transitional records between doo-wop and soul, from Chicago and Detroit are especially popular. The term has its origin in the practice of Mexican-American youths of modifying their automobiles so that the body is low to the ground.

Major, one of the six or seven record companies that have dominated the industry since the 1930s. A characteristic of a major is it owns its own pressing plants and distribution branches. During the soul era, the majors were RCA, Columbia, Capitol, Decca, MGM, Mercury, and WEA (Warner Brothers/Electra/Atlantic). *See also* **independent**.

Master, the original recording. In modern recording, the master is on a multitrack tape, which when **mixed** becomes the finished tape.

MC, an acronym for "master of ceremonies," and, as related to **rap**, the performer who recites the lyrics to the beat. Hence, some rap artists have taken such names as MC Hammer, MC Shan, MC Smooth, and MC Lyte.

Melisma, the practice, common in gospel and soul singing, of stretching a syllable over several notes.

Merseybeat, rock music from Liverpool, England, that gets its name from the Mersey River which flows through the city.

Middle-of-the-road, *see* **MOR**.

Mix, the process of converting a multitrack tape to a finished tape, or **master**.

Mixer, a club **deejay** who, using multiple turntables and electronic mixing devices blends two or more records into a seamless whole. "Mixer" also refers to the electronic equipment used to blend the records (*see also* **mix**).

Mom-and-pop, refers to a small enterprise, often owned by a married couple, hence "mom-and-pop."

MOR, acronym for "middle-of-the-road" music, also called "easy listening." Artists such as Frank Sinatra, Al Martino, Barbra Streisand, and the Ray Charles Singers, who represented the type of mainstream music that dominated the charts before the advent of rock-and-roll, are now considered MOR acts. The term arose in the 1960s to differentiate those artists from the rock and soul artists who had taken over the **charts**.

New jack swing, a style of **rhythm and blues** that combines **hip-hop** with conventional soul singing and structure, and often features **rap** interludes. New jack swing was created by producer/performer Teddy Riley with his group Guy around the turn of the 1990s.

Noodling, improvising on an instrument, usually informally while practicing or warming up.

Northern soul, the type of soul music that appealed to young people in the northern counties of England. Most of this music, which generally originated from Detroit and Chicago and dated from the late 1960s, was introduced by **deejays** in dance halls rather than on radio. A steady, fast beat and forceful African American vocals seemed the dominant characteristics of Northern soul records.

Oldie but goodie, or **oldie**, a **hit** record from the past. *See also* **dusties**.

One-hit wonder, used either derisively or affectionately to refer to a performer who only had one **hit** to his or her career. The hit may have been in the **pop chart**, **rhythm-and-blues** chart, or country-and-western chart. Some one-hit-wonders in the pop charts had long and distinguished careers with numerous hits in other charts.

One-nighter, a booking in which an artist plays just one night, common in the 1950s when a recording artist was forced to play many dates to make a living in the business.

Overdub, refers to adding a **track** to an existing track on a recording.

Platinum record, a **single** that sells two million or more copies or an **album** that sells a million copies or more. *See also* **gold record**.

Playlist, the list of records that radio stations choose to broadcast.

Polyrhythmic, refers to two or more rhythmic patterns played at the same time. In soul music, the style known as funk was often polyrhythmic.

Pop, a term to refer to the mainstream popular music to differentiate it from jazz, **rhythm and blues**, country and western, folk, and other vernacular forms. In its early days, rock-and-roll was differentiated from the mainstream music in the same manner.

Pop soul, *see* **soft soul**.

Psychedelia, a style of popular music that evokes the feeling of an hallucinatory drug experience. It arose in rock, but some soul performers employed psychedelic effects in their music.

R & B, or **r & b,** an abbreviation for **rhythm and blues**.

Rap, an African American musical style in which performers, instead of singing the lyrics, rhythmically recite them over a percussive, heavy, often rudimentary instrumental track. "Rap" also refers to the practice in soul music of giving a long recitation in a song, usually at the beginning as an introduction to the body of the song.

Raver, or **rave-up,** a slang term used in soul or rock for an aggressive, up-tempo recording.

Reggae, a syncopated Jamaican music with a heavy, chunk-alunk beat. It arose out of **ska,** which combined **calypso** and American **rhythm-and-blues** influences.

Remake, *see* **cover**.

Rhythm and blues, a synonym for black popular music. Often used to refer to the black popular music of the 1940s and 1950s that preceded the soul era.

Rhythm section, in contemporary popular music, the part of the band that consists of rhythm guitar, bass guitar, drums, and other percussion. Sometimes piano is considered a part of the rhythm section depending on how it is used – to drive the rhythm or to lead on the melody.

Riff, in popular music, a rhythmic phrase repeated over and over, usually to accompany an instrumental solo or a vocalist.

Rockaballad, a term from the 1950s which referred to a **ballad** done rock-and-roll style. Most ballads of the era were associated with the smooth **pop** style of Frank Sinatra, Tony Bennett, the Ames Brothers, and Patti Page, and "rockaballad" enjoyed a brief vogue when there was a need to differentiate rock-and-roll from pop music. Most rockaballads of the 1950s would be called **doo-wops** today.

Rockabilly, refers to a 1950s style that was thought to combine elements of country and western and those of rock-and-roll.

Roll, a rapid series of beats on a percussion instrument.

Salsa, an up-tempo hybrid music of jazz and Cuban rhythms. It first became popular in the United States in Spanish Harlem in the early 1970s. Salsa means literally "sauce," a reference to the hot, spicy sauces used in Latin American cooking.

Sampling, to incorporate into a recording a previously recorded piece of music, usually a **riff**, a drum beat, a bit of lyric, or a section of a song. MC Hammer, for example, took from Rick James's *Superfreak* the lead riff and made it the dominant riff for his giant hit, *U Can't Touch This*. He also credited James as co-writer.

Scat, a term of jazz origin that refers to the practice of singing nonsense syllables in place of lyrics to imitate an instrumental solo.

Scratching, the practice by club **deejays** of manually manipulating the turntable to create a rhythmic scratching sound with the needle, or to repeat a beat over and over again. A deejay who practices scratching is sometimes called a "scratcher."

Secular gospel, a song, generally in soul music, that is a gospel number in every respect stylistically except for the lyrics, which are non-religious, or secular, in content. Mitty Collier's *I Had A Talk With My Man*, a remake of James Cleveland's *I Had A Talk With God Last Night*, was a secular gospel song.

Shuffle, a blues based beat, usually mid-tempo to up-tempo.

Single, a record with two songs, one to a side. During most of the soul era, an artist's career was measured in terms of **hit** singles. By the mid-1970s, at the end of the soul era, **album** sales became more important and soul artists thereafter defined their recording success by their hit albums.

Ska, a syncopated Jamaican music based on **calypso** and **rhythm and blues**. It is lighter and more rhythm-and-blues flavored than the style that succeeded it, **reggae**.

Soft soul, a style that owes as much to the esthetic considerations of mainstream popular music as to **rhythm-and-blues** traditions. The music tends to emphasize a strong melody and obvious **hooks**, vocals tend to be more "correctly" sung, and the instrumentation is more formally arranged and fuller (often using strings for "sweetening"). Artists endemic to the soft-soul style are vocal groups, balladeers, and girl sopranos. Soft soul may also be called **pop** soul and uptown soul. *See also* **hard soul**.

Soul-blues, a style of soul that became popular in the 1970s, especially in the South, where blues had lost much of its African American constituency but where there was still a demand for a style of music that had some of the blues feeling and expression.

Southern soul, *see* **hard soul**.

Stable, an old record-industry term that refers to the group of recording artists that is signed to a label.

Standard, a song that after it has been popular enters the repertoire of many singers.

Steppin', an African American term that gained currency in the 1980s for a dance that resembles a mid-tempo version of the jitterbug. During the soul era, "steppin" was known as "the bop."

Stop-time rhythm, a term of jazz origin that refers to a series of short **breaks** of a bar or two by the rhythm section.

Street funk, a raw style of funk that combines rigid James Brown **riffing** formulas with free-form jazz stylings.

Supper-club jazz, a frequently disparaging term for a type of jazz that sounded smooth and sophisticated, not jarring or dissonant. One could listen to it while digesting one's meal, and follow with a few cocktails afterwards. It usually featured a **combo** of pianist, acoustic bass player, and drummer. Such combos were endemic in the African American community in the 1940s and 1950s. The Ramsey Lewis Trio began as a supper-club jazz outfit, but during the soul era changed their style to play instrumental versions of soul hits.

Swing music, jazz-oriented, big-band dance music.

Switch-off, in popular music, the practice in vocal ensembles of changing the lead vocals during the song.

Techno, a style of **house** music that owes little to **disco** or soul antecedents. The sound, influenced by German rock bands such as Kraftwork and Tangerine Dream, is highly electronic, and vocals are minimal and devoid of soul styling. The music has a sinister or forbidding atmosphere. Techno was developed in Detroit by Juan Atkins, Derrick May, and Kevin Saunderson in the late 1980s.

Teenybop, a term indicating that a song or recording artist appeals to juveniles.

Tin Pan Alley, originally a reference to a district of Manhattan around 52nd street where the songwriters and music publishers plied their trade. Gradually the term was extended to mean the entire popular music establishment, in opposition to rock-and-roll and such vernacular musics as **rhythm and blues** and country and western.

Torch song, an emotional **ballad** sung with an aching, yearning, somewhat sad feeling. A classic of the style is Julie London's *Cry Me A River*.

Tracks, the selections on an **album**.

Turntable hit, a record that receives a lot of play on radio but which garners few sales in the stores. Some recording-industry trade publications measure the amount of radio play in compiling their **charts** of the most popular records, so having a turntable **hit** is not actually a bad thing. It is better than having no hit at all.

Underdub, an incomplete **master** of a released record, usually missing certain instrumental or vocal accompaniments that were **overdubbed** for the completed recording.

Uptown soul, *see* **soft soul**.

Vamp, a chord pattern repeated endlessly. In many soul shows, a vocalist will close his or her show with a vamp, during which the brass section adds embellishments while the vocalist extemporizes variations on the song and exhorts the audience into a **call-and-response** participation. *See also* **improvisation**.

Vinyl, a slang term for a phonograph recording, from when records were made of vinyl plastic.

Vocalese, in jazz, a style in which the lyrics are sung in imitation of a jazz instrumental solo.

Vocoder, an electronic device to make the voice sound robotic or other-worldly. It is also used to change the pitch of a voice.

Wah-wah, a technique used originally in big-band music by trumpet players who created a "wah-wah" sound by waving their hand over the bell of the horn. Rock musicians created a "wah-wah" sound on their guitar by using a wah-wah foot pedal. The wah-wah guitar sound was common in many soul bands of the early 1970s.

Wax, to record a song. The term is from the early days of the record business, when a recording was cut on a wax disc.

Index

Entries in **bold** refer to albums; entries in *italics* refer to song titles.